A Dictionary of Late Egyptian

Second Edition

Volume II

A Dictionary of Late Egyptian

Second Edition

Volume II

Leonard H. Lesko, Editor

Barbara Switalski Lesko, Collaborating Editor

B C

B. C. Scribe Publications
P.O. Box 2453
Providence, RI 02906

Printed in the United States of America

by

Fall River Modern Printing Co.
798 Plymouth Avenue
Fall River, MA 02721

ISBN 0-930548-15-9

Preface to Volume II

This volume of *A Dictionary of Late Egyptian* includes all the entries of both volumes III and IV of the original five volume set, and in addition has an updated index of the English meanings found in the two new second edition volumes. Of course, there are a few entirely new entries, many more references, and twenty-five pages of new meanings that we encountered in more recent publications and referenced here.

In addition to the many, many hours that Barbara S. Lesko spent searching for additional references, she also continued to coordinate the efforts of several student assistants--for this volume notably Mariam Ayad, Jessica Levai, Marie Passanante, and Emily O'Dell. Jonathan Keiser meanwhile took over much of the production end of the work, seeing to it that the best glyph was used in each case, that there was greater consistency in formatting and clarity in abbreviations. While he had the earlier work of Stephen E. Thompson and Lee Payne as a solid basis on which to build, he, like Barbara, continued to search and question right down to the last minute. I indeed owe a great debt of gratitude to all those who have contributed to the success of this project.

It is always disappointing to encounter typographical errors, so even more time and effort went into proofreading this volume. Even so some variant British and American spellings turned up from different sources, and some of these were allowed to stand to reflect the fact that they came from different authors. I felt that we did not have to insist on total conformity.

Again, it has been a pleasure to work with our friends, Ray and Don Schenck at Fall River Modern Printing, but in spite of the fact that they have by now become totally engrossed by Egyptology, I am sure that they are as glad as I am to see this project successfully completed.

Providence, Rhode Island
January 5, 2004

Leonard H. Lesko

LIST OF ABBREVIATIONS

A 1	Alan H. Gardiner, *Egyptian Hieratic Texts,* (Series 1: Literary Texts of the New Kingdom, Part 1, The Papyrus Anastasi and the Papyrus Koller, together with the parallel texts), Leipzig, 1911.
AEO	See Gard. *AEO*
Äg. Studien	*Ägyptischen Studien*, ed. O. Firchow, Berlin, 1955 = Deutsche Akademie der Wissenschaften zu Berlin. Institut für Orientforschung Veröffentlichung Nr. 27.
AJSLL	*American Journal of Semitic Languages and Literatures* (Chicago 1884-1942); see *JNES* for continuation.
Akten...München	*Akten des Vierten Internationalem Ägyptologen Kongressen München*, 1985 (SAK, Beihefte) Hamburg, 1988.
Albright, "Notes on Eg. – Sem. Etymology"	William F. Albright, "Notes on Egypto-Semitic etymology", *JAOS* 47 (1927) 198-237.
A.Lex.	*Année Lexicographique*, Paris, 1980- .
Amarna	N. De G. Davies, *The Rock Tombs of El Amarna*, 6 Vols., London, 1903-08.
Amduat	see Hornung, *Amduat*
An 3	P. Anastasi 3, cf. *LEM*
Anc. Eg.	*Ancient Egypt*, London, 1914-35.
ANET	*Ancient Near Eastern Texts* relating to the Old Testament, 2nd edition ed. by James B. Pritchard, Princeton, 1955.
Arch. Orient.	*Archiv Orientálni, Journal of the Czechoslovak Oriental Institute*, Prague, 1929- .
ASAE	*Annales du Service des Antiquités de l'Égypte*, (Cairo, 1900-)
Assmann, *Ägyptische Hymnen*	Jan Assmann, *Ägyptische Hymnen und Gebete*, (Die Bibliothek der Alten Welt, Reihe der Alten Orient) Zurich, München, 1975.
Assmann, *Zeit und Erwigkeit*	Jan Assmann, *Zeit und Ewigkeit im alten Agypten: ein Beitrag zur Geschichte der Ewigkeit*, Heidelberg, 1975.
Bakir	Abd el-Mohsen Bakir, *Egyptian Epistolography from the Eighteenth to the Twenty-first Dynasty.* Cairo, 1970.
BAR	James H. Breasted, *Ancient Records of Egypt*, 5 vols, Chicago, 1900-07.
BdE	*Bibliothèque d'Étude, Institut Français d'Archéologie Orientale*, Cairo

Beit el-Wali	Herbert Ricke, George R. Hughes and Edward F. Wente, *The Beit el-Wali Temple of Ramesses II*, (Oriental Institute Nubian Expedition, Volume 1) Chicago, 1967.
Ber.	Berlin.
BES	*Bulletin of the Egyptological Seminar*, New York, 1979-.
Bib. Or.	*Bibliotheca Orientalis*, Leyden, 1943- .
BIE	*Bulletin de l'Institut d'Égypte,* Cairo, 1920- .
BIFAO	*Bulletin de l'Institut français d'archéologie orientale*, (Cairo, 1901-).
BM	British Museum.
BN	Bibliothèque Nationale.
Borghouts	Joris F. Borghouts, *The Magical Texts of Papyrus Leiden I 348*, Leiden, 1971.
Bremner-Rhind	see P. Bremner-Rhind
Brunner, *Geburt*	Hellmut Brunner, *Die Geburt des Gottkonigs* (Studien zur Überlieferung einen altägyptischen Mythos). (Ägyptologische Abhandlungen Bd. 10) Wiesbaden, 1964.
BSEG	*Bulletin de la Société d'Égyptologie Genève*, Geneve
CAH²	*Cambridge Ancient History*, (2nd & 3rd editions), Cambridge, 1971-77).
Cairo CG	Cairo *Catalogue Général*
Cairo Love Songs	Georges Posener, *Catalogue des ostraca hiératiques littéraires de Deir el Médineh*, II/3 pp. 43-44; pls. 74-79a. Cairo, 1938-52.
Caminos, *LEM*	Ricardo A. Caminos, *Late Egyptian Miscellanies*, (Brown Egyptological Studies) London, 1954.
Caminos, *Lit. Frags.*	Ricardo A. Caminos, *Literary Fragments in the Hieratic Script*, Oxford, 1956.
Caminos, *Tale of Woe*	Ricardo A. Caminos, *A Tale of Woe from a Hieratic Papyrus in the A.S. Pushkin Museum of Fine Arts in Moscow*, Oxford, 1977.
CB 1	Alan H. Gardiner, *The Chester Beatty Papyrus No. 1*: The Library of A. Chester Beatty, London, 1931.
CB 4	see *HPBM* below (3rd series) No. 1.
CdÉ	*Chronique d'Égypte*, Brussels, 1925- .

CDME	Raymond O. Faulkner, *A Concise Dictionary of Middle Egyptian*, Oxford, 1962.
Černý, *Coptic*	Jaroslav Černý, *Coptic Etymological Dictionary*, Cambridge, 1976.
Černý, *O.H.* (1970)	Jaroslav Černý, *Ostraca Hiératiques*, Cairo, 1930-35, 37, 39, 57, 70.
Černý, *Prices*	Jaroslav Černý, "Prices and wages in Egypt in the Ramesside Period," *Cahiers d'histoire mondiale*, Paris 1 (1954) 903-921.
Černý, *Workmen*	Jaroslav Černý, *A Community of Workmen at Thebes in the Ramesside Period*, Cairo, 1973.
CGC	Cairo General Catalogue
Charpentier, *Recueil*	F. Charpentier, *Recueil de materiaux epigraphiques relatifs à la botanique de la Égypte antique*, 1981.
Claessen, *The Early State*	J. M. Claessen, *The Early State*, The Hague, 1978.
Clère	J.J. Clère, "Un mot pour 'mariage' en egyptien de l'époque ramesside," *Rd'É* 20 (1968) 171-175.
Crevatin	F. Crevatin in *Incontri Linguistici* 9, 189-190.
Crum	Walter E. Crum, *A Coptic Dictionary*, Oxford, 1939.
CS	Jaroslav Černý, "Papyrus Salt 124 (British Museum 10053)," *Journal of Egyptian Archaeology*, 15 (1929) 243-258.
Darnell, "Two Notes"	John Darnell, "Two Notes on Marginal Inscriptions at Medinet Habu," in B. Bryan & D. Lorton eds. *Essays in Egyptology in Honor of Hans Goedicke*, San Antonio, 1994, 35-55.
Davies, *Deir el Gebrawi*	N. de Garis Davies, *The Rock Tombs of Deir el Gebrawi*, London, 1902.
DE	*Discussions in Egyptology*, Oxford, 1985-.
DFIFAO	*Documents du fouilles de l'Institut français d'archéologie orientale*, Cairo, 1938- .
Dem. Gloss	W. Erichsen *Demotisches Glossar*, Kopenhagen, 1954.
DLE	L. H. Lesko and B. S. Lesko, *A Dictionary of Late Egyptian*, Berkeley and Providence, 1982- .
DM	Deir el-Medineh
E-W	Wm. F. Edgerton and John A. Wilson, *Historical Records of Ramses III*: The Texts in *Medinet Habu Volumes I and II*, (Studies in Ancient Oriental Civilization, No. 12), Chicago, 1936.

Eg. Hier. Texts	Alan H. Gardiner, *Egyptian Hieratic Texts*, Series 1, Literary Texts of the New Kingdom, Leipzig, 1911.
Eretz Israel	*Eretz Israel*, Hebrew University, Jerusalem (1951-)
Erman, *N.A. Gram.*	Adolph Erman, *Neuägyptische Grammatik*, 2. Aufl., Leipzig, 1933.
Essays...Goedicke	*Essays in Egyptology in honor of Hans Goedicke*, ed. by Betsy Bryan & David Lorton, San Antonio, 1994.
Essays...Kantor	*Essays in Ancient Civilization Presented to Helene J. Kantor*, SAOC 47, Chicago, 1989.
Fairman Festschrift	*Glimpses of ancient Egypt: Studies in honor of H.W. Fairman*, ed. by John Ruffle, G.A. Gaballa, & Kenneth A. Kitchen, Warminster, 1979.
Festgabe...Derchain	*Religion und Philosophie im alten Ägypten; Festgabe für Philippe Derchain zu seinem 65. Geburtstag am 24. Juli 1991*, ed. by Ursula Verhoeven und Erhart Graefe, Leuven, 1991.
Festschrift...Fecht	*Beiträge zur Literatur, Sprache und Kunst des alten Ägypten; Festschrift für Gerhard Fecht zum 65. Geburtstag am Februar 1987*, ed. by Jürgen Osing und Gunter Dreyer, Wiesbaden, 1987.
Fischer, *Varia*	Henry George Fischer, *Varia* (MMA Egyptian Studies 1), New York, 1976.
Flor	Florence.
Fox	Michael V. Fox, *The Song of Songs and the Ancient Egyptian Love Songs*, Madison, University of Wisconsin Press, 1985.
Frandsen	Paul Frandsen, "Divine Kingship and Grammar," *Akten des Vierten Internationalem Ägyptologen Kongressen München*, (1985) 151-155.
Gard	Alan H. Gardiner.
Gard. *AEO*	Alan H. Gardiner, *Ancient Egyptian Onomastica*, 3 vols., Oxford, 1947.
Gard. Anas.	Alan H. Gardiner, *Egyptian Hieratic Texts*, Series 1, Literary Texts of the New Kingdom, Part 1, The Papyrus Anastasi I and the Papyrus Koller, Leipzig, 1911.
Gardiner, *Admonitions*	A.H. Gardiner, *The Admonitions of an Egyptian Sage from a Heiratic Papyrus in Leiden*, Leipzig, 1909.
Gardiner *Vizier*	Alan H. Gardiner, "The Installation of a Vizier," *Rec. de Trav.* 26, 1-19.

Gardiner & Sethe	*Egyptian Letters to the Dead: mainly from the Old & Middle Kingdom*, copied, translated, & edited by Alan H. Gardiner & Kurt Sethe, Oxford, 1975.
Gedenkschrift…Behrens	*Ägypten im Afro-Orientalischen Kontext Gedenkschrift Peter Behrens*, ed. by Daniela Mendol und Ulrike Claudi, Köln, 1991.
Giornale	Giuseppe Botti e T. Eric Peet, *Il giornale della necropoli di Tebe*, (I papiro ieratici del Museo di Torino) Torino, 1928.
Gleanings	*Gleanings from Deir el-Medina*, ed. by R.J. Demarée and Jac. J. Janssen, Leiden, 1982.
Gloss. Gol.	Golénischeff "Onomasticon of Amenope" in Gard. *AEO*
GM	*Göttinger Miszellen*. Beiträge zur ägyptologischen Diskussion, Göttingen, 1972.
G*NS*	Alan H. Gardiner, *Notes on the Story of Sinuhe*, Paris, 1916.
Goyon	Jean-Claude Goyon, *Confirmation du Pouvoir Royal au Nouvel An*, [Brooklyn Museum 47.218-50] (Text: Bibliothèque d'Étude III. Cairo, 1972; Plates: Wilbour Monographs VII, Brooklyn Museum), 1974.
Grandet	Pierre Grandet, *Le Papyrus Harris I.* (IFAO Bibliothéque d'Étude 109 & 129, Cairo, 1994-99).
Grdseloff, *Les Debuts*	B. Grdseloff, *Les Débuts du culte de Rechef en Égypte*, Cairo, 1941.
Groll. *Eg. Studies*	*Egyptological Studies*, ed. by Sarah Israelit-Groll (Scripta Hierosolymitana, XXVIII), Jerusalem, 1982.
H 1	W. Erichsen, *Papyrus Harris I*, [Bibliotheca Aegyptiaca V (Bruxelles, 1933)].
Harari	in *The Archaeology, Geography and History of the Egyptian Delta in Pharaonic Times: proceedings of Colloquium*, Oxford, 1988.
Haring	B. Haring, *Divine Households: Administrative and Economic Aspects of the New Kingdom Royal Memorial Temples in Western Thebes*, Leiden, 1997.
Harris, *Minerals*	John R. Harris, *Lexicographical Studies in Ancient Egyptian Minerals*, Berlin, 1961 = (Deutsche Akademie der Wissenschaften zu Berlin, Institut für Orientforschung, Veröff. Nr. 54).
Hierat. Pap.	*Hieratische Papyrus der Königlicher Museum zu Berlin*, Leipzig, 1911.
Helck *Bez*	Wolfgang Helck, *Die Beziehungen Ägyptens zu Vorderasien im 3. und 2. Jahrtausend v. Chr.*, (Ägyptologische Abhandlungen 5) Wiesbaden, 1962.

Helck *Bier*	Wolfgang Helck, *Das Bier im Alten Ägypten*, Berlin, 1971.
Helck *Mat*	Wolfgang Helck, *Materialien zur Wirtschafts-geschichte des Neuen Reiches* Teil 1-6 Wiesbaden, 1961-69 = Akademischer Wissenschaften und der Literatur in Mainz, Abh. der Geistes und sozialwiss. Klasse 1 Jhrg. 1960-69 + Inge Hofmann, *Indices* Wiesbaden 1970 (=Abh. 1969, Nr. 13).
Helck, *Verwaltung*	Wolfgang Helck, *Zur Verwaltung des Mittleren und Neuen Reichs*, Leiden, 1958.
H.I. Tut	Jaroslav Černý, *Hieratic Inscriptions from the Tomb of Tutʿankhamūn*, (Tutʿankhamūn Tomb Series) Oxford, 1965.
H.O.	Jaroslav Černý and Alan H. Gardiner, *Hieratic Ostraca I* (London, 1957).
Hoch	James E. Hoch, *Semitic Words in Egyptian Texts of the New Kingdom & Third Intermediate Period*, Princeton, 1994.
Hoffmeier, *Sacred*	James Karl Hoffmeier, *Sacred in the Vocabulary of Ancient Egypt: the term ḎSR, with special reference to Dynasties I-XX*, Freiburg, 1985.
Hommages…Daumas	*Hommages à François Daumas*, Montpellier, 1986.
Horemhab	The Decree of Horemhab, see *Urk.* 4, 2140-62.
Hornung, *Amduat*	Erik Hornung, *Das Amduat, Die Schrift des verborgenen Raumes*, Teil I, II, (Ägyptologische Abhandlungen, Band 7) Wiesbaden, 1963.
Hornung, "*Ewigkeitsbegriff*"	Erik Hornung, "Zum ägyptischen Ewigkeitsbegriff", Forschungen und Fortschritte, Berlin (1965) 334-336.
HPBM	British Museum. *Hieratic Papyri* . . . Third Series Chester Beatty Gift, 1 = Text; II = Plates; Edited . . . by Alan H. Gardiner (London, 1935); Fourth Series, *Oracular amuletic decrees of the late New Kingdom.* I = Text; II = Plates; Edited … by I.E.S. Edwards (London, 1960).
Inscribed…Abydos	William Kelly Simpson, *Inscribed material from the Pennsylvania-Yale excavations at Abydos*, New Haven, 1995.
Jacquet-Gordon, *Noms*	Helen Jacquet-Gordon, *Les noms des domaines funéraires sous l'ancien empire égyptien.* Cairo, 1962.
Janssen	Jac. J. Janssen, *Commodity Prices from the Ramessid Period*, Leiden, 1975.
Janssen, *LRL&C*	Jac. J. Janssen, *Late Ramesside Letters and Communications* (*HPBM*^{6}) London, 1991

Janssen, *Ship's Logs*	Jac. J. Janssen, *Two Ancient Egyptian Ship's Logs*, (Oudheidkundige Mededelingen, "Supplement" to XLII [Leiden, 1961]).
Janssen Supp. OMRO	see preceding entry.
JAOS	*Journal of American Oriental Society*, New Haven, 1943/49- .
JARCE	*Journal of the American Research Center in Egypt*, Boston/New York, 1962- .
JEA	*Journal of Egyptian Archaeology*, London, 1914- .
JEOL	*Jaarbericht Ex Oriente Lux*, Leiden, 1938-.
Jequier, *Frises*	Gustave Jéquier, *Les frises d'objects des sarcophages du moyen empire*, Mémoires publies par les membres de l'Institut français d'archéologie orientale du Caire 47, Cairo, 1921.
JESHO	*Journal of The Economic and Social History of the Orient*, Leiden, [1958]-.
JNES	*Journal of Near Eastern Studies*, Chicago, 1942- .
D. Jones, *Glossary...*	Dilwyn Jones, *A Glossary of Ancient Egyptian Nautical Titles and Terms,* New York, 1988.
JSSEA	*The Journal of the Society for the Study of Egyptian Antiquities*, Toronto, 1970- .
J-W	Karl Jansen-Winkeln *Ägyptische Biographien der 22. und 23. Dynastie* (Ägypten und Alten Testament, 8), Wiesbaden, 1985.
Keimer, *Gartenpflanzen*	Ludwig Keimer, *Die Gartenpflanzen im Alten Ägypten*. Ägyptologische Studien. Mit einem Geleitwort von Georg Schweinfurth, Hamburg, 1924.
Kemi	*Kêmi: Revue de Philologie et d'archéologie égyptienne et coptes*, Paris, 1928- .
Khonsu	University of Chicago, Oriental Institute, Epigraphic Survey, *The Temple of Khonsu*, 2 vols. (OIP 100 & 103) Chicago, 1979 & 1981.
K*RI*	Kenneth A. Kitchen, *Ramesside Inscriptions: Historical and Biographical*, Oxford, 1970- .
K*RI T&A*	Kenneth A. Kitchen, *Ramesside Inscriptions Translated and Annotated*, Oxford, 1993- .
Kruchten, *Decret*	Jean-Marie Kruchten, *Le décret d'Horemheb: traduction, commentaire épigraphique, philologique et institutionnel*, Bruxelles, 1981.

Kush	*Kush: Journal of the Sudan Antiquities Service, Khartoum*, 1953-1968.
L	London.
LAE	William Kelly Simpson, *The Literature of Ancient Egypt*, New Haven, 1972.
Lange *Amenemope*	Hans Ostenfeldt Lange, *Das Weisheitsbuch des Amenemope aus dem papyrus 10.474 des BM*, København, 1925.
Lefebvre *Parties du Corps*	Gustave Lefebvre, *Tableau des parties du corps humain mentionnées par les Égyptiens*, La Caire, 1952.
LEM	Alan H. Gardiner, *Late Egyptian Miscellanies*, (Bibliotheca Aegyptiaca VII), Bruxelles, 1937.
LES	Alan H. Gardiner, *Late-Egyptian Stories*, (Bibliotheca Aegyptiaca I), Bruxelles, 1932.
Lex. der Äg.	*Lexikon der Ägyptologie*, Edited by Wolfgang Helck and Eberhard Otto, 7 vols., Wiesbaden, 1975-92.
Lichtheim	Miriam Lichtheim, *Ancient Egyptian Literature: A Book of Readings* Vol. II: The New Kingdom, Berkeley & Los Angeles, 1976.
Lichtheim, *Moral Values*	Miriam Lichtheim, *Moral Values in Ancient Egypt*, Fribourg, 1997.
Lingua Aegyptia	*Lingua Aegyptia: Journal of Egyptian Language Studies*, Göttingen.
Livre du Centenaire	*Livre du Centenaire*, Cairo, 1980.
Louvre Leather Roll	see K*RI* 2,794,5
LRL	Jaroslav Černý, *Late Ramesside Letters*, (Bibliotheca Aegyptiaca IX [Bruxelles, 1939]).
Lucas-Harris	Alfred Lucas, *Ancient Egyptian Materials and Industries*, 4th ed. (rev. by J. R. Harris), London, 1962.
Marciniak, *DB*	Marek Marciniak, *Les Inscriptions Hiératiques du Temple de Thoutmosis III*, Warsaw, 1974.
Mariette, *Karnak*	Auguste Mariette, *Karnak: Étude topographique et archéologique…*, Leipzig, 1875.
MÄS	*Münchener Ägyptologische Studien*, Berlin.
Max d'Ani	see Papyrus Boulaq IV below.
Mayer A and B	T. Eric Peet, *The Mayer Papyri A and B*, London, 1920.

McDowell	A.E. McDowell, *Hieratic Ostraca in the Hunterian Museum Glasgow*, Oxford, 1993.
MDAIK	*Mitteilungen des Deutschen Archaeologischen Instituts Abteilung Kairo*, 1930-.
Med. Habu	Medinet Habu
Meeks	Demitri Meeks, *Année Lexicographique*, Paris, 1977- .
Megally, *Recherches*	Mounir Megally, *Recherches sur l'économie, l'administration et la comptabilité égyptiennes à la XVIIIe dynastie : d'après le papyrus E. 3226 du Louvre*, Cairo, 1977.
Mélanges	*Mélanges Maspero 1. Orient ancien*, 4 fascicules, Le Caire, 1934-61.
Mélanges...Mokhtar	*Mélanges Gamal Eddin Mokhtar*, 2 vols., Cairo, 1985.
Mes	Alan H. Gardiner, *The Inscription of Mes*, (Untersuchungen zur Geschichte und Altertumskunde Ägypten IV 3 [Leipzig, 1905]).
MH	University of Chicago, Oriental Institute, Epigraphic Survey, *Medinet Habu VIII*, (Oriental Institute Publication XCIV) Chicago, 1970.
MIFAO	*Mémoires publiés par les Membres de l'Institut Français d'Archéologie Orientale du Caire*, Cairo, 1902- .
Mich	Hans Goedicke and Edward F. Wente, *Ostraka Michaelides*, Wiesbaden, 1962.
Morenz, *Schicksals* ASAW	S. Morenz and D. Müller, *Untersuchungen zur Rolle des Schicksals in der ägyptischen Religion* (ASAW 52,1), Berlin, 1960.
Montet, *Scenes*	Pierre Montet, *Les scenes de la vie privee dans les tombeaux égyptiens de l'ancien empire*, New York, 1925.
Naun	Jaroslav Černý, "The Will of Naunakhte and the related documents," *Journal of Egyptian Archaeology*, XXXI (1945) 29ff.
O	Ostracon
O. Ash.	Ostracon Ashmolean
O. Ber.	Ostracon Berlin
OC	Ostracon Chicago
O. Edinb.	Ostracon Edinburgh
O. Flor	Ostracon Florence
O. Gard.	Ostracon Gardiner

O.H.	Georges Posener, *Catalogue des Ostraca hiératiques littéraires de Deir el Médineh*, Cairo, 1938-51.
O. IFAO	Ostracon, Institut français d'archéologie orientale
OLZ	*Orientalistische Literaturzeitung*, Berlin/Leipzig, 1898- .
OM	*Oudheidkundige Mededelingen*, Rijksmuseum van Oudheden, Leiden.
On. Am.	Onomasticon of Amenope, see Gard. *AEQ*
Onom.	Alan H. Gardiner, *Ancient Egyptian Onomastica*, 3 vols., Oxford, 1947.
O. OI	Onomasticon Oriental Institute, Chicago.
Orbis bibl. et orientalis	Orbis biblicus et orientalis
Oriens Ant.	*Oriens Antiquus*, Rome, 1962-.
Orientalia	*Orientalia*, Rome, 1932-.
Osing, *Nominalbildung*	Jurgen Osing, *Die Nominalbildung des Ägyptischen*, Mainz/Rhein, 1976
O. U. Col	Ostracon University College London
P	Papyrus
P. Boulaq IV	Auguste Mariette, *Les Pap. de Boulaq* I, Paris, 1871; Emile Suys, *La Sagesse d'Ani*, (Analecta Orientalia 11) Rome, 1935.
P. Boulaq XIII	Auguste Mariette, *Les Pap. de Boulaq* II, Paris, 1876.
P. Bremner-Rhind	R.O. Faulkner, "The Bremner-Rhind Papyrus," *Journal of Egyptian Archaeology* 1936-8: Vol. 22,[121]-140; Vol. 23,[10]-16, 166-185; Vol. 24, 41-52.
P. Brooklyn 47.218.50	see Goyon above
P. Geneva MAH	Papyrus Genève (Musée d'art et d'histoire) 15274
P.H. 500	W. Max Müller, *Die Liebespoesie der Alten Ägypter*, Liepzig, 1899.
P. Harris I	BM 9999, see *H* 1 & Grandet
P.I.H.	K. Piehl, *Inscriptions hiéroglyphiques recueilles en Europe et Égypt*, Liepzig & Stockholm, 1886-1903.
P. Jumilhac	Jacques Vandier, *Le Papyrus Jumilhac*, Paris, 1961.
P. Lansing	BM 9994, see *LEM*

P. Lee	Hans Goedicke, "Was Magic Used in the Harem Conspiracy against Ramesses III?" *Journal of Egyptian Archaeology* Vol. 49, 1963.
P. Leiden 1,348	See Borghouts
P. Leiden 1,350	See Janssen, *Ship's Logs*.
P. Leopold 2	J. Capart and Alan H. Gardiner, *Le Papyrus Leopold II aux Musee royaux d'art et d'histoire de Bruxelles et le Papyrus Amherst a la Pierpont Morgan library de New York*, New York, 1939.
P. Lythgoe	Metropolitan Museum of Art, NY, 09.130.535
P. Mag. Brooklyn	S. Sauneron, *Le papyrus magique illustré de Brooklyn, Brooklyn Museum 47.218.156*, Brooklyn, 1970.
P. Mallet	Louvre E 11006
P. Onom. Golenischeff	See Gard. *AEO*
P. Ram	Papyrus Ramesseum; see Gardiner, *The Ramesseum Papyri*, Oxford, 1955.
P. Rollin	Hans Goedicke, "Was Magic Used in the Harem Conspiracy against Ramesses III?" *Journal of Egyptian Archaeology* Vol. 49, 1963.
P. Turin 1907+1908	Jac. J. Janssen "A Twentieth Dynasty Account Papyrus," *Journal of Egyptian Archaeology*, Vol. 52, 1966.
P. Turin 2008+2016	See Janssen, *Ship's Logs*.
P. Valençay	See Gardiner, *RAD*
Parker, *Calendars*	Richard A. Parker, *The Calendars of Ancient Egypt*, Chicago, 1950.
Parker, *Oracle Pap.*	Richard A. Parker, ed., *A Saite Oracle Papyrus from Thebes in the Brooklyn Museum*, Brown Egyptological Studies 4, Providence, 1962.
Peden	A.J. Peden, *Egyptian Historical Inscriptions of the Twentieth Dynasty*, Jonsered, 1994.
Pestman, *Marriage*	P.W. Pestman, *Marriage and Matrimonial Property in Ancient Egypt*, (Papyrologica Lugduno-Batava No. 9) Leiden, 1961.
PHDM	*Papyrus hiératiques de Deir el Medineh.*
Piankhy	Hans Goedicke, *Pi(ankh)y in Egypt : a study of the Pi(ankh)y Stela*, Baltimore, 1998.
Pleyte-Rossi	W. Pleyte & F. Rossi, *Papyrus de Turin*, Leiden, 1869-76.

Posener, les douanes — "Les douanes de la Méditerranée dans l'Égypte Saïte," *Revue de Philologie, de Littérature et d'Histoire anciennes*, Paris (1947) 117-131.

Posener, *L'enseignement* — Georges Posener, *L'enseignement loyaliste: sagesse égyptienne du Moyen Empire*, Geneva, 1976.

PSBA — *Proceedings of the Society of Biblical Archaeology*. London, 1878-1918.

Push — Papyrus Pushkin 1,6,127 & 128 in the State A.S. Pushkin Museum of Fine Arts in Moscow published by Richardo A. Caminos as *A Tale of Woe*, Oxford, 1977.

Pyr. St. — *Pyramid Studies and Other Essays Presented to I.E.S. Edwards*, (ed. by John Baines et al., (Occasional Publications 7), London: Egypt Exploration Society, 1988.

QC — Queens College

RAD — Alan H. Gardiner, *Ramesside Administrative Documents*, London, 1948.

Rd'É — *Revue d'Égyptologie*, Paris, 1933- .

Redford, *History & Chronology* — Donald B. Redford, *History and Chronology of the Eighteenth Dynasty of Egypt: Seven Studies*, Toronto, 1967.

RIDA — *Revue internationale des droits de l'antiquité*, Brussels, 1954- .

Rocznik Orientalistyczny — *Rocznik Orientalistyczny*, Warsaw, 1914- .

RT — *Recueil de Travaux Relatifs à la Philologie et à l'Archéologie Egyptiennes et Assyriennes*, Paris, 1870- .

S.A. — Shafik Allam, *Hieratische Ostraka und Papyri aus der Ramessidenzeit + Hieratische Ostraka und Papyri* (transcription by J. Černý) (Urkunden zum Rechtsleben im Alten Ägypten, Band 1), Tübingen, 1973.

SAK — *Studien zur Altägyptischen Kultur*, Hamburg.

SAOC — *Studies in Ancient Oriental Civilization*, Chicago.

Sauneron OH — *Catalogue des ostraca hiératiques non-littéraires de Deir el-Médineh*, Kairo 1959.

Sauneron, *Rituel* — S. Sauneron, *Rituel de l'embaumement Pap. Boulaq III Pap.* Louvre 5.158, Cairo, 1952.

Schott, *Denkstein* — Siegfried Schott, *Der Denkstein Sethos' I. für die Kapelle Ramses' I. in Abydos*, Göttingen, 1964.

Schott, *Kanais* — Siegfried Schott, *Kanais, Der Tempel Sethos I. im Wadi Mia*, Göttingen, 1961.

Schreiber	in *Gedenkschrift...Behrens*
Serapis	*Serapis: The American Journal of Egyptology*, Chicago, 1969- .
Sethe, *Dram. Texte*	Kurt Sethe, *Dramatische texte zu altaegyptischen mystereinspielen, herausgegeben und erlautert*, Leipzig, 1928.
Sitz.B	Sitzungsberichte der königlich Preussischen Akademie der Wissenschaften, Berlin, 1918-21.
Spencer, *Egyptian Temple*	Patricia Spencer, *The Egyptian temple: A Lexicographical Study*, London, 1984.
Studien Westendorf	Friedrich Junge, *Studien In Sprache und Religion Ägyptens*, 2 vols., Göttingen, 1984.
Studies in Ancient Egypt, the Aegean and the Sudan	*Studies in Ancient Egypt, the Aegean and the Sudan: essays in honor of Dows Dunham on the occasion of his 90th birthday, June 1, 1980*, ed. by William Kelly Simpson and Whitney M. Davis, Boston, 1981.
Studies...Gordon	*The Bible World: essays in honor of Cyrus H. Gordon*, ed. by Gary Rendsburg, New York, 1980.
Studies ... Griffith	Egypt Exploration Society of London, *Studies Presented to F.Ll. Griffith*, London, 1932.
Studies ... Lichtheim	*Studies in Egyptology Presented to Miriam Lichtheim*, ed. by Sarah Israelit-Groll, Jerusalem, 1990.
Sweeney	Deborah Sweeney, "Intercessary Prayer," *Pharaonic Egypt*, ed. by Sarah Israelit-Groll, Jerusalem, 1995.
Szpakowska	Kasia Maria Szpakowska, *The Perception of Dreams and Nightmares in Ancient Egypt: Old Kingdom to Third Intermediate Period*, UCLA (dissertation), 2000.
T	Turin
TR	Thomas Eric Peet, *The Great Tomb-robberies of the Twentieth Egyptian Dynasty*, 2 volumes, Oxford, 1930.
UC	University College, London
Urk. 4	Kurt Sethe, *Urkunden der 18. Dynastie*, 2. verbesserte Auflage, 4 volumes, Leipzig, 1927-30; Wolfgang Helck, Heft 17-22, Berlin, 1955-58.
VA	*Varia Aegyptiaca*, San Antonio, 1992- .
Valbelle, *Cat. Poids*	D. Valbelle, *Catalogue des poids à inscriptions hiératiques de Deir el-Médineh nos. 5001-5423* (Documents de Fouilles 16), Cairo, 1977.
Valbelle, *Ouvriers*	D. Valbelle, *Les ouvriers de la tombe: Deir el-Medineh a l'epoque Ramesside*, Cairo, 1985.

Village Voices	*Village Voices: proceedings of the Symposium "Texts from Deir el-Medina and their Interpretation,"* ed. by R.J. Demarée & A. Egberts, Leiden, 1991.
Visible Religion	*Visible Religion*, Leiden, 1982-.
Vogelsang, Kommentar	Friedrich Vogelsang, *Kommentar zu den Klagen des Bauern*, (Untersuchungen zur Geschichte und Altertumskunde Ägyptens, Bd. 6) Leipzig, 1913.
Von Deines, *Drogennamen*	H.v.Deines and Hermann Grapow, *Wörterbuch der ägyptischen Drogennamen* (*Grundriss der Medizin der Alten Ägypter*, 6), Berlin, 1959.
Wallert, *Die Palmen*	I. Wallert, *Die Palmen im alten Ägypten* (*MÄS* 1), Berlin, 1962.
Warburton	David Warburton, *State and Economy in Ancient Egypt: Fiscal Vocabulary of the New Kingdom*, Fribourg, 1997.
Wb.	A. Erman und H. Grapow, *Wörterbuch der ägyptischen Sprache*, Leipzig, 1926-53 (5 Bande + Belegstellen).
Wb. med. Texte	H.v.Deines and W. Westendorf, *Wörterbuch der medizinischen Texte,* (*Grundriss der Medizin der Alten Ägypter*, 7), Berlin, 1961.
Wente, *LAE*	Edward F. Wente, Jr., in *The Literature of Ancient Egypt*, edited by William Kelly Simpson, New Haven 1972.
Wente, *Letters*	Edward F. Wente, Jr., *Letters from Ancient Egypt* (Society of Biblical Literary Writings from the Ancient World), Atlanta, 1990.
Wente, *LRL*	Edward F. Wente, Jr., *Late Ramesside Letters*, (Studies in Ancient Oriental Civilization, 33), Chicago, 1966.
Wil	*The Wilbour Papyrus*, Edited by Alan H. Gardiner, Oxford & Brooklyn, 1941-52 (4 volumes).
Wolf, *Bewaffnung*	Walther Wolf, *Die Bewaffnung des altägyptischen Heeres*, Leipzig, 1978 (originally 1926).
WZKM	*Wiener Zeitschrift für die Kunde des Morgenlandes*, Wien
Žabkar	L.V. Žabkar, *Study of the Ba Concept* (SAOC 34), 1968.
Zandee, *Death*	J. Zandee, *Death as an Enemy, According to Ancient Egyptian Conceptions* (Studies in the History of Religions 5), Leiden, 1960.
ZÄS	*Zeitschrift für ägyptische Sprache und Altertumskunde*, Berlin-Leipzig, 1863- .
ZDPV	*Zeitschrift des Deutschen Palästina-Vereins*, Leipzig & Wiesbaden, 1879- .

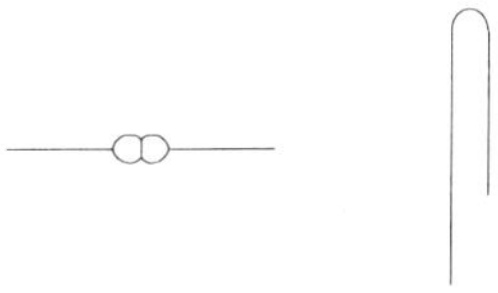

s	**she, her, it, its**	*CB* 1,C1,V1	
s	**man**	*LES* 4,3,1	
		LRL 12R12	
		RAD 10R5	
	s nb **every one**	K*RI* 5,20,4	
	s ꜥꜣ **older person, adult, grownup**	*LES* 1,4,7	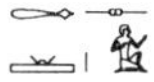
	s iwty ḥꜣty.f	*LEM* 1,3,6	
	s n mšꜥ **soldier**	*MÄS* 6,49	
st	**woman**	K*RI* 5,53,5	
	woman, wife	Push 127,2,7	
st-ḥmt	**woman, marriageable woman, wife**	*LES* 2,9,6	
	female	*LRL* 15V3	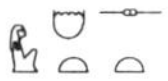
		TR 10052 (Pl.34) 15,8	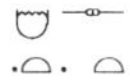
		K*RI* 1,53,1	
		LEM 1,10,1	
	virgin (?)	*Rd'É* 24,156	
	ḥmt-st **maidservant**	*LES* 9,F11	
	st nt ḳnbt **"female member of a judicial council"**	*GM* 100 (1987) 81-84	
st	**place**	*LRL* 9V19	
	throne	K*RI* 2,334,15	
	tomb	*LRL* 28V10	
		TR Abbott (Pl.3) 5,1	
		TR 10052 (Pl.26) 3,1	
		LES 2,17,8	
		K*RI* 5,10,10	
		Wil (1) 2Rx+1	
		K*RI* 2,329,1	

seat	K*RI* 1,111,3	
position	*LES* 5,2,52	
spot (cf. Wente, *Letters* p.218)	*H.O.* 80	
sty **double throne**	*H* 1,42,8	
	LEM 5,4,9	
enclosures	*LEM* 8,9,7	
landed property, properties	*JESHO* 11,158	
office	*Wil* (7) 16R18 P.Leopold II,3,3 *JEA* 22,181	
bureau (cf. Wente, *Letters* p.37)	K*RI* 6,518,16	
size, shape (?)	*Rd'É* 26,170	
tomb, abode	*A* 1,8,5	
sanctuary, "holy of holies" (cf. Wente, *Letters* p.219)	*JEA* 35,70	
mark	K*RI* 5,49,6	
st ib **affection**	K*RI* 3,393,5	
st ir sḫrw **marshalling place**	*LEM* 3,7,5	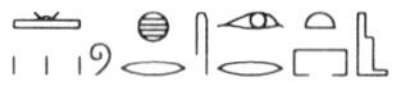
st ꜥḥꜥ **standpoint**	*RAD* 18,4R10	
st wrt **Great Seat**	*Wil* (18) 39R38	
(part of temple)	*TR* 10053 (Pl.21) 4V18	
bark shrine	*JEA* 62,72	
st pr-ꜥꜣ **royal necropolis, tomb of living king** (?)	*JEA* 15,248,24	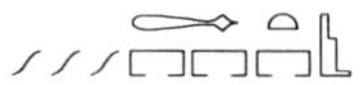
st mꜣꜣ **site, scene**	*A* 1,22,6	
st mꜣꜥt **place of truth, tomb, necropolis**	Černý, *Workmen* p.29ff	
	Černý, p.34	
	Černý, p.37	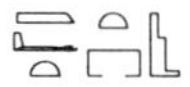
	Černý, p.39	 SIC
st n ḥtp **resting place**	*TR* Abbott (Pl.1) 1,4	
st ḥms **living room**	*TR* 10052 (Pl.30) 8,9	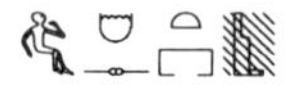
st ḥnkt **parlor**	*LEM* 10,8,6	
st ḥr **authority**	K*RI* 1,30,12	

	sway, supervision	K*RI* 5,97,14
		K*RI* 1,88,15
		K*RI* 2,328,10
	st ḥsyw **place of the praised ones**	*JEA* 65,66
	st smtr **court of examination** (cf. *Studies…Gordon* p.69)	K*RI* 5,351,12 (P.Jud.Turin IV,1)
	st sḏr **bed**	CS 1V2
	st šꜥt **dispatch office**	*Wil* (7) 16R18
		Wil (29) 61R38
	st ḳrs **place of burial**	*TR* Abbott (Pl.2) 3,4
	st ḏrt **business**	*LEM* 2,3,8
sty	**successor, follower** (cf. J-W 6.5.9 p.106; *Wb.* 4,8)	K*RI* 3,176,7
	replacement (cf. Grandet n645, "*stty*")	P.Harris I 42,8
sꜣ	**son**	*LES* 4,6,9
		LRL 33R4
		LES 4,2,1
		K*RI* 5,13,6
		K*RI* 5,7,13
		K*RI* 2,334,14
	boy	*P.Leiden* 1,348,2R9
	son (commoner – son of a god)	*JEA* 48,30
	pupil, son-in-law	*JEA* 66,101f
	sꜣ mr.f **loving son**	CB 4,2V9 *HPBM*^{3} 18
	sꜣ n s **man of good birth**	*JEA* 22,104
	sꜣ nsw **King's son**	*LRL* 28R2
		P.Leiden 1,350,4V4
	Viceroy	K*RI* 1,50,13
		K*RI* 5,29,3
	sꜣ-nḥmw (see *snḥmw* below) **grasshopper**	K*RI* 5,26,63
	sꜣ Rꜥ **Son of Re**	*LES* 4,14,10
	sꜣ ṯꜣy **male-son**	*LES* 1,4,2

s3t	**daughter**	*H* 1,30,4	
		TR 10054 (Pl.7) 2V20	
		TR 10054 (Pl.7) 2V19	
	daughter-in-law	*JEA* 66,101	
	s3t wrt **adopted daughter** (?)	*DE* 4,15-16	
	s3t-nsw	*P.Leiden* 1,350,4V5	
s3	**1/8 arura**	*RAD* 21,B7	
s3	**protection** (cf. *JEA* 16,17 for discussion of the sign)	K*RI* 5,11,11	
		K*RI* 5,67,9	
		K*RI* 5,60,14	
		H 1,26,6	
		K*RI* 5,100,13	
		K*RI* 5,16,13	
		K*RI* 2,99,3	
		HPBM[4] L2,R97	
	protection, safe conduct	*HPBM*[4] L5,V34	
	amulet (cf. Janssen p.310)	*HPBM*[4] T2,V96	
s3	*stp-s3* **royal court**	K*RI* 1,50,12-13	
s3w	**corps**	*LEM* 3,7,7	
	phyle	*LEM* 4,3	
	contingents	*LEM* 10,2,5	
	company (cf. *MÄS* 6,26-29)	*LEM* 13,2V7	
	troop	K*RI* 5,114,13	
	regiment	*JEA* 39,41&45 CB 4,5V8 *HPBM*[3] 20	
s3	**back**		
	m-s3 **after**	*LRL* 28R22	
		K*RI* 2,228,20	
	to	K*RI* 1,55,11	
	about	*LRL* 11V1	

		in pursuit	K*RI* 5,24,8
		pestering	*JEA* 26,159
		afterwards	*CB* 1,G1,V2
	m-s3	**in pursuit**	*LEM* 6,20,5
		to back up (cf. Wente, *Letters* p.35)	*LEM* 5,11,2
		in quest of	*LES* 5,2,4
		behind	*LES* 2,10,6
		tending	*LES* 4,5,10
	m-s3 dw3	**in the near future** (cf. Wente, *Letters* p.116)	K*RI* 1,324,14
	ḥr-s3	**after**	*LES* 2,8,8
		subsequently	*LES* 2,16,8
		hereafter	K*RI* 2,227,4
		following	*LES* 3,2,4
s3		**door** (cf. E-W 82,36B)	K*RI* 5,63,15
		surface (of stone)	CB 4,2V10 *HPBM*[3] 18
		surge, wall (of water)	K*RI* 5,97,16
s3		**to be satisified** (with)	*LRL* 29R6
			H 1,78,11
			HPBM[4] L6,R19
		to be sated (with)	*LEM* 10,8,6
			K*RI* 3,83,11
		to enjoy	K*RI* 1,113,10
			K*RI* 1,99,3-4 (SIC)
		to sate oneself	*A* 1,3,1
s33		**sage, wise**	J-W A9,d,1
s3i3		**evil moments** (?)	*TR* 10052 (Pl.34) 14,8
s3y		**plank, beam** (cf. Janssen p.372-374)	K*RI* 2,326,13-14 *LEM* 9,2V8

		O.Glasgow D1925,70R13
		A 1,14,3
		A 1 (Turin 7)
		Sauneron OH 554,3
s3y	**satisfaction**	K*RI* 5,22,2
s3yt	**enfeebled, broken, bruised**	*A* 1,8,8
		A 1 (O.Louvre 5)
	weak	K*RI* 3,296,8
	weakling	K*RI* 3,336,13
s3w	**to have a care**	*LEM* 11,4,7
		LEM 13,3V6
	to guard	*LRL* 5V3
	to withstand	*TR* Abbott (Pl.3) 6,7
	to protect	*LRL* 14V4
	to preserve	*LRL* 28V10
	to ward off	K*RI* 1,68,4
	to take care	K*RI* 2,87,6
	to beware of	CB 4,5V2 *HPBM*[3] 20
	to tend	*LES* 3,7,5
	to keep (cf. *JEA* 54,19)	K*RI* 2,230,11
	to restrain	*LES* 4,15,12
	to watch	*A* 1,25,4
	beware!	K*RI* 5,653,14
	take heed of me!	K*RI* 1,323,8
s3w	**guarded man, prisoner**	*TR* Amherst (Pl.5) 4,2
s3w	**defender**	*LEM* 2,3,7
	herdsmen (or *mniw*)	*H* 1,29,10
	guard, guardian	P.Turin 2008+2016,2R9
		LRL 30R16
	(cow)**herd**	*P.Leiden* 1,350,4V28
		RAD 15Rx+4

	(record) **keeper**	*LEM* 7,3,13
		BIFAO 73,195,7
		Wil (43) 88V3
s3w	(cf. *s3yt* above) **feeble**	*A* 1,9,3
s3w	**to break**	CS 2R13
	to split	CS 1V9
		K*RI* 5,24,6 (sic)
	to cut off	*Mes* 20-21,56
	to break off	*TR* 10403 (Pl.36) 1,20
	to split	*H.O.* 88,5
	to demolish, to cut up	*Rd'É* 10,66,7m
s3wy	**of his** (cf. *ZÄS* 50,114; *Serapis* 6,59)	*LEM* 1,9,6
		TR 10053 (Pl.19) 1V10
		LRL 28R29
		LRL 37R17
	belonging to him	K*RI* 2,228,7
	property	*HPBM*[4] P2,R35
	his own, of his	*JEA* 13 (Pl.14) 3,11
s3wt	(cf. *s3wy*) **his**	CS 1R4
s3wt	**total wealth, property**	*JEA* 26 (Pl.5) 4
s3wty	**guardian** (cf. Janssen p.48,53,78)	Černý, *Workmen* p.44
	archivist (cf. Grandet Vol. 1 p.97 n38-39; Peden p.191)	K*RI* 5,233,3
s3b	**jackal**	K*RI* 5,89,11
		K*RI* 5,61,6
		A 1,18,5
s3b	**dignitary**	K*RI* 1,17,16
	judge	*MÄS* 6,58-59,154

s3b	**speckled snakes**	*P.Leiden* 1,348,8R8	
s3b	**to flow** (cf. *Wb.* 3,420,3)	K*RI T&A* 1, p.22	
s3b-šwty	**multicolored of plumage** (cf. *Serapis* 6,76)	K*RI* 1,17,16	
	variegated of plumage	K*RI* 5,87,6	
s3p	**to put on, to found, to establish, to build**	J-W A13,i6	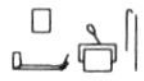
s3mt	**to mourn**	*P.Leiden* 1,348,4R5	
s3r	**to be smart**	J-W A10,d2	
s3r	**wish, desire** (cf. J-W p.604)	J-W B22,B,z4	
s3ryw	(unknown)	*MDAIK* 15,178,10	
s3rt	**wisdom, knowledge**	*A* 1,2,4	
	understanding (cf. Lichtheim, *Moral Values* pp.16-17)	*JEA* 39,16,h	
s3ḥ	**big toe**	*P.Leiden* 1,348,3R1	
s3ḥ	**to occupy** (oneself)	*LES* 9,V,8	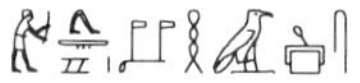
	to move close	*Rd'É* 38,70,n30	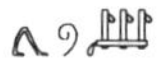
s3ḥ	**neighbor**	*LEM* 10,4,3	
	vicinity	K*RI* 1,112,12	
	neighbor	P.H. 500 (Pl.4) 2,10	
	track	*A* 1,24,2	
	neighbor	*CB* 1,C1,V8-9	
		LEM 8,6,8	
	neighborhood	K*RI* 3,329,8	
s3ḥ	**shrine** (?) (or *sḥ* pavillion ?)	*Melanges…Mokhtar* 2,357,17	
s3ḥw	**knife** (or *sḥ*) (cf. Helck, *Bez* 568,202)	*H.O.* 32,4,4	

	awl	K*RI* 3,541,4
sꜣḫ	**to glorify**	*H* 1,3,1
	to beautify	*LEM* 10,13b,1
	to bless, to beautify	CB 4,6V11 *HPBM*^{3} 20
sꜣḫꜣrꜥꜣ	(see *sḫr* below)	Helck, *Bez* 568,203
sꜣḫw	**praises**	*H* 1,6,10
	recitations	*H* 1,57,1
		K*RI* 1,112,13-14
	performance of service (cf. *LAE* p. 307)	P.H. 500 (Pl.12) 6,9
	praises	*H* 1,2,13
	illumination, transfiguration	*JEA* 65,57-58,a
sꜣsꜣ	**to overthrow**	*Wil* (70) B 23V8
	to turn about, overthrow (cf. E-W 93,45a)	K*RI* 5,71,8
sꜣsꜣrr	(or *ssrr*) (tree) (cf. *Wil* 2, p.32)	*Wil* (44) 90V6
sꜣḳ	**to fit together, to put together**	*H* 1,29,11
	to collect, to assemble (cf. J-W p.604)	J-W A22,A,4
sꜣḳ	**incense roaster**	*TR* 10052 (Pl.28) 4,25
		RT 19,93
		RT 19,93
sꜣḳ	**to protect**	*A* 1,1,5
sꜣḳti	**stone-patcher**	*LRL* 5V15
	"stone patchwork" (cf. Wente, *Letters* p.181)	*TR* 10052 (Pl.28) 4,25
	stone mason (cf. Grandet p.285)	*H* 1,29,11

s3k3k3	(cf. *sksk* below) (cf. Helck, *Bez* 568,205)	*H.O.* 65,2V3	
s3kt	(see *skt* below)	Helck, *Bez* 569,206	
s3g3	(see *sgn* below)	*Wil* (60) B13,V25	
s3g3	(see *sg* below)	Helck, *Bez* 569,207	
s3g3rṯ	(see *sgrṯ* below)	Helck, *Bez* 569,210	
s3t	**pavement, floor, ground**	*JEA* 46 (Pl.13a) 21R4	
		ZÄS 70,110	
	beams (of roof) (cf. *s3y*)	*P.Leiden*_1,348,12V3	
	ground, floor	*JEA* 22,167,17	
		J-W B22,B,4	
	soil, ground	*LEM* 3,6,10	
		LEM 5,8,9	
		K*RI* 1,107,14	
		K*RI* 2,324,14	
		K*RI* 5,70,7	
	dust, ground	K*RI* 2,326,8	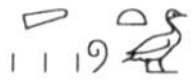
	earth, ground	K*RI* 2,325,15	
	sm3-s3tw **verge**	*LEM* 10,12,1	
	hn-s3t **pavement line**	*H* 1,7,1	
s3t	**to soil, to contaminate, to foul** (cf. J-W p.604)	J-W A4,c,20	
s3ty	(cf. *sti* below) (unknown)	Helck, *Bez* 569,211 *Wb.* 4,334,4	
s3(t)	**to detest** (cf. *Wb.* 4,27)	*JEA* 54,119	
s3drt	**hall**	Helck, *Bez* 569,212	
s3ḏr	**origin, descent** (cf. Helck, *Bez* 569,213)	*H.O.* 14,5R7	

sꜣḏr	(cf. *sḏr* below) **to twist, distort**	Helck, *Bez* 570,214	
siꜣ	**to recognize**	K*RI* 1,46,12	
	to notice	*A* 1 (O.Berlin 8)	
		A 1,10,3	
		A 1,25,5	
	to understand	Push 127,4,2	
	to perceive (cf. McDowell p.27)		
siꜣ	**perception, knowledge, insight, wisdom, shrewd one**	K*RI* 3,288,2	
siꜣt	(see *sꜣ* above) **to become full, oversized, oversatisfied**	*P.Leiden* 1,348,12V7	
siꜥr	**to make a regulation, to give authority** (cf. J-W p.604)	J-W A1,b,10	
siwt	**sheep**	K*RI* 5,54,4	
	mniw siwt **shepherd**	*Wil* (8) 18R21	
sibyn	**shelters, huts, camp** (cf. *isb*) (cf. Hoch p.255)	*ASAE* 42,pl.1,14	
sip	**to inspect, to examine**	*RAD* 23,3R12	
	to test	*A* 1,18,5	
	to control	*JEA* 59,145,8	
sipw	**disappearance, faint**	CB 4,3R12 *HPBM*³ Pl.13	
sipt	**inspection**	*H* 1,25,8	
	"inspecting" (?)	*JEA* 82,103	
	inventory, allotment	*H* 1,37b,3	
	plan, investigation	*H* 1,57,7	
		RAD 25,2R1	
	examination	*TR* Abbott (Pl.3) 6,2	
		TR Ambras (Pl.38) 2,4	
sif	**impure, unclean**	J-W A7,e,2-3	

sin	**to wear**	K*RI* 5,26,6
	to chop	*LEM* 2,7V2
	to crush, obliterate	Push 127,4,12
	to efface	P.Brooklyn 47.218.50 Goyon (Pl.14) 20,11
	to rub out, trample on	*JEA* 23,175
sin	**to wait**	P.Turin 2008+2016,2R23
		P.Turin 2008+2016,3R14
	to wait for	*LEM* 5,5,1
	(cf. McDowell p.7 nt.5)	O.Glasgow D1925.69,5
	to delay	*A* 1,15,6
sint	**clay**	Push 127,1,10
siswt	*mḥ-siswt* **sixth**	*CB* 1,C3,V10
sikr	**to decorate**	*LEM* 5,VC,7
	to enrich, make splendid	K*RI* 1,67,4
	to make excellent	O.Munich 4 *Rd'É* 9,111
sikn	**to destroy**	*JEA* 46,20
sid	**tray**	*LEM* 5,13,11
		LEM 5,17,6-7
	heaps	*H* 1,78,4
sy	**she, her**	
		CB 1,C3,V6
sy	(cf. *sby* below)	*A* 1 (P.Turin 6)
syf	(cf. *syf* below)	K*RI* 5,41,10
syḥ	**excitement, rapture**	*JEA* 49 (Pl.11) 78,84
	madness (cf. *Studies…Gordon* 75)	P.Lee 1,3
sꜥi	**to writhe** (in birth pangs)	*CB* 1B,V32

	to be in travail	K*RI* 5,15,8	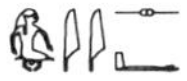
sꜥiw	**thole-boards, gunwales**	*LEM* 5,7,11	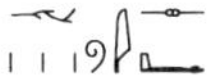
sꜥꜣ	**to enlarge**	*A* 1,1,4 *LEM* 10,1,7	
		K*RI* 5,59,2	
	to magnify	*LEM* 10,14,4	
		H 1,79,8	
	to be rich	*LEM* 10,14,6	
	to aggrandize	*LEM* 6,22,7	
	to celebrate a triumph	K*RI* 2,79,1	
	to cause to be great	*H* 1,42,5	
	to make great	*LEM* 6,9,4	
	to exalt	*Melanges...Mokhtar* 2,350,19	
	to ennoble	*LAE* p.308	
		K*RI* 1,118,7	
	to extol	K*RI* 2,75,3	
sꜥb	**to be equipped**	*H* 1,57,11	
	to be accoutered	CB 4,5V9 *HPBM*³ 20	
	to make preparations	*JEA* 25,128	
sꜥb	(bread, cake) (cf. Janssen p.346)	*LEM* 1,8,10	
		O.BM 5637,V2 *JEA* 12,Pl.37	
		P.Leiden 1,350,2V8	
		P.Leiden 1,350,1V,x+19	
	sꜥb-**cakes**	K*RI* 3,544,10	
sꜥb	**to castrate** (cf. Wente, *Letters* p.169)	*PHDM* pl.26	
sꜥb	**castrated**	*LEM* 5,15,5	
	sawed off	*RAD* 18D1,1V,a	

sꜥbw	**equipment**	*LES* 2,12,1	
sꜥm	**overlaid, inlaid**	*H* 1,45,5	
		JEA 82,108,13	
sꜥm	**to cause to eat**	*H* 1,3,6	
	to swallow	*H* 1,44,9	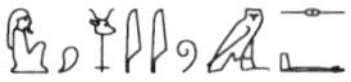
	to wash down food	*Wb.* 4,44,10	
	to drink	J-W A1,b,7-8	
sꜥnḫ	**to cause to live, to support**	*H* 1,31,7	
	to make live	*LEM* 2,9,3	
	to foster	CB 4,2V4 *HPBM*[3] 18	
	to nourish	*JEA* 26,24	
	to sustain, to revive	*LES* 4,14,12	
	to sculpture	K*RI* 5,21,12	
	to bestow life, to perpetuate	*JNES* 22,31,4	
		H 1,4,9	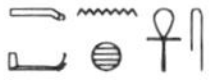
		K*RI* 1,65,9	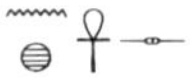
		K*RI* 1,111,15	
	sꜥnḫ t3wy **who causes the Two Lands to live**	K*RI* 1,14,2	
		K*RI* 1,40,11	
sꜥnḫw	**endowment, revenue producing property**	*JEA* 58,263	
sꜥnḫw	(portrait) **sculptor, maker of statues** (cf. *JEA* 23,6,1)	*LEM* 16,10V7	
sꜥr	**thicket** (cf. Helck, *Bez* 567,187)	*LEM* 3,6,9	
	barley field or **scrub country** (cf. Hoch p.255)	*O.H.* 1675 v10	
sꜥr	**to send up, make rise**	*H* 1,27,10	
	to present, to sacrifice	K*RI* 1,49,6	
		K*RI* 2,330,12	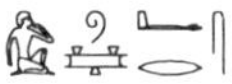
	to send up	K*RI* 2,331,14	

	to cause to ascend, to come near	Push 127,1,14	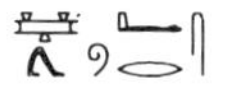
sʿrḳ	**"to bring to completion"** (cf. McDowell p.28,7,f)	O.Glasgow D1925.87,7	
sʿrt	**wool, hair** (cf. Hoch p.256; Helck, *Bez* 568,188)	K*RI* 3,500,2	
sʿḥ	**eternal image**	*ZÄS* 98,132-40	
sʿḥ	**mummy**	*TR* 10054 (Pl.6) 1R1	
		P.H. 500 (Pl.12) 6,4-5	
		P.Leopold 2,2,14	
	mummy, deceased	*TR* Amherst (Pl.5) 2,10	
	deceased, nobility	K*RI* 1,113,8	
	noble	K*RI* 3,176,7	
	rank, dignity	J-W A10,f,2	
sʿḥt	**mummy chamber**	Push 127,2,2	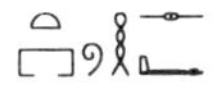
sʿḥʿ	**to raise**	K*RI* 2,231,6	
		K*RI* 2,232,1	
	to establish, to set up	K*RI* 1,107,10	
	to erect	K*RI* 1,43,4	
	to cause to stand, to penalize	*LEM* 13,3V5	
	to erect, to build	*JEA* 37,51,r	
	to accuse, stand against (cf. *ZÄS* 106,19)	*TR* 10052 (Pl.30) 8,22	
	to stand	*TR* 10052 (Pl.31) 10,16	
	to restore	*LES* 4,10,10	
	m sʿḥʿ **in** (a) **restoration**	*JEA* 82,117	
sʿḫ	**to cause to raise**	*H* 1,44,5	
sʿḳ	**to enter, to drive in**	*LES* 7,1,4 *LEM* 9,10V4	
		LRL 5R14 *RAD* 17,2R6	

	to deliver	*TR* 10068 (Pl.12) 5R19	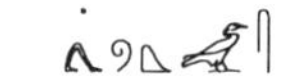
		RAD 17,5R4	
	to introduce	*LEM* 16,7V7	
sʿḳꜣ	**to direct, to test**	*LEM* 3,1,5	
		K*RI* 2,326,14	
	to set (on way)	*JEA* 47,102	
sʿšꜣ	**to repress**	*LEM* 2,3,7	
	to repel	*JEA* 14,282	
	to exclude	*H* 1,57,13	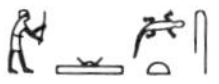
sʿšꜣt	**policeman**	*H* 1,28,8	
		K*RI* 5,12,13	
		K*RI* 3,207,10	
	escort, guard	K*RI* 5,13,10	
sʿšꜣt	**to make abundant**	*H* 1,4,7	
	to increase, to multiply	K*RI* 1,87,10	
		H 1,7,2	
		K*RI* 1,42,8	
		J-W A12,c,8	
sʿšꜣt	**protective rite**	*JEA* 22,134,3,23	
sʿd	**to make hale**	K*RI* 3,492,1	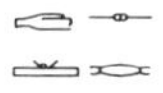
sʿḏꜣ	**to ruin**	K*RI* 5,15,1	
		K*RI* 5,22,5	
		A 1,13,3	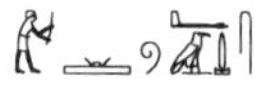
	to do harm, injustice	*A* 1 (P.Turin 2)	
sʿḏꜣ	**wrongdoing**	K*RI* 5,22,14	
	deprived	K*RI* 1,68,4	

sw	(dependent pronoun) **he, him**	*LRL* 4R8	
		K*RI* 2,227,11	
		LES 4,15,8	
		LES 4,5,6	
sw	**neighborhood**	*LEM* 2,1,4	
	vicinity (cf. Wente, *Letters* p.45)	K*RI* 3,31,10	
	region	*RAD* 24,1V5	
	neighborhood	*LEM* 10,9,2	
		LEM 10,12,9	
	region	*RAD* 23,1R4	
sw	**day**	*LRL* 2R5	
		LEM 10,8,10	
		HPBM[4] L1,V47	
	dates	K*RI* 1,49,5	
		K*RI* 1,114,4	
	sw mḏ **week** (cf. *ZÄS* 101,151)	*LEM* 8,4,11	
	decade	*LRL* 16R13	
sw-m-stt	**brush** (?)	*LRL* 36V5	
sw3	**to pass by, to elapse**	*LES* 1,4,11	
		LEM 5,11,3	
		Lange *Amenemope* 18,7	
		CB 1,C3,V10	
	to disappear, to pass away	J-W A22,B,8	
sw3	**to cut off, cut down, to fell** (cf. *Wb.* 3,427,1)	K*RI* 1,54,3	
	to train (cf. Wente, *Letters* p.192)	*LRL* 20,7	
sw3	**loincloth** (cf. Wente, *Letters* p.160)	Sauneron OH 554,3	
		H.O. 69,3	
sw3w	(cf. *sw* above) **site, plot of ground**	K*RI* 1,112,13	

	region	*HPBM*[4] L5,V42
swꜣb	(cf. *swbb* below)	
swꜣt	(unknown)	CB 7,5R8 *HPBM*[3] (Pl.34)
swꜣr	(cf. *swr* below) (chariot part) (cf. *JSSEA* 16,43)	Helck, *Bez* 568,190 *LEM* 5,17,1
swꜣḥ	**to endure**	K*RI* 1,110,9
	to abide	K*RI* 3,283,15
	to enclose	K*RI* 1,114,11
	to become hard, to become durable	J-W A20,b,2-3
swꜣš	**to praise**	K*RI* 5,34,12
		K*RI* 5,51,10
	to respect, to honor	J-W A2,e,2
		H 1,1,3
	to praise, to honor	K*RI* 5,84,8
		K*RI* 1,2,12
		K*RI* 1,10,5
	to extol	*CB* 1,C3,V5
		K*RI* 3,366,10
	to praise	K*RI* 2,285,7
		K*RI* 2,285,3
	to applaud	*H* 1,79,8
	to pay honor to	*H* 1,25,3
		K*RI* 3,284,6
	to glorify	K*RI* 1,48,13
	to invoke (?)	K*RI* 2,90,6
	to extol	*Melanges...Mokhtar* 2,348,3
swꜣḏ	(see *swḏ* below) **to assign, to hand over**	*LEM* 7,2,12

sw3d̠	**to make flourish**	CB 4,5V5 *HPBM*[3] 20	
sw3d̠-wy	**"how fortunate"**	K*RI* 3,405,2	
swʿb	**to make clean**	*H* 1,25,10	
	to purify	K*RI* 1,48,3	
	to purify, consecrate	K*RI* 1,118,5	
	to make pure	*H* 1,30,3	
	consecration (cf. Peden p.191)		
swbb	**to draw back** (cf. Hoch p.256)	*A* 1,23,4	
swbḫ	**to shine, to ilumine, to be iluminated**	K*RI* 1,113,14	
swmstt	**brush**(?) (cf. *sw-m-stt* above)		
swn	(or swnw) **pond**	*LEM* 10,12,7	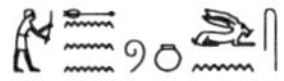
		LEM 10,12,7-8	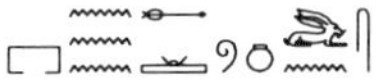
		K*RI* 1,52,2-3	
	fishing pool	K*RI* 1,54,6	
		K*RI* 2,333,7	
swn	(see *swnwn* below) **to flatter**	*LEM* 1,10,5	
swn	**to recognize**	*TR* 10383 (Pl.22) 3,1	
swn	**to buy** (cf. *BIFAO* 27,177,5; 41,130)	*TR* Ambras (Pl.38) 1,3	
	to trade, to sell	*A* 1,25,6	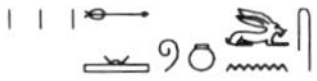
		O.Gard. 165,V12-13 S.A. p. 183	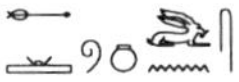
	to convert into (cf.Wente, *Letters* p.114)	K*RI* 1,239,12	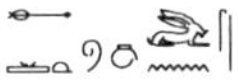
	to purchase	K*RI* 7,184,13	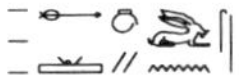
	to pay	K*RI* 3,534,1	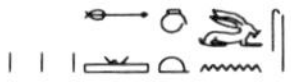

swnw	**physician**	*TR* 10053 (Pl.19) 7R10
		Wil (47) 96V22
		P.H. 500 (Pl.4) 2,11
		P.Leiden 1,350,2V21
		TR 10068 (Pl.15) 4V12
		RAD 18c,5V3
		HPBM[4] L5,V3
swnw	**tower**	K*RI* 2,325,1
swnw	**arrow**	*RAD* 25,1R3
swn(*t*)	**price**	*TR* 10052 (Pl.31) 10,20
		TR 10053 (Pl.21) 5V6
		O.Glasgow D1925,83R4
		RAD 25,1V3
		JEA 26,24,16
		K*RI* 3,658,12
	purchase price	*O.H.* 361,6
swnwn	**to flatter**	*LEM* 12,4V8
	to speak flatteringly of	*LEM* 2,2,3 *LEM* 5,6,8
	to coax	*LRL* 1V6
	to coax, to cajole	*JEA* 42,18,4
	to coax	Push 127,4,6
		A 1 (O.Louvre 6)
swnḫ	**dispute**	*Rd'É* 11,178
swr	**to drink**	*LES* 1,6,13
		LEM 10,5,6
		RAD 25,1R9
		BIFAO 76,19,1-2
swr	**to augment, to multiply** (cf. J-W p.605)	J-W A15,d,5
		J-W A22,A,3 (SIC)

swr	(unknown chariot part) **"trapper"** (horse's skirt) (cf. Hoch p.257) **reins** (cf. Grandet p.286)	*LEM* 5,17,1
swrḥ	**to spread ointment**	K*RI* 5,74,2
	to anoint	*BIFAO* 83,13,4
swrd	**to make to flourish, to perpetuate**	*H* 1,42,6
	to plant	*H* 1,57,6
swh	**to break up**	K*RI* 5,17,9
swh	**to boast, to vaunt,** "**to help**" (cf. *LAE* 91,8)	*LES* 1,8,13
		K*RI* 5,584,1
	to extol, to boast	*A* 1,15,2
		CB 1,C2,V8
		K*RI* 1,39,7
	to roar	K*RI* 5,61,4
	to bellow	K*RI* 5,62,6
		K*RI* 2,75,9
		K*RI* 2,75,8
		K*RI* 5,91,7
		K*RI* 1,102,8-10
	to praise, to boast	K*RI* 2,334,12
	to rage	*JEA* 68,177,36
swḥ	(garment) **shroud** (?) (cf. *JEA* 21,143,12; Janssen p. 290)	*H* 1,14b,2
		BIFAO 83, Boulaq XIII Frag. 17,5
swḥt	**egg**	*LEM* 2,2,7
		K*RI* 5,37,11
		K*RI* 5,59,10
		LEM 8,4,1
	shrine, shroud	*TR* 10052 (Pl.26) 3,5 *TR* 10052 (Pl.25) 1,18
	"**innermost coffin**" (cf. Janssen pp.213-214)	*MÄS* 37,20,4

swsr	**to enrich**	*CB* 1,A1,V3	
	to strengthen	J-W A20,a,6	
swsḫ	**to extend**	K*RI* 5,15,4	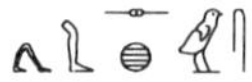
	to widen	*H* 1,22,8	
	to make wide, extensive	*H* 1,49,5	
	to make wide, spacious	K*RI* 1,40,14	
	to stretch wide	K*RI* 5,32,14	
		H 1,78,9	
	to outstretch	K*RI* 5,73,14	
	to extend	K*RI* 1,39,10	
	to enlarge, to widen	K*RI* 1,112,1	
	to extend	K*RI* 1,74,10	
	to widen	K*RI* 1,15,11	
	to stretch out	K*RI* 5,70,2	
swš	**to be twisted**	*P.Leiden* 1,348,4R8	
swgꜣ	**silly**	*LES* 5,2,22	
	fool	*LEM* 9,5V7	
	foolish	*LEM* 12,5V1	
	foolish	*A* 1,9,6	
	stupefied	K*RI* 3,169,7	
swgꜣ	**to inflict**	*Rd'É* 24,156,15,6	
swt	(cf. *sꜣwy* above) **of his, his own**	*LES* 8,3R1	
		CS 1R4	
swt	**wheat**	*LEM* 5,8,10	
		LEM 10,11,4	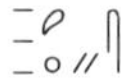
		JEA 27,27	
swt	**reeds**	*LEM* 5,8,12	
	plank (see *iswt* above)	*H.O.* 63,1,II,3	
	wooden plank	O.Glasgow D1925.70,2R3	

swt	**but, however** (cf. *Cd'É* 58,91)	CB 4,2V5 *HPBM*[3] 18
	ḫr-swt **but, if**	K*RI* 1,57,11
	however, nevertheless	K*RI* 1,111,3
swtwt	**to walk about, to stroll, to jaunt over**	*LEM* 3,4,10 *LEM* 5,11,1
		K*RI* 1,47,16
		P.H. 500 (Pl.14) 7,9
	to stroll about, promenade (cf. *Rd'É* 23,156,2) **take a walk**	*LES* 1,7,12
		LES 1,8,7
swtwt	**excursion**	*LEM* 12,3V6
	strolling	*H* 1,8,3
	procession (cf. Wente, *Letters* p.219)	*JEA* 35,70
	st-swtwt	*A* 1,21,8
	promenade, avenue (cf. *GM* 1979,23,8)	*ZÄS* 50,54
swḏ	**to assign**	*LES* 4,16,8
		LRL 28R25 *TR* 10052 (Pl.29) 6,12
	to deliver	*RAD* 17,4R2
		RAD 17,4R8
	to assign, yield	*RAD* 22,2R1
	to hand over, assign, yield	*LEM* 5,7,7 *LEM* 7,2,12
		LRL 12V6
	to hand over	*LEM* 10,8,2 P.Leopold 2,4,1
	to turn over	*ZÄS* 53,21
	to convey, assign to transmit (cf. Grandet nt.456)	*H* 1,25,5
	to hand over	*RAD* 25,1R8
	to assign	K*RI* 5,47,3
	to commit	*ZÄS* 53,11
	to entrust	*LRL* 19V1
	to deliver	*RAD* 17,2R10

	to remit	*BIFAO* 46,119,8
	to transfer, remit	P.Ashmolean 1945.96 S.A. #261
	to bequeath	*JEA* 26,23,5
	to leave, to bequeath	O.Glasgow D1925.77,1
	to restore	*ZÄS* 53,108
swḏ	**bequest**	*JEA* 26,24,11
swḏꜣ	**to keep safe**	*LEM* 11,5,4
		H 1,9,4
	to make sound	*LEM* 10,8,8
		K*RI* 3,492,1
	to keep safe, prosper	*H* 1,44,5
	to save	K*RI* 1,65,8
	to invigorate	K*RI* 5,20,10
	to make prosperous	*H* 1,57,3
swḏꜣ	**to go away**	J-W A10,e,7
swḏꜣ	**to provide**	*LEM* 10,15,5
swḏꜣ-ib	**to greet**	*LEM* 1,2,7
	to inform	*LEM* 10V2
		LEM 10,7,5
	to send greetings	*RAD* 24,1R1
		K*RI* 2,91,2
	to say	*JEA* 16,150
swḏꜣ-ib	**message, communication, greeting**	*LEM* 5,6,10 K*RI* 3,29,11
sb	**joint**	*P.Leiden* 1,350,2V5
sbw	**boards**	*LEM* 9,2V7
		JEA 49,33 (P.Berlin 10463)
	beams, rafters	*JEA* 66,160-61
sbi	**to send**	K*RI* 5,11,3

	to send on one's way	*A* 1,17,3
	to go, to travel	*LES* 10B,R7
	to pass	*LEM* 5,3,3
		P.H. 500 (Pl.12) 6,3
		K*RI* 1,26,10
		H 1,1,2
	to traverse	K*RI* 3,1,13
	to span	K*RI* 3,29,3
	to pass time	K*RI* 1,113,10
	to pass away	K*RI* 2,330,10
	to spend (time)	K*RI* 3,845,10
	to dispatch	*A* 1 (P.Turin 6)
	to surpass	K*RI* 3,346,14
	to be admitted to, **to have access to** (cf. Wente, *Letters* p.219)	*JEA* 35,70
	to vanish, to go	*LEM* 5,12,6 *LEM* 5,12,8
	sb-n-t3 **crumpled to dust**	CB 4,3V3 *HPBM*[3] 19
sb	**load**	*LEM* 10,4,10
	shipload	K*RI* 2,333,8
	cargo	K*RI* 2,332,15
		K*RI* 4,79,15
	set	*LEM* 5,16,10
sb3	**star**	*LEM* 2,6,2
		K*RI* 1,111,9
		K*RI* 2,151,9
		LES 4,15,7
		K*RI* 2,333,11
		K*RI* 5,37,15

sb3	**door, portal**	*LES* 2,5,5	
		LES 2,6,1	
		LEM 9,1V4	
		LEM 1,11,3	
		H 1,45,5	
		K*RI* 1,108,14	
		P.H. 500 (Pl.10) 5,8-9	
	gate	*TR* Abbott (Pl.4) 7,1	
		TR 10383 (Pl.22) 2,3	
		LEM 3,3,3	
		H 1,7,13	
		CS 1R9	
		RAD 18,4R19	
	doorways	K*RI* 2,325,2	
		K*RI* 3,200,7	
	doorframe	K*RI* 1,121,2	
	doors	*JEA* 13,4	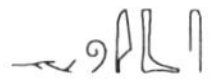
	sb3-ḥry **upper portal**	*LEM* 9,1V4	
sb3	(cf. *sbḳ* below)	*A* 1,1,4	
sb3	**to instruct, to teach** (**to guide, lead**; cf. *JEA* 13,281)	*LEM* 1,3,8 *A* 1,28,1	
		LES 5,2,21	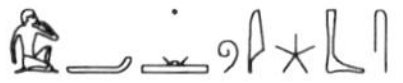
	to tend	*LEM* 10,6,5	
		Melanges...Mokhtar 2,348,3	
		LEM 9,16V2	
		LEM 6,22,7	
	to bring up, to educate	J-W A5,d,8	
	ʿt sb3 **school**	*LRL* 5V5	
		LES 3,5,1	
sb3	**school**	*Melanges . . . Mokhtar* 2,348,4	
sb3w	**teacher**	*A* 1,1,2 (O.Petrie 3)	
	instructor	*LEM* 6,23,6	

sb3yt	**instruction, guidance** (cf. *Rd'É* 9,112;10,62)	*LEM* 8,3,4	
	training	*LEM* 1,3,9-10	
	lesson, teaching	K*RI* 5,62,2	
	education	*LEM* 1,3,7	
	lesson	K*RI* 5,65,5	
	teaching	K*RI* 1,111,6	
	learning	*LES* 5,2,21	
	lore	*A* 1,11,2	
	punishment	*LES* 4,7,12	
		CS 2R17	
		TR Amherst (Pl.5) 4,3	
		TR 10052 (Pl.30) 8,19	
		TR 10052 (Pl.25) 2,16	
		TR 10052 (Pl.32) 12,11	
		P.Lee 1,7	
	chastisement	*Rd'É* 24,156,6	
	penalty	*BIFAO* 83,240	
sb3yt	**book**	CB 4,3V10 *HPBM*^{3} 19	
	book of instruction	CB 4,2V9 *HPBM*^{3} 18	
sbi	**to laugh**	*LES* 6,2x+17	
		LES 4,12,4	
sbi	**joke**	*LRL* 46R5	
	laughing	*LEM* 8,8,11	
	sporting	*LRL* 46R11	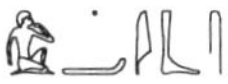
	humor	*LRL* 46R6	
	laughter	*A* 1,1,5	
sbi	**to return** (cf. Hoch p.258)	P.BM 10056,4V3	
		A 1,27,5	

sbi	**rebel, enemy**	K*RI* 5,30,10
	“The Rebel” (=Akhenaten)	K*RI* 3,158,15
	fiend (?)	K*RI* 5,63,13-14
		K*RI* 5,93,15
		K*RI* 1,77,10
	rebellion	K*RI* 5,69,14
		K*RI* 2,87,5
		K*RI* 2,87,1
sbi	**chair, throne** (see *isbt* above)	
sbn	**to diverge, to steer off course**	K*RI* 1,69,7
		K*RI* 1,110,15
	to slacken, relax, yield, waver, stagger	J-W A1,b,10
sbn	**constriction**	*HPBM*[4] T1,V62
sbnbn	**to let down**	J-W A22,b,7
sbr	**twigs, shoots, clusters** (cf. Hoch pp.258-9)	*LEM* 3,2,12
		LEM 10,13a,1
	“strong smelling beer” (cf. Hoch p.259)	*LEM* 5,13,1
sbḥ	(see *sḥb* below) **to gladden**	*LEM* 10,12,6
sbḥ	**leprosy**	*HPBM*[4] L1,R10
		HPBM[4] L2,R49-50
sbḥ	**to cry out**	P.H. 500 (Pl.8) 4,7
	to sob	P.H. 500 (Pl.14) 7,1
	to mourn	P.H. 500 (Pl.12) 6,12
	to low	*LEM* 10,12,9
sbḫt	**portal, door frame** (cf. Janssen p.389)	K*RI* 1,101,7
	porch (?)	*TR* 10053 (Pl.21) 4V12
	pylon-shaped receptacle	CB 2,49,4 *HPBM*[3]
	crypt (?)	K*RI* 3,11,16

	portal, doorway, screen, "wooden or movable screen" (cf. Wente, *Letters* p.52)	*JEA* 66,161
		K*RI* 4,86,12
sbḳ	**to find, discover**	K*RI* 1,111,7-8
sbḳ	**legitimate, legal, lawful** (cf. J-W p.605)	K*RI* 5,21,13
		K*RI* 5,37,12
	precious	*LEM* 10,2,3
		LEM 10,4,10
	excellent	K*RI* 2,80,8
	excellent, clever	*HPBM*[4] L2,R48-49
	splendid	K*RI* 1,10,12
		K*RI* 2,335,14
	fortunate	*LEM* 3,3,11
	felicitous	*A* 1,11,3
	wise	*A* 1,1,4
		K*RI* 2,336,6
	wise	*BIFAO* 45,158,11
	fortunate (cf. Wente, *Letters* p.36)	*RAD* 2,2R3
sbḳ	(cf. *sḳbb* below) **cool places**	*LEM* 10,12,9
sbg	(?)	*LEM* 8,5,10
sbgs	**to injure, cause injury**	*JEA* 52,47
sbty	**wall, rampart**	*LEM* 2,4,8
		H 1,57,12
		H 1,58,5
		A 1,27,8
	fortification	K*RI* 5,32,5
		K*RI* 5,26,11
		K*RI* 5,21,11
		K*RI* 5,18,3
	girdle wall (of temple)	*JEA* 68,131

	rampart	*H* 1,4,2	
		H 1,59,2	
	walled enclosure	*JEA* 68,fig.1,16	
	bulwark	K*RI* 2,91,15	
sbtyw	(cf. *sb* above) **oppressors, burdeners**	Push 127,5,6	
sp	**time**	*LRL* 4R6	
		LES 4,14,7-8	
		H 1,44,4	
		K*RI* 1,58,11	
	case, instance	K*RI* 5,15,2	
	act	K*RI* 3,503,15	
	actions (cf. Wente, *Letters* p.51)	K*RI* 5,564,1	
	event, misdeed, fault	*LEM* 8,7,8	
	deeds, times	K*RI* 1,60,6	
	matters, acts, times	K*RI* 1,126,5	
	occasion	K*RI* 1,90,3	
	times, themes, matter	*A* 1,7,7	
	acts	*LES* 4,3,2	
	wḥm-sp **once again**	*TR* 10054 (Pl.6) 1R7	
	p3-wʿ-sp **just this once**	*TR* 10052 (Pl.34) 14,20	
	n-sp **together, simultaneously**	P.H. 500 (Pl.14) 7,10	
		K*RI* 5,38,8	
	nn-spw **never**	Push 127,3,10	
	rnpt-sp	K*RI* 5,59,1	
sp-sn	(intensifying particle)	*LES* 2,3,9	
		LES 2,8,1	
		LES 4,15,2	
		LRL 2V7	
sp-snw	**duplicity**	K*RI* 3,362,12	
sp-tp	**beginning**	K*RI* 2,285,6	
		A 1,8,2	
	primeval	K*RI* 1,43,3	

spt	**lip**	*LEM* 5,3,3
		H 1,6,11
		CB 1,C1,V3
		HPBM[4] T2,V12
spt	**border, shore, bank**	*LES* 5,1,x+13
		LES 5,2,14
		LES 5,2,62
	beach	K*RI* 5,41,2
	rims	*H* 1,7,1
	base (of a column) (cf. Grandet p.286 n.138)	
	bank, brink (of river)	*A* 1,3,8
	edge (of *ptrỉ*)	*LEM* 5,6,11
spỉ	**to spare**	K*RI* 1,9,8
	to occur	Push 127,3,10
	to live on, continue	Push 127,2,1
	to remain	K*RI* 5,64,15
	to survive	*JARCE* 30,66-67
spyt	**remainder**	*RAD* 19,2
	remnant	*TR* 10053 (Pl.20) 2V17
	remainder	*TR* 10053 (Pl.21) 3V22
	remains	*A* 1,20,3
	remnant, left-over	*LEM* 5,8,4
		H 1,77,4
		TR 10054 (Pl.6) 3R10
		Push 127,5,1
	survivor	K*RI* 5,62,14
	remainder	*JEA* 61,127,30
	reserves (cf. Wente, *Letters* p.116)	K*RI* 1,325,1
spꜣ	(?)	*RAD* 4,1R7
		RAD 7a,2V13
spꜣt	**nome**	K*RI* 5,25,1

	district, quarter	*LEM* 9,5V1
		H 1,8,2
	district	*H* 1,58,7
	quarter	*TR* 10068 (Pl.12) 6R22
	district, nome	K*RI* 1,108,7
		K*RI* 1,50,6
	necropolis area (cf. Darnell, "Two Notes" p.38)	
sp3	**sword, blade**	*MDAIK* 39,257
spp	**exception** (cf. *BIFAO* 41,112)	*MH* 8,14 (Pl.640,4)
	shortcoming	*JEA* 41,93
		P.Turin 139,36 Pleyte-Rossi
spr	**to reach**	*LRL* 1V5
	to petition	CB 4,2V2 *HPBM*[3] 18
	to arrive	*LEM* 3,6,6
		LES 4,3,5
	to fall victim	Push 127,3,10
	to reach	Push 127,4,16
		LRL 3R4
		LRL 18V1
		RAD 24,1R7
	to succeed (cf. Wente, *Letters* p.196)	*LRL* 36V11
	to proceed, approach	*LEM* 3,5,12
	to near	*LEM* 3,5V2
	to continue	K*RI* 3,251,14
spr	**rib**	*HPBM*[4] T2,V33-34
spr	**arrival**	*LES* 5,1,3
		Naun 1,5R9
	visit	K*RI* 3,374,5

sprw-msḥ	**tender** (approacher) **of crocodiles**	*Wil* (39) 81R32
sp(r)t	(?)	*Rd'É* 30,168
		Rd'É 30,170
sp(r)t	**carob beans**	*LEM* 5,14,4
sp(r)ti-r	(part of temple) (?)	*TR* 10383 (Pl.22) 2,3
spr	**report**	*H* 1,42,3
	petitions	*LES* 2,6,6
		CB 1,C3,V6
	appeal, petition	Push 127,1,5
		K*RI* 1,66,12
	appeal	K*RI* 3,464,13
	favors	K*RI* 2,58,11
		K*RI* 2,58,8
	prayer	K*RI* 1,43,9
sprw	**petitioner**	*Rd'É* 11,178
		J-W A21,NR.1,7
sprt	**imprecation**	*HPBM*[4] T2,R88
		HPBM[4] C1,52
spḥ	**to avert, to stop**	Push 127,1,9
spẖr	**to copy, to register** (cf. *Gleanings* p.134-5)	*JEA* 27,20
	to enroll	*A* 1,12,1
	to enregister	*LRL* 5R8
		LRL 5R13
		LEM 10,7,2
	to copy	*JEA* 12,126;23,2,1
		LEM 6,15,7
		LEM 8,6,5
	to copy (cf. *ZÄS* 107,154)	*H.O.* 22,1

	to inscribe	*JEA* 42,10
spẖr	**registration**	*LEM* 8,6,2
sps	**to dominate**	K*RI* 3,300,2
spt	(cf. *špt* below) **judge** (cf. Hoch p.260)	P.Harris A6,17
spd	**sharp**	*A* 1,17,2
	acute, sharply defined	*LEM* 2,4,7
		K*RI* 5,36,10
		K*RI* 5,71,14
		K*RI* 1,16,11
	sharp, clever	*HPBM*[4] P1,R21-22
	sharp, well-prepared	K*RI* 1,80,12
	ready	K*RI* 5,38,15
	in readiness	K*RI* 3,337,10
	sharp	K*RI* 5,59,4
	keen	K*RI* 5,59,9
	spirited, fiery (cf. Grandet p.643)	
	spd-ns **sharpness of tongue, witty**	*JEA* 64,155
	spd-ḥr **keen of wit**	*A* 1,2,6
	alert	K*RI* 1,12,1-2
		K*RI* 1,78,13
	keen	*A* 1 (O.BN 7)
spd	**to equip**	*H* 1,57,8
	to set in order	*H* 1,75,8
	to provide	*HPBM*[4] L2,V23
	to restore to order	*JEA* 19,24,3
	unwavering (?)	*MDAIK* 39,64
	to equip, to prepare	K*RI* 2,333,8
spdw	**grain rations**	*LEM* 10,9,9
	rations	*A* 1,6,4
		H 1,76,9

sf	**flint knife** (cf. *sft* below)	*Rd'É* 33,39-45	
sf	**to mix**	*RAD* 9R1	
sft	**froth**	*LES* 2,8,6	
	resin	*LEM* 5,15,10	
		RAD 15V8	
sf	**to be merciful**	*LES* 5,1,x+15	
sf	**yesterday**	*LEM* 10,5,3	
		LES 2,5,4	
		Push 127,3,14	
	old	Push 127,2,10	
sfy	**child, boy, stripling**	*CB* 1,C4,V1	
		CB 1,B1,V13	
		K*RI* 5,25,15	
	youth	K*RI* 5,41,10	
		K*RI* 5,58,3	
	lad	K*RI* 5,59,7	
		K*RI* 2,327,15	
	child	*H* 1,79,7	
sfn	**kindly, merciful**	K*RI* 2,329,10	
sfr	***sifi*-oil**	K*RI* 3,550,14	
sfr	**dowery** (cf. *JEA* 13,35,18)	*JEA* 54,152	
sfry	**fine linen** (?)	*LEM* 4,4	
		LEM 5,16,5-6	
sfḫ	**to cut up**	*TR* 10053 (Pl.21) 4V21	
	to loosen, disengage	*JEA* 65,179	
	to negotiate	K*RI* 3,252,9	
	to unbind	*LRL* 9R22	
	to let go, to release	*LES* 4,9,2	
		P.H. 500 (Pl.8) 4,5	

	to cast off	K*RI* 3,6,12
	to descend	K*RI* 3,382,10
sfḫ	**blunt**	Janssen 312,4
sfḫy	**guardhouse**	*P.Leiden* 1,350,4V26
	watch	*LEM* 5,20,4
		LEM 5,18,6-7
sfḫw	**thongs** (of sandal) (cf. Janssen p.298)	O.Turin 9781+9801,6
		O.Gard. 162,8
sfḫw	**seven**	*CB* 1,C4,V6
	mḥ-sfḫt **seventh**	*CB* 1,C4,V6
sft	**to slay**	K*RI* 5,62,8
	to slaughter	*CB* 1,17R10
	to slaughter (cf. *JEA* 65,87)	*LES* 2,7,9
	to clear (field) (cf. Wente, *Letters* p.127)	K*RI* 6,66,8
sft	**butcher**	*RAD* 9R1
		TR 10052 (Pl.27) 4,3
		LEM 16,10V4
sft	**knife, sword** (cf. Janssen p.324)	K*RI* 5,53,7
		MDAIK 39,258
		A 1,25,7
		LES 2,7,9
		LES 3,7,5
		LEM 5,17,1
		LEM 5,3,8
sft	(oil) (cf. Grandet nt.852) (juniper-oil cf. Wente, *Letters* p.163)	K*RI* 6,448,15
sft	**place of slaughter**	*CB* 1,16R10

sm	**case**	*LRL* 46R7
sm	**vegetables**	*LEM* 9,15V5
	herbage	K*RI* 2,37,9
		RAD 18,2R4
		Wil (69) B22,V5
		Wil (49) 101V9 [sic]
		K*RI* 1,60,13
		K*RI* 2,37,8
	grass	*LEM* 8,4,8
	herbs (?)	*LEM* 6,21,6
	pasturage	*LRL* 32R3
	vegetables	*LES* 2,1,10
	herbage	*LEM* 8,4,3
		LEM 9,2V6
	herbs, vegetables	*P.Leiden* 1,350,1Vx+20
		RAD 18B,3V12
		Wil (65) B18V2
		Wil (49) 90V18
	plants	*H* 1,7,9
		K*RI* 1,43,7
		K*RI* 1,55,4
	vegetables	K*RI* 1,61,3
		K*RI* 1,56,5
sm	*sm*-**priest**	*LRL* 37V17,44R13
		P.Leiden 1,350,1Vx+9
		Wil (23) 49R41
		TR Abbott (Pl.4) 7,3
		TR Amherst (Pl.5) 4,4 P.Leopold 2,4,5
		TR 10068 (Pl.11) 4,14
	temple administration	S.A. # 277, p. 314,8
smꜣ	**to unite**	K*RI* 1,112,11
		A 1,2,8

	to take part in, receive	Push 127,2,2-3	
		K*RI* 2,32,10	
		K*RI* 2,32,9	
	to join	*A* 1 (O.QC.6)	
		K*RI* 5,26,15	
		K*RI* 1,119,1	
		K*RI* 1,17,14	
smꜣ	**alloy**	*H* 1,6,9	
		LEM 5,16,12	
	combinations	K*RI* 2,25,12	
	six-fold alloy	*H* 1,59,3	
	mix, alloy	*H* 1,47,4	
smꜣ	**temple** (of head)	*P.Leiden* 1,348,3R6	
smꜣ-m-snb	**enjoyment of health**	K*RI* 3,841,12	
smꜣ-sꜣtw	**verge**	*LEM* 10,12,1	
	embankment (?)	*JEA* 11,294,1	
smꜣ-tꜣ	**burial** (cf. *OLZ* 27,190)	CS 1R4	
		CS 1V11	
		CS 1R8	
		CS 1R6	
	interment, being interred	K*RI* 3,832,10	
	burial-priest	*LEM* 10,13b,3	
smꜣy	**companion**	K*RI* 3,137,5	
		HPBM[4] L2,R70	
		HPBM[4] L2,R71	
	confederates	*JEA* 46,69,5	
smꜣyt-n-grḥ	**night party**	CS 1V4	
smꜣw	**joinery** (?), **fittings** (?) (cf. Wente, *Letters* p.180)	*LRL* 5R15	

smꜣw	**cloth**	*JEA* 49,69,g
smꜣw	**sepulcher**	*LES* 9V4
smꜣty	**crossroads**	CB 11,1R9 *HPBM*[3] 64
	road	P.Brooklyn 47.218.5 Goyon (Pl.14) 20,5
smꜣ	**to slay**	*LES* 1,6,14
	to murder	*HPBM*[4] T3,R76
	to slaughter	*LRL* 42V7
		CB 1,B1,V15
	to sacrifice	*H* 1,28,4
		K*RI* 5,9,5-6
		K*RI* 5,10,13
		K*RI* 5,25,1
		K*RI* 5,14,5
		LEM 3,7,2
		K*RI* 5,47,14
		K*RI* 2,52,8
		K*RI* 1,77,2
	to kill, to destroy	K*RI* 1,60,1
smꜣw	**wild bulls**	K*RI* 5,112,16
smꜣ	**statue**	K*RI* 2,326,2
smꜣʿ	**to pray**	*LRL* 3R11
	to offer	*LEM* 10,13b,3
		H 1,48,5
	to present	*H* 1,27,4
	to present, to offer	K*RI* 1,48,12
		LRL 16R7
	to pray	*LES* 2,6,4
	to thrust	*JEA* 59,128,6
	to put in order, direct	K*RI* 1,48,14
	to present	*H* 1,8,11

sm3ʿ ḫrw	**to vindicate**	K*RI* 3,487,13
sm3ʿw	**presentation**	*H* 1,56b,2
	prayer	*CB* 1,C3,V8
	praises	*LEM* 2,10,4
	praises	*HPBM*[4] L1,R20
sm3ʿw	**sounding poles** (?)	*MÄS* 37,20,6
sm3wy	**to renew**	K*RI* 1,1,10
		Wil (4) 11R7
		K*RI* 5,74,10
		BIFAO 28,180,2 K*RI* 1,126,4
		K*RI* 2,326,2
	to make ready (?)	K*RI* 1,43,1
	to restore	*H* 1,29,11
	to renovate, restore	*A* 1,24,6
sm3wy	**restoration**	K*RI* 2,324,27
	renewal	*JNES* 42,44,1
	restoration	*H* 1,59,8
smi	**to complain**	*LRL* 38R6
	to proclaim	*RAD* 10R2
	to report	*LRL* 48R7,30R3
	to appeal	*CB* 1,C3,V6
	to address an oracle	*BIFAO* 75,109
	to denounce	*LEM* 6,13,5
	to charge, to accuse, to bring a plaint against	CS 2R17
	to announce	J-W B22,A19
smiw	**complaint, proposition**	*LES* 2,11,9
		LES 8,2,7
		K*RI* 2,117,4
		RAD 18,4R18

	utterance	CB 9B,13V8 *HPBM*[3] 60
	reputation	*A* 1,12,3
	proposition	*HPBM*[4] L1,V64
	revelation	*LES* 2,16,1
	story	K*RI* 2,326,9
	smiw-n-mdt **complaint**	*LES* 8,1,6
smit	(cf. *smiw* above) **report**	*LRL* 28R23
	charge (*sḫ3* ?)	CS 2R1 *TR* 10053 (Pl.21) 4V9
smi	**cream**	*LEM* 5,15,10
	curd (cf. Von Dienes, *Drogennamen* p.439-40)	*H.O.* 85,2,4 Janssen 353,111
	(cf. Wente, *Letters* p.122)	K*RI* 3,505,16
		RAD 22,1R1
	milk	*RAD* 22,2R2
		RAD 15V5
	cream	*RAD* 22,2R10
smity	**to chasten, to adjust, to chastise**	K*RI* 2,326,14
smꜥr	**to make fortunate, lucky**	J-W A1,b,3-4
smyt	**edge**	*LEM* 16,8V6
	mat	*LES* 6,2,x+18
	desert necropolis	K*RI* 3,455,5
smwn	**assuredly, probably, surely**	K*RI* 1,89,6
		K*RI* 1,110,15
smn	**to remain**	*LRL* 5R11
	to retain (cf. Wente, *Letters* p.180)	
	to stay	*LES* 5,1x+11
	to make definitive, fit	*LEM* 3,4,6
		H 1,3,8
	to establish	K*RI* 5,21,5

	to fasten	K*RI* 2,328,8
	to be steadfast	K*RI* 2,69,3
	to stand firm	K*RI* 5,68,12
	to stand fast	K*RI* 5,114,12
	to station (oneself)	K*RI* 6,521,2
	to fix	Push 127,4,6
	to halt	K*RI* 2,65,1
	to set on record	K*RI* 5,59,2
	to record, to affix	*H* 1,47,8
	to place	*H* 1,22,6
	to erect	K*RI* 2,325,2
		CS 2R6
	to be firmly established, solid	CB 4,3V1 *HPBM*[3] 19
	to stay put	K*RI* 3,464,4
	to hold fast	K*RI* 3,471,3
	to confirm	CS 1R14
	to stop	*LES* 2,11,2
	to set	*LES* 4,8,6
	smn-ib **to take heart**	*A* 1,5,8
	smn-ḥr **to stop at, to halt at** (cf. *JNES* 27,77)	*MDAIK* 14,147-8
smn	**remainder** (cf. Wente, *Letters* p.192)	*LRL* 9V19
smn	**Nile goose**	*LEM* 10,3,5
		K*RI* 1,50,5
		K*RI* 1,91,1
smn	(jewelry or amulet) "**carnelian**"	Janssen p.308 *Mich* V8
smn	(ailment)	*HPBM*[4] T1,V31
smnmn	**to let move, to induce to move**	K*RI* 1,54,2
smnḫ	**to establish**	*H* 1,25,12

	to make perfect, to confirm	CB 4,1V10 *HPBM*[3] 18	
	to embellish	*H* 1,45,6	
	to confirm, to advance	*H* 1,42,4	
	to be perfected	K*RI* 5,34,3	
		K*RI* 1,121,3	
		K*RI* 5,48,3	
		K*RI* 5,47,13	
	to be established	K*RI* 1,113,2	
	to advance, to endow	K*RI* 1,76,1	
	to be embellished	*H* 1,25,12	
	to be endowed	*H* 1,29,8	
smnḫt	**plans**	K*RI* 5,33,10	
		H 1,3,10	
	endowment	*H* 1,5,7	
smntyw	**gold prospectors**	*BIFAO* 84,4	
smr	**to cause pain** (cf. *Wb.* 4,139,9)	*BIFAO* 83,237f Boulaq frag. 10,5	
smr	**companion**	K*RI* 5,33,11	
	friends	K*RI* 5,14,15	SIC
	courtiers	K*RI* 1,50,13	
	royal companions	*JEA* 61,129	
		K*RI* 1,103,1	
		K*RI* 5,28,9	
		K*RI* 5,27,15	
		K*RI* 5,15,6	SIC
smḥ	**left side**	*LES* 4,10,9	
		K*RI* 3,563,9	
	left hand	*Wil* (34) 72R13	
		K*RI* 2,44,12	
		K*RI* 5,64,8	

	left arm	K*RI* 5,16,8
		P.Brooklyn 47.218.50; Goyon (Pl.10) 12,22
		A 1,23,4
	left	*H* 1,4,9
smḥ	(demon)	*P.Leiden* 1,348,2R3
smḫ	**image**	K*RI* 5,27,1
smḫ	**to forget**	*LEM* 5,12,1
		LRL 49R4,1R8
		CB 4,2V7 *HPBM*[3] 18
		CB 4,2V12 *HPBM*[3] 18
	to be fallen	K*RI* 1,113,11
	to forget, to ignore	K*RI* 1,22,5
		K*RI* 2,330,8
		HPBM[4] L1,V54-5
		K*RI* 3,773,7
	to be forgetful	*CB* 1,C4,V7
smḫ-ib	(cf. *sḫmḫ-ib* below) **pleasure**	Berlin P10630 pl.39
sms	**splash** (cf. *JEA* 11,294,6)	*LEM* 10,12,2
sms	**to make, to manufacture**	J-W B20,Z2
sms	**nestling** (cf. *JEA* 11,294,6)	*LEM* 10,12,4
	hatched	K*RI* 2,333,7
smsw	**elder, eldest**	K*RI* 2,327,14
		LES 5,1,1
		K*RI* 1,42,3
		K*RI* 5,39,3
		Černý, *Workmen* 46
	senior	*JEA* 65,180

	smsw-hyt **elder of the doorway**	*JEA* 4,134,7	
	s3-nsw-smsw **heir apparent**	*JEA* 68,121	
smsm	(?)	K*RI* 1,74,14	
smkt	**beam, rafter, girder** (cf. Hoch p.261)	Helck, *Bez* 568,193	
smt	**to scout, to engage in reconnoitering** (cf. Wente, *Letters* p.35)	*LEM* 5,10,11	
smty	**investigator, judge**	*LES* 5,1,14	
smt	**ear**	Push 127,1,14	
smt	(cf. *smyt* above)	O.Glasgow D 1925,77	
smtr	**to attend to**	*LEM* 6,23,1	
	to examine	*RAD* 25,1R13	
		TR Amherst (Pl.5) 3,6	
		TR Abbott (Pl.3) 6,7	
	to investigate (cf. Wente, *Letters* p.125)	K*RI* 4,79,12	
	to give testimony	K*RI* 1,12,6	
		K*RI* 2,116,14	
	to investigate, examine	*LEM* 3,6V5	
		P.Lee 1,5	
		K*RI* 2,116,16	
		RAD 25,1V2	
		TR 10052 (Pl.25) 1,13	
smtr	**inquiry, investigation**	*Rd'É* 7,55	
		O.DM. 126,4 *Orientalia* 45,11,e	
	trial	*TR* Amherst (Pl.5) 3,9	
	investigation	P.Leopold 2,1,3 *JEA* 22 (Pl.12)	

	testimony, examination	*TR* 10053 (Pl.17) 1R6	
		TR Ambras (Pl.38) 2,5	
		TR Abbott (Pl.2) 3,6	
		TR 10054 (Pl.7) 1V2	
		TR 10052 (Pl.26) 3,1	
		TR 10052 (Pl.27) 4,15	
		TR 10052 (Pl.30) 7,14	
smdt	**border**	K*RI* 2,232,3	
		K*RI* 2,232,9	
smdt	**slab** (cf. *GM* 33,25,2)	K*RI* 5,27,4	
smdt	**beads**	*LEM* 1,2,2	
smdt	**service-personnel**	*LRL* 45R12	
	staff, dependents	*LEM* 10,14,1	
	subordinates, subjects	*LEM* 6,10,4	
		LEM 6,26,6	
		H 1,47,9	
	underlings	K*RI* 1,52,4	
	compulsory, labor (cf. Černý, *Workmen* 50)	*RAD* 22,1R8a	
		RAD 22,1R15	
	personnel	K*RI* 2,333,10	SIC
	employment	O.Berlin 12654,V3 S.A. # 15	
		O.Berlin 12654,V5	
	serfs	Černý, *Workmen* 184,3	
	smdt-(n)-bnr (hired hands ?)	Janssen, *Ship's Logs* 23	
sn	**to pass by, surpass, to outstrip**	*LRL* 1R4	
		LRL 17R4	
		LEM 11,5,1	
	to pass	Push 127,3,14	
		TR 10052 (Pl.33) 13,12	

	to swerve	K*RI* 2,42,10
		K*RI* 1,65,8
		LES 1,5,7 *LEM* 6,21,3
		CB 1,C2,V8
	to pass by	*LEM* 3,6,3-4 *CB* 1,17R7
		K*RI* 3,357,5
		LEM 6,19,8
		LRL 24,R3
		LRL 24V2
		LEM 1,5,4
		LRL 23R3
		LRL 7R2
		K*RI* 3,159,6
	to meddle with	*LEM* 5,11,3
sn	**they, their, them**	*LRL* 22R4
		K*RI* 1,126,6
		K*RI* 1,126,6
sn	**brother**	*LRL* 5V17
		LES 2,13,4
		LES 4,8,7
		LES 4,9,7
		TR 10052 (Pl.30) 7,11
	brethren	*Wil* (8) 18R6
		Wil (22) 47R40
		K*RI* 2,104,5
		K*RI* 2,105,2
		K*RI* 2,51,11
		K*RI* 2,51,9
		LEM 6,18,3
	colleague (cf. Wente, *Letters* p.49)	K*RI* 4,88,4

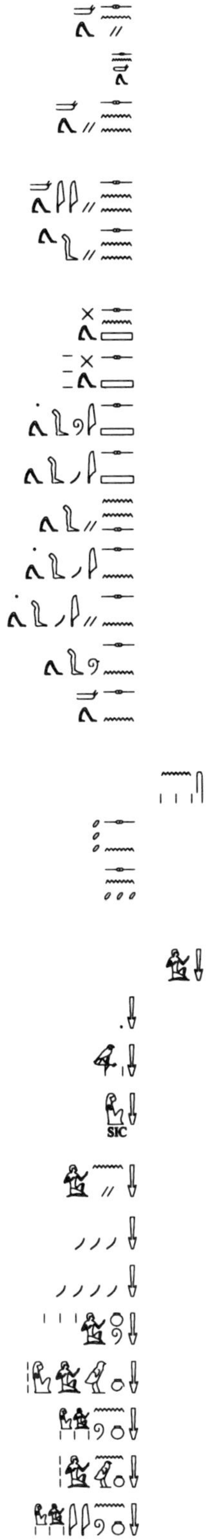

	siblings	*Mes* 11,6
	relatives	*P.Leiden* 1,348,1R6
	brother-in-law	*JEA* 66,104
	nephew	*JEA* 66,106
	brethren	*JEA* 26,23,R6
snt	**sister**	*LRL* 8V2 *CB* 1,C1,V1
		LES 4,9,4
		TR 10052 (Pl.35) 16,13
		TR 10052 (Pl.27) 3,9
		K*RI* 2,285,8
		JEA 26,24 (Pl.5) 12
sn-n-mwt	**maternal uncle**	*LES* 4,4,7
snt-nt-mwt	**aunt**	*P.Leiden* 1,348,3R9
snty	**two-sisters**	*LEM* 2V4
sn	**two**	*LES* 6,1x+1
	m-p3-s-snw **both together**	Černý, *Coptic* 157
		P.DM 39 *Livre du Centenaire* 141
sn-nw	**second**	*LRL* 23R1
		K*RI* 1,21,3
	equal	K*RI* 5,38,4
	peer	*LEM* 3,1,1
	fellow	*LEM* 3,3,5
	equal, like	*LEM* 3,4,6
	neighbor	*H* 1,75,4
	fellow	K*RI* 1,9,5
	companion	K*RI* 2,52,15
	second, brother	K*RI* 1,18,10
	image	Goyon p.54
	mḥ-snwt	*CB* 1,C1,V8

sn-nw	**bad, mean**	*HPBM*^{4} L1,R27	
		HPBM^4 L2,R15	
sny	**two of them**	K*RI* 1,97,14	
sny	(cf. *snn*) **copy**	*Mes* p.22,69	
snt	**interference** (cf. *sn* above)	*HPBM*^{4} L5,V13	
snt	**senet**	*A* 1,11,8	
		K*RI* 3,761,8	
sn	**to kiss**	*CB* 1,C4,V4	
		LES 1,5,13	
	to breathe	K*RI* 3,310,10	
	to touch, to join	Goyon p.114,278	
	sn-t3 **to kiss the earth**	K*RI* 2,285,8	
		K*RI* 5,9,9	
		K*RI* 1,78,13	
		H 1,78,1	
		K*RI* 2,327,13	
		H 1,79,8	
	to bow down, bend down	K*RI* 2,88,11	
	to make obeisance	*JNES* 39,305,a	
		K*RI* 5,25,3	
		K*RI* 5,68,11	
	to pay homage	K*RI* 3,6,15	
sniw	**ring, piece** (unit of value, 1/12 deben)	Černý, *Wages* 910f	
	weight	*JEA* 65,183f	
	piece of silver	Janssen p.102	
sny	**offerings, gifts**	*H* 1,66b,4	
	food offerings	Push 127,2,3	
		K*RI* 3,19,1	
snwy	**basis**	K*RI* 1,123,5	

snw	**flagstaff**	*LEM* 7,6,3
		K*RI* 2,38,1
		K*RI* 2,38,4
		K*RI* 1,123,5
		K*RI* 1,13,9
snw	**receipt, payment**	Janssen 508
		O.DM 1,113,62 S.A. #58
		K*RI* 3,555,9
snwt	(palace) (cf. *Wb.* 4,152)	K*RI* 2,286,13
snt	**foundation** (cf. *snṯ*)	*TR* 10053 (Pl.21) 4V23
	podium	*JEA* 46,46
snty	**testicles**	*HPBM*[3] CB 10,1R9 (Pl.62) 115,2
snb	**to be healthy, well**	*LES* 4,2,11
		LRL 37V8
	to be alive, to be in health	*LEM* 2,4V2
	to be cured (cf. Borghouts p.39,10)	*P.Leiden* 1,348,1R6
	to heal	O.Glasgow D1925,77V8
	to refresh, to greet	K*RI* 3,496,10
snb	**health**	*LES* 5,2,29 *LRL* 10V5
		Push 127,1,6
		K*RI* 5,11,15
		LRL 1R4
	nfr snb.k **fare you well**	*LEM* 1,1,2
		K*RI* 3,490,1
snbꜣ	**to come to, to belong to**	J-W A1,b,12
snf	**blood**	*LEM* 10,4,6
		H 1,77,3

		LES 2,16,9
		K*RI* 5,70,7
	blood-relation	*Rd'É* 38,68,20
snf	**to comfort**	Push 127,3,9-10
	to let breathe, relieve	*JEA* 48,34
snfr	**to rejoin**	K*RI* 1,113,1
	to heal, make well	*Wb* 4,163,1
	to ameliorate, improve	*JEA* 64,157
		Rd'É 20,p.11,14
	acceptability	K*RI* 1,67,10
snm	**to be sad**	O.Borchardt R4 S.A. #19
snm-rnpt	**contagion or pestilence of the year, epidemic**	*GM* 49,81-82
snmḥ	**prayer, supplication**	*LEM* 2,10,4
		H 1,2,13
		Push 127,1,5
		JEA 61,148,11
	petition	K*RI* 5,80,2
		K*RI* 5,68,10
		K*RI* 3,754,9 (SIC)
		K*RI* 3,832,14
snn	(cf. *sn* above) **to kiss**	*LES* 1,5,13
snn	**copy**	*Mes* 22,69
	document, list	*P.Leiden* 1,350,4V4
	guise	*LEM* 8,9,8
	likeness	K*RI* 1,27,5
	image	K*RI* 3,137,9
	likenesses, statues	K*RI* 2,332,6
	document, list, copy	*LEM* 7,6,2

	likeness	*LES* 4,5,5
		K*RI* 1,5,13-14
		K*RI* 1,118,11
	snn-n-sd **tabular document**	*LEM* 7,5,3
snn	**decan star**	K*RI* 5,108,16
snnt	(cf. *snt* above) **senet draughts** (?)	*A* 1,11,8
snnt	(cf. *snṯ* below) **layout**	*LEM* 17,3
snn-tꜣ	(cf. *snṯ*) **founder-of-the-earth**	*Wil* (71)B24V2
snny	**chariot-soldier, warrior** (cf. *MÄS* 6,59-62; *JSSEA* 10 (2)134; Helck *Bez* 568,195), **chariot-soldier, archer** (cf. Hoch p.262-3)	*H* 1,31,8
		K*RI* 2,81,12
		K*RI* 2,33,5
		K*RI* 2,64,4
		LES 1,5,11
		LES 1,6,9
	chariot warrior	K*RI* 5,22,10
		LEM 3,6,3-4
	chariot officer	*A* 1,23,6
		K*RI* 5,40,21
	chariot officer	K*RI* 1,239,8
snny	(cf. *sn* above) **to pass by** (cf. *JEA* 65,87)	CS 2R7
		TR 10052 (Pl.34) 14,24
		A 1,10,4
	to surpass	*LEM* 6,18,4
snrw	(unknown)	*LEM* 11,4,5
snrt	**sudden blindness** (?)	*HPBM*[4] L6,V29
snh	**to collect**	*LEM* 3,6,10
	to acknowledge, to assemble	*LEM* 10,9,10

	to do the registering	*LEM* 7,3,5
	to register, to muster	*LEM* 6,10,4
	(cf. *JEA* 27,75)	*LEM* 8,3,7
	to muster	Černý, *Workmen* 103
	(cf. *JEA* 46,45)	
	to make census	*LEM* 5,4,8
	to inspire	J-W A11,k
snh	**registry**	*LEM* 7,2,11
	revision	*LEM* 7,2,16
snhp	**to promote sexual activity**	*HPBM*[3] 114,1
snhm	(cf. *snh* above) **register**	O.Berlin 12654,R2 S.A. #15
snhs	**to awaken**	K*RI* 2,335,12
		K*RI* 1,48,11
snḥ	**to bind, to fasten**	*A* 1,7,4
		LEM 10,7,3
		LEM 10,7,4
	to bind fast	*LEM* 12,5V8
		K*RI* 1,19,2
snḥm	**locust, grasshopper**	*LEM* 6,16,2
		LEM 8,6,3
		K*RI* 2,19,13
		K*RI* 2,19,14
		K*RI* 1,43,7
		K*RI* 5,13,12
		K*RI* 5,26,6
snḫt	**to strengthen**	K*RI* 1,39,8
sns	**worship, laudation**	*H* 1,3,1
		H 1,2,13
	prayers	*H* 1,3,4

snsn	**to take as a friend, to befriend**	*LEM* 10,2,2	
	to associate with	K*RI* 2,333,15	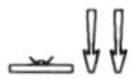
	to fraternize	*LEM* 10,1,3	
	to make friends with	*A* 1,25,4	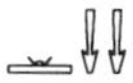
		LEM 10,8,7	
	to join, to associate	K*RI* 1,47,13	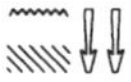
snsn	**brotherhood**	K*RI* 2,227,12	
		K*RI* 2,227,7	
snsn	**close friend**	Push 127,1,2	
snḳ	**to milk feed, suckle** (cf. *JEA* 57,85)	*LRL* 36V6	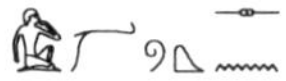
		A 1,4,2	
snk	(or *skn* ?) **to be reserved**	*Rd'É* 7,76	
snk	**darkness**	*P.Leiden* 1,348,5R2	
	obscurity	*BIFAO* 83,154	
sng3	**to spoil** (?)	*P.Leiden* 1,348,3R4	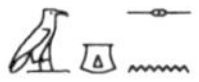
snty	**likeness** (cf. *snn* above)	K*RI* 1,5,13-14	
		K*RI* 1,118,11	
		LES 4,5,5	
	copy	*LEM* 7,6,2	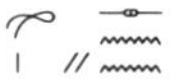
		K*RI* 1,123,12	
snṯ	**to found**	*H* 1,25,12	
	to organize, to be organized	K*RI* 5,24,2	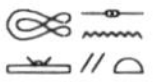
		H 1,48,2	
	to plan out	*JEA* 61,132,56	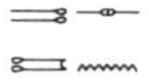
	to settle	*H* 1,76,8	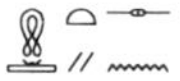
	to copy, to found	*H* 1,44,5	
snṯ	**ground plan**	*LEM* 3,2,1	
	lay out	*LEM* 17,3	

	snṯ-t3 **foundation of an enclosure wall**	*H* 1,58,5
		H 1,77,7
	foundation	*H* 1,57,12
snṯr	**incense** (cf. Janssen 445; *JEA* 23,28)	*LEM* 16,7V5
		H 1,6,2
		K*RI* 5,74,6
		K*RI* 5,93,6
		TR 10052 (Pl.25) 2,4&5
		TR 10052 (Pl.27) 3,26
		LEM 5,15,2
		H 1,7,4
		K*RI* 2,328,9
		K*RI* 1,11,3
		CS 1R10
snḏ	**to be fearful**	*LRL* 29R11
		LES 2,4,5
		LES 4,16,4
		LEM 3,5,4
	to fear	*A* 1,24,2
		K*RI* 1,40,15
	to be afraid	K*RI* 5,24,8
		K*RI* 2,105,12
		LES 2,3,9
	to be timid, deferential	*JSSEA* 8,133
	to be anxious	K*RI* 2,927,5
snḏw	**fear**	K*RI* 5,15,7
		K*RI* 2,13,9
		HPBM[4] L6,R101
		GM 33,23,1
	terrors, bad dreams	K*RI* 2,99,4

snḏt	**fear**	K*RI* 5,49,3
		K*RI* 5,25,12
		K*RI* 2,8,7
		K*RI* 2,13,6
snḏm	**to rest**	K*RI* 5,29,16
	to sit	K*RI* 5,38,11
	to be situated	*H* 1,77,1
	to sit down	*A* 1,4,6
		K*RI* 2,117,14
		K*RI* 2,117,15
		K*RI* 5,66,8
		K*RI* 5,76,4 (SIC)
		K*RI* 5,83,12
		K*RI* 3,382,2
		K*RI* 1,112,1
		K*RI* 5,18,3
	to dwell	K*RI* 5,60,9
snḏm	**to make pleasant**	K*RI* 1,66,13
	easy	*A* 1,10,9
snḏm-ib	**to inform**	*LES* 1,6,7
		LES 7,2,13
	to delight	*LEM* 10,3,1
	to tell good tidings	*CB* 1,B1,V29
	to please	*LEM* 5,3,2
	to rejoice	*A* 1,15,2
sr	**to foretell**	K*RI* 5,47,13
	to promise	K*RI* 5,74,13
		H 1,22,5
		Wil (48) 99V27
	to show	K*RI* 1,68,7
		CB 4,2V6 *HPBM*^{3} 18
	to reveal	*GM* 33,23,9

	to announce	*JEA* 68,135
	to spread abroad, to challenge	*JEA* 21,222,e
	to prophesy	*CB* 1,B1,V30
	to proclaim	*JEA* 68,135
srt	**proclamation**	*JEA* 26,23
sr	**official**	*LRL* 46V1
		LEM 3,3,11
	nobleman	*LEM* 2,9,3
		H 1,28,11
	noble	*HPBM*[4] L1,R46
	magistrates, court	*LRL* 37V10
	highborn	K*RI* 5,21,6
		LES 2,19,4
		K*RI* 5,14,15
		LEM 16,10V3
		Wil (11) 25R11
		Wil (36) 76R40
	princes	*H* 1,7,4
	notables	*TR* Abbott (Pl.3) 5,2
	grandees	*LEM* 5,17,6
sr	**to reach down**	*LEM* 5,2,12
srt	**thorn, spike, pin** Coptic ⲥⲟⲩⲣⲉ	*JEA* 65,95
	thorn prick	*H.O.* 78,3
sri	**cough**	*HPBM*[4] L5,V48
		JEA 87,177 (P.Berlin 3038)
srit	**goose**	*LEM* 5,2,2
		CB 1,17R10
		LEM 10,12,4
		MÄS 37,2,88,3

	srit-ḏriw **fatted goose**	*JEA* 65,87	
	ꜥḏ-srit **goose fat**	*LEM* 5,15,10	
sryt	*ṯ3y sryt* **standard bearer**	*LEM* 1,1V5 K*RI* 3,254,15	
	fan (bearer)	*TR* 10054 (Pl.6) 2**R4**	
	sun shade	*Wil* (9) 20R5	
srwi	**to remove**	*LRL* 9R12	
srwy	(?)	*LEM* 14,1V3	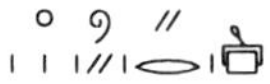
srwd	**recruits**	*ZÄS* 99,131,2 *JEA* 1,27	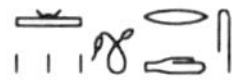
srbt	(unknown)	Helck, *Bez* 568, 196	
		H.O. 23,1R5	
srpt	**leaf, lotus-fan**	*LES* 5,2,45	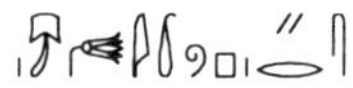
	lotus leaf	Helck, *Bez* 568,197	
		P.H. 500 (Pl.4) 2,7-**8**	
srf	**measure**	*LEM* 9,15V7	
srf	**to spare, to rest**	*LEM* 10,9,9-10	
srf	**breathing space**	*CB* 1,G1,V4	
	relief	*JEA* 59,81,bb	
	rest	*A* 1,17,2	
srf	**inflammation, fever**	*HPBM*[4] L2,V19	
		HPBM[4] T3,R25	
srmt	**sermet-brew** (beverage)	*LEM* 3,3,5	
		LEM 4,5 *LEM* 5,16,4	
	date-brew (cf. Wente, *Letters* p.164)	*H.O.* 56,4	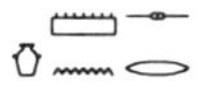
		H.O. 50,2	
	ale (?)	O.Glasgow D1925.66,9	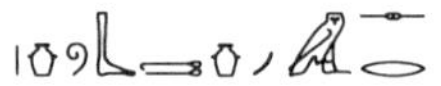

	yeast (?)	*JEA* 87,179	
srḥ3t	**shoot, sprig** **stalks, branches** (cf. Hoch p.263)	Helck, *Bez* 568,198 *H* 1,16b,6	
srẖ	**to strip off**	P.Cairo 58033,47	
srẖ	**palace façade**	K*RI* 3,288,7	
srẖw	**accusations**	*Rd'É* 7,83	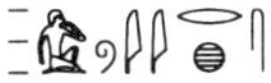
srḳ	**to inhale, to permit to breathe**	*H* 1,44,6	
		A 1,4,1	
	to breathe	Albright, “Notes on Eg.-Sem. Etymology” 2,245	
srḳ	**catfish**	*JEA* 14,30	
srḳw	**snow**	Helck, *Bez* 568,199 *ASAE* 25,187f	
srti	**captive woman** (cf. *JEA* 11,292,16) (cf. Hoch pp.265-266)	*LEM* 10,10,5	
srty	(or *srd*) **to glean**	*LEM* 8,5,1	
		Wb 4,204,17	
srd	**to renew, increase, revive** (?)	*Rd'É* 7,83	
	to cause to grow	*H* 1,29,4	
	to be restored	*H* 1,59,4	
		P.H. 500 (Pl.14) 7,7	
		K*RI* 1,109,16	
	to be refreshed	*A* 1,1,7	
		A 1(O.BN 3)	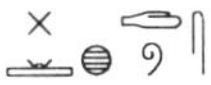
		HPBM^{4} T1,V47	
	to make grow	*Kemi* 2,10	
	to plant	K*RI* 3,298,14	
	to affirm	K*RI* 3,167,6	

srdm	**boughs, leaves** (green product of Persea)	*JEA* 12,202,1 Helck, *Bez* 569,201
srdd	**foliage** (cf. Janssen 431; *ZÄS* 99,131f)	*LES* 9,F13
		P.H. 500 (Pl.4) 2,5
		TR 10068 (Pl.9) 2R6
	shoot, growth	P.Ebers 741
shꜣ	**turmoil**	*LEM* 6,6,3
	confusion, clamoring	K*RI* 1,9,5
	boast	K*RI* 5,584,1
shꜣ	**to bring down, confound, confuse, to deceive**	*H* 1,23,4
		H 1,75,9
		K*RI* 1,9,12
		H.O. 80V21
	to be defrauded, cheated	*TR* 10052 (Pl.30) 8,9
shꜣt	**drummer**	*LEM* 9,4V1
shꜣb	**messenger**	J-W A7,d,11
shr	**to content**	K*RI* 1,58,12
	to bring contentment	K*RI* 3,17,10
	to be content, satisfied	J-W A14,z.2
shr-ib	**to take pleasure**	*LEM* 12,3V7
		K*RI* 1,48,6
		K*RI* 1,126,2
	to pacify	*Rd'É* 20,6
	to propitiate	*HPBM*[4] L1,V31
		HPBM[4] L6,V57
	to bring contentment	K*RI* 4,86,10
shrt	**sehret-stone** (?)	*LEM* 3,5,1

	gum (?), **resin** (?) (cf. Harris, *Minerals* 8,130) (cf. *BIFAO* 83,1-31)	CB 9B,18V8
		HBPM^{3} 61
		K*RI* 2,621,3
		ZÄS 96,7-8
shdt	**to curb, to restrict, to combat**	Push 127,5,1
	punishment	*JEA* 61,152,108
sḥ	**pavilion**	*LES* 4,4,1
	tent (cf. *JSSEA* 7(3)18)	*LES* 4,6,3
		K*RI* 5,52,3
	chapel, sanctuary	*HPBM*^{4} L1,R60
	sḥ-nṯr **divine booth**	*LEM* 9,1V10
	shrine	K*RI* 5,42,11
	sḥiw-nṯr (priest)	J-W p.607
sḥy	**counselor, man of good counsel**	K*RI* 2,150,13
		K*RI* 5,21,8
		K*RI* 5,84,10
sḥw	**counsels, advice**	K*RI* 5,15,2
		K*RI* 5,59,9
		K*RI* 5,68,15
		K*RI* 5,68,8
sḥꜣp	**to conceal, to bury**	K*RI* 5,31,5
	to be hidden	K*RI* 5,69,13
		K*RI* 5,93,11
		K*RI* 1,114,11
	to bury	Push 127,3,11
	to hide	Push 127,5,3
	to shelter	K*RI* 5,32,5
sḥwy	**to gather together**	K*RI* 2,16,12

	to list, to collect	*H* 1,50,4
	to assemble	K*RI* 1,26,13
		H 1,30,6
	to summarize	*H* 1,9,8
		LEM 5,7,1
	to collect	*A* 1,28,5
		K*RI* 5,80,7
	to unite	*H* 1,1,6
		K*RI* 2,16,15
sḥwy	assemblage	*TR* 10054 (Pl.6) 2R16
		LEM 7,6,6
	catalogue	*LEM* 16,10V1
	collection, list, assemblage	*H* 1,31,1
	summary	*H* 1,60,10
sḥwr	to vilify, to reproach	*LES* 3,5,4
	to slander, to heap invective	*LRL* 46R5
sḥwr	curse	*LEM* 1,11,7
	maledictions	Boulaq XIII 9,3 *BIFAO* 83,213-248
	insults, curses	*A* 1,4,8
sḥwr	Delta marshes	P.H. 500 (Pl.4) 2,3
sḥb	to make festive	K*RI* 5,39,2
		H 1,5,6
		K*RI* 1,47,2
	to make holiday	*CB* 1,B1,V2
sḥn	to command	K*RI* 1,66,9
	to order	*A* 1,16,3
	to instruct	Černý, *Workmen* 104
	to authorize	*LEM* 12,3V4
	to regulate	*RAD* 22,2R7
	to organize	K*RI* 5,40,6-7

	to employ	*LEM* 8,5,4
		LEM 7,4,9
	to command	*RAD* 22,2R1
		RAD 22,2R4
		H 1,59,11
	to regulate	K*RI* 5,38,15
	to be busy	*LEM* 10,4,9
	to be in charge	*LEM* 12,2V3
	to require, to command	K*RI* 3,530,5
sḥn	**order**	*LRL* 5V18
	business	*LES* 5,2,11
	commission	*LRL* 28R20
		LRL 47V3-4
		LRL 3R12
	labor	*LRL* 5V4
		LRL 16,9V9
		K*RI* 5,68,15
		K*RI* 1,74,12
		K*RI* 5,40,6-7
	commands	K*RI* 5,60,8
		CB 4,4V3 *HPBM*[3] 19
	assignment, task (cf. *Rd'É* 33,51,v2)	*LEM* 1,4,9 *RAD* 22,1R6
	duties	*RAD* 25,3V9
	task	*LEM* 10V9
	commission	*RAD* 25,1V12
sḥn	**commander**	K*RI* 5,22,7
		H 1,75,10
		K*RI* 1,66,9
		A 1,13,6
		A 1,22,2
	commander, captain	P.H. 500 (Pl.4) 2,6

sḥnw	(part of a building) (cf. *Rd'É* 26,171)	*LRL* 28V4	
sḥnnt	**office**	*LEM* 9,4V5	
sḥnḥn	**to hinder**	K*RI* 5,44,2	
sḥr	**to drive away, avert**	K*RI* 5,19,10	
	to avert, drive away	K*RI* 5,31,10	
		K*RI* 5,42,13-14	
	to remove	*H* 1,22,9	
	to spread, to separate (cf. Grandet n.433)	K*RI* 5,71,6	
	to banish	*CB* 1,C5,V2	
		K*RI* 1,81,10	
	to expel	J-W p.607	
	to exorcise	K*RI* 2,286,7	
	to smite	K*RI* 2,286,1	
sḥs	**to press hard, to oppress**	J-W A1,6,4	
sḥḳ3	**to cause to rule**	*H* 1,42,4	
	to make to rule	*H* 1,76,3	
sḥty	(fish)	Valbelle, *Cat.Poids* 24	
sḥtp	**to make content** (cf. *JEA* 52,29f)	K*RI* 5,37,5	
	to pacify (cf. *JSSEA* 9(2)102)	*H* 1,27,9	
		H 1,49,7	
		K*RI* 1,46,14	
	to propitiate	*P.Leiden* 1,348,1R8-9	
	to appease	*JEA* 22,106	
		JNES 22,32	
	to pacify	K*RI* 1,43,10	
	to satisfy	*H* 1,28,10	
sḥtp-nmst	**offering table**	*H* 1,28,12	

sḥtpy	**censer**	*LEM* 10,13a,9
		H 1,49,8
		KRI 2,325,8-9
sḥtm	**to destroy, to eliminate** (cf. Peden p.191)	*KRI* 5,19,4
		KRI 5,31,7
	to annihilate	*KRI* 5,71,41
		KRI 5,78,9
		KRI 5,101,12
		KRI 1,58,6-7
sḥḏ	**to illumine**	*LES* 4,1,3
		LES 4,2,10
	to brighten	*KRI* 5,89,10
		KRI 5,108,16
		LEM 10,4,7
	to shine	*KRI* 1,27,5
	to clear, to prune (cf. Wente, *Letters* p.180)	*LRL* 5V8
		LRL 36V4
	to make bright	*KRI* 1,80,14
	to illuminate	*KRI* 2,325,10
	to light	*A* 1,17,3
	to enrich	*JNES* 21,306f
	to instruct, to explain	*Rd'É* 47,155,i
sḥḏ	**illumination**	*JEA* 60,193
	sun-beams	*KRI* 3,693,12
sḥḏ-tꜣ	**dawn**	*LES* 4,10,4
sḥḏyt	**palace**	J-W A8,c
sḥḏw-n-irt	**leucoma**	*HPBM*[4] T1,V56
sḫ	**to beat**	*KRI* 5,30,11
		LEM 8,7,11
	to forge	*LRL* 16V2
	to scourge	*A* 1,18,1

	to punish	*A* 1,18,2
	to acquire (cf. *sẖt* below)	*JNES* 28,138
	to beat	*LEM* 6,17,5
	to hit, to clap	K*RI* 1,112,14
sẖ	**blow**	K*RI* 1,53,7
		K*RI* 1,55,10
		K*RI* 1,57,1
	blows, lashes	*P.Leiden* 1,350,1Vx+10
		LEM 3,6,10
		K*RI* 1,56,6
	strokes	K*RI* 1,58,10
		Naun 1,5R12
		LEM 3,5,7
		O.Berlin 12654,R10 S.A. #15
		TR 10052 (Pl.29) 6,10
sẖ	**to be deaf**	*HPBM*[4] T1,V65-66
sẖy	**deaf**	*LEM* 5,2,7
		LEM 11,2,5
	deaf man	*A* 1,6,6
sẖyw	**plans** (cf. *sẖr*)	K*RI* 5,60,10
		K*RI* 5,70,2
		K*RI* 5,73,11
sẖt	**field** (cf. *JEA* 27,87,7; Černý, *Workmen* 84)	*LRL* 5V4
		P.H. 500 (Pl.8) 4,7
	district, countryside	K*RI* 2,331,13
	fields	*LEM* 10,5,4
		LRL 8R10
	country districts	K*RI* 1,51,10
		Wil (16) 35R24
	plains	K*RI* 2,74,11

	burial ground	*Rd'É* 33,55,ap
		LES 2,2,8
		LES 2,2,4
		LEM 16,6V3
		K*RI* 2,74,10
		Wil (4) 10R6
		LEM 3,2,2
sḫty	**fowler, peasant** (cf. *JEA* 29,4,f; *JSSEA* 4,1,2)	*TR* 10052 (Pl.26) 2a,5
		LEM 5,3,9
sḫꜣ	(?)	*Rd'É* 38,73,n.30
sḫꜣ	**to recall, to remember**	*LEM* 6,15,7
	to recount	*A* 1,27,4
	to recall	*LES* 2,8,2
	to mention	*LRL* 46V3
		LRL 42R7
		LEM 10,9,4
		RAD 25,2R12
		P.H. 500 (Pl.2) 1,3
		P.H. 500 (Pl.6) 3,4-5
		P.H. 500 (Pl.10) 5,12
		K*RI* 5,24,4
		K*RI* 5,41,3
	to commemorate	K*RI* 1,113,13
	to remember	CB 4,3V11 *HPBM*[3] 19
	to be satisfied (cf. Wente, *Letters* p.135)	K*RI* 3,210,13
		K*RI* 6,156,9
sḫꜣ	**records**	*TR* Ambras (Pl.38) 1,7-8
	reminder	O.Berlin 12630,R1 S.A. #14
	memorandum	*RAD* 18,3R19
	documents	*RAD* 25,1R1
	memoranda	*TR* Abbott (Pl.4) 6,23

	memory	K*RI* 5,45,13	
	remembrance	K*RI* 3,422,6	
	(see *smit* above) **charge**	*RAD* 25,1R2	
sḫ3ḫy	**to hurry**	*A* 1,6,3	
*sḫ*ᶜ	**to adorn**	K*RI* 1,112,3	
	to arise	*JEA* 38,51,4	
	to cause to appear	*H* 1,8,9	
		H 1,76,2	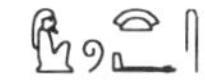
	to crown	K*RI* 5,38,12	
	to make appear	K*RI* 1,114,5	
	to be on parade, in procession	*BIFAO* 75,104	
*sḫ*ᶜ	**procession**	*Rd'É* 20,12,7	
sḫwy	**bitter gall**	P.H. 500 (Pl.10) 5,2	
sḫwy	**slaughter house**	*H* 1,4,8	
sḫw3	**to deny, to disclaim responsibility** (cf. Wente, *Letters* p.125)	K*RI* 4,80,6 & 9	
sḫwn	**dispute** (cf. *ASAE* 21,14; *JEA* 5,13,2 (Pl.21); Parker, *Oracle Pap.* 50,k)	*Rd'É* 7,82,e	
	dispute, quarrel, strife	J-W A1,c,6	
sḫwd	**to enrich**	K*RI* 1,42,7	
sḫbḫ	**to ensnare, to snare**	K*RI* 5,25,7	
		K*RI* 5,64,12	
	to catch	K*RI* 5,33,5	
sḫpr	**to train, to rear**	*LES* 1,7,7	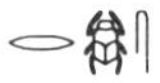
		LES 2,3,10	
	to bring up	*LEM* 5,8,7 *LEM* 5,3,6	
	to perpetuate	*LEM* 10,10,8	

	to rear, to train	*H* 1,5,9 CS 2R14	
	to foster	*CB* 1,B1,V6	
	to bring up	Naun 1,2,2	
	to bring into being	Push 128,1,2 (cf. Push 127, p.14)	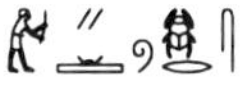
	to create	*HPBM*[4] L4,31	
		K*RI* 5,26,12	
	to fashion, to make	K*RI* 2,326,15	
	to cause to be	K*RI* 1,75,8	
sḫpr	**ward**	*LRL* 8R8	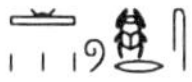
	offspring	*HPBM*[4] L1,V21	
	trainer	*A* 1,1,8 (O.BN 4)	
	ward	*ZÄS* 53,13,9	
sḫprw	**increment**	*H.O.* 64,2V3	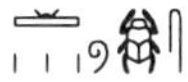
	acquisitions	*LEM* 5,3,6	
		JEA 42,17	
		RIDA 3,11,47	
	responsibility (cf. Wente, *Letters* p.149)	K*RI* 6,156,1	
sḫm	**to take possession of, to have power over**	*LES* 1,7,15	
	to be powerful	K*RI* 5,62,4	
	to be mighty	K*RI* 5,23,11	
		LEM 2,3,8	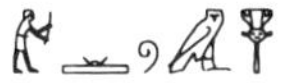
	to be strong	K*RI* 3,174,6	
	to overwhelm (cf. Wente, *Letters* p.30)	K*RI* 2,93,14	
	to be terrible of, possessed of	K*RI* 5,13,6	
	to have power	*CB* 1,B1,V21	
	to be powerful	K*RI* 1,62,7	

	to be stout	K*RI* 5,87,8	
		K*RI* 5,15,10	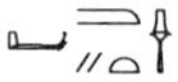
		K*RI* 2,7,8	
		K*RI* 1,11,15	
		K*RI* 5,22,10	
	to be terrible	K*RI* 1,12,3	
		K*RI* 2,120,6	
		K*RI* 2,88,16	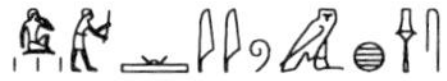
		K*RI* 5,49,5	
	sḫm-pḥty **to be very great of strength**	K*RI* 1,44,4	
	to be great of strength	K*RI* 1,41,11	
sḫm	**might**	K*RI* 2,120,2	
	fury	K*RI* 5,83,2	
		K*RI* 5,61,6	
sḫm	**mighty one**	K*RI* 1,17,13	
	controller	K*RI* 3,210,8	
sḫm	**image**	P.Brooklyn 47.218.50 Goyon (Pl.11) 16,5	
sḫm	(causative of *ḫm*, cf. *smḫ* above) **to forget**	K*RI* 3,210,8	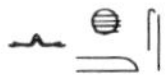
sḫm-ib	**courageous**	K*RI* 1,6,15	
		K*RI* 1,18,1	
sḫmyt	**sistrum player**	*HPBM*[4] L2,R2	
	musician	K*RI* 3,50,10	
sḫmty	**double crown**	K*RI* 5,38,10	
		H 1,42,5	
		K*RI* 1,116,6	
		MÄS 37,35,7,1	
sḫmḫ-ib	**to entertain**	K*RI* 1,113,3	

sḫmḫ-ib	**entertainment**	P.H. 500 (Pl.8) 4,1
		P.H. 500 (Pl.14) 7,3
	sport	*A* 1,8,7 (O.Louvre 4)
	pleasure (cf. Wente, *Letters* p.166)	K*RI* 5,565,5
sḫmḫ-ib	**entertainer**	*CB* 1,C1,V1
sḫn	**to contend**	*LEM* 6,14,4
	to go to law	*LES* 6,14,4
		K*RI* 1,39,9
	to meet	*LES* 4,14,3
	to dispute	*HPBM*[4] C1,43-44
	sḫn ḥnꜥ **to plead one's case against**	*Mes* 14,14
sḫn	**cake, loaf**	*JEA* 46,36 (Pl.10) 10R5
sḫn	**thymus** (?), **pancreas** (?)	*HPBM*[4] L6,R21
		HPBM[4] T2,V43
sḫn	**swelling**	*HPBM*[4] T1,V69
sḫnwt	**supports** (of heaven)	K*RI* 2,150,8
sḫni	**to avert, to ensnare** (?)	*MÄS* 37,III,88,2
sḫny	**to rest, to halt**	K*RI* 1,66,1
	to repose	*A* 1,3,8
		A 1,4,6
	to alight, to rest	K*RI* 1,39,9
	to dwell	K*RI* 1,69,7
		K*RI* 1,123,12
sḫny	**to swell**	K*RI* 1,112,8
sḫnš	**to stir up, to provoke** (cf. Hoch p.267)	K*RI* 5,22,10

sḫnty	**to travel upstream, to return**	K*RI* 2,325,6
	to advance	K*RI* 3,492,5
		K*RI* 3,17,4
sḫr	**to overthrow, to cast down, to throw down**	K*RI* 5,16,15
	to cast down	K*RI* 5,20,1
	to overthrow	K*RI* 5,41,12
		K*RI* 2,101,10
	to banish	K*RI* 5,107,5
	to lay low	K*RI* 5,43,14
	to overthrow	*H* 1,76,7
	to reproach (cf. Wente, *Letters* p.154)	Sauneron OH pl.20,518
sḫr	**to plan, to contrive**	K*RI* 2,327,5
sḫr	**plan**	CS 2V7
		LEM 3,6,7
		LES 2,7,5
		K*RI* 1,51,13
		K*RI* 5,25,15
	plans	K*RI* 1,74,11
		K*RI* 1,114,1
	matter	K*RI* 2,124,2
	means	K*RI* 1,56,9
		K*RI* 1,69,2
	nature	*LRL* 46V5
	counsels	K*RI* 2,39,5
	preparations	*LES* 2,2,5
	practice	*LES* 1,5,7
	habit	*LES* 2,10,4
	authority	*LES* 4,1,7
	parallel, equal	*LES* 2,14,5-6
	purposes (cf. Wente, *Letters* p.49)	K*RI* 3,43,11
	plans, dispositions	K*RI* 1,99,10

	dispositions	Gardiner & Sethe pl.7
	condition	*LRL* 1V4
	custom	*LRL* 4R7
	mood	*O.H.* pl.25
	fashion	*LEM* 1,3,8
	behavior (cf. Wente, *Letters* p.154)	*O.H.* pl.27, nr.446
	manner	*LRL* 12R7
	attitude	K*RI* 3,354,8; O.DM 303
	way	*LRL* 28R21
	concern	*LES* 5,2,69
	situation	K*RI* 2,227,2
	governance	*LES* 2,9,3
	state	K*RI* 5,22,5
	estate	*JEA* 41,89
	advice	*LEM* 9,5V1
	story	*TR* 10053 (Pl.20) 3V6
	course	K*RI* 2,35,6
	admonitions	K*RI* 3,536,13
	designs	*HPBM*[4] L6,R68
	advice, arguments	P.H. 500 (Pl.4) 2,5
	instructions	*O.H.* pl.3,116; K*RI* 3,540,9
	decisions, measures	*JEA* 68,135,5
	arrangements	O.Glasgow D.1925,87
	dealings	CB 4,1V5 *HPBM*[3] 18
	projects	K*RI* 4,86,13
	contrivances	*LEM* 2,6,1
		RAD 23R3
	sḫr m dwn **custom**	*TR* 10054 (Pl.7) 1V6
	p3 sḫr nty how (cf. Wente, *Letters* p.166)	*O.H.* pl.20,419
sḫr	(?) (cf. *sḫry*) **to heed** (cf. Helck, *Bez* 568,203)	*ZÄS* 106,176

	to be contemptuous, to scorn (cf. Hoch p.267)	*LEM* 3,6,4	
		K*RI* 5,46,12	
	to hold in contempt	K*RI* 5,57,8	
sẖrt	**papyrus** (scroll)	*LRL* 45V3	
		A 1 (O.Cailliaud 4)	
		A 1,4,8	
	volume, papyrus	*A* 1,8,7	
sẖry	**plan maker**	K*RI* 5,59,9	
	those who govern	K*RI* 2,151,5	
sẖẖ	**to drag**	*LEM* 10,7,9	
sẖẖ	**couriers**	O.Glasgow D.1925,77,1	
sẖs	**courier**	*LEM* 5,11,8	
sẖs	**to rush**	P.H. 500 (Pl.10) 5,12	
sẖsẖ	**to flee, to run**	*LES* 1,8,9	
	to run	*LEM* 10,3,9	
	to overrun	*Wil* (57) B10,V21	
	to hasten, to flee	K*RI* 1,74,14	
		P.H. 500 (Pl.6) 3,4	
	to run beyond, overrun	*JEA* 27,39,1	
	to run ahead of (cf. Wente, *Letters* p.46)	K*RI* 3,42,1	
sẖt	**to weave**	*LRL* 9R18	
	to trap, to catch	*LRL* 9V6	
		Max. d'Ani 1,65	
	to ensnare	K*RI* 5,33,5	
		K*RI* 5,64,11	
		K*RI* 5,71,7	
		CS 2R20	
		Wil (21) 46R27	
	to weave	*LEM* 11,4,7	

	to catch	*TR* 10052 (Pl.25) 1,7
	to mould (with sticks)	O.Berlin 11247 K*RI* 3,533,6
	to forge (cf. Wente, *Letters* p.193)	*LRL* 16V2
	to gather	Meeks 78,378
	to make bricks	*LEM* 3,3V1
sẖt	(?)	*RAD* 7,1R12
sẖt	**trap, snare**	K*RI* 5,40,5
sẖty	**weaver**	*TR* 10068 (Pl.11) 4R24
		TR 10053 (Pl.17) 2R2
		TR 10068 (Pl.12) 6R14
sẖty	**to repel**	K*RI* 1,111,10
sẖtẖt	**to hold back** (cf. *JEA* 65) **"to entrap", "ensnare"**	P.H. 500 (Pl.8) 4,8
sẖd	**disordered**	*RAD* 18,1R7
	upside down	*JEA* 10,196
		K*RI* 3,178,14
	reversed, inside out	*BIFAO* 85,241
sẖi	**to be deaf**	*A* 1,26,3
	to be neglectful (cf. *JEA* 39,53)	K*RI* 1,58,8
	sẖi ḥr **to be neglectful** (cf. *JEA* 60,70)	K*RI* 1,70,3
		CB 4,4V9 *HPBM*[3] 19
	to make deaf	*Rd'É* 7,83
sẖꜣ	**to pull**	P.H. 500 (Pl.4) 2,6
sẖnw	**to arouse, to stir up,** **to divert from duty** (cf. also Groll, *Studies…Gordon* p.77)	P.Rollin 1 *JEA* 49,74

sẖnn	**to overthrow, demolish**	K*RI* 1,69,2	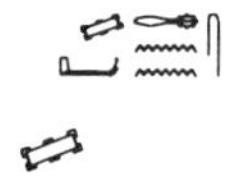
		K*RI* 5,16,9	
sẖnkt	**sifting vessel** (cf. Janssen 431,167)	*H* 1,6,11	
sẖr	**timber** (cf. D. Jones, *Glossary...* p.187)	*LEM* 10,5,6	
sẖry-ꜥ	**to underestimate, to deem insignificant**	*A* 1,7,1	
		A 1(O.Turin 5)	
	to undervalue	*A* 1,8,8	
	to despise	O.Glasgow D.1925,90,5	
sẖrrt	**bulbs** (?)	*LES* 4,10,4-5	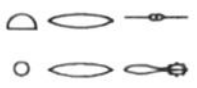
sẖkr	**to adorn, to decorate**	*H* 1,4,6	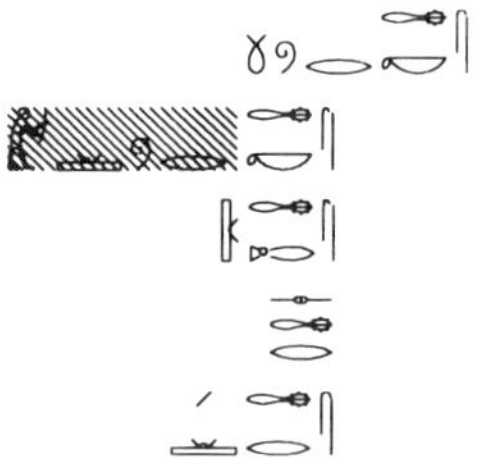
		LEM 9,3V4	
		K*RI* 1,47,7	
	to plaster	*PSBA* 22,91	
	to protect (with armor)	*JEA* 57,157,3	
ssꜣꜣ	**to satisfy, to sate**	K*RI* 1,69,1	
ssꜣḳ	**to reassemble**	K*RI* 3,167,5	
ssw	**stockade**	K*RI* 5,41,1	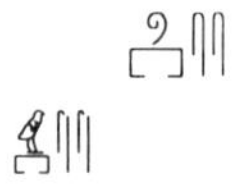
	enclosure	K*RI* 5,113,10	
sswt	**metal inlays, bolts** (?)	*H* 1,45,5	
sswn	**to destroy**	K*RI* 5,97,10	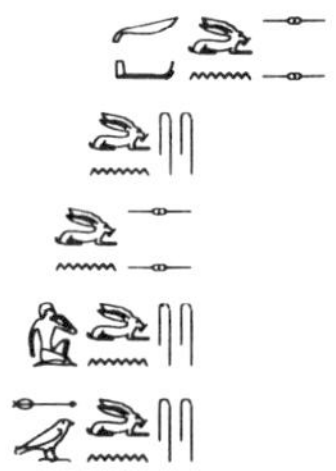
		K*RI* 1,26,14	
	to punish, to blot out	K*RI* 1,58,6	
	to be parched	K*RI* 1,66,3	
	to destroy	K*RI* 1,69,5	

ssfy	**ashes**	K*RI* 5,60,7
		K*RI* 5,23,8
		H 1,76,7
		K*RI* 5,42,9
ssmt	(unknown) (cf. E-W 81,34A)	K*RI* 5,63,10
ssmwt	**horses**	K*RI* 5,8,8
		K*RI* 5,16,16
		K*RI* 5,57,14
		K*RI* 5,37,15
		LEM 3,4,2
		K*RI* 2,286,16
		H 1,77,4
ssmt	**horsemanship**	K*RI* 5,84,14
ssny	**to breathe**	K*RI* 5,20,7
		K*RI* 5,36,15
		H 1,66b,3
	to take a breath	K*RI* 2,80,8
		K*RI* 5,82,1
		K*RI* 5,105,15
ssnb	**to keep healthy, to keep well**	*LEM* 6,12,1
	to preserve the health	*Rd'É* 6,118,c
	to preserve	*RAD* 24,1R3
ssnḏm	**costly wood**	*JEA* 50,25
	tamarisk	Janssen p.373
ssd	(plant)	Janssen pp.367-8
sš	**to write**	*TR* Abbott (Pl.23) A,1
		HPBM[4] T2,V88

	to inscribe	*H* 1,58,12
	to decorate	K*RI* 1,113,4
		K*RI* 6,672,9
	to write down	*JEA* 26,23,4
sš	**writing**	*LRL* 5V5
	books	*LES* 3,5,1
	written instructions	K*RI* 4,361,6
	writing, documents	*A* 1,1,3
		Naun 5,10
	document, piece of paper	P.Lee 1,3
	hand-writing	*LRL* 9V11
	text	*LES* 1,9,9
	painting	*H* 1,13a,2
	decorating (cf. Wente, *Letters* p.168)	P.DM 9,4
	letters	CB 4,7V3 *HPBM*[3] 21
		LEM 1,1,4
	writing	*LEM* 10,3,4
		CB 1,B1,V4
	records	K*RI* 1,42,14
	r-sš **drawing** (cf. Wente, *Letters* p.166)	*O.H.* pl.20,419
	s3w-sšw **record keeper**	*LEM* 7,3,13
	sš-n-ḥk3w **magical writing**	*Studies...Gordon* p.77
sš	**scribe**	*LEM* 7,3,13
		LES 8,2,2
	accountant	*Inscribed...Abydos* p.20
	sš-wdḥw **scribe of the offering table**	*RAD* 8R2
	sš-mšʿ **scribe of the army**	*LES* 7,3,14
	sš-n-tm3 **scribe of the mat**	*RAD* 18,2R2
	sš-nfrw **scribe of the elite troops**	*MÄS* 6,63-64,159
	sš-nsw **royal scribe**	*LRL* 28R1

	sš ḥwt-nṯr **scribe of the temple**	*RAD* 17,4V2	
	sš-ḥsb **scribe of accounts**	*RAD* 17,3R2	
	sš-sḥn **administrative scribe**	*ZÄS* 53,9	
	sš-šꜥt **letter writer**	*LEM* 6,9,2	
	dispatch	*Wil* (13)29R30	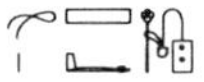
	sš-ḳd **draughtsman**	*JNES* 14,162	
		LEM 3,7,1	
		Naun 1,1R10	
	painter	O.Berlin 12654,R8 S.A. # 15	
		O.Berlin 12654,R9	
	sš-ḳdwt **draft, sketch**	O.DM 246,2,6 *Gleanings* p.195,i	
sš	(or *sn* ?) **to spread out**	*LES* 4,11,2-3	
	to pass	K*RI* 5,13,3	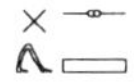
	to extend	J-W A7,e,6; A7,d,12	
	to stretch, to expand	Push 127,1,6	
	to cross	*A* 1,21,6	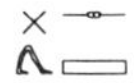
	to give fair passage	CB 4,6R2 *HPBM*[3] 14	
	to open	K*RI* 5,93,5	
	to set, to spread	*JEA* 32,49	
sš	**cakes** (*sšrt* ?)	K*RI* 3,550,6	
sšywt	**inscription, paintings**	K*RI* 1,67,4	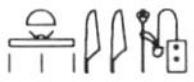
sšy	**nest**	*P.Leiden* 1,348,7R1	
	trapping marshes	K*RI* 1,49,2	
	marsh	K*RI* 1,17,15	
	bird pool	*LEM* 10,12,4	
	nest	*LEM* 3,4,2	
		LEM 8,8,1	
		K*RI* 1,26,11	
		RAD 7a,1R10	

sš3	(cf. *šs3* below) **bubalis**	*LEM* 10,3,8	
sšs3	(cf. *šs3* below) **to be skilled**	*LEM* 6,9,4	
	to make wise	K*RI* 3,336,5	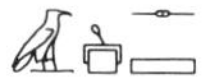
sšw	**to evacuate, unload**	*Rd'É* 33,55	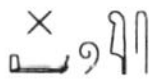
		K*RI* 1,128,13	
sšpw	(cf. *šsp*) **images** **sphinxes** (cf. K*RI T&A* I p.21) (cf. Grandet nt.118)	*H* 1,26,3	
sšpwt	(cf. *šspt* below) **cucumbers**	*LEM* 5,9,2	
sšpt	(or *šspt*) **sheen, brightness, splendor**	*CB* 1,C1,V2	
	light	J-W A10,d,12	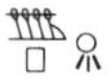
sšm	**to lead, guide, govern**	K*RI* 5,12,13	
		H 1,44,7	
	to reveal	*A* 1(O.BN 8-9)	
	to marshal	*A* 1,28,7	
	to show (the way)	*LEM* 2,4,8	
	to direct	*LEM* 10,14,2	
		K*RI* 3,295,14	
	to conduct	CB 4,4V2 *HPBM*[3] 19	
	to conduct investigation (?) (cf. Wente, *Letters* p.46)	K*RI* 3,42,10	
	to find out about	K*RI* 3,532,5	
sšm	**leader**	*Melanges...Mokhtar* 2,351,10	
	sšm-n-imn **festival-leader of Amun**	K*RI* 3,39,10	
sšm	**statue**	K*RI* 1,106,8	
		K*RI* 2,326,4	
	images, schemes	K*RI* 1,114,11	

	image	*H* 1,3,4
		K*RI* 1,107,10
	dealings	CB 4,5V2 *HBPM*[3] 20
	lead, guidance	*H* 1,66b,3
	protective images	*H* 1,67,5
	possession, rule	*H* 1,28,2
	procession	*A* 1(O.BN 6)
	retinue, guide	K*RI* 5,112,8
	procedure, guiding principle	*JEA* 17,59,38
	condition, state, nature	*JEA* 42,15,2,8
	statue	K*RI* 2,331,6
	figure, form, manifestation	*P.Leiden* 1,348,11V8
	performance, accomplishment	J-W A5,e,5; A18,c,9
	sšm(-šm) **heir** (cf. J-W p.126 nt.12)	J-W A18,c,4
		J-W A10,c,4
sšm	**bark**	K*RI* 1,115,16
sšmw	**tabernacle** (?)	*Wil* (18)40R44
		Wil (42)86V4
		Wil (40)83V26
		Wil (16)34R21
sšm-ḫs	**ritual directions**	*JEA* 32,79
sšny	**lotus**	*LES* 4,10,5
	lotus flowers	*LEM* 3,2,6
		H 1,5,3
	lotus	K*RI* 1,47,15
		CB 1,C1,V4
		P.H. 500 (Pl.4) 2,8
sšr	**work, business**	CB 4,4V3 *HPBM*[3] 19

	concern	CB 4,5V3
		HPBM[3] 20
	everything	*JEA* 17,98,19
	material things, actions, course of action	*BIFAO* 30,176
sšr	*m-sšr* **all right, in perfect order, properly, closely** (cf. Wente, *Letters* p.180)	*LRL* 6V2
		LRL 5R7
		LRL 6R5
	in proper way, in good order	K*RI* 2,330,9
	in short order	*LRL* 21R5
	well	*LRL* 5V4
		LEM 16,6V3
	well off	*LRL* 16R9
	with zeal	*LEM* 11,5,6
	with utmost zeal	*LEM* 1,1,4
	zealously	*LEM* 1,1,6
	in good condition	*LEM* 3,2,1
	m-sšr-ḏriw **quite assiduously**	K*RI* 4,86,4
sšr	**corn, grain**	*H* 1,34b,6
		RAD 19,1
	grain	Push 127,4,13
		K*RI* 1,91,4
		K*RI* 2,331,10
sšrw	**linen**	*H* 1,13,a,1
		H 1,29,6
		K*RI* 5,74,5
		K*RI* 1,60,14
	woven materials	K*RI* 2,333,10
	sšr-nsw **royal linen** (cf. Janssen p.256)	K*RI* 1,48,8
		H 1,33,2
	byssus	*LEM* 7,6,7
		TR 10068 (Pl.10) 3R23

	nʿʿ-sšr-rwḏ (?)	*RAD* 25,1V2	
		TR 10068 (Pl.13) 1V6	
		TR 10052 (Pl.26) 2,25	
	smooth cloth (cf. Wente, *Letters* p.49)	K*RI* 4,87,14	
sšrt	(loaves or fruit)	*LEM* 5,14,1	
		LEM 9,15V8	
	sšrt-**cake**	K*RI* 3,773,12	
sšs3t	(cf. *šs3t* below) **night, starry firmament**	*ZÄS* 96,111-13	
sšš	**to fete, to entertain**	*BIFAO* 27,183,2	
sšš	**exultation**	K*RI* 3,155,6	
sšši	**to spread** (a bed)	P.Turin (Pl.98) 2,5 Pleyte-Rossi	
sšt3	**secrets** (cf. *ḥry-sšt3* above)	Černý, *Workmen* 47	
		A 1(O.BN 7)	
		LEM 10,13b,1	
		LEM 10,13b,2	
	"mystery", "seclusion" (cf. Wente, *Letters* p.219)	*JEA* 35,70	
	secretly (cf. K*RI T&A* 1,128)	K*RI* 1,191,10	
sšd	**window**	*LES* 1,5,4	
		LES 5,1,49	
	royal window of appearances, balcony	*A* 1(P.Turin 6)	
sšd	**to save**	*LEM* 2,10,6	
sšd-šwty	**double-feathered crown**	K*RI* 2,355,2	
sšdw	**shooting, flashing**	K*RI* 5,37,15	
	shooting star	K*RI* 5,64,10	
	thunderbolt	K*RI* 5,109,1	

	lightening flash	*JEA* 54,40: 56,194
	meteor, shooting star	*JEA* 59,219
	flash, thunderbolt	K*RI* 1,27,6
sḳꜣ-tꜣ	**to present bread**	*MDAIK* 39,255
sḳꜣ	**to exalt**	*LES* 1,8,6
		H 1,3,3
		CB 1,C3,V5
	to set up	*RAD* 22,2R14
		K*RI* 5,59,12
	to raise	K*RI* 1,126,2
	to magnify	K*RI* 3,284,6
	to set up, exalt, prolong, to make high	K*RI* 1,97,9
	to make high (cf. *Wb* 4,302)	*JEA* 65,80
sḳꜣyḳt	**boomerang**	P.H. 500 (Pl.8) 4,3
sḳb	**to double**	K*RI* 1,66,14
sḳb	**to be exalted** (cf. Hoch p.268)	*A* 1,27,6
		K*RI* 1,7,6
sḳbb	**to calm**	K*RI* 5,84,1
	to refresh, to give cool water, to pour refreshment	K*RI* 1,66,10
sḳn	**to go to ruin, harm** (cf. Wente, *Letters* p.46)	K*RI* 3,42,7
sḳnn	(cf. *sgnn* below) **oil**	*RAD* 18,3R21
sḳnd	**to enrage**	K*RI* 5,32,11
	to infuriate, enrage	K*RI* 5,98,1
sḳniḫ	(unknown)	*HPBM*[4] L6,R102
sḳr	**to smite, to beat**	K*RI* 1,21,8
		K*RI* 5,93,1

	to hammer	*JEA* 10,195
	to pluck	*JEA* 46,54
	to decorate (cf. Wente, *Letters* p.47)	K*RI* 3,43,9
sḳr-ʿnḫ	**captive**	K*RI* 5,9,16
	bound-captive	*GM* 2,43-45
		K*RI* 5,44,11
		K*RI* 1,19,6
	living captive	K*RI* 1,22,9
		K*RI* 1,99,1
		K*RI* 1,80,9
		K*RI* 5,19,4
	living prisoner	K*RI* 1,9,8
sḳḥ	**to plaster, to white wash**	*LES* 4,13,5
	to plaster, to stucco	*TR* 10068 (Pl.12) 6R11
sḳh	**stamp, seal**	*AJSLL* 34,215f
sḳsn	**arduous**	*A* 1,10,9
sḳdy	**to convey**	K*RI* 1,48,1
sḳdyt	**voyage, shipment**	K*RI* 2,325,10
sḳdd	**to navigate**	*BIFAO* 45,159,24
sḳdd	**to let sleep, to cause to sleep**	*LES* 6,2,x+5
sk	(or *skt*) **ass's foal** (cf. Wente, *Letters* p.192)	*LRL* 9V15
sk	**to destroy**	K*RI* 2,150,16
		H 1,22,9
		K*RI* 5,79,1-2
		K*RI* 5,79,13
	to wipe out	K*RI* 1,24,13

	to destroy	K*RI* 1,77,10
		K*RI* 1,99,10
	to fell, to destroy	*JEA* 50,28
	to perish	*H* 1,29,10
	iḫmw-sk (?)	K*RI* 3,164,12
sk-nhm	(unknown)	*LEM* 5,17,1
sk-hm	(unknown)	*LEM* 11,1,5
ski	**fray, battle**	K*RI* 5,24,10
		K*RI* 5,57,4
		K*RI* 5,16,7-8
		K*RI* 5,37,14
		K*RI* 5,37,16
		K*RI* 5,59,14
		K*RI* 5,64,8
		K*RI* 2,77,1
		K*RI* 2,77,3
		K*RI* 2,77,4
		K*RI* 2,86,1
		K*RI* 5,77,4
		K*RI* 1,16,5
		K*RI* 1,13,14
		A 1,16,1
		A 1,22,6-7
		K*RI* 1,16,5
sky	**slaughterer**	K*RI* 2,85,15
		K*RI* 5,29,14
skw	**troops, battle line** (cf. *JSSEA* 11,11-13)	K*RI* 2,23,14
		K*RI* 1,80,12
		JEA 19 (Pl.26) 8
	irt sk **to draw up in line of battle**	*JEA* 21,223
	ṯs skw **to draw up troops**	*JEA* 21,223

sk3	**to plow**	*LES* 2,1,3	
	to cultivate, to till	*LRL* 8R11	
		LES 2,2,2	
		LEM 10,5,9-6,1	
		RAD 17,4R11	
		K*RI* 1,51,6	
		RAD 24,1V3	
		RAD 1,4Vx+4	
		LRL 5V9	
		LRL 3R12	
		LEM 7,4,3	
sk3	**cultivation**	*LRL* 42V2	
sk3w	**crops**	K*RI* 3,431,1	
sk3wt	**plough-land**	Push 127,4,16	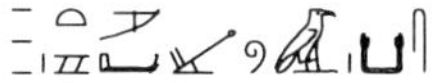
	tillage-rights	*ZÄS* 53,108	
sk3	(pedestal type stone)	*ZÄS* 100,97/99	
sk3p	**to cover**	K*RI* 5,106,7	
skm	**to complete**	*LES* 1,4,2	
	to finish out, spend	*LES* 4,8,3	
	to finish	K*RI* 5,16,10	
	to bring to an end	K*RI* 5,61,8	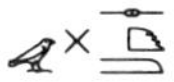
		K*RI* 5,64,2	
		K*RI* 5,69,14	
	to complete	*LEM* 3,4,8	
	to complete, to blacken	Push 127,4,10	
		K*RI* 5,40,15	
		ZÄS 57,9,43	
skm	(bird)	*LEM* 5,2,3	

skmkm	**destruction**	K*RI* 5,22,5
		K*RI* 5,25,6
		K*RI* 5,40,15
sksk	**to destroy**	*CB* 1B,V7
		K*RI* 5,10,10
		K*RI* 5,28,10
		K*RI* 5,55,7
		K*RI* 5,55,2
		H 1,16,9
		K*RI* 5,11,4
sksk	(cf. Helck, *Bez* 569,205)	*H.O.* 65,2V3
skt	**military officer, "scout** (?)**", "guard** (?)**"** (cf. Hoch p.268; Helck, *Bez* 569,206; *OLZ* 27,184; *MÄS* 6,57-8 "assault officer")	*Wil* (47) 56V17
		Wil (38) 80R30
		LEM 10,9,5
		O. Flor ZÄS 18,pp.96-97
		K*RI* 1,246,1
skty	**ship**	*LEM* 5,8,5
	sekty-bark	*LRL* 46V7
		LEM 10,14,6
		LEM 10,13a,2
		K*RI* 1,74,13
		LEM 5,7,10
sktt	**boat, ship**	P. Lansing 12,4 *JEA* 11,294,15
	sun-bark	K*RI* 5,93,15
	night-bark	K*RI* 5,30,11
		K*RI* 5,42,3
	evening-bark	K*RI* 5,106,8
sg	**to overstep, to step out** (cf. Helck, *Bez* 569,207)	*A* 1,23,2
	to command (cf. Hoch p.269)	*JEA* 42,32,21

sg	**woolen cloth** (?) **inferior cloth, sackcloth** (cf. Hoch p.259)	*A* 1,25,6
sg	(tree)	*Wil* (55) B8,V25
sg3	**silence**	*LEM* 3,1,2
sg3	**to become stupified, confused**	*LES* 8,2,6
	to be torpid, lethargic, to be dumbfounded	*LEM* 6,6,2
sgb	(or sgp) **to shriek, cry, to shout** (cf. *ZÄS* 102,64)	P.H. 500 (Pl.8) 4,6
	to clamor	K*RI* 1,49,2-3
		HPBM[4] P.Ch.40
	to lament	K*RI* 2,41,4
		K*RI* 2,41,5
		LES 4,2,1
		LES 5,2,13
	ʿš-sbg **to cry aloud**	*CB* 1,B1, V31-2
sgb	**cry**	K*RI* 3,561,12
sgbyn	**waters, body of water** (cf. Hoch p.278)	*LEM* 3,3,7
sgn	**to make weak, loosen**	K*RI* 5,91,11
sg(n)	(cf. *sgr* below) **keep**	*Wil* (13)28R6
sgnn	**oil, ointment** (cf. Janssen 336,103)	*LES* 2,10,10
		LES 4,11,7
		LEM 3,3,7
		LEM 13,1V8
		RAD 22,1R1
		LRL 4R11
		RAD 22,1R1

		RAD 18,3R21
		LEM 9,3V1
		LRL 37V17
	tallow (cf. Wente, *Letters* p.51)	K*RI* 6,79,7
	fat	Naun 1,3R11
	unguent (cf. Wente, *Letters* p.157)	K*RI* 6,266,5
sgnn	**to annoint**	*LEM* 5,15,4
		LEM 13,4V1
	to rub	*LEM* 8,4,10
		LES 1,5,9
sgr	**keep, fortress** (cf. Helck, *Bez* 569,209) **fort, magazine** (cf. Hoch p.270)	*LEM* 6,19,7
		Wil (70)B23V15
		Wil (62)B15V26
	keep	*Wil* (60)B13V25
		Wil (71)B24V14
		Wil (13)28R6
		Wil (15)33R35
		Wil (65)B18V10
sgr	**to keep silence**	K*RI* 1,114,13
sgr	**silence** (cf. *JSSEA* 8,133)	CB 4,5V2 *HPBM*[3] 20 J-W A6,e,12;All,h,4
sgrḥ	**pacification**	K*RI* 3,703,1
sgrṯ	(tool) (cf. Helck, *Bez* 569,210)	*LEM* 5,17,3
st	**them** (dependent pron.)	*LRL* 1V1
	they	*LRL* 8R15
	it	*LRL* 5R6
		LRL 4R11
st	(a measure) (cf. Grandet n.364)	*H* 1,19a,8

st-r-st.w	**legal** (?)	*LES* 4,3,3
sti	**to shoot, to hurl** (cf. *ZÄS* 70,110,121)	*LEM* 2,3,8
		K*RI* 5,24,13
		K*RI* 2,44,15
		K*RI* 2,65,9
		K*RI* 2,44,14
		K*RI* 2,44,12
		K*RI* 1,27,6
	to sprinkle water	K*RI* 1,48,5
	sti-mw **to pour water**	K*RI* 2,332,9
	to pour out, to shine	*P.Leiden* 1,348,2R2
sty	**red pigment**	*LEM* 11,4,3
		CB 3 (Pl.7) 9R13 *HPBM*[3] p.18,n.5
	ochre	K*RI* 3,533,5
		K*RI* 5,97,9
	Nubian yellow ochre	K*RI* 3,44,2 (sic)
sty	**odor**	*LES* 2,10,8
	scent	*Rd'É* 20,12,13
	fragrance	*H* 1,49,6
	perfume	*JEA* 65,81
		O.DM 696,V3
	smelling	P.H. 500 (Pl.8) 4,5
	odor	K*RI* 5,70,1
	smelling	*MÄS* 37,II,21,1
	odor, fragrance	J-W B22,B,2; B22,B,4
sty	**to reek**	*LEM* 8,9,11
		LEM 5,11,9
sty	(fruit ?)	*JEA* 49,67,9 Janssen pp.355-6
		JEA 52,86,y

styw	**jar stands**	*H* 1,6,1
		H 1,28,11
styw	(unknown) (cf. *Wb* 4,334,4)	Helck, *Bez* 569,211 P.Turin 510
styw	(see *sty* above)	*MÄS* 37,III,88,8
stt	(see *sw n stt* above)	*LRL* 36V5
st3	< *sṯ3* **to drag**	*LEM* 2,3,1
	to draw, to attract	*LEM* 13,5,4
	to pull, to bring	P.H. 500 (Pl.2) 1,8
	to convey, to usher in	*H* 1,7,7
	to bring	*H* 1,27,8
		H 1,29,8
		J-W A15,c,7
	to conduct	*H* 1,28,2
		K*RI* 2,96,5
	to carry	K*RI* 1,68,1
		K*RI* 2,109,15
	to drag, to bring	K*RI* 2,326,7
	to drag off	K*RI* 5,60,3
	to drag, to pull	K*RI* 5,49,7
	to bring	K*RI* 5,42,3
	st3-mw **water-pourer**	*LEM* 10,13b,8
st3	**to kindle, to light**	*LES* 2,4,9
		LES 9,F1
st3	**lamp, flame**	*RAD* 18,3R21
	st3-ḫbs **lighted candles**	*JEA* 22 (Pl.13) 178 P.Leopold 2,8
		K*RI* 3,44,3
st3	**well water**	*H* 1,7,11
st3	**passage**	*LEM* 7,6,3

	ramp	*A* 1,14,2
		A 1(P.Turin 7)
	r-st3 **tomb**	CS 1R17
st3	**to claim** (cf. *JEA* 19,25)	K*RI* 2,38,10
		K*RI* 2,38,15
st3w	**glances**	CB 1 (Pl.18) A1V4
st3st3	**to burn, to brown** (?) (cf. Grandet n.508)	*H* 1,48,2
st3ḥ	**to trouble**	*CB* 1 (Pl.22) C1V8
stwr	**to frighten**	J-W A13,m,2
stwh	**to pervert (?), to cause confusion** (cf. *JEA* 49,74) (see *sth* below) **to create bewilderment**	P.Lee 1,5
stwt	**to illumine**	*LEM* 3,5,1
stwt	**rays**	*LEM* 2,5,8
		LEM 5,5,8
		K*RI* 5,64,6
		H 1,42,2
		H 1,22,2
		H 1,47,1
		H 1,66b,3
		K*RI* 2,87,1
		K*RI* 2,87,2
		K*RI* 5,108,16
		K*RI* 1,47,3
		K*RI* 1,118,8
		Push 127,1,6
	radiance	K*RI* 3,693,12
stwt	**to liken**	K*RI* 2,326,9
	to make similar	J-W A1,b,6;A1,b,7

	to resemble, to smooth	*JSSEA* 3,8,10
		Sethe, *Dram. Texte* 69
	to heap up	*MÄS* 37,89,7
stwt	**to stroll** (cf. *swtwt* above)	K*RI* 3,185,6
stp	**to choose, to pick, to select**	*H* 1,27,2
	picked man	K*RI* 5,40,10
	to pick	K*RI* 5,29,4
	to choose	K*RI* 5,36,11
	to select, to choose	K*RI* 5,39,11
	to select	*LEM* 10,14,10
		LEM 5,8,4
	to choose	*H* 1,42,5
	honored	*A* 1,42,9
	chosen	K*RI* 1,19,12
	select	K*RI* 1,48,6
	choice things	K*RI* 1,101,14
	picked	*CB* 1 (Pl.29) G1V5
	choicest portions	*CB* 1,17R11
	outstanding	*CB* 1,C4V1
		P.Leiden 1,350,1Vx+20
	noble, choice	*A* 1,(O.BN 12)
		A 1,2,3
	select	*A* 1(O.BN 6)
	choicest	*A* 1,5,1
	choice words	*A* 1,7,8
		CB 4,6V13 *HPBM*[3] 20
		A 1 (O.BN 15)
		O.Berlin 12654,V2 S.A. #15
stp-s3	**to extend** (protection)	K*RI* 5,100,13
stp	**to fall to ruin, to fall apart**	*JEA* 32,54,f

stp-s3	**palace**	K*RI* 1,50,12-13	
		K*RI* 2,91,3	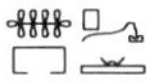
		K*RI* 2,91,4	
stf	**bad, spoiled**	*LES* 2,12,9	
		JEA 24,51	
stm	(see *sm* above)	*MDAIK* 37,322,3	
stm	**to quell, to still**	P.H. 500,12,8	
stn	**to make a distinction**	*LEM* 5,13,5	
		LEM 8,7,7	
	to remove	*LRL* 14V2	
	to distinguish	*LEM* 2,7,7	
	to be distinguished	*CB* 1 (Pl.29) G1V6	
	to be eminent	*A* 1 (O.BN 1)	
	to be distinguished	*LEM* 10,13b,5	
	to compare, to measure	*A* 1,2,5	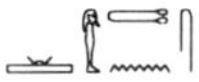
	to emulate	*JEA* 42,12	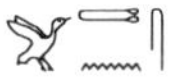
	mischievous (?)	*LEM* 10,4,6	
stn	**to keep company** (cf. *JEA* 65,84)	*CB* 1,17R5	
stnw	**squad** (cf. Wente, *Letters* p.114)	K*RI* 1,322,11	
stn	(part of the head ?)	*HPBM*^{4} L5,R10	
		HPBM^4 T1,R44	
stnw	(cf. *wstnw* above) **boldness**	*TR* 10052 (Pl. 29) 6,9	
stnm	**to lead astray**	*P.Leiden* 1,348,3R1	
str	**to go out**	*Rd'É* 24,157,40-45	
sth	**to pervert, to cause obstruction**	CB 9B,12V6-7 *HPBM*^{3} 60	
		P.Leiden 1,348,11V1	

stḥn	**dazzling**	*H* 1,8,4
	radiant	K*RI* 1,109,16
Sttyw	**Asiatics**	K*RI* 5,9,6
		K*RI* 5,22,4
		K*RI* 5,34,2-3
		K*RI* 5,57,6
stkn	**to execute, to cause to approach**	K*RI* 1,69,9
	to chase away	*BIFAO* 45,159,34
sṯ	**to pluck**	*LEM* 3,5,12
sṯ	< *sꜣt* **libation**	K*RI* 3,364,16
sṯyw	(cf. *styw* above) **vases, jars**	*H* 1,48,5
sṯꜣ	(cf. *stꜣ* above)	*H* 1,29,8
sṯꜣ-nṯr	(cf. *stꜣ* above) **corridor** (in a tomb)	*JEA* 48,58,1
sṯꜣt	**board**	*TR* 10053 (Pl.21) 4V7
		TR 10053 (Pl.21) 4V11
sṯꜣt	**aroura** (of land)	*LEM* 10,11,7
		LRL 36R6
		LEM 8,9,2
		LEM 5,9,2
		K*RI* 1,4,3
		Mes 20,52
		JEA 64,56-64
stpw	"**springer**"	*Orientalia* 49,204-7
stf	**to clean, to purify**	*JEA* 65,80

sṯn	(cf. *stn* above) **to be distinguished**	*A* 1,1,6	
sṯrty	**gleaming eyes** (cf. *Wb* 4,332,11)	*JEA* 59,126,7	
sṯs	**prop**	*H* 1,44,5	
	supports	KRI 1,47,13	
	(heavenly) **vault**	KRI 3,288,7	
sṯs	**to carry aloft**	*A* 1 (O.QC 10)	
	to remove, to lift up	KRI 1,66,10	
	to raise	KRI 3,55,14	
sd	**cloth** (of god or deceased) (cf. Janssen 272,62)	*Rd'É* 19,175	
sd-ḥw	(fish)	Valbelle, *Cat. Poids* 25	
sd	**tail**	KRI 1,56,14	
		KRI 5,41,2	
		KRI 5,63,1	
		KRI 5,30,11	
		LES 3,9,2	
		LEM 5,13,4	
	r sd r ḏ3ḏ3 **heels over head**	KRI 5,16,15	
sd	(cf. *ḥb-sd*)	*LEM* 1,4,4	
sdt	**section, column**	*A* 1,7,8	
sd	< *sḏ* **to break, penetrate**	KRI 5,21,9	
		KRI 5,32,10	
		LEM 10,10,2	
	to inflict	*LEM* 5,11,12	
		BIFAO 45,158,16	
		KRI 5,80,1	

	to smash	K*RI* 5,83,2
		K*RI* 5,91,14
	to beat	K*RI* 5,97,16
	to hew	K*RI* 1,44,5
	to pierce	K*RI* 1,53,7
	to bore	*ZÄS* 72,109
	to penetrate	K*RI* 5,92,16
		K*RI* 1,30,8
	to break	K*RI* 5,12,7
	to stop (fighting)	*JEA* 28,18
	to tear, to rend	*LES* 6,2x+19
sd-ḥrw	**face fractures**	*P.Leiden* 1,348,2R5
sd	**to clothe oneself**	*Rd'É* 24,156,5
sdt-i3dt	(part of temple)	*TR* 10053 (Pl.20) 2V12
sdw3	**to make an early start**	*JEA* 11,289,9
sdwnt	**to stretch apart, to go to pieces**	*LEM* 5,8,1
sdb	**to repress** (see *sḏb*)	Gardiner *Admonitions* 82
	to block	*ASAE* 27,227
		ZÄS 63,75,5
sdbḥ	**to furnish, to equip**	*LEM* 10,4,9
	to supply, make ready	K*RI* 5,60,4
		LEM 5,12,6
		LEM 5,13,10
	to outfit (cf. Wente, *Letters* p.168)	*PHDM* p.24
	to supply	*LEM* 5,CV6
		BIFAO 37.261
	to equip	*H* 1,7,8

	to command	*H* 1,77,9	
		K*RI* 2,11,14	
	to furnish, to equip	*RAD* 6A,1V1	
sdbḥ	**needs**	*GM* 98,13	
	gear	K*RI* 3,501,7	
	requirements	K*RI* 3,501,12	
sdbt	**hall, court** (cf. Hoch p.271)	Med. Habu 478	
	(cf. Darnell, "Two Notes" p.50)	P.Turin Cat. 1885	
sdf	(cf. *sḏf* below?) **to provide** (?)	K*RI* 1,69,10	
	to endow	*H* 1,31,4	
sdf	(a measure)(cf. Grandet n.582)	*H* 1,36b,6	
sdf	**ownership** (cf. *JEA* 34,20,4)	*H* 1,10,12	
	foundation	*Wil* (13) 29R17	
	land sustained by water	*JEA* 27,90	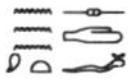
	"provision" (cf. Haring p.385)		
	"endowment" (cf. Warburton p.199)		
sdm	**eye-paint**	*CB* 1,C3,V1	
sdḫw	**plunder, victims** (?)	K*RI* 1,113,9	
sdgꜣy	**to conceal**	K*RI* 1,39,10	
sdt	**trainees** (cf. Lichtheim, *Moral Values* p.95)	K*RI* 3,296,7	
sdd	**to tremble**	K*RI* 5,25,11	
sdd	**terror, trembling**	*A* 1,24,8	
sḏ	(cf. *sd* above) **to break**	K*RI* 5,12,7	
sḏ	**to apportion**	*Wil* (5) 12R3	
		Wil (7) 16R31	
		Wil (9) 20R4	

sḏt	**apportionment**	*Wil* (4) 10R9
sḏ	(garment) (cf. Janssen p. 272; *Rd'É* 19,175; *JEA* 23,187,5)	*LEM* 6,13,4
	apron	*LES* 7,1,11
	sḏy-**garment**	*LEM* 5,3,1
	garment	*RAD* 6C,R3
		H.O. 33,1R3
		P.Vienna 34,2&5
		O.DM 198,2 S.A. #75
		H.O. 28,4R5
		O.Berlin 12647,3
		H.O. 52,2V13
sḏꜣ	**to take recreation, relax**	*LES* 1,8,7
	to be excited	P.H. 500 (Pl.14) 7,9
	sḏꜣ-ḥr **to divert oneself**	K*RI* 1,31,1
sḏꜣyt	**happiness**	P.H. 500 (Pl.2) 1,2
	sḏꜣyt-ḥr **joke, amusement**	*A* 1,(O.Louvre 4)
	"jest, joke, amusement"	*A* 1,8,7
	enjoyment	O.Glasgow D1925, 69R1
sḏꜣwty-bity	**Sealbearer of L.E.** (see *ḫtmw*) (cf. *JEA* 60,109; 61,250)	K*RI* 2,326,6
sḏwi	**to make wretched, poor**	J-W A4,c,20
sḏb	**obstacle** (cf. *ASAE* 27,227; *ZÄS* 63,75-76)	*Rd'É* 24,201-208
		Rd'É 24,205,i
sḏfꜣ(y)	**to endow, to provide**	*H* 1,46,5
		K*RI* 2,37,1
		K*RI* 1,47,7
	to supply with offerings	*JEA* 33,27,9
	to supply	K*RI* 1,42,5
	to give abundance	*CB* 1,B1,V2
	to furnish	K*RI* 1,112,4

sdf3w	**provisions**	*H* 1,7,2
	endowment	K*RI* 1,87,8
	foundation	K*RI* 1,110,1
		K*RI* 2,325,1
	endowment, foundation	*H* 1,47,11
sdf3-tr	(type of oath) (cf. *JARCE* 25,93-103)	CS 1R16
	to swear	*RAD* 18,4R3
	to substantiate (cf. *JEA* 49,79; 50,179)	P.Lee 1,1
sḏm	**to hear**	*LES* 2,7,4 *LRL* 1R6
		P.H. 500 (Pl.4) 2,5
	to listen	*LES* 2,1,10
		K*RI* 5,23,3
		LES 4,4,9
		LRL 47,R10
		LRL 24V4
	to receive (letter)	*LEM* 16,6V5
		LRL 21R2
		K*RI* 2,81,2
		K*RI* 2,114,10
		P.H. 500 (Pl.14) 7,10
	to acknowledge	*LEM* 3,3V2
	to comprehend, to have knowledge	*Rd'É* 24,205
	to hearken	*LRL* 28R27
	to understand	*JEA* 16,69,17
	to note	*LRL* 18R2
	to take notice	K*RI* 3,234,4
	to make note of	K*RI* 2,910,16
	to read	*A* 1,12,7
	to hear, obey	K*RI* 1,99,6
	to learn	*LES* 3,8,4
	to grant	*LES* 1,17,10
	to understand	*LES* 5,2,77

	sḏm-mdw **to investigate**	*JEA* 48,33	
		LEM 5,2,7	
sḏmw	**hearing**	*LEM* 10,13b,10	
	examination, judgment	O.Berlin 11241,2 S.A. #13	
sḏm	(see *sgr*) **keep**	*Wil* (62) B15V26	
sḏm	(cf. *sdm* above) **eye-paint**	*CB* 1,C3V1	
sḏmy	**hearer**	K*RI* 1,50,13	
	judge	*RAD* 8R2	
		RAD 18,6V2	
		JEA 42,9;41(Pl.7)1,4	
	servant	*TR* 10052 (Pl.27) 4,15	
		LEM 4,2	
	st-sḏmyw **audience hall**	*MÄS* 37,88,8	
sḏm-ꜥš	**servant** (cf. *ZÄS* 101,81,89)	*LRL* 43R1	
		LEM 10,15,1	
		RAD 2,2R10	
		TR Abbott (Pl.24) B12	
		Wil (10) 22R15	
		JEA 54,145	
		BIFAO 28,201,1	
		LRL 23R10	
		ZÄS 101,81-89 #44	
		ZÄS 101,81,89 #30	
sḏr	**to sleep, to go to bed**	*LES* 1,4,2	
	to lie	*LES* 2,13,2	
		LES 4,2,12	
	to sleep	O.Glasgow D.1925,79R6	
	to be bedridden	K*RI* 3,542,12	
	to prostrate	Gardiner & Sethe pl.7,16	
	to sleep together	Schreiber 315-335	

		LES 5,2,53	
	to spend the night	*LEM* 1,3,7	
	to lie down	*ZÄS* 106,17	
	to stretch out	K*RI* 2,89,6	
	to be inert, inactive	*JEA* 16,68	
	to sleep with	P.DM 21,R6 S.A. p.272	
	to be idle	*LEM* 13,3V1	
	st-sḏr **bed**	CS 1V2	
sḏrt	**prostration**	*LEM* 5,9,12	
		LEM 3,6,1	
	resting place	*LEM* 10,10,8-9	
	sleeping mat	Janssen p.158	
	night camp, bivouac (cf. *JEA* 24,191,6)	*A* 1,18,1	
	campsite	*A* 1,25,2	
sḏr	**at nighttime**	*LES* 7,3,6	
sḏr	**perseverence**	CB 4,1V7 *HPBM*^{3} 18	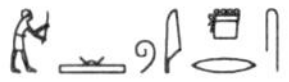
sḏr	**to writhe**	K*RI* 5,73,8	
sḏrw	**strong people**	*LEM* 12,5V8	
sḏḥ	**skin**	*HPBM*^{4} L1,V8-9	
		HPBM^{4} L6,R40	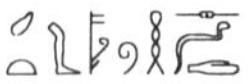
sḏḥy	**to be exhausted**	*LEM* 8,5,8	
sḏsr	**to sanctify** (cf. *JEA* 32,51)	K*RI* 1,126,2	
		H 1,28,7	
sḏt	**flame, fire**	K*RI* 5,16,8	
		K*RI* 1,18,2	

sḏd	**to relate**	*LEM* 2,1,1	
		LRL 26R6	
	to quarrel, argue, discuss	*TR* 10052 (Pl.30) 8,9	
sḏd	**tale**	Push 124,4,9-10	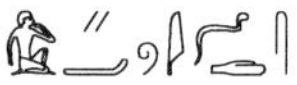
	recital	*LEM* 5,6,1	
		K*RI* 3,771,15	
	conversation	*LES* 1,5,10	
	adage (cf. Wente, *Letters* p.178)	*LRL* 41,15	
sḏdt	**report**	K*RI* 2,81,1	
sḏd	**to make permanent**	K*RI* 1,67,6	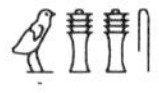

š	**pool, pond, lake**	*LES* 4,14,4
		LEM 10,12,8
		LEM 6,11,4
		K*RI* 1,13,11
		RAD 2,2R12
		Wil (18) 40R43
		Wil (16) 34R8
		LEM 3,2,2
		LEM 17,6
		LEM 9,2V6
		HPBM[4] L1,V25
	š-šʿf **reservoirs**	*LEM* 5,15,9
	imy-r-š **sea-captain**	*JEA* 4,34,9
š	(vessel)	Push 127,1,10
šꜣ	(fruit)	*LEM* 5,12,8
		H 1,9,4
	(trees, dategroves)	*H* 1,8,3
	(flowers)	*A* 1,25,3
	(bushes)	K*RI* 1,49,12
šꜣ	**meadow, marsh**	K*RI* 2,333,6
	papyrus thicket	P.H. 500 (Pl.8) 4,2
	meadow	*Wil* (54) B7V1
šꜣ	**pig, swine**	*P.Leiden* 1,348,4R9
	(cf. Janssen p.177; *JNES* 6,222,12)	K*RI* 1,55,1
	swine	K*RI* 1,54,12
	sow (cf. Wente, *Letters* p.115)	K*RI* 1,324,1
šꜣ	**to ordain**	*LES* 3,6,1
		K*RI* 2,56,14
	to owe	*LRL* 9V17

	to determine, foretell	*LES* 1,4,3	
š3	**worthy** (cf. *š3y*)	CS 2V1	
	m-š3 **as is fitting** (cf. Wente, *Letters* p.175)	*LRL* 37V11	
	p3-š3 **what ought**	Bakir pl.26,7	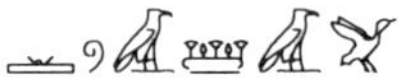
š3	**to go around**	*BIFAO* 45,159,25	
	to founder	CB 7,5R5 *HPBM*[3] 34	
š3y	**destined**	K*RI* 5,42,5	
		CB 1,17R9	
		K*RI* 1,113,10	
		K*RI* 1,114,12	
	victim of fate	*HPBM*[4] L2,R75	
	worthy of (death)	S.A. #217, p.216,19	
	predestined	K*RI* 3,339,10	
š3y	**fate** (cf. Morenz, *Schicksals* ASAW 52)	*LES* 5,2,58	
		LES 1,4,3	
		LEM 6,9,7	
	destiny	*LEM* 12,5V6	
		H 1,44,6	
		P.H. 500 (pl.12) 6,3	
		CB 4,6V6 *HPBM*[3] 20	
	fate, doom	*TR* Amherst (Pl.5) 3,9	
	condemnation	P.Leopold 2,3,19 *JEA* 22,182	
		JEA 65,87	
		K*RI* 2,227,9	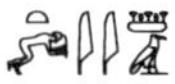
		K*RI* 2,228,13	
		K*RI* 2,326,12	
		HPBM[4] T2,R19	
	disposition (cf. Wente, *Letters* p.154)	Sauneron OH pl.20,518	
	iri-š3yt.s **to make arrangements for her**	Pestman, *Marriage* 100	

šꜣyt	**taxes**	*H* 1,12a,1 *LEM* 3,6,12
	dues	*LEM* 6,17,2-3
		H 1,28,5
		H 1,32,7
		JEA 27,20,3
šꜣꜥ	**to begin, to start** (cf. *JEA* 29,12; 57,114)	*A* 1,8,2
		K*RI* 1,112,2
	to elapse	K*RI* 3,546,5
šꜣꜥ	**until**	*H* 1,9,5
	till	*LRL* 47R11
	up to	*LES* 5,1,6
	from	*LRL* 28V8
	since	K*RI* 5,59,4
	šꜣꜥ-m **beginning from**	K*RI* 5,43,9
	from	*H* 1,13a,3
	m-šꜣꜥ **from**	K*RI* 2,16,14
	m-šꜥꜥ-n-ḏr	H.O. 70,2,9
	r-šꜣꜥ **from**	*LES* 4,16,2
	from, since	*LEM* 10,12,7
	down to	*LEM* 12,1V2
		LRL 30R11
		K*RI* 5,21,2
	till, up to	*JNES* 28,186
	unto	*TR* Abbott (Pl.3) 6,7
	down to, as far as	*TR* Abbott (Pl. 3) 5,11
		TR Abbott (Pl.14) 2V2
šꜣꜥ	**beginning**	*H* 1,44,4
šꜣꜥ	(unknown)	*LEM* 3,3,5
šꜣꜥ	(cf. *šrꜥ* below) **keep**	*TR* Amherst (Pl.5) 4,3
šꜣꜥt	(property ?)	*Rd'É* 9,113

š3ʿ3r	(cf. *šʿr* below)	Helck, *Bez* 570,216	
š3ʿ-n-ḫpr	**first to come into existence**	*HPBM*[4] L1,V18	
		HPBM[4] L2,R54	
š3w	**worth, value** (cf. *JEA* 42,14)	*LES* 2,3,4	
	fit, worthy of, suitable	*LEM* 4,3	
		LES 10,8,1	
	fitting	K*RI* 3,502,15	
	proper	Gardiner & Sethe pl.8,36	
	weight	K*RI* 1,126,5	
	weight	*TR* 10383 (Pl.22) 1,9	
	equivalent	*LES* 4,11,7	
	weight	K*RI* 1,97,10	
	capacity	*LEM* 5,9,1	
	m-š3w **properly**	K*RI* 1,42,3	
	n-š3w **properly**	*LEM* 5,16,5	
š3wt	**fitting things** (cf. *Wb.* 4,409,17)	*MÄS* 37,75	
š3wt	**coriander**	*LEM* 4,1	
		LEM 10,11,5	
		P.Leiden 1,348,3V4	
		O.Glasgow D1925,88	
š3w3bti	**shawabti** (cf. *JEA* 23,188)	O.Chicago 16,987,V1 Janssen p. 243	
		A 1,4,3	
		BIFAO 28,200	
		K*RI* 3,154,2	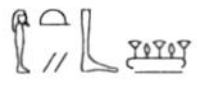
		K*RI* 3,475,9	
š3b	(measure)	*LEM* 9,15a,V5	
š3bwy	(or *šb*) (stone) (cf. Harris, *Minerals* 183)	Helck, *Bez* 570,218	
	necklace (cf. Wente, *Letters* p.145)	K*RI* 4,416,14	

š3bwty	(cf. *šwbt*) (a wooden implement) (cf. Wente, *Letters* p.137)	*MDAIK* 37,10R8 O.Berlin P.12398 K*RI* 7,194,6	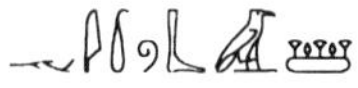
š3bd	(cf. *šbd* below) **stock**	Helck, *Bez* 570,220 *JEA* 19 (Pl.19) 5	
š3p	(cf. *šp* below) **bouncing**	*LEM* 5,12,3	
šꜥpt	(cf. *špt* below) **to judge**	*ZÄS* 53,28,45	
š3fd	(cf. *šfd* below) **to be apprehended**	*TR* 10068 (Pl.9) 1R8	
š3m	(cf. *šm* below)	Helck, *Bez* 570,221	
š3mw	(cf. *šm* below) **to traverse**	K*RI* 5,24,9	
š3nrfy	(cf. *šnrf* below)	Helck, *Bez* 570, 222	
š3nš	(cf. *šnš* below) **smelly** (?)	*LEM* 5,9,10	
š3rꜥ	(cf. *šrꜥ* below)	Helck, *Bez* 570,223	
š3rm	(cf. *šrm* below) **peace**	K*RI* 5,68,12-13	
š3rmꜥti	(cf. *šrmt* below) **provisions**	Helck, *Bez* 571,226	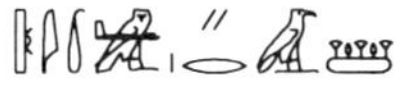
š3rg3ḥ	(cf. *šrgḥ* below) **senses**	*JEA* 65,79-80,8	
š3ḥ3ḳ3	(cf. *šḥḳ* below)	Helck, *Bez* 571,227	
š3sw	(bedouin)	*A* 1,20,4 K*RI* 6,520,13	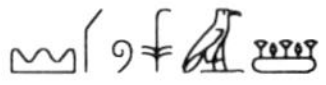 
š3š3	(cf. *šš* below) **silly**	*TR* 10052 (Pl.31) 10,8	
š3ḳ	(or *šḳ3*) (unknown)	*LES* 6,1x+4	

š3ḳw	(or *šk*) **column drums** (cf. *JNES* 28,1)	*TR* 10054 (Pl.6) 3R9	
	pole rings (cf. Janssen 201,14)	*TR* 10403 (Pl.36) 1,24	
	bracelet (cf. Wente, *Letters* p.156)	*O.H.* pl.6,125	
š3k3n3	(cf. *škn* below) **watering place**	Helck, *Bez* 571,228	
š3k3rʿ	(cf. *škrʿ* below) **basket**	*TR* 10068 (Pl.12) 5R17	
š3g3r	(cf. *šgr* below) **chest**	Helck, *Bez* 571,230	
š3g3r	(see *šgr* below) **trench**	*Onom.* A40	
š3ti	(cf. *šti* below) **haft**	*LES* 3,10,4	
š3d	(cf. *šd* below) **to pillage**	*A* 1,20,5	
š3dyrwtit	(cf. *šdrt* below) **abyss**	Helck, *Bez* 571,232	
šʿ	**to cut off, to diminish**	*HPBM*[4] L2,R89	
šʿt	**barley meal**	*H.O.* 69,2 S.A. #195	
šʿt	**knife**	K*RI* 1,103,4	
šʿt	**terror**	*Eretz Israel* 5,80,h	
	massacre	*Rd'É* 24,202,5	
	murderousness	*LEM* 2,3,4	
	slaughter	K*RI* 1,103,6	
		K*RI* 3,491,2	
	dread, terror	K*RI* 5,93,1	
šʿt	**letter, dispatch**	*LRL* 1R7	
		LEM 5,11,7	
		LES 5,2,68	
		LRL 9R8	

		LRL 1V5
		LRL 6V4
		LES 5,1,x+17
		LRL 25R4
		LRL 8V8
		LRL 51R8
		RAD 25,3V10
	letter	*A* 1,4,5
	dispatch	*Wil* (7) 16R18
	correspondence	K*RI* 3,206,8
	letter	Push 127,1,1
	message (cf. *JEA* 61,149)	*HPBM*[4] L6,V44
	st-šꜥt **dispatch office**	*Wil* (19) 42R8
šꜥy(t)	**storeroom**	*RAD* 17,5R4
šꜥy(t)	**sand**	*A* 1,16,6
		LEM 5,9,3
		LEM 17,8
		H 1,4,4
		H 1,8,4
		H 1,29,12
		Melanges... Mokhtar 2,349,13
		H 1,76,8
		K*RI* 2,112,7
		K*RI* 2,25,5
		K*RI* 1,87,10
šꜥyt	(cake)	P.H. 500 (Pl.10) 5,1
		LES 8,2,9
		RAD 2,1A,V6
	date cake	*LEM* 16,10V5
šꜥwt	**letter writing**	*LEM* 8,3,4

šʿf	(in *š-šʿf*) **reservoirs**	*LEM* 5,15,9
šʿr	**promise** (cf. Helck, *Bez* 570-216) **calculation, scheme** (cf. Hoch p.272)	*LEM* 1,2,5
	promise, threat (cf. *JEA* 42,17)	*JEA* 41 (Pl.9) 3,8
	market price (cf. Hoch p.273)	O.Cairo 25604,2
	protest	Push 127,4,5-6
	protest	*ZÄS* 94,134
šʿr	**to scheme** (cf. Hoch p.274)	P.Bologna 1094,2,5
šʿr	(cf. *šrʿ* below) **keep**	Helck, *Bez* 570,215
šʿrt	**vixen** (cf. Hoch p.274)	P.Mag.Brooklyn 4,2
šʿty	**silver-piece, money** (cf. *JNES* 24,105; *JEA* 24,139; Janssen 102,8)	O.Gard 123
šʿd	**to cut off**	*LES* 2,7,9
	to cut down	*LES* 5,2,43
	to fell	*LES* 5,2,56
		RAD 18a,1V12
	cutters	*RAD* 18d,2V13
		CS 1R7
	to slaughter	K*RI* 5,71,9
	to break, to crush (cf. Grandet p.288; *JEA* 37,29)	*H* 1,15b,9
	to cut	K*RI* 2,150,15
		K*RI* 1,13,8
	to cut down	*LES* 2,8,4
	to cut off	*HPBM*[4] T2,R92
	to part	*RAD* 25,1R2
	to part with	*JEA* 15,247
	to cut	*LRL* 36V3
	m šʿd **to be mutilated**	*ASAE* 43,79,d

šʿd	**piece**	*JEA* 49,173,6	
šʿd-ḫt	**wood cutter** (cf. Janssen pp.40 & 52)	*RAD* 18,2V13	
		TR 10068 (Pl.16) 6V6	
šʿd	**log, wood**	Janssen p.371	
šw	**sun**	*LES* 1,7,12	
	sunlight	*LES* 9,F12	
		K*RI* 5,21,15	
		K*RI* 5,38,5	
		K*RI* 1,113,14	
šw	**to be dry**	*Wil* (59) B12V8	
		Wil (11) 25R3	
	to be dried up	Push 127,4,10	
	to be deprived of	Push 127,4,13	
		Naun 5,12	
	to be lacking	*JEA* 61,152,13	
	to be empty, void	*LES* 5,2,7	
		K*RI* 3,502,13	
	to be idle	*LES* 5,2,28	
	to be free from, empty, void	*LEM* 2,6,1	
		LEM 13,3V8	
	to be devoid	*LEM* 5,5,9	
		H 1,75,4	
	idly	*LEM* 6,7,4	
		TR Abbott (Pl.2) 2,4	
	to be vacant	*LES* 4,3,10	
		K*RI* 2,335,14	
	to be needy	Push 127,4,8	
	šw-ʿw **to be avaricious, greedy**	J-W A10,e,8-9	

šw	**waste, desert**	*A* 1,26,2	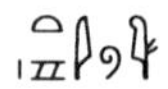
šwt	(cf. *š* above) **lakes**	*LEM* 9,2V6	
šwy	**rushes**	*LEM* 5,2,11	
	"dry grass," "hay" (cf. Janssen 154)	*LEM* 10,11,6	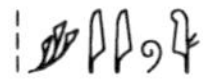
	dried grass (cf. Wente, *Letters* p.164)	Černý, *OH* (1970) pl.6,123	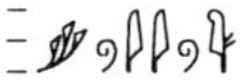
	woods	*LES* 3,10,3	
šwy	**to trade, to sell**	*TR* 10052 (Pl.27) 3,19	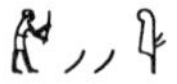
		TR 10403 (Pl.37) 3,4	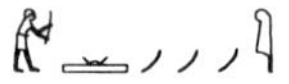
		TR 10403 (Pl.37) 3,6	
		TR 10403 (Pl.37) 3,13	
šwyt	**selling, merchandising** "**barter**" (cf. Megally, *Recherches* 254f)	K*RI* 2,333,1	
	tp-šw **distribution**	K*RI* 2,325,14	
šwyty	**merchant, trader** (cf. *JEA* 68,127,6)	K*RI* 2,8,40	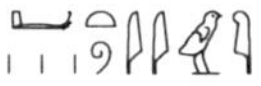
		K*RI* 2,333,1	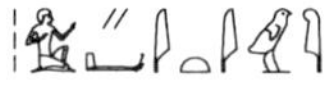
		LEM 1,5,5	
		LEM 10,4,8	
		LEM 10,7,1	
		TR 10068 (Pl.11) 4,18	
		TR 10053 (Pl.17) 1R10	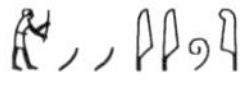
		TR 10053 (Pl.17) 1R15	
		TR 10053 (Pl.18) 4R4	
		TR 10053 (Pl.18) 4R5	
		TR 10052 (Pl.28) 5,1	
		H 1,46,2	
šwtyw	**merchandise** (?)	*JEA* 36,24 (Pl.7a)	
	occupation, trade	K*RI* 3,138,11	
šwt	**sun shade**	*Wil* (3) 9R1	
		Wil (48) 98R17	
		Wil (49) 100R9	

	shadow or shade (of a person)	*KRI* 3,216,8	
	(or *ḫ3ybt*) **shadow**	*KRI* 5,27,16	
	sunshade	*Wil* (18) 40R21	
	šwty-Rʿ **sunshade of Re**	*Wil* (63) B16,V22	
		Wil (70) B23,V4	
		Wil (8) 19R27	
	(cult place of the sun god) **shade of Re**	*MDAIK* 25,159	
šwty	**plumes**	*LES* 4,4,11	
		H 1,44,3	
	two plumes	*KRI* 5,38,10	
	double plumes	*H* 1,76,4	
	two feathers	*KRI* 5,77,10	
		RAD 25,1V9	
	feathers	*KRI* 2,151,12	
		KRI 5,89,8	
		KRI 1,114,2	
	s3b-šwty (see above) **variegated of plumage**	*KRI* 1,11,11	
šw3	**to become impoverished**	*LRL* 13R5	
	to be small, unimportant	J-W A1,b,9	
šw3	**poor man**	*KRI* 5,21,6	
		ZÄS 70,114	
		KRI 3,336,13	
šwb	**persea tree**	*LES* 2,16,10	
		LEM 1,11,2	
		P.H. 500 (Pl.6) 3,13	
šwbt	(cf. *šbd* below & *š3bwty* above) **stick, staff, rod** (cf. Hoch p.275)	*JEA* 23,188	
	baton	*MDAIK* 37,10R8 O.Berlin P.12398	

šwbty	(vase or vessel) (cf. Hoch p.275)	Helck, *Bez* 570,219	
šwbyt	(for *ḫ3ybt* ?) **shadow, shade** (?)	CB 4,6V5 *HPBM*[3] 20	
		K*RI* 5,26,11	
		K*RI* 5,39,4	
		K*RI* 5,58,1	
		H 1,78,8	
šwšt	**administration** (?) (cf. Hoch p.275)	Louvre Leather Roll 4,6	
šb	**to send out**	K*RI* 5,28,10	
šb	**to exchange**	K*RI* 1,55,2	
		BIFAO 83 P.Boulaq XIII 8a,1	
	to change, to replace	*HPBM*[4] L7,19	
		HPBM[4] L5,V7	
	to possess, be master of	*HPBM*[4] T2,V107	
šb	**condiments** (cf. Wente, *Letters* p.39)	K*RI* 6,522,4	
šb(*t*)	**equivalence, value**	K*RI* 1,44,13	
		K*RI* 5,86,4	
	price	*JEA* 14,299 (Pl.35)	
	value, price	O.Glasgow D.1925,81R10	
	wages	*Studies ... Griffith* 56,2	
	payments	K*RI* 3,548,5	
	substitution, exchange	*HPBM*[4] T1,R90	
	dit m šb **to sell**	*JNES* 6,224,42	
		JEA 12,71,8	
		RAD 25,1R2	
	dit šb **value**	K*RI* 1,44,13	

šbt	**gourds, cucumbers**	*LEM* 4,1	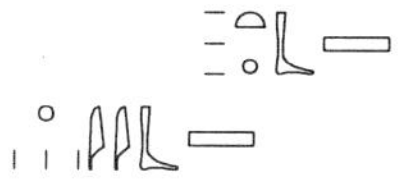
		P.Turin 2008+2016,1V8	
		LEM 5,15,11	
šbt	**offerings** (in a temple)	*SAK* 7,65-74	
šby	(a precious stone, agate?) (cf. Hoch p.275)	CB 4,7V12	
šbw	**meal**	LEM 10,14,1	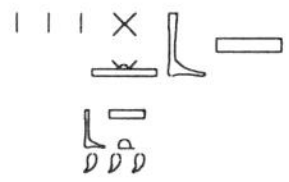
	repast	K*RI* 3,136,13	
šbb	**meal, food**	*A* 1,26,2	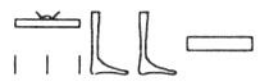
šbb	(granulated substance)	*RAD* 18,5V14	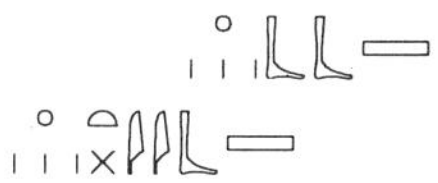
	beads (cf. Janssen p.304)	*JEA* 49,173,5	
šbn	**to mingle with, mix with**	*LEM* 17,13	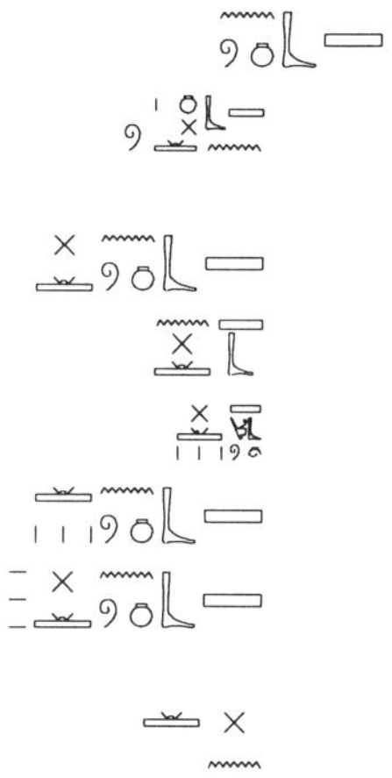
	to associate with	*Melanges...Mokhtar* 2,352,23	
	to consort with	*H* 1,3,5	
	to mingle	K*RI* 2,336,2	
		K*RI* 3,380,15	
	to mingle with	*LEM* 2,9,3	
	to combine	CB 4,7V5 *HPBM*[3] 21	
		LEM 5,14,2 *H* 1,11,5	
šbn	**assorted**	*LEM* 5,17,6	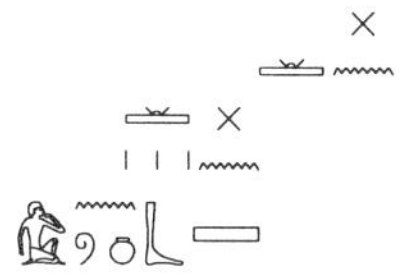
	various types	*A* 1,17,6	
	various	*JNES* 14,162	
šbrt	**flowing stream, torrent**	Shishak List 73&75	
šbd	**staff, rod** (cf. Janssen 382-4; Hoch pp.276-7; *Essays...Kantor* p.302) Coptic **ϣⲃⲱⲧ**	*LEM* 6,16,6	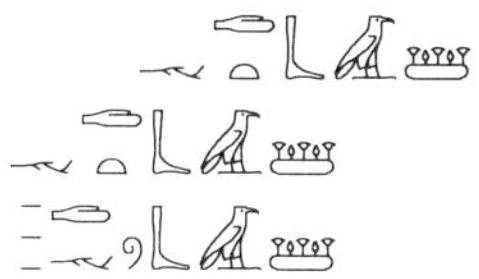
		RAD 18c,5V7	
		LEM 8,6,6	

		LEM 10,7,2
		LEM 13,1V9
		P.H. 500 (Pl.4) 2,3-4
šp	**to erect** (cf. *JEA* 11,285,10)	K*RI* 2,329,1
šp	**to smell, to inhale**	K*RI* 3,410,14
šp	**to break out**	*P.Leiden* 1,348,3R3
šp	**bouncing**	*LEM* 5,12,3
	boomerang	*LEM* 10,2,1
šp-n-st-ḥmt	**donation for the wife**	*JEA* 67,118
šps	**to establish, to endure**	J-W A5,d,3; 4,2,27
		J-W A1,c,2
šps	**noble, splendid, rich**	*LRL* 42V3
		LRL 5R1
		H 1,3,1
		P.Turin 2008-2016, 1R13
	venerable, august	*BIFAO* 75,104
	valuable	K*RI* 1,101,12
		LRL 1R1
		K*RI* 5,39,9
	august	K*RI* 5,17,13
		K*RI* 5,41,7
		LRL 6R1
		K*RI* 1,38,10
	precious	*H* 1,8,1
	august	K*RI* 1,26,12
		K*RI* 1,66,16
	magnificent	K*RI* 1,112,3
	costly	K*RI* 5,97,7
		K*RI* 1,74,9
		LRL 23R2

	nobles	CB 8,7R10 *HPBM*^{3} 41	
		K*RI* 3,845,5	
	špsy n-nsw **king's nobles**	K*RI* 2,326,6-7	
špsy	**nobleness, nobility**	*H* 1,26,5	
špsy	**lady**	*P.Leiden* 1,350,2V7	
	noble ladies	*LEM* 9,4V3	
		LES 2,12,3	
		LES 2,18,4	
		HPBM^4 C1,55	
		LES 2,15,8	
		HPBM^4 C1,56	
špssw	**riches**	K*RI* 1,48,7	
špssw	**to enrich** (cf. *JEA* 39,20)	K*RI* 1,126,4	
šf	**laceration**	CB 4,5V10 *HPBM*^{3} 20	
šft	(unknown)	*LEM* 9,4V6	
šfy	**to be contemptible,** **to be maligned** (?) (cf. Wente, *Letters* p.173)	*LRL* 46R4	
šfyt	**terribleness**	K*RI* 5,47,14	
	awfulness	*LEM* 2,4,3	
	worth	*LES* 1,7,1	
	respect, fear	*H* 1,22,8	
		H 1,66b,7	
		K*RI* 2,92,5	
		K*RI* 2,8,14	
	awe	K*RI* 5,57,6	

	awe, dread	K*RI* 5,35,12
		K*RI* 5,36,14
		K*RI* 5,29,12
		K*RI* 5,85,2
		K*RI* 5,38,13
	renown	K*RI* 3,173,9
	terror	K*RI* 5,21,4
	awe, majesty	K*RI* 5,13,3
		K*RI* 5,20,6
	dignity	*JEA* 27,45
	authority	P.Lee 1,2 *JEA* 49,78
	respect, honor	K*RI* 5,110,6
	awestruck	K*RI* 5,24,8
	wrath	K*RI* 5,13,6
šfy	**skilled, schooled**	K*RI* 3,480,13
šfʿ	**to seize upon**	K*RI* 5,69,9
	to fight	K*RI* 1,21,2
	to fight, to seize upon	K*RI* 1,102,10
	to cut, to attack	K*RI* 2,26,15
šfw	(small bird) **sparrow** (?)	*JEA* 50
	(small fowl) (cf. E-W 60,4a)	K*RI* 5,44,8
šfnw	**bushes**	K*RI* 5,65,1
	undergrowth, underbrush (cf. *Rd'É* 38,p.67,9)	CB 5,7R1 *HPBM*³ 25
šfšf	**awe, respect**	*H* 1,22,10
	renown	K*RI* 3,484,8
šfšf	**to swell up**	*JEA* 29,13,k
šfšf	**to look upon, regard, to consider**	*ZÄS* 85,36,2

šfd	**to grasp**	*A* 1,4,3	
	to apprehend, seize	*TR* 10068 (Pl.9) 1R8	
šfdiꜣ	**chest**	*TR* 10403 (Pl.36) 2,3	
		TR 10403 (Pl.36) 1,13	
šfdw	**book**	*LEM* 6,18,4	
		CB 4,2V12 *HPBM*[3] 18	
šm	**to go** (cf. *Orientalia* 45,401-2; *ZÄS* 106,20)	*LES* 6,3y-1	
		LEM 5,4,5	
		LRL 28V4	
	to go along	*LEM* 2,11,2	
	to go	*LES* 5,1,12	
		P.H. 500 (Pl.14) 7,9-10	
	to depart	*LES* 2,14,9	
	to return	P.H. 500 (Pl.8) 4,8	
	to go off	*LES* 3,8,1	
		K*RI* 5,31,5	
	to move, to come & go	*A* 1,10,3	
	to march	K*RI* 2,15,3	
	to come to pass	*LES* 9,F9	
	to walk, to emerge	K*RI* 2,7,2	
	to proceed	*LES* 1,6,2	
		K*RI* 1,40,14	
	to go forth	K*RI* 5,85,15	
		K*RI* 2,31,3	
	to set apart, to leave	K*RI* 1,114,7	
	to set out	*LES* 1,6,11	
	šm ii **going & coming**	*LRL* 8V7	
	di šm **to send**	*LES* 2,16,7	
	šmt r ꜥḥꜥ **an opposing stand** (cf. Wente, *Letters* p.128)	K*RI* 6,66,13	
šm	**to whirl around**	*LEM* 5,11,8	
	to whirl	*LEM* 6,15,6	

	to reel, to whirl around	CB 1,G2,V2
		Helck, *Bez* 570,221
šm	**business**	*TR* 10052 (Pl.31) 11,6
	travel, business	*TR* 10052 (Pl.25) 6
šm	**father-in-law** (cf. Fischer, *Varia* 19-27)	*JEA* 66,100
šmt	**route**	*A* 1,21,7
	passageway	*JEA* 46,48 (Pl.13) R21
šm3	(?) (disease)	*HPBM*[4] T2,R82
	demons, disease bearing demons	K*RI* 2,285,15
		K*RI* 2,286,7
		HPBM[4] L1,R48-49
		HPBM[4] L3,B45-46
		HPBM[4] L6,R49
		HPBM[4] T1,V7
		HPBM[4] P2,R15-16
šmyt	**storehouse**	*RAD* 17,2R5
		RAD 17,5R3
šmꜥ	**to hear** (cf. Hoch p.279)	*ZÄS* 50,122
šmꜥw	**Upper Egypt**	*H* 1,33b,2
		H 1,45,8
		K*RI* 5,101,1
		K*RI* 5,38,11
	it šmꜥw **U.E. barley**	*JEA* 17,154
	t3 šmꜥw **southbound**	K*RI* 2,336,8
šmꜥyw	**Upper Egyptians, southerners**	K*RI* 2,332,12
šmꜥ(t)	**thin, fine material** (cf. Janssen 140,43)	O.Berlin 14214,V6 S.A. #16
	linen	*LES* 5,2,40

	fine	O.Glasgow D1925,89,2,2	
		K*RI* 6,522,1	
šmꜥ	**spare, slender** (cf. *OLZ* 58,245)	*LEM* 10,7,8	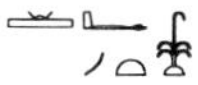
šmꜥt-ḥtp	**bundles of sedge**	P.Turin 2008+2016,1V12	
šmꜥy	**singer**	*TR* 10054 (Pl.7) 2V1	
	chantress (see *šmꜥyt*)	*LEM* 1,8,5	
šmꜥyt	**songstress, chantress, singer** (cf. *JEA* 7,8)	*LRL* 5R1	
		TR 10052 (Pl.25) 1,12	
	singer	*A* 1 (O.BN 10)	
		LRL 8R13	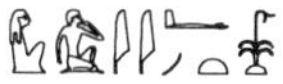
		TR Abbott (Pl.2) 3,17	
		LEM 9,1V1	
		LEM 1,9,7	
		LRL 14R9	
		LRL 6R2	
		TR 10068 (Pl.11) 4R13	
	female musician	*RAD* 17,2R10	
šmꜥwt	**chants**	K*RI* 3,657,10	
šmw	**Third Season, Summer**	*LES* 9,F4	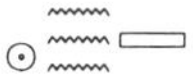
		LRL 9R6	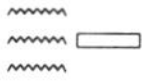
		HPBM[4] L3,B13	
		LES 5,1,6	
		LRL 16R14a	
	harvest	*LRL* 26V6	
		MÄS 37,3,88,6	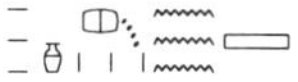
	harvest	*RAD* 12A,2R9	
	harvest taxes	*Wil* (7) 16R14	
		RAD 17,2R4	
	harvest tax (cf. *JEA* 27,20 & 56,109)	*LEM* 6,16,5	

	grain import (cf. Warburton pp.282-286)	K*RI* 3,157,1	
šm(*m*)	**hot, warm**	*LEM* 6,6,5	
	passionate (cf. *JSSEA* 8,134)	*LEM* 8,8,6	
		Lange *Amenemope* 4,17 p.35	
		P.Leiden 1,350,6R7	
	hot	O.Berlin 10645+46,V2 S.A. #9	
	"the hot one"	*GM* 38,21-28	
	burning	*LEM* 3,7,7	
šm(*m*)	**fever, heat**	CB 4,8R4 *HPBM*[3] 15	
		HPBM[4] L1,R50	
		HPBM[4] L5,V45-6	
		HPBM[4] T1,V72	
		CB 4,6V5 *HPBM*[3] 20	
		RAD 22,1R2	
šmmt	**storehouse**	*RAD* 25,1V4	
	chambers	*A* 1,4,7 & 16,7	
	stable	*LEM* 10,12,4	
šmrt	**bow**	K*RI* 5,82,12	
		K*RI* 5,16,8	
šms	**to follow**	CB 4,6V10 *HPBM*[3] 20	
		P.Leiden 1,350,2V24	
		P.H. 500 (Pl.12) 6,9	
		H 1,79,8	
	ḥr šms **itinerant**	*JEA* 23,161	
	šms-ib **to follow the conscience**	*JARCE* 7,41-54; 8,55,57	
šmsw	**follower**	*A* 1(O.BN 4)	
	retainer, servant	*LRL* 26R8	

	attendant	*TR* 10054 (Pl.8) 5V2	
		K*RI* 3,210,1	
	messenger	*LRL* 5R5	
	henchman	*LRL* 15R12	
	apparitor	*LEM* 8,5,7	
		A 1,1,8	
	retainer	*LEM* 5,11,7	
	followers	*LEM* 2,8,7	
	retainers	*LEM* 6,11,5	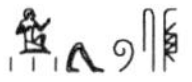
	guards	K*RI* 5,31,11	
	bodyguard	K*RI* 5,83,11	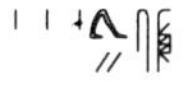
		LEM 3,6V1	
	escort	*LES* 1,5,10	
	followers	*LRL* 17R8	
		LRL 45V6	
	retainer	*LEM* 12,4V2	
		K*RI* 2,10,9	
šms	**following**	*RAD* 25,2R5	
	service	*LEM* 8,7,1	
		K*RI* 3,542,13	
	train	*A* 1 (O.QC 6)	
	train of, retinue	*A* 1,3,4	
	šms-nsw **royal retinue**	K*RI* 1,9,12	
		K*RI* 5,91,7	
	šms-ḥr **Following of Horus** (biennial tour of country) (religious standard) (cf. *ZÄS* 85,118f.)	Claessen *The Early State* 1978, 221	

šn	**tree**	*LRL* 5V8
		LES 4,6,2
		H 1,27,11
		P.H. 500 (Pl.6) 3,9
		HPBM[4] L2,V9
		MÄS 37,20,2,3
		H 1,60,7
		LEM 5,8,9
		H 1,27,9
		K*RI* 1,47,16
		K*RI* 3,463,15 (SIC)
šnyw	**garden enclosure**	*H* 1,31,1
	fowl yard, pool	P.H. 500 (Pl.8) 4,10
	groves	*H* 1,11,6
šni	**to encompass**	K*RI* 5,92,15
	to encircle	K*RI* 5,22,4
	to embrace, surround, around (cf. Wente, *Letters* p.196)	*LRL* 29R10
		K*RI* 1,1,9
		K*RI* 1,34,9
	to encircle	K*RI* 5,66,5
	to encircle, surround	K*RI* 1,30,7
	to survive	K*RI* 4,81,11
	šn-wr **ocean**	CB 4,10R10 *HPBM*[3] 16
		K*RI* 5,97,14
šnw	**circuit**	K*RI* 5,26,1
		H 1,25,6
		K*RI* 5,84,12
	enclosure	K*RI* 5,35,2
		K*RI* 1,49,6
šnw	**nets**	P.H. 500 (Pl.8) 4,8
	net	*JEA* 28,14

šnw	(vessels)	*LEM* 11,4,3	
		LEM 14,1V1	
	bags	*LEM* 11,1,2	
šni	**to curse**	*LES* 2,5,4	
	to plot	K*RI* 1,9,4	
	to conjure	*P.Leiden* 1,348,12V4	
	to enchant	*LES* 1,6,2	
	to conjure	*LES* 4,6,4	
	to invoke	*A* 1,8,2	
šnt	**conjurer** (cf. *JEA* 70,71)	*P.Leiden* 1,348,12V10-11	
šni	**to inquire**	*LEM* 12,4V5	
		LEM 13,2V10	
	to question, to plot, to utter sedition	K*RI* 1,9,4	
	to investigate	O.DM 114,5	
	to call in question, to feel agrieved at (?)	*JEA* 22,44 (32)	
	to ask for	K*RI* 3,510,9	
šny	**inquirer, sufferer** (?) **supplicator**	Push 127,4,8	
šnw	**examination, inspection**	*TR* Ambras (Pl.38) 1	
	survey, list, inventory	*JEA* 45,14	
	(legal) **disquisition**	K*RI* 3,337,2	
šni	**to be vexed**	*LES* 2,16,5	
	to become troubled	*LRL* 29R11	
	to be ill	*HPBM*[4] L5,V2	
	to take offense, to be angry	*LES* 4,3,10	
	to suffer	*P.Leiden* 1,348,12V6	
	to grieve	*LES* 2,8,1	
	to vex (cf. Wente, *Letters* p.216)	Gardiner & Sethe	
šni	(waters ?)	*LEM* 5,15,6	

šni	(cf. *šnꜥ* also) **to rain, to storm**	K*RI* 5,109,1	
	rainstorm	K*RI* 5,109,3	
šnw	**hair** (cf. *JEA* 65,82)	K*RI* 1,49,8	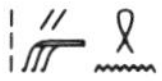
		CB 1,17R2	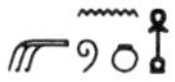
		HPBM[4] T1,V47-8	
		P.H. 500 (Pl.4) 2,1	
		P.H. 500 (Pl.6) 3,13	
		LES 2,10,9	
	wool	Janssen 444,46	
	woolen (?)	*LEM* 1,1,1	
	(fabric ?)	*LEM* 11,1,2	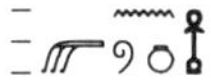
	lack of hair	*Rd'É* 11,128	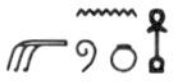
šnw	(cf. *šni* above) **to conjure**	*P.Leiden* 1,348,12V4	
šnwt	**court**	K*RI* 2,326,6	
	entourage	K*RI* 5,39,6	
	courtiers	*Melanges...Mokhtar* 2,352,23	
		Lange *Amenemope* 13,1 (68)	
		LEM 9,5V5	
		K*RI* 2,326,6	
		LEM 8,5,11	
	court, royal household	J-W A1,b,10	
šnꜥ	**warehouse** (cf. *JEA* 12,136)	*LEM* 1,8,10	
	storehouse (cf. *JEA* 64,152)	*H* 1,27,3	
		H 1,27,2	
	ergastulum	*LRL* 4V2	
		Wil (47) 96V26	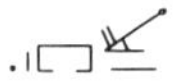
		Wil (38) 80R5	
	workhouse	*JAOS* 105,13,24	
	labor camp	K*RI* 3,140,7	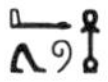
	magazine	K*RI* 5,26,13	

	storehouse	K*RI* 5,86,5	
		K*RI* 1,41,4	
		H 1,46,3	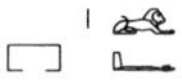
		SAK 5,289	
	underworld, tomb (cf. *JEA* 50,178)	Lange *Amenemope* 10,3	
šnꜥ	**storekeeper, warehouseman**	K*RI* 5,26,13	
šnꜥ	**to turn back**	*A* 1 (O.QC 7)	
	to turn	*LEM* 5,4,6	
	to turn back	*A* 1,3,5	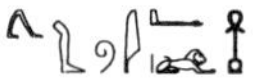
	to reject, to stop	K*RI* 1,53,11	
	to detain	K*RI* 1,51,8	
	to repel	K*RI* 1,80,11	
	to hinder	K*RI* 3,19,4	
		K*RI* 3,391,3	
šnꜥ	**hinderance**	K*RI* 3,278,11	
šnꜥ	**clouds**	K*RI* 2,230,11	
	storm	*ZÄS* 12,140	
šnꜥ	(fish) (cf. Janssen 349,37)	*LEM* 5,15,7	
		LEM 9,13a,V1	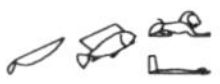
		LEM 10,12,10	
		RAD 8R3	
šnꜥy	**patrol, detainer** (cf. *JEA* 38,29 (police))	K*RI* 1,51,8	
šnꜥyw	**laborers** (?) (cf. Wente, *Letters* p.115) (or attendants, detainees ?)	K*RI* 1,323,4	
šnꜥti	(?) (unit of value)	O.H. 25572,R2-3 S.A. # 31	
šnwt	**granary**	*TR* 10053 (Pl.19) 7R9	

	double granary	*TR* 10053 (Pl.19) 7R9	
		LRL 5R9	
		LEM 3,2,4	
		RAD 1,4V, x+9	
		Wil (58) B11V3	
		Wil (25) 53R32	
		A 1 (O.Turin 2)	
		H 1,25,7	
		LRL 37R9	
		LEM 10,8,9	
		TR Abbott (Pl.2) 3,3	
		CB 1,B1V2	
		K*RI* 1,87,10	
		K*RI* 1,74,10	
		Melanges...Mokhtar 2,348,8	
		K*RI* 1,61,4	
	shed, barn	J-W A20,d	
šnwsᶜ	(tree)	*LES* 4,10,2	
šnb	**trumpet** (cf. Hoch p.281)	*CB* 1,B1,V27	
	ḏd m šnb **trumpeter**	*TR* 10052 (Pl.26) 3,3	
šnb	(malady)	*HPBM*[4] L2,V21	
		HPBM[4] T3,R34	
šnbt	**breast**	*H* 1,26,5	
	breast, flesh	K*RI* 5,30,12	
		K*RI* 5,33,6	
		H 1,6,3	
		H 1,47,5	
		K*RI* 1,111,12	
šnn	**grief, sorrow**	J-W A16,e,3	
šnrf	(chair)	*A* 1,24,1-2	

šnrf	**ruffled, disorderly**	*A* 1 (O.Berlin 8)
	to be disheveled (cf. Hoch p.283)	*A* 1,10,3
šns	**smelly**	*LEM* 3,5,11
	brackish, foul (cf. *JEA* 11,292,9)	*LEM* 10,10,1
		LEM 5,9,10
šntꜣyt	**widow**	J-W B22,b,6
šnty	(malady of the liver)	*HPBM*[4] T1,V92
šnty	< *šnḏt* (? *šndt* ?) **acacia tree**	*LEM* 5,7,10
		LES 4,6,14
		H 1,11,9
		LEM 10,11,4
		K*RI* 3,753,5-6
	acacia wood	*LEM* 5,8,2
šntyw	**opponents** (cf. Wb 4,519,9-10)	K*RI* 1,26,11
šnṯt	**dispute, battle**	J-W B13,z.2
šndy	(?) (garment)	*RAD* 7a,2R12
šndyt	**kilt** (cf. *MÄS* 8,220)	*H.O.* 54V4 Janssen 289,71
	apron (cf. Wente, *Letters* p.153)	K*RI* 3,534,4
		K*RI* 3,54,12
šr	**to close off, block up**	K*RI* 2,325,1
	to stop up	K*RI* 5,62,9
	to stop up, to block	*H* 1,75,9
		K*RI* 5,63,2
	to be dry	*JEA* 59,230
	to rebuild	K*RI* 2,328,16
šri	**to be young**	*LRL* 15V10
	young	*LES* 1,4,10

	child	*LEM* 8,7,1	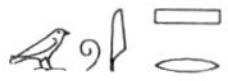
	child	*TR* Abbott (Pl.3) 6,7	
		Naun 4R3	
	little	*LEM* 12,4V5	
	insufficient (cf. Wente, *Letters* p.154)	Sauneron OH pl.20	
	small	*TR* Abbott (Pl.3) 6,8	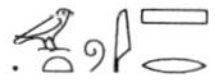
	youngest	*LRL* 28R14	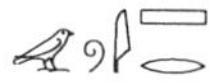
	junior, the younger (cf. Wente, *Letters* p.113)	KRI 1,237,3	
	lad	*LES* 1,5,10-11	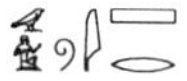
	son	*LRL* 9V4	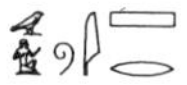
	puppy	*LES* 1,7,8	
	son	CS 1R1	
	lesser men	*LES* 6,3y	
	to be small	*LRL* 8Rn2	
	ꜥḏdi šri **baby boy, youth**	*LES* 3,4,5	
šrit	**daughter**	*LRL* 49R3	
		LRL 4R12	
		LRL 5V10	
		RAD 25,2R11	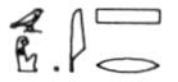
	maiden	*A* 1,25,3	
	girl, maiden	*JEA* 65,87	
	ꜥḏdit šrit **daughter**	*LRL* 3R14	
		LRL 2R8	
šri	(flowers)	*LEM* 5,2,10	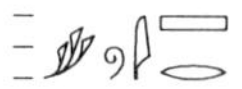
		LEM 6,5,1	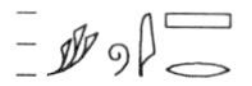
šrit	**barley**	*H* 1,27,12	
		H 1,28,8	

šrit	**nose, nostrils**	*H* 1,7,12
		H 1,49,6
		HPBM[4] T2,V71
		P.Leiden 1,348,5R4
šrʿ	**lodge**	*TR* 10053 (Pl.18) 4R13
	keep, prison	P.Leopold 2,4,11
	(cf. *JEA* 22,183)	Helck, *Bez* 570,215
	keep	*TR* Amherst (Pl.5) 4,3
		P.H. 501,1V7
		H 1,4,13
šrm	**peace, to sue for peace** (cf. Helck, *Bez* 570,225; Hoch p.285)	K*RI* 5,68,12-13
	shalom, to beg peace, to make obeisance	K*RI* 5,38,8
	to lay down (arms), **to seek peace**	*H* 1,78,11
	shalom, peace, greetings	*H* 1,42,7
	to beg peace	K*RI* 5,70,4
	to beg for peace	K*RI* 5,25,11
šrmt	**levy, contribution, delivery** (cf. Hoch p.286)	*TR* 10068 (Pl.13) 1V1
	complimentary gift, provision	*A* 1,17,5
šrš	**to make haste (to succor)**	Push 127,1,7
	swift	*A* 1,18,5
šršr	**to be perturbed**	*A* 1,5,8
šrgḥ	**excited feelings, passion, senses** (cf. Hoch p.287)	*CB* 1,16R11 *GM* 38,85-7; 47,21-2
šḥḳ	**dust, dust cloud, pulverized grain** (cf. Hoch p.288)	*A* 1 (O.Berlin 7)
		A 1,10,2
šḥḳ	**chaff**	CB 9,B18,V10 *HPBM*[3] 61

šs	(or *š* see above) (vessel)	*LRL* 44R9
šs	**alabaster**	*LEM* 9,15V3
		TR 10052 (Pl.34) 14,3
		K*RI* 1,39,13
		LES 9,F5
šsy	**alabaster worker**	*Wil* (11) 24R12
šs	(see *sšr* above) **corn** (cf. Janssen 119)	Push 127,4,15
šs-nsw	(cf. *sšr-nsw* above) **royal-linen**	*RAD* 4,1R5
šst	**skein of thread** (cf. Janssen 289)	*TR* 10068,3R28
	rope (cf. J-W p.609)	J-W A11,k
šsꜣ	**to be skilled**	*LEM* 6,9,4
	clever	*A* 1 (O.Turin 4)
	experienced	CB 4,4V9 *HPBM*[3] 19
	clever	*LEM* 6,9,3
		RAD 2,1B,V7
		A 1 (P.Turin 7)
	versed, skilled	CB 4,2V5 *HPBM*[3] 18
	to be witty, clever	Push 127,1,12
	skilled, competent	*A* 1,28,2
	skilled	K*RI* 1,48,6
		K*RI* 5,32,5
šsꜣ	**cleverness**	*LES* 4,6,14
		LEM 3,3,12
		LEM 6,8,4
		LEM 10,3,1
		JEA 60,81,1

šsꜣ-ḥr	**cleverness**	*LES* 4,6,14-7,1
šsꜣ	**to take counsel, mediate, consider, think about**	*Rd'É* 30,120
šsꜣ	**bubalis, antelope**	*LEM* 5,2,6
		LEM 10,3,8
		LEM 12,1V8
šsꜣ	**prescription**	*HPBM*[4] T1,V18
šsꜣt	**night, starry firmament**	*ZÄS* 96,111-113
šsꜣw	**slaughter knife**	*P. Leiden* 1,348,5R6
šsy	(?) (mineral)	*LEM* 11,4,2
	green frit (cf. Wente, *Letters* p.47)	K*RI* 3,44,3
šsp	**to take**	*LRL* 3R5
	to receive	K*RI* 5,29,1
	to take back	K*RI* 2,229,4
	to take over, accept	*LEM* 2,2,4
	to take hold of	*LES* 5,2,81
	to hold (cf. Wente, *Letters* p.191)	*LRL* 9R6
	to grasp	*LEM* 10,9,2
	to attain	*TR* 10053 (Pl.21) 4V10
	to suffer, to endure	Push 127,3,5-6
	to buy, purchase	*JEA* 50,83
	to initiate (cf. Wente, *Letters* p.45)	K*RI* 3,410,12
	to commence	*LES* 2,13,5
	to succeed (to someone)	*Mes* 18,38
	to secure	*LEM* 3,6,5
	to receive	*RAD* 25,1V8
		K*RI* 1,120,13
	to receive, exact	*LEM* 3,6,12

	to accept	*HPBM*[4] L5,V32
	to start (a journey)	*JEA* 33,26
	to reckon	*LEM* 7,2,12
	to accept	K*RI* 2,325,9
	to take	*A* 1,17,2
	to accept, sell for	*TR* 10052 (Pl.25) 1,9
	šsp-iwr **to become pregnant**	*LES* 2,18,5
šsp	**receipt**	*TR* Ambras (Pl.38) 2,2
		RAD 17,1R3
	šsp-snw **receipt of offerings**	*Serapis* 6,77,fig.2,3
	commencement (of perpetuity)	K*RI* 1,41,10
	beginning (of a date in time)	*ZÄS* 66,2-3
	crack (of dawn)	*LES* 5,3,6
šsp	**loaf** (cf. McDowell p.3,nt.a)	O.Glasgow D1925,66R9
šsp	**handful, palm of hand**	P.H. 500 (Pl.6) 3,10
šsp(*t*)	**cucumber**	*LEM* 5,9,2 O.Cairo 25553 S.A. # 28
šsp-r	**interrogation, deposition**	*TR* 10053 (Pl.19) 7R13
šspw	**sphinx**	K*RI* 1,16,6
	images	*H* 1,26,3
šsmt	**malachite** (?)	CB 9,B18,V8 *HPBM*[3] pl.61
šsr	**arrow**	K*RI* 5,13,7
		K*RI* 5,17,9
		K*RI* 1,77,1

šsr	**monkey** (?)	CB 3,3R12 *HPBM*[3] 5	
	sacrificial ox (?)	*JEA* 31,61,5	
šš	**doddering, silly** (cf. *JEA* 15,25,50)	*TR* 10052 (Pl.27) 3,**16**	
		TR 10052 (Pl.31) 10R8	
	madman	CS 2V3	
	(?)	*Wil* (43) 88V16	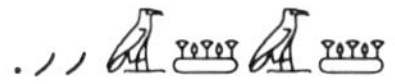
	twisting, braiding	*LEM* 10,6,1	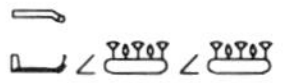
	fool	*LEM* 6,7,4	
šsm	(?)	*TR* 10053 (Pl.21) 5V**5**	
šḳw	**earrings, bracelets**	K*RI* 3,543,8	
šḳr	(?)	Naun 3,1V13	
		Janssen 200,40	
		RAD 18C,5V16	
		RAD 18C,5V11	
	(wooden container)	O.Berlin 14214, V5 – S.A. #16	
šḳrḳb	(?) (Nubian word ?)	*LEM* 11,4,1	
šḳb rkb	**upper & lower millstones** (cf. Hoch p.289)	O.Cairo 25759,4	
škn	**watering place** (cf. Hoch p.289)	K*RI* 4,3,6	
škrʿ	**basket**	*TR* 10068 (Pl.12) 5R**17**	
	basketry (cf. Janssen 161,25)	*H.O.* 20,2,5-6	
	hamper (cf. Wente, *Letters* p.155)	Černý, *OH* (1970)pl.**21**	
šgnn	**quarrel**	*HPBM*[4] C1,44-45	
šgr	**chest**	Helck, *Bez* 571,230	

šgr	**trench, ditch**	Onom. A40	
št	**tortoise**	K*RI* 3,58,11	
št	**assessment** (cf. *JEA* 27,67)	*LEM* 7,3,2	
		Wil (36) 75R1	
		RAD 23,1R14	
	impressment (cf. Wente, *Letters* p.115)	K*RI* 1,324,12	
	tax payer	*LEM* 6,27,6	
	tax master	*TR* Ambras (Pl.38) 1,2	
		LRL 32R3	
		LRL 33R1	
		LRL 36V3	
	(body of) **tax gatherers**	CB 5,8R1 *HPBM*³ 26	
št3	**mysterious**	*LES* 4,1,1	
	hiding	*H* 1,3,3	
	mysterious	*H* 1,3,4	
		H 1,9,3	
	secret, hidden	*H* 1,44,8	
		K*RI* 5,89,12	
		K*RI* 1,18,1	
	difficult	K*RI* 1,65,9	
	mysterious	*A* 1,20,7	
	secret place	K*RI* 2,330,4	
		TR 10053 (Pl.20) 2V13	
	quiet, composed	O.Louvre E2425,R3 S.A. #205	
	chamber	K*RI* 3,547,12	
št3	**copse**	*Wil* (23) 49R29	
		Wil (31) 65R4	
	brierwood (cf. *JEA* 50,26)	*Wil* 2,29,1	
	branches	*Rd'É* 29,101	

štꜣ	**region**	*HPBM*[4] L2,R27	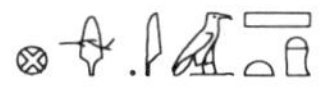
		HPBM[4] L2,R25	
		HPBM[4] T2,R25	
		HPBM[4] T3,R47-8	
štꜣyt	**shrine of Sokar**	CB 4,6V10 *HPBM*[3] 20	
štꜣyt	**cellar, cave**	*BIFAO* 72,60-1	
	hidden room	*JESHO* 11,163	
šti	**haft** (axe or knife handle) (cf. *SAK* 5,290-2; *Rd'É* 29,189-93)	*LES* 3,10,4	
	staff	O.Berlin 12654,R10 S.A. #15	
	handle	O.DM 133,R5-6 *SAK* 5,29	
šti	**gravid** (?) (sow) (cf. Wente, *Letters* p.115)	K*RI* 1,324,1	
štm	**treason, rebellion** (cf. *ZÄS* 72,109)	*JEA* 12,218,4	
šṯ	**to wear, to adorn**	*JEA* 27,131,b	
šṯyt	**grave, tomb**	J-W A23,c,2	
šdi	**to read**	*LEM* 3,3,10	
	to recite (cf. *JSSEA* 10,71)	CB 7,4R4 *HPBM*[3] 34	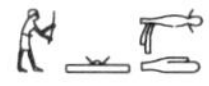
		LEM 6,8,3	
		LEM 10,1,4	
	to read	*LEM* 8,3,6	
	to save, to preserve	*RAD* 25,2V12 *LRL* 14V2	
	to restore	*TR* 10068 (Pl.12) 6R13	
	to recover	P.H. 500 (Pl.14) 7,1	
	to keep safe	*ZÄS* 106,19	
	to withdraw	*RAD* 12a,2R3	
	to drag	K*RI* 5,64,15	

	to draw forth (water) (cf. Wente, *Letters* p.29)	K*RI* 2,359,12
	to deliver	*A* 1,6,4
	to secure	*LEM* 10,6,3
		K*RI* 5,40,22
	to recover	*TR* 10068 (Pl.13) 1V25
		H 1,7,10
	to exact, to collect	*JEA* 23,187
		K*RI* 1,54,9
	to remove	*LES* 10b,R13
	to rescue	Push 127,5,4
	to save	*P.Leiden* 1,348,12V6
	to let resound	*JEA* 5,33
	to greet	CB 4,2V1 *HPBM*³ 18
	to levy	*TR* 10052 (Pl.25) 1,12
	to break, rescue, take away	K*RI* 2,151,4
	to extract	*LES* 2,8,4
	to pull, to rescue	*A* 1 (P.Turin 1)
	to maintain, secure, recover	K*RI* 2,333,7
	to take away, cut out	K*RI* 2,151,6
	to reserve	*LEM* 14,2V3
šdi	**to dig**	*H* 1,4,3
		A 1 (P.Turin 4)
		K*RI* 1,72,9
	to carve, excavate	*Melanges...Mokhtar* 2,352,16
	to hollow out (with an adze) (cf. *JEA* 72, 185-7)	
šdi	**to suckle**	K*RI* 1,40,12
	to bring up	K*RI* 1,42,2
	to suck	J-W B22,B,3
šdi	**to convey**	*LEM* 8,4,12

	to bring, to procure	*JEA* 45,9	
šdi	**withdrawers of rations**	*RAD* 21d,2,3	
šdt	**well**	*LEM* 10,7,3	
		K*RI* 2,22,5	
		P.Leiden 1,348,12R11	
		LEM 6,22,5	
		HPBM[4] L1,V23	
		LRL 5V10	
šdyt	**lump, mass**	*JEA* 12,183,5	
	plinth	K*RI* 3,795,5	
šdw	**pelt, skin**	*JEA* 50,32	
		K*RI* 1,56,8	
šdw	**dough**	*JEA* 12,183,5	
šdw	**rafts**	*JEA* 50,27	
šdwy	**kidneys** (?) (cf. K*RI* T&A p.77)	K*RI* 1,94,12	
šd3	**to assault, invade, to pillage**	*A* 1,20,5	
šdrt	**ravine, chasm** (cf. Hoch p.291)	*A* 1,24,3	
		A 1,23,3	
šdḥ	**pomegranate wine** (?)	*LEM* 5,12,1	
		P.H. 500 (Pl.10) 5,1	
		LEM 5,7,4	
		LEM 10,2,2	
		K*RI* 1,61,2	SIC
		H 1,27,8	
šdšd	**to ambush, to lie in wait for**	P.H. 500 (Pl.10) 5,9	
šdt	**plot**	K*RI* 1,45,4	

	conspiracy	K*RI* 5,39,14	
šdd	**to drag** (see *šdi* above)	K*RI* 5,64,15	
šddr	**low country** (?) (cf. *šdrt* above)	*Rd'É* 33,57	
šdt	**plot of land**	K*RI* 3,492,10	

ḳ3	**high, exalted** (cf. *JEA* 47,104)	*Rd'É* 9,113	
	long (cf. *Rd'É* 6,117 = P. Valençay 1R4)	*LRL* 1R4	
		LEM 5,7,10	
		LEM 8,8,11	
		LEM 10,7,8	
		K*RI* 5,26,10	
		K*RI* 5,17,5	
		CB 1,22,3	
		K*RI* 5,22,1	
	to be long (of time)	*Khonsu* 2,185,3	
	to emphasize	O.DM 126,9 (*Or*. 45,397)	
ḳ3(y)	**height**	K*RI* 5,15,3	
	height	K*RI* 1,48,5	
	length	*JEA* 67,95 n.v	
	rising grounds	Push 127,2,14	
ḳ3	**loudness**	*HPBM*³ CB 4,5V5	
ḳ3i	(cf. *ḳr* and *ḳri* below) **visiting, near** **to dwell, to take temporary residence** (cf. Hoch p.292)	*LES* 5,21&22	
	to take lodging (cf. *Wb*. 5,6-7,1-3)	*LES* 4,7,5	
ḳ3i	**effigy, likeness**	*LEM* 2,5,8	
	background	*LES* 1,7,2	
	nature	*A* 1,5,5	
		LEM 5,5,8	
	manner	*A* 1,24,6	
ḳ3iw	(cf. *ḳri* below) **vagabond, visitor**	*LES* 4,7,6	

ḳ3yt	**to uphold**	*LEM* 5,7,11	
ḳ3yt	**arable land** (cf. *JARCE* 1,40)	*LEM* 9,10V2	
	high ground (cf. *JEA* 54,53,n.d)	K*RI* 1,50,2	
		LEM 10,12,6	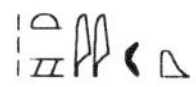
		Wil (38) 80R13	
		Wil (40) 82V26	
		Wil (42) 87V42	
		Wil (52) B5V13	
		Wil (53) B6V24	
		P.H. 500 (Pl.4) 2,4	
		RAD 23,2R14	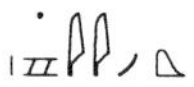
		RAD 23,2R7	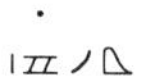
		BIFAO 86,198,3V3 (P.BM 10474)	
ḳ3ꜥ	**to vomit** (cf. *JEA* 65,84,6)	*CB* 1,17R6	
		Wb. 5,7,5	
ḳ3b > *ḳb* (?)	(see below)		
ḳ3bt	(see *ḳbyt* below) **breast**	P.H. 500 (Pl.10) 5,3	
ḳ3fyk	(see *ḳfḳ* below) **to be agape at**	*A* 1,11,4	
ḳ3r	(see *ḳr* below) **bolt**	*CB* 1,17R8	
ḳ3rrt	(see *ḳrrt* below) **cavern**	*LEM* 2,6,1	
ḳ3rw	(see *ḳwr* below)	K*RI* 1,67,16	
ḳ3riw	(see *ḳri* below) **visitor**	*LES* 4,7,10	
ḳ3rmꜥti	(see *ḳrmt* below) **ashes, embers**		

ḳꜣrnꜣti	(see *ḳrnt* below) **foreskin**		
ḳꜣrr	(see *ḳrr* below)		
ḳꜣrḏn	(see *ḳrḏn* below) **hoe**		
ḳꜣḥ	(see *ḳḥ* below)		
ḳꜣḥꜣ	(see *ḳḥ* below)		
ḳꜣs	(?) (of boat)	*LEM* 5,7,11-8,1	
ḳꜣs	**to bind** (cf. E-W 92,31)	*Wb.* 5,13	
	to tie	*JEA* 54,160,n.bb P.BM 10731,V6	
		K*RI* 5,70,9	
		K*RI* 3,7,6	
ḳꜣḳꜣ	**prey**	K*RI* 5,64,12	
ḳꜣḳꜣ	**to eat**	*A* 1 (O.QC 2)	
ḳꜣḳꜣ	**to look** (up), "**to tower**"	*H* 1,4,1	
ḳꜣḳꜣ	(tree)	*Wil* (60) B13V8	
ḳꜣdꜣrti	(see *ḳdrt* below) **incense**		
ḳꜣḏꜣ	(see *ḳḏ* below) **plaster**		
ḳꜣḏꜣwꜣr	(see *ḳḏwr* below)		
ḳꜣḏꜣm	(see *ḳḏm* below) **handful**		
ḳꜥ	**to disgorge, to render up**	*A* 1 (P.T.6)	 SIC
ḳi	**form, nature**	K*RI* 5,16,7	

	image	K*RI* 5,64,5	
		K*RI* 5,38,4	
		LEM 1,4,1	
	condition	*LEM* 6,15,7	
		LEM 8,6,2	
	state	*LEM* 10,14,4	
	like	*CB* 1,16,10	
	form	*A* 1,4,5	
	manner	*JEA* 41,101,10-11	
	aspect	K*RI* 3,275,2	
ḳꜥ	(metal)	*MH* 81 (Pl.648) 3	
ḳꜥḥ	**to extend, to bend** (cf. *JEA* 33,23,n.i)	K*RI* 1,42,12	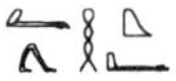
ḳꜥḥ	**shoulder**	*LES* 4,12,7	
		HPBM[4] T1V76	
		HPBM[4] L5R18	
	"**arm**" (cf. *JEA* 65,83), "**shoulder**" (cf. Fox B17,4)	*CB* 1,17R4	
	shoulder	*LES* 4,12,8	
	arm	*A* 1,10,8	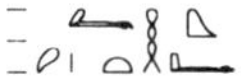
ḳꜥḥw	**corner pieces**	*TR* 10068 (Pl.10) 3R6	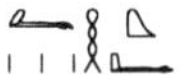
		TR 10068 (Pl.10) 3R21	
		TR 10068 (Pl.12) 6R3	
ḳꜥḥt	(vessel) (cf. Janssen p.430, §166)	*TR* 10053 (Pl.18) 5R6	
		TR 10053 (Pl.18) 5R7	
ḳꜥḥt	**tract**	*LRL* 13R4	
	districts	*LEM* 5,2,1	
	arable tract	*Wil* 10,22,11	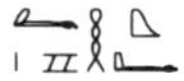
	tract	*RAD* 23,1Rx+13	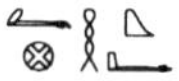
	(cf. *ZÄS* 72,48 n.1)	*ZÄS* 35,14,1.2	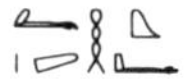
		K*RI* 2,229,7	

ḳwr	**staff of people, gold workers** (cf. *JNES* 6,222,21)	K*RI* 1,52,8	
		K*RI* 5,91,9	
	miner	*Khonsu* 2,133,35	
ḳwrw	**barges, ships**	*H* 1,4,12	
ḳwrw	**caravaneers**	K*RI* 1,67,16	
		K*RI* 1,70,1	
ḳwḳw	**nuts, dom-palm nuts** (cf. Janssen p. 356; Wallert, *Die Palmen* p. 52f.)	*LEM* 8,8,4	
ḳwt	**knot**	*LEM* 11,1,5	
ḳb	**to multiply**	*H* 1,28,5	
		LES 2,2,1	
		LEM 5,9,1	
		K*RI* 1,118,5	
		K*RI* 2,285,10	
	to double	K*RI* 5,37,12	
	to increase	K*RI* 5,84,5	
	to fold over	*H* 1,29,10	
	to turn around	*TR* 10053 (Pl.20) 2V8	
		K*RI* 5,77,6	
	to double	*Melanges... Mokhtar* 2, 349,1.12	
ḳb	*m-ḳb* **midst**	*Rd'É* 20,10,2 Louvre stele C.256,1.2	
	inside	K*RI* 3,583,4	
	m ḳb **outside**	*Wb.* 5,10,16	
ḳb	**intestine**	*JEA* 66,146	
ḳb	**calm, calmness**	*LEM* 10,14,3	
	calm	*CB* 1 (24) C3V3	
	idle, useless	*LEM* 5,11,2	
	to become cool, to find refreshment	*HPBM*[3] (Pl.37) CB7,5V7	

	to be secure, quiet	*JEA* 3,103-4
ḳb	**cool**	*LES* 2,14,2
		K*RI* 5,21,5-6
		LEM 6,11,4
		K*RI* 1,43,1
ḳb	**to cool**	P.H. 500 (Pl.14) 7,8
ḳb	**cool** (place)	K*RI* 1,116,10
ḳb	**idly, cooly, impassively, calmly**	*LEM* 1,4,7
		LES 6,15,4
	meaningless, in vain, to no purpose	*A* 1 (O.T 6) (*A* 1,p.9*, n.7)
	cooly, vain, meaningless	*A* 1,5,4
ḳbꜥ	**to jest, to tease, to mock** (cf. Hoch p.292)	*LRL* 46R13
		LRL 46V2
	to joke, jest	*Wb.* 5,25,9
ḳbw	**jars**	*LES* 9,F5
		P.Leiden 1,350,1Vx+19
		K*RI* 3,569,4
		TR 10068 (Pl.12) 6R23
		TR 10053 (Pl.17) 1R9
		K*RI* 3,773,11
	ḳbw n wt **canopic jars**	Janssen p.243,54
ḳbw	(woodwork) (?) (cf. *Wb.* 5,22,4)	Janssen p.218
ḳbyt	**breast, nipple** (cf. *ZÄS* 99,139)	*CB* 1(22) C1V4
	(cf. Fox p.22, n.b) *g3b* "**arm**"	P.H. 500 (Pl.10) 5,3
ḳbyt	**foundations**	Harris, *Minerals* 29

ḳbḥ	**bird of the marshes**	*LEM* 10,12,8
		K*RI* 1,49,1
		K*RI* 1,49,3
	cataract region	*LEM* 3,3,1
	pool	*H* 1,28,2
		H 1,37b,2
ḳbḥ	**libation**	*LEM* 5,4,5-6
		LEM 5,11,2
		LEM 10,13b,5
		K*RI* 1,125,2
		K*RI* 1,44,10
		K*RI* 1,11,13
		K*RI* 3,362,13
ḳbḥ	**libation vessel**	Janssen, p.433 §169 O.C 25692,3
ḳbḥ	**to refresh oneself**	*BIFAO* 83,232 P.Boulaq XIII,frag. 16,1.3
ḳbḥ	**sinew**	*HPBM*[4] T2V45
ḳbḥw	**body of water, cool water**	*LES* 5,2,66
		K*RI* 5,35,2
		MÄS 37,p. 11,22,1.8
ḳbs	(see *ḳ3s* above) **to bind**	K*RI* 5,70,9
ḳbḳb	**rubble** (cf. *Wb.* 5,164,12-13)	Černý, *Workmen* 90 O.Gardiner 221,2-4
ḳbḳb	**to strike down**	*HPBM*[4] L1,R15-16
ḳbḳbyt	**prostrate**	K*RI* 5,15,10
ḳf3t	**fame, victory** (cf. Borghouts p.39-40, n.11)	*P.Leiden* 1,348,1R6

ḳfn	**to bake** (cf. Janssen p.327)	*Wb.* 5,32,11-12
		LEM 2,8,3
		K*RI* 1,250,13
		LEM 8,7,7
ḳfḳ	**to be agape at**	*A* 1,11,4
ḳfḳft	(cult vessel)	*Wb.* 5,33,5
ḳfd	(?) for *ḳdf* (?) see below	*JEA* 62,62; 66,168
ḳm3	**to create**	K*RI* 5,11,12
		LEM 6,2,2
		LEM 5,4,2-3
		LEM 6,6,3
		H 1,3,3
		H 1,25,3
		P.H. 500 (Pl.8) 4,2
		K*RI* 5,21,7
		K*RI* 5,36,11
		K*RI* 5,74,9
		K*RI* 1,74,13
		K*RI* 1,97,9
		K*RI* 1,121,12
	to produce (cf. *Rd'É* 11,18)	K*RI* 1,111,5
ḳm3	**creator**	K*RI* 5,15,5
		K*RI* 3,387,10
	producer	K*RI* 3,685,10
ḳm3	**creation**	K*RI* 1,87,8
	hammered, beaten (work) (cf. Janssen p.431, n.147)	*H* 1,5,12
		TR 10068 (Pl.10) 2R6

ḳm3	**reeds**	*Wil* (52) B5V4
		Wil (23) 50R34
		Wil (31) 65R21
		Wil (24) 51R20
		Wil (28) 60R4
		LEM 10,11,6
		Wil (22) 47R8
ḳm3	**to move**	*A* 1,9,5
ḳm3	**ox, cow, bull**	*H* 1,30,3
	calf (cf. *JEA* 10,120,2)	*RAD* 25,1R3
		RAD 225,1R2
ḳm3ḥ	**leaves**, (?) **branches**	P.Turin 1966,2,2 Fox T2,2
ḳmi	*m ḳmi* **in sum**	K*RI* 5,97,9
ḳmy	**ointment, pomade of gum** (cf. Janssen p. 446 § 181; Harris, *Minerals* 158f.)	*LEM* 5,3,8
		LEM 9,3V5
		LEM 11,4,2
		P.H. 500 (Pl.2) 1,7
		P.H. 500 (Pl.8) 3,13-4,1
		K*RI* 1,26,13
	resin	Push 127,p.55
	anointing oil	K*RI* 6,353,7
ḳn	**to complete, bring to an end**	*LEM* 7,2,11
	to finish off	*LEM* 10,6,8
		K*RI* 1,19,1
	to cease	K*RI* 5,14,5
		K*RI* 5,86,11
		K*RI* 5,71,8
ḳn	*n-ḳn* **of the first quality** (cf. Janssen, p.416, n.54)	*H.O.* 56,2,3

ḳn	**at an end**	*LEM* 6,16,3
ḳn	**mat**	*LES* 5,2,40
ḳn	(injury?)	*HPBM*[4] L1,R30
ḳn	**fatty condition**	*HPBM*[4] L6,V30
ḳn	< *gn* **to weaken** (cf. Wente, *LRL* 16c (?))	*LRL* 16R7
		K*RI* 1,87,6
ḳn	**fat smoke** (cf. Borghouts, n.131)	*P.Leiden* 1,348,4R10
ḳni	**to be valiant, mighty, strong, capable, brave, active** (cf. *HPBM*[3] p.1 20,2)	K*RI* 1,62,12
		K*RI* 5,15,15
		K*RI* 5,40,20
		LEM 5,6,10
		LEM 10,10,4
		K*RI* 2,76,10
		LEM 9,4V2
		K*RI* 2,79,1
		Wil (21) 46R12
	eager	*Khonsu* 2,143,2
ḳn(*t*)	**valor**	K*RI* 5,11,2
		LEM 2,2,5
		K*RI* 5,109,4
		K*RI* 1,99,1
		A 1,1,2 (O.Petrie 2)
	victory, might	K*RI* 1,23,4
ḳnw	**feats**	*LEM* 6,9,8
		K*RI* 5,81,9
		Wil (72) B25V20
	brave deeds	*Wil* (10) 22R4

ḳnw	**many**	*LRL* 4R3
		LES 3,2,4
		LEM 1,6,2
		H 1,46,2
		Push 127 (Pl.8) 3,13
	many things	*A* 1,7,8
	long time	*LRL* 8R5
	plentiful, numerous	K*RI* 1,60,13
		K*RI* 2,31,14
	very many	P.Turin 2021,4R3 S.A. (Pl.119)
		LRL 23V3
	ḳn sp sn **many more**	*JEA* 65,87,4
ḳn	**to embrace**	*LES* 1,6,6
		K*RI* 2,232,9
		K*RI* 2,232,1,3
ḳni	**embrace**	*LRL* 29R4
		LES 7,2,5
		P.H. 500 (Pl.14) 7,4
	embrace	*LRL* 14R7
	arms	*Melanges... Mokhtar* 1, Pl.2 Cairo CG 58056,4
		LRL 13R5
ḳniw	**sheaves**	K*RI* 5,23,8
		K*RI* 5,64,10
ḳniw	**armchair** (cf. Janssen, p.187,§35) **"chair, seat"**	*LES* 3,6,3
	palanquin	K*RI* 3,844,12
	portable shrine	*RAD* 17,3R7
		RAD 17,3R4
	portable shrine (cf. Janssen, p.248,§57)	*RAD* 1,6Vx+1
	chapel	*TR* 10053 (Pl.18) 4R10

	throne	*JEA* 52,91,f
	baggage, pack, bundle (cf. S.A. p.16)	O.Ber. 14214,R4 *LEM* 1,7,2
ḳni	(bird)	*LEM* 5,15,6
ḳniw	**orpiment, yellow pigment** (cf. Harris, *Minerals* 153f.)	Janssen, p.217,n.66 Lucas-Harris, pp.248-250
ḳny	**shield bearer**	*Wil* (25) 53R22
ḳnb	**to subjugate, "to fetter"** (cf. Fox p.73, n.e; *JEA* 65,82 n.3)	*CB* 1,17R3 *Studies...Griffith* p.72 CB 9,13R12
ḳnb	**corner**	*TR* 10054 (Pl.6) 1R5
ḳnby	**naos, shrine, vault**	*Rd'É* 24,177
ḳnbt	**court**	*LES* 6,1,x+9 *LRL* 37V8 K*RI* 1,57,15 Push 127,4,11
	tribunal	*HPBM*[4] T3,R62
	ḳnbt ꜥꜣt **Great Tribunal**	P.Leopold 2,4,1 *JEA* 22, Pl.5
	ḳnbt sḏmyw	O.Cairo 25227,R1 S.A. Pl. 28
	judicial council (cf. *JNES* 6,220,6)	K*RI* 1,50,13
	court	*JEA* 17,62-4
ḳnn	(cf. *ḳn* above) **valor**	*LEM* 11,5,4 K*RI* 5,57,15 K*RI* 5,19,5
ḳnni	(oil) (cf. Janssen p.365; Lucas-Harris, p.89)	*LEM* 5,15,3

ḳnr(*t*)	**desert**	*TR* Abbott (Pl.2) 4,3
	desert edge	Push 127,3,11
		Push 127,4,10-11
ḳnḳn	**to beat**	*LRL* 26V2
	to assault	*LES* 2,4,6
		LEM 6,22,5
	to be beaten	K*RI* 3,503,6
ḳnḳn	**castigation**	*LEM* 5,2,6
	blows	P.H. 500 (Pl.4) 2,3
ḳnt	<*kntw* **wine press** (cf. Hoch p.293)	K*RI* 2,217,98
ḳnd	**to be enraged**	K*RI* 2,228,7
	to become furious	*LES* 4,3,7
	to rage	*LES* 5,2,80
		K*RI* 5,13,6
		P.H. 500 (Pl.4) 2,12
	to be angered	*LES* 1,6,10
ḳnd(*t*)	**rage**	*LES* 2,3,8
ḳr	(cf. *ḳri* below) **in the company of**	*LRL* 2R7
	near	*LES* 5,2,45
	r-ḳr **next to**	*LRL* 36R6-7
	r-ḳr	*LRL* 28R16
ḳr	(cf. *ḳrr* below) **ship**	*LEM* 9,9V3
		LEM 10,8,9
ḳryw	**crews**	*LEM* 10,12,6
ḳr	**finis**	*A* 1,7,5
ḳri	**to come near to, to visit, to attend, to draw nigh, to approach** (cf. Hoch pp.296-7)	Push 127,2,7
		JEA 39,16 n.g

ḳri	**visitor, newcomer, stranger** (cf. Hoch pp.295-6)	*ZÄS* 93,37
		LES 4,7,10
ḳri	**bolt** (cf. *JEA* 65,87)	*CB* 1,17R8
	locks (cf. Janssen p.394)	*LEM* 5,13,3
		H 1,77,8
ḳri	**thunderbolt**	*HPBM*[4] L1,R9
		HPBM[4] P3,R27
	storm	*BIFAO* 86,190, I,15,10
		P.BM 10474,1V15
ḳrty	**two sources of the Nile**	KRI 1,89,4
		KRI 1,66,12
ḳrꜥ	**shield** (cf. *MDAIK* 39,259; Hoch pp. 298-9)	KRI 2,6,6
		KRI 2,6,7
		KRI 2,6,10
		Wil (7) 17R17
ḳrꜥw	**shieldbearer** (cf. *MÄS* 6,67-8) (one of two men on chariot) (cf. Hoch pp.299-300)	*LEM* 1,9,5
		LEM 12,4V1 Caminos, *LEM* p.508
		KRI 5,8,12
		KRI 5,12,12
		KRI 5,44,13
		KRI 2,68,14
		KRI 2,66,4
		KRI 2,68,15
		KRI 2,83,16
	(cf. *Wil* 1, p.81)	*Wil* (15) 33R5 (SIC)
		Wil (14) 31R21 (SIC)
ḳrf	**chest, bag** (cf. Janssen, *Gleanings* 147,20)	P.Turin 2072/142,1R4 S.A. Pl. 128, p. 330 n.2
ḳrmt	**ashes, cinders, embers** (cf. Hoch p.301)	Mariette, *Karnak* 55,62
		Helck, *Bez* 571,235

ḳrn	(weapon, tool)	*JEA* 65,96
ḳrnt	**foreskin, uncircumcised phallus** (cf. Helck, *Bez* 571,236; Hoch p.302)	Mariette, *Karnak* 54,51/5
	phalli (cf. *JEA* 25,229,n.c)	K*RI* 5,18,12
		K*RI* 5,23,12
		K*RI* 5,15,13
ḳrr	**ship, boat**	*H* 1,11,8
		H 1,7,8
	(corn) **barges**	*H* 1,29,1
		H 1,48,6
		K*RI* 1,49,15
		K*RI* 2,333,4
ḳrr	**humble approach**	K*RI* 5,71,10
	vagrant	K*RI* 3,336,13
ḳrr	(?)	*HPBM*[4] L2,R74
ḳrr	**holocaust**	*Rd'É* 31,40
ḳrrt	**cavern**	*LEM* 2,6,1
	cavern, hole	*LEM* 5,5,9
		Khonsu 2 (Pl.112) 1
	burial chamber	*JEA* 5,27,12
	hole, (part of the Netherworld)	*ZÄS* 64,25,1.78 P.Ber.3048,7,4
ḳrḥ	(false) **friend, ally, associate**	*HPBM*[4] L6V15
	false friend, ally	*Khonsu* 2,132,3,9
ḳrḥt	**vessel, ceramic** (cf. Valbelle, *Ouviers*, p.265 n.8)	O.DM 5,5 Janssen p.426
ḳrs	**to bury, to wrap up** (cf. *JEA* 3,204,3)	CS 1R12

	to entomb	P.H. 500 (Pl.12) 6,5	
		A 1 (O.Louvre)	
		TR Abbott (Pl.3) 5,3	
	to bury	K*RI* 3,818,1	
ḳrst	**burial, interment**	*Khonsu* 2,133,35	
	burial	K*RI* 3,22,5	
	st-ḳrs **burial chamber**	*TR* Abbott (Pl.2) 3,4	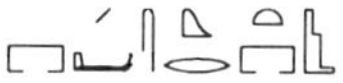
ḳrst	**coffin** (box-shaped sarcophagus)	*JEA* 65,92	
ḳrḏn	**hoe** (cf. Janssen, p.321) (a heavy) **hoe** (cf. *Essays…Kantor* p.302)	CS 2R9	
	hatchet	Helck, *Bez* 571, 237	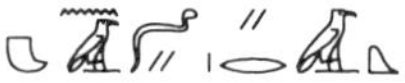
ḳh	**glow**	*HPBM*[3] CB4,6V4	
	bright	*RAD* 22,1R2	
	light	*BIFAO* 86,190,II,1,6 P.BM 10474 2V1	
		AEO (Pl.14/15) pp.29-30 P.BM 10202,1,6	
ḳh	**manacles** (cf. *JEA* 21,31,7)	*LES* 4,15,12	
		LES 7,2,5	
	bonds	*CB* 1,15,12	
	fetters	*Rd'É* 26,9-12	
		P.H. 500,2,3	
ḳh	**to tame**	*LEM* 1,3,10	
		LEM 4,4,2	
		LEM 6,8,8	
ḳh	**stone-breaking** (punishment) (cf. *Wb.* 5,67,1) (type of stone)	P.DM 27 V9-10 S.A. Pl.99	
ḳhwt	**windows**	*H* 1,5,3	

ḳḥn	**cauldron** (cf. Janssen, p.415-16; *JEA* 31,35 n.y; *Wb.* 5,67,4)	Naun 1,5R3 P.Mayer B11 *P.Leiden* 1,343-345, 9,11&12
ḳḥḳḥ	**metal work** (cf. *Anc.Eg.* 10,74)	*H* 1,6,5
ḳḥḳḥ	**quarrying**	O.Ber. 12654,R10 S.A. Pl. 13, p.36
	cutting stone (punishment)	*Gleanings* p.138-9, n.p
ḳs	**bone**	*LEM* 10,7,8 *A* 1,3,6
	frame	*LEM* 5,12,10 *LEM* 6,10,7 *A* 1 (O.QC.8) *LEM* 8,3,9 *LEM* 14,1,7-8 *H* 1,42,6 K*RI* 5,80,2 Push 127,3,11 K*RI* 5,62,13 K*RI* 5,69,6
ḳsn	**irksome, difficult**	*LEM* 8,5,8 *LEM* 10,10,8 K*RI* 1,69,3
ḳsnw	**annals**	*A* 1,1,7 *A* 1 (O.BN) 2
ḳsnty	(?) (astringent earth)	*Wb.* 5,71,5
ḳḳ	**to strip, to peel, to pare** (cf. *JEA* 11,46,2)	*TR* 10054 (Pl.6) 1R9 *TR* 10054 (Pl.7) 3R11
ḳḳi	**foil, casing**	*TR* 10054 (Pl.6) 3R7
	copper lining	*TR* 10403 (Pl.36) 2R3

ḳḳt	**transports**	K*RI* 2,286,4	
ḳd	**to build**	*LEM* 10,12,1	
		LES 1,5,4	
		LES 8,1,3	
		LEM 10,9,1	
		LEM 10,12,1	
		K*RI* 1,8,2	
	to fashion, mould	K*RI* 2,324,10	
	r-ḳd.i **to build** (me) **up**	*Melanges...Mokhtar* 2,349,11	
ḳd	**wall**	*LEM* 3,1V9	
ḳd	**potter, creator** (cf. Janssen, p.485ff.)	*TR* 10054 (Pl.8) 4V10	
	builders	K*RI* 2,331,4	
		H 1,29,11	
ḳd	**kite** (measurement) (cf. *ZÄS* 99,138f.)	*TR* 10068 (Pl.10) 3R2	
		TR 10068 (Pl.9) 4R23	
		TR 10053 (Pl.20) 3V9 *LRL* 3V2,36V9	
ḳd	**form, nature** (see *mi-ḳd*)	K*RI* 5,33,12	
	condition, disposition	*LEM* 9,1V3	
	character	K*RI* 5,32,12	
		K*RI* 1,97,16	
	duty	*ZÄS* 94,68,n.c	
	irt ḳd **to make one's reputation**	*JEA* 17,60,45 (MK)	
	w3ḥ ḳd **happy of nature**	*JEA* 5(Pl.21) C4	
	mi-ḳd **just as**	*LRL* 12V4	
		LRL 5V1	
	like	*LRL* 49 V2-3	
		LRL 43V5	
		LRL 50R21	
	(*mi*)-*ḳd.f* **entire** (?)	*LRL* 37V13	

ḳd	(cf. *ḳdi* below) **inverted** (?) (water) (cf. *GM* 10,13-16)	*H* 1,77,10
ḳd	**drawings, designs**	*H* 1,60,2
	outlined figures	*H* 1,26,9
		K*RI* 1,113,5
	outlines	*JEA* 4,139
	sš-ḳd **draughtsman** (see above)	
ḳd	**contours**	*LEM* 5 V,C6
ḳd	**circumference**	*H* 1,59,3
ḳdi	**to walk around, surround**	*LEM* 5,12,3
	to surround	*A* 1,26,4
	to go around	Push 127,2,14
	to stroll	*LES* 2,10,5
		K*RI* 1,113,7
	to promenade, to circulate	*Rd'É* 11,129 (Pl.8) P.Chassinat I,RX+2
	to describe a curve (of water)	*JSSEA* 10,68-69
ḳdy	(wood)	*TR* 10068 (Pl.11) 4R26
		TR 10068 (Pl.12) 5R16
		TR 10053 (Pl.20) 2V7
ḳd(*t*)	**sleep**	*LEM* 10,11,2
	sleep, slumber	*LES* 1,7,15
	sleep	*LES* 6,2,x+6
	sleep	*LRL* 2V3
	dream (cf. Szpakowska)	*HPBM*[4] L2 V44
	sleep	*A* 1,25,7
ḳdf	**to pluck, cull, collect,**	Gardiner, *Admonitions*, p.96-7
	to pick	*JEA* 66,168
ḳdf	**gleanings**	Push 127,4,7

ḳdrt	**incense** (cf. Hoch p.305)	*H* 1,64c,10 & 70b,11 Helck, *Bez* 572,239	
	(Semitic קְטֹ֫רֶת)	*JEA* 49,69 n.o	SIC 
ḳdḳd	**loitering, walking leisurely**	*LEM* 2,11,2	
ḳdd	**to make a round of inspection**	*LEM* 12,2V8	
	to circle, to go around	P.H. 500 (Pl.8) 4,10	
ḳdd	(see *ḳd*(*t*) above) **sleep**	*A* 1,25,7	
ḳḏ	**plaster** (cf. Helck, *Bez* 572,240; Hoch p.307) **gypsum, plaster**	*RAD* 18B,4V6	
		TR Amherst (Pl.5) 2,2	
		P.Leopold 2,11 *JEA* 22, Pl.13	
		*HPBM*³ CB,4V9	
		*HPBM*³ p.25 n.8	
		LES 4,13,5-6	
		O.Cairo J 49866,R1 *ASAE* 27,184	
		RAD 22,2R3	
		RAD 22,1R3	 SIC
		RAD 22,1R15	 SIC
ḳḏ	**plasterer** (cf. *BdÉ* 61,35-41)	*RAD* 22,2R3 & 1R10	
		RAD 22,2R11	
	gypsum-worker	*RAD* 22,1R11	
ḳḏ	**to hasten, to go around, to run** (cf. Hoch p.309)	*MDAIK* 15 (Pl.31) 179,n.G P.Geneva MAH 15274,5R8	
ḳḏw	**brambles, thorns** (cf. Helck, *Bez* 572,241) **thornbush** (cf. Hoch p.310)	*A* 1,24,3	
ḳḏt	**back of the hand**	*HPBM*⁴ T2 V21	

ḳḏwr	(oil of Hatti) (cf. Helck, *Bez* 572,242)	*LEM* 5,15,2	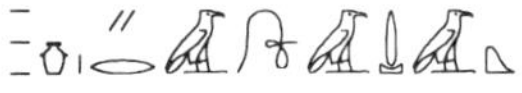
ḳḏm	**glance, vision**	*HPBM*[4] L5,V18 *HPBM*[4] L1,R29-30	
ḳḏm	**to view, to regard** (with evil intent)	*HPBM*[4] L2,R82	
ḳḏm	(measure for resin) (cf. Helck, *Bez* 572,243) **handful** (cf. Hoch p.310)	*H.O.* 35,1,II,12	
ḳḏmr	(clothing), "**tunic**"	*H* 1,63b,12	
ḳḏr	**fledgling, young bird** (cf. Hoch pp.311-12)	Mayer A and B Av13c9	
ḳḏḥ	**to crush, to grind** (cf. Helck, *Bez* 572,245) **to cut off, to break** (cf. Hoch p.313)	K*RI* 5,70,6-7	
ḳḏḏ	**to stretch out** (cf. Helck, *Bez* 572,246) **to gash** (cf. Hoch p.313)	K*RI* 5,60,12 E-W 77,16g	
ḳḏḏ	(see *ḳḏ* above) **plaster**	*ASAE* 27,185 O.Cairo J 49866,R5	
ḳḏḏ	(bread)	*Wb.* 5,82,16 Helck, *Mat* 676,60	

k3	**bull**	*LES* 2,14,5 K*RI* 5,23,5
		LEM 8,4,4
		H 1,22,1
		LEM 2,3,7
		LES 2,9,4
		LEM 9,17V5
		K*RI* 5,89,14
	ox	*LES* 3,8,1
		LEM 16,4V1
	ox	*LES* 5,1,10
	cattle	*LES* 3,8,1
		K*RI* 5,54,1
	k3-nḫt **mighty bull**	K*RI* 5,15,9
	ms-k3 **male calf**	*LRL* 42V6
k3	**personality, name**	*JEA* 50,81
		H 1,23,1
		LEM 6,11,7
	soul	*LEM* 1,4,6
	good pleasure, good will	*LEM* 1,8,3
	will	K*RI* 3,848,13
	pleasure	K*RI* 3,148,9
	genius	K*RI* 3,248,6
		K*RI* 1,11,2
	benefit	*LEM* 1,11,9
	(*n*) *k3 n* **for the benefit of**	*HPBM*[3] p.31 CB4,7R1
	soul	K*RI* 5,100,10
		LEM 13,1V2
	soul	K*RI* 1,126,4

k3	**to say**	*CB* 1 (Pl.23) C2V8	
		LES 2,17,10	
	to plot, to plan	K*RI* 5,26,1	
		K*RI* 2,81,1	
	to reflect	*LES* 4,6,8	
	to plan, "to pour forth (from mind)" (cf. *Rd'É* 24,202,3)	K*RI* 1,102,15	
k3	**then shall** (particle, future result) (cf. Erman, *N.A. Gram.* 675)	K*RI* 5,41,4	
	thus, and	*LES* 2,3,7	
	thus, so	*A* 1,12,4	
k3w	**food, sustenance**	*LEM* 3,2,10	
		H 1,79,11 *LEM* 2,1,2	
		K*RI* 5,21,12 K*RI* 1,88,10	
		K*RI* 1,68,14	
		LEM 10,12,5	SIC
	bounty	K*RI* 3,648,7	
		LEM 9,3V6	
		H 1,23,5	
		K*RI* 5,27,2	
	nourishment	*Khonsu* 1,24,4	
k3wy	**the public, foreigners**	*H* 1,30,2	
	strangers, crowd	*H* 1,78,9	
	foreigners	*JEA* 50,26	
	people, public	K*RI* 2,327,15	
	others	*A* 1,2,5	
	other people	*LEM* 9,5V1	
	foreigners	*H* 1,78,13	
k3-ḥr-k3	**Khoiak feast** (cf. *ASAE* 43,159; *Rd'É* 10,14 n.3) "attribute added to attribute"	*LEM* 3,3,4 *LEM* 3,1,7	

k3-ḥr-k3	(temple vase) (cf. Janssen, p.409)	*H* 1,6,11	
k3-ḏd	**in other words** (cf. *JEA* 24,243f.)	P.H. 500 (Pl.10) 5,11 Fox H5,11	
k3t	**vagina**	*LES* 2,7,8	
		LES 4,4,2	
	vulva	*HPBM*[3] p. 18,3 CB 3,9R9	
		HPBM[4] T2 V49	
k3t	**arts** (of war)	*LES* 3,5,1	
		LES 4,12,3 *LEM* 16,10V2	
	work	*LEM* 8,6,10	
		K*RI* 2,42,2	
		K*RI* 1,105,11	
		K*RI* 5,74,6	
		K*RI* 2,328,16	
	actions	*HPBM*[4] L7,48	
	duties	*HPBM*[3] CB4,5V7	
k3i	**prostitute** (?) *Wb.* 5,101,14 *Wb.* 5,107,10-11	*JEA* 70,96,34	
k3y	**sycamore fig**	*Giornale* (Pl.27) 4	
		ASAE 40,534-5	
		P.Turin 1881,5V2-3 K*RI* 6,617,5	
		K*RI* 6,617,6	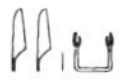
k3wšn	(cf. *kwšn* below)	Helck, *Bez* 572,247	
k3wty	**porter** (cf. Gardiner, *AEO* 1, 59*,#132)	*LRL* 36V8	
		K*RI* 1,57,7	
		K*RI* 1,66,9	
	worker	*Wb.* 5,102,4f.	

	workman	K*RI* 2,331,3	
		K*RI* 1,67,2	
		TR 10068 (Pl.16) 8V3	
k3p	**to hide, take shelter, cover** (cf. *JEA* 22,38)	K*RI* 5,28,4	
		K*RI* 5,29,12	
		LEM 8,7,5	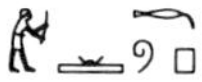
		K*RI* 2,115,8	
		K*RI* 5,69,7	
		K*RI* 5,71,10	
		K*RI* 1,22,6	
		K*RI* 5,61,4	
k3p	**roof, lid** (cf. *JEA* 46,46) "**veneer**" (?) (cf. Janssen, p.392 n.22)	*TR* 10068 (Pl.10) 3R8	
		TR 10068 (Pl.11) 3R26	
k3pw	**fowlers**	*A* 1,5,6	
k3pw	**those of the nursery** (?), **harem**, or "**trapped ones**" (cf. Fox B,C2,9) **royal nursery** (military or paramilitary unit)	*CB* 1 (Pl.23) C2V9	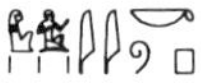
		Rd'É 31,140-141	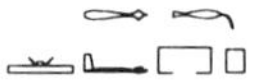
k3my	**vintner, vineyard keeper** (cf. *JEA* 38,29)	P.Leopold 2,4,7 *JEA* 22, Pl.16	
		P.Turin 2008+2016,3R5	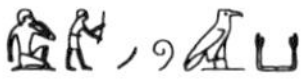
		K*RI* 1,59,6	
		K*RI* 1,59,8	
		K*RI* 1,52,7	
		LEM 5,7,1	
		H 1,7,10	
		H 1,29,4 *H* 1,27,10	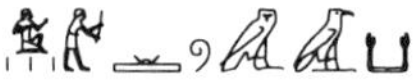
k3mw	**vineyard** **garden** (cf. Haring pp.348-9)	*LEM* 5,7,2 *TR* Abbott (Pl.1) 2R4	

		LEM 3,3,6	
		LEM 5,7,2	
		LEM 3,2,12 *H* 1,27,9 *A* 1,25,4	
		H 1,5,2	
		H 1,10,1	
k3mn	**to be blind** (cf. *CdÉ* 53,15; *Rd'É* 21,102ff.; Hoch p.319)	*LRL* 15V9,46R7 *RAD* 25,2R11	
	to blind, make blind (cf. *JEA* 10,122,4)	*LES* 3,10,7 *LES* 3,6,6	SIC
k3mn	**blind man**	*LES* 3,5,8	
	the blind	P.DM 39R8 *MIFAO* 104 (Pl.10) 139-40, n.q	
k3mn	**blindness** (cf. Hoch p.320)	*HPBM*[4] L1,R10-11 *HPBM*[4] L2,R50,76	
k3r	**shrine**	*LES* 4,3,10	
		LEM 5,11,11	
		H 1,4,10 & 6,4	
		H 1,45,8 & 58,2	
		H 1,25,8	
		TR 10053 (Pl.21) 4V21	
		K*RI* 1,58,13	
		K*RI* 1,42,5	
	chapel (cf. Valbelle, *Ouvriers*, 145) **naos, portable shrine** (cf. Spencer, *Egyptian Temple*, pp.125-130)	P.Turin cat. 1903,2V12	
	cabin (of Sun-Bark)	*P.Leiden* 1,348 (Pl.1) 1R3 p.35f., n.3 *P.Leiden* 1,348 (Pl.15) 11V6	
k3r	**boat, vessel** (cf. *kr* below)		

k3r	**weapons**	Helck, *Bez* 573,254
k3ry	**gardener**	*LES* 4,11,9
		K*RI* 1,52,7
		RAD 18D,2V14
		RAD 18B,3V15
		RAD 18B,3V13
		RAD 18D,4V13
		RAD 18,3R16
	or *k3my* (?) **vintner**	*TR* 10403 (Pl.36) 1R16
		TR 10068 (Pl.11) 4R28
		TR 10068 (Pl.13) 1V13 (SIC)
	(cf. Valbelle, *Ouvriers* p.110 n.13)	P.Turin cat. 1900, 1V16-18
k3rwt	(cf. *krì* below) **prison** (?) (cf. Helck, *Bez* 573,255)	On. Am. 451
k3ḥrk3	(see above *k3-ḥr-k3*)	
k3k3	**brush** (cf. *JEA* 29,10 n.b; Janssen, p.334)	K*RI* 5,64,9
		K*RI* 5,23,7
		K*RI* 5,35,15
	vegetation	K*RI* 3,288,6
k3kmn	(vessel) (cf. Janssen, 409&411)	*LES* 5,2,40
		O.Cairo 25,588,10
k3tmt	(see *kṯmt* below)	
k3ṯ3	(see *kṯ* below)	
k3ṯ3n3	(see *kṯn* below)	
ky	**another, other**	*LRL* 1V1
		LES 5,2,1
		Wil (2) 4RY+14
		LES 2,12,10

		K*RI* 2,228,3	
		K*RI* 2,232,7	
		LRL 21R8	
		LES 2,11,5	
		LES 1,5,12	
		LEM 1,10,9	
		LES 5,1,x+7	
	next, other	*LES* 2,6,1	
		LRL 46R8	
		LEM 10,4,9	
		P.H. 500 (Pl.12) 6,3	
		P.H. 500 (Pl.10) 5,11	
	(see *kt<u>h</u>w* for additional plural entries)	*LRL* 8V8	
	also, or "**the second**" (cf. *Rd'É* 26,169)	*LRL* 4V4	
	again	*Wil* (2) 6Rx+6	
	others	K*RI* 1,50,6	
	ky ḏd **another saying** (cf. *JEA* 53,97f.)	*LRL* 8V10	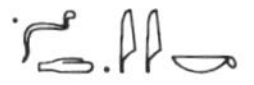
	m-ky ḏd **in other words, in short**	*JEA* 24,243-4	
	nn ky **unaccompanied**	*JEA* 65,81	
ky	**to cry out, to scream**	Push 127,3,6	
kyy	(or *kyky*, cf. *Wb.* 5,116) **monkey**	Urk. 4,2152,17	
	(cf. *HPBM*³ p.18, n.12)	*HPBM*³ CB3,9R27	
kwšn	**girth** (chariot part) (cf. Helck, *Bez* 572,247) (cf. *JSSEA* 16,34-35 n.133) (part of chariot harness) **reins** (cf. Hoch p.314)	*A* 1,24,5	
kb	(jar, jars for *šdḥ*)	P.Turin 2008+2016,1V4 *TR* 10068 (Pl.12) 6R8	
		TR 10068 (Pl.10) 3R27	
		H 1,15a,14	

kbnt	**war galley**	*JEA* 58,272
	(ship for trade to Punt)	*JEA* 64,71
	"**Byblos Boat**" (cf. *JEA* 46,67f.)	P.Lythgoe R4 *JEA* 46 (Pl.15)
kbrt	**jaundice** (?) **sulpher, brimstone** (cf. Hoch p.319)	*HPBM*[4] L6 R104-5
kbs	**grain basket** (2 oipe) (cf. Janssen p.133, 121; Helck, *Bez* 572, 248) "**footstool**"(?) (cf. Hoch pp.316-17)	O.DM 299,6
		H 1,18b,15
		H.O. 28,2,8 & 86,3,3
		O.DM 233,5
kp	**sole** (of foot), **palm** (of hand) (cf. *Wb.* 5,119,1)	P.Turin P.R. 125,11
		HPBM[4] L6 R41,42
		HPBM[4] T2,V22
	hands	K*RI* 5,18,11
		K*RI* 5,23,12
		K*RI* 5,53,2
		K*RI* 5,15,13
	(cf. Helck, *Bez* 572,249)	
kpw	(see *k3pw* above) **fowlers**	*A* 1,5,6
kpw	(see *k3pw* above) "**trapped ones**" (?) (cf. Fox B,C2,9)	*CB* 1,2,9
kpnt	(see *kbnt* above)	
kps	(?)	*LEM* 5,1b,9
kfi	**to uncover**	*LRL* 46V7
	to emerge	*LES* 4,8,10
		LES 6,1,x+3-4
		LES 4,1,11
		LES 4,4,2
		RAD 18,4R5

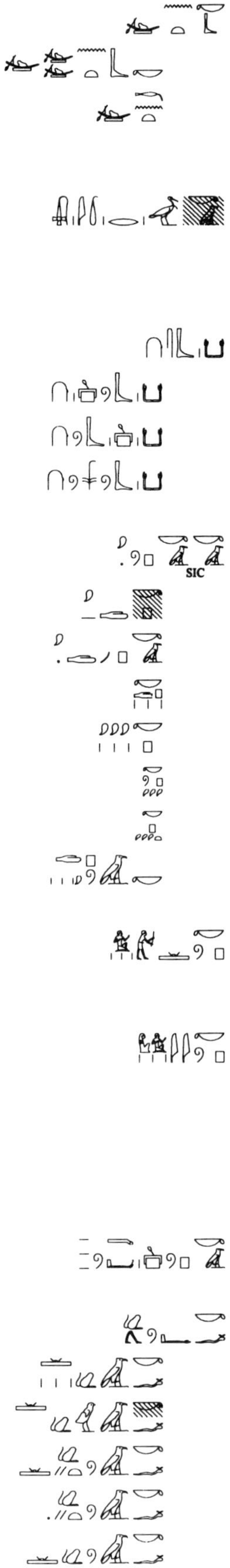

		K*RI* 1,113,15	
kf3	**back parts, hindquarters**	K*RI* 1,47,11	
	kf3-t3wy **bottom of the Two Lands**	*LEM* 13,1V8	
	m-kf3 **at all** (cf. Fox B,C3,1)	*CB* 1,3,1	
kf3t	**pedestal** (?)	*HPBM*[3] p.13 n.9 CB 3,3R20	
*kf*ꜥ	**to plunder, to take captive**	K*RI* 5,44,9	
		K*RI* 5,32,11	
		K*RI* 5,60,7	
		LEM 1,1V5	
		LEM 6,7,1	
		CS 2R7	
	to take booty	Horemhab 23	
		K*RI* 5,112,16	
		K*RI* 1,55,7	
		K*RI* 1,53,2	
		K*RI* 1,102,10	
	to capture (cf. *HPBM*[4] I, p.4-5, n.30)	*HPBM*[4] L1,R38-9	
	(cf. *kfi* above, also)	*HPBM*[4] L4,21	
*kf*ꜥ	**grasp**	K*RI* 5,85,10	
		K*RI* 5,106,13	
*kf*ꜥ*w*	**captives**	K*RI* 5,34,8	
		LEM 13,3V9	
		K*RI* 1,12,1	
km	**space, completion** "**twinkling**"	*LES* 2,18,5	
		K*RI* 5,29,13	
		LEM 2,3,4	
		K*RI* 1,42,15	
	completion, conclusion	*HPBM*[3] CB4,6V11	

km	**to be complete, full**	K*RI* 2,286,4	
km	**to be dark** **to be blind** (cf. Hoch p.319) **to be black**	*H* 1,45,5 *RAD* 25,1R2 *H* 1,7,13 K*RI* 1,73,11 P.Turin 2008+2016, 1V7	
kmyt	**herd of cattle, "black cattle"**	*H* 1,30,3 *H* 1,49,4	
kmyt	(cf. *km* above) **completion, conclusion**	*HPBM*[3] CB4,6V11	
kmir	(?) (Helck, *Bez* 573,251)	*H.O.* 8,7V3	
kmri	**tusk, ivory** (cf. Hoch p.321)	*RAD* 25,2R6 K*RI* 6,577,14	
kmrw	**dancer** (cf. Hoch p.320-21)	(cf. Helck, *Bez* 572,250) Onom. A 218	
kmḥ	(loaves) (?) **flour**	*LEM* 5,14,2 *LEM* 5,17,6 *A* 1,17,6	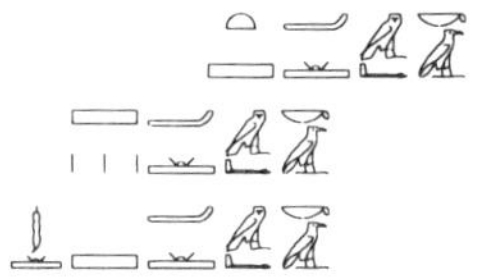
kms	(?) **weakness, error** (cf. Helck, *Bez* 573,252) **cowardice** (cf. Hoch pp.321-22)	K*RI* 5,65,13	
kmti	(tool?) (cf. Janssen p.325)	O.DM 579,14-15	
kni	**to protest, to preserve,** **to guard** (cf. Hoch p.323)	K*RI* 2,223,6	
knmy	**complainers**	Push 127,4,2	
knnr	**lyre** (cf. Hoch p.324)	*LEM* 5,12,2	
kns	**vagina** **perineum** (?)	*HPBM*[3] CB12,3 *HPBM*[4] T2,R72-3	

	vulva	*P.Leiden* 1,348,12V6	
kns	(?), **ochre** (?)	P.Brooklyn 47.218.50	
		Goyon 90,59	
knt	(garment) **cloak** (?) (cf. Hoch p.326)	P.Mayer A 4,7	
		P.BM 10068,1V4	
knt	**testicles, perineum** (cf. *HPBM*[4] p.37,24) **kidneys** (cf. Hoch p.325)	*HPBM*[4] L6,R38	
kr	**boat, ship** (cf. *JEA* 27,30 n.2; *Mélanges... Mokhtar* 1,21 n.11; *BIFAO* 101,93)	*LRL* 37V13	
		LES 5,3,3	
		LEM 11,3,7	
		LEM 16,8V5	
		RAD 10R3	
		RAD 12,2R11	
		RAD 17,3R9	
		RAD 17,3R9	
kr	**dwelling** (cf. Hoch p.328)	*TR* (P.BM 10052,7,15)	
kri	**prison** (?) (cf. Hoch p.328)	On. Am. 451	
kry	**ape**	*LEM* 1,3,9	
		LEM 3,4,1	
		LEM 6,6,7	
		LEM 6,8,7	
krb	**dog** (PN)(cf. Hoch pp.329-30)	*Wil* A32,35	
kri	**to be restrained, caged** (cf. Hoch p.328)	*Wil* B17,29	
kri	**prison** (cf. Hoch p.328)	Gloss. Gol. 6.2	
kri	**fellow**	*LEM* 10,2,3	
krp	**to efface, to erase** (cf. Hoch p.329)	Amarna 5,28	

krm	**vineyard, orchard** (cf. Hoch p.330)	*MH* 101 K*RI* 5,95,74
		K*RI* 2,156,16
	(?)	K*RI* 7,427,4
krmt	**bracelets** (cf. *GM* 74,7-9)	*LEM* 11,4,6 *LEM* 4,7 *LEM* 5,16,6
krr	(vessel for unguent)	*BIFAO* 83 (Pl.48) p.244 P. Boulaq XIII,frag. 11,3
krrt	**kidneys** (see *grt*)	*HPBM*[4] L5,24-25
krḥt	**basket, bushel** (container for fruit) (cf. Janssen, p.143; Hoch p.331)	*LEM* 5,7,5 *H* 1,40a,15
	(type of container)	*JEOL* 19,447f. *H.O.* 50,1,9
	bundles (cf. Warburton p.209)	O.DM 551V3
krs	**to skip, to caper, to dance, to jump** (cf. Helck, *Bez* 573,258; *OLZ* 28,5) **to frisk, to leap** (cf. Hoch p.312)	*LEM* 10,12,9 *JEA* 11,210ff. P.Lansing 1V9
krs	**sack** (cf. Helck, *Bez* 573,250)	P.Turin P.R. 102,1,4
	basket (?)	*JEA* 2,206,3 Mayer A and B B,14,10
kršt	**kyllestis bread** (cf. Valbelle, *Ouvriers* 271,20-1)	*LEM* 5,14,1 *LEM* 5,21,5 *LEM* 11,1,3 *P.Leiden* 1,350,2V22 *P.Leiden* 1,350 5V14 *TR* 10054 (Pl.8) 4V2 K*RI* 3,146,3
krt	(?) (cf. Janssen, p.143-4)	Naun 2V2-3

krt	**carnage, massacre, slaughter, murder** (cf. Hoch p.335)	*HPBM*^{4} T3,R77
krtbi	(?)	*LEM* 11,4,4-5
		LEM 15,1,8
krṯ	**straps** (fabric)	*LEM* 5,17,2
	whip-lash (?) (cf. *TR* p.101,n.32)	*TR* 10068 (Pl.13) 1V4
krk(*r*)	**couch, bed** (cf. *Essays…Kantor* p.302)	O.Gard. 158,6 Janssen p.185
		Urk. 4,667,2
krkr	**heap of stones** (cf. Helck, *Bez* 573,260) **rubble**	*JEA* 19,172 O.Edinb. 916,V3-4
kh	**to throw out**	K*RI* 5,16,11
		K*RI* 5,58,10
		K*RI* 5,101,2
	to hurtle (cf. *Eretz Israel* 5,81,n.dd)	K*RI* 2,151,12
	to cast a shadow	K*RI* 5,26,11
	to toss about (cf. E-W p.83)	K*RI* 5,64,9
kh	**difficult, strong, wild** *Wb*. 5,137	*A* 1,12,6-7
		A 1 (P.Turin 1)
khb	**to harm**	K*RI* 3,337,12
kḥn	**kettle, cauldron, large crock**	Janssen p.415-16 *P.Leiden* 1,343-345,IX,11&12
kḥn	<*knḥ* **darkness, gloom of night** (cf. Hoch p.315)	*H.O.* 89,9
kḥrk	(cf. *k3-ḥr-k3* above) **Khoiak, Fourth month of Akhet**	*ASAE* 43,159 O.BM 563 ga,18

kḥs	(part of a bird trap)(?) **chair** (cf. Hoch p.337)	O.DM 39R3 Helck *Bez* p.573,263	
kḥkḥ	**to grow old** (cf. *JEA* 44,74)	*LES* 9,F13	
		Push 127,1,8	
kḥkḥ	**old man**	*A* 1 (O.BN 5)	
ksy	**bowing, obeisance**	*LEM* 5,17,9	
		K*RI* 5,27,5	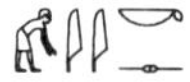
		K*RI* 1,99,5	
		K*RI* 2,285,2	
		K*RI* 1,18,11	
		K*RI* 1,30,12	
		K*RI* 2,99,15	
		K*RI* 5,108,12	
		K*RI* 2,150,15	
	m ksy **in obeisance**	*CB* 1 (Pl.24) C3V8	
		Khonsu 2,179,20	
	m ksw **in submission**	K*RI* 3,484,11	
ksb	(tree)	*LEM* 5,2,11	
		LEM 11,2,9	
		MÄS 37, p.14,20,1,8	
ksb	**grain basket**	K*RI* 3,543,12	
ksfn	(see *gsfn* below)		
ksks	**to play, perform**	*LEM* 3,4,1	
ksks	(Nubian) **dancer**	Kush 7,86&90	
ksks	**hobble**	*LES* 4,5,7	
kskst	**basket** (expensive) (cf. Janssen, p. 151,20)	*TR* 10052 (Pl.27) 3R20	
kšn	(cf. *kwšn* above) (saddle pads? reins?) (cf. Hoch pp.314-15)	P.Brooklyn 47,218.135,2,14	

kk	(see *k3k3* above) **brush**	K*RI* 5,35,15
kkw	**darkness**	*A* 1,25,4 *LES* 2,4,9
		LES 5,1x+9
		LES 9,F2
		LEM 2,5,8
		K*RI* 1,113,15
		K*RI* 5,21,9
		K*RI* 5,64,15
	twilight	*P.Leiden* 1,348,5R2
	kkw-sm3 **primeval darkness**	*P.Leiden* 1,348,4R5
		BIFAO 86,190,1,16,13 P.BM 10474,1V16
		O.Cairo JE 67100
kkt	**worm**	*LEM* 3,6,1
	weevil	*JEA* 20,187
kt	**little one**	K*RI* 5,23,2
	short (moment)	K*RI* 5,76,14
	common people	K*RI* 5,68,7
	small	*HPBM*[3] CB4,2V10
	little girl	P.Turin 1966,2,6 Fox T2,6
	small ones	K*RI* 3,363,10
kt	< *nkt* **anything** (cf. Wente, *LRL* 28au)	*LRL* 28V14
kt	(see *ky* above) **another**	K*RI* 5,74,10
ktmt	(see *kṯmt* below) **gold**	*H* 1,5,12
ktḥw	(plural of *ky*) **others, remainder**	*LES* 5,1,15
		LEM 5,11,3
		LEM 6,6,2

		LEM 6,16,1	
		H 1,4,9	
		H 1,48,4	
		K*RI* 2,58,4	
		K*RI* 2,333,6	
		TR 10054 (Pl.6) 1R6	
		Push 127,2,8	
		A 1,22,3	
		Push 127,4,13	
ktkt	**"springer"**	*LES* 1,4,10	
ktkt	**to stir, tremble**	*LES* 2,16,8	
	to totter	*HPBM*[4] T1R60	
	to move	P.CGC 58053,R9 *ASAE* 71 (Pl.1) I.9	
	to shift	K*RI* 5,68,11	
	to quiver	*JNES* 28, p.10	
	nn ktkt **unshaken** (cf. *JEA* 42,9,1,2)	P.Turin 1882,1R2 *JEA* 41, Pl. 7	
kṯ	**safflower**	*RAD* 4,2V5	
		Fox C23, p.387	
kṯ	(vessel) **cup, gobblet** (cf. Hoch p.339; *Wb.* 5,148,9-10) (metal cup)(cf. *Essays…Kantor* p.302)	*H.O.* 86,1 2V6 *LEM* 9,3V3	
	drinking vessels	K*RI* 5,53,7	
		Janssen p.408-9	
kṯt	**covering, garment** (cf. Hoch p.341)	*LEM* 5,17,1	
		RAD 4,1R5	
		RAD 5,2,13	
		H 1,14b,4	
kṯm	(see *kḏm* above) **glance**	*HPBM*[4] L1 R29-30	

kṯmw	**threats** (?), **divination, omen** (cf. Hoch p.338)	K*RI* 5,60,11	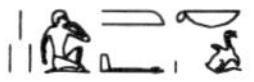
		HPBM^{4} L1,29-30	
		HPBM^{4} L5,v 17-18	
kṯmt	**goldsmith**	Helck, *Bez* 574,264	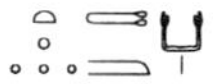
kṯmt	**gold** (cf. Hoch p.338)	*H* 1,5,12	
		K*RI* 5,74,4	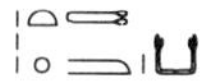
		Lange *Amenemope* 18,12	
kḏn	< *kṯn* **charioteer** (cf. Hoch pp.340-41)	K*RI* 5,1,8,12	
	equerry (cf. *JEA* 39,43; *JEA* 23,2; *JARCE* 2,88f.; *JSSEA* 10,134)	K*RI* 1,53,3	
		K*RI* 5,12,12	
		K*RI* 5,33,3	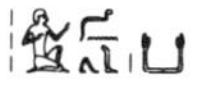
		K*RI* 2,32,12	
		K*RI* 2,64,2	
		K*RI* 5,91,9	
		K*RI* 1,51,14	
		LES 7,2,10	
		P.Leiden 1,350,2V9	
		Wil (14) 30R46	
		Wil (21) 45R12	
		K*RI* 2,83,10	
	groom	K*RI* 2,32,16	

gt	(cf. *g3wt* below) **shrine** (cf. *TR* p.69, n.28)	*TR* 10054 (Pl.7) 3R11
g3	**to chant**	*LEM* 5,12,2
	to whistle (?)	*Rd'É* 11,128 n.3&Pl.8 (P.Chassinat I,x+2R,x+9)
g3	(see *g3wt* below) **chest**	*TR* 10053 (Pl.18) 5R6
g3i	**to calumniate, to lie** *TR* 166, n.77 *TR* 168, n.98	*TR* 10052 (Pl.34) 14R17
		TR 10052 (Pl.33) 12V21
		TR 10052 (Pl.32) 11R21
		TR 10052 (Pl.32) 12V18
g3it	**chapel, shrine**	*H* 1,46,8
g3y	**jar, bowl, flask** (cf. Janssen p.426,162; Janssen, *Ships Logs*, 25; Caminos *LEM* 194f.) (wide) **cup**	*P.Leiden* 1,350,2V4
		P.H. 500 (Pl.4) 2,9
		LES 2,8,1
		LES 2,8,5
		LES 2,14,2
		LES 2,14,2 (SIC)
g3w	**to gaze**	K*RI* 5,24,1
g3w	**to lack** (also cf. *wgg*)	*LEM* 5,14,9
g3w	**to be narrow, to squeeze**	P. Edinburgh 912, face B,1.9 *Oriens Ant.* 6,50 (Pls. 18-19)
	to hem in	K*RI* 5,41,1
		K*RI* 5,69,9
	to be crowded	K*RI* 1,49,15

g3w	**oppressions**	*P.Leiden* 1,348,6R7
g3wt	**bundle**	K*RI* 5,97,6
	“bridewealth” (cf. *Gleanings* p.120)	*P.Leiden* 1,350 1V x+20
	“tax, tribute” (?) (cf. S.A. p.301; *ZÄS* 106,19,34)	P.DM 27,R11 S.A. Pl.98
		LES 10,B,11
g3wt	**sight, gaze** (cf. *g3w* above)	K*RI* 5,63,8
g3wt	**narrow road, defile**	*A* 1,23,7
		K*RI* 2,13,14
		K*RI* 2,13,11
		K*RI* 2,13,12
g3wt	**chest, box**	*H.O.* 24,1,3
		TR 10068 (Pl.12) 6R11
		P.Turin cat. 1907+1908, 3R1 *JEA* 52,87 n.oo
		H 1,13b,10
		TR 10053 (Pl.18) 5R6&14
		Naun 3R12 *JEA* 31,38
		Naun 3V11
		Naun 2V13
g3wy	(cf. *gw* below) **steed**	*CB* 1 (Pl.29) G1,V5-6
g3w3n	(cf. *gwn*) **sack**	Helck, *Bez* 574,270
g3b	(see *gb* below)	
g3by	(cf. *gbi* below) **weak**	K*RI* 3,653,7
g3bw	(cf. *gb* below) **cheat**	K*RI* 3,542,3
g3bw	**basket**	*H.O.* 28,1V3-4 Janssen p.357
g3bwy	**dreary** (?)	*A* 1,20,1

g3bt (*n*) *šrt*	**nostril**	*HPBM*[4] L6R25	
g3f	(cf. *gf* below) **monkey**	*LEM* 11,4,3	
g3f	**to be amazed**	*LEM* 6,7,2	
g3f	(see *ḳfn*) **to bake**	*LEM* 8,7,7	
g3ḫ	**to become easily tired**	*LEM* 10,7,7	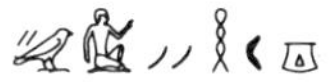
	to be faint	*CB* 1 (Pl.30) G2V2	
	to be soft	*HPBM*[3] CB4,4V3	
g3ḫy	(unknown)	K*RI* 5,64,13	
g3s	**mourning**	*LES* 2,8,8	
	sorrow (cf. Fox H7,6)	P.H. 500 (Pl.14) 7,6	
		P.Turin 1882,5R7 *JEA* 41 (Pl.11) 5,7	
g3s	**to be partial**	K*RI* 3,438,7	
g3sr	(cf. *gsr* below) (cf. Helck, *Bez* 575,275)	*H* 1,13a,6	
g3š	**to spill**	*JEA* 12,183 (Pl.37) O.BM 5637,R3-4	
g3š	**rush, reed** (cf. Janssen p.365, § 117; *OLZ* 30,145,2; *JEA* 52,88 n.ss; Helck, *Mat* V,814)	*LEM* 5,14,7	
		LEM 5,1b,3	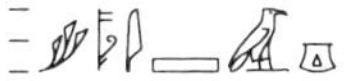
g3g3	**to cackle**	K*RI* 5,91,14	
g3g3	**to dazzle** ("to gaze") (cf. Fox H5,11)	P.H. 500 (Pl.10) 5,11	
	to be dazzled (cf. *ZÄS* 81,14-15)	*JEA* 29,57	
	to be dumbfounded (cf. Borghouts nt.411)	*P.Leiden* 1,348 11V5 (Pl.15)	
g3t	(measure)	*LEM* 5,14,4	

g3t	(see *g3wt* above) **box**	Naun 2V13	
g3ty-nṯr	(see *ḫrty-nṯr* stonemason?)	K*RI* 3,754,10	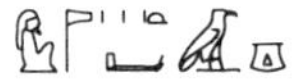
g3tr	(see *g3wt* above) **box**	*JEA* 31,38	
gw	**steed** (Helck, *Bez* 574,269; *JEA* 19,202; Hoch p.347)	*LEM* 3,6,5 *CB* 1 (Pl.29) G1V5-6	
gww	**to be amazed** (cf. *ZÄS* 81,14-17)	*Khonsu* 2,140,1 *Khonsu* 1,23,15	
gwn	**sack**	K*RI* 4,14,8 Helck, *Bez* 574,270	
gwš	**to turn aside** **to be crooked** **to be askew, bent, twisted** (cf. *JEA* 42,19,5,2-3), **crookedness** (cf. Hoch p.348) **to be distracted**	K*RI* 5,22,15 *LEM* 5,11,10 *HPBM*[3] CB 4,1V8-9 P.Turin 1882,5R3 *JEA* 41 (Pl.11) 5,3	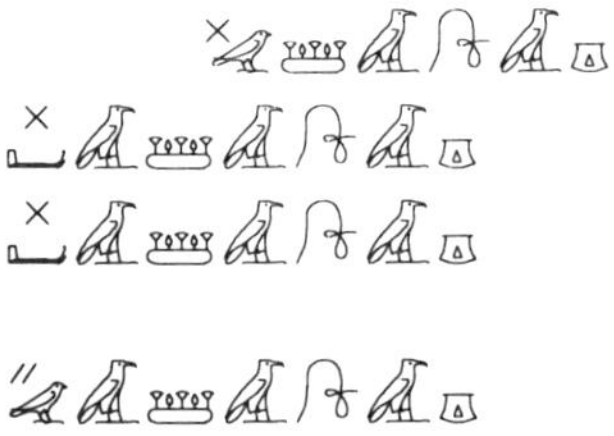
gwt	**to pack, replenish**	*LEM* 10,12,3	
gwtn	(cf. *g3wt* above) **chest**	*TR* 10068 (Pl.12) 6R11	
gwtn	**to bind** **to bind together, to tie**	*LEM* 5,3,1 *A* 1,24,7	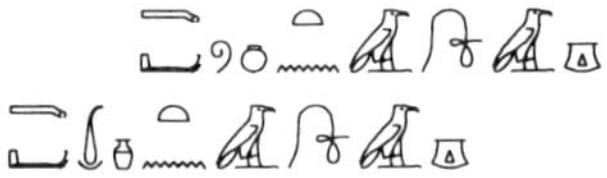
gbi	**to be weak, lame, deprived** (cf. *ZÄS* 113,79-81) **to be short** (deficient)	*HPBM*[3] CB 4,2V3 *LEM* 1,6,8 K*RI* 3,653,7 *A* 1,6,7 *LEM* 3,1,8 *LEM* 10,10,6 K*RI* 2,334,7	

	to be defrauded	Push 127,2,4
	to be parted from	*A* 1,7,1
gb	**affliction**	*LRL* 3V5
	harm, deficiency, debt (?)	*LRL* 3V14
	damage	Janssen p.320
	debt	*LES* 5,2,37
	cheating	*LES* 4,4,9
gb	**arm** (cf. *ZÄS* 43,42)	P.H. 500 (Pl.10) 5,3
		HPBM[3] CB 8,7R9
		K*RI* 5,14,3
		K*RI* 5,23,5
		K*RI* 5,43,15
		K*RI* 5,17,10
		CB 1 (Pl.22) C1V4
		O.H. (2,3) Pl.76,14 Fox C14
		HPBM[4] T2V38
gb	**blade, leaf**	*LEM* 10,6,9 (SIC)
		A 1,10,6
gb	**wild goose**	P.H. 500 (Pl.8) 4,7&9
		P.H. 500 (Pl.4) 2,1
gbw	**stick** (cf. Wb. 5,154,7 *g3bt*)	*BIFAO* 83 P.Boulaq XIII, frag. 18,1
gbgb	(cf. *gb*) **to make lame**	*HPBM*[3] CB7,8R3
gbgb	**weakness** (cf. *ZÄS* 113,79-81)	K*RI* 5,15,10
		JEA 41,Pl.17,9 P.Turin 1940+1941,**2R9**
	lameness	Push 127, p.34 n.9
	prostrate (?)	K*RI* 5,14,4
		K*RI* 5,55,7

	heaps (?)	K*RI* 2,89,5	
		K*RI* 2,89,10	
		K*RI* 2,122,10	
gp	**to catch** **to perforate, to skewer** (?), **to cut off, to pluck** (?) (cf. Hoch pp.348-349)	*LEM* 11,2,8 *LEM* 5,2,10	
gf	**monkey**	*LEM* 11,4,3	
	ape	*A* 1,10,1	
		A 1,5 (O.Berlin)	
	ape, monkey	*HPBM*[4] L6R59	
		HPBM[4] T3R54-55	
gm	**to find**	*LRL* 26V1 *LES* 2,5,1 *LEM* 6,12,6	
		LRL 4R5	
		LEM 5,10,5	
		LES 4,10,3	
		H 1,78,3	
		LRL 5R16	
		K*RI* 5,52,3	
		K*RI* 2,41,9	
		K*RI* 5,35,15	
		RAD 18,3R4	
		RAD 25,3V7	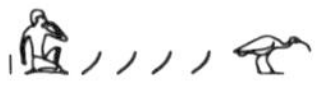
	to find, to pick out	*HPBM*[4] L1R40	
	to acquire, to appropriate	*JEA* 47,105	
	to verify, prove, to judge	*Rd'É* 21,95 n.5	
	to establish *Rd'É* 30,132	*Rd'É* 30,130	
	to find innocent	K*RI* 6,809,12 P.Mayer A,3,13	
	to notice	K*RI* 3,92,10	
	to invent	K*RI* 3,194,6	
	to recognize	*HPBM*[3] CB4,4V8	
		Rd'É 10,65-66,j	

	gm ḏrt **capable**	K*RI* 5,16,15 K*RI* 5,29,8	
	gm...r **to find fit**	*LEM* 6,17,7	
gm	**perchance, maybe** (cf. Caminos, *LEM* p.58)	*LEM* 2,8,7 *LEM* 5,10,3	
gmy	(cf. *km3* above) **reeds**	*LEM* 5,8,12	
gmyt	(female) **creator**	K*RI* 3,710,12	
gmw	(unknown) **precious stones** (?) (cf. *JEA* 34,42 (8); Harris, *Minerals* p.30)	*LEM* 11,3,8	
gmt	**black ibis**	*LEM* 5,2,1	
gmḥ	**to look at, to catch sight of**	*LEM* 5,3,4 *CB* 1 (Pl.22) C1V2-3	
	to espy	*LES* 1,4,7	
	to behold	K*RI* 5,80,14	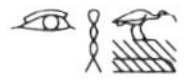
	to spy on	K*RI* 5,113,11	
		K*RI* 2,119,9	
	to look, to stare, to search out	Push 127,1,13	
		K*RI* 1,113,1	
	gmḥ r ḥ3ty **to look into hearts**	*JNES* 22,33 1.5	
gmgm	**to tear asunder**	K*RI* 5,61,10	
	to crush, to run over	P.Brooklyn 47.218.50,20,15 Goyon 80,364	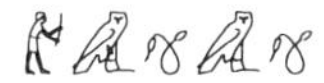
	to grope, to finger	*A* 1,28,3	
	to massage, to rub, to caress	P.H. 500 (Pl.2) 1,2	
	to seek	*ZÄS* 72,112 n.2	
gnw	(for *ḳnw*) **many**; or **oriole** (?) (cf. Fox p.76 n.1)	*JEA* 65,87,4 *CB* 1,17R10	

gnw	**wine jars**	*H* 1,49,8
gnwt	**annals, records** (cf. *Studien Westendorf* 327-41)	K*RI* 1,114,12
gnn	**to grow weak**	*LES* 2,8,1
		LEM 2,3,2
	to be weak	*LEM* 10,7,7-8
		LEM 11,5,3
	to be tender (?)	*CB* 1,17R10
		K*RI* 2,46,9
		K*RI* 2,46,8
		K*RI* 2,54,4
		JEA 23,61,5
	di gnn **to enfeeble**	P.Rollin 1 *JEA* 49,72
gnn	(plant) (cf. Caminos, *LEM* 166,8,11)	*LEM* 5,8,11 *LEM* 10,11,5
gnn	**vase stand**	*TR* 10383 (Pl.22) 1R4
gnrg	**to gossip**	*LEM* 1,7,7
gns	**outrage**	Push 127,3,6
	violence, injustice (cf. Hoch p.349)	*HPBM*[4] L6V47
		Lange *Amenemope* 8,20
gngnt	(vessel)	*Khonsu* 1,53,41
gr	**to be silent**	*LRL* 50R18
		CB 1,17R6
		LES 4,15,4
	to stop	P.H. 500 (Pl.6) 3,4
	to be silent	P.H. 500 (Pl.10) 5,10
		LEM 1,11,7
	to be quiet, still (cf. Borghouts n.458)	*P.Leiden* 1,348,2V7
		LES 5,2,8
		LRL 16R14

	to be peaceable (?)	K*RI* 3,75,1
	to be discreet	K*RI* 3,297,11
gr(*t*)	**also**	*LRL* 9V14
	still	*LRL* 29V1
		P.CGC 58053,R4
		ASAE 71 (Pl.1) 1.4
	any more (after neg.)	*TR* 10052 (Pl.27) 4R1
	too, also	*P.Leiden* 1,348,12V1
		TR 10403 (Pl.37) 3V21
		K*RI* 2,56,14
	too, either	*LRL* 12V4
		LRL 20V4
		LEM 5,8,2
		K*RI* 1,66,8
	nty nb gr **anything else**	*TR* 10052 (Pl.28) 5,8
	gr ink **in my turn** (cf. *JEA* 54,119; 31,33 n.h)	Naun 1,2R5
gr	**stream**	*Wil* B12,16
		Wil B13,22
gry	**bird** (cf. Fox H4,9)	P.H. 500 (Pl.8) 4,9
grw	**silent one** (cf. *GM* 38,25-6)	*LEM* 8,8,5
		LEM 8,8,6
	self controlled	*JSSEA* 8,69
grb	**to trim**	*LEM* 5,16,11
		LEM 11,2,1
	to shape, to shave, to plane (cf. Hoch p.351)	*A* 1,26,5
grḥ	**to finish**	*LRL* 36V4
		RAD 22,2R11
	to finish (decoration) (cf. *JEA* 4,137)	K*RI* 2,332,10

grḥ	**ending**	*CB* 1 (Pl.30) G2V1
		CB 1 (Pl.29) G1V5
grḥ	**night**	*LRL* 2V3
		LES 5,1x+5
		LEM 10,9,8
		CB 1,17R8
		P.H. 500 (Pl.4) 2,7
	evening	*LES* 1,7,15
		K*RI* 1,39,7
		LRL 34R6
		LES 3,4,4
		LEM 8,8,11
grg	**to organize**	*LES* 11,2,2
	to make ready	*LRL* 28V12
	to establish	*LEM* 9,17V2
	to curb	K*RI* 3,105,12
	to arrange	K*RI* 5,93,8
	to furnish	*HPBM*[4] T3R91-2
		K*RI* 3,18,14
	to provide, to equip	*Rd'É* 20,20,c
	to equip	*LEM* 2,1,4
	to found	*LEM* 12,5V4 Caminos *LEM* p.510
	to prepare, to set (cf. Fox H4,2,6,9)	P.H. 500 (Pl.8) 4,2; 4 4,6; 4,9
		K*RI* 2,108,5
		K*RI* 2,108,3
		K*RI* 1,30,12
	to put in order (cf. *ZÄS* 96 p.17) "founder of the Two Lands"	Coptos stela, 1.2
grg	**readiness**	*LEM* 15,1,2
		LEM 17,3

grg	**falsehood**	*LES* 3,2,1
		LES 2,17,6
		LES 2,7,8
		LES 3,7,3
	false one, imposter	*LES* 4,1,11
		LES 4,15,7
		LES 5,2,79
		LEM 8,8,10
		K*RI* 1,68,6
	falsehood	*Melanges…Mokhtar* 2,350,21
	m grg **unjustly, falsely**	Push 127,2,4
grg	**settlement**	*Wil* (54) B7V25
		Stele Ash. Mus. 1894.1076 *JEA* 54,169 (Pl.25) 8
	settlements	*CB* 1, 18V2
	equipment, founding	K*RI* 1,66,15
	equipment	*JEA* 4,139,3
grgt	**dowry** (cf. Coptic ϭⲣⲏϭⲉ)	*Rd'É* 20,174-5
grg-pr	**outfit**	Naun 1,2R3
	furniture	*JEA* 22,180 P.Leopold II,2,18
	house furnishings	*JEA* 42,18
grgwty	**rumors** (see *gnrg* above)	*LEM* 5,10,10
grt	**kidney**	*HPBM*[4] L2V43
grḏ	**morsel of meat** (cf. Hoch p.354)	*O.H.* 1406,2,x+1
gḥs	**gazelle**	*LEM* 5,10,5
		LES 4,10,7
		LEM 11,3,6
		H 1,4,8

		CB 1 (Pl.30) G2V1	
		K*RI* 1,49,4	
gs	**ointment** (cf. *JEA* 64,86; Push 127 p.57 n.2)	*JEA* 64 (Pl.14) R7	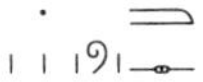
gs	**side, half** (cf. *GM* 52,43-46)	K*RI* 2,325,14	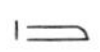
		LEM 6,16,1	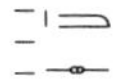
	m gs **partly**	*LRL* 9V5	
	r gs **at the side of**	*LES* 1,4,4	
	beside	Push 127,3,8	
		LES 8,1,3	 SIC
	r gswy **beside, near**	*HPBM*³ CB4,6V11	
	in the neighborhood of	K*RI* 3,436,9	
	ḥr gswy **on both sides**	*ZÄS* 103,1-4	
gs-pr	(small religious structure) **portable chest** (cf. *TR* 173 n.3)	*TR* 10403 (Pl.36) 1,9	
	workshop (cf. Helck, *Verwaltung* 297,1)	*JEA* 46,48 n.1	
gs-m3ʿ	**headache**	*HPBM*³ CB5,4V10	
		*HPBM*⁴ L2V37	
		*HPBM*⁴ L5V51	
gs-tp	**headache, migrane** (cf. *ZÄS* 11,14)	*HPBM*³ CB5,4V1	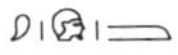
gs-ḏbw	(chariot appurtenance)	*LEM* 5,16,12	
gs3	**to bend, to make crooked, to ruin**	*HPBM*³ CB4,2V3	
gsfn	(mineral or vegetable) **chalcopyrite** (cf. *Wb*. 5,206,9-11) (variety of black eye paint)	*BIFAO* 84,4-18	
gsm	**stormy lake**	*LEM* 5,1b,2	

gsr	(measure)	*LEM* 5,14,3	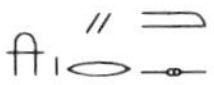
		LEM 5,15,10	
		LEM 5,15aV6	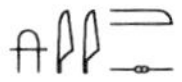
gsr	**ring, finger-ring** (cf. Helck, *Bez* 575,275; Hoch p.355)	*H* 1,13a,6	
gsgs	**to overflow**	*LEM* 12,5V9 Caminos *LEM* 511	
		H 1,4,4	
	to regulate, to put in order	Lange *Amenemope* I,15	
	m gsgs **rushing forth**	Push 127,4,8-9	
gst	(fish)	*RAD* 8R3	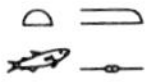
gsti	(scribe's) **palette**	*LEM* 6,11,1	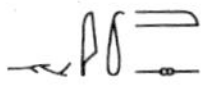
gši	**reed** (?)	*LES* 2,7,9	
		H 1,19b,10	
		H 1,72,1	
gšw	**geese**	*LES* 5,2,65	
gg	(see *gng* & *g3g3* above)		
ggt	**kidneys**	*HPBM*[3] CB7,4V5	
		HPBM[4] P4,48	
gt	(loaves)	*LEM* 5,14,2	
gt	(see *g3wt* above) **shrine**	*TR* 10054 (Pl.7) 3R11	
gt	(oil)	*LEM* 5,15,3-4	
gtr	(see *g3wt* above) (box)	Naun 2R11	
gdfdf	(?)	*LEM* 14,2V6	

t	**bread**	*LEM* 1,8,10	
	(cf. Janssen p.345)	*LRL* 3R8	
		K*RI* 1,74,11	
	t-ḥḏ **white bread**	*P.Leiden* 1,350,2V20	
	t-ḥry **celestial bread**	*JEA* 54,159	
	t-ẖry **excrement**	*JEA* 54,158 (P.BM 10731,V1)	
	t-r (or *trit* ?) **cakes of pigment** (cf. *Wb.* 5,209,11)	Harris, *Minerals* 141	
tꜣ	(fem. def. art.) **the**	*LRL* 3R12	
	"belonging to", "pertaining to"	*JEA* 58,189,9	
tꜣ	**land**	*LEM* 3,5,1	
		K*RI* 2,232,12	
		LRL 4R2,21R9	
	clay (material for bricks)	K*RI* 1,75,10	
	tꜣ ḥḏ **dawn**	*LES* 1,8,14	
	tꜣ-ḏr.f **the entire land**	*LES* 2,12,2	
	rmṯ nb n pꜣ tꜣ **anybody whatsoever**	*LRL* 21R8	
	tꜣ-wy **Two Lands**	*H* 1,43,1	
		LES 4,2,13	
		LES 4,2,10	
		LES 5,2,20	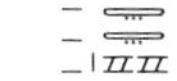
		LES 5,1,15	
		K*RI* 2,226,2	
		K*RI* 5,68,14	
		K*RI* 2,101,10	
		K*RI* 5,13,14	
		K*RI* 5,11,10	
		K*RI* 5,26,1	

	plains	K*RI* 5,22,1	
		H 1,49,12	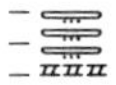
		LEM 2,2,7	
t3	**heat**	K*RI* 5,65,10	
t3-ʿbt	**offering festival** (1st month of winter) (cf. *ASAE* 43,173-81)	*Rd'É* 10,12	
t3-wr	**starboard**	Černý, *Workmen* 100	
	east side (of building)	Montet, *Scenes* 350,351	
t3-mri	**Egypt** (cf. *Cd'É* 58,134,1.4)	*Khonsu* 2,139,3	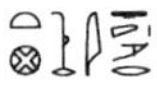
		K*RI* 5,672,2	
t3-mḥty	**Northland**	K*RI* 2,336,8	
t3-n-ḥḏ	**floor of silver**	*TR* 10053 (Pl.21) 4V15	
t3-n-ḫry-nṯr	**gods acre, cemetery, necropolis**	*HPBM*3 CB4,4V10-11	
t3-nnt	**shrine**	K*RI* 3,176,11	
t3-nt-ʿ3mw	**bubonic plague** (?)	*SAK* 11,91-105	
t3-nṯr	**god's land**	*H* 1,29,1	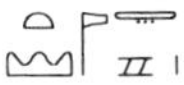
		K*RI* 2,285,3	
t3-šmʿ	**Upper Egypt**	K*RI* 2,336,8	
t3-tmw	**all mankind**	*LEM* 1,4,1	
		LEM 3,6,3	
	the masses	*HPBM*3 CB4,7V4	
	(cf. Lichtheim 2,177)	*HPBM*3 CB4,3V10	
	the whole world	*Khonsu* 1,21,26	

t3-ḏsr	**necropolis**	K*RI* 5,65,6
		K*RI* 2,325,13
	sacred territory	K*RI* 3,137,12
t3y	**this** (fem. sing.)	*LRL* 2V1
	these	*LRL* 30R11
	(with suffixes for possessive adj.)	*LES* 2,19,5
t3y	**to resist**	Stele Louvre C256,1.15 *Rd'É* 20,22,C
		K*RI* 2,97,10
t3yt	**door, covering, shroud**	*H* 1,45,7
	shroud, or shrine	*TR* 10053 (Pl.21) 4V11
t3ḥ	**to souse**	*LEM* 6,16,7
		LEM 10,7,3
	to dive (cf. Fox p.20, n.b)	P.H. 500 (Pl.8) 4,10
	to fall in	*ZÄS* 80,73-74
t3ḥt	**dregs**	*Wb.* 5,233-234
		JEA 63,176
	prostitute (?)	*JARCE* 6,99 n.17
t3š	**boundary, frontier, district, regions**	*H* 1,57,13
		K*RI* 5,77,3
		K*RI* 5,20,15
		K*RI* 5,24,2
		K*RI* 1,16,6
		K*RI* 1,99,11
		K*RI* 1,15,11
		H 1,22,8
		K*RI* 1,6,16
		JEA 47,105
		K*RI* 2,326,6

ti	(particle with the dependent pronoun)	K*RI* 1,113,10	
		K*RI* 2,93,5	
		K*RI* 1,48,1	
tit	**image**	K*RI* 1,39,4	
		LEM 9,4V8	
		K*RI* 1,71,4	
		K*RI* 5,109,15 K*RI* 3,12,2	
	tit-Rᶜ	*JEA* 62,78	
		Khonsu 8,11	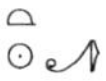
	tit ḥmt **image** (model) **of a wife**	*JEA* 68,242	
tiw	**verily, yes, certainly** (?)	*ZÄS* 43,42 n.7	
tiwy	**of yours, thine** (cf. *JEA* 20,16; *ZÄS* 50,114ff.)	*LEM* 1,4,9	
		LEM 5,10,9	
		LRL 9R6	
		LEM 5,11,7	
		K*RI* 5,86,11	
		K*RI* 5,48,10	
		LRL 11V1	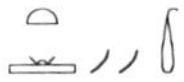
tiwt	(see *ṯbwt* below)	*LES* 6,2,x+19	
tiwrit	(see *twrit* below)	*LEM* 5,3,4	
(*ti*)*-nt-ḥtri*	**chariotry** (cf. *MÄS* 6,14-16)	*LES* 2,11,10	
		LEM 3,1,9	
		K*RI* 2,226,6	
		K*RI* 1,63,13	
		LEM 5,15,5	
ti3	**to clamor, cry out**	*Rd'É* 11,128 P.Chassinat 1, X+2RX+8-X+9	
ti3	(pharmaceutical)	*LEM* 10,4,1	

tinr	(cf. *tnr* below)	*LES* 2,3,6	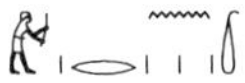
tis	**to become hard, to fix, to mount, to bind**	*H* 1,64a,9	
		K*RI* 1,47,11	
		K*RI* 3,654,5	
tišpss	**tree spice, scented wood, cinnamon** (?) (cf. Janssen p.366)	P.Turin 1907+1908,2R15 *JEA* 52,86-87 n.ff.	
	(oil from tree) (cf. Fox C9,18)	*LEM* 13,1V8	
titi	**to trample on**	K*RI* 1,7,10	
		K*RI* 5,87,7	
ty	(cf. *t* above ?) **bread**	*LEM* 13,1V10	
tw	(archaic demon. pronoun?) **this, you**	*CB* 1, C3,3 Fox B C3,3	
tw	(dep. pronoun) **you** (?) (cf. Erman, *N.A. Gram.* 357)	*LRL* 36V9	
	you (cf. Wente, *LRL* p. 77,a)	*LRL* 43R2	
	you	*LRL* 12R5	
	one, the king	*LES* 2,15,2	
	one	CS 1V3	
twt	(or *twi*, cf. *tbw* & *ṯbwt.y*) (cf. Janssen 292 §75)	*LEM* 10,9,10	
tw.i	(pron.compound) **I**	*LRL* 1R3	
	you	*LES* 4,3,7	
	I	*LES* 2,17,1	
		LES 4,15,5	
twꜣ	**wrong, wicked thing**	Push 127,4,11	
	harm, evil	*JEA* 58,216	
twꜣ	**tumor**	*HPBM*[4] T1,V68	

twꜣ	(cf. *dwꜣ* below) **door post, lintel** Coptic ⲧⲟⲩⲁ	Osing, *Nominalbildung* p.634 ff., n.659	
twn	**prize, reward** (cf. *JEA* 42,17)	*JEA* 41 (Pl.9) 8-9 P.Turin 1882,3R8-9	
		*HPBM*³ CB4,8R6	
		Naun 1,3,4	
twr	**to cleanse, purify**	*HPBM*³ CB4,4V12	
		Mélanges... Mokhtar 2,349,10	
	to be cured	Lange *Amenemope* 27,12 *JEA* 12,224,2	
twrit	**wand**	*LEM* 5,3,4	
	cane	*JEA* 23,188,2	
twh	(cf. *thꜣ* below) **to repel**	*LEM* 5,11,9	
		K*RI* 5,60,11	
twhꜣw	**recess** (?)	*JEA* 22,178 P.Leopold 2,2,9	
twhr	**Hittite troops**	*TR* 10068 (Pl.11) 4R16	
	("clean", "pure"?)	Helck, *Bez* 575,280	
twt	(cf. *tiwy* above) **of yours, your**	K*RI* 5,48,10	
twt	**to be assembled, collected together**	*H* 1,8,3	
		A 1,14,4	
		K*RI* 5,68,10	
		K*RI* 5,29,7	
		LRL 12R9	
		LEM 16,7V7	
		LRL 22V1	
		K*RI* 5,21,6	
		K*RI* 1,113,6	
		K*RI* 2,96,9	
		K*RI* 5,12,3	

	complete	K*RI* 3,484,13	
	twt m rmṯ **people around one**	*HPBM*[3] CB5,2V7	
twt	**statues, likeness, like**	*H* 1,47,7	
		A 1,1,3	
		LEM 6,14,4	
		K*RI* 2,232,1	
		LEM 3,3,5	
	statue	*RAD* 19,1	
	image	*Wil* (36) 76,23	
		TR Abbott 2,10	SIC
		H 1,28,10	
		K*RI* 1,5,14	
		K*RI* 1,16,6	
		K*RI* 2,329,4	
	image, likeness	*Wil* (48) 98V5	
	wooden statue	Janssen p.246-8	
	pupil (of eye)	*P.Leiden* 1,348,2R2 Borghouts p.46, n.27	
twt	**pleasing, agreeable, delightful** (cf. *JEA* 12,252,1)	*A* 1,1,6	
		K*RI* 5,74,12	
	lovely (cf. Fox B,C1,5)	*CB* 1 (Pl.22) C1V5	
tb	**cage**	Naun 2R12	
	box	K*RI* 3,555,11	
tbw	(see *ṯbwty* below) **sandals**	*LES* 7,2,6	
		H 1,56b,7	
		K*RI* 2,101,10	
tby	**to be shod** (cf. *JEA* 38,19,4) **to provide with sandals**	*LEM* 4,6	
		LEM 5,16,11	

tbn	**head, top**	*RAD* 18,4R5 *LEM* 5,10,12	
		LEM 9,3V5	
		P.BM 10731,V1 *JEA* 54,158	
	skull	*HPBM*[3] CB4,5V10	
	forehead	*HPBM*[3] CB7,1V7	
	head, top	*HPBM*[4] T2V82	
tbs	**heel**	*HPBM*[4] T2V54-5	
tbtb	**to mound, to draw out** (metal)	*TR* 10068 (Pl.9) 2R10	
		TR 10068 (Pl.10) 2R25	
tp	(? cf. *tpt* below)	Naun 2R13	
tp	(?) **to make, manufacture**	O.DM 131 S.A. #69, p.99 n.5	
tp	**head**	*LES* 4,12,11	
	top	*LEM* 5,2,11	
	head	*LES* 4,13,1	
	person	*H* 1,79,10	
	persons	*LEM* 5,7,3	
	individuals	K*RI* 5,53,6	
		H 1,31,3	
	chiefs (Asiatic)	K*RI* 1,30,9	
	head	*HPBM*[4] L1V12	
	m-tp-ʿ **in advance**	*JEA* 21,222 n.j	
	r-tp **in front of**	*JEA* 4,124,3	
tp	**over, upon**	*H* 1,56b,3	
	tp.f **on his own behalf**	*Wil* (7) 17R21	
	tp.f ḏs.f **by himself**	K*RI* 5,38,5	
tp-3bd	**New Crescent Day**	*Khonsu* 2,115b,9	
tp-i3t	(appointed) **time**	*MÄS* 37, p.8 1.8	

tp-ʿ	**in former time, before** (see *tpy-ʿ*)	*JEA* 67,95 n.u	
		JEA 68,176	
	original state	K*RI* 3,12,4	
tp-ʿnḫ	**prisoner of war, slave**	K*RI* 1,60,10	
tp-n	**on account of**	P.Turin 2008+2016,2R14	
	details of	K*RI* 3,547,14	
tp-n-i3wt	**head of cattle, small animals**	K*RI* 1,55,12	
		K*RI* 1,51,12	
		LEM 6,14,2	
	animal	*HPBM*^{4} T3R98	
	small game	*LES* 1,5,2-3	
		Max. d'Ani 9,2	
tp-n-idr	**head of cattle** (cf. *JEA* 38,30)	K*RI* 1,54,14	
tp-n-sḥn	**duty roster** (cf. *JNES* 10,142 n.40) **"tableau de service"**	*RAD* 18B3V2	
		Janssen p.19 n.18	
tp-nfr	**favorable, right moment**	*BIFAO* 30,101	
tp-r	**base** (of triangle)	*JEA* 12,132 & 15,174 n.1	
tp-rnpt	**annual**	*Khonsu* 1,21,21	
tp-rd	**plan, rule, instruction, directive**	K*RI* 1,49,1	
		K*RI* 1,101,6	
		H 1,25,8	
	directions	*LEM* 5,14,9	
	rules	*A* 1,6,2	
	order (of progress)	*A* 1,28,8	
	position, principle, rule	*A* 1,27,6	
		K*RI* 2,9,12	
		K*RI* 2,11,13	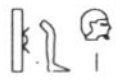
		K*RI* 2,9,15	

	orders (for work)	*Khonsu* 2,139,1	
tp-ḥwt	**roof**	*LES* 1,4,7	
		LES 10b,4	
tp-ẖt	(cf. *tpt* below) **stake**	*ZÄS* 68,27 n.82	
tp-ḫ3swt	**best of the lands** (cf. *tpy* below) (cf. *JEA* 13,197,10) **"fresh"**	K*RI* 1,47,8	
(*tp*)*-smdt*	**Half-Month Day** **15th lunar day**	*Khonsu* 2,115a,9	
		Khonsu 2,190,15	
tp-š	**quay** (?) (*tp-mri*) (cf. *JEA* 50,82)	*JEA* 38 (Pl.7) 1,69,p.16 **n.8**	
tp-šw	**destitution, ruin** (cf. *JEA* 32 (Pl.6) 26)	K*RI* 2,325,14	
tp-ḳsn	**misery**	*A* 1,21,2-3	
tp-t3	(cf. *tp* above) **upon earth**	P.H. 500 (Pl.12) 6,12	
		K*RI* 1,110,3	
tp-trw	**calendar festivals**	*LEM* 3,2,11	
		H 1,16b,13 & 7,4	
		H 1,27,5	
tp-dw3yt	**dawn**	*H* 1,27,3	
		H 1,7,7	
		H 1,78,1	
		H 1,48,5	
		K*RI* 1,111,15	
		K*RI* 2,335,1	
		K*RI* 1,48,11	
		K*RI* 1,27,3	
		K*RI* 5,84,9	

tp-ḏrt	**tax due, internal revenue** (cf. Warburton pp.287-290)	K*RI* 3,160,9	
tpi	**to spew out**	*HPBM*[3] CB7,5V10 *HPBM*[3] p.64 n.9	
	to be spat upon	*JEA* 23,175	
tpi	**to breathe** (< *tpr*)	*HPBM*[4] T1R83	
		HPBM[4] T2R23	
		K*RI* 1,18,11	
		K*RI* 2,53,16	
		K*RI* 2,53,15	
tpy	**first**	*LES* 2,16,7	
	foremost	*LES* 4,2,11	
	(**"picked," "chosen," "best,"** cf. *JSSEA* 11,13 n.58)	*H* 1,27,10	
		LES 4,8,4	
		LES 5,1,52	
		K*RI* 2,15,15	
		LRL 47R2	
	ḥm-nṯr tpy **high priest**	*LRL* 28R1	
	chief	K*RI* 5,16,14	
	best	P.H. 500 (Pl.14) 7,7	
	finest	*LES* 2,17,1	
	those upon	*JEA* 42,11,1R2 *JEA* 41 (Pl.7) 2	
tpy-ʿ	**those of former times, ancestor** (see *tp-ʿ* above) (cf. *JEA* 68,176 n.33)	Caminos, *Lit. Frags*. (Pl.2a) 2,12	
		K*RI* 3,6,10	
tpy-rnpt	**first day of lunar month, beginning of the year** (cf. Parker, *Calendars* p.306)	*JEA* 56,115	
tpy-š	**"paysan"**	Caminos, *Lit. Frags*. p.14 B,14,1.3 (Pl.3)	
tpy.w	(see *tpt* below) **yards**	*LES* 5,2,18	

tpy(wt)	**fish**, (little) **fish** (cf. Valbelle, *Ouvriers* p.274 n.1)	*RAD* 2,1Vb2 *LEM* 5,15,8 *HPBM*^{4} T1R41
tpyw-tꜢ	**heads**	K*RI* 1,69,1
tpw-r	**utterance, speech, expression**	*LES* 1,8,8 *LEM* 12,5V7 K*RI* 1,110,6 K*RI* 5,39,8 *LEM* 12,5V1 *H* 1,79,10 K*RI* 5,66,7 *A* 1,7,5 K*RI* 5,83,11
tpyw	(?)	O.Gardiner 171,8-9 Janssen p.198
tp	(see *tpy* above) **first**	K*RI* 2,324,12
tpt	**stake** (cf. *ZÄS* 68,27,82; *JNES* 6,224-5) **top of a stake**	Janssen p.376-7, 129
	(boat part) **prow** (?) (cf. Caminos, *LEM* p.134)	*LEM* 5,2,8 *LEM* 13,2V1 *LEM* 11,3,7
tpt	**yardarms**	*TR* 10383 (Pl.22) 3R1
tpt	**cord, thread**	O.DM 233,R S.A. #81
tpty	**in front of, first of**	*A* 1,27,1
	foremost, best	*A* 1,5,2
tpnn	**cumin** (cf. *Wb.* 5,296,9)	Push 127, p.62 n.2 *JEA* 87,176

tpr	(see *tpi* above) **to breathe**	*CDME* 298	
tpḥ	(see *dpḥ* below, apple)		
tpḥt	< *ṯpḥt* **hole**	*LES* 1,8,2	
	hole, cave	*KRI* 1,66,11	
	cavern	*KRI* 1,86,1	
	cavern	*P.Leiden* 1,348,5R4	
	mouth cavity, esophagus, oral cavity (cf. *JEA* 22,105)	*HPBM*[3] CB8,5V8	
	cavern (of Nile)	*KRI* 3,133,15	
tptyw	**headpiece**	*JEA* 22,179,2,14	
tf-mnꜥt	**male nurse, tutor**	*JSSEA* 9,118,6	
tfi	**to be in motion, to leap, to flatter**	*LEM* 5,10,9	
		KRI 5,12,2	
	to remove, move away	*KRI* 5,25,8	
		HPBM[4] L2V29	
	to dislodge	*HPBM*[3] CB3,5R14 p.14 n.9	
	to get agitated	*KRI* 5,28,3	
	to remove	*KRI* 5,93,11	
	to jump out, depart (cf. Fox C4,5)	*CB* 1 C4V5 *CB* 1 (Pl.23) C2V10	
tf	**agitation**	*HPBM*[4] L2 R87	
tfy	**yonder, that**	*CB* 1 (Pl.22) C1V7	
		O.H. (2,3) Pl. 76,11	
tftf	(?) **to be perturbed** (cf. *JEA* 69,131,106)	*LEM* 11,4,5	
tm	(negative verb)	*LES* 2,9,6	
		LRL 1V4	
		H 1,76,8	

			LRL 1V1
			LES 2,15,10
			LES 5,1,x+7
			LRL 2V5
			K*RI* 2,230,14
			K*RI* 5,40,9
			LES 8,1,3
			LES 4,15,12
			LRL 50V9
	lest		*HPBM*[3] CB 4,1V13
	r tmi dit	**to prevent**	*LES* 2,5,3
	tm wnt	**nonexistent**	K*RI* 5,8,7
			K*RI* 5,33,15
	tm wnw	**those who exist not**	*H* 1,76,8
tm	**ineffectiveness** (?)		*HPBM*[4] T1V64
	failure		K*RI* 3,503,1
tm	**to be complete**		*H* 1,22,6
			H 1,57,7
			RAD 8R4
			RAD 9R3
	whole (ungutted fish)		P.Turin 2008+2016 2R5
			P.Leiden 1,350,3V4
	whole (ungutted fish) (cf. Janssen p.348)		*JEA* 52,85 n.k P.Turin 1907+1908 1R21
			Push 127,1,12
	entire		*Khonsu* 2,179,19
	entire		K*RI* 1,42,3
			K*RI* 3,491,14
tmw	**everyone, totality of people** (see *tꜣ-tmmw* above)		K*RI* 1,61,1
			K*RI* 1,86,11
			K*RI* 1,97,8
			K*RI* 2,151,7
			K*RI* 1,39,5
			K*RI* 1,86,14

	people	K*RI* 3,310,7	
tmꜣ	**mat**	*RAD* 2,1aV2	
		LEM 6,23,3	SIC
		LEM 2,8,7	
		RAD 18,2R2	
		K*RI* 3,823,15	
tỉmm.t	(?) *tmyt* (?) **skin disease**	*HPBM*[4] L1V42	
tmm.t	**ritual of amulets**	*Rd'É* 28,95,4	
tmmw	(see *tꜣ-tmmw* and *tmw* above) **people, everyone**	*HPBM*[3] CB4,7V4	
		K*RI* 1,85,14	
tmm	**to keep silence**	*P.Leiden* 1,348,4R6	
tmmw	(see *tm* above) **entire, complete**	*Khonsu* 2,179,19	
tmrgn	(?) **warriors**, (soldiers of a special class), **recruits** (?)	Push 127,5,5	
tmḥy	(cf. *ṯmḥy* below)	Harris, *Minerals* p.154	
tms	(cf. *ṯms* below) **to bury**	*LES* 4,10,4	
tmsw	(cf. *ṯms* below)	*HPBM*[3] CB, 10R14	
tn	< *ṯn* **you** (pl.)	*LRL* 1V5	
tn-my	**yours**	Naun 1,2R2	
	(*n.tn-imy*)	*LRL* 30R11	
tnỉ	**to be revered**	*H* 1,44,3	
	towering	*H* 1,58,10	
		K*RI* 5,83,6	
		K*RI* 5,69,7	

tni	(cf. *tnw* below)	K*RI* 1,42,6	
tnw	**every**	*LRL* 14V3,45R5	
		LEM 11,4,7	
		A 1,16,5 *LES* 2,1,5	
		LES 1,5,7	
		LEM 11,4,7	
		LEM 16,6V8	
		H 1,6,3	
		K*RI* 1,50,3	
		K*RI* 1,90,15	
		K*RI* 2,83,3	
		K*RI* 2,285,2	
	every time	*Melanges... Mokhtar* 2,349,10	
	whenever (cf. Fox H4,8)	P.H. 500 (Pl.8) 4,8	
	m-tnw-nb **of all sorts**	*LEM* 11,4,7	
		LEM 15,2,1	
		A 1,2,5	
	r-tnw **as often as**	*LEM* 5,12,12	
tnw	**where?**	*LES* 3,5,6	
		LES 5,1,51	
		P.H. 500 (Pl.2) 1,1	
	from where, whence?	*LES* 6,2,x+18	
	when?	K*RI* 2,110,12	
tnw	**to grow up, mature**	*LES* 1,4,11	
	to be infirm, become decrepit	*Wil* 2, p. 28-29, n.1	
	tired land	*Wil* (58) B11V30	
tnw	**senility** (?)	*HPBM*[4] C1,30 p.96 n.19	
tnw	*tnw*<*ṯnw* *šri tnw* **to be low in elevation**	*LRL* 47R13	

tnw	<*ṯnw* **number**	*KRI* 1,49,4-5	
		KRI 1,49,9	
		KRI 1,49,2	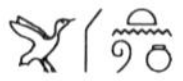
	number, quantity	*KRI* 1,80,13	
	number	*KRI* 1,43,7	
		H 1,77,4	
tnbḫ	**to shrink back**	*KRI* 2,49,10	
		LEM 11,5,3	
	to run at random	*JEA* 50,32	
tnm	**to wander, go astray**	*KRI* 5,62,11	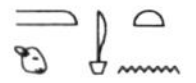
		KRI 5,65,13	
		KRI 5,73,14	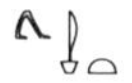
tnmmt	(skin disease) (cf. *tmmt* above)		
tn-nbw	(bronze or gold debased with bronze)	Lange *Amenemope* 18,12 Harris, *Minerals* 37	
tnr	**powerful**	*LES* 2,3,6	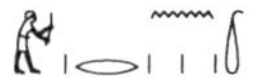
	opulent	*LEM* 10,14,5	
		KRI 2,232,5	
		KRI 2,232,6	
		KRI 5,16,15	
		KRI 5,21,7	
	strong, mighty	*A* 1,28,4	
	energetic	*LES* 7,3,5	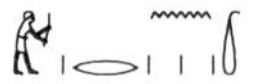
	heroic, mighty	*KRI* 5,54,8	
	potent, mighty	*KRI* 5,31,9	
		LEM 2,4,6	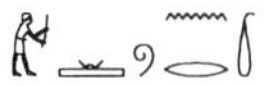
	effective	*KRI* 5,59,9	
		KRI 5,78,8	
		KRI 2,91,8	
tnr	**to persevere**	*LEM* 6,8,4	
	to grow strong	*KRI* 5,42,12	

tnr	**mighty deeds**	*H* 1,6,12
		H 1,43,14
tnr	**hillock, mounds, heaps** (cf. Hoch p.356-357)	*LEM* 9,2V6
tnrk	(wine?)	*LEM* 5,12,1
tnt-š3	"**the** (district) **of the marsh**"	*MÄS* 37,88,1 (p.12)
tr	(?)	*LEM* 3,2,5
tr	(enclitic particle) **pray, forsooth**	K*RI* 2,80,8
		LES 2,15,9
		P.Leiden 1,348,12,8
		K*RI* 3,503,14
tri	**to respect, to esteem**	K*RI* 1,113,10
	to revere	K*RI* 3,818,6
		K*RI* 1,114,13
	to adore	K*RI* 1,113,4
	sḏf3-tryt **oath** (cf. *JARCE* 25,95-96)	CS 1R16
tr	**time**	*LES* 2,2,2
		LEM 8,5,1 (sic)
	seasons (?) (cf. *tp-trw* above)	*H* 1,7,4
	fated time	Push 127,1,3
	moment	*BIFAO* 75,107
	(see *tr-n-dw3t* below)	K*RI* 1,99,2
		K*RI* 2,103,2
tr-n-mtrt	**afternoon**	*P.Leiden* 1,350 3V1
tr-n-rwh3	**evening** (cf. *SAK* 5,284-5)	*P.Leiden* 1,350 5V22
	(*rwh3*)	*TR* Abbott (Pl.3) 5,12
tr-n-rnpt	**annually**	*HPBM*[4] L5R44

tr-n-grḥ	**nighttime**	*P.Leiden* 1,350,4V32
tr-n-dw3t	**morning**	*P.Leiden* 1,350,1Vx+9 *BIFAO* 75,107 stele Cairo JE 91927,2
tri	**portal, door, door-leaves** (cf. *JEA* 60,170)	*LES* 2,16,10 *H* 1,5,5 *H* 1,58,10 K*RI* 5,74,4
	great doors	K*RI* 3,350,6
tri	(*t3i* in parallels) **to repulse, oppose**	K*RI* 2,97,15
tri(*t*)	**willow tree**	*HPBM*[3] (Pl.47) CB8,11V1 *LEM* 3,1V8
trit	(see *t-r* above)	*Wb.* 5,209,11
trp	(goose)	*LEM* 5,14,4 *LEM* 5,1b,10
trmg	**to roar, to thunder** (cf. Hoch p.358)	*LEM* 3,6V3
trr	**to race** (cf. *Orientalia* 32,432) **"to move about freely"** **to sail around, cruise about** **to go for an outing** (cf. Hoch p.359)	*LES* 4,13,4 *JEA* 19,200
trr	**oven** (cf. Hoch p.359)	*LEM* 2,8,4 *LEM* 8,7,8
trr	(?)	*LEM* 10,12,1
trš	(part of a house)	O.BM 5625,R9 *JEA* 12 (Pl.36)
trt	(see *trit* above) **willow**	*LEM* 3,1V8

thꜣ	<*thi* **to do wrong** **to transgress**	*LES* 2,8,6 *LEM* 1,1V6
		LEM 6,27,5
		LEM 7,4,7
		LRL 1V1,7R6
	to violate	*TR* Abbott (Pl.1) 2R6-7
		TR 10068 (Pl.12) 6R20
	to transgress	K*RI* 5,15,10
		K*RI* 5,12,6
	to offend	K*RI* 3,773,4
	to violate	K*RI* 5,83,13
		K*RI* 1,16,6
		K*RI* 1,51,15
	to violate	*TR* 10068 (Pl.9) 1R4
	to damage	*TR* 10403 (Pl.36) 1R8
		K*RI* 3,542,14
	to disobey	*JEA* 38,28
	to mislead	*JEA* 42,31 (10)
	to interfere with	K*RI* 1,52,4
	thi r **to rebel against** (cf. *RIDA* 22,p.120,n.124 & p.128)	K*RI* 2,228,12
thꜣ	**fault, interference**	*TR* 10383 (Pl.22) 2R5
		K*RI* 1,51,9
thꜣ	**assailant, aggressor**	*BIFAO* 87,256,262 n.h
thm	**to call up**	*LEM* 10,9,9
	to commandeer, to summon together	*LEM* 12,4V2 Caminos *LEM* p.508
	to incite, to drive	K*RI* 1,16,9
	to commandeer	K*RI* 1,49,12
		K*RI* 1,50,6
	to knock (at door) (cf. *JEA* 65,87)	*CB* 1, 17R8
	to commandeer	*LEM* 7,6,3
	to claim	*LRL* 27V4

	to attack (cf. E-W p. 40 n.6a)	K*RI* 5,31,7	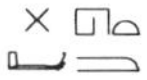
		JEA 13,39,1.8	
	to move, go forward	P.CGC 58055,R2&3 *ASAE* 71 (Pl.5)	
thm	**arrival, entry**	K*RI* 3,255,5	
thm	(disease) **perforation**	*HPBM*[4] T1V59	
thnt	(see *dhnt* below) **top, forehead** or **sketch**	*LRL* 9V19	
thr	**charioteer, warrior** (class) (cf. *JSSEA* 11,12)	*CB* 1 (Pl.29) G1V8	
	foreign troops (cf. *MÄS* 6,21-22)	*TR* 10068 (Pl.11) 4R4	
		JSSEA 11,12 n.36	
thr	(cf. *trr* above) **oven**	*LEM* 8,7,8	
thh	(cf. *th3* above) **to trespass**	K*RI* 1,68,5	
tḥw	**peas** (?), **garlic** (?) (cf. *JARCE* 16,186-9)	*LEM* 4,1,1	
		LEM 5,8,11	
		LEM 10,11,5	
tḥn	<*ṯḥn* (see below) **to gleam**	K*RI* 3,176,5	
		K*RI* 3,203,13	
tḥnt	**glaze, faience**	*LES* 4,14,8	
		K*RI* 5,74,11	
	mineral (cf. Harris, *Minerals* p.135-38)	Goyon, p.86 n.25 P.Brooklyn 47.218.50,1,9	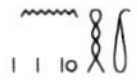
	gleaming ones	*MÄS* 37,21,4 (p.10)	
tḥs	**to pulverize** Coptic **ⲧⲱϩⲥ** (cf. Hoch p.361)	K*RI* 5,26,10	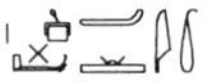
		K*RI* 5,70,7	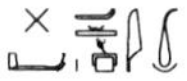
	to crush	*MDAIK* 15,178,11 P.Geneva MAH 15274,5R4	

tḫ	**beer** (cf. Fox H2,2 no.52,2)	P.H. 500 (Pl.9) 2,2
		O.DM 1078 V2
tḫỉ	**to become intoxicated** (cf. *JEA* 65,81)	*LES* 1,8,3
		LEM 10,13a,1
		CB 1,17R1
		P.H. 500 (Pl.14) 7,12
		K*RI* 1,99,4
	drunk	K*RI* 3,560,11
tḫy	**First month of year**	*Rd'É* 10,25
tḫw	**drunkenness, intoxication**	*Khonsu* 2,115A,6
tḫb	**to be steeped in**	*A* 1,1,7
	to soak	*LRL* 36V1
	to immerse	*LRL* 42R6
		LEM 2,7,7
		LEM 5,12,4
		LEM 8,7,7 (SIC)
		LEM 10,5,8-9
	to be flooded, to be irrigated	*RAD* 24,1V5
	to inundate	*A* 1 (O.QC 14)
tḫbst	**basket**	*LES* 7,2,12
		LES 7,2,4
		P.H. 500,2R12
		H.O. 47,2,5-6
		O.Gardiner 67,5-6
tḫp	**yon**	K*RI* 3,176,8
tḫn	**to injure**	K*RI* 5,32,6
		K*RI* 5,44,2
		K*RI* 1,68,4

tḫnw	**obelisk**	*A* 1,15,3
		K*RI* 2,38,8
		K*RI* 2,38,9
		K*RI* 2,38,6
		K*RI* 1,3,8
		K*RI* 1,74,12 *BIFAO* 73,122,1
		K*RI* 1,115,16
	pair of obelisks	*JEA* 61,128,44
		K*RI* 1,118,8
tḫr	(chariot part, "siding" or "paneling" ?) (cf. Helck, *Bez* 575,282; *JSSEA* 16,43f.; Hoch p.363)	*LEM* 5,16,9 O.Turin 9588,2; 57365,2
tḫtḫ	**to confuse, to confound**	*LEM* 5,10,2
		CB 1,16R10
		K*RI* 5,65,4
	to intoxicate, to confuse	*GM* 38,86
tḫtḫ	**confusion** (cf. *JNES* 28,6)	*A* 1,28,3
	disorder	*HPBM*[4] L1,R24-25
tsm	(*tsm*-boat)	*LRL* 4R5
tš	**frontier district** (cf. *tȝš* above)	*LRL* 5V10
		LRL 5V10
		K*RI* 5,36,5
		K*RI* 5,15,10
tš	**to crush** (cf. *Wb.* 5,329,17 *tsȝ*)	K*RI* 5,91,11
tši	**to separate**	K*RI* 1,50,9
	to flee	*TR* Amherst (Pl.15) 4,2
		TR 10052 (Pl.25) 1R19

	to be absent	Fox C25 (O.DM 1266+Cairo 25218)	
	to evade, to be missing	*JEA* 22,183,4,10 P.Leopold 2,4,10	
tšw	**deserters, wanderers**	*LEM* 10,10,7	
tšw	**fragments** (?)	*JEA* 22,180,3,1 P.Leopold 2,3,1	
tk	(see *tkk* below) **to injure**	*Rd'É* 30,123,1.14 (p.126, n.62)	
	to interfere, to harm	K*RI* 3,336,16	
tkꜣ	*tkꜣ*-**vessel**	*LRL* 30V6	
tkꜣ	**to illumine**	*JEA* 5,27,n.11 P.Skrine 2	
tkꜣ	**torch, flame**	*A* 1,17,3	
		K*RI* 5,62,15	
tkꜥ	**purpose**	*LEM* 6,23,1	
	design, intent	*HPBM*[4] L6V8	
		HPBM[4] T1,R31,31	
tkn	**to reach**	*LEM* 12,5V10 Caminos, *LEM* p.511	
		H 1,45,6	
	to counter	*LRL* 41R5	
	to approach	K*RI* 5,74,8	
	to attack	CS 2R21	
	to draw near	*HPBM*[3] CB4,1V13	
	to reach	*Khonsu* 2,143,1	
		K*RI* 1,7,2	
		K*RI* 1,27,8	
	to have access to	K*RI* 3,108,15	
	to oust, chase away	Push 127,2,10	

	to approach	*Melanges… Mokhtar* 2,348,7	
	tkn ḥr **to drive from** (cf. *JNES* 6,222,19)	K*RI* 1,52,1-2	
	tkn ib **to be patient, self-controlled**	*JEA* 69,92-93 n.38	
tks	**to be fixed, settled, to be stigmatized** (?)	*Rd'É* 6,119 n.g P.Valençay 1,R7	
tkšš	(from *Wb.* 5,336,1) **to trample, to seize** (cf. Grandet p.267 nt.961)	*H* 1,79,3	
tkk	**to assail**	K*RI* 5,23,5	
		K*RI* 1,22,3	
		K*RI* 1,41,3,7	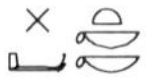
	to fall to	*ZÄS* 96,27,36	
	to injure, to cause prejudice	*Rd'É* 30,123,1.14	
tkk	**violator**	K*RI* 5,80,15	
tktk	**to violate**	K*RI* 1,11,2	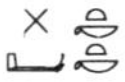

ṯt	**lumber, woodwork**	*LES* 5,1,2
		LES 5,2,4
ṯt	**gang, people**	*TR* 10052 (Pl.29) 7R3
		K*RI* 2,285,9
ṯꜣ	**to carve, to engrave**	*LEM* 5,16,9
		LEM 11,1,7
		H 1,47,8
		K*RI* 1,113,5
ṯꜣ	**nestling, youngling**	*LEM* 10,8,4
		LEM 12,1V7 Caminos, *LEM* p.507
		LEM 15,2,7
	cub, young animal (cf. Fox H2,2)	P.H. 500 (Pl.4) 2,2
	fledgling	P.BM 10416,V6 (*Pyr.St.* p.136 n.r)
ṯꜣ	**vase, vessel**	Push 127,1,11
ṯꜣ	(part of chariot, "handgrip" ?) (cf. *JSSEA* 16,32f.)	*JEA* 19,171 O.Edinb. 916,R6
ṯꜣy	**male**	*LRL* 42V6
		LES 1,4,3
		LES 3,4,6
		H 1,49,4
		H 1,78,13
		CB 1 (Pl.22) CV6
		K*RI* 5,86,4
		K*RI* 1,103,12
	men	K*RI* 1,52,6
	ḥmt-ṯꜣy (cf. *DLE* II,113)	*RAD* 18,4R8

ṯꜣy	**basket**	*LEM* 5,14,6
	box	*LEM* 10,3,1
	(cf. Janssen p.204)	*H* 1,18b,16
	ṯꜣy-drf **writing container, book case** (cf. *JEA* 65,78; *MDAIK* 15,117,4) (scroll) **box** (cf. Fox p.69)	*CB* 1,16R9
ṯꜣy	**to take**	*LRL* 47R14
		LES 5,1,10
		RAD 25,1V11
		K*RI* 1,77,1
		TR 10383 (Pl.22) 1R1
		K*RI* 2,6,14
	to acquire	*JEA* 48,66
	to wear, to don, **to be clad in**	*LRL* 15R7
	to hold	*A* 1,28,2
	to bear, to carry	K*RI* 5,65,3
		LRL 36V6
	to lay hold on, **to steal** (cf. Fox B,C1,5)	*CB* 1 (Pl.22) C1V8
	to take, to assume	*HPBM*[4] L1R43
	to seize	Push 127,2,5-6
		K*RI* 5,65,13
	ṯꜣy-ḥꜥty **to seduce, captivate**	Max d'Ani 9,6-7
	ṯꜣy-rd **to impede, to restrain**	*GM* 41,68-9
ṯꜣy	**tracking, tracker**	K*RI* 3,306,6
ṯꜣy-ꜣbw	**brander of cattle** (cf. *JEA* 27,32 n.3; *Wb.* 1,6,23)	*RAD* 17,4R7 *Wil* (A) 37R18
ṯꜣy-irt	**eye-tweezer** (?)	*JEA* 65,97 O.Wien Aeg. 1,1.9
ṯꜣy-bš	**stone worker**	*LEM* 16,10V6
	chisel bearer	Černý, *Workmen* **46 n.18**

		K*RI* 3,387,12	
ṯꜣy-mḏꜣt	**sculptor**	*LEM* 16,10V6	
	(cf. Janssen p.318 n.30)	Černý, *Workmen* 46 n.18	
	chisel bearer, sculptor	*Rd'É* 27,76	SIC
ṯꜣy-ḫw	**fan bearer**	*LEM* 9,18V1	
	(cf. *Rocznik Orientalistyczny* 41,97-100)	*LEM* 3,1,9	
		RAD 17,1R4	
		LEM 16,8V7	
	(or *ṯꜣy-sryt*)	*TR* 10052 (Pl.25)1R5	
ṯꜣy-sryt	**standard bearer**	*LEM* 6,13,3	
	(cf. *JSSEA* 10,135)	*H* 1,11,1	
	MÄS 6,69-71	K*RI* 1,52,12-13	
		TR 10054 (Pl.6) 2R14	
		TR Abbott (Pl.4) 7,5	
		Wil (10) 23R20	
		Wil (29) 61R44	
ṯꜣy-tkm	*tkm*-**bearer**	K*RI* 5,40,11	
	(class of chariot soldiers) (cf. *MÄS* 6,71-72)	*H* 1,8,10	
ṯꜣy	**diminution**	K*RI* 2,97,13	
	reproach	*LRL* 9R14	
	fault, evil deed	*Melanges...Mokhtar* 2,348,1.8 & p.354 n.r	
		RAD 18,4R4	
ṯꜣwt	**penalty**	*JEA* 23,186 *P.Leiden* 352,10	
	theft	*LEM* 6,6,2	
	forfeit, fine, penalty	K*RI* 1,54,10 *JEA* 23,186-89	
	confiscation, forfeit (cf. *JNES* 6,225)	K*RI* 1,57,5	
	m-ṯꜣwt **furtively, secretly**	*LEM* 5,4,11	

ṯꜣt	*tjꜣt*-**flowers**	P.H. 500 (Pl.14) 7,11
	vegetables	*RAD* 25,2R6
	bundles of palm leaves	Helck, *Mat* 5,815
	(vegetable)	*JEA* 10,122,3
ṯꜣw	**wind, breath**	*LES* 5,2,74
		LEM 12,5V8 Caminos, *LEM* p.511
		H 1,1,6
		K*RI* 5,20,7
		K*RI* 5,37,3
		K*RI* 1,99,7
	breezes	*JEA* 70,71
	breath	*HPBM*[4] T1V32
	liberty	*TR* 10052 (Pl.27) 4R14
	storming (cf. *JEA* 65,80,3)	*CB* 1,16R9
ṯꜣw	**fan-shaped leaves**	*LEM* 14,1V1
		LEM 11,4,3
ṯꜣw	**bearer** (cf. *ṯꜣy* above)	*LEM* 16,8V7
		LRL 28R1
		K*RI* 1,14,2
ṯꜣw	(see *ṯꜣt* above) **vegetables**	*RAD* 25,2R6
ṯꜣwrrw	(ailment, flatulence ?)	*HPBM*[4] L1V43
ṯꜣ-mri	**to speed** (?)	*A* 1,25,9
ṯꜣr	**to fix, make firm, make fast**	Posener, L'*enseignement* 37,6
ṯꜣrt	**cabin** (of boat) (cf. *ZÄS* 68,20-22)	*HPBM*[3] (Pl.25) CB 5,6R6
	cabin, forecastle, enclosed structure, fortress (?) (cf. Fox no.53,7 & p.81 n.f)	*BES* 1,29-40 O.DM 1079,71

	ḥmw-ṯꜣrt **cabinet maker**	*ZÄS* 66,5* P.BM 10056,14R12	
ṯꜣrt	**silo, granary**	Jacquet-Gordon *Noms* 46 & 287,7	
ṯꜣrynꜣ	(cf. *ṯrn* below) **corselet**	K*RI* 2,119,15	
ṯꜣgꜣ	(trees)	*LEM* 10,13a,4	
		LEM 11,1,5	
ṯꜣty	**vizier**	*LRL* 44R7	
		K*RI* 5,51,10	
		GM 98, p.12 P.DM 24,1.3	
ṯꜣtn	(see *ṯnṯꜣt* below) **throne, dais**	*LEM* 2,5,5	
ṯiṯi	**to trot**	*LEM* 4,8,8	
	to paw	*LEM* 10,11,2	
	to trot	*A* 1,24,8	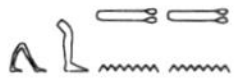
	"pawing horse," "impatient man"	Gardiner & Sethe 9,2,3 p.27	
ṯyṯy	(see *ḏyḏy* below) **to scold, to tease**	P.H. 500 (Pl.10) 5,6	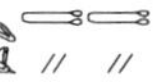
ṯwi	**little bird** (cf. *ṯwṯw* & *ṯṯw* below)	K*RI* 3,542,8	
ṯwf	**papyrus marsh** (cf. Helck, *Bez* 575,286)	*LES* 3,9,2-3	
	reed swamps (cf. *JEA* 5,186,1)	*LEM* 5,15,6	
		LEM 8,4,9	
	papyrus flowers	*H* 1,27,11	
		K*RI* 1,47,15	
ṯwrḥ	**to mock**	*H.O.* 1,R2 Helck, *Bez* 576,291	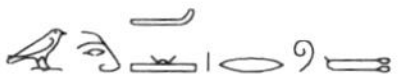
ṯwṯw	(see *ṯṯw* below) **swallow**	*LEM* 8,6,4	

ṯbw	**beaker, bowl** (cf. Valbelle, *Ouvriers* 265, 278; Janssen p.433) (*ṯ3bw*) (cf. *JEA* 49,68 n.c)	*LES* 2,8,6
		LES 4,5,9
		P.Leiden 1,350,1VX+16
	(vase)	*TR* 10052 (Pl.28) 5R14
		TR 10052 (Pl.28) 5R22
	jar	K*RI* 3,569,4
ṯbw	**sandalmaker**	*LEM* 3,6,8
		RAD 15,1RX+3
		LEM 10,4,5
		A 1,26,4
		TR 10068 (Pl.13) 1V19
ṯbw(*t*)	**sandals** (cf. Janssen *twt* or *twy* p.292, n.201)	*LES* 7,2,6
		LEM 4,7
		LEM 10,9,10
		H 1,56b,7
		K*RI* 2,101,10
		LEM 6,23,1
		Naun 4R8
		LEM 3,6,8
		LEM 8,7,4
		H 1,66b,9
		RAD 25,2R6
		RAD 18,5V6
		LES 6,2X+19
		K*RI* 5,9,10
		K*RI* 5,55,8
		K*RI* 2,328,7
	sole of foot	*HPBM*[4] L1V12
	soles of feet, footsteps	K*RI* 2,326,14
ṯbt	**rod**	*LEM* 3,7,2
	utensil (for the cult)	Jequier, *Frises* 80,n.1
ṯbṯb	**drum**	*LEM* 5,12,5

ṯpr	**chariot**	*LEM* 3,1V3	
		Helck, *Bez* 575,284	
ṯpr	**large drinking bowl, crater**	K*RI* 4,9,9	
ṯpr	**scribe**	*A* 1,10,7	
ṯpḥt	(cf. *tpḥt* above) **hole, cave, cavern**	*P.Leiden* 1,348,5R4	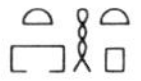
ṯpg	**barracks** (cf. Helck, *Bez* 575,285; Hoch p.365)	*LEM* 3,5,7	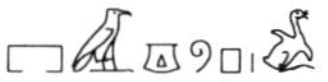
		HPBM[3] CB4,5V7	
		LEM 5,9,5	
ṯft	**chapel**	Jacquet-Gordon, *Noms* 262	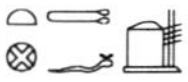
ṯfy	(cf. *ṯtf* below) **to scramble**	*LEM* 12,1V7 Caminos, *LEM* p.507	
	to overflow	K*RI* 3,370,3	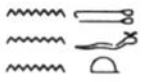
ṯmt	**healing bandages**	K*RI* 3,167,11	
ṯm3-ʿ	**strong-armed**	K*RI* 5,55,6	
ṯmḥy	(species of red ochre)	Harris, *Minerals* p.154 *Wb.* 5,369,4	
ṯms	**filthy, colored red** (cf. E-W 46,8b,p.51) **"evil injuries"** **violet, red** ("hue," "color") (cf. Harris, *Materials* 236)	*HPBM*[3] CB3,10R14	
	fury, rage (cf. Zandee, *Death* 292)	P.Brooklyn 47.218.50,20 1.10 Goyon 123,347	
ṯms	**to bury, cover** (cf. *RIDA* 16,131f. n.114)	*LES* 4,10,4	
		A 1,26,2	
ṯm-ṯm	(a measure) (cf. Warburton p.207)	*H* 1,18a,5	
ṯni	**to raise, exalt**	K*RI* 5,36,7	
		K*RI* 5,73,5	

	to lift up (in rivalry) (cf. E-W p.76 n.13a)	K*RI* 5,60,3 K*RI* 5,12,4 K*RI* 5,114,3
ṯniw	(?) **to be feeble** (cf. Lichtheim 2,155 1.11)	Lange *Amenemope* 14,11
ṯnf	**drinking** (cf. *Wb.* 5,380,10)	*BIFAO* 83 (Pl.47) P.Boulaq XIII, frag k,2
ṯnf	**to appraise** (cf. *Rd'É* 26,172) **to check, to value** Coptic ϫⲛⲟⲩϥ	*LRL* 37R11
	to put in sack	*JSSEA* 8,61
ṯnfyt	**sack, bag** (basket?) Coptic ϫⲛⲟϥ *JSSEA* 8,60-62	*LEM* 10,10,8 *RAD* 4,1R2 *LRL* 37R12 *LEM* 12,1V4
	tackle, equipment	*JEA* 63,108
	tent (?) (cf. Kruchten, *Decret* pp.33-37)	Urk. 4,2143,16 *RAD* 5,2,11 *Rd'É* 33,48 P.Cairo 5202,R15
ṯnr	(see *tnr* above) (adj.) (cf. *GM* 68,53-55)	K*RI* 5,78,1
	(subs.)	*H* 1,43,6
ṯnrḥ	**to forgive** (?) (cf. Helck, *Bez* 576,287) **to mock** (cf. *ṯhr* below) (cf. Hoch p.366)	*A* 1,9,7
ṯnḥ	**to wink, to blink**	Lange *Amenemope* 16,20
ṯnṯ3t	**throne, dais** (cf. *JEA* 13,197,2)	K*RI* 1,111,4 K*RI* 1,47,2 *LEM* 2,5,5 K*RI* 5,90,16

		H 1,76,4	
	court	*H* 1,49,10	
		Khonsu 2,182,13	
ṯr	**door** (cf. *JEA* 65,87)	*CB* 1,17R8	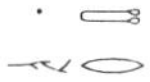
ṯry	**seed** (cf. *Orientalia* 32,435)	*H.O.* 59,1R1	
ṯrb	(vessel of metal ?) (cf. Helck, *Bez* 576,286; Janssen 338 & 435 §172; Hoch p.367)	*H.O.* 86,1R8	
		O.Cairo 25695,3	
		O.DM 625,10	
		P.Mallet 1,5	
ṯrp	**to stumble**	*LEM* 5,12,5	
ṯrf	**dance**	Montet, *Scenes* 210,367	
ṯrn	**corslet, coat of mail, body armor** (cf. Helck, *Bez* 576,288; Wolf, *Bewaffnung* 96F.; *MDAIK* 39,259)	K*RI* 2,119,15	
		K*RI* 2,28,12	
		K*RI* 2,28,10	
ṯrr	**sacrifical animal, bread** (?) (cf. Helck, *Bez* 576,290)	*H.O.* 91,1V1	
ṯrr	**siege-mound** (cf. Hoch p.365)	Piankhy 32	
		Piankhy 91	
ṯrr	**vessel** (for measuring fat) (cf. Janssen p.338)	O.DM 46,V10; 393V3	
		O.Cairo 25678,39	
ṯrst	(part of a body)	Helck, *Bez* 576,292	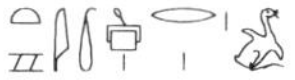
		HPBM[4] T2,V44	
ṯrt	**skiff**	*LEM* 5,1B,3	
	boat, hull	*H* 1,12b,11	

ṯrt	(flour)	*LEM* 5,13,12-14,1	
		LEM 5,17,4	
ṯḥ	**lame**	*LEM* 2,7,4	
ṯḥṯḥ	**cripple** (?) (cf. *ṯḥ*)	*TR* 10053 (Pl.19) 7R12	
ṯḥi	**to come into contact with**	*LEM* 6,6,7	
ṯḥw	(see *ṯḥḥ* below) **jubilation, joy**	*CB* 1 (Pl.25) C4V2	
	ṯḥwt-ib **exultation**	*HPBM*[3] CB4,8R13-9R1 p.32,n.7	
ṯḥb	**horse stall** (?) (cf. Helck, *Bez* p.576,255; *JAOS* 40,71)	*LEM* 5,2,5	
ṯḥn	**glistening, gleaming**	K*RI* 5,21,1	
	faience (cf. Janssen p.432; *JEA* 6,160)	K*RI* 1,39,9	
ṯḥn	**to meet, to engage with**	*LES* 2,9,2	
	to encounter	*LRL* 15R7,16R6	
	to approach, to meet, to touch	P.H. 500 (Pl.10) 5,5	
	to touch	*LES* 4,3,3	SIC
	to twitch (muscles)	*LES* 5,13,6	
		LRL 50R9	
	to move quickly, grapple with	*JEA* 3,102	
ṯḥn-nfr	**beautiful encounter**	*JNES* 20,256,c	
	good welcome	Bakir p. 57	
ṯḥr	**to disregard, treat disrespectfully**	*P.Leiden* 371,19V26 Gardiner & Sethe 8,19 & 8,26	
	to mock, to deride, offensive (cf. Hoch p.366 & 370)	*A* 1,9,7	
	to spurn, to reject	P.Brooklyn 47.218.135,4,11	

ṯḥḥ	**exultations, joy**	*H* 1,56b,6
	delight	*LEM* 3,4,5
		CB 1 (Pl.21) BV28
	delight	*A* 1,2,8
	joy	*CB* 1 (Pl.29) G1V4
		K*RI* 1,47,8
		K*RI* 2,335,2
		K*RI* 5,68,7
		K*RI* 1,48,1
		HPBM[3] CB4, 8R13-9R1
ṯs	**to tie, to bind**	*LES* 4,8,13
	to gather	*LEM* 10,7,6
		H 1,6,3
	to attack	*A* 1,3,6
	to marshal	K*RI* 2,85,2
		K*RI* 1,103,9
	to make contact with, to engage, to join	*Rd'É* 24,202,6
	to join up	K*RI* 3,167,1
	to be coherent (?)	*LEM* 12,5V1 Caminos, *LEM* p.510
	to secure	K*RI* 3,484,16
	to appoint	*LEM* 12,2V3
	to confirm, to allot	*H* 1,22,11
	to appoint (cf. *JEA* 42,16)	
	to administer	K*RI* 1,111,11
	to furnish, to provide	*HPBM*[4] L1V64
ṯs	**order, appointment** (of seed)	*LEM* 1,6,9
ṯs	**to model**	*JEA* 57,122, n.c P.BM 10800,1

ṯs	**saying**	*A* 1,11,3
		K*RI* 5,22,7
	proverbs	*A* 1,11,1
	speeches	*LEM* 10,14,10
	phrases	K*RI* 1,48,6
		K*RI* 1,112,15
	words	*Rd'É* 7,79
	utterances	*HPBM*³ CB4,6V13
		*HPBM*³ CB4,6V8
	sentences	*Rd'É* 10,64,A; p.62 + (Pl.4,1) O.BM 41541
	pronouncements, precepts	*JEA* 61,125 n.6
		CB 1,16R9
ṯs	**headman, commander**	*HPBM*³ CB4,1V9
	headman	*LEM* 16,10V3
	(or "who ties together")	K*RI* 5,89,13
	ṯs-pḏwt **commander, "group marshaller"**	*A* 1,17,8
	(cf. *MÄS* 6,72-3; *SAK* 15,143-48)	K*RI* 5,11,7
		K*RI* 5,29,4
ṯs-pẖr	**vice-versa**	*HPBM*⁴ L1R41
ṯs	**to raise up** (cf. *JEA* 58,221)	*CB* 1, (Pl.25) C4V9
	to lift up	*LES* 1,4,7
	to go up	*LRL* 4R8
	to mount	*HPBM*⁴ P2V9
	to rise up	*LEM* 5,2,3
	to muster	K*RI* 3,284,13
	to go up	*LEM* 3,6V1
		LES 9,L3
		K*RI* 3,510,8

	to exalt	P.H. 50(Pl.14) 7,6
		K*RI* 2,330,12
		K*RI* 1,24,14
		LEM 10,10,9-10
		K*RI* 5,13,13
		K*RI* 2,120,2
		K*RI* 2,120,4
		LEM 10,2,7
		LEM 8,7,4
	to climb	*A* 1,19,4
	ṯs pdt **to wield the bow**	K*RI* 3,848,3
ṯs	**ascent**	*A* 1,19,6
ṯs	**district**	K*RI* 1,50,4
ṯsw	**female mourner**	*MDAIK* 37,325,9
		K*RI* 1,112,13
		K*RI* 3,672,14&15
ṯsw	**teeth**	*P.Leiden* 1,348,2R3
ṯsw	(cf. *ṯst* "gang" below) **droves** (of cattle) (cf. *JEA* 11,293,17)	*LEM* 10,11,7
		LEM 5,9,1
ṯst	**shoal, shallows**	*BIFAO* 45,159,25
ṯst	**hill**	K*RI* 2,102,15
		K*RI* 2,14,15
		LEM 5,9,8
		LEM 10,10,1
		LEM 3,6V5
	mountain ranges	K*RI* 1,9,4
	tell	*JEA* 50,66
	hilltop	*JEA* 66,87

ṯst	**gang, troop, battalion** (cf. *JSSEA* 9,98 n.60) **"requisitioned labor"** (cf. *Serapis* 6,60)	K*RI* 1,42,8 K*RI* 1,49,10 *CB* 1 (Pl.19) BV11
ṯst	**vertebrae, ligament**	*HPBM*[4] T1V98
ṯst	**woven knots**	*LEM* 11,4,6
ṯst	**transport** (?) (Schott, *Kanais* p.141 n.10)	K*RI* 1,65,10
ṯst	*tjst*-**piece** (?) (cf. *JSSEA* 16,33) **"knob"**	*LEM* 5,16,10
ṯsm	**dog, hound**	*LES* 1,4,7 *CB* 1 (Pl.30) G2V2 *TR* Abbott (Pl.1) 2R10 K*RI* 1,99,7 (SIC)
ṯsmw	**battlements, bastion**	*H* 1,57,13 *H* 1,58,5
	surrounding walls	*H* 1,77,7
	rampart	K*RI* 3,498,15
ṯss	(fish)	Valbelle, *Ouvriers* 274
ṯk	(weight = 76 gr.)	Valbelle, *Cat. Poids* 17
ṯkm	(?)	*ZÄS* 96,16 fig. 2,1.19
ṯkr	**fortified gate** (cf. Helck, *Bez* 576,297)	*H* 1,4,2 *H* 1,57,13 *H* 1,58,5
ṯg	(wood)	*LEM* 4,17,2
ṯt	**to untie, to let loose**	*LES* 6,4,y *A* 1,20,2
	to relax	*HPBM*[4] L7,32n

ṯt-ḫnr	**rein-looser**	*LEM* 11,1,6	
ṯtb	(vases)	*MÄS* 37, p.10, 21,1.5	
ṯtf	**to pour out, to overflow**	*LEM* 5,10,7	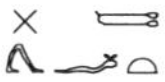
		LEM 3,5,2	
	to scramble	*LEM* 5,11,11	
	to surge	*LEM* 10,14,2	
	to overflow	*LEM* 16,1V2	
	to pour out	*A* 1,7,8	
	to stream down	K*RI* 3,7,8	
ṯtf	**bounty**	*LES* 4,14,10	
ṯtr	(?)	*LEM* 5,14,7	
ṯtṯt	**to quarrel**	*TR* Abbott (Pl.3) 5R22	
		LRL 9V3	
	to put up a fuss	*LRL* 46V3	
		LRL 3R6	
		H.O. 1,49,3R5	
		LES 4,2,4	
		LES 4,11,1	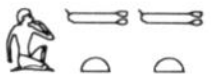
		LES 5,2,72	
		LEM 9,9V2	
		RAD 25,2R12	
		H.O. 1,70,2,4 O.Prague 1826,4 S.A. #249	
	iry-n-ṯtṯt **enemy**	*TR* 10052 (Pl.27) 4R**9**	
ṯtw	**sparrow**	*LEM* 6,16,2	
		LEM 8,6,4	
		Push 127,5,1	
ṯdw	(?)	*LEM* 9,3V2	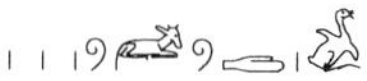

d	**yearling calves** (cf. E-W p.67,37c)	K*RI* 5,54,1	
		K*RI* 5,54,1	
dt	**collar piece** (or *drt* "hand?" of chariot, cf. *JSSEA* 16,34)	*A* 1,24,5	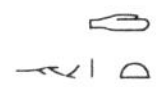
dꜣiw	**loin-cloth** (cf. Janssen 265-271; Valbelle, *Ouvriers* 152 & 281 n.3)	*LEM* 6,13,4	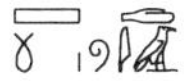
		LEM 10,6,6	
		RAD 25,2R6	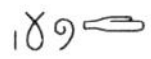
		P.DM 26R14 S.A. Pl. 93 *RAD* 25,2R1	
		P.Turin 2008+2016,2R15	
		LEM 1,1,1	
		LRL 9R18	
	kilt	K*RI* 3,534,2	
dꜣbw	**figs**	*LEM* 5,14,6	
		LEM 17,10	
		K*RI* 1,61,2	
		LEM 9,4V5	
		LEM 9,15V7	
dꜣwꜣr	(cf. *dwr* below) (fruit-measure)	*H* 1,36b,2	
dꜣdꜣ	**to be lascivious, amorous, lustful, to make love, to have sexual intercourse** (cf. Fox p.11, n.c; Hoch pp.378-80) **"lovemaking", "copulation"** (cf. *Wb.* 5,419,4-5; *JEA* 11,297,8 "bawdy")	P.H. 500 (Pl.4) 2,2	
		LEM 10,14,8	
		O.H. 1038V1	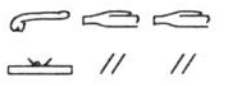

di	**to give, grant, to let, to allow, to cause, to make**	*LEM* 1,1,2	
		LRL 4R14	
		K*RI* 2,226,2	
		K*RI* 2,231,6	
		LES 5,2,63	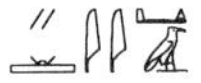
		K*RI* 5,14,3	
		LEM 13,4V8	
		Melanges...Mokhtar 2,348,6	
		LEM 5,7,11	
		K*RI* 5,58,1	
		K*RI* 2,227,5	
		LRL 4R13	
		LES 1,6,2	
	di-ꜥnḫ **given life**	K*RI* 1,65,15	
	di-ḥr **to apply oneself**	*LEM* 11,5,5	
	to watch over, to guard	*HPBM*^{4} P2,V1	
diw	**rations, grain rations**	*LRL* 9V6	
		RAD 1,1R8	
	"gift" (cf. Fox p.54)	*CB* 1 (Pl.24) C3V9	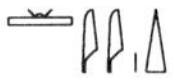
		K*RI* 5,84,3	
		P.Ashmolean 1960.1283,V3 *JEA* 66,116,bb	
	gift	K*RI* 5,28,5	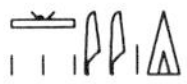
	wages, rations	*JEA* 27,23	
	income in grain	*JEA* 31,41 n.i	
diwt	**fifth**	*CB* 1 (Pl.24) C3V4	
diwt	**roar** (cf. E-W p.12, n.11a)	K*RI* 5,16,11	
disꜣ	**setting**	*TR* 10052 (Pl.29) 6R13	
		H 1,52b,6	
didi	**Nubian haematite**	*LEM* 11,4,2	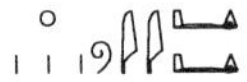

dy	**there**	*LRL* 5R18
		RAD 2,2R4
		LEM 1,5,8
		K*RI* 2,286,12
	from here	*LRL* 27R5
	here (cf. *JEA* 42,12)	P.Turin 1882,1R4 *JEA* 41 (Pl.7)
	here	*LRL* 12R3
		K*RI* 1,47,1
dydy	**vessel, flat dish, bowl, cauldron** (cf. Janssen pp.423-24)	*H.O.* 22,2R10 *H* 1,37a, 2&3
		BIFAO 27,177 O.Berlin 10629,4
dydy	(cf. *dd* below) **garden**	P.DM 26,B,R9 S.A. Pl.95
dydy	(cf. *dꜣdꜣ* above) **obscene**	*LEM* 10,14,8
dwꜣ	**to worship, praise, adore** (cf. *Serapis* 6,30,b)	*LES* 1,8,6
		LES 6,1,x+2
		LES 9,F2
		H 1,1,3
		Push 127,1,6
		CB 1 (Pl.24) C3V4
		K*RI* 1,14,5
		K*RI* 1,97,14
		K*RI* 5,35,3
		H 1,2,6
		K*RI* 3,366,14
dwꜣw	**adoration**	*LEM* 2,10,4
		H 1,6,10
		H 1,57,1
	hymns	K*RI* 3,654,7
		K*RI* 3,655,4

dw3	**door, gate, pylon**	*TR* 10053 (Pl.20) 2V12
		TR 10053 (Pl.21) 3V21
	doorway	*ASAE* 71, fig. 2a,1.8 stele Cairo JE 49113,1.8
dw3t	**praiseworthy** (?) (cf. *A* 1, p.7, n.5)	*A* 1 (O.BN 14)
dw3-nṯr	**to thank, to praise god for**	K*RI* 1,66,5
dw3-nṯr **(*n-imn*)**	**Divine Adoratress, Votaress**	*TR* Abbott (Pl.2) 4R7
		TR Abbott (Pl.2) 3R17
		RAD 24,1R6
		Khonsu 2,113,17
dw3	**to rise at dawn**	*HPBM*[3] CB4,5V9
dw3yt	**dawn, morning**	*H* 1,42,2
		K*RI* 5,38,11
		H 1,6,1
		K*RI* 5,87,7
		K*RI* 2,103,2
		K*RI* 5,27,7
	tomorrow	*LRL* 1R6
		LRL 14R11
		LES 5,1,12
	m-dw3yt **in the future**	Naun 4R5
	m dw3 s3 dw3 **henceforth**	*BIFAO* 46, 102,5-6
	ḫr r-ʿ dw3 **immediately**	*TR* Abbott (Pl.4) 6,24
	s3 dw3 **after tomorrow**	P.CGC 58055,R2 *ASAE* 71 (Pl.5)
	tp-dw3yt **dawn**	*H* 1,49,6
	tr-n-dw3 **morning**	*P.Leiden* 1,350,1Vx+8
dw3wt	> *tw3* (door part) (cf. Coptic ⲧⲟⲩⲁ)	*LEM* 3,1V8 Osing, *Nominalbildung* 634ff. n.659

dw3t	**Duat**, (place in the sky), **“netherworld”**, **“underworld”**	*LES* 4,15,4	
		H 1,1,2	
		H 1,44,5	
		K*RI* 1,48,7	
		K*RI* 1,111,2	
		A 1,11,5	
	abyss	*A* 1,24,5 K*RI* 2,333,12	
	(underground burial chamber)	*JEA* 22,178 P.Leopold 2,2,8	
dwn	**to stretch out**	*A* 1,25,9	
		K*RI* 5,113,2	
		Push 127 (Pl.4) 1,8	
		LES 4,3,9	
	to get up	*LES* 5,1,12	
	to present (?) S.A. p.323, n.16	P.Turin 2021,2,5 S.A. Pl.115	
	m-dwn **straight up**	*LES* 7,1,11	
dwn	**to recover**	*LEM* 8,5,7	
dwn	**henceforth** (cf. *JEA* 22,175-6) **continually, regularly** (cf. *JEA* 42,14)	*LRL* 18R5 CS 1V4	
dwr	(fruit-measure)	*H* 1,36b,2	
db	(see *d3bw* above) **sweet fig**	Valbelle, *Ouvriers* 276 n.9	
db	**horn**	*LES* 3,9,3	
		LEM 5,17,8	
		K*RI* 1,77,1	
db	**hippopotamus**	*LEM* 5,1b,4	
		LES 4,8,9	
		LEM 6,16,1	
		LES 4,13,9	

		LES 8,1,8
		LES 8,2,5
dbt	< *ḏbt* **brick**	*LEM* 3,3V1 *LEM* 5,12,6
	brick or **lump** (of salt)	Janssen p.440 § 175
	target, shooting mark	*HPBM*[3] CB, 2R7
	"**bricks**" (of natron)	O.Brussels E 6311,R10 S.A. Pl. 25, p. 54
	cushion, pillow (cf. Borghouts, p.56 n.55)	*P.Leiden* 1,348,2R9
	birth brick	K*RI* 3,339,11
db(t)	**tool box** ? (cf. Caminos, *LEM* p.384f.)	*LEM* 10,5,5
	box (cf. Janssen 203-4; *JEA* 65,95)	*LEM* 10,5,6
	"**cage**" (?) (cf. *JEA* 31,38)	Naun 2,V3
		Naun 3,R15
		Naun 3,R19
		O.Brussels E6339,7 Janssen p.203
	(or *ṯbw*?) **cage** (cf. Fox p.17 n.c)	P.H. 500 (Pl.8) 4,3
dbꜣr	**shrine, naos, inner sanctuary** (cf. Hoch p.376)	*AEO* I,66 Helck, *Bez* p.577,301
dbit	**blocked off** (see *ḏbꜣ*)	K*RI* 5,62,9-10
dby	(cf. *tby* above) **to fit with leather**	*LEM* 5,16,11
dby	**hippopotamus thongs**	*LEM* 6,17,5
dbywt	"**yoke arms**" (cf. *JSSEA* 16,33)	*A* 1,26,6
dbyt	**foliage**	*LEM* 3,3,3
		LEM 9,4V3

dbyt	(drink, beverage)	*LEM* 3,3,5	
		LEM 9,4V5	
dbyt	**pedestal**	*A* 1,15,3	
	base	Janssen p.248	
	(cf. Harris, *Minerals* 216)		
	sand, mud		
dbwy	**bank**	P.BM 10474,2V17	
	(cf. *BIFAO* 86,193; Meeks 1,77.5011)	Onom.Pushkin	
		P.BM 10375	
dbn	**deben** (a weight)	*LRL* 8Rn2	
	(cf. Janssen 101-2)	*LES* 4,8,12	
		A 1,11,5	
	(monetary unit)	*Khonsu* 2,133,9	
dbn	**to travel, go round**	K*RI* 5,13,6	
dbnbn	**to travel, go round, encircle**	K*RI* 1,66,8	
dbnbn	**vicissitudes**	Push 127,3,15	
dbn	**dung**	P.BM 10731 V2	
	(cf. Von Deines, *Drogennamen*, p.577)	*JEA* 54,159 n.m	
	"clay", "mud"		
dbn-ḫrp	**mind** (?) **of the Governor**	P.Brooklyn 47.218.50,1,15	
	(cf. Goyon, 87 nt.31)		
dbḥ	**to ask, beg, pray for**	*LES* 6,5,y	
		LEM 10,6,7	
		LES 5,2,57	
		Push 127 (Pl.10) 4,5	
	to request	K*RI* 3,18,5	
		K*RI* 2,226,10	
		K*RI* 5,12,5	
		LES 1,4,1	
		K*RI* 2,58,8	

		K*RI* 2,334,15	
		K*RI* 5,22,15	
dbḥw	**requirement**	*LEM* 5,12,7 *LEM* 6,3,2	
	needs	P.DM 24 (S.A. Pl. 87,4) *GM* 98,12	
	requisites	*LEM* 1,2,2	
	requirements	K*RI* 3,470,15	
dbḥt-ḥtp	**offering meal**	*Khonsu* 1,53,37	
dbs	**to prick**	*HPBM*^{3} CB 3,7R27	
dbt	(cf. *dꜣbw* above) **figs**	*LEM* 9,15V7	
dp	**to bite**	*LES* 4,9,1	
	to taste	*LEM* 3,2,3-4	
		LEM 10,10,1	
		LEM 16,10V5	
		HPBM^3 CB4 5V3	
	dp m **to fasten oneself to, to bite into**	*CB* 1, 9R1	
dpt	**flavor**	*LES* 4,3,8	
dpt	(piece of meat, kidney?)	Valbelle, *Ouvriers* p.277 n.8 O.Berlin P12337,7 *Hierat. Pap.* vol.3, Pl.31	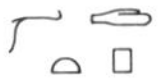
	loin	K*RI* 3,146,8	
dp	(stone object?)	*LEM* 13,2V7-8	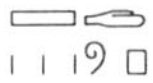
dp	(cf. *tpy* above) (fish)	*HPBM*^{4} T1R41	
dpy	(vessel)	Valbelle, *Ouvriers* 266 n.8 O.DM 3,4	

dpy	**crocodile**	K*RI* 5,109,3
		O.H. 76,12
		K*RI* 1,27,8
		K*RI* 1,68,4-5
		K*RI* 5,97,16
dpw	**mast wood** (cf. *BAR* "coffers" (*dbt* ?))	*H* 1,27,1
dpḥw	**apples**	*LEM* 3,2,5
		LEM 5,17,5
		LEM 17,9
dpẖ	**fenced in, enclosed** **"execution block"** (cf. *Orientalia* 32, 434)	P.Berlin 10496 V4 S.A. p.279, n.12 (Pl.83)
dfdf	**trickle**	K*RI* 5,38,1
dfdf	(?) (cf. E-W p.93,40b)	K*RI* 5,71,4
dm	**to sharpen, to be sharp**	*LES* 2,5,5
		K*RI* 5,23,5
	to pronounce	K*RI* 3,265,10
		K*RI* 3,307,12
		K*RI* 3,848,13
dm(*t*)	**knife**	K*RI* 5,63,8
		LEM 2,3,4
	blade	K*RI* 5,105,10
	knife	*LES* 2,9,9
	sword	K*RI* 5,62,8
		K*RI* 5,78,9
		K*RI* 5,86,2
		K*RI* 1,18,13
dmi	**to join**	K*RI* 5,70,7
	to touch, to be diligent	*H* 1,25,6

	to attach	*H* 1,79,7	
	to cleave fast to	*LEM* 3,4,5	
		LEM 10,14,5	
	to apportion to	K*RI* 5,352,14	
	to befall, to overtake	*TR* 10052 (Pl.27) 3R15	
		TR 10052 (Pl.25) 1R21	
	to befit	*MÄS* 37,22,7 (p.28)	
	to mix (cf. Fox C5)	O.DM 1266+O.Cairo 25218 *DFIFAO* 18, Pl.79	
	to stick	*LEM* 12,2V6	
		RAD 25,3V5	
dmi	**town, village**	*LRL* 3V7	
		H 1,10,12	
		LEM 6,22,2	
		LEM 5,6,3	
		CS 1V15	
		RAD 1,2Vx+9	
		LES 2,2,9	
		LRL 29R6	
		Push 127,2,6	
		LES 3,7,6	
		K*RI* 1,12,11	
		K*RI* 1,24,15	
		RAD 22,2R13	
		HPBM[4] L1R41	
	settlement	K*RI* 3,433,10	
	quay	*JEA* 22,104	
	landing place	*JEA* 50,84	
	quarter (of a city)	*JEA* 33,26,3	
	p3 dmi **the village** (Deir el Medineh)	Valbelle, *Ouvriers* 89, 114 n.3	
dm3	**to bind together, to clasp** (cf. *JEA* 36,69 (35) & 37,31)	K*RI* 5,93,1	
		Khonsu 1,21,11	
dm3t	**stretcher** (of bows)	*HPBM*[3] (Pl.14) CB4,6R8	

dmḏ	**to unite**	K*RI* 5,47,15
	to assemble	K*RI* 5,12,3
	to collect	K*RI* 5,12,4
		LEM 2,3,7
		H 1,9,3
		H 1,56b,9
		CB 1 (Pl.20) BV17
		K*RI* 1,2,12
		K*RI* 2,334,5
		K*RI* 5,22,2
dmḏwt	**mixture** (cf. Fox C15)	O.DM 12664+O.Cairo 25218,15
	total	*LRL* 8Rn2
		K*RI* 5,10,10
dmḏyt	(compendium of medicine) **pharmacopoeia, collection**	*CB* 1 (Pl.25) C4V10
dni	**to allot, to share out**	*CB* 1 (Pl. 23) C2V9
		A 1,13,2
		RAD 18,3R5
	to share (or *dni* below) "**to block up**" (?) (cf. Fox B17,7; *JEA* 65,85 n.3) **to stay aloof from, to keep oneself from**	*CB* 1 (Pl.17) 17R7
	to distribute	*LEM* 5,8,7
dni	**to dam, to dyke, to block up**	*LEM* 16,9V7
	to be checked, stopped	K*RI* 5,61,5
	to parry, to hold back, dam up (cf. *JEA* 6,104,5)	Push 127,4,9
dni	**wovenwork** (cf. Helck, *Mat* 5,918f.)	O.Berlin 14214,V6 S.A. Pl.19
dni	**land register**	Lange *Amenemope* 2,2

dni(t)	**share, portion, part**	*RAD* 18C,5V5
		TR 10068 (Pl.9) 1R11
		TR 10068 (Pl.9) 1R16
		TR 10068 (Pl.12) 6R21
	(?) (or *diw*) **share, portion, grand total** (?)	*SAK* 14,294 & 296-7
	share	*TR* 10052 (Pl.25) 2R17
		TR 10052 (Pl.26) 3R6
	list	*A* 1,15,5
		P.Cairo 58092,V9 S.A. Pl. 91, p.290
	part, share	*Khonsu* 2,133 1.20, n.R, p.19
	fragment, fraction, part	P.Leopold 2,3;3,5 *JEA* 22,180,2,19-3,1
	part (of an investment) (cf. S.A. p.260 n.11) "**property, possessions**"	P.Ashmolean 1945.96, R7 *JEA* 26, Pl.5
	iry dnyt **register**	*A* 1,17,7
dnit	**dyke** (cf. *ZÄS* 39,15,1)	*LEM* 2,8,2
		LEM 16,9V8
		Wil (40) 82V38
		Wil (49) 101V12
		Wil (23), 50R15
		K*RI* 1,9,15
		LEM 8,7,3
dnit	**used land** (cf. Gard. *AEO* pl.26,1.14)	*BIFAO* 86,194,II,2,#54 P.BM 10474,3V2
		P.Onom.Golenischeff
		P.BM 10202
dnit	**bowl, vase** (cf. Janssen p.140 §14) **basket** (cf. Warburton pp.206 & 212)	*H* 1,48,4
dniwt	**shriek, bellow** (cf. *Wb*. 5,466-7)	K*RI* 1,113,15
dni3w	**jars**	*H* 1,28,12

dnw	*dnw*-**stone**	*JNES* 20,257 n.N O.OI 16991,V9	
dnm	**furrow** (cf. Hoch p.378)	Lange *Amenemope* 7,16;8,15	
dnrg	**to be deaf**	*LEM* 5,2,5-6	
dnrg	**carob**	*LEM* 3,2,3	
	gourds (*dlg*) (cf.Janssen p.476 n.88) **sweet melon** (cf. Hoch p.378)	Helck, *Mat* 5,804 ff. *Mich* pl. 78,5	
	squash or **gourd**	*BIFAO* 46,117 f.	
	melon	Valbelle, *Ouvriers* 274 n.J	
dnḥ	**pinion**	*H* 1,76,10	
		K*RI* 5,9,5	
		K*RI* 5,57,14	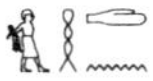
		K*RI* 5,33,6	
		LEM 8,8,1	
		LEM 6,8,1	
		LEM 6,7,5	
		LEM 2,5,4	
		LEM 3,4,2	
		LEM 5,10,4	
dnḥwy	**wings**	K*RI* 5,26,3	
		K*RI* 1,16,12	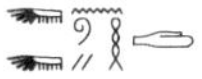
		K*RI* 1,39,9,8	
dns	**to be heavy**	*LEM* 6,21,6	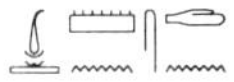
		LEM 10,14,8	
		LEM 10,2,4	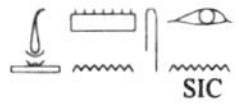
	burdensome	K*RI* 2,94,5	
	serious	*LES* 5,1,17	
	weighty	K*RI* 5,46,13	
	important	*TR* Abbott (Pl.3) 6R4	
		K*RI* 2,94,3	
	cautious (of speech) **prudent**	*JEA* 35,38f.; 37,112f.	

	courageous, resolute	*JEA* 12,210,2	
	impatient, angry	*Mes* p. 17 n.2	
dndn	**wrath** (cf. *HPBM*[4] 1,108,n.24)	*HPBM*[4] Ch.37	
dr	**to delimit, to demarcate**	*Rd'É* 33,55 n.ao	
		Cairo JE 52001,R12	
		H.O. 22,1,R2	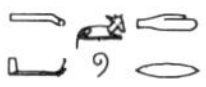
dr	**to subdue, repel** **to banish**	K*RI* 5,15,7 K*RI* 3,484,15	
	to overwhelm	*LEM* 8,8,9	
	to remove, expel	Push 127,1,6	
	to dispel	*P.Leiden* 1,348,4R7	
	to resist, deter	*Rd'É* 20,10,6	
	to cast down	*Khonsu* 2,139,3	
		TR Abbott (Pl.1) 2R9	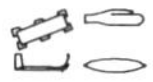
		K*RI* 1,62,7	
dr	**dressed, drawn** (cf. Valbelle, *Ouvriers* 277, n.16; *JNES* 10,91)	*H.O.* 32,5,III 3	
	dried (meat)	K*RI* 3,146,7	
dr	**shawl** (cf. Janssen p.284-86)	*Khonsu* 2,133,10,33,36 p.19 n.h	
drp	**to offer**	K*RI* 1,124,2	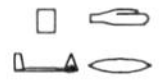
	to make offerings	K*RI* 3,370,4	
drpw	**offerings, provisions**	Push 127,2,3	
	meal, sustenance	*HPBM*[3] (Pl.20) CB4,6V1	
		BIFAO 83,237 P.Boulaq XIII,frag. 2,1	
drf	**papyrus** **scroll, writing** (cf. Fox B16,9) **records, documents** (cf. *JEA* 65,78)	*CB* 1,16R9 K*RI* 3,54,4	 

drt	(bird)	*LEM* 5,1b,9	
dhn	**to convey**	*H* 1,8,3	
	to promote	P.Turin 1882,3R4 *JEA* 41 (Pl.9) 3,4	
		H 1,42,8	
	to assign	*H* 1,59,1	
		K*RI* 5,23,3	
		K*RI* 5,84,3	
		K*RI* 5,76,5	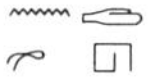
		K*RI* 1,39,6	
	to appoint	*LES* 2,18,10	
		LES 2,12,3	
		LES 4,8,4	
	to bow down, to bow low	K*RI* 1,322,7	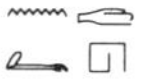
dhnt	**mountain top, peak** **summit** (cf. *AJSLL* 34,255 #132)	*LEM* 5,4,4	
		LES 4,13,8	
	top, promontory	*LRL* 15,R5	
	hilltop	*JEA* 67,158 n.17	
	peak	K*RI* 3,19,10	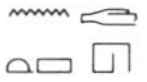
		K*RI* 3,712,14	
dhnt	**forehead**	*HPBM*[4] T1,V52	
dhnt	**sketch** (?) (cf. *Rd'É* 26,170) "**top**" (cf. Wente, *LRL* p.39) (see above)	*LRL* 9V19	
dḥ	**to be discouraging**	*Rd'É* 9,112	
		O.Ch.&O.IFAO 1207	
	to be low (cf. *Wb.* 5,480)	*LEM* 12,2V2	
dḥw	(metal) (cf. Caminos, *LEM* p.218)	*LEM* 5,17,7	
dḥ3	**to advance**	K*RI* 5,12,4	

	to support	K*RI* 5,23,3	
		K*RI* 5,69,9	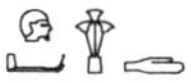
dḥ3	**straw** (cf. *JEA* 12,222,8; Helck, *Mat* 5,808)	K*RI* 5,63,15	
		K*RI* 5,71,12	
		K*RI* 2,72,11	
		K*RI* 2,120,14	
		LEM 5,12,6	
		LEM 6,3,1	
		K*RI* 2,72,12	
dḥn	**wing**	*Khonsu* 2,142,C,1 *Khonsu* 2,161,D,6	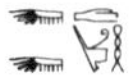
dḥr	**to embitter**	*JEA* 41,90 Cairo board 46891,15	
dḥr	**bitter**	*A* 1,5,2	
	bitter, harsh	*HPBM*[4] L1,R26	
dḥr	**hide** (cf. Janssen p.398, §148)	*LES* 5,2,41	
		LEM 10,6,6	
		LES 7,2,1	
		RAD 25,3V11	
		K*RI* 1,56,15	
	leather	*JEA* 27,62,3 O.Petrie 37R2	
dḥrt	(sickness)	*HPBM*[4] L1R49-50	
		HPBM[4] L6R105	
		HPBM[4] T2R79-80	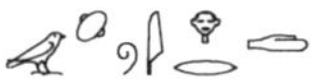
dḥt	< *ḏḥ* (?) **tin**	*LRL* 30V6	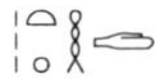
	< *ḏḥty* (?) **lead**	*LRL* 36V7	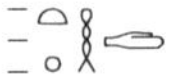
	lead	Lange *Amenemope* 18,13	
dḥtt	**testicles** (cf. *HPBM*[3] p.115,2)	*HPBM*[3] CB10,R9	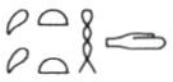

dḫ	**to overthrow**	K*RI* 5,15,4
	to defeat	K*RI* 5,28,2
		K*RI* 5,73,9
	to cast down	*Khonsu* 1,71,12
dḫwt	**boulders** (cf. Harris, *Minerals* p.30)	*A* 1,23,3
		A 1,24,2
ds	(jar) (cf. Janssen p.472-4)	*LEM* 9,15V9
		P.Leiden 1,350,1VX+17
	beer jug	*HPBM*3 CB4 5V4
	crock (for beer)	*Rd'É* 27,76
ds	**flint**	*LES* 4,9,10
	knife	K*RI* 1,10,8
		K*RI* 1,16,12
dšr	**wood**	*LEM* 5,16,9
dšr	**red**	*LEM* 12,2V6
		LEM 5,13,4
		LEM 17,11
		K*RI* 1,73,12
		LEM 3,2,6
	dšr-ib **furious**	*JEA* 35,72
	dšr-ḥr **furious**	*JEA* 35,72
dšrt	**red pot**	*JEA* 41,16
	red vessel	*Khonsu* 1,53,40 & 49
dšrt	**red crown**	K*RI* 5,58,4
		K*RI* 5,77,9
dšrt	**red land, desert**	K*RI* 5,110,8
dḳ	**to hack up**	K*RI* 5,30,12

dḳ(r)w	**fruit**	*LEM* 10,12,11	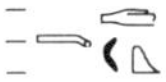
		LRL 36R7,36R11	
		H 1,48,7	
		K*RI* 2,328,9	
		H 1,8,4	
		LEM 16,7V5	
		Khonsu 1,70,2	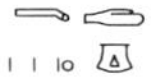
dg3	**to plant**	*LRL* 8R12	
	to plant	*LEM* 5,8,9	
	to plant	*H* 1,4,3	
		K*RI* 3.496,16	
	to plate	*LEM* 5,17,3	
	to overlay	*LRL* 9V19	
	to cover	*TR* 10054 (Pl.7) 3R16	
	to hide, cover	*TR* Amherst (Pl.5) 2V5	
	to erect (cf. Wb. 5,499,8)	*Gleanings* p.103,9	
	to be covered, be decked	P.Leopold 2,2,14 *JEA* 22,179	
dg3	**to behold, see**	*H* 1,42,6 K*RI* 3,848,10	
		A 1 (O.QC 11-12)	
		P.Leiden 1,348,2R7	
		K*RI* 3,1,11	
		K*RI* 3,366,10	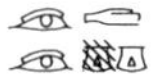
		K*RI* 1,47,10	
	to look, to stare	Push 127,1,13	
dg3	**razor** (cf. *JEA* 65,95; *WZKM* 59/60, (Pl.1,1.7))	*JEA* 63,107 ff.	
		JEA 63,109-10	
dg3	**to walk, to march** **to take steps**, but (cf. *JEA* 69, 178 "**go to see**")	Push 127,4,2	
	to go barefoot	Push 127, p.50	

dg3yt	**cuts of red meat** (cf. Valbelle, *Ouvriers* p.278)	*LEM* 5,14,3	
		K*RI* 3,146,8	
dg3wt	(fruit) (cf. Valbelle, *Ouvriers* p.275 n.12; Fox T2,11)	O.DM 134,11	
		P.Turin 1966,2,11	
dgm	**speechless** (?)	K*RI* 3,92,9	
dgm	(fruit, castor oil, *ricinus*) (cf. Janssen 334; *Drogennamen* p.583f.)	P.Ebers 25	
		P.Ber. 58	
dgs	**to tread, to set foot**	*A* 1,19,4	
	to demarcate	*LEM* 8,9,6	
	to trespass	*TR* 10052 (Pl.25) 1R2	
		TR 10052 (Pl.25) 1R2	
		TR 10052 (Pl.34) 14V4	
		LEM 3,5,3	
		K*RI* 2,74,10	
		K*RI* 5,15,2	
		K*RI* 5,69,12	
	to tread	*Melanges…Mokhtar* 2,349,15	
dgdg	**to walk over, to tread**	K*RI* 1,99,9	
	to trample down	K*RI* 5,71,8	
		K*RI* 5,110,8	
dt	(plant) (cf. Fox H 1,9) **"papyrus marsh"** (cf. *LAE* p.298)	P.H. 500 (Pl.2) 1,9	
dd	**grove** (cf. *Wb*. 5,502,1)	*LEM* 3,2,5	
		P.DM 26, B,R9 S.A. Pl.95	
	"garden" (cf. Fox p.15 n.m)	P.H. 500 (Pl.6) 3,12	
dd	(see *di* above) **given, banished**	*LEM* 13,4V8	
		P.DM 27V4 S.A. Pl.99	

dd	(see *d3d3* above) **lovemaking, copulation**	P.H. 500 (Pl.4) 2,2	
dd-r	**reciter** (cf. Lichtheim 2, p.177)	*HPBM*[3] CB4,3V4	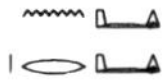
dd(t)	(cf. *dydy* also) **dish, bowl** (cf. *Wb*. 5,501,14ff.)	*LEM* 4,3 *LEM* 5,16,2	 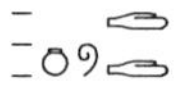

ḏt	**body, person** (cf. *JEA* 39,20,3g)	K*RI* 5,100,13	
		Push 127,2,1	
	self	*LEM* 2,10,7	
	ḏt.f	*LEM* 10,10,3	
	ḏt.f	*LEM* 10,9,4	
	"own" (cf. *GM* 141 [1991] 39-42)	Push 127,3,8	
	form (cf. Schott, *Denkstein* p.28 n.5)	K*RI* 1,113,9	
ḏt	**eternity, everlastingness** (cf. *JEA* 60,252; Hornung, "*Ewigkeitsbegriff*" (*FuF* 39) pp. 334-6; Assmann, *Zeit und Ewigkeit* 1975)	*H* 1,44,6	
		K*RI* 5,20,7	
		K*RI* 5,10,10	
		Push 127,2,4	
	n-ḏt **forever**	K*RI* 5,11,11	
ḏt	**flood**	*H* 1,48,10	
ḏꜣ	**to show forth, to reveal, to "extend," "to carry over"** (cf. Fox B,C1,5) (*ḏꜣi* below?)	*CB* 1 (Pl.22) C1V5	
ḏꜣ-rd	**to stunt growth**	*Melanges...Mokhtar* 2,348,9	
ḏꜣ-mꜣʿt	**"to spread righteousness"** (rather than Djeme) (cf. Bakir p.58)	*LRL* 15R6 & 16R4	
ḏꜣ	**fire-boring**	*HPBM*[3] CB9, 15R7-8	
ḏꜣ	**head, skull** (cf. *HPBM*[4] p.48 n.31)	*HPBM*[4] L7,56	
ḏꜣ	**crane** (bird)	P.Brooklyn 47.218.50,20,22 Goyon n.380	

ḏꜣi	**to ferry across, to cross, to sail over**	*LRL* 28R12
		LES 9 L3
		TR 10052 (Pl.31) 10V4
		K*RI* 2,15,8
		Push 127,3,1
		Khonsu 1,20,34
	to ferry	*LES* 4,5,8
		Push 127,3,1
	to cross over	*LES* 2,8,1
	to ferry	*RAD* 22,2R14
	to cross	*A* 1,3,4
		TR 10052 (Pl.34) 14V13
		TR 10052 (Pl.33) 13V2
	to cross	K*RI* 5,91,6
	to ferry over	*LES* 1,5,1
		K*RI* 2,118,10
		K*RI* 3,20,7
		K*RI* 2,118,9
	to convey	K*RI* 3,313,2
	to oppose	*P.Leiden* 1,348,3R2
	to block	*P.Leiden* 1,348,5R4
	iry-ḏꜣy **passenger**	*HPBM*^{3} CB4,1V3
	ḏꜣi tꜣ r **to oppose... to oppose, interfere with** (cf. *JNES* 6,222,22)	K*RI* 1,52,11
ḏꜣi	**ferry boat**	*LEM* 10,12,4
	ferry boat (or *wḏꜣi* ?)	*TR* 10052 (Pl.26) 2,31
ḏꜣi	(part of abdomen ?)	*HPBM*^{4} T1,V89-90
ḏꜣi	**to violate** (?)	CS 1R19
	to be ill	K*RI* 5,41,13
ḏꜣt	**remainder**	*LRL* 27aV1
		LEM 12,1V1
		RAD 17,2R11

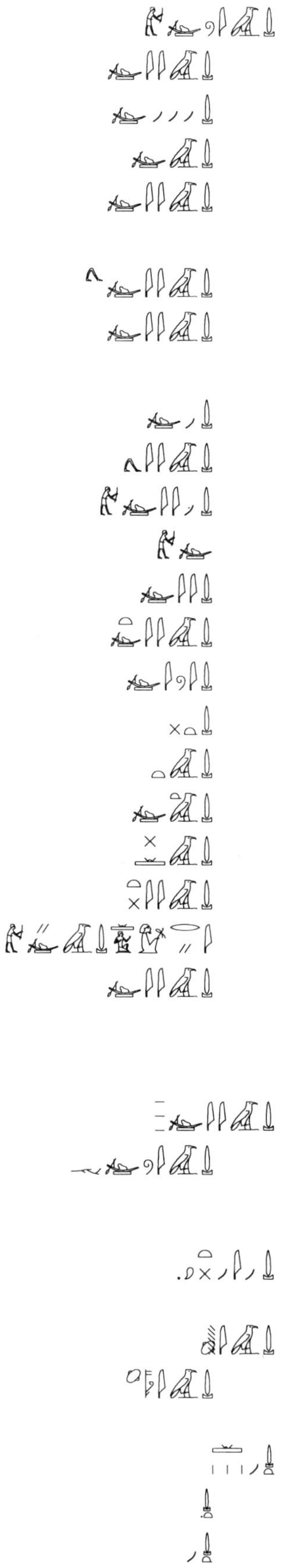

		RAD 25,1V2
		RAD 25,1V13
	deficit	*RAD* 17,4R3
		K*RI* 3,563,8
ḏ3iw	**foe**	*LEM* 8,7,5
	transgressor	*HPBM*[4] T2, V101
		HPBM[4] T2V101-102
ḏ3y	**violently**	*HPBM*[3] CB3 2R13
ḏ3y-ḫr	(for *sḏ3y-ḫr* ?) **to take pleasure** (cf. *BdE* 64/1, p.140 n.3) **to content oneself**	Lange *Amenemope* 23,16
ḏ3yt	**robe, cloak** (cf. Janssen 278)	*RAD* 6R4
		TR 10052 (Pl.29) 7R4
ḏ3yt	**ill, harm, wrong**	*LEM* 3,4,6
		K*RI* 5,42,14
		K*RI* 5,36,12
	transgression	K*RI* 4,408,1
	offense	K*RI* 3,818,2
ḏ3ir	(fruit?) (cf. Valbelle, *Ouvriers* p.275,12)	*HPBM*[3] (Pl.26) CB5,8R3
ḏ3is	**straw** (?) (cf. *CB* 1 p.38 n.2; [plant] Fox p.77 n.o)	*CB* 1,17R12
ḏ3is	**hostility**	*HPBM*[3] CB3,7R9
ḏ3ʿk	(see *ḏʿk*[*t*] below) **cry** (cf. Helck, *Bez* 577,302)	K*RI* 5,70,5
ḏ3w3ti	**sandfly**	Helck, *Bez* 577,304
ḏ3b	(cf. *ḏb* below)	

ḏ3f	**burning**	*RAD* 25,2V15	
ḏ3m3ᶜ	(see *ḏmᶜ* below)		
ḏ3mw	**young man**	*H* 1,4,5	
		CB 1 (Pl.19) BV11	
		LEM 9,4V1	
		K*RI* 1,66,6	
		K*RI* 1,74,9-10	
		K*RI* 1,65,10	
	troops	*JEA* 39,40f.	
	(military or labor classes) E-W p.52 n.13a	K*RI* 5,39,7	
	generations	K*RI* 5,62,2	SIC
	generations	*A* 1,12,5	
	throngs	*JEA* 50,84,1.11	
	young men, generations	*Khonsu* 2,132,22	
	descendants	*HPBM*[3] CB5,2V7	
	youthful	K*RI* 5,73,4	
ḏ3nn	(cf. *ḏnn* below) **shuddering** (cf. Helck, *Bez* 577,309)	*A* 1,24,1	
ḏ3r	**helper, adjutant** (cf. Hoch p.392)	*A* 1,23,9	
ḏ3r(*t*)	**necessity, provisions, rations** (cf. Helck, *Bez* 578,315)	*A* 1,12,4	SIC
		RAD 22,2R12	
ḏ3rᶜ	(see *ḏrᶜ* below) **to throw down**	Helck, *Bez* 578,314	
ḏ3ḥt	**pit**	K*RI* 3,749,7	
ḏ3ḏ3	**head**	*LES* 2,8,7	
		LRL 9R7-8	
	bulb	*LEM* 5,14,12	
		LES 4,9,10	
		K*RI* 5,30,11	

		HPBM[4] L2V36	
	summit	*A* 1,14,3	
ḏꜣḏꜣ	(djadja-jar)	*LRL* 44R9	
	pot	*LES* 4,11,8	
	drinking mug (cf. Valbelle, *Ouvriers* 265 n.12)	*LEM* 10,5,6	
ḏꜣḏꜣy	(cf. *ḏꜣi* above) **to ferry, to carry**	*LES* 4,5,14	
ḏꜣḏꜣw	**pavilion, kiosk, landing stage**	*JEA* 46,36 n.1	
	(cf. Spencer, *Egyptian Temple* 130-133)	*ZÄS* 95,119, fig.161.5	
	portico	K*RI* 3,298,13	
	(cf. *BdE* 37,39-42)	Banishment stela	
	"**colonnade**"?	K*RI* 6,535,6	
ḏꜣḏꜣwt	**courses** (?)	*H* 1,57,12	
		H 1,77,7	
		H 1,58,5	
		Rd'É 23,171 n.3	
	"**surface plane**"	*VA* 3,67-79	
ḏꜣḏꜣt	**judges, magistrates**	*H* 1,48,10	
		K*RI* 1,80,6	
		K*RI* 1,87,2	
		K*RI* 1,88,3	
		K*RI* 1,110,8	
		RAD 22,1R13	
	(cf. *ZÄS* 73,74)	*HPBM*[3] CB8,1R1	
	conclave (cf. *JEA* 42,9 & 12)	*JEA* 41 (Pl.7) P.Turin 1882,1R3	
	tribunal	K*RI* 3,771,2	
		K*RI* 3,11,13	
ḏꜣḏꜣt	**lyre**	*Melanges* 1,457-64	
	harp	*GM* 66,28 n.88	

ḏyḏy	**to scold, to tease**	P.H. 500,5,6
ḏꜥ	**storm**	*A* 1,18,5
	whirlwind	K*RI* 5,62,10
		K*RI* 5,101,2
	storm, tempest	K*RI* 5,93,19
	gale	*JEA* 47,103
	windstorm	*Rd'É* 20 (Pl.11) 1.14,p.21 n.d
	whirlwind	K*RI* 5,32,8
ḏꜥwt	**to spear fish** (?)	*LEM* 5,1b,2
ḏꜥbw	**charcoal**	*LRL* 5R16
		LEM 5,17,5
	black pigment	Harris, *Minerals* 159-60
ḏꜥm	**to faint**	*LEM* 10,10,4
ḏꜥm	**electrum**	*H* 1,4,1
		LES 2,17,4
		K*RI* 2,109,2
		K*RI* 1,47,8
		K*RI* 1,112,9
		Khonsu 2,143 C1
ḏꜥm	**scepter**	*LES* 4,5,2
ḏꜥr	**to seek out**	*LEM* 5,2,8
		LEM 11,2,6
		K*RI* 1,39,7
		K*RI* 2,77,3
		K*RI* 2,77,4
	to research (cf. *JEA* 61,125)	*JEA* 60,144,1.3
	to devise	*Khonsu* 2,142a,1
	to probe, to investigate	*Wb.med.Texte* 2,998f.

ḏʿdd	**sticks**	*LEM* 5,17,4
ḏʿḳ(*t*)	**cry for help** (cf. Helck, *Bez* 577,302&3) **to cry out** (cf. Hoch p.381)	K*RI* 5,79,2-3 K*RI* 5,70,5
ḏw	**mountain, hill**	*H* 1,77,7
		H 1,58,10
	hill	*A* 1,8,6
		LEM 5,10,7
		LES 3,9,4
		K*RI* 5,43,10
		LRL 50R3
		LRL 2R3
		LRL 15R6
		LRL 16R5
ḏw	**evil**	*A* 1(O.L.4)
	sad	*LES* 4,4,1
	ḏw ḥr **evil-faced one**	*P.Leiden* 1,348,7R3
	ḏw ḳd **evil of character**	K*RI* 5,32,12
ḏw(*t*)	**evil**	*LEM* 5,5,4
	dirt	*H* 1,27,7
	fault	*A* 1(O.BN 13)
	difficulty	*Rd'É* 30,121f.
	evil	K*RI* 5,68,14
	ill, badness (cf. Fox 21G)	O.DM 1266+O.Cairo 25218
	r ḏw ʿ3 wr **most lecherously**	*LES* 4,6,5
ḏwt	**midge**	*LEM* 5,12,9
ḏwyw	(vessel) *Wb.* 5,551,6	*A.Lex.* 77.5175
	(capacity)	*Rd'É* 11,69
ḏb	**to argue, rebut, reply**	*ASAE* 69,242-3

ḏbꜣ	**to reimburse, to turn over to**	*BIFAO* 46,108,8
	to replace	*LEM* 8,5,9
	to repay	*LES* 5,1,19
	to substitute	P.CGC 58055,R9 *ASAE* 71 (Pl.5)
ḏbꜣ	**exchange** (cf. *Serapis* 7,48 n.1)	*Studies...Griffith* Pl.10,8
	instead of	*LES* 5,2,30
	exchange	P.Turin 2008+2016,1V19
	reward	*A* 1,3,2
		K*RI* 1,67,15
	compensation	O.Berlin 12630,R3 S.A. p.35, Pl.11
	payment	*Khonsu* 2,113,25
		RAD 1,6Vx+6
		K*RI* 3,555,14
	r-ḏbꜣ **on account of**	Cairo Board 46891,1.12 *JEA* 41,89,4
		LRL 25R3
		Naun 4R9
	in exhange for	K*RI* 3,552,1
ḏbꜣ	**to provide** (for)	*H* 1,50,2
	to clothe	*H* 1,76,4
	to attire	*LEM* 10,8,10
ḏbꜣ	**vestments**	K*RI* 3,11,16
ḏbꜣ	**to stop up, to block**	*H* 1,57,5
	to block *P.Leiden* 1,348 n.188	*P.Leiden* 1,348,7R3
ḏbꜣw	**leaves**	*LEM* 8,5,6
	foliage	*A* 1,10,6
ḏbꜣw	**payments, rewards**	K*RI* 1,126,6

ḏbꜣt	**sarcophagus** (cf. Janssen p.23 §50) **coffins** (outer)	*LES* 9,F5
		K*RI* 3,58,11
		TR Abbott (Pl.2) 4,3
		TR Amherst (Pl.5) 2,3
		TR 10054 (Pl.6) 2R10
	outer sarcophagus (cf. *JEA* 10,239,2)	*JEA* 22,179 P.Leopold 2,2,12
		K*RI* 1,26,5
	robing room	K*RI* 5,100,10
ḏbiw	**armies, troops** (cf. Helck, *Bez* 577,305; Hoch p.382)	K*RI* 5,26,13
		A 1,27,1
	army, combatants	*A* 1,23,9
ḏbꜥ	**10,000**	*LRL* 28R27
	20,000	*H* 1,46,5
		H 1,28,1
	myriads	*H* 1,4,5
		K*RI* 5,26,7
		K*RI* 5,22,11
ḏbꜥ	**finger**	*LEM* 2,6,6
	fingers	*A* 1,15,5
	fingers	*LES* 7,3,14
		LEM 10,2,1
		LEM 12,5V6
		LEM 3,7,7
	toes (cf. *JEA* 39,117)	*HPBM*[4] L1,V2
ḏbꜥ	**to seal up**	*LEM* 5,7,3
		H 1,57,4
		CS 1R5
		RAD 12a,2R10
	to reproach	*LEM* 9,5V1
	to blame	*Oriens Ant.* 6,p.50 n.p (Pl.18) Edinburgh stone 912.15

ḏbꜥ	**marked men**	P.CGC 58054,V6 *ASAE* 71 (Pl.4) 1.6	
ḏbꜥty	**twenty**	*Khonsu* 2,132,11,15	
ḏbw	(chariot-part) **"adornment"**	*A* 1,26,7	
	"appliqué" (cf. *JSSEA* 16,44)	*LEM* 5,10,12	
ḏbb	(?)	*BIFAO* 86,193,38 P.BM 10474,2V12	
ḏbg	**head long dipping, dunking, soaking** (cf. *ZÄS* 80,74; Hoch p.383)	*LEM* 8,6,7	
	plunge head over heels	*LEM* 10,7,3-4	
		LEM 6,16,7-8	
ḏbḏb	**to destroy**	*JEA* 19 (Pl.29) 7 O.Turin 9588,1.7	
ḏpr	**bird** (?) (cf. Hoch p.384) (in personal name)	An. 3,6V1	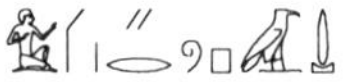
ḏprt	(cake)	*H* 1,35b,1	
ḏprt	(vessel) (cf. *BIFAO* 101,90)	Janssen p.432 O.Cairo 35677,23	
ḏpḥ	(boat part) **"plank"** or **"panel"** (cf. Hoch p.385)	Janssen p.380 §133 *Giornale* 13,2,2	
ḏpḳ	**dancer, acrobat** (cf. Hoch p.385)	*Onom.* A. 219, *AEO* 1,p.25*	
		LEM 9,4V2	
ḏfꜣw	**provisions, sustenance, food**	*LES* 4,14,10	
		LEM 2,1,2	
		LEM 5,6,2	
		A 1 (O.QC 3)	
		K*RI* 5,41,10	
		K*RI* 5,42,12	

		K*RI* 1,3,16	
		K*RI* 1,48,16	
		K*RI* 1,88,10	
		HPBM[4] P1,V14	
	abundance	*JEA* 31,66 (48)	
	victuals	Push 127, p.50	
	food offerings	*ASAE* 71, fig. 2a,4 Stele Cairo JE 49113,1.4	
ḏft	(oil)	*LEM* 5,15,2	
ḏfḏ	**pupil** (of eye)	*HPBM*[4] T2,V74	
ḏfḏ	**to drop, drip**	*LES* 2,16,9	
ḏfḏ	**drops**	K*RI* 5,22,11	
ḏmꜥ	**papyrus rolls** (cf. Janssen p.447 §182)	*LES* 10B,V9	
		TR Ambras (Pl.38) 1,7	
		JEA 22,182,4,3 P.Leopold 2,4,3	
		LEM 6,23,2	
		LEM 8,3,10	
ḏmꜥ	**to be thirsty, parched** (cf. Hoch p.386)	*P.Leiden* I,343,7,7	
		P.Leiden I,343,V spell 12	
ḏmꜥ	**misery**	*HPBM*[4] L6,V46	
ḏnw	**threshing area**	*LEM* 9,10V1	
		LEM 8,4,12	
		RAD 1,4R1	
		RAD 1,1R3	
		RAD 1,1R11	
ḏnm	(?)	*LEM* 9,3V5	
ḏnn	**torment, flogging** (cf. Hoch pp.188-9)	*HPBM*[3] CB4,5V8-9	
		LEM 2,7,2	

		LEM 5,9,5	
		LEM 10,10,9	
	hardships	*HPBM*^{3} CB4,3V13	SIC
	arduous tasks, endeavors	*LEM* 7,6,7	
	(or *ḏnḏn*)	*TR* 10052 (Pl.27) 3,17	
	(or *ḏnḏn*)	*HPBM*^{3} CB5,6R13	
ḏnn	**to be tormented**	*LEM* 3,6,10	
	to strive, to exert oneself (cf. Helck, *Bez* 577,310)	*JEA* 48,61,13	
	to conspire	*Mes* 21,3	
ḏnn	**shuddering** (cf. Helck, *Bez* p.577,309 bristling)	*A* 1,24,1	
ḏnr	**self-bent rods**	*LEM* 5,17,4	
	twigs, branches	*LEM* 12,2V4	
ḏnr	**to repay** (cf. *ḏnrm*?)	*H* 1,23,3	
ḏnrm	(*ḏlm*?) **to yield**	Push 127,4,15	
ḏnḥ	(part of a rudder)	Helck, *Bez* 577,311	
ḏnḥ	**upper arm** (?)	*HPBM*^{4} T2,V17-18	
ḏnḏn	**swan** (?), **stork** (?)	*GM* 19,57f.	
ḏnḏn	(or *ḏnn* see above) **birch** (torture instrument)	*TR* 10052 (Pl.27) 3R17	
		TR 10052 (Pl.28) 5R16	
ḏnḏnrt	(wood?)	Helck, *Bez* 577,312	
	(fuel? faggot?) (cf. Janssen, p.483; *Rd'É* 7,182 ff.)	*JEA* 66,115 n.t P.Ashmolean 1960.1283,R9	
ḏr	**since**	*H* 1,7,7	

	m-ḏr **because of** (for *m-di* ?)	*LES* 5,2,67
	m-ḏr **after**	*LES* 5,2,51
ḏrtyw	**ancestors** (cf. *JEA* 33,31,19)	K*RI* 1,42,14
		TR Abbott (Pl.2) 4R1
	duly mourned over (?)	*JEA* 17,259
ḏr	**side**	K*RI* 5,114,10
	"loins" (cf. Fox p.74)	*CB* 1,17R6
		HPBM^3 CB4,4V8
	flanks	K*RI* 3,146,8
		P.Leopold 2,2,10
		TR Abbott (Pl.1) 2R13
	flank	*Wil* (8) 19R22
		Wil (43) 88V8
		Wil (66) B19V20
	walls (cf. also *ḏrwt* below)	*LEM* 10,12,3
		RAD 18,1R6
ḏrw	**limits**	K*RI* 2,150,7
	r-ḏrw **all**	K*RI* 5,24,9
		LES 3,8,7
		LES 5,2,20
	all	CS 1R4
	entirety	Černý, *Workmen* 99
ḏr-ꜥ	**before**	K*RI* 5,23,3
	previously	K*RI* 5,60,14
	formerly	K*RI* 5,68,7
	since before	*H* 1,57,7
	ḏr-ꜥ ḏr	*H* 1,27,7
ḏr-b3ḥ	**before, aforetime**	K*RI* 1,42,6

ḏri	**to be firm** (cf. Janssen 230) **to make strong**	*LRL* 41R6
		LEM 7,5,8
		LEM 1,1,10
	to hold firmly	K*RI* 3,413,2
	stout	*LEM* 10,5,4
	harsh	K*RI* 2,95,6
	firm	K*RI* 2,6,8
		K*RI* 1,111,5
	difficult, tough, painful	*Rd'É* 24,205,n.d p.202,1.3
	severe	*TR* Abbott (Pl.3) 5R5
	strictly	*TR* Abbott (Pl.3) 6R8
	strenuously	Push 127 (Pl.6) 2R11
	to impose restrictions, to obstruct	Push 127 (Pl.10) 4,6
ḏrt	**hand**	*LRL* 9R6
		LES 4,6,1
		LES 4,11,7
		LEM 10,9,4
		LEM 10,13B,6
		RAD 25,3V10
		K*RI* 5,19,10
		HPBM[4] L5R34
		LEM 9,4V3
	trunk (of elephant)	*JEA* 30,75
	hand (?) (of chariot) (or *ḏt*, cf. *JSSEA* 16,34)	*A* 1,24,5
	ḏrt.w **their hands** (status pronominalis)	*H* 1,59,11
	m-ḏrt **through**	*LRL* 3V8
	m-ḏrt.i **in my charge**	*LRL* 9V5
	m-ḏrt **in the possession of**	*Khonsu* 2,133,41
	n-ḏrt	*LES* 5,1x+19
	n-ḏrt **handy**	*LEM* 3,7,3
	ḥr-ḏrt **independent**	*JEA* 4,248,4
	handful	Janssen p.439

d̲rỉw	**firmness**	_LEM_ 1,1,5	
d̲rỉw	**tanned hide** (cf. Janssen p.218)	Push 127,4,11	
d̲rỉt	**kite**	_LES_ 4,6,13 _LEM_ 10,4,7	
_d̲ry_	**carefully, closely**	_RAD_ 24,1V8	
_d̲rw_	(see _d̲rỉ_ above) **difficult, tough, painful**	_Rd'É_ 24, p.202,1.3,205,n.d	
_d̲rw_	(cf. _d̲r_ above) **side boards** (of coffins) (cf. Janssen p.233 n.135)	_H.O._ 63,3,8	
_d̲rw_	(cf. _d̲r_ above) (meat from side)	O.Berlin 12337,7 Valbelle, _Ouvriers_ p.277 n.7	
d̲rww	**"back"** or **"rind"**	_H_ 1,17a,12	
d̲rwt	**chamber** (cf. _d̲r_ above) **room, dwelling** **wall**? (part of house)	_TR_ 10053 (Pl.21) 4V9 Push 127, p.53 _H.O._ 65,2V6 _S.A._ p.204,n.9	
_d̲rꜥ_	**to lay low**	_KRI_ 5,21,14 _KRI_ 5,71,49	
d̲rꜥt	**plank** (cf. Hoch p.394) (ship's part)	Janssen p.380 §134 _Giornale_ 13,2R13-14	
_d̲rm_	**papyrus** (cf. _HPBM_[4] text xvii, 1;21;38)	_HPBM_[4] L2,V53	
_d̲lm_	(see _d̲nrm_ above) **to yield** (?)	Push 127,4,15 (cf. _JEA_ 69,176)	
_d̲rd̲r_	**strange, foreign** (cf. _CdÉ_ 54,208) (cf. _Rd'É_ 16,43 n.1) **stranger**	_LES_ 4,9,6 _LES_ 4,6,10 Lange _Amenemope_ 26,11	

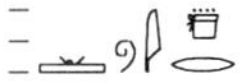

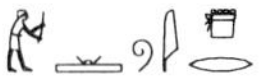

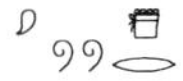

	p3 ḏrḏr **aggressor**	Max d'Ani 7,1
	s ḏrḏr **hostility**	Max d'Ani 7,2
ḏḥ	(cf. *dḥt* above) (metal) (cf. Harris, *Minerals* p.67)	*H* 1,68a,11
ḏḥw	**winnowed kernels**	*Melanges...Mokhtar* 2,348,8 & p. 355 n.y
ḏḥty	(cf. *dḥt* above) **lead**	Harris, *Minerals* 68
	ḏḥty ḥḏ **tin**?	Harris, *Minerals* 150
ḏḥwty	**first month of Akhet**	*ASAE* 43,174
ḏs	**own, self**	*LEM* 9,5V4
		CB 1 (Pl.25) C4v7
		LES 4,6,14
		LES 6,2,x+12
		K*RI* 5,39,6
		RAD 23,2R3
	ourselves	K*RI* 5,65,3
		K*RI* 1,44,7
ḏsr	**holy, sacred**	*LRL* 45R4
	(cf. Hoffmeier, *Sacred*, 1985; *Orbis bibl. et orientalis* 59)	*LES* 9,L4
	consecrated (cf. *JEA* 8,110) **set apart, separate** (cf. *JEA* 32,51 n.1)	K*RI* 5,110,5
		H 1,27,8
	sanctity	*LES* 4,14,9
	ḏsr-st **Holy of Place**	*LRL* 9R16
	glorious	*H* 1,3,4
		K*RI* 1,90,8
ḏsr	**to clear the way before..., to raise** (cf. *ZÄS* 51,120)	*JEA* 53,65 n.h
ḏsr	(oil) (cf. Fox T1,9)	P.Turin 1966,1,9

ḏsr	**strong ale**	*LEM* 10,15,2	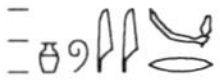
		CB 1,16R10	
ḏsrt	**holy ground,** **sacred area** (cf. Push 127, p.23)	*A* 1,3,3	
		A 1 (O.BN 8)	
ḏss	(fish)	*LEM* 10,12,10	
ḏsḏs-ib	**to be down hearted** (?)	*LEM* 12,2V4	
ḏd	**to say**	*LRL* 2V12	
	to relate	*LRL* 26R6	
		LES 4,3,10	
	("what I have said")	*LEM* 3,4,1	
	to dispute	*H.O.* 45,1R2	
		S.A. #230, p.230-1,n.1	
	to answer, assent	*HPBM*[4] L1R20	
	to say, to command	*Mes* p. 21, n.59	
	to assert, to maintain	*H.O.* (Pl.74) 1.14 O.Ash. 1945.37+1945.33,R14 S.A. p.21	
	"speakers"	K*RI* 1,101,10	
	"she who sang"	*CB* 1,17R13 *JEA* 65,87	
		JEA 65,170	
	m-ḏd **as follows**	*LES* 2,3,5	
	that	K*RI* 2,232,3	
	r-ḏd **to wit, saying, that,** (quote)	*LRL* 4V3	
	ḏd mdw in	K*RI* 5,10,12	
		K*RI* 5,10,9	
	ḏd n.f **called, named**	K*RI* 3,333,13	
	ḏd...smi **to denounce**	*LEM* 6,13,5	
ḏd	**topic**	*LEM* 6,24,3	
	deposition	*TR* 10053 (Pl.17) 1R8	
	statement	Naun 4,R1	
		K*RI* 3,272,9	

	commissions	*H* 1,79,4
	pronouncement	K*RI* 3,395,10
ḏd m ꜥꜣ nn	(?)	*LEM* 5,12,2
ḏd m šnb	**trumpeter** (cf. *Wb.* 5,514)	*TR* Abbott (Pl.23) A,4
		TR 10052 (Pl.27) 3R22
		TR 10053 (Pl.19) 7R6
ḏd	**to be established**	*A* 1,2,7
	to be stable, to endure	K*RI* 1,114,10-11
	to abide	K*RI* 2,284,14
ḏd	**stability, endurance**	K*RI* 5,16,13
	duration, stability	K*RI* 5,72,12
ḏd	**column**	*H* 1,46,9
	djed-column (cf. *GM* 109,41-51)	*LEM* 9,1V7
ḏd	**fat** (?)	*Wb.* 5,626,8
ḏd	**to pierce**	*LEM* 10,3,8
	to penetrate	K*RI* 1,99,11
	to dazzle (cf. *JEA* 11,287)	*A* 1,11,4
ḏdw	**olives, olive trees, olive oil** (cf. Hoch p.395)	*LEM* 3,2,5
		LEM 17,10
		H 1,8,5
		P.Turin 2008+2016,1V5
		P.Turin 2008+2016,2V11
	oil	Helck, *Bez* 578,316
		HPBM[3] (Pl.26) CB5, 8R10

ḏdw	**haematite**	*MÄS* 37,21,3 (p.10)	
ḏd3	**fat**	*H* 1,4,7	
		Davies, *Deir el Gebrawi* I, Pl.14	
ḏdb	**to sting**	*A* 1,21,3	
ḏdft	**snake**	*JEA* 34,118	
		HPBM[4] L5V39-40	
		HPBM[4] T1R75	
ḏdmt	**heaps**	*LEM* 4,2	
		LEM 5,13,11	
		K*RI* 1,48,8	
		K*RI* 1,48,10	
ḏdḥ	**to be confined, imprisoned**	*LES* 5,2,63	
		LEM 3,5,7	
		LRL 47R12	
		LEM 10,10,7	
		TR Abbott (Pl.2) 4R10	
	to imprison (cf. Push 127, p.53)	P.Leopold 2,3,3 *JEA* 22 (Pl.14)	
ḏdḥ	**prison**	*HPBM*[4] L6V46	
ḏḏ	**blossoms** (cf. Helck, *Bez* 578,317) **flower, rosette** (cf. Hoch p.396)	*LEM* 5,16,9 O.U.Col. 2V8	
ḏḏ	(cf. *ḏyḏy* above) **to tease, to bother**	P.H. 500,5,6	
ḏḏ	(wood) (cf. Harris, *Minerals* p.160; *Arch. Orient.* 3,397,n.i)	O.Leningrad 2973,5 *Arch. Orient.* 3,396	

A

a	*wꜥ*	I,93
abandon	*ḫꜣꜥ*	I,346
abashed(?)	*ḥnrg*	I,319
abdomen	*mhn*	I,196
abdomen	*hn*	I,288
abdomen	*ẖt*	I,379
abhorrence	*bwt*	I,133
abide	*swꜣḥ*	II,18
abide	*ḏd*	II,276
abiding	*mn*	I,183
ability	*mnḫ(t)*	I,189
abjure	*ꜥrḳ*	I,73
able	*rḫ*	I,275
abode	*msḫn(t)*	I,206
abode	*ḫnw*	I,362
abode	*st*	II,2
abomination	*bwt*	I,133
abound	*ꜥšꜣ*	I,79
abound	*bꜥḥ*	I,132
abound	*bng*	I,135
abound(?)	*bng*	I,135
about	*im*	I,26
about	*m*	I,167
about	*m-im*	I,167
about	*m-sꜣ*	I,171
about	*ḥr*	I,321
about	*ḥr-ḥr*	I,323
above	*ḥr(t)-tp*	I,327
abroad	*rwty*	I,268
abroad	*r-ḫꜣ*	I,295
abroad	*r-ḫꜣt*	I,297
abscess	*ḫsd*	I,375
abscond	*wꜥr*	I,95
absence	*ḫmt*	I,360
absent	*wꜣi*	I,87
absent	*tši*	II,220
absorb	*ꜥm*	I,66
abundance	*wꜣḥyt*	I,90
abundance	*ḏfꜣw*	II,269
abundant	*bꜥḥ*	I,132
abuse	*bwt*	I,133
abuse	*nrḥ*	I,240
abuse	*ḫnrfy*	I,366
abuse (vb.)	*nṯꜥ*	I,253
abuse (verbally)	*nrḥ*	I,240
abyss	*dwꜣt*	II,243
abyss	*šꜣdyrwtit*	II,110
acacia tree	*šnty*	II,131
acacia wood	*šnty*	II,131
accept	*šsp*	II,136
acceptability	*snfr*	II,51
access	*ꜥḳ*	I,80
access have	*ms*	I,203
acclaim (vb.)	*ḥꜥy*	I,300
acclamation	*iꜣwt*	I,12
acclamation	*ḥknw*	I,335
accomplice	*iry*	I,39
accomplice	*wꜥ-irm*	I,93
accomplish	*ꜥrꜥr*	I,72
accomplish	*mḥ*	I,197
accomplished	*ḫꜣꜥ*	I,347
according to	*m*	I,167
according to	*mi*	I,178
according to	*n*	I,223
according to	*ḫft*	I,359
according to instructions	*m-nḫb*	I,244
accordingly	*m-mitt*	I,169
accordingly	*mitt*	I,180
account	*ipw*	I,25
account	*ꜥ*	I,58
account	*ḥsb*	I,332
accountant of grain	*sš ḥsb it*	I,332
accounting	*ḥsb*	I,332
accoutered	*sꜥb*	II,13
accuracy	*ꜥḳꜣw*	I,81
accurate	*ꜥḳꜣ*	I,81
accusation	*mdt*	I,217
accusation	*ḫnw*	I,362
accusations	*srḫw*	II,59
accuse	*sꜥḥꜥ*	II,15
accuse	*smi*	II,40
achieve	*iri*	I,38
acknowledge	*snh*	II,52
acknowledge	*sḏm*	II,101
acknowledge(?)	*hn*	I,288
acquainted with	*rḫ*	I,275
acquiesce	*irt-m-mitt*	I,39
acquire	*iri*	I,37
acquire	*sḫ*	II,66
acquire	*gm*	II,188
acquire	*ṯꜣy*	II,224
acquisitions	*sḫprw*	II,69
acquit	(see find innocent)	
acquitted	*mꜣꜥ-ḫrw*	I,175
acrobat	*ḏpḳ*	II,268
act	*iri*	I,38
act	*sp*	II,30
act as	*iri*	I,38
act promptly	*pwy-ḥr-ḫrw*	I,372
action	*irt-ḫt*	I,38
actions	*sp*	II,30
actions	*sšr*	II,82
actions	*kꜣt*	II,167
active	*pr-ꜥ*	I,150
active	*ḳni*	II,152
active man	*pr-ꜥ*	I,150
acts	*sp*	II,30
acts of grace	*mnḫw*	I,189

acute	*spd*	II,34
adage	*sḏd*	II,104
addition	*ḥꜣw*	I,296
additionally	*n-hꜣw*	I,285
address	*ꜣw(i)*	I,2
address	*wšd*	I,115
address	*mdw*	I,216
address (vb.)	*ꜣw(i)*	I,2
address (vb.)	*wšd*	I,115
address (vb.)	*mdw*	I,216
address an oracle	*smi*	II,40
adept	*ꜥrḳ*	I.73
adept one	*ip-ib*	I,25
adhere	*ḫꜣm*	I,348
adjudication	*wpt*	I,98
adjust	*wꜣḥ*	I,89
adjust	*smity*	II,41
adjutant	*idnw*	I,54
adjutant	*ḏꜣr*	II,262
administer	*iri*	I,38
administer	*ṯs*	II,233
administration (?)	*šwšt*	II,116
administrator	*ꜣṯ*	I,10
administrator	*wꜥrtw*	I,95
administrator	*rwḏ*	I,269
admit into	*bsi*	I,139
admitted	*ms*	I,203
admonitions	*sḫr*	II,73
adopt	*iri*	I,38
adopted daughter(?)	*sꜣt wrt*	II,4
adoration	*iꜣwt*	I,12
adoration	*iꜣw*	I,12
adoration	*hꜣy*	I,284
adoration	*dwꜣw*	II,241
adore	*iꜣw*	I,12
adore	*tri*	II,214
adore	*dwꜣ*	II,241
adorn	*wnḫ*	I,103
adorn	*sḫꜥ*	II,68
adorn	*sḫkr*	II,76
adorn	*šṯ*	II,139
adorning	*wnḫw*	I,103
adornment	*ḏbw*	II,268
adornments	*ḫkrw*	I,389
adult	*s ꜥꜣ*	II,1
advance	*ini*	I,31
advance	*rdḥ*	I,282
advance	*smnḫ*	II,43
advance	*sḫnty*	II,72
advance	*dḥꜣ*	II,253
advantage	*ꜣḫw*	I,7
advantage	*nkt*	I,252
advantageous	*ꜣḫ*	I,7
adversary	*iry-n-ꜥḥꜣt*	I,40
adverse	*nḥꜣ*	I,242

advice	*mtr*	I,215
advice	*nḏwt-r*	I,256
advice	*sḥr*	II,61
advice	*sḫr*	II,73
advise	*mtr*	I,214
adze	*ꜥnt*	I,69
affable	*ꜣms-ib*	I,6
affair	*mdt*	I,217
affair	*ḫrt*	I,371
affairs	*ḥnw*	I,316
affection	*st ib*	II,2
affirm	*iri*	I,37
affix	*wdn*	I,118
affix	*smn*	II,42
affliction	*mntḫ*	I,190
affliction	*nḳmt*	I,251
affliction	*gb*	II,187
affluence	*rsf*	I,278
aforetime	*ḏr-bꜣḥ*	II,271
afraid	*nri*	I,239
afraid	*snḏ*	II,55
after	*m*	I,167
after	*m-ḫt*	I,170
after	*m-sꜣ*	I,171
after	*m-ḏr*	I,172
after	*ḥr-sꜣ*	I,323
after	*m-ḫt*	I,376
after	*m-sꜣ*	II,4
after	*ḥr-sꜣ*	II,5
after	*m-ḏr*	I,172
after all	*m-r-ꜥ*	I,169
after tomorrow	*sꜣ dwꜣ*	II,242
afternoon	*tr-n-mtrt*	II,214
afterwards	*ḥr-sꜣ*	I,323
afterwards	*m-sꜣ*	II,5
again	*ꜥn(n)*	I,68
again	*wḥm*	I,108
again	*m-wḥm*	I,108
again	*m-wḥm*	I,168
again	*ky*	II,171
again and again	*wnwt-wnwt*	I,101
against	*n*	I,223
against	*r-r*	I,263
agape at	*ḳꜣfyḳ*	II,144
agape at	*ḳfḳ*	II,150
age (vb.)	(see grow old)	
aged	*imꜣḫy*	I,30
agent	*rwḏ*	I,269
aggrandize	*sꜥꜣ*	II,13
aggressor	*thꜣ*	II,216
aggressor	*pꜣ ḏrḏr*	II,274
agitation	*tf*	II,209
agree	*ir-wꜥ*	I,39
agree	*hn*	I,288
agreeable	*nḏm*	I,256
agreeable	*twt*	II,203

agreement	*brṯ*	I,137
Ah!	*yꜣ*	I,11
ahead	*n-ḥr*	I,225
aid (vb.)	*wꜣḥ-ḏrt*	I,90
ailment	*smn*	II,42
ailment	*ṯꜣwrrw*	II,226
ailment type	*hḳ*	I,292
ailment type	*ḥmkt*	I,314
alabaster	*šs*	II,134
alabaster worker	*šsy*	II,134
Alas!	*wy*	I,92
ale(?)	*srmt*	II,58
alert	*spd-ḥr*	II,34
alfa-grass	*ꜥnb*	I,69
alight	*ḫni*	I,362
alight	*sḫny*	II,71
alive	*ꜥnḫ*	I,69
alive	*ꜥnḫ*	I,70
alive	*snb*	II,50
all	*r-ꜣw*	I,3
all	*nb*	I,232
all	*r-ḏr.*	I,265
all	*r-ḏrw*	I,265
all	*r-ḏrw*	II,271
all	*ḏrw*	II,271
all at once	*m-bw-wꜥ*	I,133
all at once	*m-bw-wꜥ*	I,168
All Lord	*nb-r-ḏr*	I,232
all mankind	*tꜣ-tmw*	II,198
all men	*ḥr-nb*	I,322
all right	*m-sšr*	I,171
all right	*m-sšr*	II,82
all those	*nꜣ r-ḏrw*	I,225
allot	*ḥtr*	I,339
allot	*ṯs*	II,233
allot	*dni*	II,249
allotment	*sipt*	II,11
allow	*hn*	I,288
allow	*di*	II,240
alloy	*smꜣ*	II,38
ally	*ḳrḥ*	II,157
alone	*wꜥ(i)*	I,93
alone	*wꜥty*	I,93
alone (vb. be alone)	*wꜥ(i)*	I,93
along (the road)	*m*	I,167
along with	*irm*	I,41
already	*ꜥn(n)*	I,68
already	*ḫft-ḥr*	I,359
also	*m-r-ꜥ*	I,57
also	*m-mitt*	I,169
also	*m-r-ꜥ*	I,169
also	*m-mitt*	I,180
also	*ky*	II,171
also	*gr(t)*	II,191
altar	*ḥtp*	I,337
altar	*ḫꜣwt*	I,346
although	*ḫr*	I,368
alum	*ibnw*	I,24
alum	*wšbt*	I,115
always	*rsy*	I,277
amazed	*gꜣf*	II,185
amazed	*gww*	II,186
ambush (vb.)	*šdšd*	II,141
ameliorate	*snfr*	II,51
amethyst	*irrt*	I,41
amethyst	*ḥmḳ*	I,314
amethyst	*ḥsmn*	I,333
amiable	*im(ꜣ)*	I,29
amiss	*ꜣty*	I,9
among	*im*	I,26
among	*m-m*	I,168
among	*m-ḫnw*	I,170
amongst	*m-ḫnw*	I,382
amorous	*dꜣdꜣ*	II,239
amount	*iri*	I,37
amount	*ꜥḥꜥw*	I,76
amount	*fꜣy*	I,163
amount	*rḫt*	I,276
amount to	*iri*	I,37
amphibian type	*r*	I,259
amphora	*mnt*	I,184
amphora	*msḫ(t)*	I,206
amulet	*wḏꜣ(w)*	I,122
amulet	*mkt-ḥꜥw*	I,211
amulet	*sꜣ*	II,4
amulet	*smn*	II,42
amusement	*sḏꜣyt-ḥr*	II,100
an	*wꜥ*	I,93
ancestor	*tpy-ꜥ*	II,207
ancestors	*it*	I,50
ancestors	*imyw-ḥꜣt*	I,297
ancestors	*ḏrtyw*	II,271
ancient	*ḥꜣ(w)tyw*	I,298
Ancient Memphis	*iꜣwt*	I,13
and	*irm*	I,41
and	*ḥnꜥ*	I,317
and	*ḥr*	I,321
and	*ḫr*	I,368
and	*ḫry*	I,386
and	*kꜣ*	II,166
and I will	*mtw*	I,213
and so on	*ḥmy-r*	I,312
anew	*m-mꜣwt*	I,169
anew	*mꜣw*	I,176
anew	*n-mꜣw*	I,224
anger	*ḥnḥ*	I,319
angered	*ḳnd*	II,155
angry	*ḥḏn*	I,342
angry	*dns*	II,252
angry	*šni*	II,127
angry with	*fnd*	I,164
anguish	*ḥr-(n)-ḥr*	I,322

animal	*tp-n-iꜣwt*	II,205
animals	*iꜣwt*	I,13
annals	*ḳsnw*	II,159
annals	*gnwt*	II,190
annihilate	*fḫ*	I,165
annihilate	*ḥtm*	I,338
annihilate	*sḥtm*	II,65
announce	*ꜣw(i)*	I,2
announce	*nis*	I,227
announce	*smi*	II,40
announce	*sr*	II,57
announcement	(see proclamation)	
annual	*tp-rnpt*	II,205
annually	*tr-n-rnpt*	II,214
anoint	*wrḥ*	I,105
anoint	*swrḥ*	II,21
anoint	*sgnn*	II,90
anointing oil	*ḳmy*	II,151
another	*ky*	II,170
another	*kt*	II,179
another occasion	*wḥm-sp*	I,109
another saying	*ky ḏd*	II,171
answer	*wšbt*	I,114
answer	*ḫnw*	I,362
answer (vb.)	*wšb*	I,114
answer (vb.)	*ḫsf*	I,374
answer (vb.)	*ḏd*	II,275
antelope	*šsꜣ*	II,135
anxious	*snḏ*	II,55
any	*nb*	I,232
any (thing)	*ḫt nbt*	I,233
any more	*m-ḫꜣw*	I,170
any more	*gr(t)*	II,191
anybody	*pꜣ nty nb*	I,233
anybody whatsoever	*rmṯ nb n pꜣ tꜣ*	II,197
anything	*nkt*	I,251
anything	*kt*	II,179
anything else	*nty nb gr*	II,191
anyway	*m-r-ʿ*	I,169
apart from	*wiꜣ.tw*	I,92
apart from	*r-ḫr-r*	I,263
apart from	*ḥrw-r*	I,327
apart from	*m-ḫmt*	I,361
apartment	*ipt*	I,26
ape	*kry*	II,175
ape	*gf*	II,188
Apiru	*ʿprw*	I,65
apparel	*ḥbs*	I,308
apparitor	*iry-ʿꜣ*	I,39
apparitor	*šmsw*	II,125
appeal (n.)	*spr*	II,33
appeal (vb.)	*smi*	II,40
appear	*ḫʿi*	I,351
appear	*ḫpr*	I,356
appearance	*ꜣbwt*	I,5
appearance	*iꜣbwt*	I,13
appearance	*inw*	I,33
appearance	*ḫpri*	I,357
appearance in glory	*ḫʿw*	I,352
appearances	*ḫʿw*	I,352
appease	*sḥtp*	II,64
applaud	*swꜣš*	II,18
apples	*dpḥw*	II,247
appliqué	*ḏbw*	II,268
apply oneself	*di-ḥr*	II,240
apply oneself	*ḫꜣm*	I,348
appoint	*ʿpr*	I,65
appoint	*nḥb*	I,242
appoint	*ḥn*	I,315
appoint	*ṯs*	II,233
appoint	*dhn*	II,253
appointed contribution	*ḥtr*	I,339
appointed time	*tp-iꜣt*	II,204
appointment	*ṯs*	II,233
apportion	*pš*	I,157
apportion	*sḏ*	II,99
apportion	*dmi*	II,248
apportionment	*pš*	I,157
apportionment	*sḏt*	II,100
appraise	*ṯnf*	II,230
apprehend	*mḥ*	I,197
apprehend	*šfd*	II,121
apprehended	*šꜣfd*	II,109
apprentice	*ḫry-ʿ*	I,387
approach	*pḥ*	I,152
approach	*ḫʿm*	I,353
approach	*ḫʿm*	I,380
approach	*ḫn*	I,381
approach	*ḫnḫn*	I,384
approach	*spr*	II,32
approach	*ḳri*	II,155
approach	*tkn*	II,220
approach	*ṯḥn*	II,232
approacher of crocodiles	*sprw-msḥ*	II,33
appropriate	*iṯi*	I,52
appropriate	*nw(i)*	I,230
appropriate	*nfr*	I,235
appropriate	*gm*	II,188
appropriation	*ḥꜣw*	I,285
approve	*hn*	I,288
apron	*mss*	I,206
apron	*ḥꜣṯt*	I,300
apron	*šndyt*	II,131
apron	*sḏ*	II,100
apropos	*ʿḳꜣ*	I,81
apt	*ʿḳꜣ*	I,81
arable land	*ꜣḫt*	I,8
arable land	*kꜣyt*	II,144

arable tract	ḳꜥḥt	II,146
arbitrate	wḏꜥ	I,122
arbor	ꜥt-nt-ḫt	I,59
archer	pḏty	I,161
archer	snny	II,52
archives	ḫꜣ-n-sš	I,343
archivist	sꜣwty	II,7
ardent	mds	I,218
arduous	(see difficult)	
arduous	sḳsn	II,85
arduous tasks	ḏnn	II,270
arena	bꜣwy	I,126
argue	mdw	I,216
argue	sḏd	II,104
argue	ḏb	II,265
arguments	sḫr	II,73
arise	ꜥḥꜥ	I,75
arise	sḫꜥ	II,68
arm	ꜥ	I,57
arm	ḳꜥḥ	II,146
arm	ḳbyt	II,148
arm	gꜣb	II,148
arm	gb	II,187
armchair	ḳniw	II,153
armies	ḏbiw	II,267
armory	ḫpš	I,358
arm-pit	ḥṯṯ	I,340
arms	ḳni	II,153
army	mšꜥ	I,207
army	mdgt	I,218
army	ḏbiw	II,267
around	m-ḳd	I,171
around	ḥꜣ	I,295
around	šni	II,126
aroura (of land)	sṯꜣt	II,96
arouse	sḫnw	II,75
arrange	nḥb	I,242
arrange	ḥn	I,315
arrange	grg	II,192
arrangement	ntꜥ	I,253
arrangements	sḫr	II,73
arrears	idn-diw	I,54
arrears	wḏꜣ	I,121
arrival	spr	II,32
arrival	thm	II,217
arrive	iw	I,18
arrive	ngi	I,252
arrive	spr	II,32
arrogant	ꜥb	I,63
arrogant	ꜥbꜥ	I,64
arrow	ꜥḥꜣw	I,74
arrow	swnw	II,20
arrow	šsr	II,136
artery	mt	I,213
artisan	rmṯ-ist	I,46
artisans(?)	ḥmww	I,313
arts (of war)	kꜣt	II,167
as	m-r-ꜥ	I,57
as	m	I,167
as	mi	I,178
as a result	m-ḫt	I,376
as a result of	m-ḫt	I,170
as directed	m-nḫb	I,244
as far as	r-šꜣꜥ	I,264
as far as	r-šꜣꜥ	II,107
as follows	m-ḏd	I,173
as follows	m-ḏd	II,275
as for	ir	I,37
as for	m-di	I,171
as for me	nnk	I,239
as often as	r-tnw	I,265
as often as	r-tnw	IV,88
as regards	ir	I,37
as soon as	wnn	I,102
as well	mitt	I,180
as well	m-r-ꜥ	I,260
as well as	m-mitt	I,169
as well as	r-ꜥ	I,260
as while	iw	I,17
ascend	ꜥḥꜥ	I,75
ascent	ṯs	II,235
ascertain	ꜥm	I,66
ascertain	ptr	I,159
ashamed	bḥnr	I,138
ashes	ssfy	II,77
ashes	ḳꜣrmꜥti	II,144
ashes	ḳrmt	II,156
Asiatics	Sttyw	II,96
ask	nḏnḏ	I,257
ask	dbḥ	II,245
ask advice of	nḏnḏ	I,257
ask for	šni	II,127
askew	gwš	II,186
aspect	ꜣbwt	I,5
aspect	inw	I,33
aspect	ḳi	II,146
ass	ꜥꜣ	I,61
ass	ḥꜣmr	I,299
assail	pḥ	I,152
assail	fiṯ	I,164
assail	tkk	II,221
assailant	pḥ	I,153
assailant	thꜣ	II,216
assault (vb.)	hsmḳ	I,292
assault (vb.)	šdꜣ	II,141
assault (vb.)	ḳnḳn	II,155
assemblage	sḥwy	II,62
assemble	nw(i)	I,230
assemble	sꜣḳ	II,9
assemble	snh	II,52
assemble	sḥwy	II,62
assemble	dmḏ	II,249

assembled	*twt*	II,202
assembly	*mw-ꜥḏ*	I,182
assent (vb.)	*wšd*	I,115
assent (vb.)	*ḏd*	II,275
assent to	*hn*	I,288
assert	*ḏd*	II,275
assess	*wꜣḥ*	I,89
assess	*ḥtr*	I,339
assessment	*št*	II,138
assign	*w(ꜣ)ḏ*	I,91
assign	*wḏ*	I,119
assign	*pš*	I,157
assign	*ḥtr*	I,339
assign	*swꜣḏ*	II,18
assign	*swḏ*	II,23
assign	*dhn*	II,253
assignment	*sḥn*	II,63
assist	*imi-ḏrt*	I,26
assist	*mtr*	I,214
assistant	*ꜥḏr*	I,84
assistant	*psdy*	I,156
assistant	*ẖry-ꜥ*	I,387
ass-load	*ꜥꜣt*	I,61
associate	*ḫbr*	I,354
associate	*snsn*	II,54
associate	*ḳrḥ*	II,157
associate with	*snsn*	II,54
associate with	*šbn*	II,117
assorted	*šbn*	II,117
ass's foal	*sk*	II,85
assume	*iri*	I,38
assume	*nbi*	I,233
assume	*ẖnm*	I,383
assume	*ṯꜣy*	II,224
assume (form)	*iri*	I,38
assuredly	*smwn*	II,41
astringent earth	*ḳsnty*	II,159
at	*m*	I,167
at	*r*	I,259
at	*ḫft*	I,359
at all	*iwnꜣ*	I,20
at all	*m-kfꜣ*	I,171
at all	*m-kfꜣ*	II,173
at an end	*ḳn*	II,152
at ease	*nḏm*	I,256
at first	*ẖry-ḥꜣt*	I,386
at head	*r-ḥꜣt*	I,297
at night time	*sḏr*	II,103
at once	*ꜣs*	I,9
at once	*m-tꜣ-wnwt*	I,101
at once	*m-tꜣ-wnwt*	I,171
at once	*ḥr-ꜥ*	I,321
at one's disposal	*m-di*	I,171
at peace	*ḥtp*	I,337
at the beginning	*m-ḥꜣt*	I,296
at the side of	*r gs*	II,194
at the time of	*ḫy-r-ꜥ*	I,351
attach	*dmi*	II,248
attach oneself	*nḏr*	I,257
attack	*ꜣw(i)*	I,2
attack	*ihy*	I,42
attack	*pḥ*	I,152
attack	*nḫnḫ*	I,245
attack	*hꜣ(i)*	I,283
attack	*hd*	I,293
attack	*šfꜥ*	II,120
attack	*thm*	II,217
attack	*tkn*	II,220
attack	*ṯs*	II,233
attack (n.)	*hd*	I,293
attacker	*pḥ*	I,153
attain	*ḫpr*	I,356
attain	*ššp*	II,135
attend	*ꜥḥꜥ*	I,75
attend	*ḳri*	II,155
attend to	*smtr*	II,45
attendant	*ḫnmw*	I,363
attendant	*šmsw*	II,125
attention	*ib*	I,22
attention	*ḥr*	I,320
attentive	*wꜣḥ-ib*	I,90
attentive	*bꜥ*	I,131
attentive	*mḥ msḏr*	I,197
attentive	*rs-tp*	I,277
attest	*mtr*	I,214
attest	*rḫ*	I,275
attire	*ḥbs*	I,308
attire (vb.)	*ḏbꜣ*	II,266
attitude	*sḫr*	II,73
attract	*stꜣ*	II,92
audience chamber	*ꜥḫnwty*	I,78
audience hall	*st-sḏmyw*	II,102
aught	*nkt*	I,251
augment	*swr*	II,20
august	*šps*	II,118
aunt	*snt-nt-mwt*	II,48
authorities	*ḥwtyw*	I,305
authority	*st ḥr*	II,2
authority	*sḫr*	II,72
authority	*šfyt*	II,120
authorize	*sḥn*	II,62
avarice	*ꜥwn-ib*	I,63
avaricious	*šw-ꜥw*	II,113
avenge	*ꜥn-wšb*	I,68
avenge	*wšb*	I,114
avenue	*swtwt*	II,23
avert	*ꜥn(n)*	I,68
avert	*msnḥ*	I,205
avert	*spḥ*	II,33
avert	*sḫr*	II,64
avert	*sḫni*	II,71
aviary	*hmw*	I,288

await	*ꜥḥꜥ*	I,75
awaiting	*r-ḥꜣt*	I,263
awake	*mnhs*	I,188
awake	*rs*	I,277
awaken	*snhs*	II,53
award	*wḏꜥ*	I,122
aware	*ꜥm*	I,66
aware	*ꜥnẖ*	I,70
away	*bnr*	I,134
away	*r-bnr*	I,134
away from here	*rwty*	I,268
awe	*nrw*	I,239
awe	*ḥryt*	I,327
awe	*šfyt*	II,119
awe	*šfšf*	II,120
awestruck	*šfyt*	II,120
awful	*bin*	I,131
awfulness	*šfyt*	II,119
awl	*sꜣḥw*	II,9
awning	*ḥtꜣw*	I,335
axe	*bšꜣ*	I,140
axe	*mrnbi*	I,194

B

ba	*bꜣ*	I,125
baboon	*ꜣꜥꜥn*	I,2
baby boy	*ꜥḏdi sri*	I,85
baby boy	*ꜥḏdi sri*	II,132
back	*ꜣt*	I,1
back	*iꜣt*	I,11
back	*pḥwy*	I,153
back	*psd*	I,156
back	*ḫꜣ*	I,295
back	*sꜣ*	II,4
back	*ḏrww*	II,273
back land	*pḥww*	I,153
back of head	*mkḫꜣ*	I,211
back of head	*ḫꜣ*	I,295
back of the hand	*ḳḏt*	II,162
back parts	*kfꜣ*	II,173
back up	*m-sꜣ*	II,5
backbone	*ꜣt*	I,1
backcountry	*pḥww*	I,153
background	*ḳꜣi*	II,143
backwater	*pḥww*	I,153
bad	*bin*	I,131
bad	*nbḏ*	I,234
bad	*sn-nw*	II,49
bad	*stf*	II,95
bad dreams	*snḏw*	II,55
bad side	*iꜣby*	I,13
badness	*ḏw(t)*	II,265
bag	*ꜥrf*	I,73
bag	*mḫrt*	I,202
bag	*ẖrd*	I,373
bag	*krf*	II,156
bag	*ṯnfyt*	II,230
baggage	*ḳniw*	II,154
bags	*rpw*	I,270
bags	*šnw*	II,127
bail out	*pnḳ*	I,149
bake	*pfsy*	I,148
bake	*ps*	I,155
bake	*mgr*	I,212
bake	*kfn*	II,150
bake	*gꜣf*	II,185
baked good	*ꜥgs*	I,82
baker	*ps*	I,155
baker	*rtḥty*	I,280
balance	*iwsw*	I,21
balance	*mꜥḫꜣt*	I,182
balance	*mn*	I,184
balance	*mḫꜣt*	I,201
balance (vb.)	*mḫꜣ*	I,201
balance due	*wḏꜣ*	I,121
balcony	*sšd*	II,83
bald	*is*	I,45

baldness	(see lack of hair)	
ba-like creatures	*bꜣyw*	I,125
balk at	*ḥḏn*	I,342
ball	*ḥmꜣ*	I,312
ball of yarn	*ḥpt*	I,309
balsam	*bki*	I,141
bandage	*ptr*	I,159
bandage (vb.)	*wt*	I,116
bandage (vb.)	*nwḥ*	I,231
bandages	*wt*	I,116
bandages	*pry*	I,151
bandages	*pdr*	I,160
banish	*rwỉ*	I,267
banish	*sḥr*	II,64
banish	*sẖr*	II,72
banish	*dr*	II,252
banished	*dd*	II,257
bank	*idb*	I,54
bank	*wꜣt*	I,88
bank	*wḏb*	I,123
bank	*mryt*	I,193
bank	*ḫꜣpw*	I,348
bank	*spt*	II,31
bank	*dbwy*	II,245
banking on	*m-ḫrt-n*	I,170
bar (n.)	*nbꜣ*	I,233
bar from	*ḫnr*	I,365
barber	*ẖꜥḳ*	I,381
bare	*ḥꜣy*	I,295
barge	*ꜥ-n-sẖw*	I,58
barge	*wiꜣ*	I,92
barge	*wsḫ*	I,112
barge	*mnš*	I,189
barges	*ḳwrw*	II,147
barges (corn)	*ḳrr*	II,157
bark	*imw*	I,29
bark	*sšm*	II,81
bark (vb.)	*bḥn*	I,138
bark shrine	*st wrt*	II,2
bark, sacred	*nšmt*	I,250
barley	*it*	I,50
barley	*šrit*	II,132
barley (U.E.)	*it šmꜥw*	II,122
barley field	*sꜥr*	II,14
barley meal	*šꜥt*	II,110
barn	*šnwt*	II,130
barracks	*ṯpg*	II,229
barren	*wšr*	I,115
barter	*šwyt*	II,114
basalt(?)	*bḫnw*	I,139
base	*pḥwy*	I,153
base	*dbyt*	II,245
base (of statue)	*p*	I,145
base (of triangle)	*tp-r*	II,205
base(?)	*nst*	I,247

basin	*ipip*	I,25
basin	*itr*	I,51
basin	*mḫnmt*	I,202
basin	*ḥn(t)*	I,320
basin	*ḫꜣꜥ-mḥ*	I,347
basin	*ẖnmt*	I,384
basin, large	*iknw*	I,50
basis	*snwy*	II,49
basket	*irḳs*	I,42
basket	*ꜥrḳ*	I,74
basket	*wdnw*	I,118
basket	*pdr*	I,160
basket	*mnḏm*	I,191
basket	*mḫr*	I,202
basket	*msti*	I,206
basket	*mgsp*	I,212
basket	*mḏt*	I,219
basket	*ḥtp*	I,336
basket	*ḫꜥw*	I,353
basket	*šꜣkꜣrꜥ*	II,110
basket	*škrꜥ*	II,137
basket	*krḥt*	II,176
basket	*kskst*	II,178
basket	*gꜣbw*	II,184
basket	*ṯḫbst*	II,218
basket	*ṯꜣy*	II,224
basket	*dnit*	II,250
basket maker	*ir-ḥtp*	I,39
basket(?)	*krs*	II,176
basket(?)	*ṯnfyt*	II,230
basketry	*ḥtr*	I,339
basketry	*škrꜥ*	II,137
baskets	*r-ꜥ-n-ḥtpw*	I,260
bastinado	*bḏn*	I,143
bastion	*ṯsmw*	II,236
bathe	*wꜥb*	I,94
bathe with light	*wrḥ*	I,105
baton	*ꜥwnt*	I,63
baton	*šwbt*	II,115
battalion	*iwꜥyt*	I,19
battalion	*ṯst*	II,235
batter	*isp*	I,46
batter (vb.)	*wꜣš*	I,91
batter (vb.)	*wšwš*	I,114
batter (vb.)	*hdhd*	I,293
battle	*ꜥḥꜣ*	I,74
battle	*ḫrw*	I,372
battle	*ski*	II,86
battle	*šnṯt*	II,131
battle cry	*hmhm(t)*	I,288
battle line	*skw*	II,86
battlefield	*bꜣwy*	I,126
battlefield	*pri*	I,151
battlefield	*pgꜣ*	I,158
battlefield	*ḥpḳ*	I,308
battlements	*ṯsmw*	II,236

bay (vb.)	*bḥn*	I,138
be	*wn*	I,100
be	*ḫpr*	I,356
beach	*spt*	II,31
bead	*inhm*	I,34
bead maker	*nšdy*	I,250
beads	*bḥbḥyw*	I,138
beads	*smdt*	II,46
beads	*šbb*	II,117
beaker	*ṯbw*	II,228
beam	*iṯyn*	I,53
beam	*sꜣy*	II,5
beam	*smkt*	II,45
beams	*iswt*	I,46
beams	*sꜣt*	II,10
beams	*sbw*	II,24
beans	*iwry*	I,21
beans	*pri*	I,151
bear	*ṯꜣy*	II,224
bear (n.)	*ḥtmt*	I,338
bear (vb.)	*ꜣtp*	I,10
bear (vb.)	*fꜣy*	I,163
bear (vb.)	*msi*	I,204
bear away	*ḥꜣḳ*	I,299
bear with	*ꜥḥꜥ*	I,75
bear witness	*mtr*	I,214
bearer	*fꜣy*	I,163
bearer	*ḥry*	I,386
bearer	*ṯꜣw*	II,226
bearing	*ḥry*	I,386
beat	*ḥwi*	I,303
beat	*sḫ*	II,65
beat	*sḳr*	II,84
beat	*sd*	II,98
beat	*ḳnḳn*	II,155
beaten (work)	*ḳmꜣ*	II,150
beaten	*ḳnḳn*	II,155
beatitude	*imꜣḫ*	I,29
beauteous	*ꜥn*	I,67
beautiful	*im(ꜣ)*	I,29
beautiful	*ꜥn*	I,67
beautiful	*nfr*	I,235
beautiful encounter	*ṯḫn-nfr*	II,232
beautiful of face	*nfr-ḥr*	I,236
beautify	*sꜣḫ*	II,9
beauty	*ꜣbwt*	I,5
beauty	*ꜥn(w)t*	I,67
beauty	*nfrw*	I,236
because	*pꜣ-wn*	I,145
because of	*n-ꜣbw*	I,4
because of	*m-di*	I,171
because of	*m-ḏr*	I,172
because of	*m-ḏrt*	I,172
because of	*n*	I,223
because of	*n-ꜣbw*	I,223
because of	*r-ḥꜣt*	I,263
because of	*m-ḏr*	II,271
because of the fact	*n-ꜣbw*	I,4
because of the fact	*n-ꜣbw*	I,223
become	*iri*	I,37
become	*ḫpr*	I,355
bed	*ḥꜥti*	I,302
bed	*ḥnkyt*	I,320
bed	*ḥtꜥ*	I,336
bed	*st sḏr*	II,3
bed	*st-sḏr*	II,103
bed	*krkỉ*	II,177
bedizened	*ḥṯ*	I,339
bedouin	*iwntyw*	I,20
bedouin	*šꜣsw*	II,109
bedridden	*sḏr*	II,102
bedroom(?)	*ḥnkyt*	I,320
bee keeper	*bity*	I,129
beer	*nbty*	I,234
beer	*ḥnḳt*	I,319
beer	*tḫ*	II,218
beer jar	*inḫt*	I,35
beer jug	*ꜥš*	I,79
beer jug	*ds*	II,255
beeswax	*mnḥ*	I,188
beetle	*ꜥpšt*	I,65
befall	*ḫpr-m-di*	I,356
befall	*dmi*	II,248
befit	*dmi*	II,248
before	*m-bꜣḥ*	I,126
before	*m-bꜣḥ*	I,168
before	*n-ḥꜣt*	I,224
before	*n-ḥr*	I,225
before	*n-ḫft-ḥr*	I,225
before	*r-r*	I,263
before	*r-ḥꜣt*	I,263
before	*r-ḥr*	I,263
before	*r-ḥr-n*	I,263
before	*r-ḥrw*	I,263
before	*r-ḫft-ḥr*	I,264
before	*ḥr-ḥꜣt*	I,297
before	*n-ḥr*	I,321
before	*r-ḥr*	I,321
before	*ḫft-ḥr*	I,359
before	*n-ḫft-ḥr*	I,359
before	*ḫnty*	I,367
before	*ḫr*	I,369
before	*ḥr-ḥꜣt*	I,385
before	*tp-ꜥ*	II,205
before	*ḏr-ꜥ*	II,271
before	*ḏr-bꜣḥ*	II,271
before hand	*ḥry-ḥꜣt*	I,386
befriend	*im(ꜣ)*	I,29
befriend	*snsn*	II,54
beg	*dbḥ*	II,245
beg for peace	*šrm*	II,133
beg peace	*šrm*	II,133

beget	*wtt*	I,117
beget	*pꜣy*	I,146
beget	*msi*	I,204
beget	*nwḥ*	I,231
begetter	*wtt*	I,117
begin	*mḥ*	I,197
begin	*ḫpr*	I,356
begin	*šꜣꜥ*	II,107
beginning	*wpw*	I,98
beginning	*msḫn(t)*	I,206
beginning	*ḥꜣt*	I,296
beginning	*ḥꜣty-ꜥ*	I,298
beginning	*sp-tp*	II,30
beginning	*šꜣꜥ*	II,107
beginning (of a date in time)	*šsp*	II,136
beginning from	*r-šꜣꜥ*	I,264
beginning from	*šꜣꜥ-m*	II,107
beginning of the year	*tpy-rnpt*	II,207
beginning of time	*pꜣwt-tpt*	I,146
behavior	*sḫr*	II,73
behind	*pḥ-n*	I,153
behind	*m-ḫt*	I,170
behind	*m-sꜣ*	I,171
behind	*n-ḥꜣ*	I,224
behind	*ḥꜣ*	I,295
behind	*n-ḥꜣ*	I,295
behind	*ḥr-pḥwy*	I,322
behind	*m-sꜣ*	II,5
behold	*ptr*	I,159
behold	*mꜣꜣ*	I,173
behold	*ḫf*	I,358
behold	*gmḥ*	II,189
behold	*dgꜣ*	II,256
being	*m*	I,167
belabor with	*ḫnm*	I,363
believe	*ib*	I,23
believe	*nḥ*	I,241
bellow	*dniwt*	II,250
bellow (vb.)	*bḥn*	I,138
bellow (vb.)	*swh*	II,21
bellow out	*nḥd*	I,244
belly	*ḫt*	I,379
belong to	*snbꜣ*	II,50
belonging to	*n*	I,223
belonging to	*nꜣy*	I,226
belonging to	*tꜣ*	II,197
belonging to him	*sꜣwy*	II,7
belongings	*ḫrt*	I,385
belongs to	*ny-sw*	I,227
belongs to	*n(y)-sw*	I,247
belongs to	*hnw*	I,289
beloved	*mri*	I,192
belt	*istn*	I,48
belt	*ꜥgs*	I,82
Benben	*bnbn*	I,134
bench	*pit*	I,147
bend	*pnꜥ*	I,148
bend	*hn*	I,288
bend	*hnn*	I,289
bend	*hd*	I,292
bend	*ḫꜣb*	I,348
bend	*ḫꜣm*	I,348
bend	*ḫnd*	I,368
bend	*ḳꜥh*	II,146
bend	*gsꜣ*	II,194
bend down	*sn-tꜣ*	II,49
bend the back	*hn*	I,288
beneath	*ḫr*	I,385
benefaction	*ḫnw-nfr*	I,363
benefactions	*ꜣḫw*	I,7
benefactions	*mnḫw*	I,189
benefactions	*nfr*	I,236
beneficent	*mnḫ*	I,189
beneficial	*ꜣḫ*	I,7
benefit	*ꜣḫw*	I,7
benefit	*ḫnw-nfr*	I,363
benefit	*kꜣ*	II,165
bent	*gwš*	II,186
bequeath	*rdi*	I,281
bequeath	*swḏ*	II,24
bequest	*swḏ*	II,24
beryl	*brgt*	I,137
beside	*r-gs*	I,265
beside	*r gs*	II,194
beside	*r gswy*	II,194
besides	*ihꜣ*	I,42
besides	*m-ḫꜣw*	I,169
besides	*m-di*	I,171
besides	*ḫr*	I,368
best	*tpy*	II,207
best	*tpty*	II,208
best of the lands	*tp-ḫꜣswt*	II,206
best oils(?)	*ḥꜣtt*	I,298
bestow life	*sꜥnḫ*	II,14
betimes	*r-nw*	I,262
between	*imy*	I,27
between	*m*	I,167
between	*n*	I,223
between	*r-iwd*	I,260
beverage	*iwry*	I,21
beverage	*dbyt*	II,245
beware of	*sꜣw*	II,6
beware!	*sꜣw*	II,6
bewitchment	*ḥkꜣ*	I,334
beyond	*wꜣi*	I,87
beyond	*m-ḥꜣt*	I,170
bg-fish	*bg*	I,141
bidding	*mrwt*	I,193
bier	*nmi*	I,237
big	*ꜥꜣ(i)*	I,59

big toe	*sꜣḥ*	II,8
bind	*ʿrḳ*	I,73
bind	*wʿf*	I,95
bind	*mr*	I,191
bind	*nwḥ*	I,231
bind	*snḥ*	II,53
bind	*ḳꜣs*	II,145
bind	*ḳbs*	II,149
bind	*gwtn*	II,186
bind	*tis*	II,201
bind	*ṯs*	II,233
bind fast	*snḥ*	II,53
bind together	*gwtn*	II,186
bind together	*dmꜣ*	II,248
birch	*bḏn*	I,143
birch (torture instrument)	*ḏnḏn*	II,270
bird	*ꜣpd*	I,6
bird	*iry-pt*	I,39
bird	*irtḏr*	I,42
bird	*ʿḫy*	I,77
bird	*msrt*	I,205
bird	*ḥꜣyt*	I,295
bird	*skm*	II,87
bird	*ḳni*	II,154
bird	*gry*	II,191
bird	*drt*	II,253
bird(?)	*ḏpr*	II,268
bird of the marshes	*ḳbḥ*	II,149
bird pool	*sšy*	II,79
bird type	*ḥꜣyt*	I,295
birds	*ḥriw*	I,323
birth	*msyt*	I,204
birth brick	*dbt*	II,244
birth place	*msḫn(t)*	I,206
biscuit	*ibšt*	I,24
biscuits	*ipt*	I,25
bite	*psḥ*	I,156
bite	*dp*	II,246
bite into	*dp m*	II,246
bit-loaves	*bi(ꜣ)t*	I,129
bit-pastry	*bi(ꜣ)t*	I,129
bitter	*mr*	I,191
bitter	*dḥr*	II,254
bitter gall	*sḫwy*	II,68
bivouac	*sḏrt*	II,103
black	*km*	II,174
black cattle	*kmyt*	II,174
black ibis	*gmt*	II,189
black pigment	*ḏʿbw*	II,264
black stone	*msḏmt*	I,207
blacken	*skm*	II,87
blade	*spꜣ*	II,32
blade	*gb*	II,187
blade	*dm(t)*	II,247
blame	*ḏbʿ*	II,267

blast	*hh*	I,292
blaze (vb.)	*nbi*	I,233
blepharitis	*ḥt*	I,335
bless	*sꜣḫ*	II,9
blessed dead	*mꜣʿtyw*	I,175
blessed dead	*ḥstyw*	I,331
blessed ones	*ḥsy*	I,330
blessed spirits	*mꜣʿtyw*	I,175
blessed state	*imꜣḫ*	I,29
blessings	*ḥst*	I,331
blind	*kꜣmn*	II,169
blind	*km*	II,174
blind (n.)	*kꜣmm*	II,169
blind (trans. vb.)	*kꜣmn*	II,169
blind man	*kꜣmm*	II,169
blindfolded	*ʿfnw*	I,65
blindness	*ʿfnw*	I,65
blindness	*kꜣmn*	II,169
blink	*ṯnḥ*	II,230
block (vb.)	*sdb*	II,98
block (vb.)	*šr*	II,131
block (vb.)	*ḏꜣi*	II,260
block (vb.)	*ḏbꜣ*	II,266
block up	*šr*	II,131
block up	*dni*	II,249
block up	*dni*	II,249
blocked off	*dbit*	II,244
blood	*snf*	II,50
blood vessel	*mt*	I,213
blood-relation	*snf*	II,51
bloom (vb.)	*ꜣḫꜣḫ*	I,8
bloom (vb.)	*prḫ*	I,152
blossom	*nḥbt*	I,243
blossom (vb.)	*ꜣḫꜣḫ*	I,8
blossoms	*ḏḏ*	II,277
blot out	*sswn*	II,76
blow	*nfy*	I,235
blow	*ḫḫ*	I,373
blow	*sḫ*	II,66
blows	*ḳnḳn*	II,155
blunt	*sfḫ*	II,36
blusterings	*ḫnrw*	I,365
board	*mr(y)t*	I,194
board	*sṯꜣt*	II,96
boards	*iswt*	I,46
boards	*sbw*	II,24
boast	*shꜣ*	II,60
boast (vb.)	*ʿbʿ*	I,64
boast (vb.)	*swh*	II,21
boastful	*ʿbʿ*	I,64
boasting	*ʿbʿ*	I,64
boat	*imw*	I,29
boat	*ihyt-mrw*	I,42
boat	*ʿḥʿw*	I,76
boat	*wiꜣ*	I,92
boat	*wsḫ*	I,112

boat	*msti*	I,206
boat	*sktt*	II,88
boat	*ḳrr*	II,157
boat	*kꜣr*	II,169
boat	*kr*	II,175
boat	*ṯrt*	II,231
boat part	*mšš*	I,209
boat part	*ḏpḥ*	II,268
boatbuilding workshop	*wḫrt*	I,110
boatman	*mḫnty*	I,202
boatmen	*ḫni*	I,382
bodies	*ẖt*	I,379
bodily	*n ẖt.f*	I,379
body	*ꜥt*	I,58
body	*ḥꜥw*	I,301
body	*ḥꜥt*	I,301
body	*ẖt*	I,379
body	*ḏt*	II,259
body armor	*ṯrn*	II,231
body of water	*sgbyn*	II,89
body of water	*ḳbḥw*	II,149
bodyguard	*šmsw*	II,125
boil (n.)	*ḫsd*	I,375
boiled	*ps*	I,155
boiler	*ps*	I,155
bold	*mn-ib*	I,23
bold	*mn-ib*	I,184
boldly	*m-wstnw*	I,113
boldness	*stnw*	II,95
bolt	*ḳꜣr*	II,144
bolt	*ḳri*	II,156
bolts (?)	*sswt*	II,76
bondage	*iṯr*	I,53
bonds	*ḳḥ*	II,158
bonds	*mḫꜣ*	I,201
bone	*ḳs*	II,159
book	*mḏꜣt*	I,219
book	*sbꜣyt*	II,27
book	*šfdw*	II,121
book case	*ṯꜣy-drf*	II,224
book of instruction	*sbꜣyt*	II,27
books	*sš*	II,78
boomerang	*skꜣyḳt*	II,84
boomerang	*šp*	II,118
boon	*ḥtpt*	I,338
boon which the king gives	*ḥtp-di-nsw*	I,337
booth	*imw*	I,29
booty	*ḥꜣkw*	I,300
border	*spt*	II,31
border	*smdt*	II,46
bore	*wtnw*	I,116
bore	*sd*	II,98
boring	*wtnw*	I,116
born of	*mstiwty*	I,205
both together	*m-pꜣ-s-snw*	II,48
both...and	*m...m*	I,168
bother	*ḏḏ*	II,277
bother (with)	*ꜣty*	I,9
bottom	*ḫrw*	I,387
bottom of the Two Lands	*kfꜣ-tꜣwy*	II,173
boughs	*srdm*	II,60
boulders	*dḫwt*	II,255
bouncing	*šꜣp*	II,109
bouncing	*šp*	II,118
bound	*ḫꜣpw*	I,348
boundary	*tꜣš*	II,199
bound-captive	*sḳr-ꜥnḫ*	II,85
bounty	*kꜣw*	II,166
bounty	*ṯtf*	II,237
bow	*pḏt*	I,161
bow	*šmrt*	II,124
bow (of a ship)	*ḥꜣt*	I,296
bow (vb.)	*wꜣḥ-tp*	I,90
bow (vb.)	*wšd*	I,115
bow (vb.)	*hnn*	I,289
bow (vb.)	*ḫꜣb*	I,348
bow down	*hn*	I,288
bow down	*sn-tꜣ*	II,49
bow down	*dhn*	II,253
bow low	*dhn*	II,253
bow string	*rwḏ*	I,268
bowing	*ksy*	II,178
bowl	*iꜥ*	I,16
bowl	*ynr*	I,34
bowl	*ꜥ*	I,58
bowl	*ḫꜣwy*	I,346
bowl	*ḫnty*	I,367
bowl	*gꜣy*	II,183
bowl	*ṯbw*	II,228
bowl	*dydy*	II,241
bowl	*dnit*	II,250
bowl	*dd(t)*	II,258
bowl, large	*iknw*	I,50
bowman	*pḏty*	I,161
bowmen	*iwntyw*	I,20
box	*ꜥ-n tbw*	I,57
box	*ꜥfdt*	I,65
box	*bꜣnyny*	I,126
box	*pds*	I,160
box	*mhn*	I,196
box	*mḫr*	I,202
box	*hn*	I,288
box	*hrit*	I,290
box	*hdm*	I,293
box	*gꜣwt*	II,184
box	*gꜣt*	II,186
box	*gꜣtr*	II,186
box	*gtr*	II,195
box	*ṯꜣy*	II,224

box	*db(t)*	II,244
boy	*iḥwn*	I,44
boy	*ꜥḏd*	I,84
boy	*nḫn*	I,245
boy	*ẖrd*	I,388
boy	*sꜣ*	II,3
boy	*sfy*	II,35
brace (vb.)	*mḥ*	I,197
bracelet	*šꜣḳw*	II,110
bracelets	*šḳw*	II,137
bracelets	*krmt*	II,176
brackish	*šns*	II,131
braided	(see plaited)	
braiding	*nbd*	I,234
braiding	*šš*	II,137
brambles	*ḳḏw*	II,162
brambles(?)	*nḥ*	I,242
branches	*srḥꜣt*	II,59
branches	*štꜣ*	II,138
branches	*ḳmꜣḥ*	II,151
branches	*ḏnr*	II,270
brand (vb.)	*ꜣb*	I,4
brand marks	*ꜣbw*	I,4
branded	*mnš*	I,189
brander	*ṯꜣy-ꜣbw*	I,4
brander of cattle	*ṯꜣy-ꜣbw*	II,224
branding iron	*ꜣbw*	I,4
brass(?)	*ḥmt*	I,314
brave	*ḳni*	II,152
brave (vb.)	*wstn*	I,113
brave deeds	*pḥtyw*	I,154
brave deeds	*ḳnw*	II,152
bravery	(see courage)	
brazier	*ꜥḫ*	I,77
bread	*ibšt*	I,24
bread	*ꜥḳ*	I,80
bread	*nẖt*	I,247
bread	*rḥs*	I,275
bread	*rdrd*	I,282
bread	*sꜥb*	II,13
bread	*ḳḏḏ*	II,163
bread	*t*	II,197
bread	*ty*	II,201
bread	*ṯrr*	II,231
bread(?)	*ḫꜣd*	I,350
bread-rations	*ꜥḳ*	I,80
breadth	*wsḫt*	I,112
break	*prṯ*	I,152
break	*ngi*	I,252
break	*ḥḏ*	I,340
break	*sꜣw*	II,7
break	*sd*	II,97
break	*sḏ*	II,99
break	*šꜥd*	II,112
break	*šdi*	II,140
break in	*ꜣw(i)*	I,2
break into	*fḫ*	I,165
break off	*sꜣw*	II,7
break open	*prš*	I,152
break out	*ḫꜣꜥ*	I,346
break out	*šp*	II,118
break through	*wtnw*	I,116
break through	*ḫm*	I,360
break up	*wšwš*	I,114
break up	*swh*	II,21
breast	*mnd*	I,191
breast	*msdt*	I,207
breast	*šnbt*	II,130
breast	*ḳꜣbt*	II,144
breast	*ḳbyt*	II,148
breath	*ṯꜣw*	II,226
breathe	*ḫnp*	I,363
breathe	*ḫnm*	I,363
breathe	*sn*	II,49
breathe	*srḳ*	II,59
breathe	*ssny*	II,77
breathe	*tpi*	II,207
breathe	*tpr*	II,209
breathing space	*srf*	II,58
bred	*rnn*	I,274
breeding cow	*bꜣkꜣ*	I,128
breeding cow	*bk*	I,141
breeze	*mꜣꜥw*	I,175
breeze	*mḥyt*	I,199
breezes	*ṯꜣw*	II,226
brethren	*sn*	II,47
brewer	*ꜥtḫ*	I,82
brewery	*ꜥt-ḥ(n)ḳt*	I,59
bribe	*fḳꜣw*	I,165
bribe	*ḫt*	I,343
bribe	*ḫrt*	I,371
bribes	*ḫsyw*	I,374
brick	*dbt*	II,244
bricks (of natron)	*dbt*	II,244
bridewealth	*gꜣwt*	II,184
brier wood	*štꜣ*	II,138
briers	*bnsꜣḥ*	I,135
bright	*wbḫ*	I,97
bright	*bꜣḳ*	I,127
bright	*bḳꜣ*	I,141
bright	*ḳḥ*	II,158
bright, make	*ḥḏ*	I,341
brighten	*wbn*	I,97
brighten	*sḥḏ*	II,65
brightness	*sšpt*	II,80
brilliant	*wbḫ*	I,97
brimstone	*kbrt*	II,172
bring	*imi*	I,26
bring	*ini*	I,31
bring	*iṯꜣ*	I,53
bring	*ms*	I,203
bring	*ḫrp*	I,372

bring	*stꜣ*	II,92
bring	*šdi*	II,141
bring a plaint against	*smi*	II,40
bring back	*ini*	I,31
bring back	*ꜥn(n)*	I,68
bring contentment	*shr*	II,60
bring contentment	*shr-ib*	II,60
bring down	*shꜣ*	II,60
bring forth	*ini r-ḫft-ḥr*	I,32
bring forth	*bsi*	I,139
bring into being	*msi*	I,204
bring into being	*sḫpr*	II,69
bring offerings	*wdn*	I,118
bring to an end	*skm*	II,87
bring to an end	*ḳn*	II,151
bring to completion	*sꜥrḳ*	II,15
bring to land	*mni*	I,185
bring to naught	*wsf*	I,111
bring to port	*mni*	I,185
bring up	*ini… r ḥry*	I,32
bring up	*sbꜣ*	II,26
bring up	*sḫpr*	II,69
bring up	*šdi*	II,140
bringer of wood	*in ḫt*	I,32
brink	*spt*	II,31
broad	*wsḫ*	I,112
broad hall	*wsḫt*	I,112
broil	*mgr*	I,212
broken	*sꜣyt*	II,6
broken up(?)	*ptt*	I,159
bronze	*ḥmt*	I,314
bronze	*ḥsmn*	I,333
bronze	*tn-nbw*	II,213
bronze (black)	*ḥmt-kmt*	I,315
bronze object?	*ḫry-wḏꜥ*	I,387
bronze vessel	*ꜥ-n-ḫꜥw*	I,57
brook	*nḫr(n)*	I,245
brook	*ḥmkꜣti*	I,314
brother	*sn*	II,47
brother	*sn-nw*	II,48
brotherhood	*snsn*	II,54
brother-in-law	*sn*	II,48
brow	*ḥꜣt*	I,297
brown(?) (vb.)	*stꜣstꜣ*	II,93
bruise (vb.)	*wšwš*	I,114
bruised	*sꜣyt*	II,6
brush	*isbr*	I,46
brush	*kꜣkꜣ*	II,170
brush	*kk*	II,179
brush (?)	*sw-m-stt*	II,17
brush aside	*wꜣḫ-r-tꜣ*	I,90
bubalis	*sšꜣ*	II,80
bubalis	*šsꜣ*	II,135
bubonic plague(?)	*tꜣ-nt-ꜥꜣmw*	II,198
bucket	*bs*	I,139
bucket	*ḫꜥw*	I,353
build	*iri*	I,38
build	*mḏḥ*	I,220
build	*ḫws*	I,354
build	*sꜥḥꜥ*	II,15
build	*ḳd*	II,160
build up	*ḫws*	I,354
build (me) up	*r-ḳd.i*	II,160
builder	*iḳd*	I,49
builders	*ḳd*	II,160
building job	*ꜥ-n-ḳd*	I,57
bulb	*ḏꜣḏꜣ*	II,262
bulbs (?)	*sḫrrt*	II,76
bull	*ḳmꜣ*	II,151
bull	*kꜣ*	II,165
bull calf	*ḥr-sꜣ-m*	I,323
bull, long horned	*ngꜣw*	I,252
bullock	*ḥr-sꜣ-m*	I,323
bullocks	*ḥrs*	I,328
bull's hide	*ḫnt-kꜣ*	I,381
bully	*nḫt*	I,246
bulti-fish	*in*	I,31
bulwark	*sbty*	II,30
bulwark(?)	*ḫꜣyt*	I,379
bunch	*mr*	I,192
bunch	*nꜥḥ*	I,229
bunch	*ḥtp(y)*	I,337
bundle	*mr*	I,192
bundle	*nꜥḥ*	I,229
bundle	*ḥtp(y)*	I,337
bundle	*ḫrr*	I,373
bundle	*ḳniw*	II,154
bundle	*gꜣwt*	II,184
bundles	*ḫrš*	I,373
bundles	*krḫt*	II,176
bundles of palm leaves	*ṯꜣt*	II,226
bundles of sedge	*šmꜥt-ḥtp*	II,123
burdeners	*sbtyw*	II,30
burdensome	*wdn*	I,118
burdensome	*dns*	II,251
bureau	*is*	I,45
bureau	*ḫꜣ*	I,343
bureau	*st*	II,2
burial	*smꜣ-tꜣ*	II,38
burial	*ḳrst*	II,158
burial chamber	*is*	I,45
burial chamber	*hꜣytt*	I,285
burial chamber	*htt*	I,292
burial chamber	*ḳrrt*	II,157
burial chamber	*st-ḳrs*	II,158
burial equipment	*ḫry-mrḥ*	I,387
burial ground	(see necropolis)	
burial ground	*sḫt*	II,67
burial-priest	*smꜣ-tꜣ*	II,38

buri-fish	*ꜥdw*	I,83
burin	*bsnt*	I,140
burn	*išf*	I,48
burn	*wbd*	I,97
burn	*nwẖ*	I,231
burn	*rḥ*	I,274
burn	*stꜣstꜣ*	II,93
burn up	*mẖꜣ*	I,201
burning	*wps*	I,99
burning	*šm(m)*	II,124
burning	*ḏꜣf*	II,262
bury	*sḥꜣp*	II,61
bury	*ḳrs*	II,157
bury	*tms*	II,211
bury	*ṯms*	II,229
bushel	*ḥḳꜣt*	I,334
bushel	*krḥt*	II,176
bushes	*bꜣi(t)*	I,126
bushes	*šꜣ*	II,105
bushes	*šfnw*	II,120
business	*wpwt*	I,99
business	*mẖrw*	I,202
business	*mdt*	I,217
business	*st ḏrt*	II,3
business	*sḥn*	II,63
business	*sšr*	II,81
business	*šm*	II,122
business partner	*ẖbr*	I,354
busy	*mḥ*	I,197
busy	*sḥn*	II,63
but	*ẖr-ir*	I,37
but	*wpw*	I,99
but	*wpw-ḥr*	I,99
but	*m-r-ꜥ*	I,169
but	*ḥrw*	I,327
but	*ẖr*	I,368
but	*ẖr-bn*	I,369
but	*swt*	II,23
but	*ẖr-swt*	II,23
but as for you	*ḥrw-r*	I,327
butcher	*mnḥ*	I,188
butcher	*sft*	II,36
butcher (vb.)	*wꜥwꜥ*	I,94
butchering	*ẖryt*	I,370
butler	*wbꜣ*	I,96
butler	*wdpw*	I,117
butler tasting the wine	*wbꜣ dp irp*	I,41
buttocks	*pḥt*	I,153
buttocks	*ẖpd*	I,358
buy	*ini*	I,31
buy	*swn*	II,17
buy	*šsp*	II,135
buyer	*mẖr*	I,201
by	*in*	I,31
by	*m*	I,167
by	*m-ḏrt*	I,172
by	*n*	I,223
by	*ḥr*	I,321
By Amun!	*wꜣḥ*	I,89
by golly!	*i-ḏd nb ꜥnẖ.ti*	I,233
by himself	*tp.f ḏs.f*	II,204
by itself	*r-ḥꜥt.*	I,263
by no means	*m-biꜣ*	I,129
by permission of	*m-dd*	I,172
by reason of	*n*	I,223
by way of interest	*r-msy*	I,204
by yourself	*ḥr-tp.k*	I,321
By!	*wꜣḥ*	I,89
Byblos Boat	*kbnt*	II,172
byre	*ihy*	I,42
byre	*hꜣy*	I,284
byres	*mḏt*	I,219
byssus	*sšr-nsw*	I,249
byssus	*sšr-nsw*	II,82
byssus-worker	*bꜣk-šs-nsw*	I,128

C

cabin (of boat)	*ṯꜣrt*	II,226
cabin (of Sun-Bark)	*kꜣr*	II,169
cabinet maker	*ḥmw-ṯꜣrt*	II,227
cackle	*gꜣgꜣ*	II,185
cadet	*mnḥ*	I,188
cage	*tb*	II,203
cage(?)	*db(t)*	II,244
caged	*kri*	II,175
cajole	*swnwn*	II,20
cake	*ꜥgs*	I,82
cake	*wḫꜣt*	I,110
cake	*bi(ꜣ)t*	I,129
cake	*mḥt*	I,200
cake	*rḥs*	I,275
cake	*sꜥb*	II,13
cake	*sḫn*	II,71
cake	*šꜥyt*	II,111
cake	*ḏprt*	II,268
cakes	*ipt*	I,25
cakes	*ꜥḳ*	I,80
cakes	*pꜣwt*	I,146
cakes	*rḥs*	I,275
cakes	*sš*	II,79
cakes of pigment	*t-r*	II,197
calamity	*iꜣdt*	I,15
calculate	*ip*	I,24
calculation	*ipw*	I,25
calculation	*šꜥr*	II,112
calculations	*ḥsb*	I,332
calendar festivals	*tp-trw*	II,206
calf	*bḥs*	I,138
calf	*ḳmꜣ*	II,151
call	*ꜥš*	I,78
call forth	*nis*	I,227
call in question	*šni*	II,127
call to account	*wḫꜣ*	I,110
call up	*thm*	II,216
call upon (for service)	*iṯꜣ*	I,53
called	*ḏd n.f*	II,275
calling	*iꜣwt*	I,13
calm	*ḳb*	II,147
calm	*wꜥb*	I,94
calm	*ḥtp*	I,337
calm	*ḥtpyt*	I,337
calm	*sḳbb*	II,84
calm your heart	*imy ꜥꜣ ḥꜣty.k*	I,60
calmly	*ḳb*	II,148
calmness	*ḳb*	II,147
calumniate	*hm*	I,287
calumniate	*ḥḏ*	I,340
calumniate	*gꜣi*	II,183
calves	*wnḏw*	I,103
calves	*rnn*	I,274
camp	*ihy*	I,42
camp	*hꜣy*	I,284
camp	*ḥwit*	I,305
camp	*sibyn*	II,11
campaign	*wḏ(yt)*	I,120
camps (bedawi)	*wḥt*	I,107
campsite	*sḏrt*	II,103
canal	*itr*	I,51
canal	*mr*	I,192
canal	*mšb*	I,208
canal	*hr*	I,290
canal	*ḥnw*	I,317
canal	*ḥn(t)*	I,320
candles	*ḫꜣbs*	I,348
candles	*ḫbs*	I,355
cane	*pgꜣ*	I,158
cane	*twrit*	II,202
canon	*nḫb*	I,244
canopic jars	*ḳbw-n-wt*	I,116
canopic jars	*ḳbw n wt*	II,148
canopy	*ḥty*	I,335
capable	*iḳr*	I,49
capable	*ḳni*	II,152
capable	*gm ḏrt*	II,189
capacity	*šꜣw*	II,108
capacity	*ḏwyw*	II,265
caper	*krs*	II,176
capital	*ꜥꜣ(i)*	I,59
capital charges	*mdt-n-mt*	I,217
capital offence	*btꜣ-n-mwt*	I,142
capsize	(see turn upside down)	
capsize	*ꜥgꜣ*	I,81
capsized	*ꜥkw*	I,80
captain	*ḥry-wsḫ*	I,112
captain	*ḥꜣ(w)tyw*	I,298
captain	*ḥw(n)tyw*	I,305
captain	*ḥry-wsḫt*	I,324
captain	*sḥn*	II,63
captain of heralds	*ḥry-wḥm*	I,109
captain of the Medjaw	*ḥry-mḏꜣw*	I,325
captains	*ḥry*	I,323
captivate	*ṯꜣy-ḥꜥty*	II,224
captive	*sḳr-ꜥnḫ*	I,70
captive	*ḥḳꜣ*	I,333
captive	*sḳr-ꜥnḫ*	II,85
captive woman	*srti*	II,59
captives	*iṯr*	I,53
captives	*ḥꜣḳw*	I,300
captives	*kfꜥw*	II,173
capture	*iṯꜣ*	I,53
capture	*mḥ*	I,197
capture	*ḥꜣḳ*	I,299

capture	ḳfꜥ	II,173
capture (vb.)	ẖfy	I,358
caravaneers	ḳwrw	II,147
care	ib	I,22
care	mḥ	I,198
care	nwyt	I,231
care	ḥꜣ-ib	I,295
care (to have a)	sꜣw	II,6
care for	ꜣty	I,9
care for	nhp	I,240
careen	hskt	I,292
career	nmtt	I,238
carefully	r-ikr	I,49
carefully	bꜥ	I,131
carefully	ḏry	II,273
caress	gmgm	II,189
caretaker	mškb	I,209
cargo	sb	II,25
carnage	wꜥwꜥ	I,94
carnage	krt	II,177
carnelian	smn	II,42
carnelian(?)	ḥmꜣgt	I,312
carnelian(?)	ḥrst	I,329
carob	idnrg	I,54
carob	dnrg	II,251
carob beans	sp(r)t	II,33
carpenter	ḥmww	I,313
carpenter lad	ms-ḥmnw	I,204
carpenter shop	wẖrt	I,110
carried off	ḥꜣkw	I,300
carrier	fꜣy	I,163
carry	ꜣtp	I,10
carry	ini	I,31
carry	fꜣy	I,163
carry	rmni	I,271
carry	ẖni	I,382
carry	stꜣ	II,92
carry	ṯꜣy	II,224
carry	ḏꜣḏꜣy	II,263
carry aloft	sṯs	II,97
carry away	ꜥr	I,71
carry off	iṯi	I,52
carry off	iṯꜣ	I,53
carry out	iri	I,38
carrying	ẖr-r	I,385
carrying	ẖry	I,386
carrying pole	mꜣwt	I,176
carrying pole	mꜣwḏ	I,176
carrying pole	ẖntt	I,367
carrying poles	nbꜣ	I,233
carrying stand	fꜣy	I,164
cartonnage	ꜥmꜥmt	I,66
cartouche	mnš	I,189
carve	mtn	I,214
carve	šdi	II,140
carve	ṯꜣ	II,223
carver	wp	I,98
carvers	ẖty	I,376
case	mdt	I,217
case	sp	II,30
case	sm	II,37
casing	ḳḳi	II,159
cast	wḏḥ	I,123
cast	nbi	I,233
cast	ẖꜣꜥ	I,346
cast a shadow	kh	II,177
cast blame	wꜣḥ-mdw	I,90
cast down	pẖd	I,155
cast down	hꜣ(i)	I,284
cast down	ḥdb	I,340
cast down	ẖr	I,370
cast down	sẖr	II,72
cast down	dr	II,252
cast down	dẖ	II,255
cast off	sfẖ	II,36
castigation	ḳnḳn	II,155
castle	bẖn	I,139
castle	ḥt-ꜥꜣt	I,335
cast-metal object	nṯk	I,255
castor oil	mrḥt	I,194
castor oil	dgm	II,257
castrate	ḥms	I,314
castrate	sꜥb	II,13
castrated	sꜥb	II,13
cat	my	I,179
catalogue	sḥwy	II,62
cataract region	ḳbḥ	II,149
catch	mḥ	I,197
catch	sẖbẖ	II,68
catch	sẖt	II,74
catch	gp	II,188
catch sight of	gmḥ	II,189
catcher	wḥꜥ	I,108
catfish	nꜥrw	I,229
catfish	srḳ	II,59
cattle	iꜣwt	I,13
cattle	iḥw	I,43
cattle	prk	I,152
cattle	mnmnt	I,187
cattle	kꜣ	II,165
cattle barge	ẖn-iḥw	I,382
cattle census	irw	I,40
cattle farmer	mnḥ-n-kꜣw	I,188
cattle ferry	ẖn-iḥw	I,382
cattle inspection	irw iḥw	I,39
cattle pen	st-iꜣwt	I,13
cattle stall	mḏt	I,219
cattle yard	mḏt	I,219
cattle, long-horned	ngꜣw	I,252
cattle, short-horned	wnḏw	I,103
cauldron	rhd(t)	I,274
cauldron	ḳhn	II,159

cauldron	*kḥn*	II,177
cauldron	*dydy*	II,241
cause	*imi*	I,26
cause	*rdi*	I,281
cause	*di*	II,240
cause confusion	*stwh*	II,93
cause delay	*wdf*	I,118
cause injury	*sbgs*	II,29
cause misery	*iȝd*	I,14
cause obstruction	*sth*	II,95
cause pain	*smr*	II,43
cause prejudice	*tkk*	II,221
cause to appear	*sẖʿ*	II,68
cause to approach	*stkn*	II,96
cause to ascend	*sʿr*	II,15
cause to be	*sẖpr*	II,69
cause to be great	*sʿȝ*	II,13
cause to eat	*sʿm*	II,14
cause to grow	*srd*	II,59
cause to jump	*ftft*	I,166
cause to know	*di-ʿm*	I,66
cause to live	*sʿnẖ*	II,14
cause to raise	*sʿẖ*	II,15
cause to rule	*sḥḳȝ*	II,64
cause to sleep	*sḳdd*	II,85
cause to stand	*sʿḥʿ*	II,15
causeway	*wȝt*	I,88
cautious (of speech)	*dns*	II,251
cave	*bgrṯ*	I,142
cave	*rryt*	I,274
cave	*štȝyt*	II,139
cave	*tpḥt*	II,209
cave	*ṯpḥt*	II,229
cavern	*ḳȝrrt*	II,144
cavern	*ḳrrt*	II,157
cavern	*tpḥt*	II,209
cavern	*ṯpḥt*	II,229
cavern (of Nile)	*tpḥt*	II,209
caves	*mgrwt*	I,212
cavity	*rryt*	I,274
cease	*ȝb*	I,3
cease	*wȝḥ*	I,89
cease	*rwi*	I,267
cease	*ḳn*	II,151
cease from	*rwi-m*	I,267
ceasing	*ȝbw*	I,3
cedar	*ʿš*	I,79
cedar	*mry*	I,193
ceiling	*hȝy*	I,284
ceiling	*hȝwt*	I,285
celebrate	*iri*	I,38
celebrate	*ir ẖȝwt*	I,39
celebrate	*ḥb*	I,307
celebrate a triumph	*sʿȝ*	II,13
celestial bread	*t-ḥry*	II,197
celestial ocean	*wȝḏ-wr*	I,91
cell	*rryt*	I,274
cellar	*ẖnw*	I,362
cellar	*štȝyt*	II,139
cemetery	*ẖrt-nṯr*	I,385
cemetery	*tȝ-n-ẖry-nṯr*	II,198
cemetery worker	*ms-ẖr*	I,204
censer	*sḥtpy*	II,65
central	*ḥry-ib*	I,23
ceramic	*ḳrḥt*	II,157
certain	*wʿ*	I,93
certain	*mn*	I,184
certainly	*iri*	I,37
certainly	*tiw*	II,200
certificate	*ḥy*	I,300
cessation	*ȝbw*	I,3
chaff	*šḥḳ*	II,133
chain	*isbr*	I,46
chair	*sbi*	II,28
chair	*šnrf*	II,130
chair	*ḳniw*	II,153
chair	*kḥs*	II,178
chalcopyrite	*gsfn*	II,194
challenge (vb.)	*sr*	II,57
chamber	*ipt*	I,26
chamber	*is*	I,45
chamber	*ʿt*	I,59
chamber	*štȝ*	II,138
chamber	*ḏrwt*	II,273
chamberlain	*wbȝ*	I,96
chambers	*šmmt*	II,124
champion	*nẖt*	I,246
champion	*nẖt-ʿ*	I,246
champion (vb.)	*nḏ-ḥr*	I,255
chancellery	*mstr*	I,207
change	*šb*	II,116
channel	*mr*	I,192
channel	*mšb*	I,208
channel	*mšdt*	I,209
channel(?)	*ẖȝrw*	I,349
chant (vb.)	*gȝ*	II,183
chantress	*šmʿyt*	II,123
chantresses	*ḥsy*	I,330
chants	*šmʿwt*	II,123
chapel	*ipt*	I,26
chapel	*r-pr*	I,262
chapel	*ẖnw*	I,362
chapel	*sḥ*	II,61
chapel	*ḳniw*	II,153
chapel	*kȝr*	II,169
chapel	*gȝit*	II,183
chapel	*ṯft*	II,229
chapel(?)	*mnḳb*	I,190
chapel-wall	*inhȝt*	I,34
chapter	*ḥwt*	I,304
character	*iwn*	I,20

character	*inw*	I,33
character	*bit*	I,128
character	*biꜣt*	I,130
character	*ḳd*	II,160
charcoal	*ḏꜥbw*	II,264
charge	*ꜥḳ*	I,80
charge	*smi*	II,40
charge (n.)	*btꜣ*	I,142
charge (n.)	*mdt*	I,217
charge (n.)	*smỉt*	II,41
charge (n.)	*sḫꜣ*	II,67
charge with	*mḥ ḥr*	I,197
charge with	*ḥn*	I,315
charge(?)	*hꜣw-tm*	I,285
charged to	*iwd*	I,22
charges	*wšbt-n-mdty*	I,115
charging (lion)	*htm*	I,292
chariot appurtenance	*gs-ḏbw*	II,194
chariot	*wrryt*	I,105
chariot	*bry*	I,136
chariot	*brr*	I,136
chariot	*mrkbt*	I,195
chariot	*ṯpr*	II,229
chariot body	*brr*	I,136
chariot donkeys	*ꜥꜣw-n-mrkbt*	I,61
chariot part	*iwm*	I,20
chariot part	*bt*	I,142
chariot part	*mḫt*	I,202
chariot part	*mṯt*	I,216
chariot part	*ḥꜣyry*	I,296
chariot part	*ḥmyt*	I,313
chariot part	*ḫꜣb*	I,348
chariot part	*swꜣr*	II,18
chariot part	*swr*	II,21
chariot part (siding?)	*tḫr*	II,219
chariot part (paneling?)	*tḫr*	II,219
chariot officer	*snny*	II,52
chariot warrior	*snny*	II,52
chariot's pole	*ꜥwnt*	I,63
charioteer	*kḏn*	II,181
charioteer	*tḫr*	II,217
chariotry	*nt-ḥtri*	I,252
chariotry	*ḥtr*	I,338
chariotry	*(ti)-nt-ḥtri*	II,200
chariot-soldier	*snny*	II,52
charm	*ꜣbwt*	I,5
charm	*iꜣbwt*	I,13
charm	*im(ꜣt)*	I,29
charming	*nꜥmw*	I,228
charms	*ḥkꜣ*	I,334
chase away	*stkn*	II,96
chase away	*tkn*	II,220
chasm	*šdrt*	II,141
chasten	*smỉty*	II,41
chastise	*smỉty*	II,41
chastisement	*sbꜣyt*	II,27
chateau	*pr-mꜣ*	I,150
chateau-de-la-reunion(?)	*ḥwt-ꜣbbḫy*	I,5
cheat	*gꜣbw*	II,184
cheated	*shꜣ*	II,60
cheating	*gb*	II,187
check	*ṯnf*	II,230
checked	*dni*	II,249
cheek	*mnd*	I,191
cheer	*nḏm-ib*	I,256
cheer	*ḥn*	I,315
cheered	*fꜣy-ḏꜣḏꜣ*	I,163
cheerful	*wnf*	I,101
cheerful	*wnf-ib*	I,101
cherish	*mri*	I,192
chest	*ꜥfdt*	I,65
chest	*bꜣnyny*	I,126
chest	*pgꜣ*	I,158
chest	*pds*	I,160
chest	*mhn*	I,196
chest	*hn*	I,288
chest	*šꜣgꜣr*	II,110
chest	*šfdiꜣ*	II,121
chest	*šgr*	II,137
chest	*ḳrf*	II,156
chest	*gꜣ*	II,183
chest	*gꜣwt*	II,184
chest	*gwtn*	II,186
chew	*wšꜥ*	I,113
chick peas	*ḥr-bik*	I,322
chief	*wr*	I,104
chief	*ḥry*	I,324
chief	*ḥry-tp*	I,326
chief	*tpy*	II,207
chief commander of the army	*ḥry-tp-n-mnfꜣt*	I,324
chief of departments	*ꜥꜣ-n-ꜥyt*	I,60
chief of stable	*ꜥꜣ-n-šmm*	I,60
chief physician	*wr-swnw*	I,104
chief spokesman	*r-ḥry*	I,264
chief taxing master	*ꜥꜣ-n-št*	I,60
chief workman	*ꜥꜣ*	I,60
chief workman	*ꜥꜣ-n-ist*	I,60
chiefs (Asiatic)	*tp*	II,204
child	*ꜥḏd-šri*	I,85
child	*ms*	I,203
child	*nḫn*	I,245
child	*ḥwn*	I,306
child	*ḫy*	I,343
child	*ḫi*	I,350
child	*ḫrd*	I,388
child	*sfy*	II,35

child	šri	II,132
child of nursery	ẖrd-n-kȝp	I,388
childhood	ḫnw	I,363
childish	nḫn	I,245
childlike	nḫn	I,245
childlike	ḫnw	I,363
children	nḏs	I,257
chin	ʿnʿn	I,69
chin	ʿrʿr	I,72
chink	ws	I,110
chisel	bsnt	I,140
chisel	mṯprt	I,216
chisel	mḏȝt	I,220
chisel	ntg	I,253
chisel	ḫȝ	I,343
chisel	ḫȝiw	I,344
chisel	ḫʿw	I,352
chisel	ḫnr	I,365
chisel bearer	ṯȝy mḏȝt	II,225
chisel bearer	ṯȝy-bš	II,224
choice	stp	II,94
choice things	stp	II,94
choice words	stp	II,94
choicest	stp	II,94
choicest portions	stp	II,94
choke	mr	I,191
choked	nty	I,253
choose	stp	II,94
chop (vb.)	sin	II,12
chore	wpwt	I,99
chorus	mȝwt	I,176
chosen	stp	II,94
chosen	tpy	II,207
Christ's thorn	nbs	I,234
cinders	ḳrmt	II,156
cinnamon(?)	tišpss	II,201
circle (vb.)	ḳdd	II,162
circuit	pẖrw	I,155
circuit	šnw	II,126
circulate	pẖr	I,155
circulate	ḳdi	II,161
circumference	ḳd	II,161
cistern	ḫnmt	I,384
citizen	ʿnḫ	I,70
citizen	rmṯ-n-pȝ-tȝ	I,272
citizeness	ʿnḫ-n-niwt	I,70
citizeness	ʿnḫ nw niwt	I,226
citizens	pʿt	I,147
citizens	ḥnmmt	I,318
city	niwt	I,226
city prefect	imy-r niwt	I,28
civil strife	ḫrw	I,372
clad in	ṯȝy	II,224
claim	thm	II,216
claim (vb.)	stȝ	II,93
claim back	wḫȝ	I,109
clamor (vb.)	sgb	II,89
clamor (vb.)	tiȝ	II,200
clamoring	shȝ	II,60
clan	bt	I,142
clap	ḥwi	I,303
clap	sḫ	II,66
clasp (vb.)	dmȝ	II,248
claw	ʿnt	I,69
claw	ʿgȝt	I,81
clay	ʿmʿmt	I,66
clay	sint	II,12
clay	tȝ	II,197
clay	dbn	II,245
clean	ḥsmn	I,332
clean	sṯf	II,96
clean cut	wʿb	I,94
cleanse	twr	II,202
clear	bȝḳ	I,127
clear (a field)	sft	II,36
clear (vb.)	sḥḏ	II,65
clear the way before	ḏsr	II,274
clearing	ḥḏ	I,341
cleave fast to	dmi	II,248
cleaver	ḥsḳ	I,333
clement	ḥtpyt	I,337
clever	rḫ-wsy	I,275
clever	sbḳ	II,29
clever	spd	II,34
clever	šs3	II,134
clever	šs3	II,134
cleverness	šs3	II,134
cleverness	šs3-ḥr	II,135
climb	ṯs	II,235
cloak	idg	I,55
cloak	ḏȝyt	II,261
cloak(?)	knt	II,175
close	(see near)	
close (vb.)	ʿẖn	I,78
close (vb.)	ḫtm	I,377
close friend	snsn	II,54
close off	šr	II,131
closed	ḥs	I,329
closed	ḫnr	I,365
closed (by a cord)	ḥst	I,333
closely	m-sšr	II,82
closely	ḏry	II,273
cloth	ḥbs	I,308
cloth	smȝw	II,39
cloth	sd	II,97
cloth strip	ptr	I,159
cloth type	mrw	I,194
clothe	wnḫ	I,103
clothe	ḥbs	I,308
clothe	ḏbȝ	II,266
clothe oneself	sd	II,98

clothes	*ḥbs*	I,308
clothing	*mnḫt*	I,189
clothing	*ḥbs*	I,308
clothing	*ḳḏmr*	II,163
clouds	*šnʿ*	II,129
club	*iʿn*	I,17
club	*ʿwnt*	I,63
club	*bḏn*	I,143
clump	*bꜣi(t)*	I,126
clusters	*sbr*	II,28
coast	*wꜣt*	I,88
coaster	*br*	I,136
coat of mail	*ṯrn*	II,231
coat with plaster	*ꜣʿʿ*	I,1
coax	*swnwn*	II,20
coerce	*ʿdd*	I,82
coffer	*pgꜣ*	I,158
coffer	*hn*	I,288
coffin	*wt*	I,116
coffin	*ḳrst*	II,158
coffin (innermost)	*swḥt*	II,21
coffin (wooden)	*ḫt-wt-šri*	I,375
coffins (outer)	*ḏbꜣt*	II,267
cognizance	*ʿm*	I,66
cognizant	*ip*	I,24
coherent(?)	*ṯs*	II,233
collapse	*hꜣ(i)*	I,283
collapse	*ḫꜣʿ*	I,347
collar	*wꜣḥt*	I,90
collar	*wsḫ*	I,112
collar	*bb*	I,133
collar	*fꜣy*	I,163
collar end-piece	*ḥty*	I,336
collar piece	*dt*	II,239
colleague	*iry-rdwy*	I,40
colleague	*ḫbr*	I,354
colleague	*sn*	II,47
colleagues	*wnḏw*	I,103
collect	*nw(i)*	I,230
collect	*sꜣḳ*	II,9
collect	*snh*	II,52
collect	*sḥwy*	II,62
collect	*šdi*	II,140
collect	*ḳdf*	II,161
collect	*dmḏ*	II,249
collected together	*twt*	II,202
collection	*sḥwy*	II,62
collection	*dmḏyt*	II,249
collusion	*ḥw(t)w*	I,305
colonnade	*ḏꜣḏꜣw*	II,263
color	*iwn*	I,20
color	*inw*	I,33
color	*ṯms*	II,229
colored gaily	*nʿʿ*	I,228
colored red	*ṯms*	II,229
column	*iwn*	I,20
column	*wḫꜣ*	I,110
column	*sdt*	II,97
column	*ḏd*	II,276
column drums	*šꜣḳw*	II,110
columns	*ʿꜣw*	I,61
comb	*pši*	I,157
comb	*mšddt*	I,210
comb	*nši*	I,250
combat	*ʿḥꜣ*	I,74
combat	*r-ʿ-ḫt*	I,261
combat	*ḥwny-r-ḥr*	I,305
combat (vb.)	*shdt*	II,61
combat soldier	*wʿw*	I,94
combatants	*ḏbiw*	II,267
combinations	*smꜣ*	II,38
combine	*šbn*	II,117
come	*ii*	I,15
come	*iw*	I,18
come	*mḳꜣ*	I,210
come and go	*ḫtḫt*	I,377
come and go	*šm*	II,121
come back	*iw*	I,18
come back	*ʿn(n)*	I,68
come back to	*hꜣ(i)*	I,283
come close	*ḫn*	I,381
come forth	*bsi*	I,139
come forth	*pry*	I,151
come into contact with	*ṯhi*	II,232
come into existence	*ḫpr*	I,356
come meekly	*ḫnḫn*	I,384
come near	*ḫʿm*	I,353
come near	*ḫn*	I,381
come near	*sʿr*	II,15
come near to	*ḳri*	II,155
come to	*snbꜣ*	II,50
come to an end	*mnḳ*	I,190
come to be	*ḫpr*	I,356
come to naught	*ꜣḳ*	I,9
come to pass	*wꜣi*	I,87
come to pass	*ḫpr*	I,356
come to pass	*šm*	II,121
come!	*my*	I,179
comeliness	*ʿn(w)t*	I,67
comeliness	*nfrw*	I,236
comely	*ʿn*	I,67
comfort (vb.)	*snf*	II,51
command	*wpwt*	I,99
command	*wḏ(t)*	I,119
command (vb.)	*wḏ*	I,119
command (vb.)	*ḥn*	I,315
command (vb.)	*sḥn*	II,62
command (vb.)	*sg*	II,88
command (vb.)	*sdbḥ*	II,99
command (vb.)	*ḏd*	II,275

commandeer	*nḥm*	I,243
commandeer	*thm*	II,216
commander	*ỉmy-r*	I,27
commander	*ꜥꜣ*	I,60
commander	*mry*	I,193
commander	*ḥry*	I,324
commander	*ḫrp*	I,372
commander	*sḥn*	II,63
commander	*ṯs*	II,234
commander	*ṯs-pḏwt*	II,234
commander of a host(?)	*ḥry-pḏt*	I,324
commander of ship's contingent	*ḥry-ḫnyt*	I,324
commander of troops	*ḥry-pḏt*	I,325
commands	*ḥnw*	I,316
commands	*sḥn*	II,63
commemorate	*sḫꜣ*	II,67
commence	*šsp*	II,135
commencement	*šsp*	II,136
commerce	*ḫbr*	I,354
commingle	*ꜣbḫ*	I,5
commission	*ipwt*	I,25
commission	*wpwt*	I,99
commission	*nḥ*	I,244
commission	*sḥn*	II,63
commissioner	*rwḏ*	I,269
commissions	*ḏd*	II,276
commissions(?)	*mšꜥw*	I,208
commit	*iri*	I,38
commit	*wḏ*	I,119
commit	*swḏ*	II,23
commit adultery	*nk*	I,251
common folk	*rḫyt*	I,276
common people	*kt*	II,179
common way	*rdt-r-sṯꜣ*	II,74
commoners	*rḫyt*	I,276
communicate	*hꜣb*	I,286
communication	*hꜣb*	I,286
communication	*swḏꜣ-ib*	II,24
companion	*iry*	I,39
companion	*ḫbr*	I,354
companion	*ḫnms*	I,364
companion	*smꜣy*	II,38
companion	*smr*	II,43
companion	*sn-nw*	II,48
companions	*wnḏw*	I,104
company	*ỉst*	I,46
company	*sꜣw*	II,4
compare	*stn*	II,95
compartments	*rgt*	I,280
compassion	*ꜥn(n)*	I,67
compassion	*ꜥnnw*	I,69
compassion	*nꜥ(w)*	I,228
compeers	*wnḏw*	I,103
compel	*ḥtr*	I,339
compelled	*mꜣwḏ*	I,176
compensate	*mḥ*	I,197
compensation	*ḏbꜣ*	II,266
competent	*šsꜣ*	II,134
complain	*nḥ*	I,244
complain	*smi*	II,40
complainers	*knwy*	II,174
complaint	*smiw*	II,40
complaint	*smiw-n-mdt*	II,41
complete	*ikm*	I,49
complete	*ꜥrḳ*	I,73
complete	*mnḳ*	I,190
complete	*mḥ*	I,197
complete	*skm*	II,87
complete	*ḳn*	II,151
complete	*km*	II,174
complete	*twt*	II,203
complete	*tm*	II,210
complete	*tmmw*	II,211
completing month	*mḥ-ꜣbd*	I,198
completion	*km*	II,173
completion	*kmyt*	II,174
complexion	*inw*	I,33
complimentary gift	*šrmt*	II,133
comply (nod compliance)	*hn*	I,288
compose	*iri*	I,38
composed	*štꜣ*	II,138
comprehend	*ꜥm*	I,66
comprehend	*sḏm*	II,101
compulsory	*smdt*	II,46
conceal	*imn*	I,30
conceal	*ḥꜣp*	I,299
conceal	*sḥꜣp*	II,61
conceal	*sdgꜣy*	II,99
conceited	*ꜥꜣ-ib*	I,60
conceive	*iwr*	I,21
concern	*ḫrt*	I,371
concern	*sḫr*	II,73
concern	*sšr*	II,82
concern, express	*ms-ỉb*	I,23
concerned	*nḥꜣ*	I,242
concerned about	*m-sꜣ*	I,171
concerned with	*bꜥ*	I,131
concerned with	*mḥ*	I,197
concerned, be	*ꜥnḫ*	I,70
concerning	*r*	I,259
concerning	*ḥr*	I,321
concerning	*ḥr-ḥr*	I,323
concerns	*ḫrt*	I,371
conclave	*ḏꜣḏꜣt*	II,263
conclave of gods	*psḏt*	I,157
conclusion	*km*	II,173
conclusion	*kmyt*	II,174

concubine(?)	*ḥbsyt*	I,308
concubine(?)	*ḥmt-ṯꜣy*	I,312
concubine(?)	*ḫnrt*	I,366
concur	*hn*	I,288
condemnation	*šꜣy*	II,106
condiments	*šb*	II,116
condition	*ꜥ*	I,57
condition	*r-ꜥ*	I,260
condition	*ḫrt*	I,371
condition	*sḫr*	II,73
condition	*sšm*	II,81
condition	*ḳi*	II,146
condition	*ḳd*	II,160
conditions	*ḫppw*	I,355
conduct (vb.)	*sšm*	II,80
conduct (vb.)	*stꜣ*	II,92
conduct investigation(?)	*sšm*	II,80
confection	*bnr*	I,135
confectioner	*bnrty*	I,135
confederates	*smꜣy*	II,38
confederation	*iwnmkt*	I,21
confer	*hn*	I,288
confidant	*mḥnk*	I,201
confidence	*mḥ-ib*	I,198
confident	*ꜥꜣ(yt)-ḥꜣty*	I,60
confident	*mḥ ib*	I,197
confined	*ḫni*	I,362
confined	*ḏdḥ*	II,277
confirm	*smn*	II,42
confirm	*smnḫ*	II,43
confirm	*ṯs*	II,233
confiscate	*iṯꜣ*	I,53
confiscation	*ṯꜣwt*	II,225
conflict	*ẖnnw*	I,384
conflict(?)	*r-pḏt*	I,262
confound	*ꜥnꜥn*	I,69
confound	*ẖnn*	I,384
confound	*shꜣ*	II,60
confound	*ṯḫṯḫ*	II,219
confuse	*shꜣ*	II,60
confuse	*ṯḫṯḫ*	II,219
confused	*wiꜣwiꜣ*	I,92
confused	*sgꜣ*	II,89
confusion	*shꜣ*	II,60
confusion	*ṯḫṯḫ*	II,219
conjure	*šni*	II,127
conjure	*šnw*	II,128
conjurer	*šnt*	II,127
conquer	*iṯi*	I,52
conquer	*hd*	I,293
conquer	*ḫpš*	I,358
conscript (vb.)	*iṯꜣ*	I,53
conscripts	*rmṯ-mšꜥ*	I,208
conscripts	*rmṯ-mšꜥ*	I,272
consecrate	*swꜥb*	II,19
consecrated	*ḏsr*	II,274
consecration	*swꜥb*	II,19
consider	*wꜣwꜣ*	I,88
consider	*šfšf*	II,120
consider	*šsꜣ*	II,135
considerate to	*di ḥꜣty*	I,298
considerate to	*imi ḥrr*	I,321
consisting of	*m*	I,167
consort with	*šbn*	II,117
conspiracy	*ꜥdt*	I,82
conspiracy	*šdt*	II,142
conspire	*wꜣ*	I,87
conspire	*ḏnn*	II,270
constant	*wꜣḥ-ib*	I,90
constriction	*sbn*	II,28
construct	*iri*	I,38
construct	*ḫws*	I,354
construction process(?)	*r-ꜥ-kꜣt*	I,261
construction site	*r-ꜥ-bꜣkw*	I,260
consult	*mdw*	I,216
consult	*nḏnḏ*	I,257
consult (an oracle)	*ꜥḥꜥ m-bꜣḥ*	I,76
consume	*wnm*	I,102
contact	*ḫbr*	I,354
contagion of the year	*snm-rnpt*	II,51
contain	*ꜥrf*	I,72
container	*ꜣꜥꜥ(w)t*	I,2
container	*wrmyt*	I,105
container	*nbd*	I,234
container type	*mhꜣ*	I,196
containing	*ẖry*	I,386
contaminate	*sꜣt*	II,10
contemptible	*šfy*	II,119
contemptuous	*sḫr*	II,74
contend	*sḫn*	II,71
content	*wnf*	I,101
content	*wnf-ib*	I,101
content	*brg*	I,137
content	*hr*	I,290
content	*hr-ib*	I,290
content	*ḥnrg*	I,319
content	*ḥtp*	I,337
content (vb.)	*shr*	II,60
content oneself	*ḏꜣy-ḫr*	II,261
contented	*hr-ib*	I,23
contented heart	*ꜣwt-ib*	I,3
contented(?)	*ḥnrg*	I,319
contentment	*hry-ib*	I,290
contentment	*hrt-ib*	I,291
contest (vb.)	*mdw*	I,216
contingent (of a ship)	*ẖni*	I,382
contingents	*sꜣw*	II,4
continually	*m-dwn*	I,172

continually	*dwn*	II,243
continue	*ḫpr*	I,356
continue	*spỉ*	II,31
continue	*spr*	II,32
contours	*ḳd*	II,161
contract	*brṯ*	I,137
contract	*ḫtmt*	I,377
contribution	*ỉnw*	I,32
contribution	*nḥb*	I,242
contribution	*ḥtr*	I,339
contribution	*šrmt*	II,133
contrivances	*sḫr*	II,73
contrive	*sḫr*	II,72
control (vb.)	*ḥn*	I,315
control (vb.)	*ḥnty*	I,320
control (vb.)	*sỉp*	II,11
controller	*rwḏ*	I,269
controller	*ḫrp*	I,372
controller	*sḫm*	II,70
controller of foreign troops	*ḫrp-ꜥ*	I,372
controversies	*mdt-ꜥḥꜣ*	I,217
controvert	*ꜥn(n)*	I,68
conversation	*sḏd*	II,104
converse	*mdw*	I,216
convert into	*swn*	II,19
convey	*nꜥy*	I,228
convey	*ẖnỉ*	I,382
convey	*swḏ*	II,23
convey	*sḳdy*	II,85
convey	*stꜣ*	II,92
convey	*šdỉ*	II,140
convey	*dhn*	II,253
convey	*ḏꜣỉ*	II,260
convey by water	*ẖnỉ*	I,382
convict	*hd*	I,293
convince	*ỉmy ḥsw(t) m ỉb*	I,331
convulsion	*nšny*	I,250
cook	*ps*	I,155
cool	*ḳb*	II,148
cool (place)	*ḳb*	II,148
cool (become)	*ḳb*	II,147
cool (vb.)	*ḳb*	II,148
cool place	*mnḳb*	I,190
cool places	*sbḳ*	II,29
cool water	*ḳbḥw*	II,149
cooly	*ḳb*	II,148
cooperate (with)	*ỉr-wꜥ-ỉrm*	I,39
copious	*wdn*	I,118
copper	*ḥmt*	I,314
copper lining	*ḳḳỉ*	II,159
copper pieces	*ḥmt*	I,314
copper scrap	*ḥmt-n-ḳnḳn*	I,315
copper tools	*ḫꜣỉw*	I,344
coppersmith	*ḥmty*	I,315
copse	*štꜣ*	II,138
copulate	*pꜣy*	I,146
copulate	*nk*	I,251
copulation	*dꜣdꜣ*	II,239
copulation	*dd*	II,258
copy	*mỉtt*	I,179
copy	*sny*	II,49
copy	*snn*	II,51
copy	*snty*	II,54
copy	*snṯ*	II,54
copy (vb.)	*spẖr*	II,33
copy of letter	*mỉtt*	I,179
cord	*fꜣy*	I,164
cord	*nwḥ*	I,231
cord	*rdt*	I,281
cord	*ḥsꜣ*	I,332
cord	*tpt*	II,208
cordage	*mtrt*	I,215
cordage	*nṯṯ*	I,255
coriander	*šꜣwt*	II,108
corn	*ỉt*	I,50
corn	*sšr*	II,82
corn	*šs*	II,134
corner	*ḳnb*	II,154
corner pieces	*ḳꜥḥw*	II,146
cornice(?)	*mnỉt*	I,185
corps	*sꜣw*	II,4
corpse	*ẖꜣwt*	I,379
correct	*ꜥḳꜣ*	I,81
correct	*mꜣꜥ(t)*	I,175
correct	*mt*	I,213
correctly	*ꜥḳꜣ*	I,81
correctness	*ꜥḳꜣw*	I,81
correspondence	*šꜥt*	II,111
corresponding to	*ḫft*	I,358
corridor	*r-stꜣ*	I,264
corridor	*sṯꜣ-nṯr*	II,96
corselet	*ṯꜣrynꜣ*	II,227
corselet	*ṯrn*	II,231
corundum	*ḫrsmr*	I,373
corvée	*bryt*	I,136
corvée	*bḥw*	I,138
corvée	*rmṯ-hꜣyt*	I,272
corvée	*ḥꜣyt*	I,295
costly	*šps*	II,118
costly stone	*ꜥꜣt*	I,61
costly wood	*ssnḏm*	II,77
couch	*krk(r)*	II,177
cough	*srỉ*	II,57
cough up	*ỉšš*	I,48
council chamber	*ỉs*	I,45
counsel	*nḏwt-r*	I,256
counselor	*sḥy*	II,61
counsels	*sḥw*	II,61
counsels	*sḫr*	II,72
count	*ỉp*	I,24
count	*ḥsb*	I,332

countenance(?)	*ḥȝwty*	I,298
counter (vb.)	*tkn*	II,220
counterpoise	*mnit*	I,185
counting	*ḥsb*	I,332
country	*w*	I,87
country	*ḫȝst*	I,349
country districts	*sḫt*	II,66
countryside	*sḫt*	II,66
courage	*ḥȝty*	I,297
courage	*ḥsȝ*	I,332
courageous	*sḫm-ib*	I,23
courageous	*sḫm-ib*	II,70
courageous	*dns*	II,252
courier	*ḥȝptyw*	I,299
courier	*sḫs*	II,74
couriers	*sḫḫ*	II,74
course	*nmtt*	I,238
course	*ḥpw*	I,308
course	*sḫr*	II,73
course (vb.)	*pḫr*	I,155
course of action	*sšr*	II,82
course of construction(?)	*r-ꜥ-bȝkw*	I,260
courses(?)	*ḏȝḏȝwt*	II,263
court	*wbȝ*	I,96
court	*wsḫt*	I,112
court	*h*	I,283
court	*ḫnw*	I,383
court	*sr*	II,57
court	*sdbt*	II,99
court	*šnwt*	II,128
court	*ḳnbt*	II,154
court	*ṯnṯȝt*	II,231
court of examination	*st smtr*	II,3
court of thirty	*mꜥbȝyt*	I,181
courtiers	*imyw-ḫnt*	I,27
courtiers	*smr*	II,43
courtiers	*šnwt*	II,128
courtyard	*ꜥrt*	I,72
covenant	*brṯ*	I,137
cover	*ꜥmḳ*	I,67
cover	*nmꜥ*	I,237
cover	*ḥbs*	I,308
cover	*kȝp*	II,168
cover	*ṯms*	II,229
cover	*dgȝ*	II,256
cover (vb.)	*ḥṯ*	I,339
cover (vb.)	*skȝp*	II,87
covered	*ꜥfnw*	I,65
covered	*ḥsȝ*	I,332
covered	*dgȝ*	II,256
covering	*ḥty*	I,335
covering	*ḳṯt*	II,180
covering	*tȝyt*	II,199
coverings	*wnr-ḫr*	I,103
coverings	*ḥbs*	I,308
covers	*inḥt*	I,35
covert	*bwȝt*	I,133
covet	*ȝbi*	I,4
covet	*mri*	I,192
covetous	*ꜥwn*	I,63
covetous	*ḥnty*	I,320
cow	*iḥt*	I,43
cow	*idt*	I,53
cow	*ḳmȝ*	II,151
cow type	*ḥr-sȝ-m*	I,323
coward	*ḥmt*	I,311
coward(?)	*ḥm*	I,311
cowardice	*kms*	II,174
cowherd	*sȝw*	II,6
cows	*ḫnrt*	I,366
crack	*ws*	I,110
crack (of dawn)	*šsp-ḥd*	II,136
craft	*ḥmt*	I,311
craftsman	*ḥmww*	I,313
crane (bird)	*ḏȝ*	II,259
cranium	*hn*	I,288
cranny	*bȝbȝ*	I,126
crate	*mgsp*	I,212
crater	*ṯpr*	II,229
cream	*smi*	II,41
create	*ḳmȝ*	II,150
create	*iri*	I,38
create	*msi*	I,204
create	*sḫpr*	II,69
create bewilderment	*stwh*	II,93
creation	*ḳmȝ*	II,150
creator	*ḳmȝ*	II,150
creator	*ḳd*	II,160
creator (female)	*gmyt*	II,189
creeper	*mꜥ*	I,181
crew	*ist*	I,46
crew	*hwtyw*	I,286
crew member	*rmṯ-ist*	I,46
crew member	*ist-mnš*	I,189
crews	*ḳryw*	II,155
crime	*isbt?*	I,47
crime	*ꜥḏȝ*	I,84
crime	*bin*	I,131
crime	*btȝ*	I,142
criminal	*nikw*	I,227
criminal	*ḫr*	I,370
cripple	*ṯhṯh*	II,232
criticize	(see find fault with)	
crock (for beer)	*ds*	II,255
crockery	*ḥnwt*	I,318
crocodile	*mryt*	I,194
crocodile	*msḥ*	I,205
crocodile	*dpy*	II,247

crook	*ḥḳꜣt*	I,334
crooked	*gwš*	II,186
crookedly (to lie)	*nwd*	I,232
crookedness	*gwš*	II,186
crops	*wꜣḥyt*	I,90
crops	*mḏꜥw*	I,220
crops	*skꜣw*	II,87
cross	*ꜣty*	I,9
cross	*ḏꜣi*	II,260
cross (adj.-vb.)	*sš*	II,79
cross over	*ḏꜣi*	II,260
crossroads	*smꜣty*	II,39
crowd	(see throng)	
crowd	*wnḏw*	I,104
crowd	*kꜣwy*	II,166
crowded	*gꜣw*	II,183
crown	*ꜣtf*	I,10
crown	*mḥw*	I,199
crown	*nws*	I,231
crown	*ḫꜥ*	I,352
crown (vb.)	*sḫꜥ*	II,68
crown prince	*r-pꜥt*	I,261
crowns	*ḫꜥw*	I,352
cruise about	*trr*	II,215
crumble	*fḫ*	I,165
crumpled to dust	*sb-n-tꜣ*	II,25
crush	*wꜥf*	I,95
crush	*ptpt*	I,158
crush	*mḏd*	I,221
crush	*nḏ*	I,255
crush	*ḫbḫb*	I,355
crush	*sin*	II,12
crush	*ḳḏḥ*	II,163
crush	*gmgm*	II,189
crush	*tḥs*	II,217
crush	*tš*	II,219
cry	*sgb*	II,89
cry	*ḏꜣꜥk*	II,261
cry (of satisfaction)	*hm*	I,287
cry (vb.)	(see weep)	
cry (vb.)	*sgb*	II,89
cry aloud	*ꜥš-sgb*	II,89
cry for help	*dꜥḳ(t)*	II,265
cry out	*iꜥnw*	I,17
cry out	*ꜥš-sgp*	I,79
cry out	*sbḥ*	II,28
cry out	*ḳy*	II,171
cry out	*tiꜣ*	II,200
cry out	*ḏꜥḳ(t)*	II,265
crying	*bgꜣw*	I,142
crypt	*ḫnw*	I,362
crypt(?)	*sbḫt*	II,28
crystal	*iwn*	I,20
crystal	*irḳbs*	I,41
cub	*ṯꜣ*	II,223
cubit	*mḥ*	I,198
cucumber	*bdt*	I,143
cucumber	*šsp(t)*	II,136
cucumbers	*bndt*	I,136
cucumbers	*sšpwt*	II,80
cucumbers	*šbt*	II,117
cudgel	*bḏn*	I,143
cuirasses	*rbšy*	I,270
cull	*ḳdf*	II,161
cult vessel	*ḳfḳft*	II,150
cultivate	*iri*	I,38
cultivate	*mḏꜥ*	I,220
cultivate	*skꜣ*	II,87
cultivated land	*iḥt*	I,44
cultivation	*skꜣ*	II,87
cultivator	*iḥwty*	I,44
cultivator	*mnity*	I,185
cumin	*tpnn*	II,208
cup	*mrsw*	I,195
cup	*ḥnwt*	I,318
cup (vessel)	*ḳṯ*	II,180
cupbearer	*wbꜣ*	I,96
curb	*wꜥf*	I,95
curb	*shdt*	II,61
curb	*grg*	II,192
curd	*smi*	II,41
cure (vb.)	*hrf*	I,291
cured	*snb*	II,50
cured	*twr*	II,202
curse	*sḥwr*	II,62
curse (vb.)	*wꜥꜣ*	I,93
curse (vb.)	*šni*	II,127
curtail	*ẖꜥḳ*	I,380
curtains	*wnr-ḫr*	I,103
cushion	*dbt*	II,244
custom	*ntꜥ*	I,253
custom	*sḫr*	II,73
custom	*sḫr m dwn*	II,73
cut	*šꜥd*	II,112
cut	*šfꜥ*	II,120
cut apart	*fdḳ*	I,166
cut down	*swꜣ*	II,17
cut down	*šꜥd*	II,112
cut off	*pns*	I,149
cut off	*fdḳ*	I,166
cut off	*ḥḥy*	I,329
cut off	*ḥsḳ*	I,333
cut off	*sꜣw*	II,7
cut off	*swꜣ*	II,17
cut off	*šꜥ*	II,110
cut off	*šꜥd*	II,112
cut off	*ḳḏḥ*	II,163
cut off	*gp*	II,188
cut out	*šdi*	II,140
cut up	*sꜣw*	II,7
cut up	*sfḫ*	II,35

cut up(?)	*nsns*	I,249
cuts of red meat	*dgꜣyt*	II,257
cutters	*šʿd*	II,112
cutting stone	*ḳḥḳḥ*	II,159
cutting(?)	*ḥṯ*	I,340
cypress	*ʿwnw*	I,63
cypress grass	*rdmt*	I,282
cypress grove	*ʿwnw*	I,63

D

dagger	*ḫrp*	I,328
daily	*m-mnt*	I,169
daily	*m-ḫrt-hrw*	I,170
daily	*m-mnt*	I,184
daily	*n-mnt*	I,224
daily	*ḫrt-hrw*	I,386
daily offerings	*imny*	I,30
daily portion	*imny*	I,30
daily ration	*imny*	I,30
daily service	*imny*	I,30
daily treatment(?)	*ḥꜣ-sꜣ*	I,295
dais	*ṯꜣtn*	II,227
dais	*ṯnṯꜣt*	II,230
dally	*wrš*	I,105
dam (of horses)	*mwt*	I,183
dam (vb.)	*dni*	II,249
dam up	*dni*	II,249
damage	*iḳw*	I,49
damage	*btꜣ*	I,142
damage	*gb*	II,187
damage (vb.)	*wh(i)*	I,106
damage (vb.)	*ḥḏ*	I,340
damage (vb.)	*ḫʿḳ*	I,380
damage (vb.)	*thꜣ*	II,216
damage(?)	*hꜣw*	I,285
damp	*mḳḳ*	I,210
damp-soil	*mḳḳ*	I,210
dance	*ṯrf*	II,231
dance (vb.)	*ḫbꜣ*	I,354
dance (vb.)	*krs*	II,176
dancer	*rwi*	I,267
dancer	*kmrw*	II,174
dancer	*ḏpḳ*	II,268
dancer (Nubian)	*ksks*	II,178
danger	*ḥty*	I,335
dangerous	*bin*	I,131
dangerous	*nḥꜣ*	I,242
dangers	*nḥꜣ-ḥr*	I,242
daring	(see boldness)	
dark	*km*	II,174
dark of night	*ḫꜣwy*	I,345
darkness	*wḫꜣ*	I,110
darkness	*wšꜣ(w)*	I,113
darkness	*ḫꜣwy*	I,345
darkness	*snk*	II,54
darkness	*kḥn*	II,177
darkness	*kkw*	II,179
dash ahead	*ḥfn*	I,309
date	*bnr*	I,135
date brew	*bnr*	I,135
date brew	*srmt*	II,58
date cake	*šʿyt*	II,111
date groves	*šꜣ*	II,105

dates	*sw*	II,17	decay	*ꜣḳ*	I,9
dates purveyor	*bnrty*	I,135	decaying	*isy*	I,45
daughter	*ꜥḏdt šrt*	I,85	deceased	*nty m ꜣw*	I,3
daughter	*sꜣt*	II,4	deceased	*mꜣꜥ-ẖrw*	I,175
daughter	*ꜥḏdit šrit*	II,132	deceased	*sꜥḥ*	II,15
daughter	*šrit*	II,132	deceit	*isft*	I,47
daughter-in-law	*sꜣt*	II,4	deceitfulness	*isft*	I,47
dawn	*ḥḏ-tꜣ*	I,341	deceive	*shꜣ*	II,60
dawn	*tꜣ-ḥḏ*	I,341	decide	*wpi*	I,98
dawn	*sḥḏ-tꜣ*	II,65	decide	*wḏꜥ*	I,122
dawn	*tꜣ ḥḏ*	II,197	decision	*wḏꜥ*	I,122
dawn	*tp-dwꜣyt*	II,206	decisions	*sẖr*	II,73
dawn	*tp-dwꜣyt*	II,242	decked	*dgꜣ*	II,256
dawn	*dwꜣyt*	II,242	declaration	*hry*	I,290
dawn (vb.)	*wbn*	I,97	declaratory	*hry*	I,290
day	*rꜥ*	I,266	decline	*ṛwi*	I,267
day	*hrw*	I,291	decorate	*ḥṯ*	I,339
day	*sw*	II,17	decorate	*sikr*	II,12
day before yesterday	*ẖmt m hrw*	I,361	decorate	*sẖkr*	II,76
			decorate	*sš*	II,78
daybreak	*wnyt*	I,101	decorate	*sḳr*	II,85
daytime	*hrw-wrš*	I,291	decorating	*sš*	II,78
dazzle	*gꜣgꜣ*	II,185	decorator	*nšdy*	I,250
dazzle	*ḏd*	II,276	decree	*wḏ(t)*	I,119
dazzled	*gꜣgꜣ*	II,185	decree (vb.)	*wḏ*	I,119
dazzling	*stḥn*	II,96	decrepit	*tnw*	II,212
ḏd-column	*ḏd*	II,276	dedicate	*mṯꜣ*	I,216
dead of night	*wšꜣ(w)*	I,113	deeds	*irwt*	I,40
dead of night	*nfrw-grḥ*	I,237	deeds	*sp*	II,30
dead one	*mni*	I,185	deem insignificant	*sẖry-ꜥ*	II,76
dead, be	*mt*	I,212	deep	*mḏ*	I,218
deaf	*sẖ*	II,66	deep darkness	*wšꜣ(w)*	I,113
deaf	*sẖy*	II,66	deep waters	*mtrw*	I,215
deaf	*sẖi*	II,75	deer	*hnn*	I,289
deaf	*dnrg*	II,251	defalcation	*wgg*	I,116
deaf man	*sẖy*	II,66	defeat	*ḥwrꜥ*	I,306
deafen	*hhi*	I,292	defeat	*dẖ*	II,255
deal with	*ir-hꜣw*	I,39	defend	*wšb*	I,114
deal with	*irt n*	I,39	defend	*ẖw*	I,353
deal with	*bꜣk*	I,127	defended	*ẖw-mk*	I,353
dealing with	*msbb*	I,205	defender	*mkw*	I,211
dealings	*ḥnw*	I,316	defender	*sꜣw*	II,6
dealings	*ẖnw*	I,362	defense	*mkt*	I,211
dealings	*sẖr*	II,73	defense	*nẖ*	I,244
dealings	*sšm*	II,81	defer	*wꜣḥ*	I,90
dear	*nꜥmw*	I,228	deferential	*snḏ*	II,55
death	*ꜣw*	I,3	deficiency	*gb*	II,187
death	*mt*	I,212	deficit	*ḏꜣt*	II,261
death's grapple	*mt*	I,212	defile	*gꜣwt*	II,184
debauch	*nk*	I,251	deflower	*wbꜣ*	I,96
debauch	*ẖꜥ*	I,380	defrauded	*shꜣ*	II,60
deben	*dbn*	II,245	defrauded	*gbi*	II,187
debt	*gb*	II,187	degenerate	*ẖpr*	I,356
debts	*wḏꜣ*	I,121	Deir el-Medineh	*pꜣ dmi*	II,248
decade	*sw mḏ*	II,17	delay (vb.)	*ꜥḥꜥ*	I,75
decan star	*snn*	II,52	delay (vb.)	*wꜣḥ*	I,90

delay (vb.)	*wdf*	I,118
delay (vb.)	*sin*	II,12
deliberate (vb.)	*wꜣwꜣ*	I,88
delight	*snḏm-ib*	I,23
delight	*ršw*	I,278
delight	*snḏm-ib*	II,56
delight	*ṯḥḥ*	II,114
delight (at)	*ḫntš*	I,367
delighted	*iꜣm*	I,14
delighted	*ḫntš*	I,367
delightful	*nḏm*	I,256
delightful	*twt*	II,203
delimit	*dr*	II,252
deliver	*fꜣy*	I,163
deliver	*nḥm*	I,243
deliver	*rdi*	I,281
deliver	*sꜥḳ*	II,16
deliver	*swḏ*	II,23
deliver	*šdi*	II,140
deliver (baby)	*pꜥpꜥ*	I,147
delivered	*iw*	I,18
delivered, be	*pri*	I,149
deliveries	*inw*	I,32
delivery	*šrmt*	II,133
delta marshes	*ḫꜣt-mḥw*	I,379
delta marshes	*sḫwr*	II,62
delta swamp	*idḥ*	I,55
demand	*wšbt*	I,114
demand (vb.)	*wḫꜣ*	I,109
demand(?)	*mri*	I,192
demarcate	*dr*	II,252
demarcate	*dgs*	II,257
demolish	*ḫm*	I,360
demolish	*sꜣw*	II,7
demolish	*sḫnn*	II,76
demolisher	*ḫmꜥ*	I,361
demon	*nbḏ*	I,234
demon	*ḫꜣyty*	I,345
demon	*smḥ*	II,44
demons	*šmꜣ*	II,122
demons (of terror)	*ḫrtiw*	I,328
demonstration	*iḥy*	I,42
demonstration	*wpwt*	I,99
denigrate	*wiꜣiꜣ*	I,92
denizen of the heavens	*iry-pt*	I,39
denounce	*smi*	II,40
denounce	*ḏd...smi*	II,275
dense	*nḥꜣ*	I,242
deny	*sḫwꜣ*	II,68
depart	*wḏi*	I,119
depart	*mšꜥ*	I,208
depart	*rwi*	I,267
depart	*hf*	I,287
depart	*šm*	II,121
depart	*tfi*	II,209
departments	*ꜥt*	I,59
departure	*wḏ(yt)*	I,120
dependents	*smdt*	II,46
dependents(?)	*nmḥ*	I,238
deposit (vb.)	*wꜣḥ*	I,89
deposited	*mn*	I,183
deposition	*r*	I,259
deposition	*šsp-r*	II,136
deposition	*ḏd*	II,275
deprive	*nḥm*	I,243
deprived	*sꜥḏꜣ*	II,16
deprived	*gbi*	II,186
deprived of	*ngꜣ*	I,252
deprived of	*šw*	II,113
depth	*mḏt*	I,219
deputy	*idnw*	I,54
deride	*fiṯ*	I,164
deride	*ṯḥr*	II,232
dermatitis(?)	*ḫḫ*	I,374
descend	*hꜣ(i)*	I,283
descend	*sfḫ*	II,36
descendant	*ms*	I,203
descendant	*mstiwty*	I,205
descendants	*ḏꜣmw*	II,262
descent	*sꜣḏr*	II,10
describe	*iri*	I,37
describe a curve	*ḳdi*	II,161
desert	*mrw*	I,194
desert	*ḫꜣst*	I,349
desert	*ḫrb*	I,372
desert	*šw*	II,114
desert	*ḳnr(t)*	II,155
desert	*dšrt*	II,255
desert (vb.)	*wꜥrt*	I,95
desert (vb.)	*wꜥr*	I,95
desert (vb.)	*nṯꜥ*	I,253
desert (vb.)	*ḫꜣꜥ*	I,346
desert dwellers	*ḫꜣstyw*	I,350
desert edge	*ḳnr(t)*	II,155
desert edge	*ꜥḏ*	I,83
desert necropolis	*smyt*	II,41
desert plateau	*wꜥrt*	I,95
deserters	*tšw*	II,220
deserve recognition	*mtr*	I,214
design	*tkꜥ*	II,220
designate	(see appoint)	
designate	*wꜣḥ-ḏrt*	I,90
designs	*sḫr*	II,73
designs	*ḳd*	II,161
desire	*ꜣbw*	I,4
desire	*ib*	I,22
desire	*mrwt*	I,193
desire	*ḥꜣty*	I,297
desire	*sꜣr*	II,8
desire (vb.)	*ꜣbi*	I,4

desire (vb.)	*iꜣb*	I,13
desire (vb.)	*ib*	I,22
desire (vb.)	*mri*	I,192
desist	*ḫty*	I,376
desolate (vb.)	*fḫ*	I,165
desolate (vb.)	*fk*	I,165
despicable	*ḥwr*	I,306
despise	*fiṯ*	I,164
despise	*msḏi*	I,207
despise	*sẖry-ꜥ*	II,76
despoil	*ꜥwn*	I,63
destined	*bh*	I,137
destined	*šꜣy*	II,106
destiny	*rnnt*	I,274
destiny	*šꜣy*	II,106
destitution	*tp-šw*	II,206
destroy	*ꜣḳ*	I,9
destroy	*fḫ*	I,165
destroy	*ḥsm*	I,332
destroy	*ḥḏ*	I,340
destroy	*sikn*	II,12
destroy	*smꜣ*	II,39
destroy	*sḥtm*	II,65
destroy	*sswn*	II,76
destroy	*sk*	II,85
destroy	*sksk*	II,88
destroy	*ḏbḏb*	II,268
destroyed	*ꜣḳ*	I,9
destroyed	*wš*	I,113
destroyed	*wḳp*	I,115
destroyed	*ḫr*	I,370
destroyer	*ḥtmt*	I,338
destruction	*iḳw*	I,49
destruction	*ḫbꜣ*	I,354
destruction	*skmkm*	II,88
details of	*wp*	I,97
details of	*tp-n*	II,205
detain	*ꜣb*	I,3
detain	*isḳ*	I,48
detain	*šnꜥ*	II,129
detainer	*šnꜥy*	II,129
deter	*dr*	II,252
deteriorate	*ꜣḳ*	I,9
determine	*wḏꜥ*	I,122
determine	*šꜣ*	II,106
determine right	*wpt-mꜣꜥt*	I,98
detest	*sꜣ(t)*	II,10
devastate	*fḫ*	I,165
devastate	*ḥnḳ*	I,319
develop	*ḫpr*	I,356
deviation	*nwd*	I,232
devise	*ḏꜥr*	II,264
devoid	*šw*	II,113
devoid of	*wš*	I,113
devoted to	*ꜣḫ*	I,7
devour	*wnm*	I,102
devouring flame	*wnmyt*	I,102
diadems	*ḫꜥw*	I,352
diarrhea	*whi*	I,106
dictate	*r*	I,259
die	*mni*	I,185
die	*mt*	I,212
die	*ḥtp*	I,337
difficult	*štꜣ*	II,138
difficult	*ḳsn*	II,159
difficult	*kh*	II,177
difficult	*ḏri*	II,272
difficult	*ḏrw*	II,273
difficulty	*ḏw(t)*	II,265
dig	*wꜥꜣ*	I,93
dig	*šdi*	II,140
dignitary	*sꜣb*	II,7
dignity	*sꜥḥ*	II,15
dignity	*šfyt*	II,120
dike	*ꜥ*	I,58
diligent	*dmi*	II,247
diminish	*šꜥ*	II,110
diminution	*ṯꜣy*	II,225
dire affliction	*ꜣdy*	I,10
dire affliction	*iꜣdt*	I,15
direct	*mꜣꜥ*	I,174
direct	*mni*	I,185
direct	*ḫrp*	I,372
direct	*sꜥḳꜣ*	II,16
direct	*smꜣꜥ*	II,39
direct	*sšm*	II,80
direct back	*ḫꜣꜥ*	I,347
direction	*wꜣt*	I,88
directions	*tp-rd*	II,205
directive	*tp-rd*	II,205
director	*ḫrp*	I,372
dirt	*iwtn*	I,22
dirt	*ḥs*	I,329
dirt	*ḏw(t)*	II,265
disaffected ones	*ẖꜣkw-ib*	I,380
disagree	*mdw*	I,216
disappear	*swꜣ*	II,17
disappearance	*sipw*	II,11
discard	*wꜣḥ*	I,89
discern	*rḫ*	I,275
discerning	*ip*	I,24
discharge (of fluid)	*ꜥḫ*	I,77
disclaim	*sḫwꜣ*	II,68
disclose	*wpi*	I,98
disclosure	*wp*	I,97
discouraged	*ft*	I,165
discouraging	*dḥ*	II,253
discourse	*mdt*	I,217
discover	*sbḳ*	II,29
discovery	*ꜥmw*	I,66
discreet	*ḥꜣp-ẖt*	I,299
discrete	*gr*	II,191

discuss	nḏnḏ	I,257
discuss	sḏd	II,104
disease	ḫꜣy(t)	I,345
disease	šmꜣ	II,122
disease bearing demons	šmꜣ	II,122
disease (of eye)	ḫr	I,369
disengage	sfḫ	II,35
disgorge	ḳꜥ	II,145
disgusted	ft	I,165
disgusted with	bḥnr	I,138
dish	rḥḏt	I,275
dish	ḥnwt	I,318
dish	dd(t)	II,258
dishes	mḥt	I,200
dishes	ḥnwt	I,318
disheveled	šnrf	II,131
dislodge	tfi	II,209
dismantle	fḫ	I,165
dismiss	rwi	I,267
dismiss	ḫꜣꜥ	I,346
disobey	thꜣ	II,216
disorder	tḫtḫ	II,219
disordered	sḫd	II,75
disordered hair(?)	msbb	I,205
disorderly	šnrf	II,131
disorders	ꜥbw	I,64
disparage	ḥḏ	I,340
dispatch	wḫꜣ	I,110
dispatch	sš-šꜥt	II,79
dispatch	šꜥt	II,110
dispatch (vb.)	wḏi	I,119
dispatch (vb.)	ḫꜣꜥ	I,346
dispatch (vb.)	sbi	II,25
dispatch office	st šꜥt	II,3
dispatch office	st-šꜥt	II,111
dispel	ḫsr	I,374
dispel	dr	II,252
dispenser of entertainment	sḫmḫt-ib	I,23
disperse	ḫnr	I,364
displace	mn	I,184
displace	mnmn	I,187
displace	rmni	I,271
displaced	mnmn	I,187
display (vb.)	iri	I,37
display (vb.)	wṯs	I,117
displeased	ḥḏn	I,342
dispose of	ꜥḳ ḥr	I,80
disposed	hꜣ(i)	I,283
disposition	biꜣt	I,130
disposition	šꜣy	II,106
disposition	ḳd	II,160
dispositions	sḫr	II,72
dispossess	ꜥwn	I,63
dispute	mdt	I,217
dispute	swnḫ	II,20
dispute	sḫwn	II,68
dispute	šnṯt	II,131
dispute (vb.)	mdw	I,216
dispute (vb.)	sḫn	II,71
dispute (vb.)	ḏd	II,275
disregard	wni	I,101
disregard	ḫꜣꜥ	I,347
disregard	ṯḥr	II,232
disreputable	wgg	I,116
dissolution	fḫt	I,165
distance	wꜣt	I,88
distant	wꜣi	I,87
distinguish	iwd	I,22
distinguish	wpi	I,98
distinguish	stn	II,95
distinguished	stn	II,95
distinguished	sṯn	II,97
distort	sꜣḏr	II,11
distracted	gwš	II,186
distraught	hꜣ(i)	I,283
distress	ꜥdd	I,82
distress	ḥr-(n)-ḥr	I,322
distressed	ind	I,36
distribute	dni	II,249
distribution	tp-šw	II,114
district	iꜣdt	I,15
district	w	I,87
district	ww	I,96
district	spꜣt	II,32
district	sḫt	II,66
district	ṯs	II,235
district	tꜣš	II,199
district governor	ḥḳꜣ-w(t)	I,334
district of the marsh	tnt-šꜣ	II,214
district officer	wꜥrtw	I,95
district(?)	ḫꜣrw	I,349
districts	ḳꜥḥt	II,146
disturb	ẖnn	I,384
ditch	šgr	II,137
dive	tꜣḥ	II,199
diverge	sbn	II,28
divert	wḏb	I,122
divert from duty	sẖnw	II,75
divert oneself	sḏꜣ-ḥr	II,100
divide	png	I,149
divide	pš	I,157
divider	pši	I,157
divination	kṯmw	II,181
divine	nṯry	I,254
Divine Adoratress	dw3-nṯr	II,242
divine booth	sḥ-nṯr	II,61
divine child	ms-nṯr	I,203
divine father	it-nṯr	I,50
divine images	rḫw	I,276

divine matters	*ḫt-nṯr*	I,343
divine offerings	*ḥtpw-nṯr*	I,254
divine offerings	*ḥtpw-nṯr*	I,337
divine record	*mḏꜣt-nṯr*	I,219
divine records	*mḏꜣt-nṯr*	I,254
divine scroll	*mḏꜣt-nṯr*	I,254
divine statue	*rḫ.n.f*	I,276
Divine Votaress	*dwꜣ-nṯr*	II,242
divine words	*mdw-nṯr*	I,218
divine words	*mdw-nṯr*	I,254
diviner	*rḫ(t)*	I,276
division	*pš*	I,157
divorce	*nṯꜥ*	I,253
divorce	*ḫꜣꜥ*	I,346
dnw-stone	*dnw*	II,251
do	*iri*	I,37
do again	*wḥm*	I,108
do harm	*sꜥḏꜣ*	II,16
do injustice	*sꜥḏꜣ*	II,16
do not allow	*m-ḏrty*	I,173
do not be anxious	*m-di-ḫꜣty.k*	I,172
do not!	*m*	I,167
do not!	*m-ir*	I,167
do not!	*m-di*	I,172
do service	*bꜣk*	I,127
do the registering	*snh*	II,53
do wrong	*thꜣ*	II,216
dock (vb.)	*mni*	I,185
dockyard	*wḫrt*	I,110
dockyard	*ḫr*	I,368
document	*mḏꜣt*	I,219
document	*r-ꜥ-sšw*	I,261
document	*hꜣy*	I,285
document	*snn*	II,51
document	*sš*	II,78
documents	*hry*	I,290
documents	*sḫꜣ*	II,67
documents	*drf*	II,252
doddering	*šš*	II,137
dog	*iw*	I,18
dog	*krb*	II,175
dog	*ṯsm*	II,236
dole out	*ḫꜣꜥ*	I,347
domain	*rmnyt*	I,271
domain lands	*rmnyt*	I,271
domesticated animal	*ptr*	I,159
dominate	*sps*	II,34
dominion	*wꜣs*	I,90
dom-palm	*mꜣmꜣ*	I,176
dom-palm nuts	*ḳwḳw*	II,147
don	*wnḫ*	I,103
don	*ṯꜣy*	II,224
don't worry about	*m di ḫꜣty*	I,298
donated land	*ḥnk*	I,320
donation	*imyt-pr*	I,27
donation	*ḥnk*	I,320
donation for the wife	*šp-n-st-ḥmt*	II,118
done out of excellence	*irt mnḫ*	I,39
donkey	*ꜥꜣ*	I,61
donkey	*ḥꜣmr*	I,299
don't be anxious	*m-di-ḫꜣꜥty.k*	I,172
doom	*šꜣy*	II,106
door	*ꜥꜣ*	I,61
door	*r*	I,259
door	*sꜣ*	II,5
door	*sbꜣ*	II,26
door	*tꜣyt*	II,199
door	*tri*	II,215
door	*ṯr*	II,231
door	*dwꜣ*	II,242
door latch	*ḥgꜣi*	I,335
door leaves	*ꜥꜣ*	I,61
door leaves	*tri*	II,215
door part	*ḏwꜣwt*	II,242
doorframe	*sbꜣ*	II,26
doorframe	*sbḫt*	II,28
doorjamb	*bnš*	I,135
doorjambs	*ḥi*	I,300
doorjambs	*ḥtrw*	I,339
doorkeeper	*iry-ꜥꜣ*	I,61
doorkeeper	*ꜥꜣ*	I,61
doorkeeper	*ḥry-ꜥꜣ*	I,61
doorkeeper	*wn*	I,101
doorkeeper	*mnty*	I,185
doorkeeper	*mnty*	I,190
doorpost	*twꜣ*	II,202
doorposts	*bnš*	I,135
doorposts	*ḥtyw*	I,336
doorposts	*ḥtrw*	I,339
doorway	*hꜣy*	I,284
doorway	*sbḫt*	II,29
doorway	*dwꜣ*	II,242
doorways	*sbꜣ*	II,26
double (vb.)	*sḳb*	II,84
double (vb.)	*ḳb*	II,147
double crown	*sḫmty*	II,70
double doors	*ꜥꜣ*	I,61
double granary	*šnwt*	II,130
double plumes	*šwty*	II,115
double throne	*sty*	II,2
double-feathered crown	*sšd-šwty*	II, 83
dough	*šdw*	II,141
dough(?)	*ḫꜣd*	I,350
dove(?)	*mnt*	I,184
dovecot(?)	*mḥi*	I,199
down below	*r-bnr*	I,261
down below	*r-ḫry*	I,386
down hearted (?)	*ḏsḏs-ib*	II,275

down to	*nfryt-r*	I,236
down to	*r-ẖry*	I,264
down to	*r-šꜣʿ*	II,107
downstream	*m-ḫd*	I,170
dowry	*sfr*	II,35
dowry	*grgt*	II,193
draft	*sš-ḳdwt*	II,79
drag	*itḥ*	I,52
drag	*sḫḫ*	II,74
drag	*stꜣ*	II,92
drag	*šdi*	II,139
drag	*šdd*	II,142
drag off	*stꜣ*	II,92
drain (vb.)	*ẖʿ*	I,380
draughtsman	*sš-ḳd*	II,79
draughtsman	*sš-ḳd*	II,161
draw	*stꜣ*	II,92
draw back	*swbb*	II,19
draw breath	*itḥ-ṯꜣw*	I,52
draw forth	*šdi*	II,140
draw near	*tkn*	II,220
draw nigh	*ḫʿm*	I,353
draw nigh	*ḳri*	II,155
draw out	*itḥ*	I,52
draw out	*tbtb*	II,204
draw through	*ḫns*	I,366
draw up (battle line)	*irt sk*	II,86
draw up troops	*ṯs skw*	II,86
drawing	*r-ʿ-itḥ*	I,260
drawing	*r-ʿ-sšw*	I,261
drawing	*r-sš*	II,78
drawings	*ḳd*	II,161
drawn	*dr*	II,252
dread	*ꜣw*	I,3
dread	*fꜣw*	I,164
dread	*nrw*	I,239
dread	*ḥryt*	I,326
dread	*šʿt*	II,110
dread	*šfyt*	II,120
dreadful	*bin*	I,131
dream	*wpt-mꜣʿt*	I,98
dream	*rswt*	I,278
dream	*ḳd(t)*	II,161
dreary(?)	*gꜣbwy*	II,184
dregs	*tꜣḥt*	II,199
dress	*idg*	I,55
dress	*mss*	I,206
dress (vb.)	*wnḫ*	I,103
dressed	*dr*	II,252
dried meat	*dr*	II,252
dried grass	*šwy*	II,114
dried up	*šw*	II,113
drink	*dbyt*	II,245
drink (vb.)	*sʿm*	II,14
drink (vb.)	*swr*	II,20

drinking	*ṯnf*	II,230
drinking mug	*ḏꜣḏꜣ*	II,263
drinking vessels	*kṯ*	II,180
drip (vb.)	*ḏfḏ*	II,269
drive	*ḥwꜣ*	I,305
drive	*thm*	II,216
drive away	*ḫsf-ʿ*	I,374
drive away	*sḥr*	II,64
drive from	*tkn ḥr*	II,221
drive in	*sʿḳ*	II,15
drive off	*hd*	I,293
drive out	*nwš*	I,231
drooping(?)	*bdš*	I,143
drop (a calf)	*pʿpʿ*	I,147
drop (down)	*hꜣ(i)*	I,283
drop (vb.)	*ḫꜣʿ*	I,347
drop (vb.)	*ḏfḏ*	II,269
drops	*ḏfḏ*	II,269
droves (of cattle)	*ṯsw*	II,235
drown	*ʿgꜣ*	I,81
drowse	*nmʿ*	I,237
drug	*ḫꜣw*	I,345
drum	*ṯbṯb*	II,228
drummer	*shꜣt*	II,60
drunk	(see intoxicated)	
drunk	*nwḥ*	I,231
drunk	*tḫi*	II,218
drunkards	*nꜣ ḥnḳt*	I,319
drunkenness	*tḫw*	II,218
dry	*šw*	II,113
dry	*šr*	II,131
dry grass	*šwy*	II,114
dry up	*ʿḫm*	I,78
dryness	*wšr*	I,115
Duat	*dwꜣt*	II,243
duck	*ꜣpd*	I,6
due	*wpwt*	I,99
due	*mn*	I,184
dues	*šꜣyt*	II,107
duly mourned over(?)	*ḏrtyw*	II,271
duly registered	*wʿrt*	I,95
dumbfounded	*sgꜣ*	II,89
dumbfounded	*gꜣgꜣ*	II,185
dung	*ḥrit*	I,323
dung	*dbn*	II,245
dunking	*ḏbg*	II,268
dungeon(?)	*ḫbt*	I,354
duplicity	*sp-snw*	II,30
durable, become	*swꜣḥ*	II,18
duration	*ʿḥʿw*	I,77
duration	*ḏd*	II,276
during	*m*	I,167
during	*n*	I,223
dusk	*rwhꜣ*	I,268

dust	*iwtn*	I,22
dust	*ḫmy*	I,361
dust	*sꜣt*	II,10
dust (vb.)	*šḫḳ*	II,133
dust cloud	*šḫḳ*	II,133
duties	*sḥn*	II,63
duties	*kꜣt*	II,167
duty	*irit*	I,40
duty	*irwt*	I,40
duty	*bꜣkw*	I,127
duty	*ntꜥ*	I,253
duty	*ḳd*	II,160
duty roster	*tp-n-sḥn*	II,205
dwarf	*nmw*	I,238
dwell	*ḥms*	I,314
dwell	*ḥtp*	I,336
dwell	*snḏm*	II,56
dwell	*sḫny*	II,71
dwell	*ḳꜣi*	II,143
dwelling	*ꜥt*	I,59
dwelling	*hin(t)*	I,286
dwelling	*ḫnw*	I,362
dwelling	*kr*	II,175
dwelling	*ḏrwt*	II,273
dye (vb.)	*wḏḥ*	I,123
dyke	*dnit*	II,250
dyke (vb.)	*dni*	II,249
dysentery	*whi*	I,106

E

each and every	*r-tnw*	I,265
eager	*ḳni*	II,152
ear	*msḏr*	I,207
ear	*smt*	II,45
earlier	*mꜥrw*	I,181
earlier	*mr*	I,192
ears	*ꜥnḫwy*	I,71
earth	*iwtn*	I,22
earth	*sꜣt*	II,10
earthquake	*mnmn-n-tꜣ*	I,187
ease	*mtn*	I,214
ease	*mdn*	I,218
easily tired	*gꜣḥ*	II,185
east	*iꜣbt*	I,14
East	*iꜣbtt*	I,14
East	*wbn*	I,97
East	*ḫꜥ*	I,351
east side	*tꜣ-wr*	II,198
eastern	*iꜣbt*	I,14
easy	*snḏm*	II,56
eat	*wnm*	I,102
eat	*ḳꜣḳꜣ*	II,145
ebony tree	*hbny*	I,287
ebony wood	*hbny*	I,287
ecstatic	*ḫꜣꜥ*	I,347
edge	*spt*	II,31
edge	*smyt*	II,41
educate	*mtr*	I,214
educate	*sbꜣ*	II,26
education	*ḫpriw*	I,357
education	*sbꜣyt*	II,27
efface	*sin*	II,12
efface	*krp*	II,175
effect	*ꜥrꜥr*	I,72
effect	*ḫpr*	I,356
effect (an arrival)	*iri*	I,38
effective	*imim*	I,30
effective	*tnr*	II,213
effeminate man	*ḥmt*	I,311
efficacious	*mnḫ*	I,189
efficiency	*ꜣḫw*	I,7
efficiency	*mnḫ(t)*	I,189
efficient	*mnḫ*	I,189
effigy	*ḳꜣi*	II,143
egg	*swḥt*	II,21
Egypt	*tꜣ-mri*	II,198
either	*m-r-ꜥ*	I,169
either	*m-mitt*	I,180
either	*m-mitt*	I,169
either	*n-mitt*	I,224
either	*gr(t)*	II,191
ejaculation	*ꜥꜣꜥ*	I,61
eject	*ḫꜣꜥ*	I,346

elapse	*ꜥḳ*	I,80
elapse	*ḫpr*	I,356
elapse	*swꜣ*	II,17
elated	*ꜥꜣ(i)*	I,59
elder	*ꜥꜣ*	I,60
elder	*wr*	I,104
elder	*smsw*	II,44
elder of the doorway	*smsw-hyt*	II,45
elderly soldier	*iꜣw*	I,13
eldest	*smsw*	II,44
electrum	*ḏꜥm*	II,264
eliminate	*sḥtm*	II,65
elite troops	*nfrw*	I,236
embalmer	*wt*	I,116
embankment	*ḫꜣpw*	I,348
embankment(?)	*smꜣ-sꜣtw*	II,38
embark	*ḥꜣ(i)*	I,283
embarrassed	*ḥnrg*	I,319
embellish	*smnḫ*	II,43
embellished	*mꜥn*	I,181
embellished	*smnḫ*	II,43
embers	*ḳꜣrmꜥti*	II,144
embers	*ḳrmt*	II,156
embezzlement	*wgg*	I,116
embitter	*dḥr*	II,254
emboss	*mgs*	I,212
embrace	*ḥpt*	I,309
embrace	*ḳni*	II,153
embrace (vb.)	*ḫnm*	I,383
embrace (vb.)	*šni*	II,126
embrace (vb.)	*ḳn*	II,153
embroidery(?)	*ḥpt*	I,309
emerge	*bsi*	I,139
emerge	*pri*	I,149
emerge	*šm*	II,121
emerge	*kfi*	II,172
emerging land	*prw*	I,151
eminent	*stn*	II,95
emissary	*ipwty*	I,25
emmer	*bty*	I,143
emphasize	*ḳꜣ*	II,143
employ	*sḥn*	II,63
employee	*ipty*	I,26
employment	*ḥnw*	I,316
employment	*smdt*	II,46
empty	*ḫꜥ*	I,380
empty	*šw*	II,113
emulate	*stn*	II,95
enchant	*šni*	II,127
enchant	*rkꜣ*	I,279
enchanted	*iꜣm*	I,14
enchantment	*ḥkꜣ*	I,334
encircle	*pẖr*	I,155
encircle	*šni*	II,126
encircle	*dbnbn*	II,245
enclose	*inḥ*	I,35
enclose	*inḳ*	I,35
enclose	*ꜥrf*	I,72
enclose	*swꜣḥ*	II,18
enclosed	*dpḫ*	II,247
enclosed structure	*ṯꜣrt*	II,226
enclosure	*inb*	I,33
enclosure	*ssw*	II,76
enclosure	*šnw*	II,126
enclosures	*st*	II,2
encompass	*inḥ*	I,35
encompass	*inḳ*	I,35
encompass	*ꜥrf*	I,72
encompass	*šni*	II,126
encounter	*ḥr-(n)-ḥr*	I,322
encounter (vb.)	*ṯḥn*	II,232
encroach	*hd*	I,292
encrusted	*mḥ*	I,198
encumber	*ḥn*	I,316
end	*ꜣt*	I,1
end	*pḥwy*	I,153
end	*r-ꜥ*	I,260
end (of life)	*nfryt*	I,236
end (vb.)	*mnḳ*	I,190
endeavors	*ḏnn*	II,270
ending	*grḥ*	II,192
endow	*smnḫ*	II,43
endow	*sdf*	II,99
endow	*sḏfꜣ(y)*	II,100
endowed	*smnḫ*	II,43
endowment	*sꜥnḫw*	II,14
endowment	*smnḫt*	II,43
endowment	*sdf*	II,99
endowment	*sḏfꜣw*	II,101
endowments(?)	*ḥtpw-nṯr*	I,337
end-piece of a collar	*ḥty*	I,336
ends	*pḥww*	I,153
ends	*ḥnty*	I,317
ends	*ḥnty*	I,320
endurance	*ḏd*	II,276
endure	*wꜣḥ*	I,89
endure	*mn*	I,183
endure	*swꜣḥ*	II,18
endure	*šsp*	II,135
endure	*šps*	II,118
endure	*ḏd*	II,276
enemies	*pšnw*	I,158
enemies	*ḫr*	I,370
enemy	*ḫfty*	I,359
enemy	*ḫr*	I,370
enemy	*ḫrw*	I,372
enemy	*sbi*	II,28
enemy	*iry-n-ṯṯṯ*	II,237
energetic	*tnr*	II,213
enfeeble	*di gnn*	II,190

enfeebled	*sꜣyt*	II,6
enfold	*bnd*	I,135
engage	*ṯs*	II,233
engage in	*nhp*	I,240
engage in reconnoitering	*smt*	II,45
engage with	*ṯḥn*	II,232
engaged (in or with)	*ḥms*	I,314
engaged, be	*ꜥḥꜥ*	I,75
engrave	*nḳꜥ*	I,250
engrave	*ḫty*	I,376
engrave	*ṯꜣ*	II,223
engraver	*ḫty*	I,376
enjoy	*sꜣ*	II,5
enjoyment	*sḏꜣyt*	II,100
enjoyment of health	*smꜣ-m-snb*	II,38
enlarge	*sꜥꜣ*	II,13
enlarge	*swsḫ*	II,22
enlightened	*wbꜣ*	I,96
Ennead	*psḏt*	I,157
ennoble	*sꜥꜣ*	II,13
enrage	*sḳnd*	II,84
enraged	*ḳnd*	II,155
enregister	*spẖr*	II,33
enregistered	*wꜥrt*	I,95
enrich	*sikr*	II,12
enrich	*swsr*	II,22
enrich	*sḥḏ*	II,65
enrich	*sḫwd*	II,68
enrich	*špssw*	II,119
enroll	*pgꜣ*	I,158
enroll	*spẖr*	II,33
ensnare	*sḫbḫ*	II,68
ensnare	*sḫt*	II,74
ensnare	*sḫtḫt*	II,75
ensnare (?)	*sḫni*	II,71
enter	*ꜥḳ*	I,80
enter	*ꜥḳꜥḳ*	I,81
enter	*hb*	I,286
enter	*ḫnḫn*	I,384
enter	*sꜥḳ*	II,15
enter in	*ḫnbb*	I,383
enterprising	*pr-ꜥ-ib*	I,150
entertain	*sḫmḫ-ib*	II,70
entertain	*sšš*	II,83
entertainer	*sḫmḫt-ib*	I,23
entertainer	*sḫmḫ-ib*	II,71
entertainment	*sḫmḫ-ib*	II,71
entire	*mi-ḳd*	I,178
entire	*r-ḏr*	I,265
entire	*tm*	II,210
entire	*tmmw*	II,211
entire land	*tꜣ ḏr.f*	II,197
entire(?)	*(mi)-ḳd.f*	II,160
entirely	*mi-ḳd*	I,178
entirely	*r-ꜣw*	I,260
entirety	*r-ꜣw*	I,3
entities	*wnḏw*	I,103
entirety	*ḏrw*	II,271
entomb	*ḳrs*	II,158
entourage	*šnwt*	II,128
entrails	*mẖt*	I,203
entrance	*ꜥrr(y)t*	I,73
entrap	*sḫtḫt*	II,75
entrust	*nḥtj*	I,244
entrust	*ḥn*	I,315
entrust	*swḏ*	II,23
envelope	*inḥ*	I,35
enveloping	*ꜥfnw*	I,65
environs	*hꜣw*	I,285
envoy	*ipwty*	I,25
envoy	*wpwty*	I,99
envoy	*mšꜥyty*	I,208
epagomenal days	*ḥryw-rnpt*	I,326
epidemic	*iꜣdt rnpt*	I,15
epidemic	*snm-rnpt*	II,51
epilepsy	*nsy*	I,247
equal	*mitt*	I,179
equal	*sn-nw*	II,48
equal	*sḫr*	II,72
equal (vb.)	*mẖꜣ*	I,201
equerry	*kḏn*	II,181
equip	*ꜥpr*	I,65
equip	*nsk*	I,249
equip	*ḥn*	I,315
equip	*sdbḥ*	II,98
equip	*spd*	II,34
equip	*grg*	II,192
equipage	*ḥtr*	I,338
equipment	*ꜥprwt*	I,65
equipment	*mndt*	I,191
equipment	*rks*	I,280
equipment	*ḫꜥw*	I,352
equipment	*sꜥbw*	II,14
equipment	*grg*	II,193
equipment	*ṯnfyt*	II,230
equipped	*sꜥb*	II,13
equivalence	*šb(t)*	II,116
equivalent	*šꜣw*	II,108
erase	*krp*	II,175
erased	*ft*	I,165
erect	*šp*	II,118
erect (vb.)	*ḥts*	I,339
erect (vb.)	*sꜥḥꜥ*	II,15
erect (vb.)	*smn*	II,42
erect (vb.)	*dgꜣ*	II,256
erect, become	*bnbn*	I,134
ergastulum	*šnꜥ*	II,128
errand	*wpwt*	I,99
errands	*mšꜥw*	I,208

error	*kms*	II,174
errors	*ꜥḏꜣ*	I,84
escape	*wꜥr*	I,95
escape	*pwy*	I,148
escape	*pri*	I,149
escape	*nh*	I,240
escape	*rwi*	I,267
escape(?)	*wh(i)*	I,106
escort	*sꜥšꜣt*	II,16
escort	*šmsw*	II,125
esophagus	*tpḥt*	II,209
espy	*gmḥ*	II,189
essence	*mw*	I,182
establish	*wꜣḥ*	I,89
establish	*sꜣp*	II,8
establish	*sꜥḥꜥ*	II,15
establish	*smn*	II,41
establish	*smnḫ*	II,42
establish	*šps*	II,118
establish	*gm*	II,188
establish	*grg*	II,192
established	*mn*	I,183
established	*smnḫ*	II,43
established	*ḏd*	II,276
estate	*pr*	I,149
estate	*mnꜥt*	I,186
estate	*sḫr*	II,73
esteem	*tri*	II,214
etc.	*ḥmt-r*	I,312
etc.	*ḥmy-r*	I,312
eternal image	*sꜥḥ*	II,15
eternity	*nḥḥ*	I,243
eternity	*r-nḥḥ*	I,262
eternity	*ḏt*	II,259
evacuate	*sšw*	II,80
evade	*tši*	II,220
even as	*mi*	I,178
even if	*ḫr-m-sꜣ*	I,369
even, make	*mḫꜣ*	I,201
evening	*wḫꜣ*	I,110
evening	*mšrw*	I,209
evening	*rwhꜣ*	I,268
evening	*grḥ*	II,192
evening	*tr-n-rwhꜣ*	II,214
evening meal	*msyt*	I,204
evening-bark	*sktt*	II,88
event	*sp*	II,30
ever since	*m-dwn-m-dwn*	I,172
everlastingness	*ḏt*	II,259
every	*iwd*	I,22
every	*nb*	I,232
every	*tnw*	II,212
every day	*rꜥ-nb*	I,266
every day	*ḫrt-hrw*	I,386
every time	*tnw*	II,212
everybody	*bw-nb*	I,133
everybody	*ḥr-nb*	I,322
everyone	*bw-nb*	I,133
everyone	*pꜣ nty nb*	I,233
everyone	*rmṯ-nbt*	I,272
everyone	*ḥr-nb*	I,322
everyone	*s nb*	II,1
everyone	*tmw*	II,210
everyone	*tmmw*	II,211
everything	*sšr*	II,82
everything beyond	*ḥꜣw-nbw*	I,296
evict	*wiꜣ*	I,92
evil	*ꜣw*	I,3
evil	*iwy*	I,18
evil	*isft*	I,47
evil	*ꜥḏꜣ*	I,84
evil	*bin*	I,131
evil	*nf*	I,234
evil	*twꜣ*	II,2
evil	*ḏw*	II,265
evil	*ḏw(t)*	II,265
evil deed	*ṯꜣy*	II,225
evil injuries	*ṯms*	II,229
evil moments(?)	*sꜣiꜣ*	II,5
evil of character	*ḏw ḳd*	II,265
evil one	*nbḏ*	I,234
evil renown	*mtn*	I,214
evil thing	*bin*	I,131
evildoer	*ḫꜣkw-ib*	I,380
evildoers	*ḫꜣk-ib*	I,23
evildoers	*isft*	I,47
evil-faced one	*ḏw ḥr*	II,265
eviscerate	*mš*	I,207
ewer(?)	*nw*	I,230
exact	*ꜥḳꜣ*	I,81
exact	*mt*	I,213
exact (vb.)	*šsp*	II,135
exact (vb.)	*šdi*	II,140
exact thing	*ꜥḳꜣ*	I,81
exactly	*ꜥḳꜣ*	I,81
exaggeration	*ꜥbꜥ*	I,64
exalt	*iꜣw*	I,12
exalt	*wṯs*	I,117
exalt	*sꜥꜣ*	II,13
exalt	*sḳꜣ*	II,84
exalt	*ṯni*	II,229
exalt	*ṯs*	II,235
exaltation	*ihy*	I,42
exalted	*sḳb*	II,84
exalted	*ḳꜣ*	II,143
examination	*ḥy*	I,300
examination	*sipt*	II,11
examination	*smtr*	II,46
examination	*sḏmw*	II,102
examination	*šnw*	II,127
examine	*mtr*	I,214
examine	*sip*	II,11

examine	*smtr*	II,45
example of	*ꜥ*	I,57
excavate	*šdi*	II,140
excavate (of stone)	*nḥm*	I,243
exceed	*iṯi*	I,52
exceedingly	*r-iḳr*	I,49
exceedingly	*r-ꜥꜣt-wrt*	I,60
exceedingly	*r-ꜥꜣt-wrt*	I,104
exceedingly	*r-iḳr*	I,260
exceedingly	*r-ꜥꜣ-wr*	I,261
excel	*iṯi*	I,52
excellence	*mnḫ(t)*	I,189
excellent	*ꜣḫ*	I,7
excellent	*iḳr*	I,49
excellent	*mds*	I,218
excellent	*nfr*	I,235
excellent	*sbḳ*	II,29
excellent things	*ꜣḫw*	I,7
excellent, be	*mnḫ*	I,189
except	*wpw*	I,99
except	*ḥr*	I,321
except	*ḥrw*	I,327
except for	*wpw-ḥr*	I,99
except for	*ḥry-ḥr*	I,325
except for	*ḥrw-r*	I,327
exception	*spp*	II,32
excess	*prw*	I,151
excess	*ḥꜣw*	I,296
exchange	*šb*	II,116
exchange	*ḏbꜣ*	II,266
excited	*sḏꜣ*	II,100
excited feelings	*šrgḥ*	II,133
excitement	*syḥ*	II,12
exclude	*sꜥšꜣ*	II,16
excluded from(?)	*ḫmy*	I,361
exclusive	*n-ḥꜣw*	I,296
excrement	(see dung)	
excrement	*ḥs*	I,329
excrement	*t-ẖry*	II,197
excursion	*swtwt*	II,23
execute	*iri*	I,38
execute	*stkn*	II,96
execution block	*dpḥ*	II,247
executioner	*mnḥ*	I,188
executioners	*ḫꜣyt*	I,345
exempt	*ḫw-mk*	I,353
exercise (authority)	*iri*	I,38
exert oneself	*pss*	I,156
exert oneself	*ḏnn*	II,270
exhaust	*wꜥb*	I,94
exhaust	*pnḳ*	I,149
exhaust	*ḫꜥ*	I,380
exhausted	*sḏḥy*	II,103
exist	*wn*	I,100
exist	*ḫpr*	I,356
exorcise	*sḥr*	II,64
expand	*sš*	II,79
expedition	*ipwt*	I,25
expedition	*wpwt*	I,99
expedition	*wḏ(yt)*	I,120
expedition	*mšꜥ*	I,208
expel	*sḥr*	II,64
expel	*dr*	II,252
expenditure	*hꜣw*	I,285
expenses	*hꜣw*	I,285
experience	*ꜥꜣy.f m di.f*	I,60
experience	*rḫ*	I,275
experienced	*ip-ib*	I,23
experienced	*šsꜣ*	II,134
expert	*ip*	I,24
expert	*ḥry-tp*	I,326
explain	*wpi*	I,98
explain	*wḥꜥ*	I,107
explain	*sḥḏ*	II,65
explanation	*wšb*	I,114
explore	*hb*	I,286
exposed as	*ḥꜣy*	I,295
express concern	*ms-ib* (*ꜣms*)	I,23
expression	*tpw-r*	II,208
extend	*ꜣw(i)*	I,2
extend	*bsi*	I,139
extend	*pgꜣ*	I,158
extend	*swsḫ*	II,22
extend	*sš*	II,79
extend	*ḳꜥh*	II,146
extend	*ḏꜣ*	II,259
extend (protection)	*stp-sꜣ*	II,94
extensive	*wsḫ*	I,112
extent	*m-ꜣw*	I,3
extent	*mḏt*	I,219
extinguish	*ꜥḫm*	I,78
extol	*wṯs*	I,117
extol	*sꜥꜣ*	II,13
extol	*swꜣš*	II,18
extol	*swh*	II,21
extra	*m-ḥꜣw*	I,169
extract (vb.)	*šdi*	II,140
extras	*rwtyw*	I,268
extreme	*pḥwy*	I,153
extremities	*pḥwy*	I,153
extremity (of a baton)	*ꜥḳt*	I,81
exult	*ꜥḏꜥḏ*	I,84
exult	*ḥꜥy*	I,301
exult	*ḫntš*	I,367
exultation	*hꜣy*	I,284
exultation	*sšš*	II,83
exultation	*ṯhwt-ib*	II,232
exultations	*ṯhh*	II,232
eye	*irt*	I,40
eye amulet	*wḏꜣ(w)*	I,122
eye balls	*bnr*	I,134

eye paint	*msdmt*	I,207
eye, damaged	*nknt*	I,251
eyebrow	*inḥ*	I,35
eyelids	*ꜥwy-n irt*	I,57
eye-paint	*sdm*	II,99
eye-paint	*sḏm*	II,102
eye-tweezer	*ṯꜣy-irt*	II,224

F

fabric	*nḏ*	I,255
fabric(?)	*šnw*	II,128
fabricate	*mnḫ(t)*	I,189
fabrication	*bꜣkw*	I,127
fabrics	*nwt*	I,231
face	*ḥꜣwty*	I,298
face	*ḥr*	I,320
face fractures	*sd-ḥrw*	II,98
faced with	*ḫft-ḥr*	I,359
faced with	*ḫft-r*	I,359
facing	*ꜥkꜣ*	I,81
fact	*mꜣꜥt*	I,175
faggot	*ḏnḏnrt*	II,270
faience	*irrt*	I,41
faience	*bꜥbꜥ*	I,132
faience	*tḥnt*	II,217
faience	*ṯḥn*	II,232
faience worker	*bꜥbꜥ*	I,132
fail	*wh(i)*	I,106
failings (?)	*iꜣw*	I,12
failure	*rwhꜣ*	I,268
failure	*tm*	II,210
faint	*sipw*	II,11
faint	*gꜣḥ*	II,185
faint	*ḏꜥm*	II,264
fair of countenance	*nfr-ḥr*	I,236
faith	*mḥ-ib*	I,23
faith	*mḥ-ib*	I,198
faithful	*ꜣḫ*	I,7
faithful	*mḥ*	I,198
faithful servant	*bꜣk-ꜣḫ*	I,128
falchion	*ḫpš*	I,357
falcon	*bik*	I,131
falcon-faced beans	*ḥr-bik*	I,322
fall	*wꜣi*	I,87
fall	*hꜣ(i)*	I,283
fall	*ḫr*	I,369
fall apart	*stp*	II,94
fall in	*tꜣḥ*	II,199
fall out (of hair)	*fkꜣ*	I,165
fall to	*tkk*	II,221
fall to lot of	*hꜣ(i)*	I,283
fall to ruin	*stp*	II,94
fall victim	*spr*	II,32
fallen	*ḫr*	I,370
fallen	*smḫ*	II,44
fallen down	*wš*	I,113
fallen one	*ḫr*	I,370
fallow field (?)	*ꜥmdy*	I,67
false	*ꜥḏꜣ*	I,83
false	*hḏ*	I,341
false friend	*ḳrḥ*	II,157
false one	*grg*	II,193

falsehood	*isft*	I,47
falsehood	*ʿḏꜣ*	I,84
falsehood	*grg*	II,193
falsely	*ʿḏꜣ*	I,83
falsely	*m-ʿḏꜣ*	I,84
falsely	*m-ʿḏꜣ*	I,168
falsely	*n-ʿḏꜣ*	I,223
falsely	*m grg*	II,193
falter	*nwd*	I,232
fame	*bꜣw*	I,125
fame	*ḳfꜣt*	II,149
family	*ꜣbt*	I,4
family	*bt*	I,142
family	*mhwt*	I,196
famished	*ispw*	I,47
famous	*pri*	I,149
fan	*bhꜣ*	I,138
fan	*ḫwy*	I,354
fan (bearer)	*sryt*	II,58
fan bearer	*ṯꜣy-ḫw*	I,354
fan bearer	*ṯꜣy-ḫw*	II,225
fancy (vb.)	*ib*	I,23
fang	*ḫnr*	I,365
fan-shaped leaves	*ṯꜣw*	II,226
far	*wꜣi*	I,87
far	*ḥri*	I,323
far away	*wꜣi*	I,87
far north	*pḥww*	I,153
far off	*wꜣi*	I,87
far reaching	*wsḫ*	I,112
far sighted	*pd-ḥr*	I,160
far striding	*pd-ḥr*	I,160
fare	*hmw*	I,288
fare north	*ḫd*	I,378
fare upstream	*ḫnti*	I,366
fare you well	*nfr snb.k*	II,50
farmer	*iḥwty*	I,44
farmland	*iḥt*	I,44
fashion	*mnt*	I,185
fashion	*sḫr*	II,73
fashion (vb.)	*iri*	I,37
fashion (vb.)	*msi*	I,204
fashion (vb.)	*nbi*	I,233
fashion (vb.)	*sḫpr*	II,69
fashion (vb.)	*ḳd*	II,160
fasten	*mnṯꜣ*	I,191
fasten	*smn*	II,42
fasten	*snḥ*	II,53
fasten oneself to	*dp m*	II,246
fat	*ʿḏ*	I,83
fat	*pdr*	I,160
fat	*ḫpn*	I,355
fat	*sgnn*	II,90
fat	*ḏdꜣ*	II,277
fat smoke	*ḳn*	II,152
fat(?)	*ḏd*	II,276
fate	*šꜣy*	II,106
fated time	*tr*	II,214
father	*it*	I,50
father in law	*šm*	II,122
father of his monument	*it-mnw.f*	I,50
fathom	*ʿm*	I,66
fatted cattle	*wšꜣ*	I,113
fatted goose	*srit-ḏriw*	II,58
fatten	*wšꜣ*	I,113
fattened	*ḫpn*	I,355
fattener	*wšꜣ*	I,113
fattener (of cattle)	*mri*	I,193
fatty condition	*ḳn*	II,152
fault	*btꜣ*	I,142
fault	*sp*	II,30
fault	*thꜣ*	II,216
fault	*ṯꜣy*	II,225
fault	*ḏw(t)*	II,265
favor	*ḥst*	I,331
favor	*ḥtpw*	I,338
favor (vb.)	*ḥsi*	I,329
favorable	*nfr*	I,235
favorable moment	*tp-nfr*	II,205
favored	*ḥsty*	I,331
favored one	*ḥsy*	I,329
favorite	*ib-ib*	I,22
favorite	*imy-ib tpy*	I,27
favorite	*mḥ-ib*	I,198
favors	*ḥsyw*	I,330
favors	*ḥswt*	I,330
favors	*spr*	II,33
fayence worker	*bʿbʿ*	I,132
fear	*mrꜣ*	I,193
fear	*nrw*	I,239
fear	*ḥr-(n)-ḥr*	I,322
fear	*ḥryt*	I,326
fear	*snḏw*	II,55
fear	*snḏt*	II,55
fear	*šfyt*	II,119
fear (vb.)	*snḏ*	II,55
fearful	*snḏ*	II,55
fearsome	*ḥty*	I,335
feast	*ʿbt*	I,64
feast	*ḥb*	I,306
feast (vb.)	*ḥb*	I,307
feather	*mḥwt*	I,199
feathers	*mḥwt*	I,199
feathers	*šwty*	II,115
feats	*ḳnw*	II,152
feeble	*wiꜣwiꜣ*	I,92
feeble	*ḫsy*	I,388
feeble	*sꜣw*	II,7
feeble	*ṯniw*	II,230
feed (vb.)	*wšꜣ*	I,113
feeder	*wšꜣ*	I,113

feeding place	*ḫryt*	I,371
feel	*ib*	I,23
feel aggrieved at (?)	*šni*	II,127
feel distaste	*ft*	I,165
feel inclined to	*hn*	I,288
felicitations	*hm-mi-nȝ*	I,287
felicitous	*sbḳ*	II,29
fell (vb.)	*swȝ*	II,17
fell (vb.)	*sk*	II,86
fell (vb.)	*šꜥd*	II,112
fellow	*iry*	I,39
fellow	*iry-rdwy*	I,40
fellow	*sn-nw*	II,48
fellow	*kri*	II,175
felspar	*nšmt*	I,250
female	*ḥmt*	I,311
female	*st-ḥmt*	I,311
female	*st-ḥmt*	II,1
female companion	*ḫnmst*	I,364
female image	*rpyt*	I,270
female member of a judicial council	*st nt ḳnbt*	II,1
female mourner	*ṯsw*	II,235
female musician	*šmꜥyt*	II,123
fence in	*inb*	I,33
fenced in	*dpḫ*	II,247
fenugreek(?)	*ḥm(ȝw)y*	I,312
ferry (vb.)	*ḫni*	I,382
ferry (vb.)	*ḏȝi*	II,260
ferry (vb.)	*ḏȝḏȝy*	II,263
ferry across	*ḏȝi*	II,260
ferry boat	*mḫnt*	I,202
ferry boat	*ḏȝi*	II,260
ferry over	*ḏȝi*	II,260
ferryman	*mḫnty*	I,202
fertile	*mḏȝ*	I,219
festal offerings	*ꜥbwt*	I,64
festal-attire	*wnḫw*	I,103
festival	*ꜥbt*	I,64
festival	*wp*	I,98
festival kiosk	*ḥb*	I,307
festival-leader of Amun	*sšm-n-imn*	II,80
festival offerings	*ḥbyt*	I,307
festival place	*ḥgȝi*	I,335
festival precinct	*ḥwt-ḥb-sd*	I,304
fetch	*ini*	I,31
fetch	*ḫni*	I,382
fete	*sšš*	II,83
fetter (?)	*mḏȝ*	I,219
fetter (vb.)	*ḳnb*	II,154
fetters	*pḫȝt*	I,154
fetters	*mꜥḫȝ*	I,182
fetters	*mḫȝ*	I,201
fetters	*ḳḫ*	II,158
fever	*srf*	II,58
fever	*šm(m)*	II,124
few	(see some)	
few	*ꜥnd*	I,71
few	*nhy*	I,240
field	*ȝḥt*	I,7
field	*iḥt*	I,44
field	*bȝwy*	I,126
field	*ḥkr*	I,334
field	*sḫt*	II,66
field worker	*iḥwty*	I,44
field-hand	*iḥwty*	I,44
fiend (?)	*sbi*	II,28
fierce	*nꜥš*	I,229
fierce	*rḳy*	I,279
fierce	*ḥsȝ*	I,331
fiery	*ꜥḫȝ*	I,74
fiery	*spd*	II,34
fiery breath	*hh*	I,292
Fifteenth lunar day	*(tp)-smdt*	II,206
fifth	*diwt*	II,240
fight	*ꜥḥȝ*	I,74
fight (vb.)	*šfꜥ*	II,120
figs	*dȝbw*	II,239
figs	*dbt*	II,246
figure	*ꜥḫm*	I,78
figure	*ḫpiw*	I,381
figure	*sšm*	II,81
figured	*ḫp*	I,355
filet	*mḫw*	I,199
fill	*ꜥpr*	I,65
fill	*mḥ*	I,197
fill (pots)	*ḫwt*	I,354
fill up	*bꜥḥ*	I,132
filthy	*ṯms*	II,229
find (vb.)	*sbḳ*	II,29
find (vb.)	*gm*	II,188
find fault (with)	*mdw*	I,216
find fit	*gm...r*	II,189
find innocent	*gm*	II,188
find out	*ꜥm*	I,66
find out	*rḫ*	I,275
find refreshment	*ḳb*	II,147
fine	*nfr*	I,235
fine	*ṯȝwt*	II,225
fine (linen)	*p(ȝ)ḳ(t)*	I,146
fine (vb.)	*hd*	I,293
fine linen (?)	*sfry*	II,35
finest	*tpy*	II,207
finger	*ḏbꜥ*	II,267
finger (vb.)	*gmgm*	II,189
finger-ring	*gsr*	II,195
fingers	*ḏbꜥ*	II,267
finis	*kr*	II,155
finish	*mnḳ*	I,190
finish	*skm*	II,87

finish	*grḥ*	II,191
finish (decoration)	*grḥ*	II,191
finish off	*ḳn*	II,151
finish out	*skm*	II,87
finish up	*ꜥrꜥr*	I,72
fir	*ꜥš*	I,79
fire	*bsw*	I,140
fire	*rkḥ*	I,279
fire	*ḫt*	I,343
fire	*ẖt*	I,375
fire	*sḏt*	II,103
fire-boring	*ḏꜣ*	II,259
fire-temple	*iꜣbb*	I,14
firewood	*ẖt-n-šmw*	I,375
firm	*mn*	I,183
firm	*ḏri*	II,272
firm of heart	*mn-ib*	I,184
firmament	*biꜣ*	I,130
firmer	*rd*	I,280
firmly established	*smn*	II,42
firmness	*ḏriw*	II,273
first	*ḥꜣt*	I,296
first	*ḥꜣ(w)tyw*	I,298
first	*tp*	II,208
first	*tpy*	II,207
first day of lunar year	*tpy-rnpt*	II,207
first into existence	*šꜣꜥ-n-ḫpr*	II,108
first month *Šmw*	*pn-ḫnsw*	I,148
first month of Akhet	*ḏḥwty*	II,274
first month of year	*tḫy*	II,218
first of	*tpty*	II,208
first prophet	(see high priest)	
first quality	*n-ḳn*	II,151
first season	*ꜣḫt*	I,8
fish	*rmw*	I,270
fish	*hwṯn*	I,286
fish	*ḫꜣ*	I,344
fish	*ḫpnpn*	I,355
fish	*šnꜥ*	II,129
fish	*gst*	II,195
fish	*tpy(wt)*	II,208
fish	*ṯss*	II,236
fish	*dp*	II,246
fish	*ḏss*	II,275
fish (type)	*sḥty*	II,64
fish (type)	*sd-ḥw*	II,97
fish (vb.)	*ḥꜣm*	I,299
fisherman	*wḥꜥ*	I,108
fishing lure	*wꜥwy*	I,93
fishing pool	*swn*	II,19
fishnet	*mkmrwt*	I,211
fit	*šꜣw*	II,108
fit (vb.)	*smn*	II,41
fit together	*sꜣḳ*	II,9

fit with leather	*dby*	II,244
fitted	*ḥṯ*	I,340
fitting things	*šꜣwt*	II,108
fittings	*ipt*	I,25
fittings	*ꜥprwt*	I,65
fix	(see repair)	
fix	*wꜣḥ*	I,89
fix	*smn*	II,42
fix	*tis*	II,201
fix	*ṯꜣr*	II,226
fixed	*mn*	I,183
fixed	*mtn*	I,214
fixed	*tks*	II,221
flabellum	*bhꜣ*	I,138
flabellum	*nḫḫ*	I,245
flagon	*rḥb*	I,274
flagstaff	*snw*	II,50
flail	*nḫḫ*	I,245
flame	*ꜣḫt*	I,7
flame	*bsw*	I,140
flame	*nswt*	I,249
flame	*nsrt*	I,249
flame	*rwy*	I,267
flame	*rkḥ*	I,279
flame	*hꜣwt*	I,285
flame	*stꜣ*	II,92
flame	*sḏt*	II,103
flame	*tkꜣ*	II,220
flame (devouring)	*wnmyt*	I,102
flame up	*nbi*	I,233
flaming	*ꜥḥꜣ*	I,74
flank	*ḏr*	II,271
flanks	*ḏr*	II,271
flash	*brḳ*	I,137
flash	*sšdw*	II,84
flashing	*sšdw*	II,83
flask	*mnḏḳt*	I,191
flask	*gꜣy*	II,183
flat dish	*dydy*	II,241
flatter	*swn*	II,19
flatter	*swnwn*	II,20
flatter	*tfi*	II,209
flatulence(?)	*ṯꜣwrrw*	II,226
flavor	*dpt*	II,246
flax	*mḥy(t)*	I,199
fledgling	*ḳḏr*	II,163
fledgling	*ṯꜣ*	II,223
flee	*ifd*	I,26
flee	*wꜥr*	I,95
flee	*bh*	I,137
flee	*pwy*	I,148
flee	*pt*	I,158
flee	*pd*	I,160
flee	*mḥy*	I,199
flee	*rwi*	I,267
flee	*ḥfḏ*	I,310

flee	*sḫsḫ*	II,74
flee	*tši*	II,219
flesh	*iwf*	I,20
flesh	*ḥꜥw*	I,301
flesh	*ḥꜥt*	I,301
flesh	*šnbt*	II,130
flight(?)	*ḥmḥm*	I,314
flint	*ds*	II,255
flint knife	*sf*	II,35
flock	*ẖpt*	I,381
flocks	*iꜣwt*	I,13
flocks	*ꜥwt*	I,62
flocks	*mnmnt*	I,187
flogging	*ḏnn*	II,269
flood	*wgꜣ*	I,115
flood	*bꜥḥ*	I,132
flood	*mḥy*	I,198
flood	*mtrw*	I,215
flood	*nwy*	I,230
flood	*nwn*	I,231
flood	*nnw*	I,239
flood	*ḏt*	II,259
flood (vb.)	*bꜥḥ*	I,132
flood (vb.)	*mḥ*	I,197
flooded	*tḫb*	II,218
flooded land	*ḥꜣyt*	I,296
floodwater	*mw*	I,182
floodwaters	*nwy*	I,230
floor	*sꜣt*	II,10
floor of silver	*tꜣ-n-ḥḏ*	II,198
floral offerings	*ḥtpw*	I,338
flounder (vb.)	*ꜥnꜥn*	I,69
flour	*ꜣḳw*	I,9
flour	*wgm*	I,115
flour	*bty*	I,143
flour	*nḏ*	I,255
flour	*kmḥ*	II,174
flour	*ṯrt*	II,231
flourish	*ꜣḫꜣḫ*	I,8
flourish	*wꜣḏ*	I,91
flourish	*rwḏ*	I,269
flourish	*rnpi*	I,273
flourish	*rd*	I,280
flow	*bsi*	I,139
flow	*hꜣ(i)*	I,284
flow	*ḥw-ny*	I,305
flow (vb.)	*ḥwi*	I,303
flow (vb.)	*sꜣb*	II,8
flower	*ḏḏ*	II,277
flower (vb.)	*prḫ*	I,152
flower type	*ḥḳꜣyt*	I,334
flowers	*mḫmḫwt*	I,201
flowers	*ḥrrt*	I,328
flowers	*ḥtpw*	I,338
flowers	*šꜣ*	II,105
flowers	*šri*	II,132
flowingly	*bsi*	I,139
fluffy	*itn*	I,51
fluid	*mw*	I,182
flute (?)	*mꜣt*	I,173
flutter	*pwy*	I,148
fly	*pꜣ*	I,146
fly	*pwy*	I,148
fly (n.)	*ꜥf(f)*	I,65
fly aloft	*ꜣꜥꜥ(t)*	I,2
fly at the voice	*pwy-ḥr-ḫrw*	I,372
fly away	*pwy*	I,148
fly away	*rwi*	I,267
fly into rage	*ḥḏn*	I,342
fly up	*ḥfd*	I,310
fodder	*wnmw*	I,102
foe	*rḳy(w)*	I,279
foe	*ḫfty*	I,359
foe	*ḫr*	I,370
foe	*ḏꜣiw*	II,261
foil	*ḳḳi*	II,159
fold over	*ḳb*	II,147
folding stool	*isbt*	I,46
foliage	*srdd*	II,60
foliage	*dbyt*	II,244
foliage	*ḏbꜣw*	II,266
follow	*nḏr*	I,257
follow	*ḫtḫt*	I,378
follow	*šms*	II,124
follow the conscience	*šms-ib*	II,124
follower	*imy-ḫt*	I,27
follower	*hnw*	I,289
follower	*imy-ḫt*	I,375
follower	*sty*	II,3
follower	*šmsw*	II,124
following	*m-sꜣ*	I,171
following	*ḥr-sꜣ*	I,323
following	*ḥr-sꜣ*	II,5
following	*šms*	II,125
Following of Horus	*Šms-Ḥr*	II,125
food	*wnmw*	I,102
food	*pꜣwt*	I,146
food	*mk(y)w*	I,211
food	*ḥꜣw*	I,296
food	*ḥw*	I,302
food	*šbb*	II,117
food	*kꜣw*	II,166
food	*ḏfꜣw*	II,268
food offerings	*sny*	II,49
food offerings	*ḏfꜣw*	II,269
fool	*ḫꜣini*	I,345
fool	*ḫiniw*	I,350
fool	*swgꜣ*	II,22
fool	*šš*	II,137
foolish	*wḫꜣ*	I,110

foolish	*ḫꜣiw*	I,344
foolish	*ḫn*	I,361
foolish	*swgꜣ*	II,22
foolish person	*rmṯ-ḫꜣi*	I,272
foolish person	*ḫꜣini*	I,345
foot	*rd*	I,281
footsteps	*ṯbw(t)*	II,228
footstool	*hr-rdwy*	I,290
footstool	*hdm*	I,293
footstool	*hdm-rdwy*	I,293
footstool	*kbs*	II,172
for	*ꜥḳꜣ*	I,81
for	*pꜣ-wn*	I,145
for	*n*	I,223
for	*r*	I,259
for purpose of	*n-ꜣbw*	I,4
for the benefit of	*(n) kꜣ n*	II,165
forbidden entry	*ḫnr*	I,365
force	*pḥty*	I,154
force	*ḫymṯꜣ*	I,351
force	*ḫpš*	I,357
force (open)	*ḫm*	I,360
force (vb.)	*wꜣš*	I,91
force one's way into	*wtnw*	I,116
forced labor	*bḥw*	I,138
forceful	*mds*	I,218
ford	*mšdt*	I,209
fore mentioned	*ḫnty*	I,367
forecastle	*ṯꜣrt*	II,226
forecourt	*wbꜣ*	I,96
forecourt	*ḫꜣti*	I,350
forefathers	*it*	I,50
forehead	*ḥꜣt*	I,297
forehead	*tbn*	II,204
forehead	*thnt*	II,217
forehead	*dhnt*	II,253
foreign	*ḏrḏr*	II,273
foreign land	*ḫꜣst*	I,349
foreign lands	*ḫꜣswt*	I,349
foreign lands	*ḫꜣstyw*	I,349
foreign nations	*ḫꜣstyw*	I,349
foreign troops	*thr*	II,217
foreign woman	*ḫꜣsty*	I,349
foreigner	*ꜣꜥꜥ*	I,2
foreigner	*ḫꜣsty*	I,349
foreigners	*ḫꜣstyw*	I,350
foreigners	*kꜣwy*	II,166
foreland	*ḫnty*	I,367
foreman	*ꜣṯ*	I,10
foreman	*ḥw(n)tyw*	I,305
foreman	*ḫry-ꜥ*	I,387
foremost	*ḥꜣ(w)tyw*	I,298
foremost	*ḫnty*	I,367
foremost	*tpy*	II,207
foremost	*tpty*	II,208

foreskin	*ḳrnt*	II,145
foretell	*sr*	II,56
foretell	*šꜣ*	II,106
forever	*nḥḥ*	I,243
forever	*r-nḥḥ*	I,243
forever	*r-šw*	I,265
forever	*n-ḏt*	II,259
forfeit	*ṯꜣwt*	II,225
forge (vb.)	*sḫ*	II,65
forge (vb.)	*sḫt*	II,75
forget	*mhy*	I,196
forget	*ḫm*	I,360
forget	*smḫ*	II,44
forget	*sḫm*	II,70
forgetful	*smḫ*	II,44
forgive	*ḥtp*	I,336
forgive	*ṯnrḥ*	II,230
forgo	*ḫꜣꜥ*	I,347
form	*ꜣb(wt)*	I,5
form	*irw*	I,40
form	*ḫpri*	I,356
form	*ḫpri*	I,357
form	*sšm*	II,81
form	*ḳi*	II,145
form	*ḳd*	II,160
form	*ḏt*	II,259
form (vb.)	*pipi*	I,147
form (vb.)	*msi*	I,204
former	*ḥꜣ(w)tyw*	I,298
formerly	*mꜥrw*	I,181
formerly	*mr*	I,192
formerly	*ḫry-ḥꜣt*	I,386
formerly	*ḏr-ꜥ*	II,271
formulas	*r-ḏdw*	I,265
formulate	*nis*	I,227
forsake	*hꜣ(i)*	I,283
forsake	*ḫꜣꜥ*	I,347
forsooth	*tr*	II,214
fort	*inbt*	I,33
fort	*mktr*	I,212
fort	*mgdr*	I,212
fort	*ḫtm*	I,377
fort	*sgr*	II,90
fortification	*inbt*	I,33
fortification	*mktr*	I,212
fortification	*sbty*	II,29
fortified gate	*ṯkr*	II,236
fortress	*itḥ*	I,52
fortress	*mnw*	I,187
fortress	*mnnw*	I,188
fortress	*nmty*	I,238
fortress	*nḫtw*	I,246
fortress	*ḫtm*	I,377
fortress	*sgr*	II,90
fortress(?)	*ṯꜣrt*	II,226
fortunate	*mꜥr*	I,181

fortunate	*mrd*	I,195
fortunate	*sbḳ*	II,29
fortune	*rnnt*	I,274
forward	*m-ḥr*	I,170
forward	*n-ḥr*	I,225
forward	*m-ḥrw*	I,321
forward	*n-ḥr*	I,321
forward	*ḥr-(n)-ḥr*	I,322
forward	*ḥr-(n)-ḥr*	I,322
foster	*sꜥnḫ*	II,14
foster	*sḫpr*	II,69
foster child of	*rnn*	I,273
foul	*ḥwꜣw*	I,305
foul	*šns*	II,131
foul (vb.)	*sꜣt*	II,10
foul fluid	*mw-ḏw*	I,183
foul humors	*ḫnt*	I,366
found	*grg*	II,192
found (vb.)	*wꜣḥ*	I,89
found (vb.)	*sꜣp*	II,8
found (vb.)	*snṯ*	II,54
foundation	*mꜣwḏ*	I,176
foundation	*ḥwt*	I,304
foundation	*snt*	II,50
foundation	*snṯ*	II,55
foundation	*sdf*	II,99
foundation	*sdfꜣw*	II,101
foundation of an enclosure wall	*snṯ-tꜣ*	II,55
foundations	*ḳbyt*	II,148
founder (vb.)	*šꜣ*	II,106
founder of Two Lands	*grg*	II,192
founder-of-the-earth	*snn-tꜣ*	II,52
founding	*grg*	II,193
fountain	*bꜥr*	I,132
four	*fdw*	I,166
four sides	*ifdw*	I,26
fourth	*mḥ-fdw*	I,166
fourth month of Akhet	*kḥrk*	II,177
4th month of *prt*	*pn-rnwt*	I,148
fowl	*ꜣpd*	I,6
fowl	*rsf*	I,278
fowl	*ḫpwt*	I,355
fowl yard	*mḥwn*	I,200
fowl yard	*šnyw*	II,126
fowler	*wḥꜥ*	I,108
fowler	*wḥꜥw-ꜣpdw*	I,108
fowler	*sḫty*	II,67
fowler of migratory birds	*wḥꜥw-gš*	I,108
fowlers	*kꜣpw*	II,168
fowlers	*kpw*	II,172
fraction	*dni(t)*	II,250
fragment	*dni(t)*	II,250
fragments (?)	*tšw*	II,220
fragrance	*ḫnm*	I,363
fragrance	*sty*	II,91
fragrant wood (?)	*ḫꜣw*	I,345
frame	*ḥꜥt*	I,301
frame	*ḳs*	II,159
frame (person's)	*hn*	I,288
fraternize	*snsn*	II,54
fray	*ski*	II,86
free (?)	*wšꜣ*	I,113
free from	*wš*	I,113
free from	*šw*	II,113
free tenants	*nmḥ*	I,238
free time	*wšꜣ*	I,113
free woman	*nmḥ*	I,238
freedom	(see liberty)	
freely	*m-wstnw*	I,113
freeman(?)	*nmḥ*	I,238
freight	*ꜣtp*	I,10
freighter	*br*	I,136
freighter	*mnš*	I,189
fresh	*mꜣw*	I,176
fresh	*n-mꜣwt*	I,224
fresh	*rnpi*	I,273
fresh lands	*nḫbw*	I,245
fresh vegetables	*wꜣḏ-smw*	I,91
friend	*ḫnms*	I,364
friendly	*ꜣms-ib*	I,6
friendly	*ꜥn*	I,67
friends	*smr*	II,43
fright	*mrꜣ*	I,193
frighten	*stwr*	II,93
frisk	*krs*	II,176
frit, blue	*ḫsbd*	I,374
frit, green	*ḥmt*	I,311
from	*m-ꜥ*	I,57
from	*m*	I,167
from	*m-ꜥ*	I,167
from	*m-šꜣꜥ*	I,171
from	*m-di*	I,171
from	*n*	I,223
from	*ḥr*	I,321
from	*ḫr*	I,369
from	*m-šꜣꜥ*	II,107
from	*šꜣꜥ*	II,107
from	*šꜣꜥ-m*	II,107
from	*r-šꜣꜥ*	II,107
from (one's) presence	*r-ḥꜣt*	I,297
from here	*dy*	II,241
from now onwards	*m-mnt-ḫr-hrw*	I,169
from where?	*tnw*	II,212
from without	*n-bnr*	I,223
front	*ḥꜣ(w)tyw*	I,298
frontier	*tꜣš*	II,199

frontier district	*tš*	II,219
froth	*sft*	II,35
fruit	*ꜥdn*	I,82
fruit	*bny*	I,134
fruit	*mhwt*	I,196
fruit	*sšrt*	II,83
fruit	*šꜣ*	II,105
fruit	*dḳ(r)w*	II,256
fruit	*dgꜣwt*	II,257
fruit	*dgm*	II,257
fruit	*ḏꜣir*	II,261
fruit(?)	*nkpt*	I,251
fruit(?)	*rrmt*	I,274
fruit(?)	*ḥḳḳ*	I,334
fruit(?)	*sty*	II,91
fruit(?)	*ḏꜣir*	II,261
fruit-measure	*dꜣwꜣr*	II,239
fruit-measure	*dwr*	II,243
frustration	*ꜣrr*	I,6
fuel	*ḏnḏnrt*	II,270
fugitive	*wꜥr*	I,95
fugitive	*mḥw*	I,199
fugitive	*mḥy*	I,199
fugitive	*nhr*	I,241
fugitives	*pdw*	I,160
full	*ꜣw(i)*	I,3
full	*bk*	I,141
full	*km*	II,174
full (to become)	*siꜣt*	II,11
functions	*irwt*	I,40
funerary chamber	*htt*	I,292
funerary chapel	*ḥwt-kꜣ.k*	I,304
funerary outfit	*ḫt-n-grgw*	I,375
furious	*ḫꜥr*	I,353
furious	*ḳnd*	II,155
furious	*dšr-ib*	II,255
furious	*dšr-ḥr*	II,255
furiously	*m-prš*	I,152
furnish	*iri*	I,38
furnish	*ꜥpr*	I,65
furnish	*ꜥrꜥr*	I,72
furnish	*fꜣy*	I,163
furnish	*sdbḥ*	II,98
furnish	*sḏfꜣ(y)*	II,100
furnish	*grg*	II,192
furnish	*ṯs*	II,233
furniture	*ipdw*	I,26
furniture	*ḥnw*	I,317
furniture	*grg-pr*	II,193
furrow	*dnm*	II,251
further	*ḥnꜥ*	I,317
further	*ḫr*	I,368
furthermore	*r-mitt*	I,262
furtively	*m-ṯꜣwt*	II,225
fury	*nšny*	I,250
fury	*sḫm*	II,70
fury	*ṯms*	II,229
future	*ii*	I,16

G

gain	*wḫꜣ*	I,109
gain mastery	*ḫꜣm*	I,348
gait	*nmtt*	I,238
gale	*ḏꜥ*	II,264
galena	*msdmt*	I,207
galley	*br*	I,136
galley	*mnš*	I,189
game (animals)	*iꜣwt*	I,13
gang	*ist*	I,46
gang	*wnḏw*	I,104
gang	*mšꜥ*	I,208
gang	*rit*	I,266
gang	*ṯt*	II,223
gang	*ṯst*	II,235
gangway	*wꜣt-n-šmt*	I,88
garden	*bꜥḥ*	I,132
garden	*ḥsbt*	I,332
garden	*kꜣmw*	II,168
garden	*dydy*	II,241
garden	*dd*	II,257
garden enclosure	*šnyw*	II,126
garden meadow	*ḥsbt*	I,332
gardener	*kꜣry*	II,170
garland	*wꜣḥt*	I,90
garlands	*ꜥnḫw*	I,70
garlands	*mꜣḫw*	I,177
garlands	*mḥy*	I,199
garlic	*ḫtn*	I,378
garlic	*tḥw*	II,217
garment	*ifd*	I,26
garment	*bndw*	I,135
garment	*rd*	I,280
garment	*ḫrd*	I,373
garment	*ḫnk*	I,384
garment	*sḏ*	II,100
garment (?)	*šndy*	II,131
garments	*ḥbs*	I,308
garrison	*iwꜥyt*	I,19
garrison captain	*ḥry iwꜥyt*	I,19
garrison commander	*imy-r iwꜥyt*	I,19
garrison commander	*imy-r iwꜥyt*	I,27
garrison leader	*ḥry-iwꜥyt*	I,324
gash (vb)	*ḳḏḏ*	II,163
gate	*nšp*	I,250
gate	*ḫtm*	I,377
gate	*sbꜣ*	II,26
gate	*dwꜣ*	II,242
gate(?)	*rryt*	I,274
gateway	*ꜥry*	I,71
gateway	*ꜥrr(y)t*	I,73
gateway	*wmwt*	I,100
gateway	*rwyt*	I,267
gateway	*rwty*	I,268
gateway	*ḫtm*	I,377
gather	*ꜥwꜣy*	I,63
gather	*nw(i)*	I,230
gather	*sḫt*	II,75
gather	*ṯs*	II,233
gather in	*fꜣy*	I,163
gather together	*sḥwy*	II,61
gaze	*gꜣwt*	II,184
gaze (vb.)	*nw*	I,229
gaze (vb.)	*gꜣw*	II,183
gazelle	*mꜣ-ḥḏ*	I,174
gazelle	*gḥs*	II,193
gear	*rks*	I,280
gear	*sdbḥ*	II,99
geese	*gšw*	II,195
geese(?)	*mst*	I,205
gems, semi-precious	*rpy*	I,270
genealogy(?)	*rn*	I,272
general	*imy-r mšꜥ*	I,28
general	*imy-r-mšꜥ*	I,208
generalissimo	*imy-r mšꜥ*	I,28
generations	*pꜣwt-tpt*	I,146
generations	*ḫt*	I,379
generations	*ḏꜣmw*	II,262
generous one(?)	*ḥry-wḏb.f*	I,325
genius	*kꜣ*	II,165
gentle	*hr-ib*	I,290
genuine	*m-wn-mꜣꜥ*	I,168
genuine	*mꜣꜥ(t)*	I,175
get agitated	*tfi*	II,209
get out	*pri*	I,149
get to bottom	*in pḥ*	I,32
get to bottom	*in-pḥwy*	I,153
get up	*ꜥḥꜥ*	I,75
get up	*fꜣy*	I,163
get up	*dwn*	II,243
gibber	*ꜣꜥꜥ*	I,2
gift	*fkꜣw*	I,165
gift	*mnḥt*	I,188
gift	*diw*	II,240
gifts	*ꜣwt*	I,3
gifts	*inw*	I,32
gifts	*brkw*	I,137
gifts	*mndt*	I,191
gifts	*sny*	II,49
gild	*nbi*	I,233
giraffe	*mmy*	I,183
gird oneself	*bnd*	I,135
girder	*smkt*	II,45
girdle wall (of temple)	*sbty*	II,29
girl	*šrit*	II,132
girth (chariot part)	*kwsn*	II,171

give	*imi*	I,26	glory	*b3w*	I,125
give	*mt3*	I,216	glory	*f3w*	I,164
give	*di*	II,240	glow	*kh*	II,158
give abundance	*sdf3(y)*	II,10	gnat	*hnms*	I,364
give authority	*si^cr*	II,11	gnaw	*wš^c*	I,113
give birth	*msi*	I,204	go	*w3i*	I,87
give cool water	*skbb*	II,84	go	*n^cy*	I,228
give fair passage	*sš*	II,79	go	*hn*	I,316
give light to	*wpš*	I,99	go	*sbi*	II,24
give praise	*i3w*	I,12	go	*šm*	II,121
give shelter	*hbs*	I,308	go along	*šm*	II,121
give testimony	*smtr*	II,45	go and come	*ii*	I,16
give up	*imi*	I,26	go around	*phr*	I,155
give up	*wh^c*	I,107	go around	*š3*	II,106
give way	*bdš*	I,143	go around	*kdi*	II,161
given	*dd*	II,257	go around	*kdd*	II,161
given life	*di-^cnh*	II,240	go around	*kd*	II,162
giving birth (to twins)	*ms-htr*	I,204	go astray	*htht*	I,377
			go astray	*tnm*	II,213
glad	*wnf-ib*	I,101	go away	*hd*	I,341
glad, be	*3w(i)*	I,3	go away	*swd3*	II,24
glad, be	*ndm-ib*	I,23	go back	*wh^c*	I,107
glad, be	*wnf*	I,101	go back on	*pn^c*	I,148
glad, be	*ndm-ib*	I,256	go barefoot	*dg3*	II,256
glad, be	*rš*	I,278	go down	*h3(i)*	I,283
glad, be	*hnm*	I,363	go downstream	*hd*	I,378
glad, make	*3ms-ib*	I,6	go for an outing	*trr*	II,215
gladden	*sbh*	II,28	go forth	*wdi*	I,119
gladness	*3wt-ib*	I,3	go forth	*pri*	I,149
gladness	*ršwt*	I,279	go forth	*šm*	II,121
glance	*irt*	I,40	go forward	*thm*	II,217
glance	*hr*	I,321	go ill	*bnd*	I,135
glance	*kdm*	II,163	go in	*^ck*	I,80
glance	*ktm*	II,180	go naked	*h3y*	I,295
glances	*st3w*	II,93	go north	*hd*	I,378
glass	*bd*	I,143	go off	*šm*	II,121
glaze	*thnt*	II,217	go out	*^cr*	I,71
gleam	*thn*	II,217	go out	*pri*	I,149
gleaming	*thn*	II,232	go out	*str*	II,95
gleaming eyes	*strty*	II,97	go round	*dbn*	II,245
gleaming ones	*thnt*	II,217	go round	*dbnbn*	II,245
glean	*srty*	II,59	go south	*hnti*	I,366
gleanings	*kdf*	II,161	go speedily	*hn*	I,316
glisten	*brk*	I,137	go through	*phr*	I,155
glistening	*^cb*	I,63	go to bed	*sdr*	II,102
glistening	*thn*	II,232	go to extremes	*ini hnty*	I,32
glitter (vb.)	*brk*	I,137	go to law	*shn*	II,71
globe	*itn*	I,51	go to pieces	*sdwnt*	II,98
gloom(?)	*ht3w*	I,335	go to ruin	*skn*	II,84
gloom of night	*khn*	II,177	go to sleep	*nm^c*	I,237
glorifications	*3hw*	I,7	go up	*ts*	II,234
glorify	*s3h*	II,9	go!	*isy*	I,45
glorify	*sw3š*	II,18	goat	*ib*	I,23
glorious	*dsr*	II,274	goat	*^cnh*	I,71
glorious one	*3h*	I,7	goat	*^cr*	I,71
glorious, be	*3h*	I,7	goatherd	*mniw-^cnh*	I,186

goats	*ʿwt*	I,62
god	*nṯr*	I,254
god of all	*nb-r-ḏr*	I,232
god's acre	*tꜣ-n-ẖry-nṯr*	II,198
god's father	*it-nṯr*	I,50
god's father	*it-nṯr*	I,254
god's land	*tꜣ-nṯr*	II,198
god's mother	*mwt-nṯr*	I,254
god's stone	*ʿꜣt-nṯr*	I,61
god's wife	*ḥmt-nṯr*	I,312
god's words	*mdw-nṯr*	I,218
goddess	*nṯrt*	I,255
going and coming	*šm ii*	II,121
gold	*nbw*	I,234
gold	*ktmt*	II,179
gold house	*ḥwt-nbw*	I,304
gold prospectors	*smntyw*	II,43
gold workers	*ḳwr*	II,147
goldsmith	*nby*	I,233
goldsmith	*ḥmww*	I,313
goldsmith	*kṯmt*	II,181
gold-washing teams	*iʿw-nbw*	I,16
good	*ꜣḫw*	I,7
good	*im(ꜣ)*	I,29
good	*nfr*	I,235
good cheer	*bw-nfr*	I,133
good condition	*m-sšr*	I,171
good lord	*nb-nfr*	I,232
good pleasure	*kꜣ*	II,165
good ripe old age	*iꜣwt ʿꜣt nfrt*	I,12
good sir	*m-pw*	I,168
good thing	*nfr*	I,235
good welcome	*ṯḥn-nfr*	II,232
good will	*kꜣ*	II,165
good youngster	*nḏs iḳr*	I,257
goodness	*nfr*	I,235
goods	*ꜣḫwt*	I,8
goods	*wnnt*	I,102
goods	*nkt*	I,251
goods	*ḥnw*	I,317
goods	*ḫt*	I,343
goods	*ẖt*	I,375
goose	*srit*	II,57
goose fat	*ʿḏ-srit*	II,58
goose type	*r*	I,259
gossip (vb.)	*gnrg*	II,190
gourd	*bdt*	I,143
gourd	*dnrg*	II,251
gourds	*bndt*	I,136
gourds	*šbt*	II,117
gourds	*dnrg*	II,251
govern	*ḥnty*	I,320
govern	*sšm*	II,80
governance	*sḫr*	II,73
governor	*ḥḳꜣ-w(t)*	I,334
governor of the south countries	*imy-r ḫꜣswt rst*	I,28
grace	*im(ꜣt)*	I,29
grace	*ḥst*	I,331
gracious	*im(ꜣ)*	I,29
gracious	*nʿ(i)*	I,227
gracious	*nʿmw*	I,228
gracious faced	*nfr-ḥr*	I,236
gracious to	*ḥtp*	I,336
graciousness	*im(ꜣt)*	I,29
grain	*it*	I,50
grain	*ʿmʿm*	I,66
grain	*wꜣḥyt*	I,90
grain	*npr*	I,234
grain	*nfr*	I,236
grain	*sšr*	II,82
grain basket	*kbs*	II,172
grain basket	*ksb*	II,178
grain bride(?)	*npr*	I,234
grain rations	*spdw*	II,34
grain rations	*diw*	II,240
grain type	*hrnt*	I,292
grain-yield	*wꜣḥyt*	I,90
granary	*šnwt*	II,129
granary	*ṯꜣrt*	II,227
grand total	*dni(t)*	II,250
grandees	*sr*	II,57
granite	*inr n mꜣṯ*	I,34
granite (red)	*mꜣṯ*	I,178
grant	*di*	II,240
grant (vb.)	*sḏm*	II,101
granulated substance	*šbb*	II,117
grapes	*iꜣrrt*	I,14
grapes	*irrt*	I,41
grapple with	*ṯḥn*	II,232
grasp	*ḫfʿ*	I,358
grasp	*šfd*	II,121
grasp	*kfʿ*	II,173
grasp (vb.)	*ꜣmm*	I,6
grasp (vb.)	*mḥ*	I,197
grasp (vb.)	*ḫfʿ*	I,358
grasp (vb.)	*šsp*	II,135
grasp meaning	*hꜣi-r*	I,284
grass	*sm*	II,37
grasshopper	*ʿpšt*	I,65
grasshopper	*sꜣ-nḥmw*	II,3
grasshopper	*snḥm*	II,53
grave	*is*	I,45
grave	*nft(t)*	I,237
grease	*ʿḏ*	I,83
grease	*mrḥt*	I,194
great	*ꜣw(i)*	I,2
great	*ʿꜣ(i)*	I,59
great	*wr*	I,104
great	*wr*	I,104

great	*wsr*	I,111
Great Bear	*ḫpš*	I,358
great court	*wbꜣ*	I,96
great crown	*wrrt*	I,105
great enchantress	*wrt-ḥkꜣw*	I,105
great green	*wꜣḏ-wr*	I,91
Great Hall	*wsḫt ꜥꜣt*	I,112
Great of Magic	*wrt-ḥkꜣw*	I,105
Great of Magic	*wrt-ḥkꜣw*	I,334
great of strength	*sḫm-pḥty*	II,70
Great One	*wrt*	I,104
great one of the portable shrine	*ꜥꜣ-n-ḳniw*	I,60
great royal wife	*ḥmt-wrt-nsw*	I,248
Great Seat (of temple)	*st wrt*	II,2
great seer	*wr-mꜣꜣ*	I,104
great sorceress	*wrt-ḥkꜣw*	I,105
great statues	*nꜣ rḫ.n.f ꜥꜣ*	I,276
Great Tribunal	*ḳnbt ꜥꜣt*	II,154
Greatest of Seers	*wr-mꜣꜣ*	I,104
Greatest of Seers	*wr-mꜣꜣ*	I,173
greatly	*r-ꜥꜣt*	I,261
greatness	*ꜥꜣ*	I,60
greed	*ꜥwn-ib*	I,23
greed	*ꜥwn-ib*	I,63
greedy	*ꜥfi*	I,65
greedy	*šw-ꜥw*	II,113
green	*ꜣḫꜣḫ*	I,8
green	*wꜣḏ*	I,91
green	*wꜣḏwꜣḏ*	I,91
green stone	*wꜣḏ*	I,91
greenery	*wꜣḏ-smw*	I,91
greet	*nḏ-ḫrt*	I,371
greet	*swḏꜣ-ib*	II,24
greet	*snb*	II,50
greet	*šdi*	II,140
greet respectfully	*nḏ-ḫrt*	I,256
greeting	*nyny*	I,227
greeting	*swḏꜣ-ib*	II,24
greetings	*iꜥnw*	I,17
greetings	*brkw*	I,137
greywacke(?)	*bḫn*	I,139
griddle-stone	*inr n gꜣf*	I,34
grief	*iꜥnw*	I,17
grief	*ḫꜣ-ib*	I,295
grievance	*bin*	I,130
grieve	*nhp*	I,240
grieve	*šni*	II,127
griffon	*ꜥḫḫ*	I,78
grind	*wḳm*	I,115
grind	*nḏ*	I,255
grind	*ḳḏḥ*	II,163
grip (vb.)	*mḥ*	I,197
gritstone	*biꜣt*	I,130
groans	*iꜥnw*	I,17
groom	*mꜥriw*	I,181
groom	*mri*	I,193
groom	*ḳḏn*	II,181
grope	*wḫꜣ*	I,110
grope	*gmgm*	II,189
grotto	*rryt*	I,274
ground	*sꜣt*	II,10
ground	*iwtn*	I,22
ground plan	*snṯ*	II,54
group	*ist*	I,46
group	*rit*	I,266
group	*ḫt*	I,379
group marshaller	*ṯs*	II,234
grove	*bꜣi(t)*	I,126
grove	*ḫt*	I,375
grove	*dd*	II,257
grove(?)	*hrw*	I,291
groves	*šnyw*	II,126
grow	*mdꜥ*	I,220
grow	*rd*	I,280
grow	*ḫꜣꜥ*	I,347
grow green	*ꜣḫꜣḫ*	I,8
grow into	*rd-m*	I,280
grow old	*iꜣwi*	I,12
grow old	*kḥkḥ*	II,178
grow strong	*tnr*	II,213
grow up	*ꜥꜣ(i)*	I,59
grow up	*rd*	I,280
grow up	*tnw*	II,212
grow weak	*bdš*	I,143
grow weak	*gnn*	II,190
grownup	*s ꜥꜣ*	II,1
growth	*srdd*	II,60
guard	*sꜣw*	II,6
guard	*sꜥšꜣt*	II,16
guard(?)	*skt*	II,88
guard (vb.)	*mni*	I,185
guard (vb.)	*mki*	I,210
guard (vb.)	*nbnb*	I,234
guard (vb.)	*rs*	I,277
guard (vb.)	*ḥr-ḥr*	I,322
guard (vb.)	*ḥrḥr*	I,328
guard (vb.)	*sꜣw*	II,6
guard (vb.)	*kni*	II,174
guard (vb.)	*di-ḥr*	II,240
guarded man	*sꜣw*	II,6
guardhouse	*inbt*	I,33
guardhouse	*sfḫy*	II,36
guardian	*mnꜥt*	I,186
Guardian	*mḥy*	I,199
guardian	*rwḏ*	I,269
guardian	*sꜣw*	II,6
guardian	*sꜣwty*	II,7
guards	*šmsw*	II,125
guidance	*sbꜣyt*	II,27
guidance	*sšm*	II,81

guide	*sšm*	II,81
guide (vb.)	*mꜣꜥ*	I,174
guide (vb.)	*sbꜣ*	II,26
guide (vb.)	*sšm*	II,80
guide rope	*ḫrpt*	I,373
guiding principle	*sšm*	II,81
guilt	*ꜥḏꜣ*	I,84
guilty	*ꜥḏꜣ*	I,84
guilty one	*ꜥḏꜣ*	I,84
guilty one	*wṯsy*	I,117
guise	*snn*	II,51
gullet	*ꜥšꜥš*	I,79
gully	*bḳꜥ*	I,141
gum(?)	*shrt*	II,61
gunnels	*ḥrit*	I,323
gunwales	*ḫꜣw*	I,345
gunwales	*sꜥiw*	II,13
gut (vb., fish)	*wgs*	I,115
gypsum	*ḳḏ*	II,162
gypsum-worker	*ḳḏ*	II,162

H

habit	*sẖr*	II,72
hack up	*bꜣ*	I,125
hack up	*fdḳ*	I,166
hack up	*dḳ*	II,255
haematite	*ḏdw*	II,277
haft	*šꜣti*	II,110
haft	*šti*	II,139
hail	*iꜣw*	I,12
hail to!	*inḏ-ḥr*	I,36
hail!	*ḫy*	I,350
hail!	*ḫy-ḳd-k*	I,350
hair	*sꜥrt*	II,15
hair	*šnw*	II,128
hairdressing	*nši*	I,250
hairy	*itn*	I,51
hale	*wḏꜣ ib*	I,121
half	*gs*	II,194
Half-Month Day	*(tp)-smdt*	II,206
hall	*ꜥrt*	I,72
hall	*wsẖt*	I,112
hall	*ḫꜣ*	I,343
hall	*sꜣdrt*	II,10
hall	*sdbt*	II,99
halt	*wḥꜥ*	I,107
halt	*smn*	II,42
halt	*sẖny*	II,71
halt at	*smn-ḥr*	II,42
hammer (vb.)	*mgs*	I,212
hammer (vb.)	*sḳr*	II,85
hammered (work)	*ḳmꜣ*	II,150
hand	*ꜥ*	I,57
hand	*ḏrt*	II,272
hand(?) (of chariot)	*ḏrt*	II,272
hand ax	*minb*	I,180
hand over	*wꜣi*	I,87
hand over	*swꜣḏ*	II,18
hand over	*swḏ*	II,23
handful	*šsp*	II,136
handful	*ḳꜣḏꜣm*	II,145
handful	*ḳḏm*	II,163
handful	*ḏrt*	II,272
handgrip(?)	*ṯꜣ*	II,223
handle	*šti*	II,139
handle (of adze)	*nw*	I,230
hands	*r-ꜥwy*	I,261
hands	*kp*	II,172
handsomely (rewarded)	*mnḫ*	I,189
handworker	*ḥmww*	I,313
hand-writing	*sš*	II,78
handy	*n-ḏrt*	II,272
happen	*ḫpr*	I,355

happiness	*ꜣwt-ib*	I,3
happiness	*ꜣwt-ib*	I,22
happiness	*wꜣḏ*	I,91
happiness	*sḏꜣyt*	II,100
happy	*iꜥi*	I,16
happy	*nḏm-ib*	I,23
happy	*wꜣḏ*	I,91
happy	*brg*	I,137
happy	*mrd*	I,195
happy	*nꜥꜥ-ib*	I,228
happy	*nfr*	I,235
happy of nature	*wꜣḥ ḳd*	II,160
happy state	*mnt*	I,185
harbor	*mniwt*	I,186
harbor	*mr*	I,192
harbor master	*imy-r mr*	I,28
hard	*n(ꜣ)ḥꜣw*	I,226
hard	*nḥꜣ*	I,242
hard, become	*tis*	II,201
hard, become	*swꜣḥ*	II,18
hardships	*ḏnn*	II,270
harem	*pr-ḫnr*	I,150
harem	*pr-ḫnr*	I,365
harem	*pr-ḫnrt*	I,366
harem	*ḫnty*	I,367
harem	*kꜣpw*	II,168
harem woman	*ḫnrt*	I,365
harlot	*msy*	I,204
harlots	*ḫnmw*	I,363
harm	*iit*	I,16
harm	*btꜣ*	I,142
harm	*gb*	II,187
harm	*twꜣ*	II,201
harm	*ḏꜣyt*	II,261
harm (vb.)	*ꜣꜥꜥ*	I,1
harm (vb.)	*sḳn*	II,84
harm (vb.)	*khb*	II,177
harm (vb.)	*tk*	II,220
harmful action(?)	*ḥtp*	I,337
harness (vb.)	*nḥb*	I,242
harp	*bnt*	I,134
harp	*ḏꜣḏꜣt*	II,263
harpooners	*msntyw*	I,205
harsh	*dḥr*	II,254
harsh	*ḏri*	II,272
harsh (of words)	*mr*	I,191
harvest	*šmw*	II,123
harvest (vb.)	*ꜥwꜣy*	I,63
harvest tax	*šmw*	II,123
hasten	*ꜣs*	I,8
hasten	*fꜣy*	I,163
hasten	*ḥn*	I,316
hasten	*sḫsḫ*	II,74
hasten	*ḳḏ*	II,162
hastily	*ꜣs*	I,9
hatched	*sms*	II,44
hatchet	*ḳrḏn*	II,158
hate	*msḏi*	I,207
hated	*ḫbd*	I,355
hateful	*ḫnw*	I,363
haughty	*ꜥbꜥ*	I,64
haul	*itḥ*	I,52
haunch	*mꜣst*	I,177
haunches	*mnty*	I,185
have a care for	*ꜣty*	I,9
have access to	*sbi*	II,25
have access to	*ms*	I,203
have access to	*tkn*	II,220
have compassion	*ḥmr*	I,313
have intercourse	*nk*	I,251
have knowledge	*sḏm*	II,101
have magic power over	*ꜣḫ*	I,7
have no regard	*ḫm*	I,360
have power	*sḫm*	II,69
have power over	*sḫm*	II,69
have recourse	*in m*	I,32
have sex with	*nk*	I,251
have sex with	*rḫ*	I,275
have sexual intercourse	*dꜣdꜣ*	II,239
have words	*mdw*	I,216
haversack	*ḫꜣr*	I,380
he	*f*	I,163
he	*mntf*	I,190
he	*mtw.f*	I,213
he	*ntf*	I,253
he (dep. pronoun)	*sw*	II,17
head	*ḥr*	I,321
head	*tbn*	II,204
head	*tp*	II,204
head	*ḏꜣ*	II,259
head	*ḏꜣḏꜣ*	II,262
head cloth	*idg*	I,55
head long dipping	*ḏbg*	II,268
head of cattle	*tp-n-iꜣwt*	II,205
head of cattle	*tp-n-idr*	II,205
headache	*gs-mꜣꜥ*	II,194
headache	*gs-tp*	II,194
headdress	*nws*	I,231
headlong(?)	*ḥfḏ*	I,310
headman	*ṯs*	II,234
headman of village	*ḥḳꜣ-ḥwt*	I,333
headpiece	*tptyw*	II,209
headrest	*wrs*	I,105
heads	*tpyw-tꜣ*	II,208
heal	*mnḳ*	I,190
heal	*hrf*	I,291
heal	*snb*	II,50
heal	*snfr*	II,51
healer	*rḫ(t)*	I,276
healing bandages	*ṯmt*	II,229

health	*snb*	II,50
healthy	*rnpi*	I,273
healthy	*snb*	II,50
heap	*ꜥḥꜥw*	I,76
heap invective	*sḥwr*	II,62
heap of corpses	*ḫꜣwt*	I,379
heap of stones	*krkr*	II,177
heap up	*brg*	I,137
heap up	*stwt*	II,94
heaps	*iwnw*	I,20
heaps	*sid*	II,12
heaps	*tnr*	II,214
heaps	*ḏdmt*	II,277
heaps(?)	*gbgb*	II,188
hear	*ꜥḏ*	I,83
hear	*sḏm*	II,101
herd of cattle	*kmyt*	II,174
hearer	*sḏmy*	II,102
hearing	*sḏmw*	II,102
hearken	*sḏm*	II,101
heart	*ib*	I,22
heart	*ḥꜣty*	I,297
heart of	*ḥry-ib*	I,325
heart's desire	*ḫrt-ib*	I,371
heat	*šm(m)*	II,124
heat	*tꜣ*	II,198
heaven	*ꜣbt*	I,4
heaven	*pt*	I,145
heaven	*hꜣy*	I,284
heaven	*ḥry*	I,324
heaven	*ḥrt*	I,327
heavy	*ꜥꜣ(i)*	I,59
heavy	*wdn*	I,118
heavy	*dns*	II,251
hedge	*inb*	I,33
heed	*ib*	I,22
heed	*hn*	I,288
heed	*sẖr*	II,73
heedful of	*ꜣty*	I,9
heedlessness	*ḫꜣḫ-ib*	I,349
heel	*tbs*	II,204
heels	*rd*	I,281
heels over head	*r sd r ḏꜣḏꜣ*	II,97
heifers	*ḥrst*	I,328
height	*ḫy*	I,350
height	*ḳꜣ(y)*	II,143
heir	*iwꜥ*	I,19
heir	*sšm(-šm)*	II,81
heir apparent	*sꜣ-nsw-smsw*	II,45
held by	*ẖr*	I,385
Heliopolitan	*iwnw*	I,20
hell-hole	*y(ꜣ)ꜥrw*	I,13
hell-hole	*yꜥr*	I,17
helm	*ḥmy(t)*	I,312
help (vb.)	*swh*	II,21
helper	*ꜥḏr*	I,84
helper	*psdy*	I,156
helper	*nḫ*	I,244
helper	*ḏꜣr*	II,262
helpless	*wiꜣwiꜣ*	I,92
hem in	*inḥ*	I,35
hem in	*gꜣw*	II,183
henceforth	*m-dwn*	I,172
henceforth	*m dwꜣ sꜣ dwꜣ*	II,242
henceforth	*dwn*	II,243
henchman	*šmsw*	II,125
her	*s*	II,1
her	*sy*	II,12
her majesty	*ḥmt*	I,311
herald	*wḥm*	I,109
herald	*wḥm-nsw*	I,109
herb	*ḫꜣw*	I,345
herbage	*sm*	II,37
herbs	*imyt-tꜣ*	I,27
herbs(?)	*rnpwt*	I,273
herbs(?)	*sm*	II,37
herd	*idr*	I,54
herd of cattle	*kmyt*	II,174
herds	*iꜣwt*	I,13
herds	*iḥw*	I,43
herds	*ꜥwt*	I,62
herds	*mnmnt*	I,187
herdsman	*mniw*	I,186
herdsmen	*sꜣw*	II,6
here	*ꜥꜣ*	I,60
here	*m-dy*	I,172
here	*mi-nꜣ*	I,178
here	*nꜣ*	I,225
here	*r-mi-nꜣ*	I,262
here	*dy*	II,241
hereafter	*ꜥn(n)*	I,68
hereafter	*ḥr-sꜣ*	II,5
hereditary noble	*r-pꜥt*	I,261
hereditary prince	*r-pꜥt*	I,147
heritage	*iwꜥ*	I,19
hero	*pr-ꜥ*	I,150
hero	*nḫt-ꜥ*	I,246
heroic	*pr-ꜥ*	I,150
heroic	*nḫt-ꜥ*	I,246
heroic	*tnr*	II,213
herpes	*mšpnt*	I,208
hew	*mšd*	I,209
hew	*mḏḥ*	I,220
hew	*sd*	II,98
hey!	*yḥ*	I,43
hidden	*imn*	I,30
hidden	*sḥꜣp*	II,61
hidden	*štꜣ*	II,138
hidden room	*štꜣyt*	II,139
hide	*ḫꜣy*	I,345
hide	*ḫnt*	I,381
hide	*dḥr*	II,254

hide (vb.)	*imn*	I,30
hide (vb.)	*ḥ3p*	I,299
hide (vb.)	*sḥ3p*	II,61
hide (vb.)	*k3p*	II,168
hide (vb.)	*dg3*	II,256
hiding	*št3*	II,138
hie!	*iḥt*	I,43
hieroglyphs	*mdw-nṯr*	I,218
high	*ḫy*	I,350
high	*ḳ3*	II,143
high ground	*ḳ3yt*	II,144
high priest	*ḥm-nṯr tpy*	II,207
highborn	*sr*	II,57
higher than	*ḫy*	I,350
highlands	*ḥ3ydbi3*	I,296
highlands	*ḥdb*	I,340
high-lying agricultural land	*w3bt*	I,88
hill	*ḫnrḏ*	I,366
hill	*ṯst*	II,235
hill	*ḏw*	II,265
hill countries	*ḫ3swt*	I,349
hill country	*ḫ3st*	I,349
hill(?)	*wpt-r*	I,98
hillock	*tnr*	II,214
hilltop	*ṯst*	II,235
hilltop	*dhnt*	II,253
him	*f*	I,163
him that has not	*p3 iwty*	I,22
himself	*r-ḥʿt.*	I,263
hinder	*inty*	I,36
hinder	*intnt*	I,36
hinder	*sḥnḥn*	II,64
hindquarters	*kf3*	II,173
hindrance	*intnt*	I,36
hin-measure	*hnw*	I,289
hinterland	*pḥww*	I,153
hippopotamus	*db*	II,243
hippopotamus thongs	*dby*	II,244
hips(?)	*mny*	I,186
hire	*ini*	I,31
hire(?)	*ʿg3t*	I,82
hired gang	*bryt*	I,136
hired hands(?)	*smdt-(n)-bnr*	II,46
his	*f*	I,163
his	*s3wt*	II,7
his own	*s3wy*	II,7
his own	*swt*	II,22
hit	*sḫ*	II,66
hither	*r-mi-n3*	I,262
Hittite troops	*twhr*	II,202
hoarse	*ḫnr*	I,365
hobble	*ḫbḫb*	I,355
hobble	*ksks*	II,178
hock	*m3st*	I,177
hoe	*iknw*	I,50
hoe	*ḳrḏn*	II,158
hold	*iri*	I,38
hold	*ḫ3m*	I,348
hold	*ẖr*	I,385
hold	*ṯ3y*	II,224
hold (of a ship)	*wnḏw*	I,103
hold at bay	*inty*	I,36
hold back	*iḥm*	I,43
hold back	*sḫtḫt*	II,75
hold back	*dni*	II,249
hold fast	*mḥ*	I,197
hold fast	*smn*	II,42
hold firm to	*mḥ*	I,197
hold firmly	*ḏri*	II,272
hold in arrears	*3sḳ*	I,9
hold in contempt	*sḫr*	II,74
hold one's ground	*ʿmdy*	I,67
hold secret	*ḥ3p*	I,299
holder	*wrmyt*	I,105
holding	*3ḫt*	I,7
hole	*iknt*	I,50
hole	*ḳrrt*	II,157
hole	*tpḥt*	II,209
hole	*ṯpḥt*	II,229
hole(?)	*prṯ*	I,152
holiday	*hrw-nfr*	I,291
hollow (n.)	*wnḏw*	I,103
hollow (n.)	*ḫ3rw*	I,349
hollow (vb.)	*mšd*	I,209
holocaust	*ḳrr*	II,157
holy	*ḏsr*	II,274
holy ground	*ḏsrt*	II,275
holy of holies	*st*	II,2
Holy of Place	*ḏsr-st*	II,274
homage	*brkw*	I,137
homage	*nḏ*	I,255
homage	*ḥf*	I,309
home	*pr*	I,149
home	*ẖnw*	I,383
honest	(see trustworthy)	
honest	*ʿḳ3-ib*	I,81
honey	*bit*	I,128
honey gatherer	*bity*	I,129
honor	*šfyt*	II,120
honor (vb.)	*sw3š*	II,18
honored	*im3ḫy*	I,30
honored	*stp*	II,94
hoof	*ʿg3t*	I,81
hook	*ẖ3ww*	I,379
horizon	*3ḫt*	I,8
horn	*ʿb*	I,63
horn	*db*	II,243
horned	*ʿb*	I,63
horns	*ḥnwty*	I,318

horror	*bwt*	I,133
horse stall(?)	*ṯḥb*	II,232
horsemanship	*ssmt*	II,77
horses	*ḥtr*	I,338
horses	*ssmwt*	II,77
host	*pḏty*	I,161
hostilities	*ḫrw*	I,372
hostility	*ḏꜣis*	II,261
hostility	*s ḏrḏr*	II,274
hot	*šm(m)*	II,124
hot breath	*hh*	I,292
hound	*ṯsm*	II,236
hour	*wnwt*	I,101
house	*iwyt*	I,18
house	*ʿt*	I,59
house	*bt*	I,142
house	*pr*	I,149
house furnishings	*grg-pr*	II,193
house of books	*pr-mḏꜣt*	I,150
house of books	*pr-mḏꜣt*	I,220
house of life	*pr-ʿnḫ*	I,70
house of life	*pr-ʿnḫ*	I,149
house of morning	*pr-dwꜣ*	I,150
household	*pr*	I,149
how	*wsy*	I,111
how	*pꜣ sḫr nty*	II,73
how are you?	*tw.k mi iḫ sp-sn*	I,44
how are you?	*ḫy-ḳd-k*	I,351
how are you? (f.)	*ḫr ʿ.ṯ*	I,369
how are you? (pl.)	*ḫr ʿ.ṯn*	I,369
how clever	*rḫ-wsy*	I,275
how fortunate	*swꜣḏ-wy*	II,19
how long?	*wr*	I,104
how many?	*wr*	I,104
how well knowing	*rḫ-wsy*	I,275
how?	*ḫr-ʿ*	I,57
how?	*mi-iḫ*	I,178
however	*ḫr*	I,368
however	*ḫr-swt*	II,23
however	*swt*	II,23
howl	*ʿwn*	I,63
hue	*inw*	I,33
hue	*ṯms*	II,229
hull	*ṯrt*	II,231
human beings	*pʿt*	I,147
human herd	*wnḏw*	I,104
humanity	*rmṯ*	I,271
humble approach	*ḳrr*	II,157
humble servant	*bꜣk-im*	I,26
humbly	*m-hms*	I,288
humility	*m-hms*	I,288
humor	*sbi*	II,27
hundred thousand	*ḥfnw*	I,309
hunger	*ḥḳr*	I,334
hungry	(see famished)	
hungry	*ḥḳr*	I,334
hungry people	*ḥḳrw*	I,334
hunt (vb.)	*bḥs*	I,138
hunt (vb.)	*nw*	I,229
hunter	*nw*	I,230
hunters	*mḥw*	I,199
hunting	*nw*	I,229
huntsman	*nw*	I,230
hurl	*ḫꜣʿ*	I,347
hurl	*sti*	II,91
hurry	*ꜣs*	I,8
hurry	*ḥpt*	I,309
hurry	*sḫꜣḫy*	II,68
hurry up!	*yḥ*	I,43
hurry(?)	*ḥfḏ*	I,310
hurtle	*kh*	II,177
husband	*hꜣy*	I,284
hut	*imw*	I,29
hut	*isbw*	I,46
hut	*ʿt*	I,59
hut	*ḫnw*	I,362
huts	*sibyn*	II,11
hyena(?)	*ḥtmt*	I,338
hyena(?)	*ḥḏri*	I,342
hymns	*dwꜣw*	II,241
ḫy-vegetable	*ḫy*	I,350

I

I	*ỉ*	I,11
I	*ỉnk*	I,36
I	*wỉ*	I,92
I	*tw.ỉ*	II,201
I (writer)	*bꜣk-ỉm*	I,128
ibexes	*nrꜣw*	I,239
ibis	*hb*	I,287
identity	*rn*	I,272
idle	*sḏr*	II,103
idle	*šw*	II,113
idle	*ḳb*	II,147
idle, be	*wsf*	I,111
idle, lie	*nnỉ*	I,239
idleness	*wsft*	I,111
idly	*šw*	II,113
idly	*ḳb*	II,148
if	*ỉnn*	I,33
if	*ỉr*	I,36
if	*wnn*	I,102
if	*m-pꜣ*	I,168
if	*hn*	I,289
if	*ḫr-swt*	II,23
if only	*hnn*	I,289
ignorance	*ḫmt*	I,360
ignorant	*ḫm*	I,360
ignorant of	*ḫm*	I,360
ignorantly	*m-ḫm(t)*	I,170
ignorantly	*m-ḫmt*	I,360
ignore	*wꜣḥ*	I,89
ignore	*mkḥꜣ*	I,211
ignore	*ḫꜣꜥ*	I,347
ignore	*ḫm*	I,360
ignore	*smḫ*	II,44
ignoring	*ḫꜣꜥ*	I,347
ill	*bỉn*	I,131
ill	*mr*	I,191
ill	*šnỉ*	II,127
ill	*ḏꜣỉ*	II,260
ill	*ḏꜣyt*	II,261
ill	*ḏw(t)*	II,265
illness	*mnt*	I,184
illness	*mr*	I,191
illness	*ḫꜣy(t)*	I,345
illuminate	*sḥḏ*	II,65
illuminated	*swbḫ*	II,19
illumination	*sꜣḫw*	II,9
illumination	*sḥḏ*	II,65
illumine	*wpš*	I,99
illumine	*swbḫ*	II,19
illumine	*sḥḏ*	II,65
illumine	*stwt*	II,93
illumine	*tkꜣ*	II,220
image	*ꜥḫm*	I,78
image	*ꜥšm*	I,79
image	*ḫpỉw*	I,381
image	*smḫ*	II,44
image	*sn-nw*	II,48
image	*snn*	II,51
image	*sḫm*	II,70
image	*sšm*	II,81
image	*ḳỉ*	II,146
image	*tỉt*	II,200
image	*twt*	II,203
image of a wife	*tỉt ḥmt*	II,200
images	*sšpw*	II,80
images	*sšm*	II,80
images	*šspw*	II,136
imagine	*mꜣṯ*	I,177
imbue	*ꜣbḫ*	I,5
immediately	*m-tꜣ-wnwt*	I,171
immediately	*ḥr-ꜥ*	I,321
immediately	*hr r-ꜥ dwꜣ*	II,242
immerse	*tḫb*	II,218
impartial	*ḥr-gs*	I,323
impassively	*ḳb*	II,148
impatience	*ḫꜣḫ-ỉb*	I,349
impatient	*dns*	II,252
impatient man	*ṯỉṯỉ*	II,227
impede	*ṯꜣy-rd*	II,224
imperishable stars	*ḫm-sk*	I,360
implements	*ḫꜥw*	I,352
implicate	*hn*	I,288
importance	*r-ꜥꜣy*	I,261
important	*ꜥꜣ(ỉ)*	I,59
important	*dns*	II,251
impose restrictions	*ḏrỉ*	II,272
impost	*ỉnw*	I,32
impost	*bꜣkw*	I,127
imposter	*grg*	II,193
impoverished	*šwꜣ*	II,115
impracticable	*nḥꜣ*	I,242
imprecation	*sprt*	II,33
impress	*ꜥḳ*	I,80
impressed labor	*bḥw*	I,138
imprint	*ḫt*	I,376
imprison	*ḥꜥḳ*	I,299
imprison	*ḏdḥ*	II,277
imprisoned	*ḏdḥ*	II,277
imprisonment	*ḫnrt*	I,366
improve	*ꜥrꜥr*	I,72
improve	*snfr*	II,51
impure	*sỉf*	II,11
in	*ỉm*	I,26
in	*m*	I,167
in	*m-ḫnw*	I,170
in	*ḥr*	I,321
in a restoration	*m sꜥḥꜥ*	II,15
in accordance with	*r-mỉtt-n*	I,180
in accordance with	*r-mỉtt-n*	I,262

in accordance with	*ḫft*	I,359
in addition	*m-ḥꜣw*	I,296
in advance	*m-tp-ꜥ*	II,204
in any way	*m-r-ꜥ*	I,169
in as much as	*r-ntt*	I,263
in charge	*m-ḥr*	I,170
in charge	*n-ḥꜣt*	I,224
in charge	*n-ḥꜣt*	I,296
in charge	*sḥn*	II,63
in charge of	*ḥr-ḥr*	I,323
in conformity with the canon	*nḫb*	I,244
in employ of	*m-di*	I,171
in exactly the same state	*r-mitt-ꜥḳꜣ*	I,180
in excess	*m-ḥꜣw*	I,169
in exchange for	*r-ḏbꜣw*	I,265
in former time	*tp-ꜥ*	II,205
in front	*n-ḫft-ḥr*	I,359
in front	*m-ḫnty*	I,367
in front of	*m-ḥꜣt*	I,170
in front of	*n-ḥr*	I,225
in front of	*n-ḫft-ḥr*	I,225
in front of	*ḫft-ḥr*	I,359
in front of	*ḫnty*	I,367
in front of	*r-tp*	II,204
in front of	*tpty*	II,209
in good condition	*m-sšr*	I,171
in good condition	*m-sšr*	II,82
in good order	*m-sšr*	I,171
in good order	*m-sšr*	II,82
in haste	*ꜣs*	I,9
in health	*snb*	II,50
in his opinion	*ib ḥr*	I,22
in humility	*m-hms*	I,288
in like manner	*m-mitt*	I,169
in midair	*ꜥḫ*	I,77
in my charge	*m-ḏrt.i*	II,272
in my turn	*ink*	I,36
in my turn	*gr ink*	II,191
in no way	*m-biꜣ*	I,129
in obeisance	*m ksy*	II,178
in one voice	*m-r-wꜥ*	I,169
in opposition to	*ꜥḳꜣ*	I,81
in order	*m-sšr*	I,171
in order that	*n-mr(t)*	I,224
in order to	*r*	I,259
in other words	*kꜣ-ḏd*	II,167
in other words	*m-ky ḏd*	II,171
in pain (be)	*ispw*	I,47
in perfect order	*m-sšr*	II,82
in person	*m-ḥꜥw*	I,301
in possession of	*m-di*	I,171
in possession of	*ḫr*	I,385
in privacy	*m-wꜥ*	I,93
in procession	*sḫꜥ*	II,68

in proper way	*m-sšr*	II,82
in pursuit	*m-sꜣ*	I,171
in pursuit	*m-sꜣ*	II,5
in quest of	*m-sꜣ*	I,171
in quest of	*m-sꜣ*	II,5
in readiness	*spd*	II,34
in short	*m-ky ḏd*	II,171
in short order	*m-sšr-sp-sn*	I,171
in short order	*m-sšr*	II,82
in spite of	*m-sꜣ*	I,171
in spite of	*ḫbꜣ-r*	I,354
in submission	*m ksw*	II,178
in sum	*m ḳmi*	II,151
in the charge of	*m-di*	I,171
in the charge of	*m-di*	I,171
in the charge of	*m-ḏrt*	I,172
in the charge of	*m-ḏrt*	I,172
in the charge of	*r-iwd*	I,260
in the charge of	*ḫry-ḏrt*	I,387
in the company of	*m-ꜥb*	I,168
in the company of	*m-di*	I,171
in the company of	*r-ḳr*	I,265
in the company of	*ḳr*	II,155
in the course of	*m ḏr*	I,171
in the future	*m-dwꜣyt*	II,242
in the heart of	*ḥry-ib*	I,325
in the manner	*m-sḫr*	I,171
in the manner of	*mi-ḳd*	I,178
in the midst	*ḥry-ib*	I,325
in the midst of	*m-ḫnw*	I,170
in the midst of	*m-ḫnw*	I,382
in the midst of	*n-ḫnw*	I,382
in the near future	*m-sꜣ dwꜣ*	II,5
in the neighborhood of	*r gswy*	II,194
in the possession of	*m-ḏrt*	II,272
in the presence of	*ꜥḳꜣ*	I,81
in the presence of	*m-bꜣḥ*	I,126
in the presence of	*m-bꜣḥ*	I,168
in the presence of	*ḫr*	I,369
in the tenure of	*ḫr*	I,385
in travail	*sꜥi*	II,13
in vain	*ḳb*	II,148
inactive	*sḏr*	II,103
incapable(?)	*ḫr*	I,370
incense	*snṯr*	II,55
incense	*ḳꜣdꜣrti*	II,145
incense	*ḳdrt*	II,162
incense roaster	*sꜣḳ*	II,9
incise	*nḳꜥ*	I,250
incite	*thm*	II,216
incline	*pnꜥ*	I,148
incline toward	*mḫꜣ m*	I,201
include	*iri*	I,38
income in grain	*diw*	II,240

increase	*ḥꜣw*	I,296
increase (vb.)	*sꜥšꜣt*	II,16
increase (vb.)	*srd*	II,59
increase (vb.)	*ḳb*	II,147
increment	*sḫprw*	II,69
incurable disease	*bṯw*	I,143
indeed	*yꜣ*	I,11
indeed	*iwnꜣ*	I,20
indeed	*m-r-ꜥ*	I,57
indeed	*mk*	I,210
indeed	*ḥm*	I,310
indefatigable	*iḫmw-wrḏ*	I,44
independent	*ḥr-ḏrt*	II,272
indigence	*ngꜣ*	I,252
individuals	*tp*	II,204
indolent	*bꜣg*	I,128
indolent	*bgꜣ*	I,142
induce to move	*smnmn*	II,42
induct	*bsi*	I,139
ineffectiveness(?)	*tm*	II,210
ineffectual	*iꜣ iꜣ*	I,11
ineptitude	*wiꜣwiꜣ*	I,92
inert	*nni*	I,239
inert	*sḏr*	II,103
infant	*ꜥḏd*	I,84
infantry	*mnfꜣt*	I,187
infantry	*mšꜥ*	I,208
infantryman	*wꜥw*	I,94
inferior cloth	*sg*	II,89
infested(?)	*nḥꜣ*	I,242
infinity	*nḥḥ*	I,243
infirm	*tnw*	II,212
inflammation	*srf*	II,58
inflammations	*wḫdw*	I,110
inflated ego	*biꜣ(t)-ꜥꜣ*	I,130
inflict	*swgꜣ*	II,22
inflict	*sd*	II,97
influence(?)	*ꜥꜣ*	I,60
influential	*ꜥꜣ(i)*	I,59
inform	*swḏꜣ-ib*	I,23
inform	*di-ꜥm*	I,66
inform	*mtr*	I,214
inform	*r-rdit-rḫ*	I,275
inform	*rdi-rḫ*	I,281
inform	*swḏꜣ-ib*	II,24
inform	*snḏm-ib*	II,56
inform against	*wṯs*	I,117
informer	*wṯsy*	I,117
infraction	*wtnw*	I,116
infuriate	*sḳnd*	II,84
ingot(?)	*ntk*	I,255
inhabitant	*ꜥnḫ*	I,70
inhale	*ḫnm*	I,363
inhale	*srḳ*	II,59
inherit	*iwꜥ*	I,19
inheritance	*iwꜥ*	I,19

initially	*m-tꜣ-ḥꜣt*	I,296
initiate	*bsi*	I,139
injure	*ꜣꜥꜥ*	I,1
injure	*iꜣd*	I,14
injure	*nṯꜥ*	I,253
injure	*ḥḏ*	I,340
injure	*sbgs*	II,29
injure	*tḫn*	II,218
injure	*tk*	II,220
injure	*tkk*	II,221
injured (country?)	*iꜣṯ*	I,14
injury(?)	*ḳn*	II,152
injustice	*gns*	II,190
ink	*nry*	I,239
ink	*ry(t)*	I,266
inlaid	*ḥṯ*	I,339
inlaid	*sꜥm*	II,14
inlay	*mḥ*	I,198
inlay (vb.)	*mḥ*	I,197
inlay (vb.)	*ḥwṯ*	I,306
inlay (vb.)	*ḥṯ*	I,339
inner arm	*ḫry-ḫpš*	I,387
inner coffin	*wt-šri*	I,116
inner sanctuary	*dbꜣr*	II,244
inner side	*wꜣt ḫnw*	I,88
innermost chamber	*nfrw*	I,237
innermost coffin	*swḥt*	II,21
innermost thoughts	*imyw-ḫt*	I,27
innocent	*wꜥb*	I,94
inquire	*nḏnḏ*	I,257
inquire	*šni*	II,127
inquire about	*rḫ*	I,275
inquire about health	*nḏ-ḫrt*	I,256
inquire after welfare	*nḏ-ḫrt*	I,371
inquirer	*šny*	II,127
inquiry	*smtr*	II,127
inscribe	*mtn*	I,214
inscribe	*nḳꜥ*	I,250
inscribe	*spḫr*	II,34
inscribe	*sš*	II,78
inscription	*wḏ(t)*	I,119
inscription	*sšywt*	II,79
inside	*m-ḫnw*	I,170
inside	*n-ḫnw*	I,225
inside	*rit-ḫnw*	I,266
inside	*m-ḫnw*	I,382
inside	*m-ḳb*	II,147
inside out	*sḫd*	II,75
insight	*siꜣ*	II,11
insignia	*ḫkrw*	I,389
insignificant	*isy*	I,45
inspect	*ptr*	I,159
inspect	*rwḏ*	I,268
inspect	*sip*	II,11

inspecting	*sipt*	II,11
inspection	*sipt*	II,11
inspection	*šnw*	II,127
inspector	*rwḏ*	I,269
inspector(?)	*ḥy*	I,300
inspire	*snh*	II,53
install	*wꜣḥ*	I,89
install	*bsi*	I,139
install	*pḥꜥ*	I,155
instance	*sp*	II,30
instant	*ꜣt*	I,1
instead of	*r-ḏbꜣw*	I,265
instead of	*ḏbꜣ*	II,266
institute (vb.)	*wꜣḥ*	I,89
instruct	*mtr*	I,214
instruct	*sbꜣ*	II,26
instruct	*sḥn*	II,62
instruct	*sḥḏ*	II,65
instruction	*wḏ(t)*	I,119
instruction	*mtr*	I,215
instruction	*sbꜣyt*	II,27
instruction	*tp-rd*	II,205
instructor	*sbꜣw*	II,27
insult	*ḫnrfy*	I,366
insults	*sḥwr*	II,62
intact	*wḏꜣ*	I,120
intelligent	*pgꜣ-ḥr*	I,158
intensifying particle	*sp-sn*	II,30
intent	*tkꜥ*	II,220
intercede	*wšb*	I,114
interested much	*ꜥnḫ*	I,70
interfere	*tk*	II,220
interfere with	*ḫn*	I,381
interfere with	*ḫnn*	I,384
interfere with	*thꜣ*	II,216
interfere with	*ḏꜣi tꜣ r*	II,260
interference	*mdt*	I,217
interference	*snt*	II,49
interference	*thꜣ*	II,216
interment	*smꜣ-tꜣ*	II,38
interment	*ḳrst*	II,158
internal revenue	*tp-ḏrt*	II,207
interred	*ḥtp*	I,337
interred	*smꜣ-tꜣ*	II,38
interrogation	*šsp-r*	II,136
intervene	*ꜥḳ*	I,80
intestine	*ḳb*	II,147
intestines	*imyw-ḫt*	I,27
intimate (vb.)	*iri*	I,38
into	*m*	I,167
into	*r*	I,259
into	*r-r-ꜥ*	I,263
intoxicate	*tḫtḫ*	II,219
intoxicated	*tḫi*	II,218
intoxication	*tḫw*	II,218
intrigues	*ḥḏ-ib*	I,341
introduce	*bsi*	I,139
introduce	*sꜥḳ*	II,16
inundate	*iwḥ*	I,21
inundate	*tḫb*	II,218
inundated lands	*bꜥḥ*	I,132
inundation	*bꜥḥ*	I,132
Inundation Season	*ꜣḫt*	I,8
invade	*šdꜣ*	II,140
invent	*gm*	II,188
inventories	*imyt-pr*	I,27
inventory	*ipw*	I,25
inventory	*sipt*	II,11
inventory	*šnw*	II,127
inverted(?)	*ḳd*	II,161
investigate	*smtr*	II,45
investigate	*sḏm-mdw*	II,102
investigate	*šni*	II,127
investigate	*ḏꜥr*	II,264
investigation	*sipt*	II,11
investigation	*smtr*	II,45
investigator	*smty*	II,45
invigorate	*swḏꜣ*	II,24
invigorated	*rnpi*	I,273
invited	*nis*	I,227
invocation offerings	*prt-ḫrw*	I,151
invoke	*šni*	II,127
invoke(?)	*swꜣš*	II,18
irksome	*ḳsn*	II,159
iron	*biꜣ*	I,130
irrigated	*tḫb*	II,218
irrigation basin	*ḫnn*	I,384
is it not so?	*is bn*	I,45
is there not?	*is n wn*	I,45
island	*iw*	I,18
issue (vb.)	*ini*	I,31
issue (vb.)	*pri*	I,149
issue (vb.)	*ḫꜣꜥ*	I,347
it	*s*	II,1
it	*st*	II,90
item	*ꜥ*	I,57
itemized	*ḥr-sꜣ-rn*	I,323
itinerant	*ḥr šms*	II,124
its	*s*	II,1
itself	*r-ḥꜥt.*	I,263
ivory	*ꜣbw*	I,5
ivory	*kmri*	II,174
ivory tusk	*nḏḥ(t)*	I,257

J

jackal	ishb	I,47
jackal	wnš	I,103
jackal	sꜣb	II,7
jail	itḥ	I,52
janitor	wn	I,101
jar	ꜣꜥꜥ(w)t	I,2
jar	mnt	I,184
jar	mḥtt	I,200
jar	mḏꜣy	I,219
jar	mḏkt	I,221
jar	nw	I,230
jar	nmst	I,238
jar	ḫꜣwy	I,346
jar	gꜣy	II,183
jar	ṯbw	II,228
jar	ds	II,255
jar	ḏꜣḏꜣ	II,263
jar stands	styw	II,92
jars	sṯyw	II,96
jars	ḳbw	II,148
jars	kb	II,171
jars	dniꜣw	II,250
jaundice(?)	kbrt	II,172
jaunt over	swtwt	II,23
javelin	mrḥ	I,194
javelin	niw	I,226
jeer at	nṯꜥm	I,253
jerboa(?)	ḫdri	I,342
jest	sḏꜣyt-ḥr	II,100
jest (vb.)	ḳbꜥ	II,148
jewelry	smn	II,42
job	iꜣwt	I,13
job	wpwt	I,99
job	ḥnw	I,316
join	ꜥḳ	I,80
join	nḥb	I,242
join	ẖnm	I,383
join	smꜣ	II,38
join	sn	II,49
join	snsn	II,54
join	ṯs	II,233
join	dmi	II,247
join up	ṯs	II,233
join up with	ir-wꜥ	I,39
joinery (?)	smꜣw	II,38
joint	sb	II,24
joke	sbi	II,27
joke	sḏꜣyt-ḥr	II,100
joke (vb.)	mnẖ(t)	I,189
joke (vb.)	ḳbꜥ	II,148
jolting	hskt	
journey	wḏ(yt)	I,120
journey	mšꜥ	I,208
journey	ḥrty	I,328
journey (vb.)	ḥn	I,316
joy	ꜣw(i)	I,3
joy	ꜣwt-ib	I,3
joy	ꜣwt-ib	I,22
joy	ihy	I,42
joy	nḏm-ib	I,256
joy	ršw	I,278
joy	ršwt	I,279
joy	ṯhw	II,232
joy	ṯhḥ	II,232
joyful	ꜣw(i)	I,3
joyful	wnf	I,101
joyful	wnf-ib	I,101
joyful	ršwt	I,278
joyful	ḥꜥy	I,300
joyfully	ršrš	I,279
joyous	wnf-ib	I,101
joys	ḥgꜣw	I,335
jubilating crowd	ihy	I,42
jubilating crowd	wpwt	I,99
jubilation	ihy	I,42
jubilation	nhm	I,241
jubilation	rnn(wt)	I,274
jubilation	ṯhw	II,232
jubilee	ḥb-sd	I,307
judge	sꜣb	II,7
judge	spt	II,34
judge	smty	II,45
judge	sḏmy	II,102
judge (vb.)	wpi	I,98
judge (vb.)	wḏꜥ	I,122
judge (vb.)	gm	II,188
judge (vb.)	šꜥpt	II,109
judges	ḏꜣḏꜣt	II,263
judgment	wpt	I,98
judgment	sḏmw	II,102
judicial council	ḳnbt sḏmyw	II,154
jug	inḥt	I,35
jug	msẖ(t)	I,206
jug	mḏꜣy	I,219
jug	mḏkt	I,221
jump	(see leap)	
jump	krs	II,176
jump out	tfi	II,209
jump up	nhp	I,240
juniper oil	sft	II,36
just	mt	I,213
just as	mi-ḳd	I,178
just as	mi-ḳd	II,160
just ones	mꜣꜥtyw	I,175
just this once	pꜣ-wꜥ-sp	II,30
justice	mꜣꜥt	I,175
justified	mꜣꜥ-ḫrw	I,175
justified	mꜣꜥ-ḫrw	I,372

K

k3-servants	*ḥm-k3*	I,310
keel	*pipit*	I,147
keel(?)	*p3[y]pt*	I,146
keen	*spd*	II,34
keen of wit	*spd-ḥr*	II,34
keep	*ḥr-ḥr*	I,322
keep	*ḥrḥr*	I,328
keep	*s3w*	II,6
keep (n.)	*sg(n)*	II,89
keep (n.)	*sgr*	II,90
keep (n.)	*sḏm*	II,102
keep (n.)	*š3ᶜ*	II,107
keep (n.)	*šᶜr*	II,112
keep (n.)	*šrᶜ*	II,133
keep apart	*3bb*	I,5
keep away from	*ḫnr*	I,365
keep back	*isḳ*	I,48
keep busy	*nhp*	I,240
keep company	*stn*	II,95
keep festival	*ir ḫ3wt*	I,39
keep healthy	*ssnb*	II,77
keep off	*ḫsf-ᶜ*	I,374
keep on	*ḫpr*	I,356
keep oneself from	*dni*	II,249
keep safe	*swḏ3*	II,24
keep safe	*šdi*	II,139
keep silence	*sgr*	II,90
keep silence	*tmm*	II,211
keep up	*ᶜḥᶜ*	I,75
keep watch	*rs*	I,277
keep well	*wḏ3*	I,120
keep well	*ssnb*	II,77
keeper	*imy-r*	I,27
keeper of plough-oxen	*ᶜ3my-n-sk3*	I,62
keeper of the stable	*imy-r iḥw*	I,28
keeping up with	*r-ᶜḳ3*	I,261
kerchief	*idg*	I,55
kernels	*inyt*	I,32
kernels	*ḫ3nn*	I,348
kettle	*kḥn*	II,177
Khoiak	*kḥrk*	II,177
Khoiak feast	*k3-ḥr-k3*	II,166
kid	*ib*	I,23
kidney	*grt*	II,193
kidney(?)	*dpt*	II,246
kidneys	*knt*	II,175
kidneys	*krrt*	II,176
kidneys	*ggt*	II,195
kill	*wᶜwᶜ*	I,94
kill	*ẖdb*	I,389
kill	*sm3*	II,39
kill (one's self)	*mt*	I,212
kilt	*mss*	I,206
kilt	*šndyt*	II,131
kilt	*d3iw*	II,239
kin	*h3w*	I,285
kind	*nᶜᶜ-ib*	I,23
kind	*im(3)*	I,29
kind	*mnt*	I,185
kind	*nᶜᶜ-ib*	I,228
kind	*nfr*	I,235
kind to	*w3ḥ-ib*	I,90
kindle	*st3*	II,92
kindly	*w3ḥ-ib*	I,23
kindly	*sfn*	II,35
kindly disposed	*im(3)*	I,29
kindness	*ᶜn(n)*	I,67
kindness	*nᶜ(w)*	I,228
kindred	*h3w*	I,285
kine	*rnn*	I,274
king	*nsw*	I,248
The King of Lower Egypt	*bity*	I,129
king of U&L Egypt	*nsw-bit*	I,129
king of U&L Egypt	*n(y)-sw-bit*	I,225
king's apartments	*ipt-nsw*	I,248
king's grace	*k3-nsw*	I,249
king's harem	*ipt-nsw*	I,248
king's induction	*bs-nsw*	I,139
king's nobles	*špsy n nsw*	II,119
king's son	*s3 nsw*	II,3
King's Son of Kush	*s3-nsw-n-kš*	I,248
king's victuals	*ᶜnḫ-nsw*	I,70
king's victuals	*ᶜnḫw-nsw*	I,248
king's wife	*ḥmt-nsw*	I,248
king's wife	*ḥmt-nsw*	I,311
kings	*nsw*	I,248
kingship	*nsyt*	I,247
kingship(?)	*nsw*	I,248
kiosk	*ḏ3ḏ3w*	II,263
kiss	*sn*	II,49
kiss	*snn*	II,51
kiss the earth	*sn-t3*	II,49
kitchen	*wᶜbt*	I,95
kite	*bik*	I,131
kite	*ḳd*	II,160
kite	*ḏrit*	II,273
knee	*pd*	I,160
knee	*m3st*	I,177
kneel	*brk*	I,137
kneel	*m3s*	I,177
knife	*itmt*	I,51
knife	*s3ḥw*	II,8
knife	*sft*	II,36
knife	*šᶜt*	II,110

knife	*dm(t)*	II,247
knife	*ds*	II,255
knife (double-edged)	*wp*	I,98
knight	*mryn*	I,194
knock (at door)	*thm*	II,216
knock down	*whn*	I,106
knot	*ḳwt*	II,147
know	*ꜥm*	I,66
know	*ꜥrḳ*	I,73
know	*rḫ*	I,275
know sexually	*nk*	I,251
know sexually	*rḫ*	I,275
knowing a craft	*rḫyw*	I,276
knowing one	*rḫ-ḫt*	I,275
knowledge	*rḫ*	I,275
knowledge	*siꜣ*	II,11
kyllestis bread	*kršt*	II,176

L

labor	*smdt*	II,46
labor	*sḥn*	II,63
labor camp	*šnꜥ*	II,118
labor service	*hꜣy*	I,284
laborer	*snꜥyw*	II,129
laceration	*išf*	I,48
laceration	*šf*	II,119
lack	*ḥnr*	I,319
lack (vb.)	*ꜣty*	I,9
lack (vb.)	*ꜣdt*	I,10
lack (vb.)	*wh(i)*	I,106
lack (vb.)	*gꜣw*	II,183
lack of hair	*šnw*	II,128
lacking	*ꜣty*	I,9
lacking	*ngꜣ*	I,252
lacking	*šw*	II,113
lad	*iḥwn*	I,44
lad	*ꜥḏd*	I,84
lad	*ms*	I,203
lad	*ẖrd*	I,388
lad	*sfy*	II,35
lad	*šri*	II,132
laden	*ꜣtp*	I,10
lady	*nbt*	I,233
lady	*špsy*	II,119
lake	*ym*	I,28
lake	*brkt*	I,137
lake	*mr*	I,192
lake	*ḥn(t)*	I,320
lake	*š*	II,105
Lake Moeris	*wꜣḏ-wr*	I,91
lakes	*šwt*	II,114
lame	*gbi*	II,186
lame	*ṯh*	II,232
lameness	*gbgb*	II,187
lament (vb.)	*nḫ*	I,244
lament (vb.)	*sgb*	II,89
lamp	*ḫꜣbs*	I,348
lamp	*ḫbs*	I,355
lamp	*stꜣ*	II,92
lance	*mꜥbꜣ*	I,181
lance	*mrḥ*	I,194
lance	*niw*	I,226
land	*ꜣḥt*	I,7
land	*ḫꜣ-tꜣ*	I,344
land	*tꜣ*	II,197
land (vb.)	*mni*	I,185
land (vb.)	*ḫꜣꜥ*	I,346
land (vb.)	*ḫpr*	I,356
land donated	*ḥm-kꜣ-tꜣ*	I,310
land mark	*wḏ*	I,120
land register	*dni*	II,249
land sustained by	*sdf*	II,99

water		
land type	ḫꜣ-tꜣ	I,344
land-cubit	mḥ-tꜣ	I,198
land-cubit	mḥ-tꜣ	I,199
landed property	st	II,2
landing place	dmi	II,248
landing place	mniwt	I,186
landing stage	ḏꜣḏꜣw	II,263
lands, fresh	nḫbw	I,245
lands, low	nḫbw	I,245
languid	wiꜣwiꜣ	I,92
languor	bgꜣ	I,142
lapidary	nšdy	I,250
lapis lazuli	ḫsbd	I,374
lapse	wn	I,101
large	ꜥꜣ(i)	I,59
large crock	kḥn	II,177
large drinking bowl	ṯpr	II,229
large vessel	mnḏkt	I,191
lascivious	dꜣdꜣ	II,239
lash	ḥꜥr	I,353
lashes	mntd	I,191
lashes	mtḏ	I,215
lashes	rwḏ	I,268
lashes	sḫ	II,66
last day	ꜥrḳ	I,73
later	(see afterwards)	
lattice(?)	ḥgꜣi	I,335
laudanum	rdn	I,282
laudation	sns	II,53
laugh (vb.)	sbi	II,27
laughing	sbi	II,27
laughter	sbi	II,27
launch	wdi	I,117
launch	ms	I,203
launch	ḫꜣꜥ	I,347
launder	rḫt	I,276
launderer	rḫty	I,277
laundryman	rḫty	I,277
lave	iꜥi	I,16
law	hp	I,287
law court	ḥwt-sr	I,304
lawful	sbḳ	II,29
lay aside	wꜣḥ	I,89
lay down	wꜣḥ	I,89
lay down	nmꜥ	I,237
lay hands on	ꜣw(i)	I,2
lay hold of	mḥ	I,197
lay hold on	ṯꜣy	II,224
lay low	sḫr	II,72
lay low	ḏrꜥ	II,273
lay on	wšwš	I,114
lay out	snṯ	II,54
lay out (bed)	nmꜥ	I,237
lay priesthood	wnwt(y)	I,101
lay waste	ḫbḫb	I,355
layout	snnt	II,52
lazy	bꜣg	I,128
lazy	bgꜣ	I,142
lead	ḥꜣt	I,296
lead	sšm	II,81
lead	dḥt	II,254
lead	ḏḥty	II,274
lead (vb.)	ꜥr	I,71
lead (vb.)	mꜣꜥ	I,174
lead (vb.)	ḫrp	I,372
lead (vb.)	sbꜣ	II,26
lead (vb.)	sšm	II,80
lead astray	stnm	II,95
lead on out	in r-bnr	I,32
lead to	ḫꜣꜥ-r	I,347
lead(?)	ḥrr	I,328
leader	imy-ḥꜣt	I,27
leader	ꜥꜣ	I,60
leader	ḥꜣ(w)tyw	I,298
leader	ḫrp	I,372
leader	sšm	II,80
leaf	srpt	II,58
leaf	gb	II,187
league	itrw	I,51
lean	rhn	I,274
lean upon	hn	I,288
leap	pwy	I,148
leap	krs	II,176
leap	tfi	II,209
learn	ꜥm	I,66
learn	sḏm	II,101
learned one	rḫ-ḫt	I,275
learning	sbꜣyt	II,27
leather	dḥr	II,254
leather bucket	msti	I,206
leather coverings	mšy	I,207
leather sack	iḫꜣ	I,44
leave	ꜥr	I,71
leave	wꜣḥ	I,89
leave	whs	I,107
leave	wḏi	I,119
leave	pri	I,149
leave	ntꜥ	I,253
leave	ḫꜣꜥ	I,346
leave	swḏ	II,24
leave	šm	II,121
leave alone	rdi-r-tꜣ	I,281
leave behind	ḫꜣꜥ	I,346
leave off	whꜥ	I,107
leave unattended	nḫꜣ	I,242
leaves	ꜥḫmw	I,78
leaves	srdm	II,60
leaves	ḳmꜣḥ	II,151
leaves	ḏbꜣw	II,266
leaving	pr	I,149

lector priest	*ẖry-ḥb(t)*	I,387
lectors	*ẖry-ḥb(t)*	I,387
leeks	*ꞽꜣḳt*	I,14
left	*ꞽꜣbt*	I,14
left	*smḥ*	II,44
left arm	*smḥ*	II,44
left hand	*ꞽꜣby*	I,13
left hand	*smḥ*	II,43
left side	*ꞽꜣby*	I,13
left side	*smḥ*	II,43
left to their own devices	*wꜣḥ ḥr ꜥw*	I,90
left-over	*spyt*	II,31
legal	*sbḳ*	II,29
legal(?)	*st-r-st.w*	II,91
legal document	*hry*	I,290
legal record	*hry*	I,290
legitimate	*sbḳ*	II,29
legs	*mnty*	I,185
lend support	*rdi-ḏrt*	I,282
length	*ꜣw(t)*	I,3
length	*iwn*	I,20
length	*ḳꜣ(y)*	II,143
lentils	*ꜥršn*	I,73
leopard	*ꜣby*	I,4
leopard-skin	*ẖnt-bꜣ*	I,381
leprosy	*sbḥ*	II,28
lesser men	*šri*	II,132
lesson	*sbꜣyt*	II,27
lest	*tm*	II,210
let	*imi*	I,26
let	*rdi*	I,281
let	*di*	II,240
let breathe	*snf*	II,51
let down	*sbnbn*	II,28
let go	*sfḫ*	II,35
let loose	*ntf*	I,253
let loose	*ḫꜣꜥ*	I,346
let loose	*ṯt*	II,236
let me	*mtw.i*	I,213
let move	*smnmn*	II,42
let resound	*šdi*	II,140
let sleep	*sḳdd*	II,85
let success be with me	*di ḫpr wn m-di.i*	I,100
lethargic	*sgꜣ*	II,89
letter	*wḫꜣ*	I,110
letter	*mḏꜣt*	I,219
letter	*hꜣb*	I,286
letter	*šꜥt*	II,110
letter writer	*sš-šꜥt*	II,79
letter writing	*šꜥwt*	II,111
letters	*mdw-nṯr*	I,218
letters	*sš*	II,78
lettuce	*ꜥbw*	I,64
lettuce	*ḫṯn*	I,378
leucoma	*sḥḏw-n-irt*	II,65
Levant	*wbn*	I,97
level	*mḫꜣ*	I,201
level with	*n-ḥꜣt*	I,224
levy	*ḥtr*	I,339
levy	*šrmt*	II,133
levy	*šdi*	II,140
liaison	*ḫbr*	I,354
libate	*iwḥ*	I,21
libation	*sṯ*	II,96
libation	*ḳbḥ*	II,149
libation vessel	*ḳbḥ*	II,149
libations	*iwḥ*	I,21
liberal	*pgꜣ-ḏrt*	I,158
liberty	*wstnw*	I,113
liberty	*ṯꜣw*	II,226
library	*pr-mḏꜣt*	I,150
library	*pr-mḏꜣt*	I,220
lid	*ḥbs*	I,308
lid	*kꜣp*	II,168
lid (coffin)	*wꜣ(t)*	I,87
lid(?)	*nḳr-mnḏm*	I,251
lie	*ꜥḏꜣ*	I,84
lie	*sḏr*	II,102
lie	*gꜣi*	II,183
lie between	*iwd*	I,22
lie crookedly	*nwd*	I,232
lie down	*nmꜥ*	I,237
lie down	*sḏr*	II,103
lie idle	*nni*	I,239
lie in wait for	*šdšd*	II,141
lie on one's back	*nmꜥ*	I,237
lies	*mdt-n-ꜥḏꜣ*	I,217
lieutenant	*idnw*	I,54
lieutenant commander	*idnw*	I,54
life	*ꜥnḫ(w)*	I,70
life of the world	*ꜥnḫ-n-tꜣ*	I,70
lifetime	*ꜥḥꜥw*	I,77
lifetime	*hꜣw*	I,285
lift	*wṯs*	I,117
lift	*fꜣy*	I,163
lift up	*sṯs*	II,97
lift up	*ṯs*	II,234
ligament	*ṯst*	II,235
light	*isy*	I,45
light	*ꜥb*	I,63
light	*wnyt*	I,101
light	*sšpt*	II,80
light	*ḳḥ*	II,158
light (vb.)	*sḥḏ*	II,65
light (vb.)	*stꜣ*	II,92
light up	*brg*	I,137
lighted candles	*stꜣ-ḫbs*	II,92
lightening flash	*sšdw*	II,84
lightweight	*isy*	I,45

like	*m-mitt*	I,169
like	*mi*	I,178
like	*mi-ḳi(-n)*	I,178
like	*mi-ḳd*	I,178
like	*mitt*	I,180
like	*m-mitt*	I,180
like	*mi-ḳd*	II,160
like (n.)	*mitt*	I,179
like (n.)	*mnt*	I,185
like (n.)	*sn-nw*	II,48
like (n.)	*ḳi*	II,146
like (n.)	*twt*	II,203
like unto	*mi-ḳi(-n)*	I,178
liken	*stwt*	II,93
likeness	*bȝyt*	I,126
likeness	*mity*	I,179
likeness	*snn*	II,51
likeness	*snty*	II,54
likeness	*ḳȝi*	II,143
likeness	*twt*	II,203
likewise	*m-mitt*	I,169
likewise	*m-r-ʿ*	I,169
likewise	*r-mitt*	I,262
lilies(?)	*mymy*	I,180
limb	*ʿt*	I,58
limbs	*ḥʿt*	I,301
limestone	*inr n ʿinw*	I,34
limestone	*ʿyn*	I,62
limit	*pḥwy*	I,153
limit	*r-ʿ*	I,260
limit (vb.)	*ḥn*	I,315
limits	*ḥnty*	I,317
limits	*ḥnty*	I,320
limits	*ḏrw*	II,271
limp	*ḥdy*	I,340
line	*mḫȝ*	I,201
line	*rdt*	I,281
linen	*mḥʿw*	I,199
linen	*mk*	I,210
linen	*sšrw*	II,82
linen	*šmʿ(t)*	II,122
linger	*inty*	I,36
linger	*isḳ*	I,48
linger	*ʿḥʿ*	I,75
lintel	*wmt*	I,100
lintel	*pḫȝ*	I,154
lintel	*ḥryw-n-ʿwy*	I,326
lintel	*twȝ*	II,202
lion	*mȝi*	I,173
lion	*rw*	I,266
lion(?)	*iȝr*	I,14
lioness	*rby*	I,270
lioness(?)	*rw-ȝbw*	I,266
lip	*spt*	II,31
liquidate	*ḥtm*	I,338
list	*ʿrt*	I,72
list	*mitt*	I,179
list	*rn-rn*	I,272
list	*rḫt*	I,276
list	*snn*	II,51
list	*sḥwy*	II,62
list	*šnw*	II,127
list	*dni(t)*	II,250
list (vb.)	*rḫ*	I,275
list (vb.)	*r-rdit-rḫ*	I,275
list (vb.)	*sḥwy*	II,62
listen	*mḥ*	I,197
listen	*sḏm*	II,101
lists	*ipw*	I,25
literature	*mdw-nṯr*	I,218
litigate	(see go to law)	
litigate	*wpi*	I,98
litigation	*wpt*	I,98
little	*nkt*	I,251
little	*šri*	II,132
little bird	*ṯwi*	II,227
little fish	*tpy(wt)*	II,208
little girl	*kt*	II,179
little one	*kt*	II,179
live	*ʿnḫ*	I,69
live	*ʿḥʿ*	I,75
live (vb.)	*wȝḥ*	I,89
live (vb.)	*wn*	I,100
live on	*spi*	II,31
livelihood	*ʿnḫ(w)*	I,70
lively youth	*rnp*	I,272
liver	*mist*	I,181
livestock	*mnmnt*	I,187
living captive	*sḳr-ʿnḫ*	II,85
living one	*ʿnḫ*	I,70
living prisoner	*sḳr-ʿnḫ*	II,85
living room	*st ḥms*	II,2
load	*ȝtp*	I,10
load	*sb*	II,25
loaf	*bi(ȝ)t*	I,129
loaf	*sḫn*	II,71
loaf type	*ht*	I,292
loan (n.)	*wšby*	I,114
loaves	*ʿḳ*	I,80
loaves	*ʿkk*	I,81
loaves	*pȝwt*	I,146
loaves	*ht*	I,292
loaves	*ḥḏt*	I,342
loaves	*ḫrps*	I,373
loaves	*sšrt*	II,83
loaves	*kmḥ*	II,174
loaves	*gt*	II,195
lock	*mȝʿyw*	I,174
lock of hair	*fʿȝ*	I,164
locks	*ḳri*	II,156
locust	*snḥm*	II,53
lodge	*šrʿ*	II,133

M

mace	*ḥḏ*	I,341
madder	*iwpꜣ*	I,19
madder	*ipꜣ*	I,25
madman	*ḫꜣini*	I,345
madman	*šš*	II,137
madness	*syḫ*	II,12
magazine	*wḏꜣ*	I,121
magazine	*mḫr*	I,202
magazine	*ḫr*	I,385
magazine	*sgr*	II,90
magazine	*šnꜥ*	II,128
magic	*ḥkꜣ*	I,334
magic power over	*ꜣḫ*	I,7
magical charms	*ꜣḫw*	I,7
magical writing	*sš-n-ḥkꜣw*	II,78
magician	*ḥry-ḥkꜣ*	I,325
magician	*ḫrp-srḳt*	I,373
magicians	*ḫry-ḥb(t)*	I,387
magistrate	*wr*	I,104
magistrate's mansion	*ḥwt-sr*	I,304
magistrates	*sr*	II,57
magistrates	*ḏꜣḏꜣt*	II,263
magnate	*ꜥꜣ*	I,60
magnate	*wr*	I,104
magnate	*bwꜣ*	I,133
magnificence	*fꜣw*	I,164
magnificent	*šps*	II,118
magnify	*sꜥꜣ*	II,13
magnify	*skꜣ*	II,84
magpie	*iꜣbt*	I,14
maiden	*ꜥḏd-šrt*	I,85
maiden	*nfrt*	I,237
maiden	*rwnt*	I,267
maiden	*šrit*	II,132
maids	*ḫnmw*	I,363
maidservant	*bꜣkt*	I,128
maidservant	*ḫnmw*	I,363
maidservant	*ḫnmt*	I,364
maidservant	*ḥmt-st*	II,1
maidservants	*ḥmt*	I,311
maintain	*šdi*	II,140
maintain	*ḏd*	II,275
majesty	*ḥm*	I,310
majesty	*šfyt*	II,120
majesty (fem.)	*ḥmt*	I,311
major domo	*ꜥꜣ-n-pr*	I,60
make	*iri*	I,37
make	*sms*	II,44
make	*sḫpr*	II,69
make	*tp*	II,204
make	*di*	II,240
make a distinction	*stn*	II,95
make a regulation	*siꜥr*	II,11
make a round of inspection	*ḳdd*	II,162
make a wonder	*biꜣ*	I,129
make abundant	*sꜥšꜣt*	II,16
make an early start	*sdwꜣ*	II,98
make appear	*sḫꜥ*	II,68
make arrangements	*iri-šꜣyt.s*	II,106
make aware	*di-ꜥm*	I,66
make blind	*kꜣmn*	II,169
make bricks	*pipi*	I,147
make bricks	*sḫt*	II,75
make bright	*sḥḏ*	II,65
make census	*snh*	II,53
make clean	*swꜥb*	II,19
make cognizant	*di-ꜥm*	I,66
make common cause with	*ir wꜥ irm*	I,93
make contact with	*ṯs*	II,233
make content	*sḥtp*	II,64
make crooked	*gsꜣ*	II,194
make deaf	*sḫi*	II,75
make definitive	*smn*	II,41
make even	*mḫꜣ*	I,201
make excellent	*sikr*	II,12
make extensive	*swsḫ*	II,22
make fast	*ṯꜣr*	II,226
make festive	*sḥb*	II,62
make firm	*ṯꜣr*	II,226
make flourish	*swꜣḏ*	II,19
make fortunate	*smꜥr*	II,41
make friends	*ḫnms*	I,364
make friends with	*snsn*	II,54
make glad	*ꜣms-ib*	I,6
make glad	*ꜣms-ib*	I,22
make great	*sꜥꜣ*	II,13
make grow	*srd*	II,59
make hale	*sꜥd*	II,16
make haste	*ꜣs*	I,8
make haste	*ḥfḏ*	I,310
make haste	*šrš*	II,133
make high	*skꜣ*	II,84
make holiday	*ir hrw nfr*	I,39
make holiday	*sḥb*	II,62
make lame	*gbgb*	II,187
make live	*sꜥnḫ*	II,14
make note of	*sḏm*	II,101
make obeisance	*sn-tꜣ*	II,49
make offerings	*wdn*	I,118
make offerings	*mꜣꜥ*	I,174
make offerings	*drp*	II,252
make one's reputation	*irt ḳd*	II,160
make one's way	*bgb*	I,142
make perfect	*smnḫ*	II,43
make permanent	*sḏd*	II,104

massacre	*ḫꜣyt*	I,345
massacre	*ḫrw*	I,372
massacre	*šꜥt*	II,110
massacre	*krt*	II,177
massage (vb.)	*gmgm*	II,189
masses	*rḫyt*	I,276
masses	*tꜣ-tmw*	II,198
mast	*ḫt-ṯꜣw*	I,375
mast wood	*dpw*	II,247
mast(?)	*pꜣ[y]pt*	I,146
master	*ꜥꜣ*	I,60
master	*nb*	I,232
master	*ḥry*	I,324
master	*ḫrp*	I,372
master (vb.)	*ḫrp*	I,372
master of	*šb*	II,116
master of largess	*ḥry-iꜥb*	I,324
mastery	*ꜣḫw*	I,7
mastery gain	*ḫꜣm*	I,348
masturbate	*nwḥ*	I,231
mat	*wꜣt-šwy*	I,88
mat	*p(s)št*	I,156
mat	*rdmt*	I,282
mat	*smyt*	II,41
mat	*ḳn*	II,152
mat	*tmꜣ*	II,211
match	*mḫꜣ*	I,201
mate	*iry*	I,39
material things	*sšr*	II,82
maternal uncle	*sn-n-mwt*	II,48
matter	*wp*	I,97
matter	*wpwt*	I,99
matter	*mdt*	I,217
matter	*ḫnw*	I,362
matter	*sp*	II,30
matter	*sḫr*	II,72
matting	*inw*	I,32
matting	*idnw*	I,54
mattock	*nꜣyḫ*	I,226
mature (vb.)	*ꜥꜣ(i)*	I,59
mature (vb.)	*tnw*	II,212
may	*iḫ*	I,44
May (he) live, be prosperous, and be healthy	*ꜥnḫ, wḏꜣ, snb*	I,70
maybe	*gm*	II,189
mayor	*imy-r niwt*	I,28
mayor	*ḥꜣty-ꜥ*	I,58
mayor	*ḥꜣty-ꜥ*	I,298
me	*i*	I,11
me	*wi*	I,92
meadow	*ꜣḫt*	I,8
meadow	*iꜣdt*	I,15
meadow	*ḥsbt*	I,332
meadow	*šꜣ*	II,105
meadow-saffron	*ḥbrḏt*	I,308
meal	*ꜥš*	I,79
meal	*šbw*	II,117
meal	*šbb*	II,117
meal	*drpw*	II,252
mean	*sn-nw*	II,49
meaning	*mdt*	I,217
meaningless	*ḳb*	II,148
means	*mẖrw*	I,202
means	*sḫr*	II,72
meanwhile	*ḫr-r-ꜥ*	I,260
meanwhile	*ḫy-r-ꜥ*	I,351
measure	*pdr*	I,160
measure	*mdy*	I,216
measure	*mdd*	I,218
measure	*mḏt*	I,219
measure	*ḥpt*	I,309
measure	*ḥḳꜣt*	I,334
measure	*srf*	II,58
measure	*st*	II,90
measure	*sdf*	II,99
measure	*šꜣb*	II,108
measure	*gꜣt*	II,185
measure	*gsr*	II,195
measure	*ṯm-ṯm*	II,229
measure (vb.)	*ḫꜣi*	I,344
measure (vb.)	*stn*	II,95
measure for resin	*ḳḏm*	II,163
measurement	*ḫꜣy*	I,344
measurement	*ẖtyw*	I,377
measurement (2 cubits)	*nbi*	I,233
measurement made	*ḫꜣy*	I,344
measurer	*ḫꜣi*	I,344
measures	*ḫꜣywt*	I,344
measures	*sḫr*	II,73
meat	*iwf*	I,20
meat from side	*ḏrw*	II,273
mechanic	*ḥmww*	I,313
meddle with	*sn*	II,47
mediate	*šsꜣ*	II,135
medicine	*pẖrt*	I,155
medicine	*ḥrw-ꜥ*	I,327
medicine type	*nḥš*	I,244
Mediterranean	*wꜣḏ-wr*	I,91
Medjaw captain	*ḥry-mḏꜣw*	I,325
Medjay	*mḏꜣw*	I,220
meet	*ḫp*	I,355
meet	*sḫn*	II,71
meet	*ṯḥn*	II,232
meet up with	*ir n (?) ḥꜣt*	I,39
melee	*ḫḫ*	I,373
melon	*dnrg*	II,251
melt	*wḏḥ*	I,123
melt	*nbi*	I,233
melt away(?)	*mrḳḥt*	I,195
melt(?)	*bꜣbꜣ*	I,126

member	*ꜥt*	I,58
member of the crew	*wꜥw*	I,94
member of tribe	*ꜣbt*	I,4
members	*ḥꜥt*	I,301
memorandum	*sẖꜣ*	II,67
memory	*sẖꜣ*	II,68
men	*pꜥt*	I,147
men	*ṯꜣy*	II,223
mend	*ꜥn*	I,68
mention	*sẖꜣ*	II,67
mercenaries	*nꜥrn*	I,229
merchandise(?)	*šwtyw*	II,114
merchandizing	*šwyt*	II,114
merchant	*mkrw*	I,211
merchant	*šwyty*	II,114
merciful	*nꜥ(i)*	I,227
merciful	*ḥtp*	I,336
merciful	*sfn*	II,35
merciful (vb.)	*sf*	II,35
mercy	*ꜥn(n)*	I,67
mercy	*nꜥ(w)*	I,228
Mesore (month)	*wpt-rnpt*	I,98
message	*swḏꜣ-ib*	I,23
message	*ipwt*	I,25
message	*wpwt*	I,99
message	*mdt*	I,217
message	*hꜣb*	I,286
message	*swḏꜣ-ib*	II,24
message	*šꜥt*	II,111
messenger	*ipwty*	I,25
messenger	*wpwty*	I,99
messenger	*mhr*	I,196
messenger	*shꜣb*	II,60
messenger	*šmsw*	II,125
metal	*ḳꜥ*	II,146
metal	*dḥw*	II,253
metal	*ḏḥ*	II,274
metal inlays	*sswt*	II,76
metal object	*in*	I,31
metal object	*nṯpts*	I,254
metal tool	*iḏdk*	I,55
metal tool	*mrḳḏn*	I,195
metal work	*ḳḥḳḥ*	II,159
meteor	*sšdw*	II,84
method	*mdt*	I,217
midday	*ꜥḥꜥw-mtrt*	I,77
midday	*mtrt*	I,215
middle	*ḥry-ib*	I,23
middle	*ḥry-ib*	I,325
midge	*ḏwt*	II,265
midst	*ḥry-ib*	I,23
midst	*mtt*	I,213
midst	*ḥry-ib*	I,325
midst	*m-ḳb*	II,147
might	*bꜣw*	I,125
might	*pḥty*	I,154
might	*sḫm*	II,70
might	*ḳn(t)*	II,152
mighty	*ꜥꜣ(i)*	I,59
mighty	*wr*	I,104
mighty	*wsr*	I,111
mighty	*pḥty*	I,154
mighty	*nḫt*	I,245
mighty	*sḫm*	II,69
mighty	*ḳni*	II,152
mighty	*tnr*	II,213
mighty bull	*kꜣ-nḫt*	II,165
mighty deeds	*tnr*	II,214
mighty one	*sḫm*	II,70
migraine	*gs-tp*	II,194
mild	*nꜥ(i)*	I,227
mild	*ḥtpyt*	I,337
military officer	*skt*	II,88
milk	*irtt*	I,42
milk	*ḥḏw*	I,341
milk	*smi*	II,41
milk (vb.)	*hr*	I,290
milk cow	*ꜥmryt*	I,67
milk feed	*snḳ*	II,54
million	*ḥḥ*	I,329
millstone	*bnwt*	I,134
mina (a weight)	*mnniw*	I,187
mind	*ib*	I,22
mind	*ḥr*	I,321
mind(?) of the Governor	*dbn-ḫrp*	II,245
mindful of	(see heedful of)	
mindless	(see senseless)	
mine	*ḫꜣt*	I,380
miner	*iꜣk*	I,14
miner	*ḳwr*	II,147
mineral	*inr*	I,34
mineral	*wꜣy*	I,88
mineral	*bk*	I,141
mineral	*ḥrr*	I,328
mineral	*tḥnt*	II,217
mineral pigment	*ikbw*	I,49
mineral(?)	*šsy*	II,135
mingle	*ꜣbḫ*	I,5
mingle	*šbn*	II,117
miracle	*biꜣyt*	I,130
mire(?)	*mḫn*	I,202
mirror	*ꜥnḫ*	I,70
miscarriage	*ms-ḏꜥt*	I,204
miscarry	*hꜣ(i)*	I,283
mischief	*wgg*	I,116
mischief	*bin*	I,131
mischievous(?)	*stn*	II,95
misdeed	*sp*	II,30
misdemeanor	*ꜥḏꜣ*	I,84
miserable	*wgg*	I,116

move	*ḳmꜣ*	II,151
move	*ktkt*	II,180
move	*thm*	II,217
move about freely	*trr*	II,215
move away	*ꜣbb*	I,5
move away	*tfi*	II,209
move freely	*wstn*	I,113
move from place to place	*iṯ-in*	I,53
move hastily	*fḳꜣ*	I,165
move quickly	*ifd*	I,26
move quickly	*ṯḥn*	II,232
mow down	*isḫ*	I,47
mow down	*wꜥwꜥ*	I,94
mr-garden(?)	*mr*	I,192
much	*ꜥšꜣ*	I,79
mud	*ꜥmꜥmt*	I,66
mud	*dbyt*	II,245
mud	*dbn*	II,245
mud-flat	*ꜥmꜥmt*	I,66
mullet	*imskꜣ*	I,31
mullet	*ꜥḏw*	I,83
multicolored of plumage	*sꜣb-šwt*	II,8
multiply	*sꜥšꜣt*	II,16
multiply	*ḳb*	II,147
multitude	*ꜥḥꜥw*	I,76
multitude	*ꜥšꜣt*	I,79
mummy	*sꜥḥ*	II,15
mummy chamber	*sꜥḥt*	II,15
mummy wrapping	*wt*	I,116
murder	*smꜣ*	II,39
murder	*krt*	II,177
murderousness	*šꜥt*	II,110
muscle	*mt*	I,212
musical instrument	*nṯḫ*	I,255
musician	*ḫnrt*	I,365
musician	*sḫmyt*	II,70
musician priestess	*ḫnwt*	I,363
must	*mrsw*	I,195
muster	*snh*	II,53
muster	*ṯs*	II,234
mutilate	*ḫšb*	I,375
mutilated	*m-šꜥd*	II,112
my	*i*	I,11
my home companion	*irt.i-n-ḫms*	I,314
my own	*pꜣy.i ink*	I,36
myriads	*ꜥšꜣt*	I,79
myriads	*ḏbꜥ*	II,267
myrrh	*ꜥntyw*	I,71
myself	*r-ḥꜥt*	I,263
mysteries	*itnw*	I,51
mysterious	*štꜣ*	II,138
mystery	*sštꜣ*	II,83

N

naked	*ḥꜣy*	I,295
name	*rn*	I,272
name	*kꜣ*	II,165
name list	*rn-rn*	I,272
name of a tree	*ꜣꜥꜥ*	I,2
named	*ḏd n.f*	II,275
namely	*wp*	I,97
namely	*m*	I,167
naos	*ḳnby*	II,154
naos	*kꜣr*	II,169
naos	*dbꜣr*	II,244
narrow	*gꜣw*	II,183
narrow road	*gꜣwt*	II,184
native (of a place)	*ms*	I,203
natron	*ḥsmn*	I,333
nature	*inw*	I,33
nature	*biꜣt*	I,130
nature	*sḫr*	II,72
nature	*sšm*	II,81
nature	*ḳꜣi*	II,143
nature	*ḳi*	II,145
nature	*ḳd*	II,160
naughty	*bin*	I,131
navel	*ḫpꜣ*	I,381
navigate	*nꜥy*	I,228
navigate	*sḳdd*	II,85
navy	*ḫni*	I,382
nay	*ḫr-bn*	I,369
near	*spr*	II,32
near	*ḳꜣi*	II,143
near	*kr*	II,155
near	*r gswy*	II,194
nearby	*ꜥrw*	I,71
neat	*wꜥb*	I,94
necessities	*ḫrt*	I,385
necessity	*ḏꜣr(t)*	II,262
neck	*nḥb*	I,242
neck	*ḫḫ*	I,374
necklace	*bb*	I,133
necklace	*šꜣbwy*	II,108
necklace(?)	*ḥty*	I,336
necropolis	*igrt*	I,50
necropolis	*ḥrt*	I,328
necropolis	*ḫr*	I,368
necropolis	*ḫrt-nṯr*	I,385
necropolis	*st mꜣꜥt*	II,2
necropolis	*tꜣ-n-ḫry-nṯr*	II,198
necropolis	*tꜣ-ḏsr*	II,199
necropolis area	*spꜣt*	II,32
need	*ꜣty*	I,10
need	*mꜣr*	I,177
needs	*ḫrt*	I,371
needs	*ḫrt*	I,385

northerners	*mḥtyw*	I,200
Northland	*tꜣ-mḥty*	II,198
northward	*m-ḫd*	I,170
northward	*m-ḫt*	I,378
north-west	*mḥt-imnt*	I,200
nose	*fnd*	I,164
nose	*šrit*	II,133
nose wings	*msdty*	I,207
nostril	*gꜣbt* (*n*) *šrt*	II,185
nostrils	*fnd*	I,164
nostrils	*šrit*	II,133
not	*bw*	I,132
not	*bn*	I,134
not acknowledge	*ḫm*	I,360
not care for	*ḫm*	I,360
not know	*ḫm*	I,360
not say	*wiꜣ*	I,92
not speak	*wiꜣ*	I,92
not yet	*ꜥn*(*n*)	I,68
not...at all	*bn...iwnꜣ*	I,134
notable	*bwꜣ*	I,133
notables	*rmṯ-ꜥꜣw*	I,272
notables	*sr*	II,57
notch	*ḫty*	I,376
note (vb.)	*rḫ*	I,275
note (vb.)	*sḏm*	II,101
notice (vb.)	*ptr*	I,159
notice (vb.)	*siꜣ*	II,11
notice (vb.)	*gm*	II,188
nourish	*sꜥnḫ*	II,14
nourishment	*ḥw*	I,302
nourishment	*kꜣw*	II,166
now	*ist*	I,48
now	*m-tꜣ-wnwt*	I,101
now	*m-tꜣ-wnwt*	I,171
now	*mk*	I,210
now	*rk*	I,279
now	*ḫr*	I,368
now after	*ḫr-ir-m-ḫt*	I,369
now regarding	*ḫr m-di*	I,369
now then	*ist*	I,48
Nubian haematite	*didi*	II,240
Nubian word(?)	*šḳrḳb*	II,137
Nubian yellow ochre	*sty*	II,91
nugget	*mḫtbtb*	I,202
nullify	*wsf*	I,111
number	*ipt*	I,25
number	*ipt*	I,25
number	*rḫt*	I,276
number	*rḫt*	I,276
number	*ḥmn*	I,313
number	*tnw*	II,213
numerous	*ꜥšꜣ*	I,79
numerous	*ḳnw*	II,153
Nun	*nwn*	I,231
nurse	*mnꜥt*	I,186
nurse (vb.)	*imḥ*	I,30
nurse (vb.)	*rnn*	I,273
nursed by	*rnn*	I,273
nurses	*ḫnmw*	I,363
nuts	*ḳwḳw*	II,147
nw-jar	*nw*	I,230

O

O that!	*h(ꜣ)n-my*	I,286
oak	*inrn*	I,34
oar	*wsr*	I,111
oasis	*wḥꜣt*	I,107
oasis	*ḥnw*	I,317
oat flakes	*iwšꜣ*	I,21
oath	*ꜥnḫ*	I,70
oath	*ꜥrḳ*	I,73
oath	*sḏfꜣ-tr*	II,101
oath	*sḏfꜣ-tryt*	II,214
obdurate	*nḫt*	I,246
obeisance	*brkw*	I,137
obeisance	*ksy*	II,178
obelisk	*tḫnw*	II,219
obey	*sḏm*	II,101
object under discussion	*ꜣpt*	I,6
objects	*ꜣḫwt*	I,8
oblations	*ꜥbwt*	I,64
oblations	*wdnw*	I,118
obligation	*irit*	I,40
obligation	*irwt*	I,40
obligation	*rḫ-st-ḏrt.f*	I,276
obligatory service	*bryt*	I,136
obliterate	*whn*	I,106
obliterate	*sin*	II,12
obscene	*dydy*	II,241
obscurities	*itnw*	I,51
obscurity	*snk*	II,54
observe	*ptr*	I,159
observe	*mꜣꜣ*	I,173
obstacle	*sḏb*	II,100
obstruct	*hd*	I,293
obstruct	*ḥn*	I,316
obstruct	*ḏri*	II,272
obstruction	*intnt*	I,36
obtain	*ini*	I,31
occasion	*sp*	II,30
occupation	*ḥnt*	I,317
occupation	*šwtyw*	II,114
occupy (oneself)	*sꜣḥ*	II,8
occur	*ii*	I,16
occur	*ḫpr*	I,356
occur	*spi*	II,31
ocean	*wꜣḏ-wr*	I,91
ocean	*šn-wr*	II,126
ochre	*sty*	II,91
ochre(?)	*kns*	II,175
odious	*ḫnw*	I,363
odor	*ḫnm*	I,363
odor	*sty*	II,91
of	*m*	I,167
of	*n*	I,223
of	*nw*	I,229
of all sorts	*m-tnw-nb*	II,212
of good cheer	*nḏm-ib*	I,256
of his	*sꜣwy*	II,7
of his	*swt*	II,22
of his body	*n ẖt.f*	I,379
of interest	*r-msy*	I,204
of Neith	*mḥt-inb*	I,200
of ours	*inn*	I,33
of thine	*tiwy*	II,200
of whom	*n-m*	I,224
of yours	*tiwy*	II,200
offend	*thꜣ*	II,216
offenders	*ḫr*	I,370
offence	*ḏꜣyt*	II,261
offense	*btꜣ*	I,142
offer	*wdn*	I,118
offer	*brk*	I,137
offer	*mꜣꜥ*	I,174
offer	*ms*	I,203
offer	*ḥnk*	I,319
offer	*ḫrp*	I,372
offer	*smꜣꜥ*	II,39
offer	*drp*	II,252
offering	(see boon)	
offering	*wdnw*	I,118
offering	*mꜣꜥ*	I,174
offering	*mnḥt*	I,188
offering cake	*wꜣḏ*	I,91
offering festival	*tꜣ-ꜥbt*	II,198
offering loaf	*wꜣḏ*	I,91
offering meal	*dbḥt-ḥtp*	II,246
offering stones	*ꜥbꜣw*	I,64
offering table	*wḏḥw*	I,123
offering table	*ḫꜣwt*	I,346
offering table	*sḥtp-nmst*	II,64
offering vessel	*wḏḥw*	I,123
offerings	*ꜣwt*	I,3
offerings	*irt-ḫt*	I,38
offerings	*ꜥꜣbt*	I,62
offerings	*ꜥbw*	I,64
offerings	*ꜥbwt*	I,64
offerings	*wdnw*	I,118
offerings	*wḏḥw*	I,123
offerings	*pꜣwt*	I,146
offerings	*ḥbyt*	I,307
offerings	*ḥtpw*	I,337
offerings	*ḫt*	I,343
offerings	*sny*	II,49
offerings (temple)	*šbt*	II,117
offerings	*drpw*	II,252
office	*iꜣwt*	I,13
office	*mstr*	I,207
office	*ḫꜣ*	I,343
office	*st*	II,2
office	*sḥnnt*	II,64

office holder	*ỉꜣwty*	I,13
officer	*wꜥw*	I,94
officer	*skt*	II,88
official	*sr*	II,57
official employee	*ỉpty*	I,26
officiate	*ỉrỉ*	I,38
offspring	*ms*	I,203
offspring	*ẖt*	I,379
offspring	*sḫpr*	II,69
ogdoad	*ḫmnyw*	I,361
ogdoad	*ḫmntyw*	I,361
oh that	*hꜣy*	I,284
oh!	*pꜣ*	I,145
oh!	*hꜣy*	I,284
oh!	*ḫy*	I,350
oil	*ynb*	I,33
oil	*ꜥnḏ*	I,71
oil	*ꜥḏ*	I,83
oil	*ꜥḏmm*	I,84
oil	*mrḥt*	I,194
oil	*mḏt*	I,219
oil	*nḥḥ*	I,244
oil	*nkftr*	I,251
oil	*sft*	II,36
oil	*sḳnn*	II,84
oil	*sgnn*	II,89
oil	*ḳnnỉ*	II,154
oil	*gt*	II,195
oil	*ḏft*	II,269
oil	*ḏsr*	II,274
oil	*ḏdw*	II,276
oil from Hatti	*ḳḏwr*	II,163
oil-man	*ꜥnṯ*	I,71
ointment	*mḏt*	I,219
ointment	*sgnn*	II,89
ointment	*ḳmy*	II,151
ointment	*gs*	II,194
oipe-measure	*ỉpt*	I,25
old	*ỉꜣyt*	I,12
old	*ỉꜣwỉ*	I,12
old	*ỉsy*	I,45
old	*ꜥꜣ(ỉ)*	I,59
old	*sf*	II,35
old age	*ỉꜣy*	I,11
old age	*ỉꜣwt*	I,12
old comrades	*ỉsyw*	I,45
old man	*ỉꜣw*	I,13
old man	*kḥkḥ*	II,178
old woman	*ỉꜣwt*	I,13
older	*ꜥꜣ(ỉ)*	I,59
older person	*s ꜥꜣ*	II,1
oldest	(see eldest)	
olive oil	*ḏdw*	II,276
olive trees	*ḏdw*	II,276
olive tree(?)	*bꜣḳ*	I,127
olives	*ḏdw*	II,276

omen	*kṯmw*	II,181
omit	*wꜣḥ*	I,89
omit	*rdỉ*	I,281
on	*m*	I,167
on	*n*	I,223
on	*ḥr*	I,321
on	*ḥr-ẖt*	I,323
on account of	*m-ḫt*	I,170
on account of	*ẖr-st-r*	I,385
on account of	*tp-n*	II,205
on account of	*r-ḏbꜣ*	II,266
on behalf of	*n*	I,223
on both sides	*m-ỉtrty*	I,52
on both sides	*ḥr gswy*	II,194
on his own behalf	*tp.f*	II,204
on my part	*ỉnk*	I,36
on one's way to	*ỉw*	I,18
on parade	*sḫꜥ*	II,68
on reaching	*r-gs*	I,265
on the contrary	*m-bỉꜣ*	I,129
on the contrary	*m-bỉꜣ*	I,168
once again	*wḥm-sp*	I,109
once again	*m-wḥm-sp*	I,109
once again	*m-wḥm*	I,168
once again	*wḥm-sp*	II,30
once before	*ꜥn(n)*	I,68
one	*wꜥ*	I,93
one	*mtw*	I,213
one	*tw*	II,201
one adept	*ỉry [n] ỉp*	I,25
one and only	*wꜥ-wꜥty*	I,93
one eighth arura	*sꜣ*	II,4
one of a kind	*ḫw-wꜥ*	I,353
one who answers	*wšbt*	I,114
one-half	*rmn*	I,271
one-sided	*nmꜥ*	I,237
onions	*ḥḏw*	I,341
onslaught	*hd*	I,293
onwards	*r-ḥry*	I,324
open	*wbꜣ*	I,96
open	*wbn*	I,97
open	*wpỉ*	I,98
open	*wn*	I,100
open	*bḳy*	I,141
open	*pgꜣ*	I,158
open	*ngỉ*	I,252
open	*sš*	II,79
open court	*wbꜣ*	I,96
open field	*pgꜣ*	I,158
open up	*ꜣw(ỉ)*	I,2
open up	*prḫ*	I,152
opener (door)	*wn*	I,101
opener of the Two Lands	*wp(t)-tꜣwy*	I,98
openhanded	*pgꜣ-ḏrt*	I,158
opinion	*ỉb*	I,22

opinion	*wšbt*	I,114
opinion	*rḫ*	I,275
opponent	*iry-n-wp*	I,40
opponent	*rḳy(w)*	I,279
opponent	*ḫfty*	I,359
opponents	*šntyw*	II,131
oppose	*ꜥḥꜣ*	I,74
oppose	*ꜥḥꜥ*	I,75
oppose	*ḥtp*	I,336
oppose	*ḫsf-ꜥ*	I,374
oppose	*tri*	II,215
oppose	*ḏꜣi*	II,260
oppose	*ḏꜣi tꜣ r*	II,260
opposing party	*nḏr*	I,257
opposite	*ꜥḳꜣ*	I,81
opposite	*r-ꜥḳꜣ*	I,261
opposite side	*ḫft-ḥr*	I,359
opposition	*ꜥḥꜥw*	I,76
oppress	*ꜥšḳ*	I,80
oppress	*sḥs*	II,64
oppression	*ꜥdd*	I,82
oppressions	*ꜥšḳ*	I,80
oppressions	*gꜣw*	II,184
oppressive	*wdn*	I,118
oppressors	*sbtyw*	II,30
opulent	*tnr*	II,213
or	*m-r-pw*	I,169
or	*r-pw*	I,262
or	*m-r-pw*	I,262
or else	*r-pw*	I,262
or not	*biꜣ*	I,129
oracle	*biꜣyt*	I,130
oracle	*nḏwt-r*	I,256
oracle	*ḫrtw*	I,371
oracle	*ḫrtw*	I,373
oral	*r-mdwt*	I,262
oral cavity	*tpḥt*	II,209
orchard	*ꜥt-nt-ḫt*	I,59
orchard	*bꜥḥ*	I,132
ordain	*wḏ*	I,119
ordain	*wḏꜥ*	I,122
ordain	*šꜣ*	II,105
order	*wp*	I,97
order	*sḥn*	II,63
order	*ṯs*	II,233
order (of progress)	*tp-rd*	II,205
order (vb.)	*ḥn*	I,315
order (vb.)	*sḥn*	II,62
orderliness	*mtr*	I,215
orders	*wpwt*	I,99
orders	*mḏꜣt*	I,219
orders	*ḥnw*	I,316
orders (for work)	*tp-rd*	II,206
ordinal	*nw*	I,230
ordinance	*mḫrw*	I,202
ordinance	*ntꜥ*	I,253
ordinances	*ḥnw*	I,316
ordinary bread	*ꜥḳw-n-wnmw*	I,80
ordinary man	*wꜥw*	I,94
organize	*ḥn*	I,315
organize	*snṯ*	II,54
organize	*sḥn*	II,62
organize	*grg*	II,192
organized	*snṯ*	II,54
origin	*sꜣḏr*	II,10
original state	*tp-ꜥ*	II,205
oriole(?)	*gnw*	II,189
ornament	*mndt*	I,191
ornament of a ship	*mḥbš*	I,201
ornament self	*bnd*	I,135
ornamental collar	*wsḫ*	I,112
ornamented	*ḫp*	I,355
ornaments	*ꜥprwt*	I,65
ornaments	*ḫkrw*	I,389
orphan	*nmḥ*	I,238
orphaned	*nmḥ*	I,238
orpiment	*ḳniw*	II,154
oryx	*mꜣ-ḥḏ*	I,174
ostentatiously	*m-wstnw*	I,113
ostracon	*nḏr*	I,257
ostrich	*niw*	I,226
ostrich	*nrw*	I,240
other	*ky*	II,170
other people	*kꜣwy*	II,166
others	*kꜣwy*	II,166
others	*ky*	II,171
others	*ktḫw*	II,179
otherwise	*m-r-pw*	I,169
otherwise	*m-r-pw*	I,262
ours	*inn*	I,33
ourselves	*ḏs*	II,274
oust	*tkn*	II,220
out	*bnr*	I,134
out	*r-bnr*	I,134
out	*r-ḫry*	I,264
out of	*m*	I,167
out of excellence	*ḥr-mnḫ*	I,189
outdoors	*m-rwti*	I,268
outer	*n-bnr*	I,134
outer	*n-bnr*	I,223
outer chamber	*ḫnty*	I,367
outer coffin	*wt-ꜥꜣ*	I,116
outer sarcophagus	*mstp*	I,206
outer sarcophagus	*ḏbꜣt*	II,267
outfit	*grg-pr*	II,193
outfit (vb.)	*ꜥrꜥr*	I,72
outfit (vb.)	*sdbḥ*	II,98
outlined figures	*ḳd*	II,161
outlines	*ḳd*	II,161
output	*bꜣkw*	I,127
outrage	*gns*	II,190
outside	*n-bnr*	I,134

outside	*r-bnr*	I,134
outside	*ḥr-bnr*	I,134
outside	*n-bnr*	I,223
outside	*r-bnr*	I,261
outside	*r-rwty*	I,263
outside	*rwty*	I,268
outside	*m-rwti*	I,268
outside	*ḥꜣ*	I,295
outside	*m-ḳb*	II,147
outsiders	*rwtyw*	I,268
outstanding	*stp*	II,94
outstretch	*swsḫ*	II,22
outstrip	*sn*	II,46
outward form	*ꜣbwt*	I,5
outworker	*pry*	I,151
oven	*mḳꜥr*	I,210
oven	*rwrw*	I,268
oven	*trr*	II,215
oven	*thr*	II,217
oven's bottom	*mḳꜥr*	I,210
oven's bottom	*mg*	I,212
over	*ḥr-ḥr*	I,322
over	*ḥr(t)-tp*	I,327
over	*tp*	II,204
over the secrets	*ḥry-sštꜣ*	I,325
overcome	*hd*	I,292
overcome	*ḫy*	I,350
overflow	*bꜥḥ*	I,132
overflow	*ngsgs*	I,252
overflow	*gsgs*	II,195
overflow	*ṯfy*	II,229
overflow	*ṯṯf*	II,236
overflowing	*msms*	I,205
overfull	*msms*	I,205
overgrown	*rd*	I,280
overlaid	*sꜥm*	II,14
overlay	*ḥṯ*	I,339
overlay (vb.)	*dgꜣ*	II,256
overpower	*nꜥš*	I,229
overrun	*sḫsḫ*	II,74
oversatisfied	*siꜣt*	II,11
overseer	*imy-r*	I,27
overseer	*mꜣ(w)*	I,175
overseer	*ḥry*	I,323
overseer of the treasury	*imy-r pr ḥḏ*	I,28
overseer of the workshop	*imy-r ḥmt*	I,28
oversized	*siꜣt*	II,11
overstep	*sg*	II,88
overtake	*dmi*	II,248
overthrow	*pnꜥ*	I,148
overthrow	*pḫd*	I,155
overthrow	*ḥdb*	I,340
overthrow	*ḫryt*	I,370
overthrow	*ẖtb*	I,389
overthrow	*sꜣsꜣ*	II,9
overthrow	*sḫr*	II,72
overthrow	*sẖnn*	II,76
overthrow	*dḫ*	II,255
overthrown	*ḫr*	I,369
overturn	*pnꜥ*	I,148
overturned	*ḫrḫr*	I,373
overwhelm	*ḥtm*	I,338
overwhelm	*ḫꜣb*	I,348
overwhelm	*ḫꜣm*	I,348
overwhelm	*sḫm*	II,69
overwhelm	*dr*	II,252
owe	*šꜣ*	II,105
own	*m-wn-mꜣꜥ*	I,168
own	*ḥꜥt*	I,301
own	*ḏs*	II,274
own	*ḏt*	II,259
own self	*r-ḥꜥw*	I,301
ownership	*sḏf*	II,99
ox	*iwꜣ*	I,19
ox	*iḥ*	I,43
ox	*ḥr-sꜣ-m*	I,323
ox	*ḳmꜣ*	II,151
ox	*kꜣ*	II,165
ox herd	*mnḥ-n-kꜣw*	I,188
ox hide	*msk*	I,206
ox-amulets	*ḫns*	I,366
oxen	*iḥw*	I,43

P

paces	*rd*	I,281
pacification	*sgrḥ*	II,90
pacify	*wꜥb*	I,94
pacify	*shr-ib*	II,60
pacify	*sḥtp*	II,64
pack	*ḳniw*	II,154
pack (vb.)	*gwt*	II,186
pack off	*ḫpp*	I,355
packs	*ps*	I,155
pail	*bs*	I,139
pain	*mr*	I,191
pain (be in)	*ispw*	I,47
painful	*mr*	I,191
painful	*ḏri*	II,272
painful	*ḏrw*	II,273
painful of action	*mr-n-sp*	I,191
paint	*ry(t)*	I,266
painter	*sš-ḳd*	II,79
painting	*sš*	II,78
paintings	*sšywt*	II,79
pair	*ꜥ*	I,57
pair	*rd*	I,281
pair (of sandals)	*ḥtr*	I,338
pair of horses	*ḥtr*	I,338
pair of nose wings	*msdty*	I,207
pair of obelisks	*tḫnw*	II,219
pair(?)	*ḥꜣity*	I,295
palace	*ꜥḥ*	I,74
palace	*pr-nsw*	I,150
palace	*pr-nsw*	I,248
palace	*ḥwt-ꜥnḫ*	I,304
palace	*snwt*	II,50
palace	*sḥḏyt*	II,65
palace	*stp-sꜣ*	II,95
palace façade	*srḫ*	II,59
palanquin	*ḳniw*	II,153
pale	*ḥḏ*	I,341
palette (scribe's)	*gsti*	II,195
palisade(?)	*ḫꜣyt*	I,379
palm (of hand)	*kp*	II,172
palm branches	*bꜣ-ꜥꜣyt*	I,125
palm fronds	*wd-mnḏm*	I,120
palm of hand	*šsp*	II,136
palm switches	*bꜣ-ꜥꜣyt*	I,125
pan type	*nmst*	I,238
pancreas(?)	*sẖn*	II,71
panel	*ḏpḥ*	II,268
panic	*ḥr-(n)-ḥr*	I,322
panic	*ḥryt*	I,326
panoply	*ḫkrw*	I,389
panther	*ꜣby*	I,4
papyrus	*isw*	I,45
papyrus	*mnḥw*	I,188
papyrus	*sẖrt*	II,74
papyrus	*drf*	II,252
papyrus	*ḏrm*	II,273
papyrus (scroll)	*sẖrt*	II,74
papyrus bundle	*wḏ-mr*	I,120
papyrus flowers	*ṯwf*	II,227
papyrus marsh	*ṯwf*	II,227
papyrus marsh	*dt*	II,257
papyrus marshes	*pꜣ-ṯwf*	I,145
papyrus roll	*ꜥrt*	I,72
papyrus roll	*mḏꜣt*	I,219
papyrus rolls	*ḏmꜥ*	II,269
papyrus rope	*wḏ-nwḥ*	I,120
papyrus scroll	*drf*	II,252
papyrus scrolls	*ꜥrt*	I,72
papyrus thicket	*ꜣḫy*	I,8
papyrus thicket	*šꜣ*	II,105
parallel	*sẖr*	II,72
parch	*nḏꜣ*	I,256
parched	*sswn*	II,76
pardon	*ḥtp*	I,336
pare	*ḳḳ*	II,159
parents	*ꜣbt*	I,4
park	*prw*	I,151
parlor	*st-ḥnkyt*	I,320
parlor	*st ḥnkt*	II,2
parry	*dni*	II,249
part	*dni(t)*	II,250
part (vb.)	*šꜥd*	II,112
part company	*idḥ*	I,55
part of a bird trap	*kḥs*	II,178
part of a body	*rꜥm*	I,266
part of a body	*ṯrst*	II,231
part of a building	*sḥnw*	II,64
part of a chariot	*ṯꜣ*	II,223
part of a house	*trš*	II,215
part of a rudder	*ḏnḥ*	II,270
part of an investment	*dni(t)*	II,250
part of abdomen	*ḏꜣi*	II,260
part of female anatomy	*ḥgꜣi*	I,335
part of sarcophagus or tomb	*mnniwt*	I,188
part of temple	*sdt i͗ꜣdt*	II,98
part of temple(?)	*sp(r)ti-r*	II,33
part with	*šꜥd*	II,112
parted from	*gbi*	II,187
partial	*nmꜥ*	I,237
partial	*gꜣs*	II,185
participate	*ꜥḳ*	I,80
partly	*m gs*	II,194
partly lost	*ḫtḫt*	I,378
parts	*psšw*	I,156
parts	*fdḳw*	I,166

party	*wnḏw*	I,104
pass (vb.)	*ii*	I,16
pass (vb.)	*ḫpr*	I,356
pass (vb.)	*sbi*	II,25
pass (vb.)	*sn*	II,46
pass (vb.)	*sš*	II,79
pass away	*sbi*	II,25
pass by	*ḫꜣꜥ*	I,346
pass by	*swꜣ*	II,17
pass by	*sn*	II,46
pass by	*snny*	II,52
pass judgment	*wḏꜥ*	I,122
pass the day	*wrš*	I,105
pass time	*sbi*	II,25
passage	*r-stꜣ*	I,264
passage	*stꜣ*	II,92
passageway	*šmt*	II,122
passenger	*iry-ḏꜣy*	II,260
passion	*ib*	I,22
passion	*šrgḥ*	II,133
passionate	*šm(m)*	II,124
pastry	*ꜥgs*	I,82
pastry	*rbk*	I,270
pastry(?)	*ḫrps*	I,373
pasturage	*sm*	II,37
pastures	*iꜣdt*	I,15
patch (vb.)	*ꜣꜥꜥ*	I,1
path	*wꜣt*	I,88
path	*mit*	I,179
path	*mṯn*	I,216
path of truths	*wꜣt-mꜣꜥt*	I,88
patient	*wꜣḥ-ib*	I,23
patient	*ꜥꜣ(i)*	I,60
patient	*wꜣḥ-ib*	I,90
patient	*tkn ib*	II,221
patricians	*pꜥt*	I,147
patrol	*šnꜥy*	II,129
pauper	*nmḥ*	I,238
pause	*ꜥḥꜥw*	I,77
pause (vb.)	*ꜥḥꜥ*	I,75
pavement	*sꜣt*	II,10
pavement line	*hn-sꜣt*	II,10
pavilion	*imw*	I,29
pavilion	*sḥ*	II,61
pavilion	*ḏꜣḏꜣw*	II,263
pavilion(?)	*sꜣḥ*	II,8
paw (vb.)	*ṯiṯi*	II,227
pawing horse	*ṯiṯi*	II,227
pay	*fꜣy*	I,163
pay	*ḫꜣꜥ*	I,347
pay	*swn*	II,19
pay (a debt)	*ḥtm*	I,338
pay attention	*imi-ib*	I,26
pay attention	*ptr*	I,159
pay homage	*sn*	II,49
pay honor to	*swꜣš*	II,18
payment	*ḥꜣw*	I,296
payment	*ḥḏ*	I,340
payment	*snw*	II,50
payment	*ḏbꜣ*	II,266
payments	*ḏbꜣw*	II,266
paysan	*tpy-š*	II,207
peace	*ḥtpw*	I,338
peace	*šꜣrm*	II,109
peace	*šrm*	II,133
peaceable	*gr*	II,191
peace be at	*ḥtp*	I,337
peace of mind	*mdn*	I,218
peak	*rš*	I,278
peak	*dhnt*	II,253
pear	*bki*	I,141
peas(?)	*tḥw*	II,217
peasant	*sḫty*	II,67
pebbles	*ꜥnr*	I,69
pedestal	*dbyt*	II,245
pedestal(?)	*kfꜣt*	II,173
pedestal-type stone	*skꜣ*	II,87
peel (vb.)	*hf*	I,287
peel (vb.)	*ḳḳ*	II,159
peer	*sn-nw*	II,48
peg	*ẖꜣww*	I,379
pellet	*ẖꜥw*	I,353
pelt	*šdw*	II,141
penalize	*sꜥḥꜥ*	II,15
penalty	*sbꜣyt*	II,27
penalty	*ṯꜣwt*	II,225
penetrate	*ꜥḳ*	I,80
penetrate	*ꜥḳꜥḳ*	I,81
penetrate	*pḥ*	I,152
penetrate	*sd*	II,97
penetrate	*ḏd*	II,276
people	*pꜥt*	I,147
people	*mhwt*	I,196
people	*rmṯ*	I,271
people	*rḫyt*	I,276
people	*ẖt*	I,379
people	*kꜣwy*	II,166
people	*tmw*	II,211
people	*tmmw*	II,211
people	*ṯt*	II,223
people around one	*twt m rmṯ*	II,203
people of	*nꜣy*	I,226
per day	*m-mnt*	I,169
perceive	*ib*	I,23
perceive	*ꜥm*	I,66
perceive	*siꜣ*	II,11
perceive a fact	*in ib*	I,32
perceiving	*ꜥmw*	I,66
perception	*siꜣ*	II,11
perceptive(?)	*ḫry*	I,370
perchance	*gm*	II,189
perfected	*smnḫ*	II,43

perfection	*nfrw*	I,236
perforate	*gp*	II,188
perforation (disease)	*thm*	II,217
perform	*ꜥrꜥr*	I,72
perform	*ksks*	II,178
perform the duties of an heir	*iwꜥ*	I,19
performance	*sšm*	II,81
performance of service	*sꜣḫw*	II,9
perfume	*nḏm-sty*	I,256
perfume	*sty*	II,91
perineum	*knt*	II,175
perineum(?)	*kns*	II,174
period	*ꜣt*	I,1
period	*ꜥḥꜥw*	I,77
period (of time)	*ḫnty-rnpt*	I,317
periplous	*ḫn*	I,382
perish	*ꜣḳ*	I,9
perish	*sk*	II,86
permanent	*mn*	I,183
permission to use	*wꜣt-n-šmt*	I,88
permit	*wꜣḥ*	I,90
permit to breathe	*srḳ*	II,59
perpetuate	*sꜥnḫ*	II,14
perpetuate	*swrd*	II,21
perpetuate	*sḫpr*	II,68
persea tree	*šwb*	II,115
persecute	*iꜣd*	I,14
perseverance	*sḏr*	II,103
persevere	*rwḏ*	I,269
persevere	*tnr*	II,213
persist	*rwḏ*	I,269
persist	*ḫꜣm*	I,348
person	*ꜥnḫ*	I,70
person	*rmṯ*	I,271
person	*ḥꜥw*	I,301
person	*tp*	II,204
person	*ḏt*	II,259
personal attention	*ḥr*	I,320
personality	*kꜣ*	II,165
personnel	*rmṯ*	I,271
personnel	*smdt*	II,46
persons	*tp*	II,204
perspicacious of heart	*ꜥrḳ*	I,73
pertaining to	*tꜣ*	II,197
perturbed	*šršr*	II,133
perturbed	*tftf*	II,209
pervade	*pḫr*	I,155
perverse (of heart)	*ḫꜣkw-ib*	I,380
pervert	*pnꜥ*	I,148
pervert	*stwh*	II,93
pervert	*sth*	II,95
pestering	*m-sꜣ*	II,5
pestilence	*iꜣdt*	I,15
pestle	*ḥmy*	I,312
petition	*spr*	II,33
petition	*snmḥ*	II,51
petition (vb.)	*spr*	II,32
petitioner	*sprw*	II,33
petty	*nḏs*	I,257
peypenen leaves	*pr-pnn*	I,152
phalli	*ḳrnt*	II,157
phallus	*ḥnn*	I,318
Pharaoh	*pr-ꜥꜣ*	I,150
pharmaceutical	*tiꜣ*	II,200
pharmacopoeia	*dmḏyt*	II,249
phoenix	*bnw*	I,134
phrases	*ṯs*	II,234
phyle	*sꜣw*	II,4
physician	*swnw*	II,20
pick	*ꜥnt*	I,69
pick	*fḳꜣ*	I,165
pick	*ḥwi*	I,303
pick	*stp*	II,94
pick	*ḳdf*	II,161
pick out	*wḫꜣ*	I,110
pick out	*ptr*	I,159
pick out	*gm*	II,188
pick up	*fꜣy*	I,163
pickax	*ḫnr*	I,365
pickaxe	*ḫꜣ*	I,343
pickaxe	*ḫꜣiw*	I,344
picked	*stp*	II,94
picked	*tpy*	II,207
picked man	*stp*	II,94
piece	*ꜥ*	I,57
piece	*sniw*	II,49
piece	*šꜥd*	II,113
piece of meat	*dpt*	II,246
piece of paper	*sš*	II,78
piece of silver	*sniw*	II,49
piece of wood	*ityn*	I,53
pieces	*psšw*	I,156
pieces	*fdḳw*	I,166
pieces of copper	*ḥmt*	I,314
pieces(?)	*rr*	I,274
pierce	*sd*	II,98
pierce	*ḏd*	II,276
pig	*ḥwt*	I,305
pig	*ḫdr*	I,378
pig	*šꜣ*	II,105
pig sty	*st-iꜣwt*	I,13
pigeon	*mnt*	I,184
pigeonnier	*mḥwn*	I,200
pigment(?)	*br*	I,136
pile	*ꜥḥꜥw*	I,76
pile (of cadavers)	*iwnw*	I,20
pilfer	*ḫbꜣ*	I,354
pillage	*šꜣd*	II,110

pillage	*šdꜣ*	II,141
pillar	*iwn*	I,20
pillar	*wḫꜣ*	I,110
pillars	*ꜥꜣw*	I,61
pillow	*dbt*	II,244
pilot	*ꜥš-ḥꜣt*	I,79
pilot	*ꜥš-ḥꜣt*	I,297
pin	*srt*	II,57
pine	*ꜥš*	I,79
pine cone	*iꜣrrt*	I,14
pinion	*ḫnd*	I,368
pinion	*dnḥ*	II,251
pint(?)	*hnw*	I,289
pipe	*w(ꜣ)ḏn*	I,92
pit	*ḏꜣḥt*	II,262
pita-bread(?)	*bi(ꜣ)t*	I,129
pitch	*mrḥt*	I,194
pitfall	*mstḥ*	I,207
pith	*bkt*	I,141
pity	*nꜥ(w)*	I,228
place	*w*	I,87
place	*bw*	I,133
place	*st*	II,1
place (vb.)	*imi*	I,26
place (vb.)	*wꜣḥ*	I,89
place (vb.)	*wdi*	I,117
place (vb.)	*smn*	II,42
place of burial	*st ḳrs*	II,3
place of slaughter	*sfṯ*	II,36
place of the praised ones	*st ḥsyw*	II,3
place of truth	*st mꜣꜥt*	II,2
placed	*mtn*	I,214
placenta	*mwt-rmṯ*	I,183
plains	*sḫt*	II,66
plains	*tꜣ*	II,198
plaited	*nbd*	I,234
plaiting	*nbd*	I,234
plan	*ḫmt*	I,361
plan	*sipt*	II,11
plan	*sḫr*	II,72
plan	*tp-rd*	II,205
plan (vb.)	*wꜣwꜣ*	I,88
plan (vb.)	*sḫr*	II,72
plan (vb.)	*kꜣ*	II,166
plan maker	*sḫry*	II,74
plan out	*snṯ*	II,54
plane (vb.)	*grb*	II,191
plank	*sꜣy*	II,5
plank	*swt*	II,22
plank	*dpḥ*	II,268
plank	*ḏrꜥt*	II,273
planking	*iswt*	I,46
planks	*iswt*	I,46
plans	*smnḫt*	II,43
plans	*sḫyw*	II,66
plant	*iꜣds*	I,15
plant	*iwfyt*	I,20
plant	*ḥmm*	I,313
plant	*ḫy*	I,350
plant	*ssd*	II,77
plant	*gnn*	II,190
plant	*dt*	II,257
plant (vb.)	*wꜣḥ*	I,89
plant (vb.)	*wꜣḏ*	I,91
plant (vb.)	*swrd*	II,21
plant (vb.)	*srd*	II,59
plant (vb.)	*dgꜣ*	II,256
plants	*isw*	I,45
plants	*mnḥw*	I,188
plants	*rnpwt*	I,273
plants	*ḫꜣw*	I,345
plants	*sm*	II,37
plaster	*ḳꜣḏꜣ*	II,145
plaster	*ḳḏ*	II,162
plaster	*ḳḏ*	II,163
plaster (vb.)	*ꜣꜥꜥ*	I,2
plaster (vb.)	*sḫkr*	II,76
plaster (vb.)	*sḳḥ*	II,85
plasterer	*ḳḏ*	II,162
plate (vb.)	*dgꜣ*	II,256
plated	*ḥṯ*	I,340
platform	*rid*	I,266
platform	*rwḏw*	I,269
plating	*ḥbs*	I,308
play	*ḥꜥb*	I,302
play	*ksks*	II,178
plead one's case against	*sḫn ḥnꜥ*	II,71
pleasant	*ꜣms-ib*	I,6
pleasant	*bnr*	I,135
pleasant	*nꜥmw*	I,228
pleasant	*nfr*	I,235
pleasant	*nḏm*	I,256
pleasantness	*bnr*	I,135
please	*iḫ*	I,44
please	*my*	I,179
please	*nḏm*	I,256
please (vb.)	*ꜣḫ*	I,7
please (vb.)	*shr-ib*	I,23
please (vb.)	*snḏm-ib*	II,56
pleased	*ꜣms-ib*	I,6
pleased	*iꜣm*	I,14
pleased	*nḏm-ib*	I,23
pleased	*hꜣ-ib*	I,23
pleased	*hꜣ-ib*	I,284
pleased	*hr-ib*	I,290
pleased	*ḥtp*	I,336
pleasing	*hr*	I,290
pleasing	*twt*	II,203
pleasure	*ꜣbw*	I,4
pleasure	*iꜣb*	I,13

pleasure	*ršwt*	I,279
pleasure	*hꜣ-ib*	I,284
pleasure	*smḫ-ib*	II,44
pleasure	*sḫmḫ-ib*	II,71
pleasure house	*pr-mꜣ*	I,150
plebians	*rḫyt*	I,276
plentiful	*ḳnw*	II,153
plinth	*inr-smꜣ*	I,34
plot	*šdt*	II,142
plot (vb.)	*wꜣwꜣ*	I,88
plot (vb.)	*šni*	II,127
plot (vb.)	*kꜣ*	II,166
plot of ground	*bkyt*	I,141
plot of ground	*swꜣw*	II,17
plough herdsman	*ꜥꜣmy-n-skꜣ*	I,62
plough land	*skꜣwt*	II,87
plough lands	*nḫbw*	I,245
plow	*hb*	I,286
plow	*skꜣ*	II,87
pluck	*wgs*	I,115
pluck	*sḳr*	II,85
pluck	*sṯ*	II,96
pluck	*ḳdf*	II,161
pluck	*gp*	II,188
plumb line	*ḫꜣy*	I,344
plumes	*šwty*	II,115
plunder	*ḥꜣḳw*	I,300
plunder	*sdḫw*	II,99
plunder (vb.)	*iṯi*	I,52
plunder (vb.)	*ḥꜣḳ*	I,299
plunder (vb.)	*ḥwrꜥ*	I,306
plunder (vb.)	*ḥwtf*	I,306
plunder (vb.)	*ḫfy*	I,358
plunder (vb.)	*ḳfꜥ*	II,173
plunge	*hꜣ(i)*	I,283
plunge head over heels	*ḏbg*	II,268
ply	*ḫni*	I,382
podium	*snt*	II,50
point (of obelisk)	*ḥwy*	I,303
point aloft	*bnbn*	I,134
point back	*ḫꜣꜥ*	I,347
point out	*wꜣḥ-ḏrt*	I,90
pointed speeches(?)	*nsḳ*	I,249
poison	*mtwt*	I,213
pole	*ꜥ*	I,58
pole	*wḫꜣ*	I,110
pole (carrying)	*nbꜣ*	I,233
pole rings	*šꜣḳw*	II,110
poles	*mꜣwt*	I,176
polestar	*msḫt*	I,206
police	*mḏꜣw*	I,220
policeman	*mḏꜣw*	I,220
policeman	*sꜥšꜣt*	II,16
polish (vb.)	*mšrr*	I,209
polish(?)	*nḳꜥ*	I,250
pomegranate	*inhrmꜣ*	I,34
pomegranate wine(?)	*šdḥ*	II,141
pommade of gum	*ḳmy*	II,151
pond	*brkt*	I,137
pond	*mḥḏrt*	I,201
pond	*mš*	I,207
pond	*ḫꜣt*	I,379
pond	*swn*	II,19
pond	*š*	II,105
pond(?)	*phrt*	I,152
ponder(?)	*ḥḥy*	I,329
pool	*brkt*	I,137
pool	*nwy*	I,230
pool	*ḫꜣꜥ-mḥ*	I,347
pool	*ḫntš*	I,368
pool	*š*	II,105
pool	*šnyw*	II,126
pool	*ḳbḥ*	II,149
poor	*nmḥ*	I,238
poor man	*iwty*	I,22
poor man	*šwꜣ*	II,115
poor ones(?)	*nmḥy*	I,238
populace	*rmṯ-n-pꜣ-tꜣ*	I,272
porch(?)	*sbḫt*	II,28
porridge	*bty*	I,143
port	*mniwt*	I,186
portable chest	*pr-n-sṯꜣ*	I,150
portable chest	*gs-pr*	II,194
portable shrine	*ḳniw*	II,153
portable shrine	*kꜣr*	II,169
portal	*hꜣy*	I,284
portal	*sbꜣ*	II,26
portal	*sbḫt*	II,28
portal	*tri*	II,215
porter	*ḥry-ꜥꜣ*	I,61
porter	*kꜣwty*	II,167
portico	*ḏꜣḏꜣw*	II,263
porticoes	*wnr-ḫr*	I,103
portion	*pš*	I,157
portion	*ḫrt*	I,371
portion	*ḫrt*	I,385
portion	*dni(t)*	II,250
portions	*ꜥḥꜥw*	I,76
portrait sculptor	*sꜥnḫw*	II,14
position	*ꜥḥꜥw*	I,76
position	*st*	II,2
position	*tp-rd*	II,205
position(?) (vb.)	*ꜥgꜣ*	I,81
possess	*ḫꜣm*	I,348
possess	*šb*	II,116
possessed of	*sḫm*	II,69
possessed one	*ḫꜣꜥ*	I,347
possession	*mnꜥt*	I,186
possession	*ḥnw*	I,317

possession	*sšm*	II,81
possessions	*ȝḫwt*	I,8
possessions	*imy-pr*	I,27
possessions	*imy-prw*	I,27
possessions	*ẖt*	I,343
possessions	*ḫrt*	I,371
possessions	*ẖrt*	I,385
possessions	*dni(t)*	II,250
possessor	*nb*	I,232
post	*iȝwt*	I,13
pot	*ḏȝḏȝ*	II,263
potency	*ȝʿy*	I,1
potent	*mnḫ*	I,189
potent	*nʿš*	I,229
potent	*tnr*	II,213
potter	*iḳd-nḏst*	I,49
potter	*ḳd*	II,160
pottery	*ḥnwt*	I,318
pottery	*ḥnḳt*	I,319
poultry yard	*hmw*	I,288
pound (vb.)	*wsr*	I,111
pour	*wȝḥ*	I,89
pour	*wḏḥ*	I,123
pour forth	*bʿḥ*	I,132
pour forth (from mind)	*kȝ*	II,166
pour forth(?)	*bȝbȝ*	I,126
pour out	*wḏḥ*	I,123
pour out	*sti-mw*	II,91
pour out	*ṯtf*	II,236
pour refreshment	*sḳbb*	II,84
pour water	*sti-mw*	II,91
poverty	*ngȝ*	I,252
power	*ȝʿy*	I,1
power	*bȝw*	I,125
power	*ḫymṯȝ*	I,351
power	*ḫpš*	I,357
power	*ḫmṯ*	I,361
power(?)	*nrw*	I,239
powerful	*wsr*	I,111
powerful	*pḥty*	I,154
powerful	*mds*	I,218
powerful	*nʿš*	I,229
powerful	*nḫt*	I,245
powerful	*sḫm*	II,69
powerful	*tnr*	II,213
practice	*sḫr*	II,72
practice (vb.)	*iri*	I,38
practice on	*ir-ḫr*	I,39
praise	*iwt*	I,18
praise	*mhrn*	I,196
praise	*hnw*	I,289
praise	*ḥst*	I,331
praise (vb.)	*iȝw*	I,12
praise (vb.)	*ḥsi*	I,329
praise (vb.)	*swȝš*	II,18
praise (vb.)	*swh*	II,21
praise (vb.)	*dwȝ*	II,241
praise god for	*dwȝ-nṯr*	II,242
praised	*ḥsy*	I,329
praised ones	*ḥsy*	I,330
praises	*iȝw*	I,12
praises	*iȝwt*	I,12
praises	*hȝrn*	I,286
praises	*ḥswt*	I,330
praises	*ḥknw*	I,334
praises	*sȝḫw*	II,9
praises	*smȝʿw*	II,40
praiseworthy(?)	*dwȝt*	II,242
prance(?)	*nsns*	I,249
pray	*my*	I,179
pray	*nḥ*	I,241
pray	*smȝʿ*	II,39
pray	*tr*	II,214
pray for	*dbḥ*	II,245
prayer	*nḥt*	I,242
prayer	*nḥbt*	I,242
prayer	*spr*	II,33
prayer	*smȝʿw*	II,40
prayer	*snmḥ*	II,51
prayers	*sns*	II,53
preceding	*ḫry-ḥȝt*	I,386
precept	*mtr*	I,215
precepts	*ṯs*	II,234
precinct	*bkyt*	I,141
precious	*iḳr*	I,49
precious	*sbḳ*	II,29
precious	*šps*	II,118
precious stone	*irḫ*	I,41
precious stone	*ʿȝt*	I,61
precious stones	*gmw*	II,189
precise	*ʿḳȝ*	I,81
precise	*mt*	I,213
precisely	*ʿḳȝ*	I,81
predestined	*šȝy*	II,106
predilection	*biȝt*	I,130
prefer	*mri*	I,192
pregnancy	*iwr*	I,21
pregnant	*iwr*	I,21
pregnant	*bk*	I,141
pregnant	*šsp-iwr*	II,136
pregnant (be)	*mḥ*	I,197
pregnant female	*idt*	I,53
preparations	*sḫr*	II,72
prepare	*ḥr*	I,321
prepare	*spd*	II,34
prepare	*grg*	II,192
prepare(?)	*nsḳ*	I,249
prepared	*iwr*	I,21
prepared	*ḥr*	I,321
prescription	*pḫrt*	I,155
prescription	*ntʿ*	I,253

prescription	*šsꜣ*	II,135
present	*ꜥḥꜥ*	I,75
present	*fꜣy*	I,163
present (vb.)	*brk*	I,137
present (vb.)	*mꜣꜥ*	I,174
present (vb.)	*ms*	I,203
present (vb.)	*ḥnk*	I,320
present (vb.)	*ḫrp*	I,372
present (vb.)	*sꜥr*	II,14
present (vb.)	*smꜣꜥ*	II,39
present(?) (vb.)	*dwn*	II,243
present bread	*sḳꜣ-tꜣ*	II,84
presentation	*mꜣꜥ*	I,174
presentation	*smꜣꜥw*	II,40
presents	*mrk*	I,195
preserve	*nḥm*	I,243
preserve	*sꜣw*	II,6
preserve	*ssnb*	II,77
preserve	*šdi*	II,139
preserve	*kni*	II,174
preserve from	*wdꜣ ḫr*	I,121
preserve the health	*ssnb*	II,77
presider over	*ḫnty*	I,367
press	*ꜥdd*	I,82
press hard	*mḏd*	I,221
press hard	*sḥs*	II,64
prestation	*ḥḏ*	I,340
presumption	*itḥ-ib*	I,23
presumption	*itḥ-ib*	I,52
prevail over	*hd*	I,293
prevent	*ḫsf-ꜥ*	I,374
prevent	*r tmi dit*	II,210
previous	*ḫry-ḥꜣt*	I,297
previously	*ḫry-ḥꜣt*	I,386
previously	*ḏr-ꜥ*	II,271
prey	*ḥwrꜥ*	I,306
prey	*ḳꜣḳꜣ*	II,145
price	*isw*	I,45
price	*mḫr*	I,201
price	*swn(t)*	II,20
price	*šb(t)*	II,116
prick	*nḳꜥ*	I,250
prick	*dbs*	II,246
priest	*wꜥb*	I,94
priest	*sḥiw-nṯr*	II,61
priest of Shu	*fkty*	I,165
priesthood	*wnwt(y)*	I,101
priestly hour	*wnwt*	I,101
primeval	*sp-tp*	II,30
primeval darkness	*kkw-smꜣ*	II,179
primeval waters	*nwn*	I,231
primeval waters	*nnw*	I,239
Primordial One	*pꜣwty*	I,146
prince	*wr*	I,104
prince	*r-pꜥt*	I,261
prince	*rpꜥt*	I,270
prince	*ḥꜣty-ꜥ*	I,298
princes	*msw-nsw*	I,205
princes	*sr*	II,57
principal	*wr*	I,104
principal favorite	*imy-ib tpy*	I,27
principal of the harem	*wrt-ḫnrt*	I,366
principal sanctuary in Heliopolis	*hwt-sr*	I,304
principle	*tp-rd*	II,205
prison	*itḥ*	I,52
prison	*ḫnrt*	I,366
prison	*šrꜥ*	II,133
prison	*kri*	II,175
prison	*ḏdḥ*	II,277
prison(?)	*kꜣrwt*	II,170
prison(?)	*kri*	II,175
prisoner	*rmṯ-sꜣw*	I,272
prisoner	*sꜣw*	II,6
prisoner of war	*tp-ꜥnḫ*	II,205
privacy	*m-wꜥ*	I,93
private	*hꜣrṯṯ*	I,286
private person	*nmḥ*	I,238
privilege	*wstnw*	I,113
privileged	*ḫw-mk*	I,353
prize	*twn*	II,202
probably	*smwn*	II,41
probe	*ḏꜥr*	II,264
procedure	*mdt*	I,217
procedure	*sšm*	II,81
proceed	*wḏꜣ*	I,121
proceed	*pri*	I,149
proceed	*nꜥy*	I,228
proceed	*spr*	II,32
proceed	*šm*	II,121
proceed to	*ḫpr*	I,356
proceedings	*irwt*	I,40
process	*mdt*	I,217
process of construction(?)	*r-ꜥ-kꜣt*	I,261
procession	*swtwt*	II,23
procession	*sḫꜥ*	II,68
procession	*sšm*	II,81
processional appearance	*ḫꜥw*	I,352
proclaim	*wṯs*	I,117
proclaim	*nis*	I,227
proclaim	*smi*	II,40
proclaim	*sr*	II,57
proclaim(?)	*[m]ꜣt*	I,177
proclamation	*srt*	II,57
procure	*wḫꜣ*	I,109
procure	*šdi*	II,141
produce	*inw*	I,32
produce	*bꜣkw*	I,127
produce	*mḏꜥw*	I,220

produce (vb.)	*ini r-ḫft-ḥr*	I,32
produce (vb.)	*ḳmꜣ*	II,150
producer	*ḳmꜣ*	II,150
product	*pyṯ*	I,147
production	*bꜣkw*	I,127
products	*ꜣḫwt*	I,8
products	*mꜣꜥ*	I,174
products	*nkt*	I,251
profession	*iꜣwt*	I,13
profession	*ḥnw*	I,316
profitable	*ꜣḫ*	I,7
profound(?)	*mḏ*	I,218
project	*bꜣkw*	I,127
project	*r-ꜥ-bꜣkw*	I,260
projects	*sḫr*	II,73
prolong	*sḳꜣ*	II,84
promenade	*swtwt*	II,23
promenade (vb.)	*swtwt*	II,23
promenade (vb.)	*ḳdi*	II,161
promise	*mdt*	I,217
promise	*šꜥr*	II,112
promise (vb.)	*sr*	II,56
promises	*nfr*	I,236
promontory	*dhnt*	II,253
promote	*dhn*	II,253
promote sexual activity	*snhp*	II,53
promptly	*rwḏ*	I,269
promptly	*rd*	I,280
pronounce	*dm*	II,247
pronouncement	*ḏd*	II,276
pronouncements	*ḫrw*	I,372
pronouncements	*ṯs*	II,234
prop	*sṯs*	II,97
proper	*mt*	I,213
proper (be)	*nfr*	I,235
proper place	*mkt*	I,211
properly	*m-sšr*	I,171
properly	*m-šꜣw*	II,108
properly	*n-šꜣw*	II,108
properties	*st*	II,2
property	*ꜣḫwt*	I,8
property	*imy-pr*	I,27
property	*imy-prw*	I,27
property	*imyt-pr*	I,27
property	*mnꜥt*	I,186
property	*nkt*	I,251
property	*ḫt*	I,343
property	*ḫrt*	I,371
property	*sꜣwy*	II,7
property	*sꜣwt*	II,7
property	*dni(t)*	II,250
property(?)	*šꜣꜥt*	II,107
propertyless person	*iwty*	I,22
prophesy	*sr*	II,57
prophet	*ḥm-nṯr*	I,254
prophet	*ḥm-nṯr*	I,310
propitiate	*ḥtp*	I,336
propitiate	*shr-ib*	II,60
propitiate	*sḥtp*	II,64
proposition	*smiw*	II,40
prosper	*wḏꜣ*	I,120
prosper	*rwḏ*	I,269
prosper	*swḏꜣ*	II,24
prosperity	*wḏꜣ*	I,121
prosperous	*wḏꜣ*	I,120
prostitute	*tꜣḫt*	II,199
prostitute(?)	*kꜣi*	II,167
prostrate	*pḫd*	I,155
prostrate	*ḥbrbr*	I,308
prostrate	*ḥbdyt*	I,308
prostrate	*ḥdb*	I,340
prostrate	*ḫtb*	I,389
prostrate	*sḏr*	II,102
prostrate	*ḳbḳbyt*	II,149
prostrate(?)	*gbgb*	II,187
prostration	*sḏrt*	II,103
protect	*mki*	I,210
protect	*nbnb*	I,234
protect	*nh*	I,240
protect	*nḫt*	I,246
protect	*nḏ-ḥr*	I,255
protect	*ḫw*	I,353
protect	*sꜣw*	II,6
protect	*sꜣk*	II,9
protect (with armor)	*sḫkr*	II,76
protected	*ḫn*	I,361
protected and defended	*ḫw-mk*	I,353
protection	*mkt*	I,211
protection	*nḫ*	I,244
protection	*ḫw*	I,353
protection	*sꜣ*	II,4
protective images	*sšm*	II,81
protective rite	*sꜥšꜣt*	II,16
protector	*mꜥwnf*	I,181
protector	*mḥ-ib*	I,198
protector	*mkw*	I,211
protector	*nmty*	I,238
protector	*nḫ*	I,244
protector	*nḫt*	I,246
protector	*nḏty*	I,256
protector	*ḫw*	I,353
protector(?)	*nby*	I,233
protectress	*ḫwt*	I,354
protest	*šꜥr*	II,112
protest (vb.)	*kni*	II,174
protrude	*pꜣy*	I,146
prove	*gm*	II,188
provender	*wnmw*	I,102
proverbs	*ṯs*	II,233

provide	*ꜥpr*	I,65
provide	*bꜥḥ*	I,132
provide	*ḥn*	I,315
provide	*swḏꜣ*	II,24
provide	*spd*	II,34
provide	*sḏfꜣ(y)*	II,100
provide	*grg*	II,192
provide	*ṯs*	II,233
provide (for)	*ḏbꜣ*	II,266
provide with	*iri*	I,37
provide with sandals	*tby*	II,203
provide(?)	*sdf*	II,99
provided that	*m-pꜣ*	I,168
province	*ꜥ*	I,58
provision	*sdf*	II,99
provision house	*wꜥbt*	I,95
provisions	*nkt*	I,252
provisions	*rsf*	I,278
provisions	*sḏfꜣw*	II,101
provisions	*šꜣrmꜥti*	II,109
provisions	*šrmt*	II,133
provisions	*drpw*	II,252
provisions	*ḏꜣr(t)*	II,262
provisions	*ḏfꜣw*	II,268
provoke	*sḫnš*	II,71
prow	*imy-ḥꜣt*	I,27
prow rope	*ḫntt*	I,367
prow(?)	*tpt*	II,208
prowess	*bꜣw*	I,125
prudent	*dns*	II,251
prune (vb.)	*shḏ*	II,65
pry	*ḫf*	I,358
ps-jar (for dates)	*ps*	I,156
ptri-waters	*ptri*	I,159
public	*kꜣwy*	II,166
public appearance feast	*wn-ḥr-ḥb*	I,100
pudenda	*ḫpꜣ*	I,381
puerile	*ꜥḏdw*	I,85
pull	*itḥ*	I,52
pull	*sḫꜣ*	II,75
pull	*stꜣ*	II,92
pull	*šdi*	II,140
pull out the tongue	*itḥ-ns*	I,52
pulverize	*tḥs*	II,217
pungent sayings(?)	*nsḳ*	I,249
punish	*hd*	I,292
punish	*sḫ*	II,66
punish	*sswn*	II,76
punishment	*sbꜣyt*	II,27
punishment	*shdt*	II,61
pupil	*sꜣ*	II,3
pupil (of eye)	*twt*	II,203
pupil (of eye)	*ḏfḏ*	II,269
puppy	*šri*	II,132
purchase	*ini*	I,31
purchase	*swn*	II,19
purchase	*šsp*	II,135
purchase price	*swn(t)*	II,20
pure	*ꜥb*	I,63
pure	*wꜥb*	I,94
pure (of gold)	*nfr*	I,235
purge	*ḥsmn*	I,332
purify	*ꜥb*	I,63
purify	*twr*	II,202
purify	*wꜥb*	I,94
purity	*wꜥb*	I,94
purify	*swꜥb*	II,19
purify	*sṯf*	II,96
purpose	*ḥnt*	I,317
purpose	*ḫmt*	I,361
purpose	*tkꜥ*	II,220
purposes	*sḫr*	II,72
purse(?)	*ḫrd*	I,373
pursue	*nḏr*	I,257
purveyor of dates	*bnrty*	I,135
push	*wꜣš*	I,91
put	*iri*	I,38
put	*wꜣḥ*	I,89
put	*wdi*	I,117
put a stop to	*in-pḥwy*	I,153
put an end to	*in pḥ*	I,31
put aside	*wꜣḥ*	I,89
put in order	*smꜣꜥ*	II,39
put in order	*grg*	II,192
put in order	*gsgs*	II,195
put in place	*pḥꜥ*	I,155
put in proper array	*nsk*	I,249
put in sack	*ṯnf*	II,230
put matters right	*irt m-sšr-sp-sn*	I,39
put on	*ir-ḥr*	I,39
put on	*nbi*	I,233
put on board	*ꜣtp*	I,10
put to use	*bꜣk*	I,127
put together	*sꜣḳ*	II,9
put up a fuss	*ṯṯṯt*	II,237
pylon	*bḫnt*	I,139
pylon	*dwꜣ*	II,242
pylon-shaped receptacle	*sbḫt*	II,28
pyramid	*mr*	I,192
pyramid-tomb	*mr*	I,192

Q

quail	*pꜥr*	I,147
quail (vb.)	*bdš*	I,143
quality	*biꜣt*	I,130
quantity	*ẖrt*	I,371
quantity	*tnw*	II,213
quarrel	*mhd*	I,197
quarrel	*sḏd*	II,104
quarrel	*šgnn*	II,137
quarrel	*ṯtṯt*	II,237
quarrel (vb.)	*mdw*	I,216
quarry	*ḥṯ*	I,340
quarry	*ẖꜣt*	I,380
quarrying	*ḳḥḳḥ*	II,159
quarryman	*nšdy*	I,250
quarryman	*ẖrty*	I,387
quarrymen	*ẖryw*	I,386
quarter	*ẖrꜥ*	I,371
quarter	*spꜣt*	II,32
quarter (of city)	*dmi*	II,248
quartermaster	*wꜥrtw*	I,95
quarters	*ipt*	I,26
quartz(?)	*m(i)nw*	I,186
quartzite	*biꜣt*	I,130
quay	*mryt*	I,193
quay	*tp-š*	II,206
quay	*dmi*	II,248
queen	*ḥmt-nsw*	I,311
quell	*stm*	II,95
quench	*ꜥḫm*	I,78
question (vb.)	*nḏnḏ*	I,257
question (vb.)	*šni*	II,127
quick	(see swift)	
quickly	*ꜣs*	I,9
quiet	*mdn*	I,218
quiet	*štꜣ*	II,138
quiet	*ḳb*	II,148
quiet	*gr*	II,190
quit	*ꜥr*	I,71
quite a number	*ꜥḥꜥw*	I,76
quite apart from	*tꜣy-rit*	I,266
quiver	*ispt*	I,47
quiver (vb.)	*nwṯ*	I,232
quiver (vb.)	*ktkt*	II,180
quota	*ipt*	I,25
quote	*r-nty*	I,253
quote	*r-nty*	I,262
quote	*r-ḏd*	I,265
quote	*ḥnꜥ-r-ḏd*	I,265
quote	*ḥnꜥ-ḏd*	I,317

R

race (vb.)	*trr*	II,215
radiance	*stwt*	II,93
radiant	*wbḫ*	I,97
radiant	*stḥn*	II,96
rafter	*smkt*	II,45
rafters	*sbw*	II,24
rafts	*šdw*	II,141
rage	*ḳnd(t)*	II,155
rage	*ṯms*	II,229
rage (vb.)	*nšny*	I,250
rage (vb.)	*ḥdn*	I,342
rage (vb.)	*ḫꜥr*	I,353
rage (vb.)	*swh*	II,21
rage (vb.)	*ḳnd*	II,155
raging	*nꜥš*	I,229
rags	*isw*	I,45
rags	*ḥtꜣw*	I,335
raiment	*mnḫt*	I,189
rain	*iꜣdt*	I,15
rain (vb.)	*ḥwi*	I,303
rain (vb.)	*šni*	II,128
rainstorm	*šni*	II,128
rainy	*ḫr-mw*	I,182
raise	*wṯs*	I,117
raise	*fꜣy*	I,163
raise	*sꜥḥꜥ*	II,15
raise	*sḳꜣ*	II,84
raise	*sṯs*	II,97
raise	*ṯni*	II,229
raise	*ḏsr*	II,274
raise one's hand (against)	*fꜣy-ꜥ*	I,163
raise one's voice	*nḥd*	I,244
raise sail	*fꜣy*	I,163
raise up	*ꜥḫ*	I,77
raise up	*ṯs*	II,234
raised terrace	*rwḏw*	I,269
ram	*iꜣywr*	I,12
ram	*rhnt*	I,274
ram(?)	*iry*	I,40
ram-headed one	*bꜣ-šfyt*	I,126
ramp	*stꜣ*	II,93
rampart	*sbty*	II,29
rampart	*ṯsmw*	II,236
rank	*iꜣwt*	I,13
rank	*sꜥḥ*	II,15
rape	*ẖꜥ*	I,380
rapid (water)	*bꜣšꜣ*	I,127
rapidly	*ꜣs*	I,9
rapids	*mw-bš*	I,182
rapture	*syḥ*	II,12
rat(?)	*inḥw*	I,35
ration	*ẖrt*	I,385

rations	*spdw*	II,34
rations	*diw*	II,240
rations	*ḏꜣr(t)*	II,262
ravaging	*htm*	I,292
ravine	*bḳꜥ*	I,141
ravine	*ḫꜣrb*	I,349
ravine	*šdrt*	II,141
rays	*stwt*	II,93
razor	*mẖḳ*	I,202
razor	*ẖr-ꜥ*	I,387
razor	*dgꜣ*	II,256
razor case	*ẖꜥw*	I,380
reach	*ini ḥnty*	I,32
reach	*pḥ*	I,152
reach	*ḥn*	I,316
reach	*ẖnm*	I,383
reach	*spr*	II,32
reach	*tkn*	II,220
reach an agreement	*ir wꜥ irm*	I,93
reach down	*sr*	II,57
reach manhood	*ip-ḏt*	I,24
reaction	*wšbt*	I,114
read	*ꜥš*	I,78
read	*sḏm*	II,101
read	*šdi*	II,139
readiness	*ḥry*	I,324
readiness	*ḥryt*	I,327
readiness	*grg*	II,192
ready	*iri*	I,37
ready	*spd*	II,34
ready (make)	*ḥr*	I,321
ready to	*m-r-ꜥ*	I,260
real	*m-wn-mꜣꜥ*	I,168
real	*mꜣꜥ(t)*	I,175
realgar	*ꜣwt-ib*	I,3
realize	*ꜥm*	I,66
really	*m-mꜣꜥt*	I,168
really barley	*it-m-it*	I,50
realm of the dead	*igrt*	I,50
realm of the dead	*ẖrt-nṯr*	I,385
reap	*isḫ*	I,47
reap	*ꜥwꜣy*	I,63
rear	*pḥwy*	I,153
rear (vb.)	*ḥwrr*	I,306
rear (vb.)	*sḫpr*	II,68
reassemble	*ssꜣḳ*	II,76
rebel	*rst*	I,278
rebel	*ḫnw*	I,363
rebel	*ḫr*	I,370
rebel	*ẖꜣkw-ib*	I,380
rebel	*sbi*	II,28
rebel (vb.)	*bšd*	I,140
rebel (vb.)	*bdš*	I,143
rebel (vb.)	*ḫsf-ꜥ*	I,374
rebel against	*thi r*	II,216
rebellion	*bštw*	I,140
rebellion	*bdš*	I,143
rebellion	*ḫrw*	I,372
rebellion	*sbi*	II,28
rebellion	*štm*	II,139
rebellious	*bšt*	I,140
rebellious	*bḳ*	I,141
rebels	*ẖꜣkw-ib*	I,23
rebels	*bšt*	I,140
rebels	*bšdw*	I,140
rebels	*bdš*	I,143
rebuild	*šr*	II,131
rebut	*ḏb*	II,265
recall	*sḫꜣ*	II,67
receipt	*snw*	II,50
receipt	*šsp*	II,136
receipt of offerings	*šsp-snw*	II,136
receive	*ẖnm*	I,383
receive	*smꜣ*	II,38
receive	*šsp*	II,135
receive (letter)	*sḏm*	II,101
receptacle	*inr*	I,34
receptacle	*wšw*	I,114
receptacle	*hn*	I,288
recess	*twhꜣw*	II,202
recital	*sḏd*	II,104
recitation	*nis*	I,227
recitations	*sꜣḫw*	II,9
recite	*šdi*	II,139
reciter	*dd-r*	II,258
recklessness	(see heedlessness)	
reckon	*ip*	I,24
reckon	*ḥsb*	I,332
reckon	*šsp*	II,136
reckon with	*ḥsb*	I,332
recognize	*wšd*	I,115
recognize	*mtr*	I,214
recognize	*siꜣ*	II,11
recognize	*swn*	II,19
recognize	*gm*	II,188
recompense	*isw*	I,45
recompense	*mtn*	I,214
reconnaissance officer	*mhr*	I,196
record	*mitt*	I,179
record (vb.)	*wꜣḥ*	I,89
record (vb.)	*smn*	II,42
record keeper	*sꜣw*	II,7
record keeper	*sꜣw-sšw*	II,78
recorded	*mn*	I,183
records	*sḫꜣ*	II,67
records	*sš*	II,78
records	*gnwt*	II,190
records	*drf*	II,252
recount	*sḫꜣ*	II,67
recourse to	*wꜣi*	I,87

recover	*šdi*	II,139
recover	*dwn*	II,243
recover from	*pri*	I,149
recruit	*iḥwn*	I,44
recruits	*ḥwnw-nfrw*	I,306
recruits	*srwd*	II,58
recruits(?)	*tmrgn*	II,211
rectum	*pẖt*	I,153
red	*dšr*	II,255
red cloth	*ins(y)*	I,35
Red Crown	*ini*	I,32
Red Crown	*nt*	I,225
Red Crown	*dšrt*	II,255
red jasper	*mẖnmt*	I,201
red jasper	*ẖnmt*	I,364
red land	*dšrt*	II,255
red ochre	*mnš(t)*	I,190
red ochre	*ṯmḥy*	II,229
red pigment	*sty*	II,91
red pot	*dšrt*	II,255
Red Sea	*wꜣḏ-wr*	I,91
red vessel	*dšrt*	II,255
reed	*ꜥrw*	I,71
reed	*mꜣt*	I,173
reed	*gꜣš*	II,185
reed brush	*ꜥrw*	I,71
reed stalks	*ꜥnb*	I,69
reed swamps	*ṯwf*	II,227
reed thicket	*isbr*	I,46
reed(?)	*gši*	II,195
reeds	*isw*	I,45
reeds	*isbr*	I,46
reeds	*wnr*	I,102
reeds	*mnḥw*	I,188
reeds	*swt*	II,22
reeds	*ḳmꜣ*	II,151
reeds	*gmy*	II,189
reek (vb.)	*sty*	II,91
reel	*šm*	II,122
refined	*wḏḥ*	I,123
reflect	*kꜣ*	II,166
refrain(?)	*mꜣwt*	I,176
refresh	*snb*	II,50
refresh	*sḳbb*	II,84
refresh oneself	*ḳbḥ*	II,149
refreshed	*srd*	II,59
regalia	*ẖkrw*	I,389
regard (vb.)	*mꜣꜣ*	I,173
regard (vb.)	*nw*	I,229
regard (vb.)	*šfšf*	II,120
regard (vb.)	*ḳḏm*	II,163
regiment	*sꜣw*	II,4
region	*iꜣt*	I,11
region	*ꜥ*	I,58
region	*w*	I,87
region	*sw*	II,17
region	*swꜣw*	II,18
region	*štꜣ*	II,139
regions	*tꜣš*	II,199
register	*ꜥ*	I,58
register	*ꜥrw mtrw*	I,72
register	*mḏꜣt*	I,219
register	*snhm*	II,53
register (vb.)	*spẖr*	II,33
register (vb.)	*snh*	II,53
register (vb.)	*iry dnyt*	II,250
registration	*spẖr*	II,34
registry	*snh*	II,53
regular	*mt*	I,213
regularly	*m-dwn*	I,172
regularly	*dwn*	II,243
regularly (handing over)	*ꜥḥꜥ*	I,75
regulate	*ḥn*	I,316
regulate	*sḥn*	II,62
regulate	*gsgs*	II,195
regulation	*wḏ(t)*	I,119
regulation	*ntꜥ*	I,253
regulation	*hp*	I,287
regulation(?)	*rḥt*	I,276
reign	*ꜥḥꜥw-nsyt*	I,77
reign	*ḥkꜣ*	I,333
reimburse	*ḏbꜣ*	II,266
reinforcement	*nẖt*	I,246
rein-looser	*ṯt-ẖnr*	II,236
reins	*ẖnr*	I,365
reins	*swr*	II,21
reins (part of chariot harness)	*kwšn*	II,171
reins(?)	*ẖrꜣḥt*	I,370
reis	*wꜥw*	I,94
reject	*bꜥ*	I,131
reject	*ẖꜣꜥ*	I,346
reject	*šnꜥ*	II,129
rejection	*bꜥ*	I,131
rejoice	*ꜣw(i)*	I,3
rejoice	*iꜥi*	I,16
rejoice	*ꜥḏꜥḏ*	I,84
rejoice	*wnf*	I,101
rejoice	*nhm*	I,241
rejoice	*nḏm-ib*	I,256
rejoice	*rš*	I,278
rejoice	*ḥꜥy*	I,300
rejoice	*ḥꜥwy*	I,302
rejoice	*ẖntš*	I,367
rejoice	*snḏm-ib*	II,56
rejoicing	*wnf-ib*	I,23
rejoicing	*ihy*	I,42
rejoicing	*ihhy*	I,43
rejoicing	*nhm*	I,241
rejoicing	*ršw*	I,278
rejoicing	*ršrš*	I,279

rejoicing	*hꜣy*	I,284
rejoin	*snfr*	II,51
rejuvenated	*rnpi*	I,273
relapse	*ʿn(n)*	I,68
relate	*sḏd*	II,104
relate	*ḏd*	II,275
relatives	*mhwt*	I,196
relatives	*sn*	II,48
relax	*mdn*	I,218
relax	*sbn*	II,28
relax	*sḏꜣ*	II,100
relax	*ṯt*	II,236
release	*wḥʿ*	I,107
release	*ntf*	I,253
release	*ḫꜣʿ*	I,347
release	*sfḫ*	II,35
relief	*wḥʿ*	I,107
relief	*srf*	II,58
relieve	*snf*	II,51
relinquish	*ḫꜣʿ*	I,347
rely	*hn*	I,288
relying	*mḥ-ib*	I,197
remain	*ʿḥʿ*	I,75
remain	*wꜣḥ*	I,89
remain	*mn*	I,183
remain	*spi*	II,31
remain	*smn*	II,41
remain firm	*rwḏ*	I,269
remain inactive	*ḥms*	I,314
remainder	*wḏꜣ*	I,121
remainder	*pḥwy*	I,153
remainder	*mn*	I,184
remainder	*spyt*	II,31
remainder	*smn*	II,42
remainder	*ktḥw*	II,179
remainder	*ḏꜣt*	II,260
remains	*spyt*	II,31
remarks	*mdt*	I,217
remedy	*pḫrt*	I,155
remedy	*hrf*	I,291
remember	*sḫꜣ*	II,67
remembrance	*sḫꜣ*	II,68
reminder	*sḫꜣ*	II,67
remiss	*bꜣg*	I,128
remiss	*bgꜣ*	I,142
remiss	*nni*	I,239
remissness	*bgꜣ*	I,142
remit	*swḏ*	II,24
remnant	*spyt*	II,31
remove	*ini*	I,31
remove	*iṯꜣ*	I,53
remove	*wiꜣ*	I,92
remove	*mn*	I,184
remove	*rwi*	I,267
remove	*rmni*	I,271
remove	*ḫbꜣ*	I,354
remove	*ḫsr*	I,374
remove	*srwi*	II,58
remove	*sḫr*	II,64
remove	*stn*	II,95
remove	*sṯs*	II,97
remove	*šdi*	II,140
remove	*tfi*	II,209
remove	*dr*	II,252
remove(?)	*nfʿ*	I,235
renaissance	*wḥm-msw*	I,109
rend	*prš*	I,152
rend	*sd*	II,98
render	*ʿn-smi*	I,68
render up	*ḳʿ*	II,145
renew	*smꜣwy*	II,40
renew	*srd*	II,59
renewal	*smꜣwy*	II,40
renewed	*mꜣʿ*	I,174
renovate	*smꜣwy*	II,40
renown	*hnhn*	I,290
renown	*šfyt*	II,120
renown	*šfšf*	II,120
repair	*ʿn*	I,68
repay	*ḏbꜣ*	II,266
repay	*ḏnr*	II,270
repeat	*wḥm*	I,108
repeated again	*wḥm-ʿn*	I,109
repeated copulation	*nknk*	I,251
repeatedly	*m-wḥm*	I,108
repeatedly	*m-wḥm*	I,168
repeating births	*wḥm-msw*	I,109
repel	*inty*	I,36
repel	*ḫsf-ʿ*	I,374
repel	*sʿšꜣ*	II,16
repel	*sḫty*	II,75
repel	*šnʿ*	II,129
repel	*twh*	II,202
repel	*dr*	II,252
replace	*šb*	II,116
replace	*ḏbꜣ*	II,266
replenish	*gwt*	II,186
reply	*wšbt*	I,114
reply (vb.)	*wšb*	I,114
reply (vb.)	*ḫsf*	I,374
reply (vb.)	*ḏb*	II,265
report	*wḥm*	I,108
report	*pri*	I,149
report	*smi*	II,40
report (n.)	*ʿn-smi*	I,68
report (n.)	*spr*	II,33
report (n.)	*smit*	II,41
report (n.)	*sḏdt*	II,104
repose	*sḫny*	II,71
reprehensible	*bin*	I,131
representation	*wšb*	I,114

repress	*ḥwỉ*	I,303
repress	*sꜥšꜣ*	II,16
repress	*sdb*	II,98
reprimand	*ꜥḥꜣ*	I,74
reprimand	*mdw*	I,217
reprimand severely	*ꜥḥꜣ ꜥꜣ*	I,74
reproach	*ṯꜣy*	II,225
reproach (vb.)	*sḥwr*	II,62
reproach (vb.)	*sḫr*	II,72
reproach (vb.)	*ḏbꜥ*	II,267
reptile	*ḥrrt*	I,328
repulse	*trỉ*	II,215
reputation	*smỉw*	II,41
request	(see ask)	
request	*nḥ*	I,241
request (vb.)	*dbḥ*	II,245
require	*wḫꜣ*	I,109
require	*sḥn*	II,63
requirement	*dbḥw*	II,246
requirements	*ḫrt*	I,371
requirements	*ḫrt*	I,373
requirements	*ḫrw*	I,387
requirements	*sdbḥ*	II,99
requirements	*dbḥw*	II,246
requisites	*dbḥw*	II,246
requisition	*nḥb*	I,242
requisition	*nḥm*	I,243
requisitioned labor	*ṯst*	II,235
rescue	*šdỉ*	II,140
research	*ḏꜥr*	II,264
resemble	*stwt*	II,94
resentful	*bḳ-ib*	I,141
reserve	*nḥm*	I,243
reserve	*ḫw*	I,353
reserve	*šdỉ*	II,140
reserved	*ḫw-mk*	I,353
reserved	*snk*	II,54
reserves	*spyt*	II,31
reservoir	*mw-ḥms*	I,183
reservoirs	*š-šꜥf*	II,105
reservoirs	*šꜥf*	II,112
reside	*ḥtp*	I,336
residence	*isbw*	I,46
residence	*ḫnw*	I,383
residing in	*ḥry-ib*	I,23
residing in	*ḥry-ib*	I,324
residing in	*ḥry-ib*	I,325
resin	*sft*	II,35
resin	*ḳmy*	II,151
resin(?)	*shrt*	II,61
resist	*ḥḏn*	I,342
resist	*tꜣy*	II,199
resist	*dr*	II,252
resolute	*dns*	II,252
resource	*wꜣt*	I,88
respect	*šfyt*	II,119
respect	*šfšf*	II,120
respect (vb.)	*bꜥ*	I,131
respect (vb.)	*swꜣš*	II,18
respect (vb.)	*trỉ*	II,214
respond	*wšb*	I,114
respond	*ḫsf*	I,374
response	*wšbt*	I,114
responsibility	*sḫprw*	II,69
rest	*srf*	II,58
rest (vb.)	*wrd*	I,106
rest (vb.)	*mtn*	I,214
rest (vb.)	*ḥtp*	I,336
rest (vb.)	*ḫnỉ*	I,362
rest (vb.)	*snḏm*	II,56
rest (vb.)	*srf*	II,58
rest (vb.)	*sḫny*	II,71
resting place	*ḫnw*	I,362
resting place	*st n ḥtp*	II,2
resting place	*sḏrt*	II,103
resting place(?)	*msḫn(t)*	I,206
resting places	*ḥtpt*	I,338
restoration	*smꜣwy*	II,40
restore	*mnḳ*	I,190
restore	*rd*	I,280
restore	*sꜥḥꜥ*	II,15
restore	*swḏ*	II,24
restore	*smꜣwy*	II,40
restore	*šdỉ*	II,139
restore to order	*spd*	II,34
restored	*srd*	II,59
restrain	*ỉnty*	I,36
restrain	*ỉhm*	I,43
restrain	*rtḥ*	I,280
restrain	*ḫnr*	I,365
restrain	*sꜣw*	II,6
restrain	*ṯꜣy-rd*	II,224
restrained	*krỉ*	II,175
restraint	*ḫbꜣ*	I,354
restrict	*shdt*	II,61
retain	*ỉsḳ*	I,48
retain	*smn*	II,41
retainer	*hnw*	I,289
retainer	*šmsw*	II,124
retinue	(see following)	
retinue	*sšm*	II,81
retinue	*šms*	II,125
retire	*ḫty*	I,376
retire	*ḫtḫt*	I,377
retreat	*ꜥn(n)*	I,68
retreat	*ḥm*	I,310
retreat	*ḫty*	I,376
return	*ỉỉ*	I,15
return	*ỉw*	I,18
return	*ỉnỉ*	I,31
return	*ꜥn(n)*	I,68
return	*wḥꜥ*	I,107

return	*ḥsi*	I,329
return	*ḫꜣꜥ*	I,346
return	*sbi*	II,27
return	*sẖnty*	II,72
return	*šm*	II,121
return of the year	*nri*	I,239
return to	*hꜣ(i)*	I,283
reveal	*wbꜣ*	I,96
reveal	*wpi*	I,98
reveal	*sr*	II,56
reveal	*sšm*	II,80
reveal	*ḏꜣ*	II,259
reveal (door)	*wmwt*	I,100
revealing of face	*wn-ḥr*	I,100
revelation	*wpt-mꜣꜥt*	I,98
revelation	*smiw*	II,41
revelers	*ẖnmw*	I,363
revenue	*bꜣkw*	I,127
revenue making property	*sꜥnḫw*	II,14
revenues	*ḥtr*	I,339
revere	*tri*	II,214
revered	*imꜣḫy*	I,30
revered	*tni*	II,211
reverse	*pnꜥ*	I,148
reversed	*sẖd*	II,75
review	*ip*	I,24
revile	*bḥn*	I,138
revile	*nrḥ*	I,240
revision	*snh*	II,53
revive	*sꜥnḫ*	II,14
revive(?)	*srd*	II,59
revolt	*ḥḏn*	I,342
revolt	*ḫrw*	I,372
revolve	*pẖr*	I,155
reward	*isw*	I,45
reward	*mtnwt*	I,216
reward	*twn*	II,202
reward	*ḏbꜣ*	II,266
reward (n.)	*fꜣy*	I,163
reward (n.)	*fḳꜣw*	I,165
reward (vb.)	*fḳꜣ*	I,165
reward (vb.)	*mtn*	I,214
reward (vb.)	*ḥsi*	I,329
reward(?)	*mtwn*	I,214
rewards	*mk(y)w*	I,211
rewards	*ḏbꜣw*	II,266
rib	*spr*	II,32
rib (of ship)	*wgꜣ*	I,115
rich	*ꜥꜣ(i)*	I,59
rich	*ꜥšꜣ*	I,79
rich	*wsr*	I,111
rich	*bwꜣ*	I,133
rich	*brg*	I,137
rich	*sꜥꜣ*	II,13
rich	*šps*	II,118
riches	*špssw*	II,119
ricinus	*dgm*	II,257
rid of	*pšn*	I,158
riddles	*itnw*	I,51
ridge	*ꜥḥꜥt*	I,77
ridicule	*ꜣbi*	I,4
right	*ꜥḳꜣ*	I,81
right	*wnmy*	I,102
right	*mꜣꜥ(t)*	I,175
right	*mt*	I,213
right away	*ꜣs*	I,9
right hand side	*wnmy*	I,102
right moment	*tp-nfr*	II,205
righteous	*ꜥḳꜣ*	I,81
righteous one	*mꜣꜥtyw*	I,175
rims	*spt*	II,31
rind	*ḏrww*	II,273
ring	*sniw*	II,49
ring	*gsr*	II,195
ring stand	*ꜥgꜣn*	I,82
ring stand	*ꜥgn*	I,82
riparian land	*idb*	I,54
riparian land	*wḏb*	I,123
riparian plots	*idb*	I,54
ripe (old age)	*ꜥꜣ(i)*	I,59
ripen	*wḏḥ*	I,123
rise	*wbn*	I,97
rise	*ḫꜥi*	I,351
rise at dawn	*dwꜣ*	II,242
rise up	*ṯs*	II,234
rising grounds	*ḳꜣ(y)*	II,143
ritual	*irt-ḫt*	I,38
ritual directions	*sšm-ḫs*	II,81
ritual of amulets	*tmm.t*	II,211
ritual priests	*ḫry-ḥb(t)*	I,387
ritual roll	*ḥbt*	I,307
rituals	*ihbw*	I,43
river	*itr*	I,51
river	*nhr*	I,241
river mouth	*ḥꜣt*	I,297
riverbank	*wḏb*	I,123
riverbank	*mꜣꜥ*	I,174
riverboat	*mnš*	I,189
road	*wꜣt*	I,88
road	*mit*	I,179
road	*mṯn*	I,216
road	*smꜣty*	II,39
roam	*wnšnš*	I,103
roar	*diwt*	II,240
roar (vb.)	*nḥd*	I,244
roar (vb.)	*ḥrr*	I,328
roar (vb.)	*swh*	II,21
roar (vb.)	*trmg*	II,215
roaring	*ḥrr*	I,328
roast	*wbd*	I,97
roast joint	*ꜣšrt*	I,9

roaster (of incense)	*ps*	I,155
roasting spit	*mḳꜥr*	I,210
rob	*ꜥwꜣỉ*	I,63
rob	*ꜥwn*	I,63
rob	*ḥꜣḳ*	I,299
rob	*ḥꜥdꜣ*	I,302
rob	*ḥwrꜥ*	I,306
rob	*ḥwtf*	I,306
robber	*ỉṯꜣy*	I,53
robber	*ꜥwꜣ*	I,62
robber's shaft	*ỉs*	I,45
robbery	*ḥwrꜥ*	I,306
robe	*ḏꜣyt*	II,261
robing room	*ḏbꜣt*	II,267
rock-cut tomb	*mꜥḥꜥt*	I,182
rock-cut tomb	*ḥrt*	I,328
rocks	*ꜥnr*	I,69
rod	*ỉꜣꜣt*	I,11
rod	*ꜥ-n-ḫt*	I,57
rod	*bḏn*	I,143
rod	*šbd*	II,117
rod	*ṯbt*	II,228
rod of palm	*bꜥỉ*	I,132
role	*ỉꜣt*	I,11
roll call	*rn-rn*	I,272
roll of testimonies	*ꜥrw mtrw*	I,72
rolls	*fdnw*	I,166
roof	*kꜣp*	II,168
roof	*tp-ḥwt*	II,206
room	*ꜥt*	I,59
room	*ḏrwt*	II,273
root	*mnyt*	I,186
rope	(see cordage)	
rope	*wꜣ*	I,88
rope	*pry*	I,151
rope	*fꜣy*	I,164
rope	*nwḥ*	I,231
rope	*rdt*	I,281
rope(?)	*ḥbr*	I,308
ropes	*mḫꜣ*	I,201
rosette	*ḏḏ*	II,277
rough	*n(ꜣ)ḥꜣw*	I,226
rough	*nḥꜣ*	I,242
rough	*ẖt*	I,379
round (vb.)	*ꜥby*	I,64
round up	*nw(ỉ)*	I,230
round up	*ẖtẖt*	I,389
rouse	*nw*	I,230
rout	*ỉfd*	I,26
route	*ꜥ-n-šmt*	I,57
route	*ꜥn-smt*	I,68
route	*šmt*	II,122
row (vb.)	*ẖnỉ*	I,382
rowers & towers	*mškb*	I,209
royal butler	*wbꜣ-nsw*	I,96
royal butler	*wbꜣ-nsw*	I,248
royal butler	*wdpw-nsw(?)*	I,248
royal children	*msw-nsw*	I,205
royal children	*msw-nsw*	I,248
royal companions	*smr*	II,43
royal court	*stp-sꜣ*	II,4
royal cupbearer	*nỉw-nsw*	I,226
royal cupbearer	*wbꜣ-nsw*	I,248
royal decree	*wḏ-nsw*	I,120
royal envoy	*ỉpwty*	I,25
royal gifts	*mrk*	I,195
royal harim	*ỉpt-nsw*	I,26
royal herald	*wḥm-nsw*	I,109
royal household	*snwt*	II,128
royal linen	*sšr-nsw*	I,249
royal linen	*ḥbs-n-nsw*	I,308
royal linen	*sšr-nsw*	II,82
royal linen	*šs-nsw*	II,134
royal mother	*mwt-nsw*	I,248
royal necropolis	*st pr-ꜥꜣ*	II,2
royal nursery	*kꜣpw*	II,168
royal records	*mḏꜣt-nsw*	I,219
royal retinue	*šms-nsw*	II,125
royal scribe	*sš-nsw*	II,78
royal scribes	*sšw-nsw*	I,248
royal window of appearances	*sšd*	II,83
royal writ	*wḏ-nsw*	I,120
rub	*sgnn*	II,90
rub	*gmgm*	II,189
rub out	*sỉn*	II,12
rubble	*ḫšḫš*	I,375
rubble	*ḳbḳb*	II,149
rubble	*krkr*	II,177
rudder	*ḥmy(t)*	I,312
ruddle	*mny*	I,186
ruffled	*šnrf*	II,131
ruin	*ỉꜣt*	I,11
ruin	*mrḥ*	I,194
ruin	*tp-šw*	II,206
ruin (vb.)	*fḫ*	I,165
ruin (vb.)	*sꜥḏꜣ*	II,16
ruin (vb.)	*gsꜣ*	II,194
ruined	*wꜣsỉ*	I,90
rule	*sšm*	II,81
rule	*tp-rd*	II,205
ruler	*ḥḳꜣ*	I,333
Ruler of Justice	*ḥḳꜣ-mꜣꜥt*	I,333
rulership	*ḥḳꜣ*	I,333
rules	*tp-rd*	II,205
rumors	*grgwty*	II,193
run	*pḥrr*	I,154
run	*pt*	I,158
run	*pd*	I,160
run	*ḥḥy*	I,329
run	*sẖsẖ*	II,74
run	*ḳḏ*	II,162

run (flow)	*nhr*	I,241
run ahead of	*sẖsẖ*	II,74
run at random	*tnbẖ*	II,213
run away	*hꜣ(i)*	I,284
run beyond	*sẖsẖ*	II,74
run off	*wꜥr*	I,95
run out	*wꜥb*	I,94
run out (of supplies)	*hꜣ(i)*	I,284
run over	*gmgm*	II,189
run(?)	*ḥpt*	I,309
runnel	*ẖꜣs*	I,349
runner	*wꜣt-šwy*	I,88
runner	*pḥrr*	I, 154
rush	*ḥfḏ*	I,310
rush	*sẖs*	II,74
rush	*gꜣš*	II,185
rush brush	*ꜥrw*	I,71
rushes	*isw*	I,45
rushes	*isrw*	I,47
rushes	*mrsyr*	I,195
rushes	*šwy*	II,114
rushing forth	*m gsgs*	II,195

S

sack	*pdr*	I,160
sack	*ẖꜣr*	I,380
sack	*krs*	II,176
sack	*gꜣwꜣn*	II,184
sack	*gwn*	II,186
sack	*ṯnfyt*	II,230
sack (of leather)	*mss*	I,206
sackcloth	*sg*	II,89
sacred	*ḏsr*	II,274
sacred area	*ḏsrt*	II,275
sacred bark	*wiꜣ*	I,92
sacred eye amulet	*wḏꜣ(w)*	I,122
sacred staff	*mdw*	I,218
sacred territory	*tꜣ-ḏsr*	II,199
sacred way	*wꜣt-nṯr*	I,88
sacred wells(?)	*nhrty*	I,241
sacrifice (vb.)	*mꜣꜥ*	I,174
sacrifice (vb.)	*sꜥr*	II,14
sacrifice (vb.)	*smꜣ*	II,39
sacrificial animal	*ṯrr*	II,231
sacrificial ox(?)	*šsr*	II,137
sacrificial tablet	*ḥtp*	I,337
sad	*ind*	I,36
sad	*snm*	II,51
sad	*ḏw*	II,265
safe	*ꜥḏ*	I,82
safe	*wḏꜣ*	I,120
safe, keep	*swḏꜣ*	II,24
safe and sound	*wḏꜣ snb*	I,121
safe conduct	*sꜣ*	II,4
safeguard	*ẖw*	I,353
safflower	*kṯ*	II,180
sage	*nfr*	I,235
sage	*sꜣꜣ*	II,5
sail	*wḏi*	I,119
sail	*ẖni*	I,382
sail around	*trr*	II,215
sail away	*ḥḏ*	I,341
sail over	*ḏꜣi*	II,260
sailors	*ẖni*	I,382
sails	*ḥtꜣw*	I,335
sally forth to battle	*bs-r-sky*	I,139
salt	*ḥmꜣt*	I,312
salutation	*nyny*	I,227
salute (vb.)	*wšd*	I,115
salvation	*wḏꜣ*	I,121
sample of	*ꜥ*	I,57
sanctify	*sḏsr*	II,103
sanctity	*ḏsr*	II,274
sanctuary	*iwyt*	I,18
sanctuary	*iwnn*	I,21
sanctuary	*wbꜣ*	I,96
sanctuary	*pr-wr*	I,149

sanctuary	*ḥwt-ꜥꜣt*	I,304
sanctuary	*sḥ*	II,61
sanctuary	*st*	II, 2
sand	*dbyt*	II,245
sand	*šꜥy(t)*	II,111
sandalmaker	*ṯbw*	II,228
sandals	*tbw*	II,203
sandals	*ṯbw(t)*	II,228
sandfly	*ḫmy-rdwy*	I,361
sandfly	*ḏꜣwꜣti*	II,261
sandstone	*inr n rwḏ*	I,34
sandstone	*biꜣt*	I,130
sandstone	*rwḏ*	I,269
sarcophagus	*ḏbꜣt*	II,267
sate	*ssꜣꜣ*	II,76
sate oneself	*sꜣ*	II,5
sated	*bꜥḥ*	I,132
sated (with)	*sꜣ*	II,5
satisfaction	*hrt-ib*	I,291
satisfaction	*sꜣy*	II,6
satisfactorily	*r-ꜣbw*	I,4
satisfactorily	*r-ꜣbw*	I,260
satisfactory	*hr-ib*	I,290
satisfied	*hr-ib*	I,23
satisfied	*mtr*	I,214
satisfied	*hr-ib*	I,290
satisfied	*ḥtp*	I,336
satisfied	*shr*	II,60
satisfied	*sẖꜣ*	II,67
satisfied (with)	*sꜣ*	II,5
satisfy	*iꜥi*	I,16
satisfy	*sḥtp*	II,64
satisfy	*ssꜣꜣ*	II,76
savage	*ḥsꜣ*	I,331
save	*nḥm*	I,243
save	*swḏꜣ*	II,24
save	*sšd*	II,83
save	*šdi*	II,139
saw	*wsy*	I,111
sawed off	*sꜥb*	II,13
say	*i*	I,11
say	*mdw*	I,216
say	*ḫf*	I,358
say	*ḫr*	I,369
say	*swḏꜣ-ib*	II,24
say	*kꜣ*	II,166
say	*ḏd*	II,275
saying	*m-ḏd*	I,173
saying	*r*	I,259
saying	*r-ḏd*	I,265
saying	*ṯs*	II,233
sayings, pungent	*nsḳ*	I,249
scabbard	*mꜣyt*	I,174
scale	*iwsw*	I,21
scale	*mꜥḫꜣt*	I,182
scale	*mḫꜣt*	I,201
scarabs	*ḫprw*	I,357
scarf	*idg*	I,55
scatter	*ḫnr*	I,364
scene	*st mꜣꜣ*	II,2
scent	*sty*	II,91
scented water(?)	*ḫrpt*	I,373
scented wood	*tišpss*	II,201
scepter	*ꜣms*	I,6
scepter	*ḥḳꜣt*	I,334
scepter	*ḏꜥm*	II,264
schemes	*sšm*	II,80
schoenus	*itrw*	I,51
school	*ꜥt-sbꜣ*	I,59
school	*ꜥt sbꜣ*	II,26
school	*sbꜣ*	II,26
schooled	*šfy*	II,120
scimitar	*ḫpš*	I,357
scold	*ṯyṯy*	II,227
scold	*ḏyḏy*	II,264
scorch	*išf*	I,48
scorch	*nwḫ*	I,231
scorn (vb.)	*sḫr*	II,74
scornful	*fiṯ*	I,164
scorpion	*wḥꜥt*	I,108
scourge	*sḫ*	II,65
scout	*ḥꜣptyw*	I,299
scout (?)	*skt*	II,88
scout (vb.)	*smt*	II,45
scow	*br*	I,136
scramble	*ṯfy*	II,229
scramble	*ṯṯf*	II,237
scrap of	*nkt*	I,251
scrap of copper	*ḥmt-n-ḳnḳn*	I,315
scrape	*nkꜥ*	I,250
scream (vb.)	*ky*	II,171
screen	*sbḫt*	II,29
screw	*mnyny*	I,186
scribe	*sš*	II,78
scribe	*ṯpr*	II,229
scribe of accounts	*sš-hsb*	II,79
scribe of army	*sš-mšꜥ*	I,208
scribe of elite troops	*sš-nfrw*	II,78
scribe of the army	*sš-mšꜥ*	II,78
scribe of the mat	*sš-n-tmꜣ*	II,78
scribe of the offering table	*sš-wḏḥw*	II,78
scribe of the temple	*sš ḥwt-nṯr*	II,79
scribe type	*mns*	I,189
script	*mdw-nṯr*	I,218
script	*mdw-nṯr*	I,254
scroll	*ꜥrt*	I,72
scroll	*mḏꜣt*	I,219
scroll	*drf*	II,252
scrub country	*sꜥr*	II,14

sculptor	*sꜥnḫw*	II,14
sculptor	*ṯꜣy mḏꜣt*	II,225
sculpture (vb.)	*sꜥnḫ*	II,14
scuttled	*bgꜣ*	I,142
sdy-garment	*sḏ*	II,100
sea	*ym*	I,28
sea	*wꜣḏ-wr*	I,91
sea captain	*imy-r-š*	II,105
Sea of Reeds	*pꜣ-ṯwf*	I,145
Sea People?	*mškb*	I,209
sea shore	*wḏb*	I,123
seal	*ḫt*	I,376
seal	*ḫtm*	I,377
seal	*sḳḥ*	II,85
Seal bearer of L.E.	*sḏꜣwty-bity*	II,100
seal up	*ḏbꜥ*	II,267
sealer	*ḫtmty*	I,377
sear	*išf*	I,48
search	*ḥḥy*	I,329
search for	*wḫꜣ*	I,109
search out	*gmḥ*	II,189
search out	*ḫdḫd*	I,390
seasonal river bed	*nḫr(n)*	I,245
seasons(?)	*tr*	II,214
seat	*ḥtmt*	I,338
seat	*st*	II,2
Seat (Great)	*stwrt*	II,2
seat	*ḳniw*	II,153
seclusion	*sštꜣ*	II,83
second	*mḥ-sn*	I,198
second	*sn-nw*	I,230
second (the)	*ky*	II,171
second	*sn-nw*	II,48
second month of *Šmw*	*pn-in*	I,148
second month of *ꜣḫt*	*pn-ipt*	I,148
second month of *Prt*	*mḫr*	I,201
second season	*prt*	I,151
secret	*imn*	I,30
secret	*hꜣrṯṯ*	I,286
secret	*ḫn*	I,361
secret	*ḫnr*	I,365
secret	*štꜣ*	II,138
secret place	*štꜣ*	II,138
secretly	*m-ṯꜣwt*	II,225
secretly	*sštꜣ*	II,83
secretly	*ṯꜣwt*	II,225
secrets	*imnyt*	I,30
secrets	*sštꜣ*	II,83
section	*sdt*	II,97
sections	*fdḳw*	I,166
secure	*wḏꜣ snb*	I,121
secure	*mni*	I,185
secure	*ḫw*	I,353
secure	*ḳb*	II,148
secure	*šsp*	II,135
secure	*šdi*	II,140
secure	*ṯs*	II,233
sedge bundles	*šmꜥt-ḫtꜣ*	II,123
seduce	*ṯꜣy-ḥꜥty*	II,224
see	*ptr*	I,159
see	*mꜣꜣ*	I,173
see	*nw*	I,229
see	*dgꜣ*	II,256
see it, see it (?)	*mks mks*	I,211
seed	*prt*	I,152
seed	*mw*	I,182
seed	*ḫmy*	I,361
seed	*ṯry*	II,231
seed (human)	*my(w)*	I,179
seed corn of emmer	*mymy*	I,180
seeing that	*ḫr r-ꜥ*	I,57
seeing that	*mi*	I,178
seeing that	*ḫr-r-ꜥ*	I,260
seek	*gmgm*	II,189
seek	*wḫꜣ*	I,109
seek out	*ptr*	I,159
seek out	*ḥḥy*	I,329
seek out	*ḏꜥr*	II,264
seer	*mꜣꜣ*	I,173
sehret-stone(?)	*shrt*	II,60
seize	*iṯi*	I,52
seize	*mḥ*	I,197
seize	*nḏr*	I,257
seize	*hꜣ(i)*	I,283
seize	*ḥꜣḳ*	I,299
seize	*ṯꜣy*	II,224
seize	*šfd*	II,121
seize	*tkšš*	II,221
seize upon	*šfꜥ*	II,120
sekty-bark	*skty*	II,88
select	*stp*	II,94
self	*n-ḥꜥw*	I,224
self	*r-ḥꜥt.*	I,263
self	*ḥꜥt*	I,301
self	*ḏt*	II,259
self	*ḏs*	II,274
self-bent rods	*ḏnr*	II,270
self-confident	*ꜥꜣ-ib*	I,60
self-controlled	*grw*	II,191
self-controlled	*tkn*	II,221
sell	*imi*	I,26
sell	*rdi*	I,281
sell	*swn*	II,19
sell	*šwy*	II,114
sell	*dit m šb*	II,116
sell for	*šsp*	II,136
selling	*šwyt*	II,114
semen	*my(w)*	I,179
semen	*mtwt*	I,213

semi-precious stones	*rpy*	I,270
send	*ii*	I,16
send	*iw*	I,18
send	*imi-ii*	I,26
send	*imi-in.tw*	I,26
send	*imi-iw*	I,27
send	*di in*	I,32
send	*issb*	I,47
send	*wḏi*	I,119
send	*hꜣb*	I,286
send	*di ḥn*	I,316
send	*sbi*	II,24
send	*di šm*	II,121
send forth	*wdi*	I,117
send greetings	*swḏꜣ-ib*	II,24
send off	*ḫpp*	I,355
send on one's way	*sbi*	II,25
send out	*šb*	II,116
send up	*sꜥr*	II,14
senet	*snt*	II,49
senet draughts	*snnt*	II,52
senility	*wgg-iꜣwt*	I,116
senility(?)	*tnw*	II,212
senior	*ꜥꜣ(i)*	I,59
senior	*smsw*	II,44
senior apprentices	*ḫrdw ꜥꜣyw*	I,388
sense	*ib*	I,22
sense	*ḥꜣty*	I,298
senseless	*iwty-ḥꜣty*	I,22
senseless	*iwty-ib*	I,22
senses	*šꜣrgꜣḥ*	II,109
senses	*šrgḥ*	II,133
sensible person	*rmṯ m-tꜣ-wnwt*	I,101
sentences	*ṯs*	II,234
sentry	*wršy*	I,106
separate	*ꜣbb*	I,5
separate	*iwd*	I,22
separate	*hf*	I,287
separate	*sḥr*	II, 64
separate	*tši*	II,219
separate	*ḏsr*	II,274
separate from	(see apart from)	
separated from	*pšn*	I,158
separation	*ꜣbw*	I,3
sepulcher	*nfr(t)*	I,237
sepulcher	*smꜣw*	II,39
serfs	*mrw*	I,194
serfs	*nḏt*	I,256
serfs	*smdt*	II,46
sergeant	*ḥty*	I,335
serious	*ꜥꜣ(i)*	I,59
serious	*dns*	II,251
sermet-brew	*srmt*	II,58
serpent	*hfꜣw*	I,309
servant	*sḏm-ꜥš*	I,79
servant	*bꜣk*	I,128
servant	*ḥm*	I,310
servant	*ḥmt*	I,311
servant	*sḏmy*	II,102
servant	*sḏm-ꜥš*	II,102
servant	*šmsw*	II,124
serve	*ꜥḥꜥ*	I,75
serve	*wꜥw*	I,94
serve	*bꜣk*	I,127
serve	*brk*	I,137
serve as pilot	*ꜥš-ḥꜣty*	I,79
servers	*mꜣdyw*	I,178
service	*hꜣy*	I,284
service	*ḥnw*	I,316
service	*šms*	II,125
servicemen	*wꜥw*	I,94
service-personnel	*smdt*	II,46
sesame oil	*nḥḥ*	I,244
set	*ḥtp*	I,336
set	*sb*	II,25
set	*grg*	II,192
set	*sš*	II,79
set	*smn*	II,42
set (on way)	*sꜥkꜣ*	II,16
set apart	*šm*	II,121
set apart	*ḏsr*	II,274
set aside	*ḫw-mk*	I,353
set down	*wꜣḥ*	I,89
set foot	*wḏi*	I,119
set foot	*dgs*	II,257
set forth	*wḏi*	I,119
set in order	*spd*	II,34
set of coffins	*wt-wꜣ*	I,116
set on record	*smn*	II,42
set out	*nmꜥ*	I,237
set out	*ḥn*	I,316
set out	*šm*	II,121
set sail	*nꜥy*	I,228
set up	*sꜥḥꜥ*	II,15
set up	*skꜣ*	II,84
set upon	*m-ḫrt-n*	I,170
setting	*disꜣ*	II,240
settle	*nh*	I,240
settle	*snṯ*	II,54
settled	*tks*	II,221
settlement	*grg*	II,193
settlement	*wḥt*	I,107
settlement	*dmi*	II,248
settlements	*grg*	II,193
seven	*sfḫw*	II,36
seventh	*mḥ-sfḫt*	II,36
seventh month	*rkḥ*	I,280
sever	*fdk*	I,166
several	*ḥmn*	I,313
severe	*ꜥꜣ(i)*	I,60
severe	*ḏri*	II,272

sexual intercourse	(see copulation)	
sexual partner	*nknk*	I,251
sexually excite	*hd*	I,293
shabby	*isy*	I,45
shade(?)	*šwbyt*	II,116
shadow	*ḫ3ybt*	I,345
shadow	*ḫ3b*	I,348
shadow	*šwt*	II,115
shadow	*šwbyt*	II,116
shaft	*ˁ*	I,58
shaft	*m3yt*	I,174
shake	*nwṯ*	I,232
shallows	*ṯst*	II,235
shalom	*šrm*	II,133
shape	*irw*	I,40
shape (vb.)	*pipi*	I,147
shape (vb.)	*ptḥ*	I,159
shape (vb.)	*grb*	II,191
shape(?)	*st*	II,2
share	*pš*	I,157
share	*ḫrt*	I,385
share	*dni(t)*	II,250
share (vb.)	*png*	I,149
share (vb.)	*pš*	I,157
share (vb.)	*dni*	II,249
share in	*ˁk*	I,80
share out	*dni*	II,249
sharp	*spd*	II,34
sharp	*dm*	II,247
sharpen	*dm*	II,247
sharply defined	*spd*	II,34
sharpness of tongue	*spd-ns*	II,34
shatter	*hd*	I,340
shave	*ḫˁk*	I,380
shave	*grb*	II,191
shawabti	*š3w3bti*	II,108
shawabti box	*itrt*	I,52
shawl	*mrw*	I,194
shawl	*dr*	II,252
shawl(?)	*rwḏ*	I,268
shawl(?)	*ḥry-kˁḥt*	I,326
she	*mtw*	I,213
she	*s*	II,1
she	*sy*	II,12
she who sang	*dd*	II,275
sheaves	*ḳniw*	II,153
shed	*ḫnw*	I,362
shed tears	*rmw*	I,270
sheen	*w(3)w(3)w*	I,88
sheen	*sšpt*	II,80
sheep	*siwt*	II,11
sheet	*ifd*	I,26
shell (vb.)	*hf*	I,287
shelter	*isbw*	I,46
shelter	*nh*	I,240
shelter (vb.)	*iwd*	I,22
shelter (vb.)	*sḫ3p*	II,61
shelters	*sibyn*	II,11
shepherd	*mniw*	I,186
shepherd	*mniw-siwt*	I,186
shepherd	*mniw siwt*	II,11
shield	*ikm*	I,50
shield	*ḳrˁ*	II,156
shield (vb.)	*ḫw*	I,353
shield bearer	*ḳny*	II,154
shield bearer	*ḳrˁw*	II,156
shift (vb.)	*ktkt*	II,180
shift (vb.)	*pnˁ*	I,148
shine	*wbn*	I,97
shine	*psḏ*	I,157
shine	*ḫˁi*	I,351
shine (vb.)	*swbḫ*	II,19
shine	*sḥḏ*	II,65
shine	*sti-mw*	II,91
ship	*imw*	I,29
ship	*ˁḥˁw*	I,76
ship	*wi3*	I,92
ship	*wsḫ*	I,112
ship	*br*	I,136
ship	*mnš*	I,189
ship	*skty*	II,88
ship	*sktt*	II,88
ship	*ḳr*	II,155
ship	*ḳrr*	II,157
ship	*kr*	II,175
ship for trade to Punt	*kbnt*	II,172
ship's bow	*ḥ3t*	I,296
ship's captain	*ḥry-wsḫt*	I,324
ship's mast	*nˁr*	I,228
ship's master	*ˁ3*	I,60
ship's part	*ityn*	I,53
ship's part	*ḏrˁt*	II,273
shipload	*sb*	II,25
shipmate	*imy-wsḫ*	I,27
shipment	*sḳdyt*	II,85
shipping trade	*ḫbr*	I,354
ships	*ḳwrw*	II,147
shipwrecked	*bg3*	I,142
shipwrights	*ḥmww*	I,313
shipyard	*wḫrt*	I,110
shoal	*m3st*	I,177
shoal	*ṯst*	II,235
shod	*tby*	II,203
shoot	*wdi*	I,117
shoot	*srḥ3t*	II,59
shoot	*srdd*	II,60
shoot	*sti*	II,91
shoot (plant)	*bkt*	I,141
shoots (plant)	*sbr*	II,28
shooting	*sšdw*	II,83

shooting mark	*dbt*	II,244
shooting star	*sšdw*	II,83
shore	*idb*	I,54
shore	*w(ꜣ)ḏb*	I,92
shore	*wḏb*	I,123
shore	*mꜣꜥ*	I,174
shore	*mryt*	I,193
shore	*npr(t)*	I,234
shore	*rwḏ*	I,268
shore	*ḫꜣpw*	I,348
shore	*spt*	II,31
short (deficient)	*gbi*	II,186
short (moment)	*kt*	II,179
shortcoming	*spp*	II,32
shorten	*ḫb*	I,354
shoulder	*rmn*	I,271
shoulder	*ḳꜥḥ*	II,146
shout	*hm*	I,287
shout (vb.)	*sgb*	II,89
shout for joy	*ḥꜥwy*	I,302
shouting	*bgꜣw*	I,142
shouting	*nhm*	I,241
show (the way)	*sšm*	II,80
show (vb.)	*sr*	II,56
show forth	*ḏꜣ*	II,259
show mercy	*ḥmr*	I,313
show off	*nsns*	I,249
shrewd	*ip-ib*	I,23
shrewd	*ip*	I,24
shrewd	*wḥꜥ*	I,108
shrewd	*wḥꜥ-ib*	I,108
shrewd one	*siꜣ*	II,11
shriek	*dniwt*	II,250
shriek (vb.)	*sgb*	II,89
shrine	*iwnn*	I,21
shrine	*ipt*	I,26
shrine	*itrt*	I,52
shrine	*pr-wr*	I,149
shrine	*ḫm*	I,360
shrine	*swḥt*	II,21
shrine	*ḳnby*	II,154
shrine	*kꜣr*	II,169
shrine	*gt*	II,183
shrine	*gꜣit*	II,183
shrine	*gt*	II,195
shrine	*tꜣyt*	II,199
shrine	*sḥ-nṯr*	II,61
shrine	*dbꜣr*	II,244
shrine of Sokar	*štꜣyt*	II,139
shrine(?)	*ḥbt*	I,307
shrine(?)	*sꜣḥ*	II,8
shrine	*tꜣ-nnt*	II,198
shrink back	*tnbḥ*	II,213
shrink in terror	*ḥfḏ*	I,310
shroud	*swḥt*	II,21
shroud	*tꜣyt*	II,199
shroud(?)	*swḥ*	II,21
shrub	*isbr*	I,46
shudder	*nš*	I,249
shuddering	*ḏꜣnn*	II,262
shuddering	*ḏnn*	II,270
siblings	*sn*	II,48
sick	*mr*	I,191
sick	*nḳm*	I,251
sick man	*mr*	I,191
sickness	*mnt*	I,184
sickness	*ḫꜣy(t)*	I,345
side	*wꜣ(t)*	I,87
side	*wꜣt*	I,88
side	*rit*	I,266
side	*rmn*	I,271
side	*gs*	II,194
side	*ḏr*	II,271
side boards	*ḏrw*	II,273
side with	*ꜥḥꜥ*	I,76
siege-mound	*ṯrr*	II,231
sieve	*m(t)rḫt*	I,215
sieve	*nḳrw*	I,251
sifi-oil	*sfr*	II,35
sifting vessel	*sḫnkt*	II,76
sight	*irt*	I,40
sight	*ptr*	I,159
sight	*mꜣꜣ*	I,173
sight	*gꜣwt*	II,184
signet ring	*ḫtm*	I,377
silence	*sgꜣ*	II,89
silence	*sgr*	II,90
silent	*gr*	II,190
silent one	*grw*	II,191
silly	*swgꜣ*	II,22
silly	*šꜣšꜣ*	II,109
silly	*šš*	II,137
silo	*ṯꜣrt*	II,227
silver	*r-ḫmt*	I,264
silver	*ḥḏ*	I,340
silver	*ḥḏ-m-ḥḏ*	I,341
silver-piece	*sniw*	II,49
silver-piece	*šꜥty*	II,112
similar	*m-mitt*	I,169
similar make	*stwt*	II,93
similar to	*r*	I,259
similarly	*mi-ḳd*	I,178
similarly	*m-mitt*	I,180
simultaneously	*n-sp*	II,30
sin	*isft*	I,47
sin	*btꜣ*	I,142
since	*yꜣ*	I,11
since	*m-šꜣꜥ*	I,171
since	*m-ḏr*	I,172
since	*n-ḏr*	I,225
since	*ḫft*	I,359
since	*šꜣꜥ*	II,107

since	r-šꜣꜥ	II,107
since	ḏr	II,270
since before	ḏr-ꜥ	II,271
since of old	ḫry-ḥꜣt	I,386
sinew	ḳbḥ	II,149
sing	ꜥnyny	I,69
sing	ḥsi	I,329
singer	ḥsy	I,330
singer	ḥst	I,331
singer	šmꜥy	II,123
singer	šmꜥyt	II,123
single	wꜥty	I,93
sink	mt	I,212
sink	hrp	I,291
sister	snt	II,48
sistrum player	sḫmyt	II,70
sit	ḥms	I,314
sit	snḏm	II,56
sit at ease	ḥms	I,314
sit down	snḏm	II,56
site	st mꜣꜣ	II,2
site	swꜣw	II,17
situated	snḏm	II,56
situation	sḫr	II,73
six great law courts	ḥwt	I,304
six-fold alloy	smꜣ	II,38
sixth	mḥ-siswt	II,12
sixth month	rkḥ	I,280
size	st	II,2
skein	ḥꜣpwti	I,299
skein of thread	šst	II,134
sketch	thnt	II,217
sketch	sš-ḳdwt	II,79
sketch(?)	dhnt	II,253
skewer(?)	gp	II,188
skiff	ṯrt	II,231
skill	ḥmt	I,311
skilled	ip-ib	I,24
skilled	wḥꜥ-ib	I,108
skilled	rḫ	I,275
skilled	hf	I,287
skilled	sšsꜣ	II,80
skilled	šfy	II,120
skilled	šsꜣ	II,134
skilled one	rḫ-ḫt	I,275
skin	inm	I,33
skin	ḥꜥt	I,301
skin	ḫnt	I,381
skin	sḏḥ	II,103
skin	šdw	II,141
skin condition	ꜥršn	I,73
skin disease	tmm.t	II,211
skin disease	tnmmt	II,213
skip	krs	II,176
skipper	nfw	I,235
skirmisher	mg(ꜣ)	I,212
skull	tbn	II,204
skull	ḏꜣ	II,259
sky	pt	I,145
sky	ḥry	I,324
sky	ḥrt	I,327
slab	smdt	II,46
slack	bꜣg	I,128
slack	bgꜣ	I,142
slack	nni	I,239
slacken	whs	I,107
slacken	nni	I,239
slacken	sbn	II,28
slackening	nnyt	I,239
slackness	wiꜣwiꜣ	I,92
slake	iꜥi	I,16
slander	ḥḏ	I,340
slander	ḫnw	I,363
slander	sḫwr	II,62
slanderer	wṯsy	I,117
slaughter	ꜥḏt	I,83
slaughter	wꜥwꜥ	I,94
slaughter	mꜣꜥ	I,174
slaughter	ḥms	I,314
slaughter	ḥnty	I,320
slaughter	ḫꜣyt	I,345
slaughter	ḫryt	I,371
slaughter	sft	II,36
slaughter	krt	II,177
slaughter	smꜣ	II,39
slaughter	šꜥt	II,110
slaughter	šꜥd	II,112
slaughter house	sḫwy	II,68
slaughter knife	ššꜣw	II,135
slaughterer	sky	II,86
slaughterer	ḥnty	I,320
slave	tp-ꜥnḫ	II,205
slave woman	ḥmt	I,311
slave-boy	ms-ḥm	I,204
slaves(?)	ḥmw-nsw	I,310
slay	fḫ	I,165
slay	ḥms	I,314
slay	ḫdb	I,389
slay	sft	II,36
slay	smꜣ	II,39
slayers	ḫꜣbb	I,348
sledge	wnš	I,103
sleep	ḳd(t)	II,161
sleep	ḳdd	II,
sleep (vb.)	ꜣꜥꜥ	I,1
sleep (vb.)	ꜥꜥw	I,62
sleep (vb.)	ꜥwn	I,63
sleep (cause to)	sḳdd	II,85
sleep (vb.)	sḏr	II,102
sleep together	sḏr	II,102
sleep with	nk	I,251
sleep with	sḏr	II,103

sleeping mat	*sḏrt*	II,103
sleeves	*ish*	I,47
slender	*šmꜥ*	II,123
slice	*fdḳ*	I,166
slide	*ḥbrbr*	I,308
slight	*wni*	I,101
slip	*wh(i)*	I,106
slip by	*ꜥḳ*	I,80
slippery ground	*ḫrḳtt*	I,373
slit (vb.)	*wgs*	I,115
slope	*isp*	I,46
sloth	*bgꜣ*	I,142
sluggish	*iꜣ iꜣ*	I,11
sluggish	*wiꜣwiꜣ*	I,92
slumber	*ḳd(t)*	II,161
slumber (vb.)	*ꜥꜥw*	I,62
small	*nḏs*	I,257
small	*kt*	II,179
small	*šwꜣ*	II,115
small	*šri*	II,132
small animals	*tp-n-iꜣwt*	II,205
small bird	*ḫpwt*	I,355
small board	*pḫꜣ*	I,154
small cattle	*ꜥwt*	I,62
small cattle	*ꜥnḫ*	I,71
small fowl	*šfw*	II,120
small game	*tp-n-iꜣwt*	II,205
small ones	*kt*	II,179
small religious structure	*gs-pr*	II,194
small window	*ws*	I,110
smaragdus	*wꜣḏ*	I,91
smart	*ꜣḫ*	I,7
smart (be)	*sꜣr*	II,8
smart	(see clever)	
smash	*wšwš*	I,114
smash	*sd*	II,98
smash	(see crush)	
smear	*wrḥ*	I,105
smell	*ḫnm*	I,363
smell	*šp*	II,118
smelling	*sty*	II,91
smelly	*šns*	II,131
smelly(?)	*šꜣnš*	II,109
smelt	*wḏḥ*	I,123
smelting furnace	*ꜥḏnt*	I,84
smite	*ir iḫt r*	I,39
smite	*ptpt*	I,158
smite	*ḥwi*	I,303
smite	*ḥwfn*	I,305
smite	*ḥfn*	I,309
smite	*sḥr*	II,64
smite	*sḳr*	II,84
smooth	*ꜣꜥꜥ*	I,1
smooth	*nꜥꜥ*	I,228
smooth (vb.)	*stwt*	II,94
smooth cloth	*nꜥꜥ-sšr-rwḏ*	II,83
smooth floor	*ḫrḳtt*	I,373
smooth yarn	*nꜥꜥ nwt*	I,228
smooth yarn	*nwt*	I,231
sm-priest	*sm*	II,37
smuggle	*ḫn*	I,381
snake	*r*	I,259
snake	*ḥfꜣw*	I,309
snake	*ḥrrt*	I,328
snake	*ḏdft*	II,277
snakes (speckled)	*sꜣb*	II,8
snap	*mšfy*	I,208
snare	*pḫꜣ*	I,154
snare	*ḥgꜣi*	I,335
snare	*sḫt*	II,75
snare (vb.)	*sḫbḫ*	II,68
snatch	*ḫnp*	I,363
sneak-thief	*nhr*	I,241
sneer	*piṯꜣ*	I,147
snow	*srḳw*	II,59
so	*kꜣ*	II,166
so and so	*mn*	I,184
so much	*rsy*	I,277
so. . .as	*ḫy...ḫy*	I,351
soak	*tḫb*	II,218
soaking	*ḏbg*	II,268
sob	*sbḥ*	II,28
sobbing(?)	*biꜣk*	I,131
socle (of temple)	*p*	I,145
sodom apple tree	*mꜣtt*	I,177
soft	*gꜣḥ*	II,185
soft(?)	*bdš*	I,143
soil	*ꜣḥt*	I,7
soil	*iwtn*	I,22
soil	*sꜣt*	II,10
soil (vb.)	*sꜣt*	II,10
solar disk	*itn*	I,51
soldier	*ꜥnḫ-n-mšꜣ*	I,70
soldier	*wꜥw*	I,94
soldier	*s n mšꜥ*	II,1
soldier scribe	*mhr*	I,196
soldiers	*mnfꜣt*	I,187
soldiers	*nꜥrn*	I,229
sole (of foot)	*kp*	II,172
sole of foot	*ṯbw(t)*	II,228
sole (of sandal)	*rd*	I,281
soles of feet	*ṯbw(t)*	II,228
sole one	*wꜥ*	I,93
solemn	*ꜥꜣ(i)*	I,60
solid	*smn*	II,42
solve	*wḥꜥ*	I,107
some	*nhy*	I,240
some	*nkt*	I,251
some(?)	*wn*	I,100
son	*pꜣ*	I,145
son	*ms*	I,203

son	*sꜣ*	II,3
son	*šri*	II,132
son-in-law	*sꜣ*	II,3
Son of Re	*sꜣ Rꜥ*	II,3
songs	*ḥst*	I,330
songstress	*šmꜥyt*	II,123
soothe	*ḥtp*	I,336
soothing	*hr*	I,290
sore	*ḫsd*	I,375
sorrow	*ihm*	I,43
sorrow	*mr*	I,191
sorrow	*ḥꜣ-ib*	I,295
sorrow	*šnn*	II,131
sorrow	*gꜣs*	II,185
sorrow(?)	*mꜣwt*	I,176
sorry	*ihm*	I,43
soul	*bꜣ*	I,125
soul	*kꜣ*	II,165
souls	*bꜣw*	I,125
sound	*wḏꜣ*	I,120
sound eye	*wḏꜣ(t)*	I,122
sounding poles(?)	*smꜣꜥw*	II,40
souse	*tꜣḥ*	II,199
south	*m-ḫnt*	I,170
south	*rsy*	I,277
south	*rst*	I,278
south (go) (vb.)	*ḫnti*	I,366
south land	*tꜣ-rsy*	I,277
south land	*tꜣ šmꜥw*	II,122
South of his Wall (Ptah)	*inb rsy*	I,33
south wind	*rsw*	I,278
south-east	*rsy-iꜣbty*	I,277
southbound	*šmꜥw*	II,122
southern	*rsy*	I,277
southern	*ḫnty*	I,366
southern province	*ꜥ-rsy*	I,58
southerners	*šmꜥyw*	II,122
southerners	*rsyw*	I,278
southerners	*rstyw*	I,278
southward	*m-ḫnt*	I,170
southward	*m-ḫnti*	I,366
south-west	*rsy-imnty*	I,277
sovereign	*ity*	I,51
sow	*ḫḏr*	I,378
sow	*šꜣ*	II,105
space	*km*	II,173
space	*ꜥḥꜥw*	I,77
spacious	*swsḫ*	II,22
span (of horses)	*ḥtr*	I,338
span (of life)	*wrš*	I,105
span (vb.)	*sbi*	II,25
span of chariotry	*ꜥ-n-ḥtri*	I,57
spare	*šmꜥ*	II,123
spare (vb.)	*wꜣḥ*	I,90
spare (vb.)	*spi*	II,31
spare (vb.)	*srf*	II,58
spare time	*wšꜣ*	I,113
sparkle	*brḳ*	I,137
sparrow	*ṯtw*	II,237
sparrow(?)	*šfw*	II,120
spat upon	*tpi*	II,207
speak	*mdw*	I,216
speak a foreign language	*ꜣꜥꜥ*	I,2
speak about	*wfs*	I,99
speak flatteringly of	*swnwn*	II,20
speaker of the army	*wḥm-n-pꜣ-mšꜥ*	I,109
speakers	*ḏd*	II,275
spear	*mꜥbꜣ*	I,181
spear	*niw*	I,226
spear fish(?)	*ḏꜥwt*	II,264
species of red ochre	*ṯmḥy*	II,229
specification	*wp*	I,97
specify	*wp*	I,97
speech	*mdt*	I,217
speech	*ns*	I,247
speech	*ḫnw*	I,362
speech	*tpw-r*	IV,83
speech, pointed	*nsḳ*	I,249
speeches	*ṯs*	II,234
speechless(?)	*dgm*	II,257
speed(?) (vb.)	*ṯꜣ-mri*	II,226
speedily	*ꜣs*	I,9
spell	*r*	I,259
spells	*r-ḏdw*	I,265
spelt	*bty*	I,143
spend	*skm*	II,87
spend (time)	*iri*	I,38
spend (time)	*sbi*	II,25
spend all day	*wrš*	I,105
spend the night	*sḏr*	II,103
spend time	*wrš*	I,105
spew	*bši*	I,140
spew out	*tpi*	II,207
sphere	*itn*	I,51
sphinx	*ḥw*	I,303
sphinxes	*šspw*	II,80
spike	*ḫꜣiw*	I,344
spike	*ḫꜥw*	I,352
spike	*srt*	II,57
spikes	*ḫnr*	I,365
spill	*gꜣš*	II,185
spirit	*ꜣḫ*	I,7
spirit (voracious)	*ꜥḫm*	I,78
spirited	*spd*	II,34
spiritless	*wiꜣwiꜣ*	I,92
spit	*bši*	I,140
spit	*pgs*	I,158

spit forth	*išš*	I,48
spittoon	*pgs*	I,158
splash	*sms*	II,44
spleen	*nš(t)*	I,249
splendid	*sbḳ*	II,29
splendid (make)	*sikr*	II,12
splendid	*šps*	II,118
splendor	*fꜣw*	I,164
splendor	*sšpt*	II,80
split	*pḫꜣ*	I,154
split (vb.)	*sꜣw*	II,7
split open	*pḫꜣ*	I,154
spoil	*iḳ*	I,49
spoil	*wh(i)*	I,106
spoil	*ḥwrꜥ*	I,306
spoil	*sngꜣ*	II,54
spoil (n.)	*ḥꜣḳw*	I,300
spoilage	*iḳw*	I,49
spoiled	*stf*	II,95
spokes	*mꜣwt*	I,176
spokesman	*wḥm*	I,109
sport	*sḫmḫ-ib*	II,71
sporting	*sbi*	II,27
sportsmen	*mḥw*	I,199
spot	*st*	II, 2
spread	*ḫnti*	I,366
spread	*sḥr*	II,64
spread	*sš*	II,79
spread (a bed)	*sšši*	II,83
spread abroad	*bꜥḥ*	I,132
spread abroad	*sr*	II,57
spread ointment	*swrḥ*	II,21
spread out	*iꜥb*	I,17
spread out	*pš*	I,157
spread out	*sš*	II,79
spread righteousness	*ḏꜣ-mꜣꜥt*	II,259
sprig	*srḥꜣt*	II,59
spring	*ꜥyn*	I,62
spring	*ḫnmt*	I,384
springer	*ktkt*	II,180
springer	*stpw*	II,96
sprinkle	*iwḥ*	I,21
sprinkle water	*sti*	II,91
spurn	*ṯhr*	II,232
spurt	*pꜣy*	I,146
spy	*ḥꜣptyw*	I,299
spy on	*gmḥ*	II,189
squad	*stnw*	II,95
squalor(?)	*ḥtꜣw*	I,335
squash	*dnrg*	II,251
squeeze	*gꜣw*	II,183
squint	*ḥnr*	I,319
sshrt-cake	*sšrt*	II,83
stability	*ḏd*	II,276
stable	*ihy*	I,42
stable	*iḥ*	I,43
stable	*mḏt*	I,219
stable	*šmmt*	II,124
stable	*ḏd*	II,276
stable master	*ḥry-iḥw*	I,324
stable master	*ḥry-iḥ*	I,325
stack	*wꜣḥ*	I,89
staff	*bꜣkt*	I,128
staff	*m(ꜣ)ḳr*	I,177
staff	*mdw*	I,218
staff	*ḥꜥw*	I,301
staff	*ḫt-šḳr*	I,375
staff	*smdt*	II,46
staff	*šwbt*	II,115
staff	*šbd*	II,117
staff	*šti*	II,139
staff of people	*ḳwr*	II,147
stag	*iꜣywr*	I,12
stagger	*wtmtm*	I,116
stagger	*sbn*	II,28
stairs	*rdw*	I,282
stairway	*r-ꜥ-rdwy*	I,260
stairway	*rwḏw*	I,269
stairwell	*ꜥt-pꜣ-rꜥ*	I,59
stake	*ḫt*	I,375
stake	*tp-ḫt*	II,206
stake	*tpt*	II,208
stalks	*isw*	I,45
stalks	*srḥꜣt*	II,59
stall	*ihy*	I,42
stallion	*ibry*	I,24
stalls	*mḏt*	I,219
stamp	*hꜣb-m-rd*	I,286
stamp	*skḥ*	II,85
stand	*ꜥḥꜥ*	I,75
stand	*sꜥḥꜥ*	II,15
stand against	*sꜥḥꜥ*	II,15
stand by	*ꜥḥꜥ*	I,75
stand fast	*smn*	II,42
stand fast	*mn*	I,183
stand firm	*ꜥmdy*	I,67
stand firm	*smn*	II,42
stand still	*ꜥḥꜥ*	I,75
stand up to	*ꜥḥꜥ*	I,75
standard bearer	*ṯꜣy sryt*	II,58
standard bearer	*ṯꜣy-sryt*	II,225
standing water	*mw-ḥms*	I,183
standpoint	*st ꜥḥꜥ*	II,2
stanza	*ḥwt*	I,304
star	*sbꜣ*	II,25
starboard	*imy-wrt*	I,27
starboard	*tꜣ-wr*	II,198
stare	*gmḥ*	II,189
stare	*dgꜣ*	II,256
starry firmament	*sšsꜣt*	II,83
starry firmament	*šsꜣt*	II,135

start	*fꜣy*	I,163
start	*ḥꜣt*	I,296
start	*šꜣꜥ*	II,107
start (a journey)	*šsp*	II,136
state	*r-ꜥ*	I,260
state	*ḫrt*	I,371
state	*ḳi*	II,146
state	*sḫr*	II,73
state	*sšm*	II,81
state of affairs	*ꜥ*	I,57
statement	*wšbt*	I,114
statement	*wdt-r*	I,117
statement	*ḏd*	II,275
station (oneself)	*smn*	II,42
statue	*rpyt*	I,270
statue	*rḫ.n.f*	I,275
statue	*ḥsy*	I,330
statue	*ẖnty*	I,385
statue	*smꜣ*	II,39
statue	*sšm*	II,80
statues	*ḫprw*	I,357
statues	*snn*	II,51
statues	*twt*	II,203
statutes	*hp*	I,287
stave	*ꜥwnt*	I,63
staves	*ẖbyt*	I,381
stay	*ꜥḥꜥ*	I,75
stay	*mnt*	I,185
stay	*ḥms*	I,314
stay	*ḥtp*	I,336
stay	*ḫꜣꜥ*	I,347
stay	*smn*	II,41
stay aloof from	*dni*	II,249
stay put	*ḥms*	I,314
stay put	*smn*	II,42
steadfast	*rwḏ*	I,269
steadfast	*smn*	II,42
steal	*iṯi*	I,52
steal	*iṯꜣ*	I,53
steal	*ꜥwꜣi*	I,63
steal	*ṯꜣy*	II,224
stealthily(?)	*n-ḏꜣyt*	I,225
stealthily(?)	*hrṯṯ*	I,292
steam	*iꜣdt*	I,15
steed	*gꜣwy*	II,184
steed	*gw*	II,186
steeds	*rks*	I,280
steeds	*ḥtr*	I,338
steeped in	*tḫb*	II,218
steer	*mni*	I,185
steer	*ḥm*	I,310
steer (laws)	*mni*	I,185
steer off course	*sbn*	II,28
steering oar	*wsr*	I,111
steering oar	*ḥmy(t)*	I,312
stela	*ꜥḥꜥ*	I,76
stela	*wḏ*	I,120
step	*ḫnd*	I,368
step by step	*nmtt*	I,238
step out	*sg*	II,88
stepmother	*ii*	I,16
stepmother	*mwt-iit-msy*	I,183
steps	*rdw*	I,282
stern	*pḥwy*	I,153
steward	*imy-r pr*	I,28
stick	*ꜥ-n-ḫt*	I,57
stick	*bḏn*	I,143
stick	*pgꜣ*	I,158
stick	*mdw*	I,218
stick	*šwbt*	II,115
stick	*gbw*	II,187
stick (vb.)	*dmi*	II,248
sticks	*pḫꜣ*	I,154
sticks	*ḏꜥdd*	II,265
stiff	*nḫt*	I,246
stiffen	*nḫt*	I,246
stifled	*nty*	I,253
stigmatized	*tks*	II,221
still	*ꜥn(n)*	I,68
still	*m-r-ꜥ*	I,169
still	*gr*	II,190
still	*gr(t)*	II,191
still (vb.)	*stm*	II,95
sting	*psḥ*	I,156
sting	*nḥs*	I,244
sting	*ḏdb*	II,277
stink	*ḫnš*	I,366
stir	*ktkt*	II,180
stir up	*nw*	I,230
stir up	*ḫws*	I,354
stir up	*sḫnš*	II,71
stir up	*sḫnw*	II,75
stock	*šꜣbd*	II,109
stockade	*ssw*	II,76
stocks	*pḫꜣt*	I,154
stomach	*ẖt*	I,379
stone	*inr*	I,34
stone	*bḥs*	I,138
stone	*mnhyw*	I,188
stone	*sꜣbwy*	II,108
stone object	*dp*	II,246
stone patch work	*bꜣk sꜣḳti*	I,128
stone worker	*ṯꜣy-bš*	II,224
stone-breaking	*ḳḥ*	II,158
stonecutter	*nšdy*	I,250
stone mason	*sꜣḳti*	II,9
stonemason	*ḫrty-nṯr*	I,254
stonemason	*ḥmww*	I,313
stonemason	*ẖrty*	I,387
stonemason	*ḫrty-nṯr*	I,388
stone-patcher	*sꜣḳti*	II,9
stones	*ꜥnr*	I,69

stop	*ꜣb*	I,3
stop	*isḳ*	I,48
stop	*ꜥḥꜥ*	I,75
stop	*wꜣḥ*	I,89
stop	*wḥꜥ*	I,107
stop	*spḥ*	II,33
stop	*smn*	II,42
stop	*gr*	II,190
stop	*šnꜥ*	II,129
stop (fighting)	*sd*	II,98
stop at	*smn-ḥr*	II,42
stop up	*ḏbꜣ*	II,266
stop up	*šr*	II,131
stopped	*dni*	II,249
stopping place	*ḫnw*	I,362
store (vb.)	*wꜣḥ*	I,89
storehouse	*wḏꜣ*	I,121
storehouse	*šmyt*	II,122
storehouse	*šmmt*	II,124
storehouse	*šnꜥ*	II,128
storekeeper	*šnꜥ*	II,129
storeroom	*wḏꜣ*	I,121
storeroom	*šꜥy(t)*	II,111
stores	*ꜥḥꜥw*	I,76
stork(?)	*ḏnḏn*	II,270
storm	*iꜣdt*	I,15
storm	*ḳri*	II,156
storm	*ḏꜥ*	II,264
storm	*šnꜥ*	II,129
storm	*ḏꜥ*	II,264
storm (vb.)	*hsmḳ*	I,292
storm (vb.)	*šni*	II,128
storming	*nšny*	I,250
storming	*ṯꜣw*	II,226
stormy lake	*gsm*	II,194
story	*mdt*	I,217
story	*ḥr*	I,320
story	*smiw*	II,41
story	*sḫr*	II,73
stout	*wmt*	I,100
stout	*sḫm*	II,70
stout	*ḏri*	II,272
stout warriors	*wmt*	I,100
stouthearted	*mn-ib*	I,23
stouthearted	*mn-ib*	I,184
stow	*wꜣḥ*	I,89
stow(?)	*ḫnr*	I,365
stowed	*mn*	I,183
straight	*ꜥḳꜣ*	I,81
straight (be)	*mḫꜣ*	I,201
straight	*mt*	I,213
straight away	*rd*	I,280
straight away	*ḥpt*	I,309
straight on	*ḥr-(n)-ḥr*	I,322
straight up	*m-dwn*	II,243
straightaway	*ḥr-r-ꜥ*	I,322

straightforward	*mt*	I,213
strainer	*m(t)rḫt*	I,215
strainer	*nḳrw*	I,251
strange	*ḏrḏr*	II,273
stranger	*ḳri*	II,156
stranger	*ḏrḏr*	II,273
strangers	*ḫppw*	I,355
strangers	*kꜣwy*	II,166
strap	*istn*	I,48
strap	*ꜥgs*	I,82
straps	*ḫꜥr*	I,353
straps (fabric)	*krṯ*	II,177
straw	*dḥꜣ*	II,254
straw(?)	*ḏꜣis*	II,261
stream	*ybr*	I,24
stream	*nhr*	I,241
stream	*ḥmkꜣti*	I,314
stream	*ḫd*	I,378
stream	*gr*	II,191
stream (vb.)	*ḥwi*	I,303
stream down	*ṯtf*	II,237
street	*iwyt*	I,18
street	*ḫꜣrw*	I,349
strength	*ꜣꜥy*	I,1
strength	*bꜣw*	I,125
strength	*pḥty*	I,154
strength	*nḫt*	I,246
strength	*rd*	I,280
strengthen	*swsr*	II,22
strengthen	*snḫt*	II,53
strenuously	*ḏri*	II,272
stretch	*ꜣw(i)*	I,2
stretch	*pḏ*	I,160
stretch	*sš*	II,79
stretch (n.)	*ꜣw(t)*	I,3
stretch apart	*sdwnt*	II,98
stretch out	*bnbn*	I,134
stretch out	*pd*	I,160
stretch out	*ḥdb*	I,340
stretch out	*swsḫ*	II,22
stretch out	*ḳḏḏ*	II,163
stretch out	*dwn*	II,243
stretch out	*sḏr*	II,103
stretch wide	*swsḫ*	II,22
stretcher (of bows)	*dmꜣt*	II,248
strictly	*ḏri*	II,272
stride	*wstn*	I,113
stride	*nmtt*	I,238
strife	*sḫwn*	II,68
strike	*wšwš*	I,114
strike	*ḥwi*	I,303
strike down	*ḳbḳb*	II,149
striking force	*ꜣt*	I,1
string	*mḫꜣ*	I,201
string	*nwt*	I,231
string	*ḥsꜣ*	I,332

strip (vb.)	*ḳḳ*	II,159
strip off	*srẖ*	II,59
stripling	*mnḥ*	I,188
stripling	*nẖn*	I,245
stripling	*ḥwn*	I,306
stripling	*sfy*	II,35
strips	*pry*	I,151
strive	*pss*	I,156
strive	*ḏnn*	II,270
strokes	*sẖ*	II,66
stroll (vb.)	*ḳdi*	II,161
stroll (vb.)	*stwt*	II,94
stroll about (vb.)	*swtwt*	II,23
strolling	*swtwt*	II,23
strong	*wsr*	I,111
strong	*wḏꜣ ib*	I,121
strong	*pḥty*	I,154
strong	*nꜥš*	I,229
strong	*nẖt*	I,245
strong	*ḳni*	II,152
strong	*kh*	II,177
strong	*tnr*	II,213
strong (vb.)	*sẖm*	II,69
strong ale	*ḏsr*	II,275
strong arm	*ẖpš*	I,357
strong man	*nẖt*	I,246
strong people	*sḏrw*	II,103
strong smelling beer	*sbr*	II,28
strong-armed	*ṯmꜣ-ꜥ*	II,229
stronghold	*mktr*	I,212
stronghold	*nmty*	I,238
strongholds	*nẖtw*	I,246
stucco (vb.)	*sḳḥ*	II,85
stuck	*mtn*	I,214
student	*ẖry-ꜥ*	I,387
stuff	*nkt*	I,252
stumble	*ṯrp*	II,231
stunt growth	*ḏꜣ-rd*	II,259
stupefied	*swgꜣ*	II,22
stupefied	*sgꜣ*	II,89
sturdy	*rwḏ*	I,269
subdue	*wꜥf*	I,95
subdue	*ḥn*	I,315
subdue	*dr*	II,252
subject to	*ẖrp*	I,372
subjects	*bꜣkt*	I,128
subjects	*smdt*	II,46
subjugate	*ḥnbs*	I,318
subjugate	*ḳnb*	II,154
sublime	*ꜥꜣ(i)*	I,59
submerge	*hrp*	I,291
submissive	*ẖr-mw*	I,182
submissiveness	*mḥy*	I,198
submit	*ꜥš*	I,78
submit	*wꜣḥ*	I,89
submit (self)	*hn*	I,288
subordinates	*smdt*	II,46
subsequently	*ḥr-sꜣ*	I,323
subsequently	*ḥr-sꜣ*	II,5
subside	*ꜥn(n)*	I,68
subside	*ꜥẖm*	I,78
substantiate	*sḏfꜣ-tr*	II,101
substitute	*ḏbꜣ*	II,266
substitutes	*iwꜣit*	I,19
substitution	*šb(t)*	II,116
subtract	*ẖbꜣ*	I,354
succeed	*ẖpr*	I,356
succeed	*spr*	II,32
succeed (to someone)	*šsp*	II,135
succeed in	*rẖ*	I,275
success	*rwḏ*	I,269
success be with me	*ẖpr-wn m-di.i*	I,356
successful	*wꜣḏ*	I,91
successful	*mrd*	I,195
successor	*sty*	II,3
successors	*ẖprw*	I,357
succor	*šrš*	II,133
such	*mitt*	I,180
such and such	*ḥmn*	I,313
such as...so	*mi-kd..mi-kd*	I,178
suck	*itḥ*	I,52
suckle	*snḳ*	II,54
suckle	*šdi*	II,140
sudden blindness	*snrt*	II,52
sue for peace	*šrm*	II,133
suffer	*iꜣd*	I,15
suffer	*nḳm*	I,251
suffer	*šni*	II,127
suffer	*šsp*	II,135
sufferer(?)	*šny*	II,127
sugar	*inw*	I,32
suitable	*šꜣw*	II,108
sulpher	*kbrt*	II,172
summarize	*sḥwy*	II,62
summary	*sḥwy*	II,62
summer	*šmw*	II,123
summit	*rš*	I,278
summit	*dhnt*	II,253
summit	*ḏꜣḏꜣ*	II,263
summon	*ꜥš*	I,78
summon together	*thm*	II,216
sun	*itn*	I,51
sun	*rꜥ*	I,266
sun	*šw*	II,113
sun disk	*itn*	I,51
sun folk	*ḥnmmt*	I,318
sun people	*ḥnmmt*	I,318
sun shade	*sryt*	II,58
sun shade	*šwt*	II,114
sun-bark	*sktt*	II,88

sun-beams	*sḥḏ*	II,65
sunder	*fdḳ*	I,166
sunlight	*šw*	II,113
sunshade of Re	*šwt-Rꜥ*	II,115
sunshine	*ꜣḫwt*	I,8
superbly	*m-ḥꜣw-ḥr nfr*	I,296
superintendent	*ꜣṯ*	I,10
superintendent	*imy-r*	I,27
superintendent of the royal harim	*imy-r ipt-nsw*	I,28
superior	*ḥry*	I,323
superiors	*ḥwtyw*	I,305
superiors	*ḫrp*	I,372
supervise	*nw*	I,229
supervision	*st ḥr*	II,3
supervision of	*r-ḥꜣt*	I,296
supervision of	*ḥr-ꜥwy*	I,322
supervisor	*ḥy*	I,300
supervisors	*wḥm*	I,109
supplication	*snmḥ*	II,51
supplicator	*šny*	II,127
supplies	*ꜣḫwt*	I,8
supplies	*rsf*	I,278
supply	*ꜥpr*	I,65
supply	*ꜥrꜥr*	I,72
supply	*bꜥḥ*	I,132
supply	*mḥ-ḏrt*	I,198
supply	*ḫrt*	I,385
supply	*sdbḥ*	II,98
supply	*sḏfꜣ(y)*	II,1000
supply with offerings	*sḏfꜣ(y)*	II,100
support (n.)	*wḫꜣ*	I,110
support (n.)	*nḫt*	I,246
support (vb.)	*rhn*	I,274
support (vb.)	*sꜥnḫ*	II,14
support (vb.)	*dḫꜣ*	II,254
supports	*ꜥmd*	I,67
supports	*sṯs*	II,97
supports (of heaven)	*sḫnwt*	II,71
suppress	*mni*	I,185
supreme chief	*r-ḥry*	I,264
surely	*mk*	I,210
surely	*smwn*	II,41
surface (of stone)	*sꜣ*	II,5
surface plane	*ḏꜣḏꜣwt*	II,263
surge	*ṯtf*	II,237
surge (of water)	*sꜣ*	II,5
surpass	*iṯi*	I,52
surpass	*sbi*	II,25
surpass	*sn*	II,46
surpass	*snny*	II,52
surpluses	*prw*	I,151
surround	*inḥ*	I,35
surround	*pḫr*	I,155
surround	*šni*	II,126
surround	*ḳdi*	II,161
surrounding walls	*ṯsmw*	II,236
survey	*ipw*	I,25
survey	*šnw*	II,127
survive (vb.)	*spi*	II,31
survivor	*ḥry-tꜣ*	I,326
survivor	*spyt*	II,31
suspend	*ꜥḫ*	I,77
sustain	*sꜥnḫ*	II,14
sustenance	*ꜥ-n-ꜥnḫ*	I,57
sustenance	*ꜥnḫ(w)*	I,70
sustenance	*r-ꜥ-ꜥnḫ*	I,260
sustenance	*kꜣw*	II,166
sustenance	*drpw*	II,252
sustenance	*ḏfꜣw*	II,268
swallow	*ꜥm*	I,65
swallow	*sꜥm*	II,14
swallow	*ṯwṯw*	II,227
swallow(?) (n.)	*mnt*	I,184
swamp	*bwꜣt*	I,133
swampy lake	*ḥn*	I,316
swampy lake(?)	*ḥnw*	I,317
swan(?)	*ꜥḫy*	I,77
swan(?)	*ḏnḏn*	II,270
sway	*st ḥr*	II,3
swear	*ꜥrḳ*	I,73
swear	*sḏfꜣ-tr*	II,101
swear (oath)	*iri*	I,37
sweating	*nḫf*	I,245
sweet	*bnr*	I,135
sweet	*nḏm*	I,256
sweet fig	*db*	II,243
sweet melon	*idnrg*	I,54
sweet melon	*dnrg*	II,251
sweetness	*bnr*	I,135
swell (vb.)	*sḫny*	II,71
swell up	*šfšf*	II,120
swelling	*sḫn*	II,71
swelling	*šfšf*	II,120
swerve	*hskt*	I,292
swerve	*sn*	II,47
swift (be)	*pḥrr*	I,154
swift (be)	*nsns*	I,249
swift (be)	*ḫyḫy*	I,351
swift	*ḫḫ*	I,373
swift	*šrš*	II,133
swift(?)	*nsns*	I,249
swift-stepped	*pd-nmtt*	I,160
swine	*šꜣ*	II,105
swollen	*bꜣkꜣ*	I,128
swollen	*bk*	I,141
sword	*ḥrp*	I,328
sword	*ḫpš*	I,357
sword	*spꜣ*	II,32
sword	*sft*	II,36

sword	*dm(t)*	II,247
sword (short)	*ḥrp*	I,328
sword bearer(?)	*ḫpšy*	I,358
sworn testimony	*hꜣy*	I,285
sycamore	*nh(ꜣ)t*	I,240
sycamore fig	*kꜣy*	II,167
sympathetic	*ỉm(ꜣ)*	I,29
Syrian	*ḫꜣry*	I,349
Syrian dignitaries	*nhry*	I,241
syrup(?)	*ḫww*	I,354

T

tabernacle(?)	*sšmw*	II,81
table	*mšr*	I,209
table of offerings	*ḫꜣwt*	I,346
tablet	*ꜥnw*	I,69
tablet	*ꜥrt*	I,72
tablet	*ḥtp*	I,337
taboo(?)	*bwt*	I,133
tabular document	*snn-s-sd*	II,52
tackle	*ṯnfyt*	II,230
tail	*sd*	II,97
take	*iṯi*	I,52
take	*iṯꜣ*	I,53
take	*mḥ*	I,197
take	*nḏr*	I,257
take	*šsp*	II,135
take	*ṯꜣy*	II,224
take (a wife)	*iri*	I,38
take a breath	*ssny*	II,77
take a walk	*swtwt*	II,23
take anew	*wḥm*	I,108
take as a friend	*snsn*	II,54
take away	*iṯi*	I,52
take away	*nḥm*	I,243
take away	*šdi*	II,140
take back	*šsp*	II,135
take booty	*kfꜥ*	II,173
take captive	*ḥꜣḳ*	I,299
take captive	*kfꜥ*	II,173
take care	*ib*	I,22
take care	*ib r.k*	I,22
take care	*sꜣw*	II,6
take care of	*ꜣty*	I,9
take care of	*mḥ*	I,197
take care of	*nw*	I,229
take charge of	*nw*	I,229
take cognizance	*ꜥm*	I,66
take counsel	*wꜣwꜣ*	I,88
take counsel	*nḏnḏ*	I,257
take counsel	*šsꜣ*	II,135
take heart	*smn-ib*	II,42
take heed of me!	*sꜣw*	II,6
take hold of	*šsp*	II,135
take lodging	*ḳꜣi*	II,143
take note	*rḫ*	I,275
take notice of	*sḏm*	II,101
take offense	*šni*	II,127
take over	*šsp*	II,135
take part in	*smꜣ*	II,38
take pleasure	*shr-ib*	I,23
take pleasure	*shr-ib*	II,60
take pleasure	*hꜣ-ib*	I,284
take pleasure	*hr-ib*	I,290
take pleasure	*shr-ib*	II,60

take pleasure	*ḏꜣy-ḥr*	II,261
take possession of	*mḥ*	I,197
take possession of	*sḫm*	II,69
take recreation	*sḏꜣ*	II,100
take shelter	*kꜣp*	II,168
take steps	*dgꜣ*	II,256
take temporary residence	*ḳꜣi*	II,143
take their own lives	*mt*	I,212
take thought	*ib*	I,22
take thought	*wꜣwꜣ*	I,88
take under coercion	*ḥwrꜥ*	I,306
take up (a case)	*iri*	I,38
tale	*sḏd*	II,104
talk	*ḫnw*	I,362
talk about	*wfs*	I,99
talker	*md(w)tyw*	I,218
tallow	*ꜥḏ*	I,83
tallow	*sgnn*	II,89
tally(?)keeper	*ḥry-wḏb*	I,324
talon	*ꜥnt*	I,69
tamarisk	*isꞽ*	I,47
tamarisk	*ssnḏm*	II,77
tame (vb.)	*ḳḥ*	II,158
tamper	*ḫn*	I,381
tan	*bḥw*	I,138
tanned hide	*ḏriw*	II,273
tap (of feet)	*hꜣb-m-rd*	I,286
target	*dbt*	II,244
tariff	*bꜣkw*	I,127
tarry	*ꜣsḳ*	I,9
tarry	*ḫni*	I,362
task	*ḥnt*	I,317
task	*sḥn*	II,63
tassels	*ꜥprwt*	I,65
taste (vb.)	*dp*	II,246
tax	*bꜣkw*	I,127
tax	*mndt*	I,191
tax	*gꜣwt*	II,184
tax (vb.)	*ḥtr*	I,339
tax due	*tp-ḏrt*	II,207
tax gathers	*št*	II,138
tax officials	*mškb*	I,209
tax payer	*št*	II,138
tax people	*htriw*	I,339
taxes	*ḥtr*	I,339
taxes	*šꜣyt*	II,107
taxing master	*št*	II,138
tax-people	*ḥtriw*	I,339
teach	*mtr*	I,214
teach	*sbꜣ*	II,26
teacher	*sbꜣw*	II,26
teaching	*mtr*	I,215
teaching	*sbꜣyt*	II,27
team	*ḥtr*	I,338
tear (vb.)	*ꜥfḳ*	I,65
tear (vb.)	*prš*	I,152
tear (vb.)	*sd*	II,98
tear asunder	*gmgm*	II,189
tear out	*nṯꜥ*	I,253
tear up	*nšd*	I,250
tear(?) (vb.)	*wtwt*	I,116
tears	*mw*	I,182
tease	*ṯyṯy*	II,227
tease	*ḏyḏy*	II,264
tease	*ḏḏ*	II,277
teenaged boy	*ḥwn*	I,306
teeth	*ṯsw*	II,235
tell	*mtr*	I,214
tell	*ḫr*	I,369
tell	*ṯst*	II,235
tell good tidings	*snḏm-ib*	II,56
temenos	*wbꜣ*	I,96
tempest	*ḏꜥ*	II,264
temple	*ꜥḥ*	I,74
temple	*pr*	I,149
temple	*r-pr*	I,262
temple	*ḥwt*	I,303
temple	*ḥwt-ꜥꜣt*	I,304
temple	*ḥwt-nṯr*	I,304
temple	*ḫnw*	I,362
temple (of head)	*mꜣꜥ*	I,174
temple (of head)	*smꜣ*	II,38
temple administration	*sm*	II,37
temple vase	*kꜣ-ḥr-kꜣ*	II,167
ten	*mḏ*	I,218
ten thousand	*ḏbꜥ*	II,267
tenant	*iḥwty*	I,44
tenant	*mnḥ*	I,188
tenant-farmer	*mnḥ*	I,188
tend	*iri*	I,38
tend	*sꜣw*	II,6
tend	*sbꜣ*	II,26
tend to	*rnn*	I,273
tender of crocodiles	*sprw-msḥ*	II,33
tender(?)	*gnn*	II,190
tending	*m-sꜣ*	II,5
tending (cattle)	*m-sꜣ*	I,171
tent	*imw*	I,29
tent	*ihr*	I,43
tent	*sḥ*	II,61
tent(?)	*ṯnfyt*	II,230
tent village(?)	*ḥwit*	I,305
tenth	*mḏ*	I,218
tents(?)	*mhrw*	I,196
termination of a tendon	*mꜣty*	I,177
terrace	*rid*	I,266

terrible	*nḥꜣ*	I,242
terrible	*ḥsꜣ*	I,331
terrible	*sḫm*	II,70
terrible of	*sḫm*	II,69
terribleness	*šfyt*	II,119
territory	*ḥḳr*	I,334
terror	*nrw*	I,239
terror	*ḥryt*	I,326
terror	*sdd*	II,99
terror	*šꜥt*	II,110
terror	*šfyt*	II,120
terrorize(?)	*rtḥ*	I,280
terrors	*snḏw*	II,55
test (vb.)	*sip*	II,11
test (vb.)	*sꜥḳꜣ*	II,16
testament	*imyt-pr*	I,27
testicles	*snty*	II,50
testicles	*knt*	II,175
testicles	*dḥtt*	II,254
testify	*mtr*	I,214
testimonial document	*ḥy*	I,300
testimonies	*ipw*	I,25
testimony	*mtr*	I,215
testimony	*smtr*	II,46
text	*r-ꜥ-sšw*	I,261
text	*sš*	II,78
thank	*dwꜣ-nṯr*	II,242
thankful	*nhm*	I,241
thanksgiving	*ḥknw*	I,335
that	*pf*	I,148
that	*nfy*	I,234
that	*nty*	I,253
that	*tfy*	II,209
that	*m-ḏd*	II,275
that one	*pn*	I,148
that which	*nt(y)w*	I,253
that which comes forth	*pry*	I,151
that which is cultivated	*iḥt*	I,44
the	*pꜣ*	I,145
the	*tꜣ*	II,197
the (plural)	*nꜣ*	I,225
the hot one	*šm(m)*	II,124
the king, "one"	*tw*	II,201
the thirty	*mꜥbꜣyt*	I,181
theft	*ṯꜣwt*	II,225
thefts	*iṯꜣw*	I,53
their	*w*	I,87
their	*sn*	II,47
their hands	*ḏrt.w*	II,272
them	*w*	I,87
them	*sn*	II,47
them (dep. pron.)	*st*	II,90
themes	*sp*	II,30

then	*isk*	I,48
then shall	*kꜣ*	II,166
there	*im*	I,26
there	*n-im*	I,223
there	*nim*	I,227
there	*dy*	II,241
there is no...	*mn*	I,183
there is not	*bn*	I,134
these	*ipw*	I,25
these	*nꜣy*	I,225
these	*nn*	I,239
these	*tꜣy*	II,199
they	*w*	I,87
they	*mntw*	I,190
they	*mtw*	I,213
they	*sn*	II,47
they	*st*	II,90
thick	*wmt*	I,100
thick walls	*wmwt*	I,100
thicket	*bꜣi(t)*	I,126
thicket	*hbḳ*	I,287
thicket	*sꜥr*	II,14
thicket (papyrus)	*šꜣ*	II,105
thickness	*wmt*	I,100
thief	*iṯꜣy*	I,53
thighs	*mnty*	I,185
thin	*p(ꜣ)ḳ(t)*	I,146
thin cloth	*ḫrd*	I,373
thin, fine material	*šmꜥ(t)*	II,122
thine	*tiwy*	II,200
thing	*wnnt*	I,102
thing	*mdt*	I,217
thing	*ḫt*	I,343
thing	*ḫnw*	I,362
things	*ꜣḫwt*	I,8
things	*nkt*	I,251
things of	*nꜣy*	I,226
think	*ib*	I,23
think	*mꜣṯ*	I,177
think about	*wꜣwꜣ*	I,88
think about	*šsꜣ*	II,135
third epagomenal day	*mswt-stẖ*	I,205
third month of *ꜣḫt*	*ḥwt-ḥr*	I,304
third month of *prt*	*pn-imn-ḥtp*	I,148
third season	*šmw*	II,123
thirst	*ibbw*	I,24
thirsty	*ibi*	I,24
thirsty	*ḏmꜥ*	II,269
this	*pꜣy*	I,146
this	*pw*	I,147
this	*pn*	I,148
this	*nꜣ(y)*	I,225
this	*nn*	I,239
this	*tꜣy*	II,199
this	*tw*	II,201

thole-boards	*sꜥiw*	II,13
thong	*ꜥgs*	I,82
thongs	*mtḏ*	I,215
thongs	*sfḫw*	II,36
thorn	*srt*	II,57
thornbush	*ḳḏw*	II,162
thorn prick	*srt*	II,57
thorns	*ḳḏw*	II,162
those	*nfy*	I,235
those before	*imyw-ḥꜣt*	I,297
those of	*nꜣy*	I,226
those of former times	*tpy-ꜥ*	II,207
those of the harem	*kꜣpw*	II,168
those of the nursery	*kꜣpw*	II,168
those upon	*tpy*	II,207
those who	*nt(y)w*	I,253
those who exist not	*tm wnw*	II,210
those who govern	*sḫry*	II,74
those who know	*rḫyw*	I,276
those who know a craft	*rḫyw-ḥmt*	I,276
those who terrify	*ꜥrḏw*	I,74
though	*ḫr*	I,368
thoughts	*imyw-ḫt*	I,27
thoughts	*ḥꜣty*	I,298
thousand	*ḫꜣ*	I,343
thrash	*wšwš*	I,114
thread	*ꜥꜣt*	I,61
thread	*nwt*	I,231
thread	*ḥsꜣ*	I,332
thread	*tpt*	II,208
threat	*šꜥr*	II,112
threats	*kṯmw*	II,181
three	*ḫmt*	I,361
thresh	*ḥy*	I,300
thresh	*ḥwi*	I,303
threshing area	*ḏnw*	II,269
threshing floor	*ḫtyw*	I,376
threshing platform	*ḫtyw*	I,377
threshold	*pnꜥt*	I,149
threshold	*pḫꜣ*	I,154
throat	*ꜥšꜥš*	I,79
throat	*ḥty*	I,335
throat	*ḫꜥb*	I,353
throat	*ḫḫ*	I,374
throne	*isbt*	I,46
throne	*wṯst*	I,117
throne	*bḥdw*	I,139
throne	*p*	I,145
throne	*nst*	I,247
throne	*sbi*	II,28
throne	*st*	II,1
throne	*ḳniw*	II,154
throne	*ṯꜣtn*	II,227
throne	*ṯnṯꜣt*	II,230
throng	*ꜥšꜣt*	I,79
throng	*wmt*	I,100
throngs	*ḏꜣmw*	II,262
through	*m-di*	I,171
through	*m-ḏrt*	I,172
through	*ḫt*	I,375
through	*m-ḏrt*	II,272
through the length of	*m-ꜣw*	I,3
throughout	*m-ꜣw*	I,3
throughout	*m-ḫt*	I,170
throughout	*ḫt*	I,375
throw	*wdi*	I,117
throw	*ḥwꜣ*	I,305
throw	*ḫꜣꜥ*	I,346
throw down	*whn*	I,106
throw down	*ḫꜣꜥ*	I,346
throw down	*sḫr*	II,72
throw down	*ḏꜣrꜥ*	II,262
throw out	*ḫꜣꜥ*	I,346
throw out	*kh*	II,177
throwing stick	*ꜥmꜥ*	I,66
thrust	*ꜥmḳ*	I,67
thrust	*smꜣꜥ*	II,39
thunder (vb.)	*trmg*	II,215
thunderbolt	*sšdw*	II,83
thunderbolt	*ḳri*	II,156
thunderbolt fall	*wgp*	I,115
thus	*m-mitt*	I,169
thus	*mi-nꜣ*	I,178
thus	*r-mitt-n*	I,180
thus	*m-mitt*	I,180
thus	*ḫr*	I,368
thus	*kꜣ*	II,166
thymus(?)	*sḫn*	II,71
tie	*nṯṯ*	I,255
tie (vb.)	*ḳꜣs*	II,145
tie (vb.)	*gwtn*	II,186
tie (vb.)	*ṯs*	II,233
tie up	*itḥ*	I,52
till	*šꜣꜥ*	II,107
till	*r-šꜣꜥ*	II,107
till (vb.)	*skꜣ*	II,87
tillage rights	*skꜣwt*	II,87
tilled land	*ꜣḫt*	I,8
timber	*sḫr*	II,76
time	*ꜣt*	I,1
time	*iꜣdt*	I,15
time	*nw*	I,230
time	*nri*	I,239
time	*rk*	I,279
time	*hꜣw*	I,285
time	*sp*	II,30
time	*tr*	II,214
time span	*ꜥḥꜥw*	I,77

times	*sp*	II,30
timid	*snḏ*	II,55
tin	*dḥt*	II,254
tin(?)	*ḏḥty ḥḏ*	II,274
tingle	*nḳꜥ*	I,250
tip(?)	*br*	I,136
tips	*ḥꜣ(w)tyw*	I,298
tire	*wrd*	I,106
tire (of a chariot wheel)	*ḫꜣb*	I,348
tired	*wrd*	I,106
tired	*bꜣg*	I,128
tired	*bgꜣ*	I,142
tired	*ft*	I,165
tired land	*tnw*	II,212
tithe	*mḏ*	I,218
title of high priest of Ptah	*wr-ḫrp-ḥm(w)t*	I,104
titulary	*nḫb*	I,244
tjꜣt-flowers	*ṯꜣt*	II,226
tjst-piece	*ṯst*	II,236
tkm-bearer	*ṯꜣy-tkm*	II,225
to	*m-ꜥ*	I,167
to	*m-di*	I,171
to	*n*	I,223
to	*r*	I,259
to	*r-mn*	I,262
to	*r-r*	I,263
to	*r-ḳr*	I,265
to	*ḫr*	I,369
to	*m-sꜣ*	II,4
to no purpose	*ḳb*	II,148
to the extent of	*m-ꜣw*	I,3
to the interior	*r-ḫnw*	I,382
to the limits	*r-ꜣw*	I,3
to wit	*r-ḫd*	II,
today	*pꜣ-hrw*	I,145
today	*m-pꜣ-hrw*	I,168
today	*pꜣ-hrw*	I,291
toes	*ḏbꜥ*	II,267
together	*n-sp*	II,30
together with	*irm*	I,41
together with	*m*	I,167
together with	*r*	I,259
toil	*bꜣkw*	I,127
toilet	*wnḫw*	I,103
tomb	*is*	I,45
tomb	*ꜥꜥi*	I,62
tomb	*ꜥḥꜥt*	I,77
tomb	*pr-ḏt*	I,150
tomb	*mꜥḥꜥt*	I,182
tomb	*nfr(t)*	I,237
tomb	*r-stꜣ*	I,264
tomb	*ḥrt*	I,328
tomb	*ḫr*	I,368
tomb	*st*	II,1
tomb	*st mꜣꜥt*	II,2
tomb	*r-stꜣ*	II,93
tomb	*šnꜥ*	II,129
tomb chamber	*mḥy*	I,199
tomb of living king(?)	*st pr ꜥꜣ*	II,2
tombs	*nꜣ ḫrw n msw-nsw*	I,368
tombstone	*wḏ*	I,120
tomorrow	*m-dwꜣt*	I,172
tomorrow	*dwꜣyt*	II,242
tongue	*ns*	I,247
too	*m-r-ꜥ*	I,169
too	*gr(t)*	II,191
tool	*minb*	I,180
tool	*ḫꜣ*	I,344
tool	*sgrṯ*	II,90
tool	*ḳrn*	II,157
tool	*kmti*	II,174
tool box(?)	*db(t)*	II,244
tool type	*ḫꜣiw*	I,344
tool(?)	*mṯprt*	I,216
tools	*ḫꜥw*	I,352
tools	*ḫnr*	I,365
tooth	*ibḥ*	I,24
tooth	*nḏḥt*	I,257
tooth	*ḫnr*	I,365
tooth	*ḫr*	I,369
top	*ḥrw*	I,327
top	*ḥrt*	I,327
top	*tbn*	II,204
top	*tp*	II,204
top	*thnt*	II,217
top	*dhnt*	II,253
top of a stake	*tpt*	II,208
top of head	*wpt*	I,98
top of the earth	*wp(t)-tꜣ*	I,98
topic	*ḏd*	II,275
torch	*tkꜣ*	II,220
torment	*ḏnn*	II,269
tormented	*ḏnn*	II,270
torpid	*sgꜣ*	II,89
torrent	*šbrt*	II,117
toss about	*kh*	II,177
total	*dmḏwt*	II,249
totality of people	*tmw*	II,210
totter	*ktkt*	II,180
touch	*wḫꜣ*	I,110
touch	*ngi*	I,252
touch	*ḫn*	I,381
touch	*sn*	II,49
touch	*ṯḥn*	II,232
touch	*dmi*	II,247
tough	*ḏri*	II,272
tough	*ḏrw*	II,273
toward	*ḥr*	I,321
tower	*mktr*	I,212

tower	*ḫtm*	I,377
tower	*swnw*	II,20
tower (vb.)	*ḳꜣḳꜣ*	II,145
towering	*tnỉ*	II,211
towing man	*mškb*	I,209
town	*dmỉ*	II,248
town	*wḥt*	I,107
trace	*ꜥ*	I,58
track	*ꜥ*	I,58
track	*sꜣḥ*	II,8
tracker	*ṯꜣy*	II,224
tracking	*ṯꜣy*	II,224
tract	*rwḏ*	I,268
tract	*ḳꜥḥt*	II,146
trade	*ḫbr*	I,354
trade	*swn*	II,19
trade	*šwy*	II,114
trader	*šwyty*	II,114
traditional	*mt*	I,213
train	*swꜣ*	II,17
train	*sḫpr*	II,68
train	*šms*	II,125
train (vb.)	*rmṯ*	I,271
train of retinue	*šmsw*	II,125
trainees	*sdt*	II,99
trainer	*sḫpr*	II,69
training	*sbꜣyt*	II,27
trample	*ptpt*	I,158
trample	*ḫnd*	I,368
trample	*tkšš*	II,221
trample down	*dgdg*	II,257
trample on	*sỉn*	II,12
trample on	*tỉtỉ*	II,201
transfer (vb.)	*swḏ*	II,24
transfiguration	*sꜣḫw*	II,9
transformation	*ḫprỉ*	I,357
transformed	*ḫpr*	I,356
transgress	*thꜣ*	II,216
transgression	*ḏꜣyt*	II,261
transgressor	*ḏꜣỉw*	II,261
transport	*fꜣy*	I,163
transport	*ḫnỉ*	I,382
transport boat	*ꜥḳꜣ*	I,81
transport officer	*mškb*	I,209
transport(?)	*ṯst*	II,236
transports	*ḳḳt*	II,160
trap	*pḫꜣ*	I,154
trap	*msṯḥ*	I,207
trap	*sḫt*	II,75
trap (vb.)	*sḫt*	II,74
trapped ones	*kꜣpw*	II,168
trapped ones	*kpw*	II,172
trapper	*swr*	II,21
trapping marshes	*sšy*	II,79
travail (to be in)	*sꜥỉ*	II,13
travel	*pḫr*	I,155
travel	*mšꜥ*	I,208
travel	*nꜥy*	I,228
travel	*nmỉ*	I,237
travel	*ḥpt*	I,309
travel	*ḥrty*	I,328
travel	*ḫt*	I,376
travel	*šm*	II,122
travel	*dbn*	II,245
travel	*dbnbn*	II,245
travel (vb.)	*sbỉ*	II,25
travel freely	*wstn*	I,113
travel swiftly	*pḥrr*	I,154
travel upstream	*sḫnty*	II,72
traverse	*pḫr*	I,155
traverse	*hb*	I,286
traverse	*ḫnd*	I,368
traverse	*šꜣmw*	II,109
traverse (vb.)	*sbỉ*	II,25
tray	*sỉd*	II,12
tread	*ptpt*	I,158
tread	*hb*	I,286
tread	*ḫnd*	I,368
tread	*dgs*	II,257
tread	*dgdg*	II,257
tread (against)	*hꜣy*	I,283
tread (vb.)	*dgs*	II,257
tread on	*ḫn*	I,381
treason	*štm*	II,139
treasure ships	*r-ḥḏw*	I,264
treasure(?)	*mꜣꜥ*	I,174
treasury	*pr-ḥḏ*	I,150
treasury	*r-ḥḏ*	I,264
treasury	*pr-ḥḏ*	I,340
treat	*ỉrỉ*	I,38
treat disrespectfully	*ṯḥr*	II,232
treaty(?)	*brṯ*	I,137
tree	*ỉmw*	I,29
tree type	*ỉšd*	I,48
tree type	*wꜥn*	I,95
tree type	*bkỉ*	I,141
tree	*sꜣsꜣrr*	II,9
tree	*ssrr*	II,9
tree	*sg*	II,89
tree	*šn*	II,126
tree	*šnwsꜥ*	II,130
tree	*ḳꜣḳꜣ*	II,145
tree	*ksb*	II,178
tree (of a plantation)	*mnw*	I,187
tree name	*ꜣꜥꜥ*	I,2
tree spice	*tỉšpss*	II,201
tree(?)	*hrw*	I,291
trees	*ḫt*	I,375
trees	*šꜣ*	II,105
trees	*ṯꜣgꜣ*	II,227

tremble	*isdd*	I,48
tremble	*pwy*	I,148
tremble	*nwr*	I,231
tremble	*nwṯ*	I,232
tremble	*nš*	I,249
tremble	*sdd*	II,99
tremble	*ktkt*	II,180
trembling	*ꜣst*	I,9
trembling	*sdd*	II,99
trench	*šꜣgꜣr*	II,110
trench	*šgr*	II,138
trespass	*thh*	II,217
trespass	*dgs*	II,257
tresses	*nbd*	I,234
trial	*smtr*	II,45
tribe	*mhwt*	I,196
tribesmen	*iwntyw*	I,20
tribunal	*ḳnbt*	II,154
tribunal	*ḏꜣḏꜣt*	II,263
tribute	*inw*	I,32
tribute	*bꜣkw*	I,127
tribute	*mnḥt*	I,188
tribute	*gꜣwt*	II,184
trickle	*dfdf*	II,247
trifle	*ꜣbi*	I,4
trim	*grb*	II,191
triumph	*ḥbnw*	I,307
triumphant	*mꜣʿ-ẖrw*	I,175
troop	*pḏty*	I,161
troop	*sꜣw*	II,4
troop	*ṯst*	II,235
troop commander	*ḥry-pḏt*	I,161
troop commander	*ḥry-pḏt*	I,325
troops	*iwʿyt*	I,19
troops	*mnfꜣt*	I,187
troops	*mšʿ*	I,207
troops	*nʿrn*	I,229
troops	*skw*	II,86
troops	*ḏꜣmw*	II,262
trot	*ṯiṯi*	II,227
trouble (vb.)	*stꜣḥ*	II,93
troubled	*pnʿ*	I,148
troubled	*nhꜣ*	I,242
troubled	*šni*	II,127
true	*mꜣʿ(t)*	I,175
true of voice	*mꜣʿ-ẖrw*	I,175
true of voice	*mꜣʿ-ẖrw*	I,372
truly	*yꜣ*	I,11
truly	*m-mꜣʿt*	I,168
trumpet	*šnb*	II,130
trumpeter	*ḏd m šnb*	II,276
trumpeter	*ḏd m šnb*	II,130
trunk (of elephant)	*ḏrt*	II,272
trunk (of tree)	*irkt*	I,42
trust	*nḥ*	I,242
trust in	*mḥ*	I,197
trust with	*mḥ*	I,197
trust(?)	*nḥ*	I,241
trustee	*rwḏ*	I,269
trusting	*mḥ-ib*	I,23
trusting	*mḥ ib*	I,197
trustworthy	*mt*	I,213
trusty one	*mḥ-ib*	I,198
truth	*mꜣʿt*	I,175
try	*wẖꜣ*	I,110
tsm-boat	*tsm*	II,219
tuft(?)	*br*	I,136
tumor	*twꜣ*	II,201
tunic	*mss*	I,206
tunic	*ḳḏmr*	II,163
tunnel (vb.)	*wtnw*	I,116
tunneling	*wtnw*	I,117
tunneling	*bꜣk-ẖrty*	I,388
turmoil	*ẖnnw*	I,384
turmoil	*shꜣ*	II,60
turn	*msnḥ*	I,205
turn	*ẖꜣʿ*	I,346
turn	*šnʿ*	II,129
turn (bad)	*iri*	I,38
turn about	*pẖr*	I,155
turn about	*sꜣsꜣ*	II,9
turn around	*msbb*	I,205
turn around	*ḳb*	II,147
turn aside	*gwš*	II,186
turn away	*msnḥ*	I,205
turn away	*rwi*	I,267
turn back	*ʿn(n)*	I,68
turn back	*wḏb*	I,122
turn back	*pnʿ*	I,148
turn back	*msnḥ*	I,205
turn back	*ḥm*	I,310
turn back	*ẖsf*	I,374
turn back	*ẖty*	I,376
turn back	*šnʿ*	II,129
turn into	*ẖpr*	I,356
turn longingly	*ḥnr*	I,319
turn one's back	*mkḥꜣ*	I,211
turn one's back	*ẖꜣʿ-hꜣ-r*	I,347
turn over to	*ḏbꜣ*	II,266
turn upside down	*pnʿ*	I,148
turn upside down	*pẖd*	I,155
turning about	*pẖrw*	I,155
turquoise	*brt*	I,136
turquoise	*mfkt*	I,183
turret	*ẖtm*	I,377
tusk	*kmri*	II,174
tutor	*tf-mnʿt*	II,209
twelfth month, Mesore	*wpt-rnpt*	I,98
twenty	*ḏbʿty*	II,268
twenty thousand	*ḏbʿ*	II,267
twig	*iꜣꜣt*	I,11

twigs	*ꜥḫmw*	I,78
twigs	*sbr*	II,28
twigs	*ḏnr*	II,270
twilight	*mšrw*	I,209
twilight	*rwhꜣ*	I,268
twilight	*kkw*	II,179
twinkling	*km*	II,173
twins	*ḥtr*	I,338
twist	*ꜥn(n)*	I,68
twist	*ḫnd*	I,368
twist	*sꜣḏr*	II,11
twisted	*mn*	I,184
twisted	*swš*	II,22
twisted	*gwš*	II,186
twisting	*šš*	II,137
twitch (muscles)	*ṯḥn*	II,232
two	*sn*	II,48
two feathers	*šwty*	II,115
two foremost ones	*ḥꜣwtywy*	I,298
Two Ladies	*nbty*	I,233
Two Lands	*tꜣ-wy*	II,197
two of them	*sny*	II,49
two plumes	*šwty*	II,115
two rows	*itrty*	I,52
two serpent goddesses	*ḥꜣwtywy*	I,298
two sides	*itrty*	I,52
two sides	*ḥnty*	I,317
two sides	*ḥnty*	I,320
two-sisters	*snty*	II,48
two sources of the Nile	*ḳrty*	II,156
two-thirds	*rwy*	I,267
tyrannize	*ꜥšḳ*	I,80
tyrannize	*ꜥšg*	I,80

U

unaccompanied	*nn ky*	II,171
unacquainted	*ḫm*	I,360
unanimously	*m-r-wꜥ*	I,169
unbind	*ntf*	I,253
unbind	*sfḫ*	II,35
uncircumcised phallus	*ḳrnt*	II,157
unclean	*sif*	II,11
uncleanness	*ꜥbw*	I,64
uncover	*wn*	I,100
uncover	*kfi*	II,172
under	*ḫr*	I,369
under	*ẖr*	I,385
under	*ẖry*	I,386
under (one's) charge	*r-ḥꜣt*	I,297
under (their) charge	*ẖry-ꜥ*	I,387
under my supervision	*ḥr ꜥ(wy).i*	I,57
under the authority of	*r-ḫt*	I,376
under the authority of	*r-ḫt*	I,264
under the charge of	*r-ḫt*	I,376
under the control of	*r-ḫt*	I,376
under the jurisdiction of	*r-ḫt*	I,376
under the supervision of	*r-ḥꜣt*	I,296
under the supervision of	*ḥr-ꜥwy*	I,322
underestimate	*sẖry-ꜥ*	II,76
undergarment(?)	*ḫnk*	I,384
underground burial chamber	*dwꜣt*	II,243
undergrowth	*šfnw*	II,120
underlings	*smdt*	II,46
underpants(?)	*ḫnk*	I,384
understand	*ꜥm*	I,66
understand	*siꜣ*	II,11
understand	*sḏm*	II,101
understanding	*wḥꜥ-ib*	I,23
understanding of heart	*wḥꜥ-ib*	I,108
undertaking	*pss*	I,156
undervalue	*sẖry-ꜥ*	II,76
underworld	*igrt*	I,50
underworld	*šnꜥ*	II,129
underworld	*dwꜣt*	II,243
unfasten	*ntf*	I,253
unfinished	*ḥr-wꜣt*	I,322
unfold	*prḫ*	I,152
unfurl	*wḥꜥ*	I,107

unguent	*bꜣs*	I,127
unguent	*ḥꜣtt*	I,299
unguent	*sgnn*	II,90
unhindered	*wstn*	I,113
unhindered	*m-wstnw*	I,113
unimportant	*nḏs*	I,257
unimportant	*šwꜣ*	II,115
uninjured eye	*wḏꜣ(t)*	I,122
unique one	*wꜥ*	I,93
unit of value	*šnꜥti*	II,129
unite	*ꜣbḫ*	I,5
unite	*ḫnm*	I,383
unite	*smꜣ*	II,37
unite	*sḥwy*	II,62
unite	*dmḏ*	II,249
universal god	*nb-r-ḏr*	I,232
unjust	*m-ꜥḏꜣ*	I,84
unjustly	*m-ꜥḏꜣ*	I,168
unjustly	*m grg*	II,193
unload	*sšw*	II,80
unmellowed wine	*p(ꜣ)wr*	I,146
unmindful	*ḫm*	I,360
unnecessary(?)	*m-bnr*	I,168
unoccupied	*wꜥb*	I,94
unrestrainedly	*m-wstnw*	I,113
unshaken	*nn ktkt*	II,180
untended	*nḫꜣ*	I,242
untie	*ṯt*	II,236
until	*ỉ-ỉr*	I,38
until	*r-mn*	I,184
until	*nfryt-r*	I,236
until	*r*	I,259
until	*r-mn*	I,262
until	*r-r-ꜥ*	I,263
until	*r-šꜣꜥ*	I,264
until	*šꜣꜥ*	II,107
unto	*r-šꜣꜥ*	II,107
unusual conditions	*ḫppw*	I,355
unwavering(?)	*spd*	II,34
unwearying ones	*ỉḫmw-wrḏ*	I,44
unworthy	*bn-sꜣw*	I,134
up	*r-ḥry*	I,264
up	*r-ḥry*	I,324
up to	*r-šꜣꜥ*	II,107
up to	*šꜣꜥ*	II,107
upbringing	*rnn*	I,274
upbringing	*ḫpriw*	I,357
uphold	*ḳꜣyt*	II,144
upon	*m-ḥr*	I,170
upon	*n*	I,223
upon	*ḥr*	I,321
upon	*ḥr-ꜥ*	I,322
upon	*ḥry-tp*	I,326
upon	*tp*	II,204
upon earth	*tp-tꜣ*	II,206
upper arm	*rmn*	I,271

upper arm(?)	*ḏnḥ*	II,270
upper chamber	*ꜥrt*	I,72
Upper Egypt	*šmꜥw*	II,122
Upper Egypt	*tꜣ-šmꜥ*	II,198
Upper Egyptians	*šmꜥyw*	II,122
upper legs	*mnty*	I,185
upper portal	*sbꜣ-ḥry*	II,26
upper rail (of chariot box)	*ḥtr*	I,377
upset	*pnꜥ*	I,148
upset	*ḫrḫr*	I,373
upset(?)	*ꜥḏ*	I,83
upside down	*sḫd*	II,75
upwards	*r-ḥry*	I,264
uraeus	*ỉꜥrt*	I,17
uraeus serpent	*ꜣḫt*	I,7
uraeus serpent	*wꜥ*	I,93
uraeus serpent	*ḥry(t)-tp*	I,326
uraeus(?)	*wꜣrr*	I,89
uraeus(?)	*wrt*	I,105
use	*ỉri*	I,38
use	*nkt*	I,252
use	*hꜣw*	I,285
use	*ḫꜣm*	I,348
used	*hꜣw*	I,285
used land	*dnit*	II,250
useful	*ꜣḫ*	I,7
useless	*ỉꜣ ỉꜣ*	I,11
useless	*ḳb*	II,147
usher in	*stꜣ*	II,92
utensil (for the cult)	*ṯbt*	II,228
utter	*wšꜥ*	I,113
utter confusion	*hrṯḳh*	I,292
utter sedition	*šni*	II,127
utterance	*wšbt*	I,114
utterance	*pry*	I,151
utterance	*nis*	I,227
utterance	*r*	I,259
utterance	*ḫnw*	I,362
utterance	*smiw*	II,41
utterance	*tpw-r*	II,208
utterances	*ṯs*	II,234

V

vacant	*šw*	II,113
vagabond	*ḳꜣiw*	II,143
vagina	*kꜣt*	II,167
vagina	*kns*	II,174
vagrant	*ḳrr*	II,157
vain	*ḳb*	II,148
valiant	*pr-ʿ*	I,150
valiant	*ḳni*	II,152
valiant arm	*ḫpš*	I,357
valley	*int*	I,32
valley	*ʿmḳ*	I,67
valor	*ḳn(t)*	II,152
valor	*ḳnn*	II,154
valuable	*šps*	II,118
value	*fꜣy*	I,163
value	*šꜣw*	II,108
value	*šb(t)*	II,116
value	*dit šb*	II,116
value (vb.)	*ṯnf*	II,230
value of hired cattle	*ʿgꜣt*	I,82
vanish	*isb*	I,46
vanish	*sbi*	II,25
vanquish	*hd*	I,293
variegated of plumage	*sꜣb-šwty*	II,8
variegated of plumage	*sꜣb-šwty*	II,115
various	*pry*	I,151
various	*šbn*	II,117
various types	*šbn*	II,117
varnish	*mrḥt*	I,195
vase	*irr*	I,41
vase	*irrḏ*	I,41
vase	*ʿnḫy*	I,70
vase	*wnr*	I,102
vase	*mḥ-bḳ*	I,198
vase	*ḫꜣwy*	I,346
vase	*šwbty*	II,116
vase	*ṯꜣ*	II,223
vase	*ṯbw*	II,228
vase	*dnit*	II,250
vase (1/2 *hin*)	*bꜣ*	I,125
vase stand	*ḫnty*	I,367
vase stand	*gnn*	II,190
vases	*sṯyw*	II,96
vases	*ṯtb*	II,236
vassal(?)	*mꜣwḏ*	I,176
vat	*ʿtḫ*	I,82
vault (heavenly)	*sṯs*	II,97
vault	*ḳnby*	II,154
vaunt	*swh*	II,21
vegetable	*wꜣḏ-smw*	I,91
vegetable garden (watered)	*ʿsb*	I,78
vegetables	*rnpwt*	I,273
vegetables	*sm*	II,37
vegetables	*ṯꜣt*	II,226
vegetables	*ṯꜣw*	II,226
vegetation	*kꜣkꜣ*	II,170
veils	*ḫrd*	I,373
vein	*mt*	I,213
veneer	*kꜣp*	II,168
veneer wood(?)	*pẖꜣ*	I,154
venerable	*imꜣḫy*	I,30
venerable	*šps*	II,118
vengeance	*wšbt*	I,114
venom	*mtwt*	I,214
vent	*pẖꜣ*	I,154
vent indignation	*pnḳ*	I,149
verbal	*r-mdwt*	I,262
verdant	*ꜣḫꜣḫ*	I,8
verdant	*wꜣḏ*	I,91
verge	*smꜣ-sꜣtw*	II,10
verge	*smꜣ-sꜣtw*	II,38
verify	*gm*	II,188
verily	*tiw*	II,200
versed	*ʿrḳ*	I,73
versed	*šsꜣ*	II,134
vertebrae	*ṯst*	II,235
very	*r-sy*	I,264
very good	*m-sšr-sp-sn*	I,171
very great of strength	*sḫm-pḥty*	II,70
very many	*ḳnw*	II,153
very much	*ʿšꜣ*	I,79
very well	*m-sšr-sp-sn*	I,171
vessel	*imw*	I,29
vessel	*irrḏ*	I,41
vessel	*iḏr*	I,55
vessel	*mꜣdydy*	I,178
vessel	*mnš*	I,189
vessel	*mrynt*	I,194
vessel	*mḥ-bḳ*	I,198
vessel	*nš*	I,249
vessel	*rhd(t)*	I,274
vessel	*ḥnw*	I,317
vessel	*š*	II,105
vessel	*ḳʿḥt*	II,146
vessel	*ḳrḥt*	II,157
vessel	*kꜣr*	II,169
vessel	*kꜣkmn*	II,170
vessel	*kṯ*	II,180
vessel	*gngnt*	II,190
vessel	*tkꜣ*	II,220
vessel	*ṯꜣ*	II,223
vessel (for measuring fat)	*ṯrr*	II,231
vessel	*dydy*	II,241

vessel	*dpy*	II,246
vessel	*ḏwyw*	II,265
vessel	*ḏprt*	II,268
vessel (blood)	*mt*	I,213
vessel (large)	*mnḏḳt*	I,191
vessel (offering)	*wḏḥw*	I,123
vessel (or measure)	*mdd*	I,218
vessel for beer	*wšm*	I,115
vessel for beer	*ps*	I,156
vessel for measuring fat	*ṯrr*	II,231
vessel for unguent	*krr*	II,176
vessel of bronze	*ꜥ-n-ḫꜥw*	I,57
vessel of metal	*irr*	I,41
vessel of metal	*ṯrb*	II,231
vessels	*šnw*	II,127
vestments	*ḏbꜣ*	II,266
veteran servant	*iꜣy-n-bꜣk*	I,12
vex	*ind*	I,36
vex	*nhḳ*	I,241
vex	*šni*	II,127
vexed	*ḥwꜣw*	I,305
vexed	*ḥḏn*	I,342
vexed	*šni*	II,127
viceroy	*sꜣ-nsw-n-kš*	I,248
viceroy	*sꜣ nsw*	II,3
vice-versa	*ṯs-pẖr*	II,234
vicinity	*mtt*	I,213
vicinity	*hꜣw*	I,285
vicinity	*sꜣḥ*	II,8
vicinity	*sw*	II,17
vicissitudes	*dbnbn*	II,245
victim of fate	*šꜣy*	II,106
victims (?)	*sdḫw*	II,99
victorious	*nḫt*	I,246
victory	*nḫt*	I,246
victory	*ḳfꜣt*	II,149
victory	*ḳn(t)*	II,152
victuals (king's)	*ꜥnḫ(w)*	I,70
victuals	*mk(y)w*	I,211
victuals	*ḏfꜣw*	II,269
view (vb.)	*ḳḏm*	II,163
vigilance	*rs-tp*	I,277
vigilant	*rs*	I,277
vigilantly	*rs-tp*	I,277
vigorous	*wꜣḏ*	I,91
vigorous	*rnpi*	I,273
vigorous men	*mꜥḥꜣw*	I,181
vile(?)	*ḫsy*	I,388
vilify	*ḥḏ*	I,340
vilify	*sḥwr*	II,62
villa	*bḫn*	I,139
villa	*pr-mꜣ*	I,150
village	*wḥt*	I,107
village	*dmi*	II,248
vindicate	*smꜣꜥ ḫrw*	II,40
vindicated	*mꜣꜥ(t)*	I,175
vinegar	*ḥmḏ*	I,315
vineyard	*krm*	II,176
vineyard garden	*kꜣmw*	II,168
vineyard keeper	*kꜣmy*	II,168
vintner	*kꜣmy*	II,168
vintner	*kꜣry*	II,170
violate	*thꜣ*	II,216
violate	*tktk*	II,221
violate(?)	*ḏꜣi*	II,260
violate (a woman)	*ḫꜥ*	I,380
violate (tomb)	*wꜣḥ*	I,89
violator	*ḥḏ*	I,341
violator	*tkk*	II,221
violence	*gns*	II,190
violence(?)	*nhꜣ*	I,242
violent	*ḫwrꜥ*	I,306
violently	*m-ḫwrꜥ*	I,170
violently	*ḥꜥt*	I,302
violently	*ḏꜣy*	II,261
violet	*ṯms*	II,229
virgin(?)	*st-ḥmt*	II,1
virility	*pḥty*	I,154
virtue	*biꜣt*	I,130
vision	*mꜣꜣ*	I,173
vision	*rswt*	I,278
vision	*ḳḏm*	II,163
visit	*ḫn*	I,316
visit	*spr*	II,32
visit	*ḳri*	II,155
visiting	*ḳꜣi*	II,143
visitor	*ḳꜣiw*	II,143
visitor	*ḳꜣriw*	II,144
visitor	*ḳri*	II,156
vitality	*ḥnḥn*	I,319
vixen	*šꜥrt*	II,112
vizier	*ṯꜣty*	II,227
voice	*r*	I,259
voice	*ḫrw*	I,371
void	*šw*	II,113
volition	*ꜣbw*	I,4
volume	*sḫrt*	II,74
voluntarily	*n-mrw.f*	I,224
vomit	*bši*	I,140
vomit (vb.)	*ḳꜣꜥ*	II,144
voracious(?) spirit	*ꜥḫm*	I,78
Votaress	*dwꜣ-nṯr*	II,242
voyage	*wḏ(yt)*	I,120
voyage	*ḫn*	I,382
voyage	*sḳdyt*	II,85
vulture	*nrit*	I,239
vulva	*kꜣt*	II,167
vulva	*kns*	II,175

W

wad	*ḫꜥw*	I,353
wady	*nḫr(n)*	I,245
wady	*ḫꜣrb*	I,349
waft	*ḥwꜣ*	I,305
wages	*bꜣkw*	I,127
wages	*ḥtr*	I,339
wages	*šb(t)*	II,116
wages	*diw*	II,240
wagon	*ꜥgrt*	I,82
wagon box	*brr*	I,136
wagon part	*inḳfḳft*	I,35
wagon part	*ꜥḏr*	I,84
wail	*rmw*	I,270
wailing woman	*wšbt*	I,114
wait	*isḳ*	I,48
wait	*ꜥḥꜥ*	I,75
wait	*sin*	II,12
wait for	*sin*	II,12
waiters	*mꜣdyw*	I,178
waiting place	*rwyt*	I,267
wake (vb.)	*nhsi*	I,241
walk	*nꜥy*	I,228
walk	*ḫnd*	I,368
walk	*šm*	II,121
walk	*dgꜣ*	II,256
walk about	*pẖr*	I,155
walk about	*swtwt*	II,23
walk around	*ḳdi*	II,161
walk away	*rwi*	I,267
walk backwards	*nꜥy n ḥꜣ.f*	I,228
walk over	*dgdg*	II,257
walking leisurely	*ḳdḳd*	II,162
wall	*inb*	I,33
wall	*sbty*	II,29
wall	*ḳd*	II,160
wall (of water)	*sꜣ*	II,5
wall in	*inb*	I,33
wall off	*inb*	I,33
wall(?)	*ḏrwt*	II,273
walled enclosure	*sbty*	II,29
wallow(?)	*ḥbnbn*	I,307
walls	*ḏr*	II,271
wand	*twrit*	II,202
wander	*wnšnš*	I,103
wander	*ḫt-tꜣ*	I,343
wander	*ḫt-tꜣ*	I,376
wander	*tnm*	II,213
wander about	*ii*	I,16
wander about	*pẖr*	I,155
wander(?)	*ḫt-tꜣ*	I,376
wanderer	*nhr*	I,241
wanderers	*tšw*	II,220
want	*wgꜣ*	I,115
want	*wgg*	I,116
want	*mri*	I,192
want	*ḥꜣ-ib*	I,295
war	*ꜥḥꜣ*	I,74
war	*ḫrw*	I,372
war galley	*kbnt*	II,172
ward	*sḫpr*	II,69
ward off	*wiꜣ*	I,92
ward off	*nh*	I,240
ward off	*sꜣw*	II,6
warehouse	*wḏꜣ*	I,121
warehouse	*šnꜥ*	II,128
warehouse keeper	*ꜥꜣ-n-wḏꜣ*	I,60
warehouseman	*šnꜥ*	II,129
warfare	*r-ꜥ-ꜥḥꜥ*	I,260
warfare	*r-ꜥ-ḫꜥw*	I,260
warfare	*r-ḫꜥw*	I,264
warfare	(see combat)	
warm	*šm(m)*	II,124
warrior	*ꜥḥꜣwty*	I,75
warrior	*mꜥhr*	I,181
warrior	*mryn*	I,194
warrior	*snny*	II,52
warrior (class)	*thr*	II,217
warrior(?)	*mhr*	I,196
warriors	*mꜥḥꜣw*	I,181
warriors	*mhwt*	I,196
warriors	*nꜥrn*	I,229
warriors	*tmrgn*	II,211
warship	*mnš*	I,189
warships	*ꜥḥꜥw*	I,76
wash	*iꜥi*	I,16
wash	*rḫt*	I,276
wash down food	*sꜥm*	II,14
washbowl	*iꜥ*	I,16
washer man	*rḫty*	I,277
washers (of gold)	*iꜥw*	I,16
waste	*fk*	I,165
waste	*šw*	II,114
watch	*ptr*	I,159
watch	*rs*	I,277
watch	*rs-tp*	I,277
watch	*rsw*	I,278
watch	*sfḫy*	II,36
watch (vb.)	*sꜣw*	II,6
watch day	*wrš*	I,105
watch for	*nw*	I,229
watch out	*bꜥ sp-sn*	I,131
watch over	*di-ḥr*	II,240
watch post	*inb*	I,33
watchful	(see vigilant)	
watchman	*wnwt(y)*	I,101
watchman	*wršy*	I,106
water	*mw*	I,182
water	*ntꜥ*	I,253
water bearer	*wꜣḥ-mw*	I,90

water carrier	*in mw*	I,32
water jars	*ḥsyw*	I,330
water pourer	*wꜣḥ-mw*	I,90
water pourer	*stꜣ-mw*	II,92
water procession	*ẖn*	I,382
water skin	*ẖnt*	I,381
water spell(?)	*ḥsy-mw*	I,330
water spirit	*nḫt*	I,246
water vases	*ḥst*	I,330
water's edge	*mꜣꜥ*	I,174
watercourse	*itr*	I,51
watercourse	*ḥnw*	I,317
watered garden	*ꜥsb*	I,78
watering jar	*wḏḥw*	I,123
watering place	*ẖnmt*	I,384
watering place	*šꜣkꜣnꜣ*	II,110
watermelon	*idnrg*	I,54
waters	*ym*	I,28
waters	*nḫr(n)*	I,245
waters	*ntꜥ*	I,253
waters	*hrnw*	I,291
waters	*sgbyn*	II,89
waters(?)	*šni*	II,127
watery depths	*mḏt-mw*	I,219
waver	*iṯ-in*	I,53
waver	*sbn*	II,28
waves	*hnw*	I,289
wax	*mnḥ*	I,188
way	*wꜣt*	I,88
way	*bst*	I,140
way	*mit*	I,179
way	*mṯn*	I,216
way	*sḫr*	II,73
way (be on)	*iw…r*	I,18
we	*inn*	I,33
weak	*ꜣhd*	I,6
weak	*wiꜣwiꜣ*	I,92
weak	*ẖsy*	I,388
weak	*sꜣyt*	II,6
weak	*gꜣby*	II,184
weak	*gbi*	II,186
weak	*gnn*	II,190
weaken	*ḳn*	II,152
weakling	*sꜣyt*	II,6
weakness	*wiꜣwiꜣ*	I,92
weakness	*wgg*	I,116
weakness	*kms*	II,174
weakness	*gbgb*	II,187
wealth	*ꜣḫwt*	I,8
wealth (total)	*sꜣwt*	II,7
wealthy	*wsr*	I,111
weapon	*ḳrn*	II,157
weapon case	*ꜥrḳ*	I,74
weapon(?)	*mḏrn*	I,220
weapons	*ꜥḥꜣw*	I,74
weapons	*ẖꜥw*	I,352
weapons	*kꜣr*	II,170
wear	*wṯs*	I,117
wear	*šṯ*	II,139
wear	*ṯꜣy*	II,224
wear	*sin*	II,12
wear a cuirass	*rbšy*	I,270
weariness	*wrd*	I,106
weariness	*bgꜣ*	I,142
weary	*wrd*	I,106
weary	*bꜣg*	I,128
weary	*bgꜣ*	I,142
weary	*ft*	I,165
weary	*nni*	I,239
weary of heart	*wrd-ib*	I,106
weasel(?)	*ḥḏri*	I,342
weave	*ndb*	I,255
weave	*sḫt*	II,74
weaver	*sḫty*	II,75
weavers	*mrw*	I,194
webbing	*ꜥꜣt*	I,61
webbing	*mtrt*	I,215
weed	*wnb*	I,101
week	*sw mḏ*	II,17
weep	*rmw*	I,270
weevil	*kkt*	II,179
weigh	*fꜣy*	I,163
weigh down	*wdn*	I,118
weigh house(?)	*ẖꜣy*	I,344
weight	*fꜣy*	I,163
weight	*nmst*	I,238
weight	*sniw*	II,49
weight	*šꜣw*	II,108
weight (76 gr.)	*ṯk*	II,236
weighty	*dns*	II,251
welcome	*ii*	I,16
well	*m-sšr*	I,171
well	*ẖnmt*	I,384
well	*snb*	II,50
well	*m-sšr*	II,82
well	*šdt*	II,141
well off	*m-sšr*	II,82
well to do	*bwꜣ*	I,133
well water	*stꜣ*	II,92
well-disposed	*mnḫ*	I,189
well-established	*mnḫ*	I,189
well-prepared	*spd*	II,34
wench	*msy*	I,204
West	*ꜥnḫt*	I,70
west	*imnt*	I,30
west (side)	*imy-wrt*	I,27
western	*imnt*	I,30
westerners	*imntyw*	I,30
wharf	*wḫrt*	I,110
what	*nt(y)w*	I,253
what exists	*wnnt*	I,102
what I have said	*ḏd*	II,275

what if	*hnn*	I,289
what is the point?	*iꜣ-iḫ*	I,44
what is the use of?	*iꜣ-iḫ*	I,44
what is this about?	*iry.tw.f iḫ*	I,39
what is to come	*ii*	I,16
what is...?	*ḫy*	I,350
what means?	*iḫ*	I,44
what?	*iḫ*	I,44
what?	*m*	I,167
what?	*ptr*	I,159
what?	*ḫr*	I,369
whatever	*nb nty*	I,232
whatever	*pꜣ nty nb*	I,233
whatever else	*nty nb*	I,233
whatsoever	*m-kfꜣ*	I,171
wheat	*swt*	II,22
wheat	(see emmer)	
when	*iw*	I,17
when	*ir*	I,37
when	*m*	I,167
when	*m-ḏr*	I,172
when	*ḫft*	I,358
when?	*tnw*	II,212
whence?	*tnw*	II,212
whenever	*tnw*	II,212
where?	*iṯ*	I,52
where?	*ptr*	I,159
where?	*tnw*	II,212
whereabouts	*hꜣw*	I,285
whereas	*iw*	I,17
whereas	*ḫr*	I,368
whether	*n*	I,223
whether it is not so	*biꜣ*	I,129
whether...or	*n...n*	I,224
whether...or	*nꜣ...nꜣ*	I,225
whetstone	*inr n dm*	I,34
which	*iṯ*	I,52
which	*nty*	I,253
which derive from	*nty ḥr*	I,321
which is in	*imy*	I,27
which?	*miṯ*	I,181
while	*iw*	I,17
while	*ist*	I,48
while	*m*	I,167
whip	*isbr*	I,46
whip	*mntd*	I,191
whip	*mḫt*	I,202
whip (vb.)	(see beat)	
whip-lash(?)	*krṯ*	II,177
whirl	*šm*	II,122
whirl away	*ḥwꜣw*	I,305
whirlwind	*dꜥ*	II,264
whistle (vb.)	*gꜣ*	II,183
white	*wbḫ*	I,97
white	*ḥḏ*	I,341
white bread	*t-ḥḏ*	II,197
white crown	*ḥḏt*	I,342
White Crown	*nfr-ḥḏt*	I,236
white wash (vb.)	*sḳḥ*	II,85
whither	*r-tnw*	I,265
who	*ỉḫ m rmṯ*	I,44
who	*nty*	I,253
who cannot be weary (stars)	*ḫm-wrdw*	I,360
who cannot rest (stars)	*ḫm-wrdw*	I,360
who causes the Two Lands to live	*sꜥnḫ tꜣwy*	II,14
who is before	*ḫnty*	I,367
who is in	*ỉmy*	I,27
who is responsible to you	*nty mntk*	I,190
who resides in	*ḥry-ib*	I,325
who ties together	*ṯs*	II,234
who?	*m*	I,167
who?	*n-m*	I,224
who?	*n(y)m*	I,227
who?	*nm*	I,237
whole	*ꜥḥꜥw*	I,76
whole	*wḏꜣ*	I,120
whole	*r-ḏr*	I,265
whole (ungutted fish)	*tm*	II,210
whole world	*tꜣ-tmw*	II,198
why?	*ḥr iḫ*	I,44
why?	*ḥr-iḫ*	I,321
wick	*ꜥḫm*	I,78
wick	*ḫbs*	I,355
wicked	*ꜥḏꜣ*	I,83
wicked	*bin*	I,131
wicked thing	*twꜣ*	II,201
wicks	*ḫꜣbs*	I,348
wide	*wsḫ*	I,112
wide hall	*wbꜣ*	I,96
widen	*swsḫ*	II,22
widow	*ḫꜣrt*	I,349
widow	*ẖrit*	I,386
widow	*šntꜣyt*	II,131
wield the bow	*ṯs pdt*	II,235
wife	*irt*	I,40
wife	*ḥwt*	I,304
wife	*ḥmt*	I,311
wife	*ḥmt-ṯꜣy*	I,312
wife	*ḫnrt*	I,365
wife	*st*	II,1
wife	*st-ḥmt*	II,1
wife(?)	*ḥbsyt*	I,308
wild	*nḫꜣ*	I,242
wild	*kh*	II,177
wild bulls	*smꜣw*	II,39
wild cattle	*ꜥwt*	I,62

wild goose	*gb*	II,187
wild pig(?)	*ḥḏri*	I,342
wild-faced one	*nḥꜣ-ḥr*	I,242
wilds	*y(ꜣ)ꜥrw*	I,13
wilds	*yꜥr*	I,17
will	*bꜣw*	I,125
will	*hry*	I,290
will	*kꜣ*	II,165
willow	*trt*	II,215
willow tree	*tri(t)*	II,215
willow(?)	*mry*	I,193
wind	*hh*	I,292
wind	*ṯꜣw*	II,226
window	*sšd*	II,83
windows	*ḳḥwt*	II,158
windstorm	*ḏꜥ*	II,264
wine	*irp*	I,40
wine cellar	*ꜥt-irp*	I,41
wine cellar	*ꜥt irp*	I,59
wine department	*ꜥt-irp*	I,59
wine jars	*gnw*	II,190
wine overseer(?)	*ḥry-bꜥḥ*	I,325
wine overseer(?)	*ḥry-kꜣmw*	I,325
wine press	*ḳnt*	II,155
wine steward	*wbꜣ dp irp*	I,41
wine(?)	*tnrk*	II,214
wing	*dḥn*	II,254
wings	*dnḥwy*	II,251
wink	*ṯnḥ*	II,230
winnow	*wḳm*	I,115
winnow	*ẖẖ*	I,373
winnowed kernels	*ḏḥw*	II,274
winnowing	*ẖẖ*	I,373
wipe out	*sk*	II,85
wisdom	*sꜣrt*	II,8
wisdom	*siꜣ*	II,11
wise	*ꜥrḳ*	I,73
wise	*nfr*	I,235
wise	*sꜣꜣ*	II,5
wise	*sbḳ*	II,29
wise one	*rẖ-ẖt*	I,275
wise woman	*rẖ(t)*	I,276
wish	*ꜣbi*	I,4
wish	*ꜣbw*	I,4
wish	*iꜣb*	I,13
wish	*ib*	I,22
wish	*wẖꜣ*	I,109
wish	*mrwt*	I,193
wish	*nḥ*	I,241
wish	*nḥt*	I,242
wish	*ḥꜣty*	I,297
wish	*ḥnr*	I,319
wish	*sꜣr*	II,8
wit (vb.)	*r-ḏd*	II,275
with	*irm*	I,41
with	*m*	I,167
with	*m-ꜥ*	I,167
with	*m-ẖnw*	I,170
with	*m-di*	I,171
with	*m-ḏrt*	I,172
with	*n*	I,223
with	*r-ḥnꜥ*	I,263
with	*r-ḥnꜥ*	I,317
with	*ẖr*	I,385
with eternity	*r-nḥḥ*	I,262
with reference to	*ẖry-st-(r)-n*	I,386
with utmost zeal	*m-sšr-iḳr-sp-sn*	I,171
with utmost zeal	*m-sšr*	II,82
with zeal	*m-sšr*	II,82
withdraw	*nḥm*	I,243
withdraw	*hꜣ(i)*	I,283
withdraw	*šdi*	II,139
within	*m-ẖnw*	I,170
within	*m-ẖnw*	I,382
within	*r-ẖnw*	I,382
within	*r-ẖnw*	I,382
without	*iwty*	I,21
without	*bn*	I,134
without	*n-bnr*	I,134
without	*r-bnr*	I,134
without	*r-bnr*	I,261
without	*m-ẖm(t)*	I,170
without	*m-ẖmt*	I,361
without	*n-r-ꜥ*	I,224
without	*ngꜣ*	I,252
without defects	*mrd*	I,195
without knowledge	*m-ẖmt*	I,361
withstand	*sꜣw*	II,6
witless	*ẖm*	I,360
witness (vb.)	*ptr*	I,159
witness, bear	*mtr*	I,214
witty	*spd-ns*	II,34
witty	*šsꜣ*	II,134
woe	*imw*	I,28
woe	*wgg*	I,116
woe	*mr*	I,191
woe to	*iꜥnw*	I,17
woe!	*ihy*	I,42
woes	*iꜣdt*	I,15
woes	*ihm*	I,43
wolf	*wnš*	I,103
woman	*st*	II,1
woman	*st-ḥmt*	II,1
woman	*ḥmt*	I,311
woman	*rmṯt*	I,272
woman diviner	*rẖ(t)*	I,276
woman of the harem	*ẖnrt*	I,365
womankind	*ḥr-nb*	I,322
womb	*ẖt*	I,379
wonder	*biꜣyt*	I,130
wonderful	*biꜣyt*	I,130

wood	*imw*	I,29
wood	*brry*	I,136
wood	*ḫt*	I,375
wood	*šꜥd*	II,113
wood	*ḳdy*	II,161
wood	*ṯg*	II,236
wood	*dšr*	II,255
wood	*ḏnḏnrt*	II,270
wood	*ḏḏ*	II,277
wood bringer	*in ḫt*	I,32
wood cutter	*šꜥd-ḫt*	II,113
wood tar	*mrḥt*	I,194
wooden container	*šḳr*	II,137
wooden plank	*swt*	II,22
wooden statue	*twt*	II,203
wooden or movable screen	*sbẖt*	II,29
woods	*šwy*	II,114
woodwork	*ṯt*	II,
woodwork(?)	*ḳbw*	II,148
wool	*sꜥrt*	II,15
wool	*šnw*	II,128
woolen cloth(?)	*sg*	II,89
woolen(?)	*šnw*	II,128
word	*mdt*	I,217
word	*r*	I,259
words	*ḫnw*	I,362
words	*ṯs*	II,234
work	*ipwt*	I,25
work	*irrt*	I,41
work	*wpwt*	I,99
work (vb.)	*bꜣk*	I,127
work	*bꜣkw*	I,127
work	*r-ꜥ-bꜣkw*	I,260
work	*sšr*	II,81
work	*kꜣt*	II,167
work out	*iri*	I,38
work the pleasure	*iꜣb*	I,13
worker	*kꜣwty*	II,167
worker (precious stones)	*nšdy*	I,250
worker in faience	*bꜥbꜥ*	I,132
workers	*r-ꜥ-bꜣkw*	I,260
workhouse	*šnꜥ*	II,128
workman	*rmṯ-ist*	I,46
workman	*rmṯ-ist*	I,272
workman	*kꜣwty*	II,168
workmanship	*bꜣkw*	I,127
workmen	*ḥsbw*	I,332
works	*irwt*	I,40
workshop	*wꜥbt*	I,95
workshop	*pr-ms*	I,150
workshop	*nḥdy*	I,244
workshop	*ḥmt*	I,311
workshop	*ḥmwt*	I,313
workshop	*gs-pr*	II,194
workshop (boatbuilding)	*wḫrt*	I,110
worm	*inr*	I,34
worm	*fn(t)*	I,164
worm	*kkt*	II,179
worms	*wꜥwy*	I,93
worn out	*whs*	I,107
worry	*ḥwꜣw*	I,305
worship	*sns*	II,53
worship	*dwꜣ*	II,241
worth	*iri*	I,37
worth	*šꜣw*	II,108
worth	*šfyt*	II,119
worthy	*ꜣḫ*	I,7
worthy	*iḳr*	I,49
worthy	*šꜣ*	II,106
worthy of	*šꜣw*	II,108
worthy of (death)	*ꜥꜣ-n-mt*	I,60
worthy of (death)	*šꜣy*	II,106
would that	*hnn*	I,289
would that!	*hꜣ*	I,295
would that!	*ḥnr*	I,318
wound	*wbn*	I,97
woven knots	*ṯst*	II,236
woven materials	*sšrw*	II,82
woven work	*nbd*	I,234
woven work	*dni*	II,249
wrangle	*ꜥḥꜣ*	I,74
wrap up	*wt*	I,116
wrap up	*bnd*	I,135
wrap up	*ḳrs*	II,157
wrath	*bꜣw*	I,125
wrath	*šfyt*	II,120
wrath	*dndn*	II,252
wreath	*mḥw*	I,199
wreathes	*mꜣḥw*	I,177
wretched	*bin*	I,131
wretched(?)	*ḫsy*	I,389
write	*iri*	I,38
write	*hꜣb*	I,286
write	*sš*	II,77
write down	*sš*	II,78
writhe	*sḏr*	II,103
writhe (in birth pangs)	*sꜥi*	II,12
writing	*mḏꜣt*	I,219
writing	*hꜣb*	I,286
writing	*sš*	II,78
writing	*drf*	II,252
writing board	*ꜥnw*	I,69
writing container	*ṯꜣy-drf*	II,224
written	*hry*	I,290
wrong	*ꜥḏꜣ*	I,83
wrong	*btꜣ*	I,142
wrong	*nf*	I,234

wrong	*twꜣ*	II,201
wrong	*ḏꜣyt*	II,261
wrong doing	*iwy*	I,18
wrong doing	*isft*	I,47
wrong doing	*šꜥḏꜣ*	II,16
wrongfully	*m-btꜣ*	I,142
wrongly	(see falsely)	
wroth	*ḥḏn*	I,342
wrought	*ḥwt*	I,304
wsrt-pole	*wsrt*	I,112

Y

yardarms	*tpt*	II,208
yards	*tpy.w*	II,207
yarn	*nwt*	I,231
year	*rnpt*	I,273
year after year	*rnpt-n-rnpt*	I,273
yearling calves	*d*	II,239
yearly	(see annual)	
yeast (?)	*srmt*	II,59
yellow ochre	*mnš(t)*	I,190
yellow pigment	*ḳniw*	II,154
yes	*tiw*	II,200
yes!	*iri*	I,37
yesterday	*sf*	II,35
yield	*ḥmḥm*	I,313
yield	*swḏ*	II,23
yield	*sbn*	II,28
yield	*ḏnrm*	II,270
yield(?)	*ḏlm*	II,273
yield (grain)	*wꜣḥyt*	I,90
yoke	*nḥb*	I,242
yoke	*nḥbt*	I,243
yoke	*ḥtr*	I,338
yoke arms	*dbywt*	II,244
yon	*tḫp*	II,218
yonder	*tfy*	II,209
you	*mtw*	I,213
you	*ntk*	I,253
you	*tw*	II,201
you	*tw*	II,201
you (plural)	*tn*	II,211
you (pl.in.prn.)	*mtwn*	I,214
you (plural)	*mntn*	I,190
you (plural)	*mtw*	I,213
you (singular)	*mntk*	I,190
young	*rnpi*	I,273
young	*šri*	II,131
young (employees)	*ms-ḫr*	I,204
young (n.)	*nḫn*	I,245
young (n.)	*nḏs*	I,257
young (n.)	*ḫy*	I,343
young animal	*ṯꜣ*	II,223
young girl	*nfrt*	I,237
young girl	*rwnt*	I,267
young god	*ms-nṯr*	I,203
young man	*iḥwn*	I,44
young man	*rnp*	I,272
young man	*ḏꜣmw*	II,262
young men	*ḏꜣmw*	II,262
young ones	*rnn*	I,274
young people	*nfrw*	I,237
young priest	*ms-wꜥb*	I,203
young slave	*ms-ḥm*	I,204
young soldiers	*ḥwnw-nfrw*	I,306

youngest	*šri*	II,132
youngling	*ṯꜣ*	II,223
younglings	*rnn*	I,274
youngster (good)	*nḏs iḳr*	I,257
your	*twt*	II,202
your attention	*ḥr-k*	I,322
yours	*tn-my*	II,211
yourself	*r-ḥʿt*	I,263
yourself	*ḥr-k*	I,322
youth	*iḥwn*	I,44
youth	*ʿḏꜣ*	I,83
youth	*ʿḏd*	I,84
youth	*ʿḏd-ʿꜣ*	I,85
youth	*ʿḏdi šri*	II,132
youth	*mnḥ*	I,188
youth	*rnpi*	I,273
youth	*ḥʿʿ*	I,302
youth	*ḥwn*	I,306
youth	*ḫnw*	I,363
youth	*ḫrd*	I,388
youth	*sfy*	II,35
youthful	*ʿḏdw*	I,85
youthful	*rnp*	I,272
youthful	*ḥwn*	I,306
youthful	*ḏꜣmw*	II,262
youths	*rnyw*	I,272

Z

zeal	*ḥr*	I,320
zealously	*m-sšr*	I,171
zealously	*m-sšr*	II,82